MARKETING STRATEGY & MANAGEMENT

Sara Miller McCune founded SAGE Publishing in 1965 to support the dissemination of usable knowledge and educate a global community. SAGE publishes more than 1000 journals and over 800 new books each year, spanning a wide range of subject areas. Our growing selection of library products includes archives, data, case studies and video. SAGE remains majority owned by our founder and after her lifetime will become owned by a charitable trust that secures the company's continued independence.

Los Angeles | London | New Delhi | Singapore | Washington DC | Melbourne

MARKETING STRATEGY & MANAGEMENT

Diane M. Phillips

SAGE

Los Angeles | London | New Delhi
Singapore | Washington DC | Melbourne

Los Angeles | London | New Delhi
Singapore | Washington DC | Melbourne

SAGE Publications Ltd
1 Oliver's Yard
55 City Road
London EC1Y 1SP

SAGE Publications Inc.
2455 Teller Road
Thousand Oaks, California 91320

SAGE Publications India Pvt Ltd
B 1/I 1 Mohan Cooperative Industrial Area
Mathura Road
New Delhi 110 044

SAGE Publications Asia-Pacific Pte Ltd
3 Church Street
#10-04 Samsung Hub
Singapore 049483

Editor: Matthew Waters
Editorial assistant: Charlotte Hanson
Production editor: Nicola Marshall
Copyeditor: Bryan Campbell
Proofreader: Leigh Smithson
Indexer: Gary Kirby
Marketing manager: Sarah Jane Silvester
Cover design: Francis Kenney
Typeset by: C&M Digitals (P) Ltd, Chennai, India
Printed in the UK

Library of Congress Control Number: 2022942254

British Library Cataloguing in Publication data

A catalogue record for this book is available from the British Library

ISBN 978-1-5297-7856-4
ISBN 978-1-5297-7855-7 (pbk)

At SAGE we take sustainability seriously. Most of our products are printed in the UK using responsibly sourced papers and boards. When we print overseas we ensure sustainable papers are used as measured by the PREPS grading system. We undertake an annual audit to monitor our sustainability.

To Jason, Caitlyn, and Evan

CONTENTS

ONLINE RESOURCES

This textbook is accompanied by online resources to aid teaching and support learning. To access these resources, visit: **https://study.sagepub.com/phillips**. Please note that lecturers will require a SAGE account in order to access the lecturer resources. An account can be created via the above link.

For Lecturers

- **PowerPoints** that can be downloaded and adapted to suit individual teaching needs.
- A **Teaching Guide** providing practical guidance and support and additional materials for lecturers using this textbook in their teaching. Each case study is accompanied by a detailed teaching note, complete with calculations and in-depth answers to case questions.
- A **Testbank** that can be used for both formative and summative student assessments.

ABOUT THE AUTHOR

Diane M. Phillips, Ph.D. is a professor of marketing at Saint Joseph's University in Philadelphia, USA. Dr. Phillips is also a Guest Professor at the Institute for Retail Management at the University of St. Gallen, Switzerland. She received her M.S. in marketing from Texas A&M University and her Ph.D. in marketing from Penn State University. Dr. Phillips has spent more than two decades teaching at the undergraduate, graduate, and executive levels. Much of her research focuses on the issue of consumer behavior, strategy, and sustainability. Her research has been published in a variety of international publications and she is a frequent speaker at international conferences, civic organizations, businesses, and universities on the topic of marketing strategy and climate change. Dr. Phillips has also traveled broadly, meeting with marketing executives in a wide variety of industries to discuss the real-life challenges that they face in the dynamic, ever-changing global marketplace. Dr. Phillips taps into these three critical experiences – teaching, sustainability, and real-world marketing applications – to create this book, *Marketing Strategy & Management.*

Case Study Author Affiliations

Joe Bogue, Ph.D., University College Cork, Cork, Ireland.
Dena Caiozzo, Wawa Corporation, Wawa, PA, USA
Conor Hyde, Hyde Whiskey, Cork, Ireland.
Kristina Kleinlercher, Ph.D., Management Center Innsbruck, Innsbruck, Austria.
Tyrha M. Lindsey-Warren, Ph.D. Baylor University, Waco, Texas, USA.
Emily Moscato, Ph.D., currently unaffiliated.
Jason Keith Phillips, Ph.D., West Chester University, West Chester, PA, USA.
Lana Repar, Ph.D., University College Cork, Cork, Ireland.
Thomas Rudolph, Ph.D., University of St. Gallen, St. Gallen, Switzerland.

ACKNOWLEDGMENTS

The author would like to express a special note of thanks to the following graduate students who assisted in the completion of this text and its peripheral materials: Francesco Melcarne, Caroline Stepchuk, Mei Fong Chan, and Ambra Caserta. In addition, a special heart-felt thank you to Emily Aznavourian for her exceptional sense of color, light, and style. Thank you to Matthew Waters, my Editor at SAGE Publishing, for taking a chance on this project and believing in the synergy of strategy and sustainability. I hope you are as pleased as I am with the final product. Thanks also to Charlotte Hanson, Editorial Assistant, for her careful attention to detail and her superb organizational skills. Thanks to my husband, Jason Phillips, for his unwavering support of this project through its many, many long months of development. Thanks to the thousands of students whom I have had the honor to teach throughout the years. You truly inspire me. Finally, I would be remiss in not thanking all of the dedicated, passionate individuals who have been working so tirelessly in addressing the issue of climate change and promoting a more sustainable world. Stay inspired – we are fighting the good fight!

1 SETTING THE STAGE: THE PURPOSE AND PROMISE OF MARKETING

LEADERSHIP INSIGHTS 1

Photo 1.1 Kate Colarulli

Source: courtesy, Kate Colarulli

Meet Kate Colarulli, VP, Retention Marketing & PR

CleanChoice Energy

Meet Kate Colarulli. After working successfully for several years in the nonprofit space and getting an MBA from Cambridge University, Colarulli landed a job at CleanChoice Energy and moved to the US. CleanChoice Energy is a renewable energy supplier (see CleanChoiceEnergy.com). "Climate change is the seminal issue of our time and we need to meet consumers where they are," she said. "We all know that we need to embrace clean energy in order to avoid catastrophic climate change, but it has been very difficult to scale. For example, if you wanted to put solar panels on your home, you would need a home with a roof, so you can't be living in a condo. You need some upfront capital, you need the roof to be situated correctly to capture the sun, and you need to have an appetite for a multi-month construction project. This rules out a lot of people. So, the thing we're trying to do is make clean energy convenient, to meet consumers where they are," she explained.

Colarulli and her team actualize "meeting customers where they are" with two distinct directives. First, the customer sign-up experience is easy. "Our signup process is two minutes or less. Its super, super simple. Our clean energy requires no construction, no interruption in your utility service. It just fits into the customer's daily life. We do all of the hard work on the back end. Second, our marketing needs to interrupt the customer. We recognize that we are all leading busy lives and few people out there are actively looking for green energy solutions. They might love green energy, they might be totally into green, or wanting to do their part in cleaning up the world, but in the end, they're not actively looking for it. We employ interruptive tactics to meet people where they are and give them what they want: a convenient, meaningful way to make the world a better place. Direct mail is a great interruptive tactic; it really is the

Photo 1.2 Renewable energy generation in Italy

Source: Pixabay

unsung hero of marketing today. Unlike digital marketing which is so easy to ignore, direct mail gets the message right in front of your customer. Direct mail brings it right to their door and they have it in their hand. Sure, people say they don't look at their mail, but at least they look at it long enough to sort it and determine what's important," explained Colarulli. "Now, for existing customers, digital marketing can be powerful – but again, it's not about passive portals, it's about cultivating an active relationship where we are providing an easy, meaningful way for the customer to green their world" (see Photo 1.2).

One of the most important lessons Colarulli has learned in her career is: rather than focusing on a particular industry or company, young marketers should focus on developing a skillset. "I tell young people who work for me that your 20s is all about developing your skills and figuring out what you don't like. Someone who is truly driven to succeed will learn how to be great in a variety of areas, for example, social media, analytics, or project management. Develop your toolkit so that no matter where your passion takes you in life, you can always add value to a team and be employable. Having a good toolkit allows young professionals to follow their passions. It allows you to do what you want to do."

1.1 THE IMPOSSIBLE DREAM

The year was 2016 and the tiny island nation of Fiji was about to make history. For the first time ever, the Fiji 7s Rugby Team had a fighting chance to qualify for the Olympics and perhaps even win a medal. No athlete from Fiji had ever won an Olympic medal (Associated Press 2016). Fiji is a developing nation of less than one million people, scattered over 334 islands in the South Pacific. The average Fijian makes $5860 per year (World Bank Data 2018). For decades, Fiji had been plagued by political unrest, corruption, grinding poverty, and a distinct lack of self-confidence. To make matters even worse, in February 2016, Fiji was hit by a category 5 cyclone, the strongest storm ever to make landfall in the Southern Hemisphere. The storm's sustained winds of 184mph ripped off roofs and the bark of trees. Forty-four people died and a huge swath of the main island was torn to shreds, leaving thousands homeless and without water, sanitation, or food (Cullinane and Ap 2016). In all, 131,000 people became homeless and 20% of the country's gross domestic product (GDP) was destroyed (Holmberg 2017). Fiji was definitely on its knees.

The Fijian people have a strong cultural heritage that centers around family and community; they are a kind, generous, and deeply religious people. To a Fijian, family is everything. People look out for one another and share what meager possessions they have. As the country was starting to rebuild after the cyclone, it started to shift its focus to its favorite pastime, rugby, and a man named Ben Ryan, the team's new coach from England. Ryan was starting to rack up some impressive wins in the 2016 Olympic qualifying tournaments. Ryan had come to Fiji just a few years before, when he learned that the head coaching job for the Fiji 7s rugby team was open. On a whim, he applied for the job and shortly after, he was hired. Little did he know what a difference that decision would make in his life, the lives of the players, or Fiji (Ryan 2018).

When Ryan moved to Fiji in 2013, his first task was to transform the rag-tag group of undisciplined players into the nation's – and indeed the world's – dream team. The overall objective was to have the team qualify for the 2016 Olympics in Rio, Brazil, and perhaps even bring home a medal for the first time in history. Almost immediately, Ryan saw that the players had the raw, explosive talent needed, but they lacked a strategy to help them fully realize their potential. Ryan's three-pronged strategy was based on a careful understanding of the culture and individual adaptation to meet the demands of the situation. First, he deeply immersed himself in the community and culture that was such a strong undercurrent in his players' lives. For example, when one particularly talented player wasn't giving his full effort in practice sessions, Ryan went to the player's village and spoke with his family. With the pressure of the entire extended family, the player was soon consistently breaking his own personal best times and goals. The British method of coaching established a strict distance between coaches and players, but in Fiji, Ryan formed close bonds with his players and embraced the community-centric culture of his new home (Ryan 2018).

Second, to fine-tune the strength and talent of the team, Ryan instituted a punishing schedule of physical conditioning for his players. He had the players run up and down towering sand dunes on the beach to strengthen their lungs, hearts, and legs. Ryan made sure that his team was ready to adapt its behavior according to the demands of the competition. Through extreme conditioning and seemingly endless execution of drills, the team became strong, capable, and ready to meet any situation it faced on the field. Once the conditioning and practice sessions were over, however, Ryan made time to socialize and get to know the players on a personal basis and to solidify the team's cohesion. The team and coaches lived together in dorms and ate all of their meals together. A typical evening would find them sitting around a campfire talking, singing, telling stories, and joking around (Ryan 2018).

Finally, Ryan adapted his strategy to the individual needs of the situation. He optimized the talents of each individual player and he shifted his strategy for each opponent. Using data to create insights about the competition, he was able to accurately anticipate the different playing styles and strategies of each team. For example, one team was known for its explosive speed, while another relied on the precise execution of a collection of different plays. Ryan employed different strategies for Argentina, the US, England, and South Africa (Ryan 2018).

In the end, this three-pronged strategy that Ryan had created and implemented was successful. Team Fiji beat all of its opponents and ended up winning the country's first-ever gold medal in a stunning 43–7 thrashing of England (Daye 2016). The entire country shut down the next day to celebrate – no one was coming to work anyway. People wept and celebrated. Once the team came back home, celebrations lasted several more days, and when the players finally made it home to their villages, even more celebrations ensued (Ryan 2018). Special recognition was given to Ryan for his strategy. Young couples named their newborn babies after him, and Fiji's prime minister awarded him with a hereditary chiefly title and a swath of land and beach on the country's biggest island (see Photo 1.3).

Photo 1.3 Fiji wins its first Olympic medal in 2016

Source: mfauzisaim/Shutterstock.com

Ryan's strategy to bring his team and Fiji to the world's biggest stage – and win – demonstrates several important characteristics of good strategy. Broadly speaking, we know that there are some fundamental principles of good strategy:

- Good strategy is personal; it considers the characteristics of the situation and context.
- Good strategy builds and nurtures the organization's strengths.
- Good strategy is flexible; it adapts to the needs of the situation.

This textbook is all about marketing strategy. Unlike other books, it takes a decidedly more hands-on approach that will allow you to take what was learned in the chapter and apply those lessons to real-life situations and case studies. In addition, this book emphasizes the broader environment and the context in which marketing strategy occurs, such that long-term sustainable benefits are achieved. Individuals utilize strategic principles every day in their efforts to achieve their goals. This is exactly what Ben Ryan and Team Fiji did, and this is the essence of what we will be discussing in this book.

1.2 LEARNING OBJECTIVES

After studying this chapter, you will be able to do the following:

1. Describe the core responsibility of marketing and its place within the organization.
2. Discuss the critical nature of the value proposition.
3. Describe how marketing strategy builds upon and extends the core principles of marketing.
4. Explain the four key developments in the evolution of our understanding of the responsibility of marketing: stakeholder theory, corporate social responsibility, shared value, and sustainability.
5. Argue for the importance of sustainability as a strategic imperative for marketing.

1.3 BEFORE WE BEGIN

If you ask the average person to define marketing, more than likely, you will hear that marketing is about selling things, it's about making products, or it's about advertising. Some people who have studied marketing may claim that marketing is all about the marketing mix: product, price, place, and promotion. Sure, marketing depends on the marketing mix to deliver products and satisfy consumer needs. However, marketing managers know that marketing is a lot more than the set of tasks it performs to deliver value to consumers. One of the early experts in the field of marketing strategy, Theodore Levitt, argued that managers often committed the mistake of defining their businesses too narrowly by what they produced. He called this problem **marketing myopia**, or the tendency to view the scope of a business in very narrow and constrained terms. Instead, Levitt called for our conceptualization of marketing to be broadened to embrace a more customer, institutional, stakeholder, and societal orientation (Levitt 1960). At the time, the call for such a broadened view, especially one that focused on consumers, was revolutionary. This new broadened view meant, for example, that Sony Pictures was no longer just a movie company, it was an entertainment company. Similarly, BP (British Petroleum) was not just an oil company, it was an energy company. To back up its broadened perspective, BP (in)famously launched "Beyond Petroleum" rebranding efforts in 2002 and 2020 (Carpenter 2020). Abandoning the previous myopic approach and broadening the view meant that managers were better able to identify a wider range of opportunities and threats. This definition certainly made sense from a consumer perspective. Consumers wanted to be entertained; they didn't necessarily need to visit a theater to see a movie, and in fact may prefer gaming or other forms of entertainment to movies. Similarly, consumers wanted energy to power their homes and cars; they didn't necessary need oil to do so.

Consider the difference between Netflix and Blockbuster's approach to marketing and what value their businesses offered to consumers. Both businesses started out renting movies to individuals. In 1985, Blockbuster started renting movies on videotapes to individuals, who had to enter the store, select a movie, and then return it when they were done. At the time, it was the only opportunity consumers had to see a movie after it left the theater (Olito 2020). Netflix was founded in 1997. It never had brick-and-mortar stores, but instead offered an online movie rental service which was a much more customer-friendly experience. Customers would go online, select a set of movies they would like to see, and Netflix would send them the movies through the postal system. Over the next few decades, as more American households gained access to high-speed broadband, streaming became the norm. Because of its established online interface, Netflix was ideally positioned to offer streaming content, and in 2016, launched its services globally to 130 countries. Blockbuster could have invested in updating its customer interface, but selected not to do so. After all, management insisted, they were in the movie rental business and they simply needed to find new and creative incentives for customers to visit their brick-and-mortar stores. Unfortunately for Blockbuster, this myopic view of their business was a critical mistake and limited their perspective about potential opportunities. Customers were simply not going to return to the stores to rent movies when Netflix offered a much simpler service without the hassle of remembering to return the movie in order to avoid a late fee. In fact, Netflix CEO Reed Hastings claimed that he started the company because he wanted to avoid paying a $40 late fee to Blockbuster. In total, Blockbuster was making about $800 million per year, or 16% of its profits, on late fees. As a consequence of not understanding the shift in the marketplace or realizing what business it was really in, Blockbuster never recovered. It filed for bankruptcy in 2010 and closed all except one of its more than 9000 stores around the world. Today, the last store is located in Oregon and is available to rent on Airbnb (Olito 2020) (see Photo 1.4).

Photo 1.4 Netflix offered better value to its customers

So, what is marketing? According to the American Marketing Association, **marketing** is the activity, set of institutions, and processes for creating, communicating, delivering, and exchanging offerings that have value for customers, clients, partners, and society at large (AMA 2017). This definition has evolved over several decades, but an important feature is that it is not at all myopic. This definition has a few important components. First, it acknowledges the critical importance of the consumer to the process. For the record, a **customer** is the person or entity who purchases the product; a **consumer** is the person or entity who uses the product. Sometimes the customer and the consumer can be the same person, as when a person purchases and consumes a coffee, or a manufacturing facility purchases new equipment to use. Sometimes, however, the customer and consumer are different. This might happen when one person in the family purchases something for others in the household to use, as when parents (customer) purchase a piece of sporting equipment for their children (consumer). Second, the AMA definition of marketing also introduces the concept of "offerings that have value." Indeed, marketers can promote products, but can also promote other offerings that provide value to customers such as ideas ("higher education is important for success"), services (medical services or financial services), people (political candidates or celebrities), or places (Paris or Tahiti). Although sometimes problematic, for simplicity, we generally use the umbrella term "products" to refer to all of these offerings. Third, the definition stresses the importance of exchange. That is, one party must give up something, while the other party gets something. In most cases, a person gives up money for a product. However, other things of value can also be exchanged, such as attention, time, personal data, a vote, or something else of value to the other party.

Strategy is the process of developing an understanding of the situation, anticipating the actions of others, and adapting to those actions in order to achieve a goal. Individuals enact strategies every day – from trying to convince your professor to push the exam back until next week, to asking your boss for a raise. You set a goal, anticipate how the other entity will react, and then adapt your own behaviors accordingly. An important component of strategy is a careful assessment of and preparation for the competition. Indeed, the "job of the strategist is to understand and cope with the competition" (Porter 2008, p. 79). The competitive landscape should be broadly defined; the firm's competitors are not simply the immediate players in the industry, they are any entity that competes for customers and profit (Porter 1996, 2008).

ENDURING INSIGHTS 1.1

"I've been up against tough competition all my life. I wouldn't know how to get along without it."
– Walt Disney

The venerable head of Disney recognized the importance of competition: it increased the quality of the product and pushed internal processes to be more efficient and effective. Disney had no opportunity to become complacent in the highly-competitive tech and media industry. Disney defined its competition quite broadly: it was in the entertainment business and it needed to deliver content to customers in the manner that was easiest for them. In 2017, Disney entered the content streaming business and purchased a portion of 21st Century Fox for $52.4 billion. Although the move would put Disney in a head-to-head competition with the well-entrenched Netflix and other streaming services, Disney executives believed their approach would lead to "more innovative and compelling ways" to deliver content to customers (Barnes 2017) (see Photo 1.5).

Photo 1.5 In 2017, Disney made a big bet on the future of streaming content

Figure 1.1 Marketing strategy in the organization

Marketing strategy is an integrated set of decisions and processes designed to deliver value to consumers in order to help the organization achieve specific objectives. In helping the organization achieve its overall objectives, marketing strategy provides an essential pillar in the organization's overall strategy. There are several other important features to this definition. First, marketing strategy is dynamic because it continually adapts to the changing environmental and competitive landscape by developing new innovations and perspectives. Second, the concept of an "integrated set of decisions and processes" indicates a careful and deliberate set of processes carried out by the management team (Varadarajan 2010). Ideally, these choices are based on sound research, and are forward thinking, long term, and sustainable. Further, these decisions should be interrelated, interdependent, and internally consistent. Third, marketing strategy is competitive in nature; we are seeking to do a better, faster, and more efficient job than the competition in delivering the value proposition. Finally, the definition recognizes the customer-centric nature of the organization; no organization could be sustainable over the long term unless it was able to deliver value to its customers (see Figure 1.1).

It is important to note that the job of the marketing manager is not just to deliver value, but to do so in such a way that is better than that of the competition. Customers in the target market need to believe that their needs are being satisfied best by the offering that *your* organization provides. Zappos is an online shoe store with a wide variety of moderately and high-priced shoes. It is known for its wide variety of styles and, most importantly, for its excellent customer service. Can customers get their shoes elsewhere at better prices? Yes. Can they get better customer service? No. The goal for Zappos and any other organization is to provide an offering that, compared to the competition, does a better job at delivering value to its target customers.

Identifying and Defining the Competition

Experts agree that healthy competition results in better quality products and services for consumers (Porter 2008). It is also better for a nation's economy when firms compete in order to be more efficient and to better meet the needs of their customers (Porter and Kramer 2011). Perhaps one of the most difficult first steps in understanding the competitive landscape is precisely determining how narrowly or broadly one must define the competition. Think about the competitive landscape for a small restaurant in town. If the restaurant defines its competition narrowly, it might conclude that all the other restaurants in town are competitors. However, customers have many options available for how they will spend their money. As discussed previously, customers want to have their needs satisfied and there are often a variety of ways in which to do that. Broadly defined, competition would also include the possibility of eating at home, so competitors would also include grocery stores, takeout restaurants, and even services like Hello Fresh, which provides more than 5.3 million customers around the world with easy-to-assemble, healthy, and tasty meals (About us 2021a). By broadly defining the competitive landscape, marketing managers can better identify not just the myriad of options that are available to customers, but they can create strategies that keep these competitive forces in check.

ENDURING INSIGHTS 1.2

"Keep your friends close, but your enemies closer." – Michael Corleone, *The Godfather II*

The origin of this quote has been attributed to both Sun Tzu (the Chinese military strategist) and Niccolo Machiavelli (the 15th century diplomat) (Aileron 2012). Legendary actor Al Pacino made it famous in his portrayal of mafia boss Michael Corleone in *The Godfather II*. Two mafia families were engaged in a bitter fight and someone had betrayed Corleone. He expanded, "I want him completely relaxed and confident in our friendship, then I will be able to find out who the traitor in my family was." The quote portrays a strategic mind; it suggests that knowledge of the competition is crucial and it is important to understand it at a deep level. At the same time, however, key pieces of information need to be kept quiet from the competition such that the competition cannot guess your organization's next move.

The Five Competitive Forces

One model for identifying the variety of competitive forces influencing the organization is the Five Forces model. Regardless of the industry we may examine – airlines vs. the art market, fashion vs. forestry products, or transportation vs. tech – any industry's underlying profit structure is still subject to the same competitive forces. Since an important part of marketing strategy is to differentiate the firm's offerings from that of the competition, a careful consideration of each of these five forces is an important first step in developing marketing strategy. **The Five Forces model** takes a broad perspective on competition by acknowledging that it can come from: (1) the threat of new entrants, (2) the bargaining power of buyers, (3) the threat of substitute products or services, (4) the bargaining power of suppliers, and (5) rivalry among existing competitors. The marketing team that understands that it is subject to competitive pressure beyond just its immediate competitive rivals will recognize a wider variety of competitive threats, will be better prepared to address them, and will be able to identify new opportunities that the organization can leverage to its own advantage (Porter 2008):

- *Threat of new entrants* – the marketing team needs to consider the ease with which a competitor can enter the market. Are there significant barriers to entry that would make entry hard, such as significant investment in technology or equipment? Perhaps the profit margins are low and would thus discourage new entrants. Has the industry created unique or proprietary processes, or distribution strategies, such that there would be a significant learning curve for new entrants? Often, just the threat of entry can keep prices and profitability down.
- *Bargaining power of buyers* – this force involves the extent to which buyers are very powerful and thus would force concessions such as lower prices or more favorable services such as buy-backs, warranties, or cooperative advertising. Powerful buyers have strong negotiating leverage, which can cut into profits.
- *Threat of substitute products or services* – this force considers the uniqueness or critical nature of the firm's offering. Does the organization have a patent or other protection for the product or process? Can competitors easily create and deliver a substitute? Can consumers have their needs easily satisfied by another product? When the threat of substitutes is high, profit and growth potential suffer.
- *Bargaining power of suppliers* – this force involves the extent to which the firm's suppliers are very powerful and might not be motivated to offer better terms such as price breaks, volume discounts, or other corollary services. The supplier might be powerful if it is very big, if your firm is small (relative to the supplier's other customers), or if it offers a unique product that cannot be easily obtained elsewhere. A powerful supplier can be especially difficult if it exists in an industry where it is difficult to pass along higher prices to your customers.
- *Rivalry among existing competitors* – this force captures the extent to which the existing competition may be frequent and fierce. Fierce competition is likely in industries where: (1) there are numerous competitors who are roughly equal in size and power; (2) exit barriers are high; and (3) the competition is highly committed to the business or leadership in the marketplace.

Understanding these disparate forces is the starting point for the marketing team as it works to create an effective marketing strategy (Porter 2008). No marketing team wants to enter a market, introduce a new product or service, or expand its offerings unless there is a reasonably good opportunity for making a profit. The Five Forces model helps the team better predict that profit potential. Scanning the competitive landscape for potential gaps and opportunities that it can leverage is part of this important first step in developing an intuitive and effective marketing strategy. The best strategies leverage more than one of the Five Forces. Several possibilities for effective strategic moves include (Porter 2008):

- *Position the company* – situate the organization within the industry so that it exists where the competitive forces are relatively weak.
- *Exploit industry change* – monitor and anticipate shifts in the industry such that the organization can stake a claim to an advantageous strategic position before the competition has a chance to do so.
- *Shape industry structure* – through innovation, lead a transformation of the industry for the better. Ideally, the innovative nature of the transformation will shift the competition in a direction in which your own organization can excel.
- *Define the industry* – draw boundary lines around the industry such that it is neither too broad nor too narrow. This will more precisely define the scope of the competition as well as sources of profit within the industry.

1.4 THE VALUE PROPOSITION

The value proposition is the set of needs a company can satisfy for its target market customers that the competition cannot (Porter and Kramer 2006, p. 89). Think about it as a bundle of benefits that the firm promises to deliver. In delivering the value proposition to the customer, it is important to deliver an objectively better product or service – the pizza must taste better, the software must perform better, or the medication must have fewer side-effects. One way or another, the product or service needs to meet the customer's needs better than that of the competition. Objectively better performance is certainly necessary. However, the marketing team must also effectively communicate these benefits to the consumer so that consumers *perceive* the performance to be better too. After all, how will the customer know which product is better? There have been numerous examples over the years about customers who insist that their favorite brand of beer, coffee, etc. is objectively better than that of the competition, only to find out that in blind taste-tests, they actually "prefer" the taste of the competition's product (McRaney 2011).

Americans like their beer, so much so, that they consume an average of 75 liters per person per year. A full 40% of Americans claim that beer is their alcoholic beverage of choice, compared to 25% who prefer wine. Sales at some of the biggest breweries have leveled off in recent years, as Americans shifted their beer-drinking preferences to smaller craft beers and Mexican imports (Andrews and Suneson 2018). However, are Americans purchasing beer that objectively tastes better than other beers? The conclusion is a resounding "no." When expert taste testers engaged in a blind test of some of the biggest-selling beers and provided their ratings on a 5-point scale, Bud Light, the best-selling beer in the US with a 15.4% market share, received the lowest quality rating (Noel 2017) (see Table 1.1 and Photo 1.6).

Table 1.1 American beer sales, market share, and quality ratings

Ranking by Market Share	Brand	Manufacturer	Market Share	Quality (Taste rating on 5-point scale)
1	Bud Light	Anheuser-Busch InBev	15.4%	3.0
2	Coors Light	Molson Coors	7.7%	3.7
3	Budweiser	Anheuser-Busch InBev	6.2%	3.3

Sources: Andrews and Suneson (2018) and Noel (2017)

Photo 1.6 Bud Light is the best-selling beer in the US

Source: iStock

In examining Table 1.1, one should not draw the conclusion that quality is immaterial to delivering the value proposition; quality is just part of the value proposition. Bud Light has twice the market share of its next closest competitor, Coors Light, because customers are deriving some sort of value from consumption of the product. A variety of influences, including image, habit, and social pressures, all contribute to a consumer's choices. Table 1.2 below provides evidence that image is a strong contributing factor for American beer purchases. Indeed, compared to its competitors, Anheuser-Busch InBev spends more money on advertising and has a commanding share of the market.

Table 1.2 Annual US advertising spending for top beer manufacturers

Manufacturer	Advertising Spending (in millions USD)
Anheuser-Busch InBev	428
Constellation Brands	359
Molson Coors	218

Source: Statista (2019)

ENDURING INSIGHTS 1.3

"The standard you walk past is the standard you keep." – Ben Ryan (2018), coach, the Fiji 7s Rugby team

Coach Ben Ryan often used this quote to motivate his team on its way to Olympic gold. To Ryan, although the overall objective was Olympic gold, integrity and a high standard of excellent performance were equally important. This quote meant that standards of performance and integrity could not be relaxed. Ever. No player could take shortcuts in training, play at a level that was below his abilities, or in any way uphold himself or his teammates to anything but the highest level of expectations. Once those standards were relaxed, they were lost. In effect, these standards of integrity and excellence provided a "true North" for the team. In the end, this quote provided tremendous motivation to the team and coaching staff.

1.5 MARKETING'S ROLE AND OBLIGATION

Marketing is in a unique position because part of its work is focused within the organization and part of its work is focused outside the organization. It has the unique obligation to monitor and understand a variety of external influences, and bring those insights back to the inner-workings of the organization where they can be used to inform marketing strategy. Similarly, marketing is tasked with the job of taking strategies that have been created by the marketing team, and implementing those strategies out into the marketplace (see Figure 1.2 below).

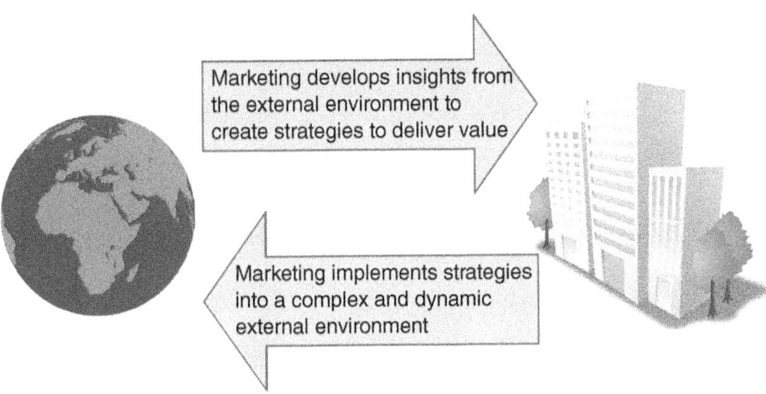

Figure 1.2 Marketing is the bridge between the organization and the external environment

What exactly is this **external environment**? It includes a wide variety of constituents and forces that influence or could potentially influence the organization. These might include any combination of the following: the legal and regulatory systems, the culture, the financial and economic system, the technological environment, the media system, the climate/weather/topography, the political system, the demographic makeup of the market, the marketing system, the network of business partners (or potential partners), and the competitive landscape. Where exactly does marketing fit within the organization? Marketing is one of the functional units of the organization and must operate within the confines of the overall organizational structure, alongside other functional units such as finance, accounting, manufacturing, operations, human resources, and distribution. Importantly, marketing needs to ensure that the strategies it enacts support and enhance the organization's mission and values. Further, because marketing has the unique role of being a bridge between the external environment and the organization, it needs to be especially careful to do this ethically and sustainably. Remember that marketing strategy emphasizes the importance of creating an integrated set of decisions and processes that are not only integrated with previous decisions, research, and priorities, but are also integrated with the activities of the organization and its other functional units. Some organizations are so large that they have several different **strategic business units**, or **SBUs**. Each one of these SBUs operates somewhat independently with its own set of functional units. Global conglomerate Unilever is an excellent example of an organization that has a set of very different SBUs that all work fairly independently to achieve their own objectives. Together, however, they support the overall objectives of Unilever. Figure 1.3 depicts Unilever's three SBUs, with a sampling of brands from each.

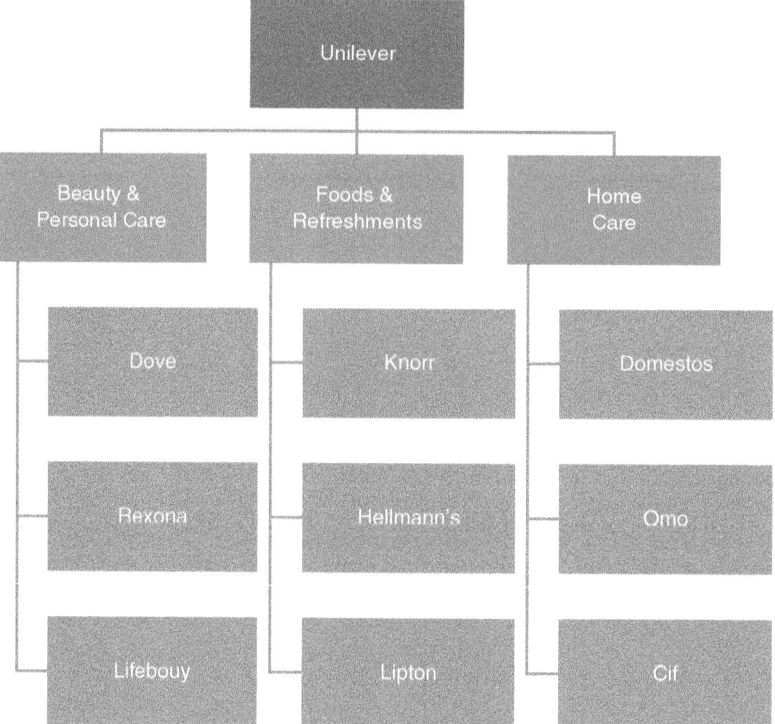

Figure 1.3 Unilever's SBU structure

Because of its role as a bridge between the external environment and the organization, marketing is often called upon to be the standard-bearer for the organization's ethical principles and standards. One such call proposed that marketing strategy should abide by three key principles (Hulland, Houston, and Hoekman 2020):

- The *Responsible* principle requires giving voice to all marketing stakeholders in order to create a shared vision about the organization's offerings. This requires forming truly collaborative partnerships among the organization, its customers, and other stakeholders to develop purposeful engagement, as well as articulating social, environmental, and economic priorities.
- The *Respectful* principle focuses on enabling different levels of aspiration within a fair society. Equality, diversity, and social inclusion underpin this principle to ensure that vulnerable, disadvantaged, and previously marginalized communities are empowered to make their own meaningful contributions in marketplaces.
- The *Resilient* principle is based on continuous improvement through self and group reflections. This is achieved through establishing highly-efficient infrastructure and supply chains, and effectively harnessing innovation and entrepreneurship.

Early economists and business professionals argued that the sole purpose of an organization is to maximize its financial and economic gains. One especially influential economist of the latter half of the 20th century, Milton Friedman, developed several economic theories that were particularly influential. Friedman argued that corporations exist in order to generate shareholder wealth; this is their singular purpose (see Feloni 2018, Friedman 1970, Winer 1966).

Managers could certainly make donations to social and environmental causes on their own, but to use the resources of the corporation to do so would be abdicating the organization's responsibility to its stockholders, the real owners of the organization (Friedman 1970). Friedman promoted the benefits of a free market, with no interference from governments (Cohen 2008). For the next few decades, this conceptualization strongly influenced business-related policies in the US, the UK, and Europe (Latapi Agudelo, Johannsdottir, and Davidsdottir 2019), as well as business education and operations around the world. His theories also guided policies at the International Monetary Fund and the World Bank in the 1980s and 1990s. In hindsight, many of these policies led to severe hardships for many people in the developing world because of their "survival of the fittest" approach to economic development (Cohen 2008). The problem with this perspective is that it assumes that business and societal benefits are a zero-sum game, which they most certainly are not. Indeed, the economy and society can both simultaneously benefit by well-designed and implemented policies (Porter and Kramer 2006). Today, enlightened experts have recognized that marketing needs to embrace the needs of *all* relevant stakeholders (Balmer 2011), must always keep the needs of the consumer at the forefront of its decisions (McDonald 2009), and must promote environmental sustainability (Latapi Agudelo, et al. 2019).

There have been four significant advancements in how our understanding of the role of marketing has evolved. Each one has moved the field closer to marketing taking more responsibility for not only the success of the organization, but also for making sustainable, long-term improvements in the health of the environment and society. The following sections will introduce four advancements that each provide a unique perspective on the responsibility of marketing: stakeholder theory, corporate social responsibility, shared value, and sustainability.

Stakeholder Theory

A **stakeholder** is any identifiable group or individual who can affect the achievement of an organization's objectives or who is affected by the achievement of an organization's objectives. (Freeman and Reed 1983). **Internal stakeholders** are those entities who have a direct connection to and relationship with the company. They include financiers, employees, and customers. **External stakeholders** are those entities who have more of an indirect connection to the organization. There may not be a contractual relationship, but these groups still have an interest in, or a stake in, what happens with the organization. These entities include business partners, society, the environment, non-governmental organizations (NGOs), the media, activists and consumer advocacy groups, competitors, and the government (Freeman 1994, Freeman and Evan 1990, Freeman and Reed 1983). It is important to note that the connections between the organization and each stakeholder will vary, depending on the industry. For example, compared to some industries, the pharmaceutical industry will likely have stronger connections with the government because of safety and regulatory procedures. By contrast, the communications industry may have stronger connections with the media (Fassin 2009).

The biggest contribution of **stakeholder theory** to our understanding of marketing strategy is that it considers the wide variety of constituencies that impact and are impacted by the actions of the organization (Fassin 2009, LaPlume, Sonpar, and Litz 2008). By looking at the external environment through the lens of stakeholder theory, the marketing team has a greater degree of flexibility in charting its strategic course. Because of this broader perspective, it is clear that the organization's economic success can coexist with the organization's ethical principles. Indeed, using the stakeholder view, the marketing team may become aware of new and more effective operations (Freeman 1994), including giving some stakeholders direct input into some of the decisions that are made (Freeman and Evan 1990). Importantly, stakeholder theory provides decision-makers greater clarity for strategic decisions because it takes into account the needs of all stakeholders, not just those of stockholders (LaPlume, Sonpar, and Litz 2008).

Stakeholder theory has not been without its critics, with the primary criticism being that there needs to be a clearer distinction between the roles, influence, and obligations of internal stakeholders and external stakeholders (cf. Fassin 2009, LaPlume et al. 2008) such that there are no areas of overlap or gaps in responsibilities and roles. One approach to solving this problem separates stakeholders into three distinct groups (Fassin 2009):

- *Stakeholders* – these entities have a genuine and concrete stake in the organization, as well as some degree of loyalty to the organization. As with the earlier definition of internal stakeholders, these entities include financiers, employees, and customers.
- *Stakewatchers* – entities in this category do not have a direct stake in the organization. However, they endeavor to protect the interests of stakeholders and notify the organization when concerns arise. Examples could be labor unions or community watchdog groups.
- *Stakekeepers* – these entities include independent regulators who exert indirect influence and control over the organization. In a way that is similar to the concept of a "gatekeeper," stakekeepers include government agencies and other certifying groups that impose regulations and hold the organization accountable.

The benefit of conceptualizing three separate spheres of influence on the organization is that it more precisely focuses the management team on the narrow conceptualization of stakeholders, who are genuinely an integral part of the organization. While other outside entities also should be monitored, communicated with, and may even present some opportunities for collaboration, their influence on the strategic direction of the organization is less important than that of stakeholders (see Figure 1.4 below).

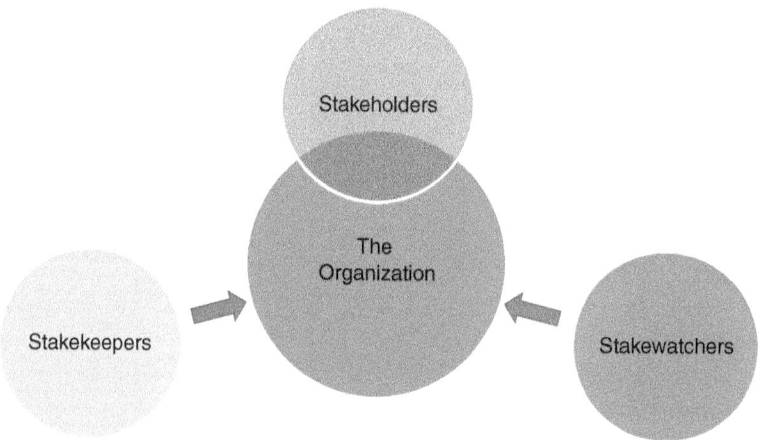

Figure 1.4 Three spheres of influence on the organization

Source: adapted, in part, from Fassin (2009)

BLUNDERS & INSIGHTS 1.1

Cultural Missteps in China

WHAT HAPPENED: In the spring of 2018, global luxury brand Dolce & Gabbana (D&G) had expected to make a big splash in the Chinese market with its upcoming fashion show in Shanghai, when it posted several culturally-insensitive videos to social media. The videos showed a Chinese woman who was attempting to eat several traditionally-Italian foods, like cannoli, pizza, and spaghetti, with chopsticks. An off-camera male voice tried to instruct her on what do to. After quite a bit of struggle, the young woman was able to take a taste of these wonderful foods. D&G executives claimed that the ad was an attempt to celebrate the upcoming fashion show and the intersection of Italian and Chinese culture. The backlash was swift, severe, and far-reaching. Far from a celebration of Chinese culture, consumers viewed the ad as condescending and insulting. Social media erupted at the "vicious attitude" shown in the ad toward China and called for boycotts and an apology from the company. D&G products were removed from several online and brick-and-mortar retailers (*The Guardian* 2018), D&G's brand ambassador in China resigned (DW News 2018), and the actress from the ad issued an apology for her participation in the ad saying she felt "guilty and ashamed" for her part in perpetuating incorrect images and perceptions of Chinese culture. She later claimed that the ad almost ruined her career (BBC 2019). In the end, D&G cancelled its Shanghai fashion show (DW News 2018).

DEBRIEF: China accounts for one third of all spending on luxury goods, with almost $100 billion spent in just 2017 (DW News 2018). A thorough external analysis would have revealed that the advertising execution was likely to be inflammatory. Beyond that, this misstep underscores two important concepts from this chapter. First, stakeholder theory suggests that key stakeholders, such as employees (including those working on the fashion show and those working at the retail stores), should have been a part of the decision-making process. Second, as the bridge between the external environment and the organization, the marketing team should have paid particular attention to the ad's execution and should have identified it as problematic (see Photo 1.7).

Photo 1.7 Fashion powerhouse D&G committed a cultural misstep in China

Source: Pixabay

Corporate Social Responsibility

Corporate social responsibility (CSR) is a strategic approach that seeks to achieve core business objectives, while also creating value for society and the environment. This conceptualization of the role of the organization and marketing is not new. In 1938, business theorist Chester Barnard argued that the purpose of the corporation was to serve society (Freeman and Reed 1983). The latter half of the 20th century and the first part of the 21st century saw a more widespread push for organizations to adopt a CSR perspective. These calls for more of an active role in addressing social and environmental issues stem from activists, NGOs, and governments who often portray organizations as the source of many social and environmental ills (Porter and Kramer 2006). The 1960s were a time of globalization, as well as social upheaval and awakening. People marched for civil rights and against the atrocities in the Vietnam War. As more families around the world got televisions, for the first time, vivid images played out in people's homes of the war as well as grinding poverty and environmental destruction in other parts of the world.

By the 1980s, the push for organizations to adopt a CSR perspective was even more insistent. This was due, in part, to several global developments and events, such as the nuclear disaster at Chernobyl in 1986, the Brundtland Commission's stark warning about climate change and the health of the planet in 1987, and the adoption of the Montreal Protocol to close the growing hole in the planet's protective ozone layer in 1987. The 1990s saw increasing concern, culminating in several historical statements and agreements designed to address climate change. The first global agreement to limit CO_2 emissions was the Kyoto Protocol in 1997. At this time, globalization was occurring at an increasing pace and organizations often came face-to-face with severe poverty and environmental degradation in the developing world (Latapi Agudelo, et al. 2019).

In 1996, CSR Europe was founded and eventually became the leading European business network for CSR. At 10,000+ members worldwide, it encourages systemic change and integrative actions to encourage sustainable growth (About us 2021b). One company at the forefront of CSR is the Nestlé Corporation, the world's largest food company, with operations in 191 countries. One of the founding members of CSR Europe, Nestlé has thoroughly incorporated CSR into its global operations. As one example, Nestlé adds extra vitamin fortification to the bouillon cubes it sells in Africa under the Maggi brand in order to address a common vitamin deficiency there. Notably, the company doesn't promote these efforts (Ewing 2019). Decision-makers at Nestlé recognize their obligation to provide economic and societal benefits in the countries in which they operate.

Shared Value

Perhaps the most important step toward acknowledging the importance of both business and economic goals was the call for a new way of thinking, or a **paradigm shift**. Specifically, business leaders and marketers started to recognize that organizations can be *more* successful than their competitors if they focus on both social *and* economic priorities. This requires a long-term investment in the firm's future competitiveness. Rather than being reactive, the shared value perspective is strategic (Porter and Kramer 2006). Specifically, the concept of **shared value** suggests that there is a synergistic effect when the organization focuses on both economic and social/environmental priorities. A shared value perspective requires "policies and operating practices that enhance the competitiveness of a company while simultaneously advancing the economic and social conditions in the communities in which it operates. Shared value creation focuses on identifying and expanding the connections between societal and economic progress" (Porter and Kramer 2011, p. 66).

In recent years, Nestlé has moved beyond a CSR perspective to adopt a shared value perspective in its work to improve the lives of farmers who grow its cocoa and coffee beans in different parts of the world. The organization has used its resources and expertise – agricultural, manufacturing, distribution, and financial – to teach farmers better irrigation and harvesting techniques. Global corporations usually try to squeeze every last penny out of local farmers in order to minimize costs, which are then passed along to consumers, thus giving the corporation a competitive edge. However, after Nestlé enacted its improvements, farmers started to produce better quality coffee beans. Nestlé not only paid better prices for those higher-quality beans, they passed along a higher price to consumers, who were happy to have a better-tasting product. Economic development for the farmers and their community improved: families were able to send their children to school, the community was able to drill wells for clean drinking water, health clinics were opened, and the living conditions for everyone improved. At the same time, the improvements in production resulted in significant cost savings for Nestlé because of less waste and greater efficiencies (Sustainable Coffee Farming 2021, Porter and Kramer 2011) (see Figure 1.5 and Photo 1.8).

The original conceptualization suggests an additive effect.

But we know that there is a synergistic effect when social value and economic value are prioritized.

Figure 1.5 The concept of shared value

Source: Porter (2013)

Photo 1.8 Nestlé uses a shared value perspective in its operations

Source: Pixabay

A critical first step in shifting to a shared value perspective is for the marketing team to identify social or environmental opportunities that fit with the nature of the business. There are three ways in which a marketing team can create opportunities for shared value (Porter and Kramer 2011, p. 65):

1 *Reconceiving products and markets* to improve consumer welfare and environmental health. The goal is to not just sell more products, but to sell products that are good for consumers. For example, traditionally-run food companies create tasty foods that encourage more consumption, which can result in obesity and other health-related problems. A shared value perspective focuses attention on taste *and* health.
2 *Redefining productivity in the value chain* to improve efficiency and effectiveness, while at the same time improving environmental performance by using fewer resources and generating less waste. Organizations can optimize trucking routes, establish just-in-time inventory systems, increase recycling, shift to renewable energy, and install low-energy equipment. Less reliance on fossil fuel-based energy also makes the organization less susceptible to volatile energy prices.
3 *Enabling local cluster development* such that key business partners are geographically located close together (banking, logistics, IT, service, etc.). Productivity and innovation see synergistic improvements from these efficiencies. Further, the entire system is more effective when it is supported by a well-run community with access to education, transportation, infrastructure, and healthcare. Deficiencies in these areas increase costs for the company (such as remedial training, health insurance, lost productivity, and higher costs for warehousing and transportation).

A shared value perspective is fundamentally different from CSR (see Figure 1.6).

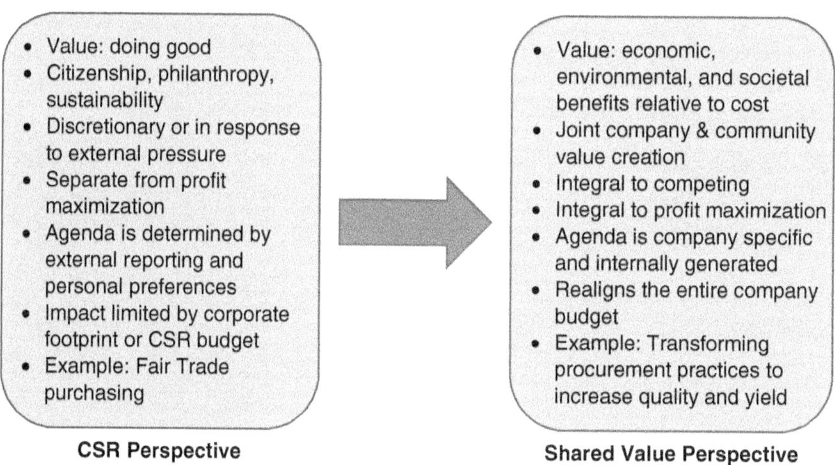

Figure 1.6 Differences between a CSR perspective and a shared value perspective

Source: Porter and Kramer (2011)

Several points need to be clarified about the concept of shared value. First, shared value is not about redistributing the value that is created among a wider array of constituents. Instead, it is about "expanding the total pool of economic and social value" (Porter and Kramer 2011, p. 65). Again, the point is that, with this shift, the number of resulting benefits for *everyone* increases; it is not a zero-sum game. Second, under a shared value perspective, management recognizes that not all profit is equal. Indeed, "profits involving a social purpose represent a higher form of capitalism – one that will enable society to advance more rapidly while allowing companies to grow even more" (p. 75). This long-term perspective uplifts both society and the organization. Finally, the vehicle by which the shared value perspective works for the organization is *profit*. Indeed, as Porter claims, "profit is magic" (2013). Why? Governments and NGOs are limited in the impact they can have because of the tax revenue they collect or the donations they receive. Once the money runs out, so does the ability to enact social and environmental change. Organizations, however, do not have such constraints. As long as the organization is able to make profit from every product it sells or service it delivers, it can continue. The solution becomes self-sustaining (Porter 2013).

BLUNDERS & INSIGHTS 1.2

Is Zuckerberg Really That Clueless?

WHAT HAPPENED: Despite his business success, Mark Zuckerberg, CEO of Facebook, sometimes seems to have an uncanny ability to be truly out of step with the world around him. Within 2 weeks in September–October of 2017, Zuckerberg engaged in two tone-deaf moves that left his public relations team trying to pick up the pieces. First, he made a bone-headed comment about the Jewish day of atonement, Yom Kippur. Religious groups and others strongly criticized the comments and an apology was issued. As if that wasn't enough, shortly thereafter, Facebook launched a promotion for its new VR app. To illustrate how "real" the new app seemed, Zuckerberg and a colleague "visited" the recently hurricane-ravaged island of Puerto Rico to "see" the devastation first-hand. "One of the things that's really magical about virtual reality is you can get the feeling that you're really in a place," Zuckerberg's avatar said. The avatars proceeded to "tour" the flooded streets and destroyed neighborhoods, all the while happily discussing the new VR app. Zuckerberg even stumbled over some of the basic facts of the storm and never actually talked about the storm's name or the extent of the devastation or human suffering. Inexplicably, the avatars even gave each other a "high five" before they left the island and moved on to their next location. Hurricane Maria was a Category 5 storm (among the strongest possible) and destroyed much of the island's infrastructure. Most people didn't get access to electricity or clean drinking water for months (Andrews 2017) and close to 3000 people died as a result of the storm and in its immediate aftermath (Newkirk 2018). Critics called the VR promotion "tone deaf," "an insensitive marketing stunt," and "the height of tastelessness" (Andrews 2017).

DEBRIEF: A shared value perspective would have clued Zuckerberg in to the real plight of the people living in Puerto Rico. Access to food, water, healthcare, sanitation, and shelter were an everyday struggle for a vast majority of the population. Such an analysis would have revealed that real lives were lost, many people were seriously injured, and the suffering was severe.

The Sustainability Perspective

Sustainable development "meets the needs of the present without compromising the ability of future generations to meet their own needs" (*Our Common Future*, Brundtland 1987, p. 16). **The sustainability perspective** builds on the shared value perspective, but places particular emphasis on the importance of the well-being of the natural environment. The sustainability perspective has some unique characteristics that collectively differentiate it from other perspectives regarding the responsibility of marketing:

- It focuses on the health of the natural environment, especially the climate. The health of the natural environment and the health of society are inextricably linked – without a thriving natural environment, neither society nor business can thrive.
- It is integrative, broadly considering a variety of challenges faced in numerous contexts, as well as potential solutions offered by different sources.
- It is flexible; it is able to meet the changing needs of different situations and contexts.
- It takes a long-term perspective, considering the long-term strategic positioning of the organization, as well as the long-term viability of society and the natural environment.
- It endeavors to outmaneuver the competition, just like any good strategy. Efforts include helping move consumers away from competitive non-sustainable choices and behaviors.
- It acknowledges that sustainability is a constantly moving target – new technologies as well as new challenges often arise.
- It nurtures and builds on the strengths of the organization and its stakeholders.
- It is objective-oriented, like any good strategy (cf. Varadarajan 2010).
- It allocates resources to achieve its objectives.

Over the last few decades, several important events and benchmarks have occurred in the evolution of thought regarding the obligation of organizations and marketing. Together, they have facilitated a move toward the sustainability framework (see Table 1.3). Importantly, these benchmarks have resulted in a paradigm shift such that influencers and everyday citizens were made more aware of the importance of the natural environment. In addition, with the establishment of several global organizations and agreements, researchers and other thought leaders have engaged in pivotal research that aids in our understanding of the natural sciences. The **Intergovernmental Panel on Climate Change (IPCC)**, for example, publishes comprehensive assessment reports and special reports on the state of the climate, its impacts, and possible mitigation strategies. This research has provided cutting-edge information that is used by governments and business leaders to enact sustainable objectives and strategies.

Table 1.3 Key benchmarks influencing the evolution of sustainability thought

Date & Event	Description
1986	The Chernobyl nuclear accident in Ukraine occurred, the worst nuclear disaster in history.
1987	The Montreal Protocol was signed, a global commitment to reduce ozone-damaging substances.
1987	The UN's Brundtland Report was released, which defined sustainable development and called for immediate action on climate change.
1988	The Intergovernmental Panel on Climate Change (IPCC) was established by the United Nations (UN) to assess and report on the science of climate change.
1995	The first annual Conference of the Parties (COP) conference was held in Berlin. COP is a collection of countries committed to reducing greenhouse gas emissions.
1995	CSR Europe, a network of business leaders committed to corporate social responsibility, was founded.
1997	The Kyoto Protocol was signed, a global commitment signed by 191 countries committed to reducing greenhouse gases.

Date & Event	Description
1999	Kofi Annan, the UN's Secretary-General, gave a speech to global business leaders calling for them to join with the UN to embrace "a global compact of shared values and principles, which will give a human face to the global market" (1999).
2000	The UN's Millennium Development Goals (MDGs) were issued. This was a list of 8 goals (regarding poverty, hunger, and health) that global leaders had hoped to achieve by 2015.
2006	*An Inconvenient Truth*, a movie that vividly depicted the damaging effects of climate change, was released.
2011	The Fukushima disaster occurred in Japan. Following a 9.0 earthquake, the nuclear plant was overwhelmed by a tsunami, resulting in the release of radioactive material.
2015	The Paris Climate Accord was signed and later ratified by 190 countries committed to reducing greenhouse gasses to limit planetary global warming to 2° C.
2016	The UN's Sustainable Development Goals (SDGs) were issued. This list of 17 items replaced the MDGs and represented a global commitment and partnership to address the planet's most pressing issues by 2030.

The front-and-center issue in the sustainability perspective is the imperative to immediately reduce carbon dioxide (CO_2) and other greenhouse gas emissions. CO_2 is released into the atmosphere with the burning of fossil fuels (oil, gas, and coal). The vast majority of climate scientists agree that accumulating amounts of CO_2 and other greenhouse gasses in the atmosphere will likely warm the planet by 1.5°C by as early as 2030 and, if left unchecked, 2.0°C by the second half of the 21st century. The results would be increased temperatures, longer droughts, sea-level rise, more intense fire seasons, and more intense storms. The social and human cost would be severe. The economic damage is inextricably linked to these devastating effects and would be just as severe, including crop and habitat loss, damaged and destroyed infrastructure, and retreat of populations from the coastlines (see IPCC 2018). Therefore, scientists, governments, and businesses agree that there is an urgent imperative to reduce CO_2 emissions.

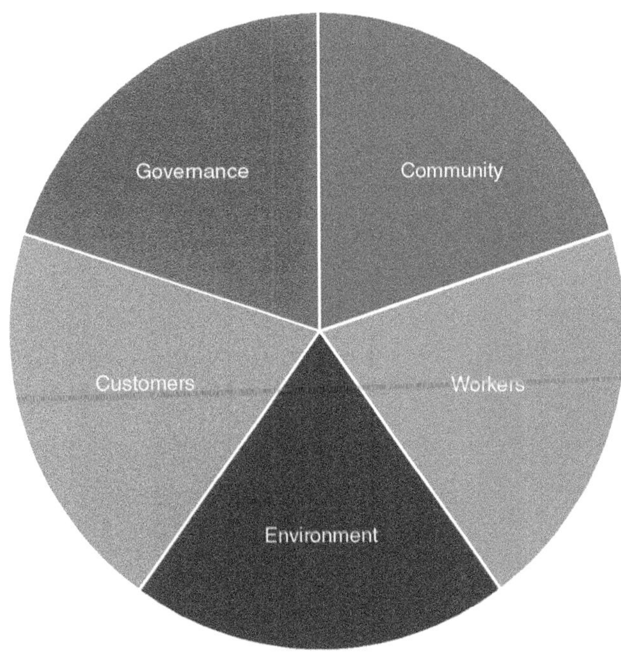

Figure 1.7 The five dimensions of B Corp™ Certification

In 2006, a new organization called B Lab was founded to respond to this call for organizations to not just exhibit greater social and environmental responsibility, but to incorporate it into the very fabric of the organization. The "B" stood for benefit and the overriding purpose of the organization was to certify companies that were operating in ways that not only had strong and transparent corporate governance, but operated to directly benefit workers, communities, the environment, and customers. Once an organization can demonstrate that it has met the minimum level of performance on each of these five dimensions, the organization becomes a "Certified B Corporation™." An organization's ratings on each of the five dimensions are available on the B Corp™ website for any interested stakeholder to see, which can attract the attention of customers and business partners. By 2022, the company had certified 6000+ organizations in 86 countries across 159 industries (A Global Community of Leaders 2022).

There are numerous benefits to B Corp Certification™, such as identifying areas where operations can become more efficient, increasing the brand's goodwill and image, attracting and retaining talented employees, and benchmarking against other like-minded organizations (Stammer 2016). There are three key strategic benefits to certification. First, B Corp Certification™ is an important differentiator in the marketplace, and brands that are differentiated from the competition perform better financially. Second, amidst a sea of greenwashing, smaller firms need to work harder to prove their sustainability credentials and certification gives them the credibility to make these claims. Third, given the prevalence of corporate misdeeds, many organizations and their leaders want to join the effort to redefine what success means in business (Kim, Karlesky, Myers, and Schiefeling 2016). Global food giant Danone, for example, received a much more favorable interest rate on a €2 billion loan because it was B Corp™ certified (Feloni 2018). Even smaller organizations can benefit from certification. Cabot Creamery is a cooperative of farmers in the Northeastern US and sells its cheeses and other dairy products to select locations around the world. It was able to leverage its B Corp Certification™ to access new markets and form important partnerships with other like-minded sustainable organizations (Stammer 2016) (see Figure 1.7).

1.6 SUMMARY

Coach Ben Ryan effectively utilized strategy to bring Olympic gold home to Fiji and, as we will find out in this book, global organizations are effectively using marketing strategy to confront some of the planet's biggest challenges, while at the same time delivering value to their customers and making a profit. This introductory chapter laid the groundwork for developing a deep understanding of marketing strategy and a skillset to help create and implement effective marketing strategies.

Marketing functions as an important bridge between the dynamics of what is happening outside the organization and those that are happening within the organization. Because of this unique position, marketing has an obligation to be particularly attuned to and responsive to some of the biggest issues facing our planet today. At its very core, the function of marketing is to deliver value to consumers. The value proposition is the set of needs that the organization satisfies for its target customers. Importantly, the organization must do this better than the competition.

Over the years, as experts and thought leaders pushed for more accountability from organizations, four key developments in the evolution of our understanding of the responsibility of marketing occurred: stakeholder theory, corporate social responsibility, shared value, and sustainability. In the end, the sustainability perspective emerged as the most strategic but also holistic and integrative way in which to approach marketing strategy. Because of this, sustainability needs to become a strategic imperative for marketing decision-makers. Indeed, there are distinct economic and competitive benefits to adopting the sustainability perspective.

Successful design and implementation of marketing strategy in the 21st century is not an easy task. Indeed, marketing decision-makers certainly have their work cut out for them – consumers can sometimes be fickle, competitors can be especially aggressive, technology is constantly changing, and reports about the health of the planet are increasingly dire. Because of this, marketing decision-makers must continuously educate themselves about their customers, competitors, trends, technological advancements, and other external threats and opportunities. In doing so, they can create and deliver effective marketing strategies.

QUESTIONS FOR REVIEW & DISCUSSION

1. Where is the marketing function located within the organization and what is its purpose? What do we mean when we say that marketing is a bridge between the internal world of the organization and the external world?
2. What exactly do we mean when we say that marketing delivers a "value proposition?" Why don't we just say that marketing delivers products?
3. Paying a higher price for a product does not necessarily mean that the customer's value proposition is higher. Discuss.
4. In what way was stakeholder theory an important first step in the evolution of our understanding of the responsibility of marketing?
5. Describe several key differences between CSR and shared value. What benefits does the shared value approach provide that CSR does not?
6. In what way is the sustainability approach *strategic*? Why do we say that sustainability is a strategic imperative for marketing?

1.7 REFERENCES

A Global Community of Leaders. 2022. Certified B Corporation. B Lab. Accessed 17 June 2022. https://bcorporation.net/?gclid=CjwKCAiAxeX_BRASEiwAc1QdkQcKKvnILqX_YKzg_LdAKMhgzNu2XoDDDnlmQfneHmGANctrRS8p7RoC4McQAvD_BwE.

About us. 2021a. CSR Europe. Accessed 13 March 2021. www.csreurope.org.

About us. 2021b. Hello Fresh. Accessed 15 March 2021. www.hellofreshgroup.com/en/about-us/.

Aileron. 2012. Keeping Your Friends Close. Forbes.com. December 27. Accessed January 10, 2021. www.forbes.com/sites/aileron/2012/12/27/keeping-your-enemies-closer/?sh=446645ff5727.

AMA. 2017. Definition of Marketing. *The American Marketing Association.* Accessed 4 January 2021. www.ama.org/the-definition-of-marketing-what-is-marketing/

Andrews,Travis M. 2017. Facebook's Mark Zuckerberg Apologizes for "Tone Deaf" Virtual Trip to Puerto Rico. *The Washington Post.* October 11. Accessed 10 January 2021. www.washingtonpost.com/news/morning-mix/wp/2017/10/11/facebooks-mark-zuckerberg-apologizes-for-tone-deaf-virtual-trip-to-puerto-rico/.

Andrews, Colman and Grant Suneson. 2018. America's 26 Top-selling Beers Show that the Country Still Likes a Cold One Now and Then. *USA Today.* 17 October. Accessed 8 January 2021. www.usatoday.com/story/money/food/2018/10/17/beer-consumption-these-americas-26-top-selling-beers/38104743/.

Associated Press. 2016. The Fijian Way: The People's Team Delivers 1st Olympic Gold. *Daily Mail.* August 11. Accessed 12 September 2019. www.dailymail.co.uk/wires/ap/article-3735149/Fiji-ensures-Olympic-medal-aims-gold.html.

Balmer, John M.T. 2011. Corporate Marketing Myopia and the Inexorable Rise of a Corporate Marketing Logic. *European Journal of Marketing, 45* (9), 1329–52.

Barnes, Brooks. 2017. Disney Makes $52.4 Billion Deal for 21st Century Fox in Big Bet on Streaming. *New York Times.* 14 December. Accessed 6 January 2021. www.nytimes.com/2017/12/14/business/dealbook/disney-fox-deal.html?smprod=nytcore-iphone&smid=nytcore-iphone-share.

BBC. 2019. "Racist" D&G Ad: Chinese Model Says Campaign Almost Ruined her Career. *BBC.* 23 January. Accessed 11 January 2021. www.bbc.com/news/world-asia-china-46968750.

Brundtland, Gro Harlem. 1987. *Report of the World Commission on Environment and Development: Our Common Future.* United Nations General Assembly. Document A/42/427.

Carpenter, Scott. 2020. After Abandoned "Beyond Petroleum" Re-brand, BP's New Renewables Push Has Teeth. *Forbes.* 4 August. Accessed 16 June 2022. www.forbes.com/sites/scottcarpenter/2020/08/04/bps-new-renewables-push-redolent-of-abandoned-beyond-petroleum-rebrand/?sh=291bd3fc1ceb.

Cohen, P. 2008. On Chicago Campus, Milton Friedman's Legacy of Controversy Continues – Correction Appended. *The New York Times.* 12 July. https://advance-lexis-com.ezproxy.sju.edu/api/document?collection=news&id=urn:contentItem:4SYT-3JD0-TW8F-G1DM-00000-00&context=1516831.

Cullinane, S. and T. Ap. 2016. Fiji: Deaths from Cyclone Winston Reach 42 as Full Scope of Disaster Unfolds. *CNN.* February 23. Accessed 18 July 2020. www.cnn.com/2016/02/22/asia/fiji-tropical-cyclone-winston/index.html.

Daye, A. 2016. Fiji Erupts into Celebration after First Olympic Gold. *CNN.* 13 August. Accessed 18 July 2020. https://edition.cnn.com/2016/08/12/sport/fiji-wins-first-olympic-gold-social-reaction/index.html.

DW News. 2018. Dolce & Gabbana Under Fire Over Racism Accusations, *DW News,* 23 November. Accessed 11 January 2021. www.youtube.com/watch?v=594Q9CJQbD4.

Ewing, J. (2019, November 18). Nestlé Says It Can Be Virtuous and Profitable. Is That Even Possible? *International New York Times,* NA. Accessed 8 January 2021. https://link.gale.com/apps/doc/A606045776/STND?u=sjuniv&sid=STND&xid=7557cccd.

Fassin, Yves. (2009). The Stakeholder Model Refined. *Journal of Business Ethics, 84,* 113–35.

Feloni, Richard. 2018. More than 2,600 Companies, Like Danone and Patagonia, are On Board with an Entrepreneur who Says the Way we Do Business Runs Counter to Human Nature and There's Only One Way Forward. *Business Insider.* 8 December. Accessed 8 January 2021. www.businessinsider.com/b-corporation-b-lab-movement-and1-cofounder-2018-11

Freeman, R. Edward. (1994). The Politics of Stakeholder Theory: Some Future Directions. *Business Ethics Quarterly, 4,* 409–21.

Freeman, R. Edward and David L. Reed. 1983. Stockholders and Stakeholders: A New Perspective on Corporate Governance. *California Management Review, 25* (3), 88–106.

Freeman, R. Edward and W.M. Evan. 1990. Corporate Governance: A Stakeholder Interpretation. *Journal of Behavioral Economics, 19,* 337–59.

Friedman, Milton. 1970. The Social Responsibility of a Firm is to Increase its Profits. *The New York Times Magazine,* September 13, 32–3.

Holmberg, A. 2017. Resilience & love in action: Rebuilding after Cyclone Winston. *The World Bank. Feature Story.* 7 November. Accessed 18 July 2020. www.worldbank.org/en/news/feature/2017/11/07/resilience-love-in-action-rebuilding-after-cyclone-winston.

Hulland, John, Mark Houston, and Anne Hoekman. 2020. Reimagining Marketing Strategy: Driving the Debate on Grand Challenges. Call for papers for a special issue and thought leadership forum for the *Journal of the Academy of Marketing Science.* 18 June. Accessed 2 January 2021. www.ama.org/listings/2020/06/18/reimagining-marketing-strategy/.

Intergovernmental Panel on Climate Change (IPCC). 2018. Summary for Policymakers. In: *Global Warming of 1.5°C. An IPCC Special Report on the impacts of global warming of 1.5°C.* Masson-Delmotte, V., lead editor. World Meteorological Organization, Geneva, Switzerland, 32 pp.

Kim, Suntae, Matthew J. Karlesky, Christopher G. Myers, and Todd Schiefeling. 2016. Why Companies are Becoming B Corporations. *Harvard Business Review,* 17 June, 1–5.

LaPlume, André O., Karan Sonpar, and Reginald A. Litz. 2008. Reviewing a Theory that Moves Us. *Journal of Management, 34* (6), 1152–89.

Latapi Agudelo, Mauricio Andres, Lara Johannsdottir, and Brynhildur Davidsdottir. 2019. A Literature Review of the History and Evolution of Corporate Social Responsibility. *International Journal of Corporate Social Responsibility, 4* (1), https://doi.org/10.1186/s40991-018-0039-y.

Levitt, Theodore. 1960. Marketing Myopia. *Harvard Business Review, 38* (4), 45–56.

McDonald, Malcolm. 2009. The Future of Marketing: Brightest Star in the Firmament, or Fading Meteor? Some Hypotheses and a Research Agenda. *Journal of Marketing Management, 25* (5–6), 431–50.

McRaney, David. 2011. *You Are Not So Smart: Why You Have Too Many Friends on Facebook, Why Your Memory is Mostly Fiction, and 46 Other Ways You're Deluding Yourself.* Gotham Books, New York.

Newkirk, Vann R. 2018. A Year After Hurricane Maria, Puerto Rico Finally Knows How Many People Died. *The Atlantic.* 28 August. Accessed 10 January 2021. www.theatlantic.com/politics/archive/2018/08/puerto-rico-death-toll-hurricane-maria/568822/.

Noel, Josh. 2017. What's Best Macro Beer in America? 3 Craft Brewers Taste Test 16. *Chicago Tribune.* 11 July. Accessed 8 January 2021. www.chicagotribune.com/dining/craving/ct-macro-beer-tasting-food-0712-20170706-story.html

Olito, Frank. 2020. The Rise and Fall of Blockbuster. *BusinessInsider.com.* 20 August. Accessed 4 January 2021. www.businessinsider.com/rise-and-fall-of-blockbuster.

Porter, Michael E. 1996. What is Strategy? *Harvard Business Review, 74* (6), 61–78.

Porter, Michael E. 2005. CEO as Strategist. *Leadership Excellence, September, 22* (9), 11.

Porter, Michael E. 2008. The Five Competitive Forces that Shape Strategy. *Harvard Business Review,* January, 79–93.

Porter, Michael E. 2013. Michael Porter: Why Business Can Be Good at Solving Social Problems. *TED.* TED Conferences, LLC. 7 October. Accessed 8 January 2021. www.youtube.com/watch?v=0iIh5YYDR2o&t=6s.

Porter, Michael E. and Mark R. Kramer. 2006. Strategy & Society: The Link Between Competitive Advantage and Corporate Social Responsibility. *Harvard Business Review.* December, 78–92.

Porter, Michael E. and Mark R. Kramer. 2011. Shared Value: How to Reinvent Capitalism—and Unleash a Wave of Innovation. *Harvard Business Review.* January–February, 62–77.

Ryan, Ben. 2018. *Sevens Heaven: The Beautiful Chaos of Fiji's Olympic Dream.* Weidenfeld & Nicholson, London, UK.

Stammer, Richard. 2016. It Pays to Become a B Corporation. *Harvard Business Review.* 6 December.

Statista. 2019. Advertising Spending of Selected Beer Manufacturers in the United States in 2019. *Statista 2021.* Accessed 8 January 2021. www.statista.com/statistics/264998/ad-spend-of-selected-beer-manufacturers-in-the-us/#:~:text=Anheuser%2DBusch%20InBev%20%E2%80%93%20the%20largest,on%20traditional%20and%20online%20media.

Sustainable Coffee Farming. 2021. Nestlé Nespresso SA. Accessed 8 January 2021. https://Nestlé-nespresso.com/views/sustainable-coffee-farming.

The Guardian, 2018. Chinese Retail Sites Drop Dolce & Gabbana Amid Racist Ad Backlash. *The Guardian*, 23 November. Accessed 11 January 2021. www.theguardian.com/world/2018/nov/23/dolce-gabbana-vanishes-from-chinese-retail-sites-amid-racist-ad-backlash.

Varadarajan, Rajan. 2010. Strategic Marketing and Marketing Strategy: Domain, Definition, Fundamental Issues and Foundational Premises. *Journal of the Academy of Marketing Science, 38*, 119–40.

Winer, Leon. 1966. A Profit-oriented Decision System. *Journal of Marketing, 30* (January), 38–44.

World Bank Data. 2018. Country Profile – Fiji. *The World Bank*. Accessed 12 September 2019. https://databank.worldbank.org/views/reports/reportwidget.aspx?Report_Name=CountryProfile&Id=b450fd57&tbar=y&dd=y&inf=n&zm=n&country=FJI.

2 MARKETING PLANNING: GOOD STRATEGY DOESN'T JUST HAPPEN

LEADERSHIP INSIGHTS 2

Photo 2.1 Bill Tierney

Source: courtesy, Bill Tierney

Bill Tierney, VP

Brian Communications

How do you plan an event for over one million people? Very carefully, that's how. When Pope Francis visited Philadelphia as part of the World Meeting of Families celebration in 2015, Bill Tierney and other experts at Brian Communications were called upon to plan the event.

Over his career, Tierney can look back at some of his most interesting and challenging projects with satisfaction. "I'm a very creatively-minded person and I worked on some pretty cool projects. One of the best was when Pope Francis made a visit to Philadelphia in 2015. This event is held every three years; one million people were expected to show up. My office had to coordinate over 2500 media people from all over the world. With extra levels of security, it was a very complex process to get reporters proper access to the events," recalled Tierney. The eyes of the world were watching.

As soon as Philadelphia was selected as the host city a full 18 months before the event, Tierney and his team started setting objectives for the event. "Our goal from the initial announcement was to create excitement from the start. We wanted everyone involved – the entire city," Tierney remembered. The team at Brian Communications had three broad objectives: (1) position Philadelphia as a world-class city; (2) achieve record attendance; and (3) achieve significant corporate sponsorships.

In order to achieve these objectives, the team created a detailed set of strategies and tactics. For example, to help achieve the objectives of record attendance and corporate sponsorships, the team knew they needed to be welcoming to everyone. "We wanted to include all religions, not just Catholics or even Christian denominations. By positioning it as a milestone moment in the history of Philadelphia and not as a religious event, large corporations such as Aramark, Campbell Soup, and Comcast were excited to support it. Prominent business leaders from all faiths were included; the budget was $54 million," he recalled.

In order to fulfill the objectives of positioning Philadelphia as a world-class city and achieving record attendance, the team engaged with locals to inform the global audience about the city, including its famed mural arts program. Philadelphia has an extensive and dynamic mural arts program with over 4000 murals throughout the city – the most of any city on earth. "Wells Fargo was one of the major sponsors and they wanted to create a new mural. We thought we could have 10 separate events – in Philadelphia, Delaware, New Jersey, and the suburbs – and at each one of the events, we created a paint-by-number system of smaller panels. People were invited to come to one of the locations and paint a panel that would later be assembled into a giant mural. Anyone could participate. The important thing was these events were in different media markets so we would have broad media coverage; we didn't want to saturate the local media. We also wanted to involve all kinds of different schools – trade and technical, public, and private schools. In the end, over 2700 people participated. Then, we realized that we qualified for recognition from the Guinness Book of World Records; they came out and certified the mural. Pope Francis even signed one of the panels of the mural while he was on stage," reported Tierney.

Under Tierney's direction, the team worked tirelessly to coordinate and enact these and other strategies to fulfill the three objectives for the event. To create further support and engagement, the team created a fully-integrated print, outdoor, and online campaign. In the end, the event brought hundreds of thousands of people to the city and placed Philadelphia at the center of global attention during the 4-day event. Importantly, Pope Francis used his platform to urge leaders to work with the global community to fight climate change (see Photo 2.2). Later in 2015, the Paris Climate Accord would be signed. In terms of key performance indicators (KPIs), the efforts resulted in over one billion global media impressions, 84 "front pages" in the US, and one million attendees of the Pope's outdoor mass.

Photo 2.2 Philadelphia, 2015: Pope Francis delivers a message on sustainability

Source: Governor Tom Wolf

To what does Tierney attribute this success? Hard work, intuition, a natural affinity for communications, and some great mentors along the way. If Tierney could give his own 20-year-old self some advice it would be: "be open to opportunities. I wanted to work in real estate and finance! While I was in college, I took a course in political science media. I really didn't know what I wanted to do with it, but it seemed kind of interesting. It was the course that changed everything for me. Once I took it, I got hooked on communications."

2.1 GOOD PLANNING RESULTS IN SYNERGIES

The Migros ("me-gro") Group is Switzerland's biggest employer. This complex organization with over 106,000 employees achieved sales of 27 billion CHF in 2019, a growth of 0.8% over the previous year (2019 in Brief 2019). Founded in 1925 as a cooperative, the Migros Group works directly with suppliers to eliminate the proverbial "middleman" and bring high-quality, fresh products to its customers at the lowest possible prices. Grocery is the biggest part of Migros' business, with additional operations in travel, financial services, education, hotels, bookstores, electronics, housewares, and convenience stores. Migros keeps its prices low on its most popular items, while increasing the quality of its store-brand items, ensuring that its customers can easily access high-quality, sustainable, and healthy products.

From the very beginning of its existence, Migros was concerned about weaving sustainability into the fabric of all the organization's operations (Phillips 2013; The History of Migros 2021).

Much of this focus on sustainability can be directly attributed to the organization's leadership. Indeed, the Swiss have a great fondness for Migros and its founder, Gottlieb Duttweiler, who stressed the importance of being financially successful, but also giving back to society. In one survey of Swiss citizens, he ranks second only to Albert Einstein as the most influential Swiss citizen of all time. Duttweiler's organizational philosophy is often quoted by admirers: "we recognize and accept the fact that the bigger a company is, the stronger it must commit itself to a greater good. A commitment that exceeds commercial aspects but is directed to finding solutions for problems faced by mankind" (Phillips 2013, p. 111).

The organization's operations are not just well coordinated, they are carefully designed to achieve synergistic effects in meeting and exceeding the needs of consumers. In 2019, the organization trimmed several businesses because of less-than-ideal fit (2019 in Brief 2019). This streamlining effort helped it better focus its efforts on finding ways to deliver value to customers. One synergy that Migros has achieved is within the transportation division and its efforts to decarbonize road traffic. Migros occupies a leading position in rail freight transport in Switzerland, and where possible, shipments have been moved from truck to rail, a low-carbon method of transportation. One consequence of this is that its trucking operations have also been made more efficient, resulting in fewer stops and a greater number of trucks running at full capacity, which also results in CO_2 savings. Another synergy is found in the operations of two of its SBUs: travel planning services and hotels. These organizations share resources and data to provide clients with the vacations they desire at reasonable prices.

Photo 2.3 Migros trucks powered with natural gas are more efficient and cleaner than trucks powered with diesel

Source: Shutterstock/Judith Linine

Careful and thoughtful planning has made it possible to achieve these synergies, while still delivering unparalleled customer value. Shortly after the Paris Climate Accord was signed in 2015, the Migros Group restructured its organizational plan such that sustainability became completely woven into the fabric of the company's organizational and marketing plans. To achieve its objectives, Migros has combined its technology, IT, and logistics departments in order to maximize these sustainability-related efficiencies and synergies throughout the entire organization. As a result, the organization was able to scale its operations and share its operational and sustainability expertise with other stakeholders. These efforts have worked. In 2019, an independent global organization examined the sustainability efforts of 243 global retailers and the Migros Group received the highest rating of all of them (2019 in Brief 2019). This chapter is about strategic planning and the synergies that can exist when a plan is well-conceived and executed (see Photo 2.3).

2.2 LEARNING OBJECTIVES

After studying this chapter, you will be able to do the following:

1 Sketch out the critical steps involved in creating a marketing plan.
2 Describe the critical importance of the value proposition to marketing planning.
3 Compare and contrast the three methods by which the marketing team can draw inspiration for the development of marketing objectives.
4 Create an argument for how the marketing strategy would benefit from utilizing the United Nations' (UN) sustainable development goals.
5 Develop a set of meaningful marketing objectives using the SMART format.

2.3 THE MARKETING PLAN

Organizational strategy and marketing strategy are inextricably linked because the activities of the marketing department fit under the overall umbrella of the organization's priorities and strategies. Once the organization has established its mission and vision, the marketing team will then operate within that framework and establish its own strategy to help achieve the organization's strategy. In short, the marketing strategy helps achieve the organizational strategy. It consists of "big ideas" and goals that the marketing team wishes to achieve, from a competitive, customer, and market standpoint. This chapter is devoted to one of the most important tasks that can be undertaken by the marketing team: creating a marketing plan. The **marketing plan** consists of a deliberate set of steps that are designed to achieve the marketing strategy; it is the marketing team's roadmap for achieving the marketing strategy (see Figure 2.1).

Figure 2.1 The Marketing Plan

The Situation Analysis

The first part of the marketing plan is an assessment of the current state of affairs, the **situation analysis**. The purpose of the situation analysis is to determine how well the organization is set up to implement a set of objectives. The marketing team will pay particular attention to its existing customers and its target market. It will also carefully examine the nature of the competitive landscape and will identify any trends that are relevant. During this process, the marketing team will likely conduct a **SWOT analysis** to identify internal strengths and weaknesses, as well as external opportunities and threats (see Figure 2.2).

The marketing team will first carefully examine the organization from an insider's perspective. **Strengths** are positive internal factors that will help an organization succeed in its efforts to achieve objectives. Strengths might include, for example, a proprietary process or patent, exclusive access to certain markets or resources, or especially strong relationships with customers. **Weaknesses** are negative internal factors that could hinder the organization's efforts toward achieving its objectives and might include, for example, high employee turnover, less-than-efficient internal processes, or financial constraints. Next, the marketing team will examine a variety of factors that are external to the organization. **Opportunities** are positive external factors that could potentially be leveraged to help the organization succeed in achieving its objectives.

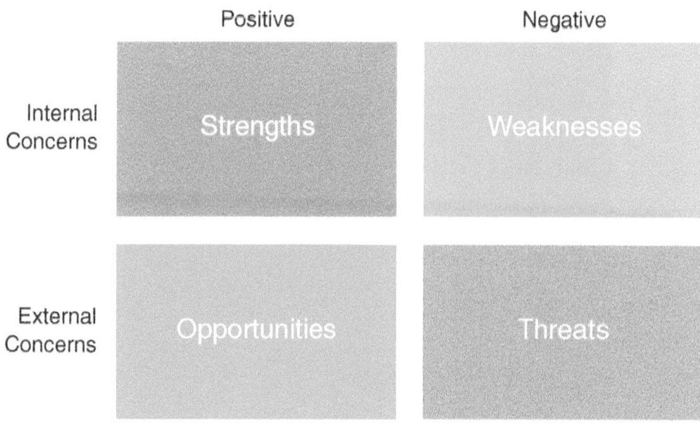

Figure 2.2 The four dimensions of a SWOT analysis

Examples of opportunities could be a shift in a demographic or cultural trend that is favorable to the organization. Perhaps a competitor has a patent that is expiring or perhaps a new market is becoming newly accessible. Any of these external developments could potentially assist the marketing team's efforts in carrying out its objectives. Finally, **threats** are negative external factors that could damage the team's ability to fulfil its objectives. Here, examples might include the implementation of a new regulation, new tariffs, new taxes, or higher interest rates. An especially aggressive competitor, restricted access to resources or raw materials, or changes in the natural environment such as increased likelihood of flooding, sea level rise, droughts, fires, severe storms, etc. could also be classified as threats.

A thorough examination of external influences will also likely include a **PESTLE Analysis**, which involves a careful consideration of the political, economic, sociocultural, technological, legal, and environmental influences on the marketing team's ability to deliver the value proposition to the consumer. By enumerating each of these external influences, the marketing team will have a more complete, multidimensional understanding of the context in which it will deploy its marketing strategy (see Figure 2.3).

Climate Change as a Threat

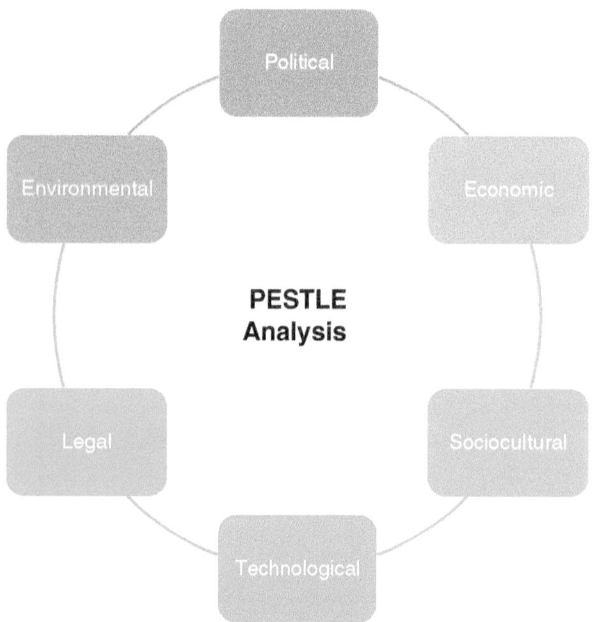

Figure 2.3 The 6 dimensions of a PESTLE Analysis

Scientists are in agreement: as a result of the burning of fossil fuels, unprecedented levels of CO_2 and other greenhouse gasses have accumulated in the atmosphere and are warming the planet. In over 800,000 years of planetary history, concentrations of these gasses in the atmosphere have never been this high. This effect is not a natural phenomenon; humankind is doing this. This increased warming has resulted in unprecedented changes to the climate system and, if left unchecked, the continued burning of fossil fuels will cause continued warming, long-lasting damage, and an increasing "likelihood of severe, pervasive, and irreversible impacts for people and ecosystems" (IPCC 2014, p. 8).

Organizations, consumers, and stakeholders exist and operate in this new era of climate upheaval. Globally, temperatures have already increased, glaciers and snowcaps have melted, and sea levels have risen (IPCC 2014). As stronger storms, droughts, fires, and other natural disasters occur in the future, disruptions to business operations and consumer lives will occur. A combination of high winds, low visibility, and human error, for example, caused a massive ship hauling

Photo 2.4 Several seasons of drought have led to intense fires throughout Australia

Source: Melanie Lazarow

close to 20,000 shipping containers that were bound for European markets to become stuck in the Suez Canal for 6 days in the spring of 2021 (Russon 2021). This blockage caused delays for almost 450 other ships, which had to wait until special diggers and higher tides could be used to free the 400-meter ship out of the sandy embankment. Experts estimated that 12% of global trade, or $9.6 billion, passes through the canal each day, most of it originating from Asia (Russon 2021). After the ship was freed, the Suez Canal Authority seized the ship and slapped the owners with a $916 million fine (Van Boom and Keane 2021). In the summer of 2021, Australia experienced a heatwave that broke records and sparked wildfires throughout the country. Temperatures inched close to 50°C in Sydney's western suburbs, with temperatures reaching 80°C on carpark surfaces and 100°C on playground equipment in the area. Experts predict that large swaths of these locations may need to be abandoned in the coming decades because the intensity of the heat will be too great for human habitation (Purtill 2021) (see Photo 2.4).

These are not isolated incidents. Indeed, every human on Earth will be directly and/or indirectly impacted in the coming decades by climate change. Over the next few decades, scientists predict that heatwaves in all parts of the planet will last longer and be more intense, extreme precipitation events will be more intense and frequent, the oceans will continue to acidify, and sea levels will rise even more (IPCC 2014). This means that coastal communities will need to be abandoned as people move away from the rising seas; as many as one billion people will need to move to higher ground by the year 2100 (Kulp and Strauss 2019). Agricultural and aquacultural systems around the world will be strained to the point of collapse; naval bases, ports, and other infrastructure at sea level will need to be abandoned; and countless non-human species will become extinct.

ENDURING INSIGHTS 2.1

"Victory comes from finding opportunities in problems."– Sun Tzu, ancient Chinese military strategist

Even against overwhelming odds, it is still possible to achieve success. In looking at the severity of the climate crisis, it is easy to become discouraged and revert to old strategies that have worked in the past. However, smart strategists will find a way to adjust their thinking, question long-held assumptions, and try things others will not try. Strategic thinking breaks with the equilibrium of our normal way of thinking and *creates* new opportunities in the marketplace (Zinkhan and Pereira 1994).

Climate Action as an Opportunity

Climate change will certainly be a threat to consumer and organizational efforts. However, efforts at *climate action* can open opportunities for the marketing team. Remember, as described in the SWOT analysis, an external opportunity is a macro-level trend that can be leveraged by the marketing team to help fulfill its objectives. How can climate action be an opportunity? First, for those organizations that are already implementing sustainability-related changes into their operations, existing environmental regulations could offer the opportunity to successfully compete for consumers. In short, for organizations that have already made the hard choices to be more sustainable, regulations could open up new markets that were not previously accessible. For example, the European Climate Law has a goal to reduce CO_2 emissions by 55% by 2030 and to become climate neutral by 2050 (Council of the EU 2020). Any organization that offers solutions to businesses, governments, and consumers to help achieve their goals will have a competitive advantage. Opportunities like this exist throughout the world for organizations that are already ahead of their competitors on the sustainability journey. Second, a pool of hard-working and highly-motivated talent exists in the sustainability space. More business schools are offering sustainable programs, including sustainable MBAs (Jack 2020). Further, once these talented individuals arrive at organizations that align with their values, they tend to stay. Across a variety of business sectors, one study found that 57% of employees were actively looking for new job opportunities, but that number dropped to 7% for those who felt that their company was making a strong positive impact in the world (WeSpire 2021) (see Photo 2.5). Third, because there is growing consensus among consumers that organizations should shoulder more responsibility in addressing the climate crisis, any organization that steps into this space will likely be rewarded for its efforts. A huge majority of UK and US consumers – 88% – believe that brands should help consumers be more environmentally friendly and ethical in their daily lives. Given this high level of expectation, organizations that do *not* offer sustainable solutions to consumers are making a risky choice (Townsend 2018).

Photo 2.5 Sustainable organizations attract and retain top talent

Source: Pixabay

Target Market Analysis

After the situation analysis is complete, the next step in developing the marketing plan is to identify the target market and conduct a target market analysis. The **target market** is the subset of individuals in the overall market to which the organization will direct its marketing efforts. Few organizations have the resources to get their message in front of every individual in the entire market. Nor should they. Despite what a marketing team may wish to think, there are some people who will never be interested in the product, so approaching these individuals with a carefully-crafted message is a waste of their time and the organization's resources. Individuals within a target market should all exhibit a similar reaction to the organization's marketing efforts and have the means to purchase the firm's offering. A **target market analysis** is an in-depth look at the individuals in the target market, with the purpose of identifying the primary forces that impact decision-making. This analysis is so important to the development of the marketing plan, that an entire chapter is devoted to it later in this textbook. However, for now, it is important to know that, just like the organization is impacted by internal and external influences, consumers are also subjected to internal and external influences. By the end of this step in the marketing plan, the marketing team should know exactly what makes its customers tick.

Internal Influences on the Consumer

In assessing the internal influences on the consumer, the team will examine a variety of psychological dimensions that are relevant to the consumer. According to the British Psychological Society, **psychology** is the "scientific study of the mind and how it influences our behavior" (BPS 2021). The marketing team might attempt to identify core values that are important to the target market. It would also be interested in identifying the target market's interests and activities. Other important questions would be: What are their attitudes on a variety of topics? What previous experience do they have with the product or service in question? What emotions do they experience when they use our product or service? What expectations do they have?

External Influences on the Consumer

The marketing team will also examine a host of sociocultural factors that may influence the target market. According to the British Sociological Association, **sociology** "seeks to provide insights into, and evidence about, the many forms of relationships among people, both formal and informal" (BSA 2021). Here, the marketing team will examine how individuals in the target market are influenced by their families, friends, cultures, subcultures, and other individuals and reference groups. The team would also likely assess the strength and nature of these influences, as well as a variety of broad cultural trends.

BLUNDERS & INSIGHTS 2.1

Moldy Whoppers? No Thanks

WHAT HAPPENED? A few months into the global pandemic of 2020, restaurants and many other customer-facing businesses around the world were shut down. Competition in the fast food and takeout category became more heated as consumers longed for a break from cooking at home. Enter Burger King. The original intent was good – to introduce customers to its new all-natural recipes, including the iconic Whopper. The execution, however, is where this campaign failed. In a time-lapse video, a beautiful, freshly-cooked Whopper was shown as it slowly decayed and turned green. The message was supposed to reinforce the notion that Whoppers do not contain any artificial preservatives.

DEBRIEF: This is an example of not knowing your target market. At the time this campaign was launched, there were a lot of unknowns with regard to the global Covid-19 pandemic. Many people were still unsure about whether they should sanitize their groceries, mail, or takeout containers, and in the very early days of the crisis, experts were providing conflicting advice. Consumers were prioritizing health, cleanliness, and safety. Understandably, at a time when consumers were hyper-concerned about viruses and germs, the moldy Whopper did not exactly instill a sense of confidence or comfort.

Marketing Objectives

The next step in the development of an effective marketing plan is the development of a set of **marketing objectives**, a clear statement of the results that the marketing team expects to achieve. In creating a set of objectives, the marketing team needs to take into account the organization's SWOT and be forward-leaning; it is not simply enough to stand still. Insights generated from the target market analysis are used to predict the behavior of customers in our target market. In creating marketing objectives, the goal is to out-maneuver the competition to serve those customers better. A well-constructed objective statement accomplishes a few things: (1) it provides clarity to the rest of the team and stakeholders; (2) it provides a rationale for the allocation of the budget; (3) it provides a benchmark for assessment – did we do what we set out to do?; and (4) it motivates the team to work hard to achieve those objectives.

ENDURING INSIGHTS 2.2

"If a man knows not what harbor he seeks, any wind is the right wind." – Seneca, Roman statesman and scholar

This quote emphasizes the importance of having an objective that guides decisions and behaviors. As applied to marketing, objectives direct the team's attention, efforts, and resources toward fulfilling those objectives. Importantly, clearly articulated objectives provide clarity and a sense of shared purpose for the team.

Creating a set of cogent objectives is not an easy task because it requires both backward thinking (What do we know about our target market? What worked or didn't work in the past?) and forward thinking (How will our target market react? What external trends and opportunities can we leverage? How will the competition react?). The following sections explore the process of creating marketing objectives. First, how do marketing managers come up with inspiration for what to do? Second, how do marketing managers construct meaningful objectives?

Generating Inspiration for Marketing Objectives

Sometimes the direction forward is an obvious one. The target market, the competition, or the environment evolves or changes in a way that the marketing department needs to respond to with a marketing plan. Sometimes, however, the way forward is less obvious.

BCG Growth Matrix

One way to generate inspiration for how a marketing team can deliver value is with a tool that was designed by the Boston Consulting Group (BCG), the **BCG Growth Matrix**, which helps identify potential areas for market growth. First, the marketing team "positions" the organization's products or product lines on a two-dimensional grid with relative market share and market growth rate as the two dimensions. Second, depending on where the products or product lines are positioned in the grid, a set of objectives is developed that is appropriate for the product and the market conditions. The underlying principle in the BCG Growth Matrix is that the value of a product depends upon obtaining a leading market share position before market growth starts to slow (Henderson

1970). **Stars** are in an ideal position in the marketplace, with high share and high growth. They generate significant sales, but also require significant resources to maintain and improve their level of performance. **Cash cows** are also in a favored position, with high market share, albeit slow growth. Basically, the resources needed to maintain these products is eclipsed by the sales they generate – certainly a good position in which to sit. **Question marks** currently have low market share, but exist in a market that is growing, so it is unclear what the future may hold. Allocating significant resources could shift these products into the star category. Alternatively, depending on the competitive landscape, it might be more prudent to only judiciously allocate resources here. Finally, **dogs** occupy a very unattractive position with low relative market share and low market growth rate. Allocating resources to these products would be futile. Instead, marketers should look elsewhere for more attractive opportunities (Hax and Majluf 1983) (see Photo 2.6).

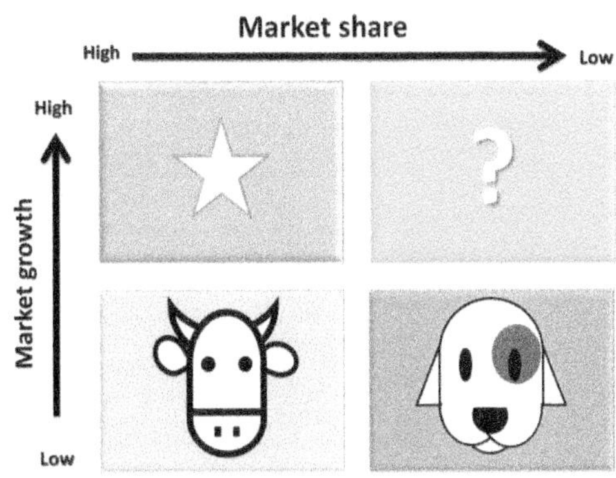

Photo 2.6 The BCG Growth Matrix

Source: mindroom14 / Shutterstock

Blue Ocean Strategy

Another tool for generating ideas for marketing objectives is through implementation of the **Blue Ocean Strategy**, which stresses the importance of avoiding direct competition in the marketplace and instead, identifying uncontested space in which to do business. This is not an easy proposition, but consider the success of Cirque de Soleil. Competing head-to-head with other circuses would have been costly and ineffective because several well-entrenched competitors were already in the marketplace and there was little room for a new entrant. Significant barriers also existed, including the upkeep and equipment necessary for the animal acts and other acts. On top of that, a variety of social trends indicated that customers were losing interest in the circus. Cirque de Soleil, however, identified a new market: sophisticated and dramatic acrobatic performances set to arresting music. This new market was created from combining elements of the circus with theater. It is important to recognize that finding a Blue Ocean is not about developing a new innovation; it is about delivering something that customers value. **Red Oceans**, by contrast, are characterized by fierce competition and downward price pressure (see Figure 2.4). If implemented correctly, a Blue Ocean Strategy will create new demand where there was none, render the competition irrelevant, and disprove the notion that customers have to pay more to get more (Kim and Mauborgne 2004) (see Photo 2.7).

There are at least four distinct advantages to the Blue Ocean Strategy. First, demand for the product is created, rather than fought over. The first entrant to a new market is the one that establishes the parameters by which value is delivered to consumers. In communicating with its customers and other stakeholders, the organization is unencumbered by any existing marketplace standards, because there are none. In a related vein, a second advantage is that it creates its own barriers to entry, including economic barriers (because of benefits of scale) and psychological barriers (because anything else would be an "imitation"). Cirque de Soleil is a "stand alone" experience and no other competitor could legitimately jump into the marketplace and copy it. Third, in the minds of consumers, organizations will enjoy long-lasting differentiation from the competition. Finally, brand equity is strengthened for organizations that utilize a Blue Ocean Strategy. **Brand equity** is the monetary value of the brand, over and above another unbranded version of the product. Consumers will likely develop a preference for the brand and may even be willing to spend more money to get it (Kim and Mauborgne 2004).

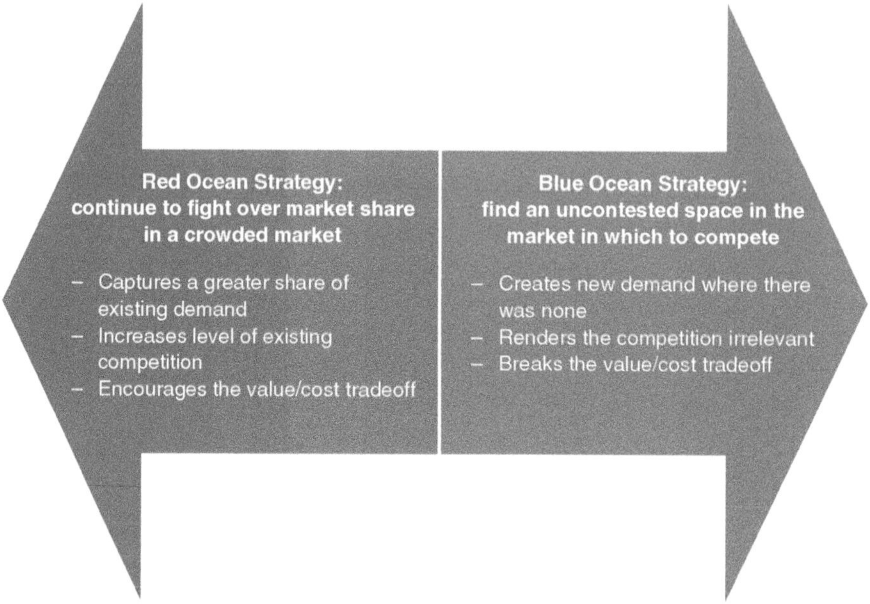

Red Ocean Strategy: continue to fight over market share in a crowded market

- Captures a greater share of existing demand
- Increases level of existing competition
- Encourages the value/cost tradeoff

Blue Ocean Strategy: find an uncontested space in the market in which to compete

- Creates new demand where there was none
- Renders the competition irrelevant
- Breaks the value/cost tradeoff

Figure 2.4 Blue Oceans vs. Red Oceans

Source: adapted from Kim and Mauborgne (2004)

Photo 2.7 Cirque de Soleil utilized a Blue Ocean Strategy

Sustainable Development Goals (SDGs)

A third possibility for generating inspiration for the development of relevant marketing objectives starts with an examination of the **Sustainable Development Goals (SDGs)** from the United Nations (UN). The SDGs are a set of 17 goals that the member states of the UN officially adopted in 2016. They are designed to promote global sustainable development and address some of the most pressing issues of our time. Importantly, these goals are interconnected with and interdependent on one another because they recognize that economic development goes hand-in-hand with tackling climate change and improving social problems (Hoek 2018, The 17 Goals 2021). Businesses, governments, and NGOs worked together to craft the 17 SDGs (Hoek 2018), representing a true partnership of thought and commitment in fostering a more sustainable planet for us all. The 17 SDGs are accompanied by a comprehensive set of 169 specific targets and 230 indicators (Hoek 2018) with the overall goal to promote and strengthen global peace and prosperity (The 17 Goals 2021) (see Figure 2.5). Experts predict that the SDGs will open up vast market opportunities. Even conservative estimates say that the SDGs will generate market opportunities of over $12 trillion per year by 2030 (Elkington 2018).

Figure 2.5 The Sustainable Development Goals (SDGs)

Source: The United Nations

The SDGs have helped direct the strategic course of action for governments, non-profit organizations, and for-profit organizations. Global communications giant Huawei has identified a set of SDGs that are particularly relevant to its work, including quality education (SDG4), good health and well-being (SDG3), and industry, innovation, and infrastructure (SDG9). Recognizing that different technologies can address different consumer needs, Huawei developed an index to assess a country's information and communications technology capabilities and then recommend specific products that can help that country make improvements. For example, when the index was used in Ghana in 2017, it became very clear that broadband access needed to be improved. Only 0.3% of people there had home broadband access and foreign direct investment had just fallen by 11% over the previous year. By deploying specific Huawei products that improved and expanded broadband access, Ghana was able to make clear and significant improvements in these SDGs (Huawei 2019), which also made the country more attractive for foreign direct investment (see Photo 2.8).

The SDGs can be particularly useful in providing direction for the development of a set of marketing objectives. Take the example of SDG10: reduced inequalities. Tommy Adaptive is a line of clothing from Tommy Hilfiger, designed to help individuals who have reduced motor capabilities. Adaptive clothing (or "inclusive fashion") includes, for example, magnet closures on shirts instead of buttons, or side seam openings on pants and shirts to fit prosthetic limbs. An important component in the line's success is the fact that the design process itself is inclusive; individuals with a range of different abilities collaborate on the styles, fabrics, and other elements. Even the online shopping experience is accessible for people living with a range of visual, auditory, and cognitive experiences. Tommy Adaptive products are available in Europe, the US, Australia, and Japan. Globally, the adaptive clothing market is estimated to be worth $64.3 billion and Tommy Adaptive was the first mainstream fashion house in this category, something that gives them a great sense of pride. Luxury powerhouse LVMH has also announced a commitment to this market (Webb 2021a), as have numerous other fashion brands. Adaptive clothing is also, by the way, a product of Blue Ocean thinking. Before Tommy Hilfiger entered the market in 2016, adaptive clothing was made by several medical garment companies that focused on functionality, to the exclusion of style.

Photo 2.8 Students in Ghana benefitted when broadband access expanded in the country

Source: Pixabay

Global style and beauty brand L'Oréal has made great strides in the last decade in developing cutting-edge chemistry to incorporate sustainable ingredients into its products. These innovations are examples of important steps toward SDG14 and SDG15 (life below water and life on land). Headquartered in Paris, the L'Oréal Group manages 35 brands and achieves €28 billion in annual sales. L'Oréal ensures that all of its global operations comply with strict European standards of product safety, where 1300 different substances are banned from use in cosmetics. L'Oréal's efforts toward sustainability have been impressive, with €1 billion invested and a global team of 4000 researchers working to help the organization reach its goals by 2030. Of special note is the goal to source 95% of its ingredients from "renewable plant sources, abundant minerals, or circular processes." Why is this a priority? Researchers have concluded that the organization's most severe environmental impacts can be attributed to the products' ingredients and packaging. The organization has already made considerable strides toward achieving its goals. In 2020, 80% of L'Oréal's ingredients were easily biodegradable and 59% were renewable.

These accomplishments have been carefully tracked, are transparent, and have been verified by external experts (Webb 2021b). One benefit of using an SDG approach for the development of marketing objectives is that it expands the range of possibilities that would be considered relevant domains for the marketing team. Table 2.1 illustrates just a sampling of the possibilities that could be considered relevant areas for the marketing team in its efforts toward developing marketing objectives (see Photo 2.9).

Table 2.1 The Sustainable Development Goals (SDGs)

SDG	Description
1 No poverty	To end poverty in all its forms everywhere by 2030. *Marketing connections: sourcing ingredients or other materials from organizations such as the Fairtrade Organization, which promotes a fair and living wage for agricultural and manufacturing workers around the world.*
2 Zero hunger	To end hunger, achieve food security and improved nutrition, and promote sustainable agriculture. *Marketing connections: using drought-resistant grains in the production of food and beverage products; a variety of food and beverage companies have already identified drought-resistant grains that can be used in food production (c.f. Siegner 2019).*
3 Good health and well-being	To ensure healthy lives and promote well-being for all at all ages. *Marketing connections: developing phone apps and wearable technology that can track key indicators of an individual's health, such as blood pressure or blood sugar levels.*
4 Quality education	To ensure inclusive and quality education for all and promote lifelong learning. *Marketing connections: designing educational laptops and Wifi service that can be solar-powered, enabling children in remote areas to access the world's libraries and online courses.*
5 Gender equality	To achieve gender equality and empower all women and girls. *Marketing connections: establishing policies to encourage partnerships with women-owned businesses; including women on new product research and design teams.*
6 Clean water and sanitation	To ensure access to safe water sources and sanitation for all. *Marketing connections: educating people about the importance of handwashing. Thousands of people in developing countries die every year from bacterial infections that can easily be prevented by better handwashing. Unilever sells a variety of soaps and detergents, some in single-use packets, to these areas.*

(Continued)

Table 2.1 (Continued)

SDG	Description
7 Affordable and clean energy	To ensure access to affordable, reliable, sustainable, and modern energy for all. *Marketing connections: developing products that require less energy or no energy to operate; creating products that are easily and conveniently recharged.*
8 Decent work and economic growth	To promote inclusive and sustainable economic growth, employment, and decent work for all. *Marketing connections: encouraging consumers to think about the long-term and sustainable implications of the products they buy, thus resulting in increased demand for well-made, long-lasting products, which results in the need for more skilled workers.*
9 Industry, innovation, and infrastructure	To build resilient infrastructure, promote inclusive and sustainable industrialization, and foster innovation. *Marketing connections: designing new products to consume less electricity; using fewer resources to manufacture products; using renewable energy to manufacture products; creating systems to collect used and broken products.*
10 Reduced inequalities	To reduce inequalities within and among countries. *Marketing connections: designing products for people with disabilities; incorporating people from marginalized groups in marketing communications; hiring people from marginalized groups for customer-facing interactions.*
11 Sustainable cities and communities	To make cities inclusive, safe, resilient, and sustainable. *Marketing connections: selecting locations for brick-and-mortar operations in geographic areas that have demonstrated a commitment to the development and maintenance of infrastructure, as well as a concentrated set of other amenities, such as housing, schools, shopping, and leisure. Concentrated operations reduce the distances needed to travel and, thus, CO_2 emissions.*
12 Responsible consumption and production	To ensure sustainable consumption and production patterns. *Marketing connections: designing new products to be easily disassembled so that the component parts can be reused or recycled; educating consumers about sustainable consumption; nudging consumers toward more sustainable choices.*
13 Climate action	Taking urgent action to tackle climate change and its impacts. *Marketing connections: manufacturing and delivering products with net zero carbon emissions. In India, Amazon announced a plan to add 10,000 fully electric delivery vehicles by 2025 (c.f. Bhalla 2021).*

SDG	Description
14 Life below water	To conserve and sustainably use the world's ocean, seas, and marine resources. *Marketing connections: to address the issue of the vast amount of plastic in the oceans, designing products with recycled plastic components; sourcing seafood from organizations that protect marine life, such as the Marine Stewardship Council.*
15 Life on land	To sustainably manage forests, combat desertification, halt and reverse land degradation, and halt biodiversity loss. *Marketing connections: sourcing wood and paper products from organizations that protect forests, such as the Forest Stewardship Council; encouraging cities and countries to expand their recycling efforts.*
16 Peace, justice, and strong institutions	To promote peaceful and inclusive societies for sustainable development, provide access to justice for all, and build effective, accountable, and inclusive institutions at all levels. *Marketing connections: avoiding ingredients and materials from conflict zones; promoting collaborations and partnerships with organizations that promote social and environmental justice.*
17 Partnerships for the goals	To revitalize the global partnership for sustainable development. *Marketing connections: fostering partnerships with global sustainability organizations in sustainability; promoting transparency in sustainability, and obtaining certification for sustainable processes from organizations such as B Lab.*

Source: The United Nations

Photo 2.9 Sustainability in Vatican City

Constructing the Marketing Objectives

As marketing objectives are being created, remember that they must be consistent with other organizational-level objectives. A number of experts have recommended step-by-step guides or standards to use when constructing compelling objectives.

Big, hairy, audacious goals (BHAGs)

One of these standards suggests that objectives should be big and bold; they should be "shoot for the moon" goals and be difficult to achieve, but inspirational for the marketing team. These types of objectives are called **BHAGs** ("bee-hags"), which stands for big, hairy, audacious goals. Think about a small player in the marketplace that sets an objective of achieving a commanding share of the market, doubling its customer satisfaction ratings, or introducing a completely new-to-the-market innovative product. When an organization works to reach these kinds of objectives, the effect is a dramatic improvement in the organization's fundamental capabilities; it becomes a stronger and more competitive player in the marketplace. Further, the leadership team gains confidence and experience to be ready for the next BHAG (Collins 1999).

Specific, measurable, attainable, realistic, and time-bound (SMART) objectives

Another standard by which objectives can be constructed is the SMART format. A wide variety of for-profit and not-for-profit organizations have utilized the SMART format to create objectives. **SMART objectives** are specific, measurable, achievable, realistic, and time-bound. More specifically, objectives should be:

- *Specific* – provide as much detail as possible about what will be accomplished.
- *Measurable* – specify a clear criterion or KPI by which the objective can be assessed.
- *Attainable* – ask: does the organization have the internal capabilities in terms of skills, time, and funding to achieve this objective?
- *Realistic* – ask: is the objective reasonable – not too high and not too low?
- *Time-bound* – provide a deadline by which the objective will be accomplished.

The closer an objective comes to satisfying each of the five dimensions, the more likely it will be able to provide clear guidance for the marketing team. The development of SMART objectives needs to take into account a variety of contextual and environmental factors (Bjerke and Renger 2017). Properly constructed, SMART objectives provide important direction and motivation to the team; everyone knows exactly what needs to be achieved and the **key performance indicators (KPIs)** – the measures by which success will be assessed, such as market share, profit, or sales – are clear. In addition, SMART objectives provide a rationale for saying "no" to projects or initiatives that do not specifically enhance the chances of achieving the objectives (Morton 2011). Table 2.2 provides an analysis of three separate objective statements, using the SMART criteria.

Table 2.2 Sample marketing objectives and SMART analysis

Objective Statement	SMART Analysis
Target women between the ages of 18 and 25 with an integrated communications campaign featuring a top celebrity endorser. ✗ Not SMART!	S – the level of focus here is too narrow (promotion). A more appropriate level of focus should be on sales, market share, or other market-related effect. Further, the objective doesn't say what effect is expected; once these women are targeted, what are they expected to do? M – nothing measurable. A – absent any other information, we can assume that the organization has the internal capabilities to pull this off. R – without a clear measurable goal, it is impossible to determine whether it is realistic. T – no deadline.
Improve the customer experience of everyone who is using our online portal. ✗ Not SMART!	S – the objective is not specific enough – how much should it be improved? How exactly is the customer experience measured? M – nothing measurable. A – absent any other information, we can assume that the organization has the internal capabilities to pull this off. R – without a clear measurable goal, it is impossible to determine whether it is realistic. T – no deadline.
Increase sales in our brick-and-mortar stores with women 25–55 by 20% by 31 December 2024. ✓ SMART!	S – sales is a very reasonable marketing-related objective and the fact that we are expecting a 20% increase is very specific. M – a sales increase of 20% is measurable. A – absent any other information, we can assume that the organization has the internal capabilities to pull this off. R – 20% is neither too high nor too low. T – the deadline is 31 December 2024.

Note that the comprehensive set of specific targets and indicators that accompany the 17 SDGs also function as KPIs. These KPIs can be easily incorporated into the marketing team's objectives. For example, among other objectives for 2030, Unilever has pledged to source 100% of its agriculturally-based ingredients from sustainable sources (SDG12) and improve the livelihoods of 5.5 million people in its supply chain with a variety of initiatives that promote safety and equality (SDG8) (Hoek 2018). If this seems like the team is spending a lot of time and attention on marketing objectives, you're right. It is necessary for the marketing team to spend a significant amount of time and effort to develop compelling and effective objectives. Indeed, it is the most important step in developing an effective marketing strategy. Why? It is equivalent to starting out on a trip without a map or GPS – you will definitely be able to go *somewhere*, but is it really where you want to go? The next step in the marketing planning process is the effective deployment of the elements of the marketing mix.

Marketing Strategy

This is where the four elements of the marketing mix – product, price, place, and promotion – combine to deliver the value proposition. Recall that the value proposition is the organization's offering that satisfies the needs of the target market better than that of the competition. The elements of the marketing mix are so important to marketing strategy that this text devotes a chapter to each one. For now, however, let's introduce them:

- **Product** – the organization's offering that is designed to fulfill a consumer's need or want. It can be a tangible product (e.g., a new iPhone), as well as a service (e.g., a haircut), an idea (e.g., don't drink and drive), a destination (e.g., Paris), an experience (e.g., a honeymoon), or a person (e.g., a political candidate or a celebrity spokesperson).
- **Price** – what the consumer gives up to get the product. Most often, this is expressed in monetary terms. However, price could also include a consumer's time, attention, data, or vote. In the case of bartering, it could include another service or item (e.g., in exchange for helping paint his garage, your neighbor will give you a case of beer). Finally, opportunity costs are also incorporated in the price; the consumer who buys a product is *giving up* the chance to buy another product.
- **Place** – the sequence of steps and services that move a product from raw materials, through processing/manufacturing, warehousing, retailing, to the consumer, and eventually to disposal. It includes the physical movement of the product as well as services such as invoicing, inspections, certifications, inventory control, tariffs, and taxes.
- **Promotion** – the communication that occurs between the organization and the target market. Once the marketing team develops a message that will resonate with the target audience, it has several tools available to convey that message.

Photo 2.10 Fiji Water is sourced in Fiji but shipped all over the world

Source: Shutterstock/Audio und werbung

At the conclusion of this step in the marketing plan, the marketing team will have an integrated plan to utilize these tools to deliver the value proposition to the target market. Decisions about one component of the marketing mix will necessarily impact the other elements. Consider the decisions that are made, for example, by the marketing team at Fiji Water. This high-end water is naturally filtered through volcanic rock and sourced from an artesian spring. The packaging has a distinctive square shape with images evoking an island paradise (product). The price is higher than the competition, consistent with its premium image (price). Fiji Water only comes from Fiji, but it can be found in cafes, grocery stores, restaurants, and other specialty stores all over the world (place). The main message for Fiji Water is that it is untouched by human hands and is "Earth's finest water." The marketing team uses a combination of print, point-of-purchase, video, and sponsorships to communicate with its target market (promotion). All parts of the marketing mix work together to convey the product's high-end, exclusive image. It should be clear that a thorough understanding of the target market is critical for each of these elements to be effective and to be seamlessly integrated with one another (see Photo 2.10 and Figure 2.6).

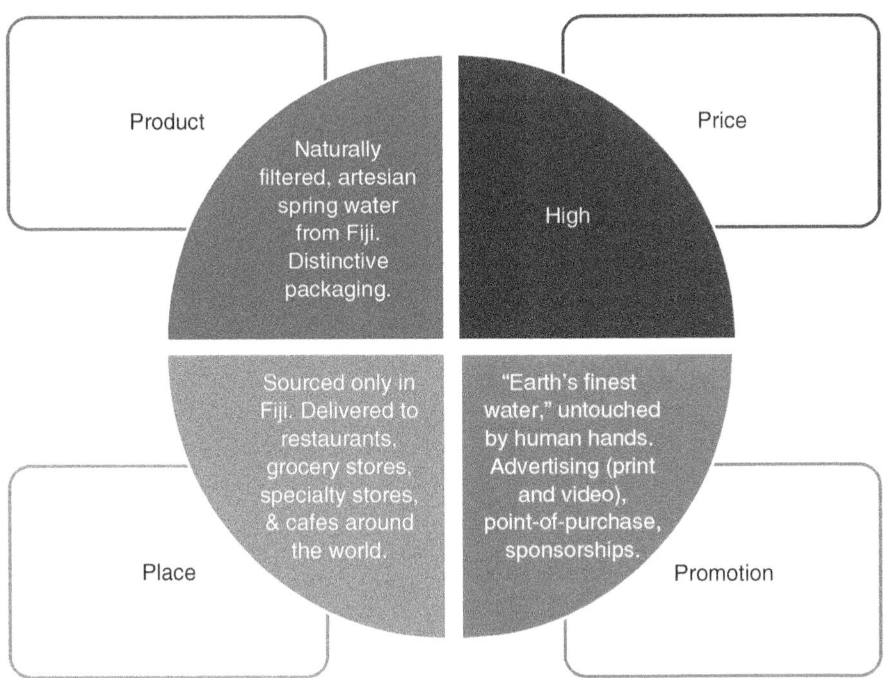

Figure 2.6 Fiji Water's integrated marketing mix

BLUNDERS & INSIGHTS 2.2

Crowdsourcing is Bad News for the Whopper

WHAT HAPPENED? Another Burger King blunder? Unfortunately, yes. In 2017, the global restaurant chain saw an exciting opportunity to launch an organic conversation about its brand with the help of newly-emerging home assistant technology. It launched a campaign to encourage people to say "Ok Google, what is the Whopper burger?" into their Google Home devices, which would take them directly to a tasty description of the burger, complete with a list of high-quality fresh ingredients. Unfortunately, the description for the Whopper was located on Wikipedia, a crowd-sourced online encyclopedia. Almost immediately, users started editing the Wikipedia entries. Some of the more amusing entries included statements that the Whopper was the "worst hamburger product," that it was made with a flame-grilled "100% medium-sized child," that it contained "cyanide," and that it was "far inferior to the Big Mac." Within 2 hours of the launch of the campaign, Google disabled the function (Tan 2017).

DEBRIEF: This failure of planning had consequences for both Burger King and Google Home. First, decision-makers at Burger King should have known that Wikipedia content is easily edited

(Continued)

by anyone who would like to have a little fun with the brand. It is a bad idea to place your brand in the hands of people who may not have its best interest in mind. Second, the reputation of Google Home was also put at risk as users started to question the privacy of their own conversations, as well as the utility of the information the device provided (Tan 2017).

Facilitating Successful Strategy Execution

The next step in the development of the marketing plan is to develop a set of procedures for the successful implementation and control of the plan. Organizations are notoriously weak at strategy execution. The marketing team could have the most compelling objectives and strategy, but when it comes to execution, things sometimes go awry. The most frequent reason for a strategy failure is inadequate or unavailable resources (21% of failures). However, when combined, poor communication accounts for 26% of the failures (poorly communicated strategy (14%) and unclear definition of actions required for execution (12%)) (Mankins and Steele 2005) (see Figure 2.7).

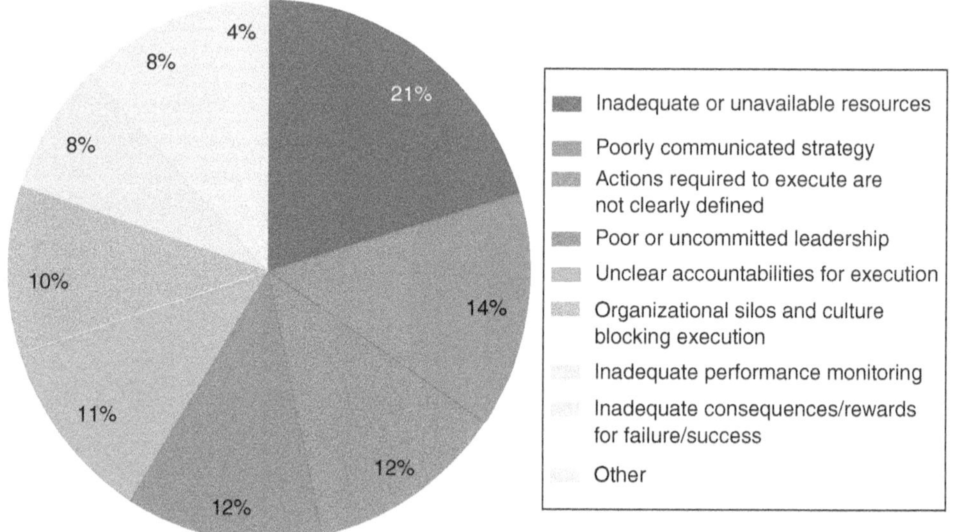

Figure 2.7 Why strategies fail

Source: Mankins and Steele (2005)

Because of these failures, especially those related to communication, the marketing team should implement two important procedures. The first is *information flow* – information about the market, the competition, and the organization's own performance must be directed quickly and efficiently to the people who need to see it. The second is *information clarity* – individuals must clearly understand the decisions and actions for which they are responsible. When this occurs, second-guessing rarely happens and individuals work to support, rather than control, the decisions of others (Neilson, Martin, and Powers 2008). In addition to these procedures, several additional communication-related tools also help increase the likelihood of successful implementation of the marketing plan (see Table 2.3). The marketing plan should be viewed as a dynamic entity and should provide for enough flexibility to accommodate new information, circumstances, or challenges so that, in the event that something goes wrong, the problem can be assessed and fixed quickly and effectively.

Table 2.3 Tools for implementation and control of the marketing plan

Communication-related Tools for Successful Implementation	What Is It?
Create a workflow map	A detailed timeline, including start and end dates, of the tasks to be completed.
Agree on key performance indicators (KPIs)	Agreement on how the team will define "success" should be achieved in the early stages of the marketing planning process. Team reminders of these KPIs throughout the process are beneficial.
Identify the person with responsibility	Assignment of individual responsibility for each task in the marketing plan. These individuals should be empowered to make decisions, not simply report problems to other members in the team.

Finally, This is Not the End

Even after the marketing team launches the marketing plan and carries it through to completion, the effort to deliver value to the target market has not ended. The team has already reaped significant benefits working within the marketplace and it has developed important insights about its target market. These experiences and insights must be leveraged to help inform the creation of the next set of objectives.

2.4 ACHIEVING SYNERGIES

Marketing planning that incorporates sustainability is, simply put, better planning. Across a wide variety of studies that have examined the linkages between sustainable business practices and business performance, 88% found that sustainable business practices led to better operational performance and 80% demonstrated higher stock performance (Clark, Feiner, and Viehs 2014). For the record, a **synergy** occurs when the combined effects are equal to more than the sum of the parts. That is, 1 + 1 = 3. The following discussion will argue that synergies in marketing performance and sustainability can be realized when traditional business paradigms are challenged.

Challenging Existing Paradigms

To create a relevant and impactful strategy, it is sometimes necessary to challenge traditional ways of thinking and behaving. One traditional paradigm, for example, is that there is a difference between for-profit and not-for-profit organizations. Historically, in accordance with the economic theory promoted by Milton Friedman, for-profit organizations were structured and operated in order to maximize shareholder wealth (1970). The primary objective was to optimize

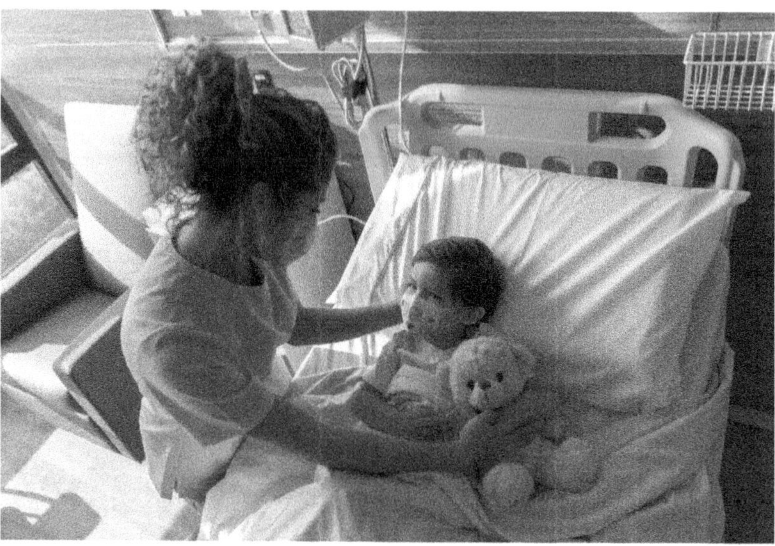

Photo 2.11 RMHC provides much-needed lodging, food, and respite to families with sick children.

Source: iStock

short-term profits, and any resources that were devoted to social or environmental causes took the form of limited-term projects, partnerships, or donations; they were not central to how the organization operated. More recently, the boundary between for-profit and not-for-profit organizations has become blurred. According to the concept of shared value, there is often a fine line between for-profit and not-for-profit endeavors, as organizations realize that they may have a greater duty than a singular focus on profits and dedicate a specific amount of their revenue to such activities (Porter and Kramer 2011). Since 1974, the Ronald McDonald House Charities (RMHC) has been helping families with sick children stay close together. Organized as a nonprofit organization, profits from McDonald's Corporation and other fundraising activities allow RMHC to offer three types of comfort to families: comfortable overnight accommodation and meals in a Ronald McDonald House located close to a hospital; quiet rest and snacks in a Ronald McDonald family room in hospitals; and medical, dental, and other health care resources in mobile Ronald McDonald Care vans. In 2019, the 365 Ronald McDonald Houses in 64 countries provided over 2.6 million overnight stays, saving families approximately $935 million in lodging and food expenses (Our Strategy 2021) (see Photo 2.11).

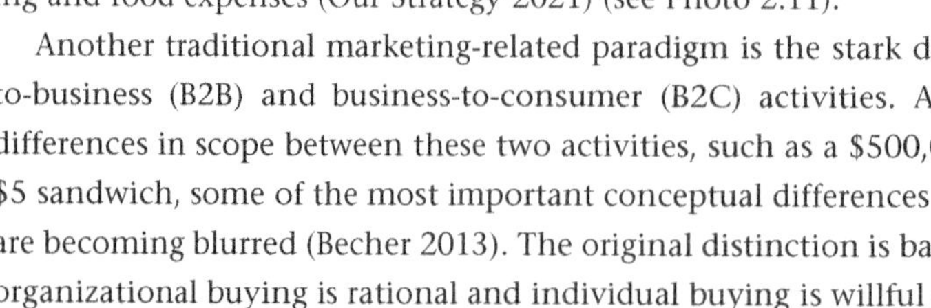

Another traditional marketing-related paradigm is the stark distinction between business-to-business (B2B) and business-to-consumer (B2C) activities. Although there are certainly differences in scope between these two activities, such as a $500,000 piece of machinery vs. a $5 sandwich, some of the most important conceptual differences between these two concepts are becoming blurred (Becher 2013). The original distinction is based on the false premise that organizational buying is rational and individual buying is willful and emotional. Instead, B2B and B2C both emphasize a value proposition, enhance engagement, and nourish relationships. *Any* customer-centric approach will emphasize how the product or service will help solve a problem for the customer and will tap into both emotional and reason-based decision-making (Wilson 2000). An important factor in this paradigm shift is the greater empowerment of the customer. Sophisticated software allows all types of buyers to become knowledgeable about the product and lessens the need for the expertise of a specialized B2B salesperson. Technology and advanced data analytics also help sellers tailor their offerings to the needs of individual customers. This is an important development because both sellers and buyers have relevant and plentiful information to make their decisions (Nath, Saha, and Salehi-Sangari 2019). Consider the enormous changes that are happening in the travel industry. Highly-informed and empowered consumers make their own bookings without the expertise of a travel agent. For their part, hotels, car rental companies, and other attractions communicate directly with customers. Further adding to the blurring of lines, C2C, or consumer-to-consumer, interactions through sites such as Airbnb are providing different and sometimes more authentic experiences for travelers. Airbnb lists over seven million properties in 220 countries around the world and had experienced impressive growth until the Covid-19 global pandemic hit. Immediately after lockdowns were imposed around the world, Airbnb cut back on many of its initiatives and laid off 25% of its workforce, as its market valuation dropped from a high of $31 billion to $18 billion (Glusac 2020). However, as lockdowns ended, individuals started to travel again and interest in short-term rentals through C2C sites like Airbnb surged (Bursztynsky 2022).

The Triple Bottom Line

The New Environmental Paradigm represents a shift in our fundamental worldview of the relationship between humankind and the environment by acknowledging that human health and welfare depend on a healthy environment (Dunlap and Van Liere 1978). Building on this, perhaps the most important paradigm that needs to be challenged is the notion that marketers need to make a choice between maximizing financial outcomes and maximizing social and environmental outcomes (c.f. Boakye, Tingbani, Ahinful, Damoah, and Tauringa 2020, Figge and Hahn 2012, Nidumolu, Prahalad, and Rangaswami 2009). Using a sustainability approach is not simply something that is nice to have, it is a strategic imperative that positions the organization to better deliver the value proposition. When an organization uses a sustainability approach, it (Loock and Phillips 2020):

- becomes more innovative
- lowers costs
- is better able to attract and retain talent
- is better prepared to comply with environmental regulations
- becomes differentiated in the minds of consumers.

The Triple Bottom Line argues that organizations should simultaneously work to benefit social, economic, and environmental objectives. There are plenty of measures that can be used to assess an organization's economic success, but this model suggests that decision-makers also need to find ways to assess the social and environmental implications of their decisions (*Economist* 2009, Elkington 2018). Think about the case of Johnson & Johnson, a pharmaceutical company that often needs to source ingredients for its life-saving drugs from environmentally-sensitive habitats. Decision-makers at Johnson & Johnson can certainly predict the amount of product trial, market share, and profit they might expect when they introduce a new drug. However, what is the environmental impact of building new roads into the forest to obtain this important

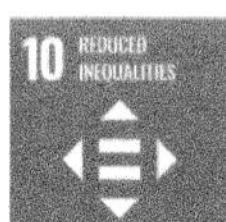

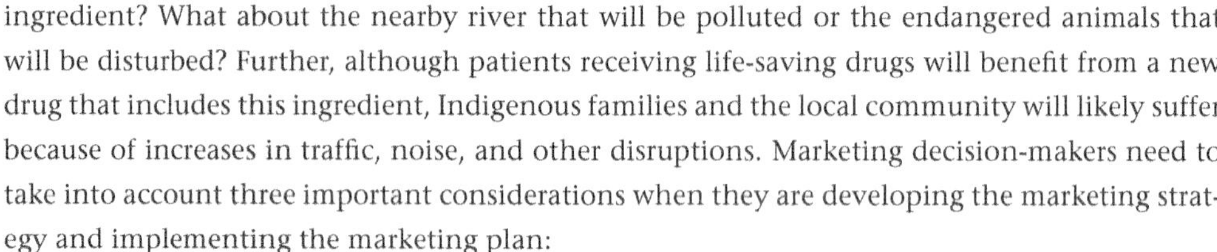

ingredient? What about the nearby river that will be polluted or the endangered animals that will be disturbed? Further, although patients receiving life-saving drugs will benefit from a new drug that includes this ingredient, Indigenous families and the local community will likely suffer because of increases in traffic, noise, and other disruptions. Marketing decision-makers need to take into account three important considerations when they are developing the marketing strategy and implementing the marketing plan:

- People – what will be the impact experienced by a wide variety of different groups of people, such as the neighboring community, workers, company employees, and customers?
- Planet – what will be the impact of this marketing initiative on a variety of natural resources, such as air quality, water quality, natural habitats, native species, and the waste stream?
- Prosperity – what will be the impact on a variety of other economic outcomes, such as profit, market position, brand equity, customer satisfaction, competitive position, innovativeness, and customer relationships?

Ideally, the organization will sit within the intersection of people, planet, and prosperity and the marketing plan will function to reinforce this position. The triple bottom line perspective seeks to achieve long-term benefits for each component of the model rather than short-term, incremental, and often meaningless gains. It is important to note that the triple bottom line perspective's three dimensions are in alignment with the 17 SDGs (Hoek 2018) and are stakeholder-driven in their focus (Elkington 2018). Because of this, the marketing plan must incorporate stakeholder input at each step of the marketing plan, from objective setting through facilitating the successful implementation of the plan (see Figure 2.8). The Sun & Earth company is a small organization located close to Philadelphia that specializes in making plant-based soaps and detergents. Founded in 1988, the company has always operated according to the principles of the triple bottom line:

- People – many of the workers at the company's facility are formally-incarcerated individuals or others who have a poor or non-existent work history. Sun & Earth invests in these individuals by providing a steady, well-paying job. For the first time for many of them, their lives have purpose. Customers appreciate the products because they are reasonably priced, they do not contain any harmful ingredients, and they work as well as, or better than, traditionally-made products.
- Planet – 71% of the ingredients for the products are sourced from plants. The products are vegan, hypoallergenic, have not been tested on animals, and most are packaged in post-consumer recycled plastic (Our Standards 2021).
- Prosperity – in 2020, Sun & Earth was acquired by Nehemiah, an organization that manufactures a variety of consumer products that have a social mission. Nehemiah is privately owned, but reports impressive results in the category of prosperity. Its 180 employees not only earn a living wage, they receive job training and development, thus improving the skills of the company's workforce. Its employee turnover rate is less than 1/2 of the industry average and it had $59.4 million in sales in 2018 (Simon 2020).

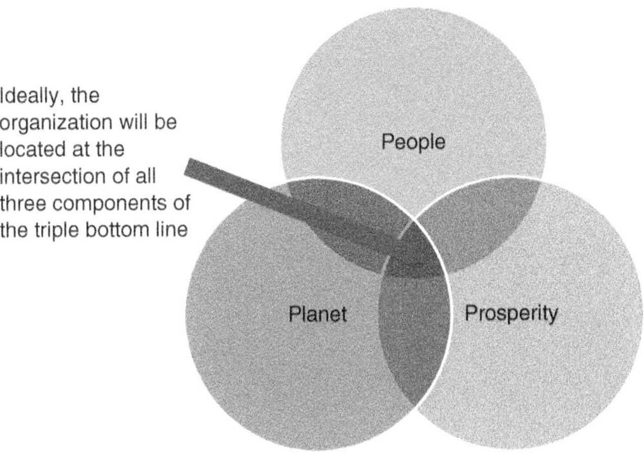

Figure 2.8 The triple bottom line

ENDURING INSIGHTS 2.3

> "It's not the will to win that matters – everyone has that. It's the will to prepare to win that matters." – Paul "Bear" Bryant

An American college football coach from 1954–82, Bear Bryant's teams broke records for their winning seasons and many of his players went on to successful professional careers in football (Britannica 2021). Bryant was known for putting his players through long hours of drills and tough training so that they could execute plays perfectly on the field, when it mattered. This quote emphasizes the importance of the team's preparation and the development of skills in order to flawlessly execute their strategies against the competition.

2.5 SUMMARY

After successfully creating and implementing a compelling marketing plan, remember that the purpose is not simply to achieve a set of objectives designed to deliver value to the target market – we want to do it *better* than the competition. The first step in developing an effective marketing plan is to conduct a thorough situation analysis, where the marketing team examines a variety of internal and external forces. The second step is developing an in-depth understanding of the target market, which will carry through to each of the remaining steps in the marketing plan. Next, the marketing team will create a set of objectives. The team can look to a variety of sources for inspiration for the development of the objectives, including the BCG matrix, Blue Ocean Strategy, and the 17 SDGs. When constructing the objectives, adherence to a SMART format will help foster clear communication throughout the remainder of the process. The next step is a careful coordination of the four parts of the marketing mix in order to deliver the value proposition. Finally, the marketing team will work to implement the marketing plan and, if necessary, make adjustments. Here, the team must commit to clear and efficient communication of information to everyone involved in the plan's implementation. In order to help the parts of the marketing plan work synergistically together to achieve our objectives, marketers need to rethink old paradigms, such as the outdated distinction between profit vs. not-for-profit operations, B2B vs. B2C perspectives, and the quest for maximization of a single bottom line, rather than a triple bottom line.

For a detailed outline of the marketing plan, refer to Appendix 1.

QUESTIONS FOR REVIEW & DISCUSSION

1. Sketch out the five steps involved in creating a marketing plan. Why do we say that the marketing plan must be flexible and dynamic? In what way does an understanding of the target market help inform each part of the marketing plan?
2. The PEZ Corporation (see case study) was founded in 1927. Its distinctive candy and creative candy dispensers are loved by children and adults all over the world. What is PEZ' value proposition for children? Adults? Why is it important to make this distinction?
3. Experts predict that the SDGs will generate market opportunities of over $12 trillion per year by 2030 (Elkington 2018). If this is the case, why aren't more companies taking advantage of these opportunities? What is holding them back?
4. As we learned from the previous chapter, CleanChoice Energy is a provider of renewable energy solutions to businesses, homes, and other organizations. Imagine that CleanChoice is attempting to target universities across southern France and Spain. Develop a set of at least three meaningful marketing objectives using the SMART format.
5. What do we mean when we say that sustainability is a strategic imperative for organizations? Construct an argument to convince your very skeptical friend or family member that this is so.
6. If so much effort goes into the creation of the marketing strategy and the careful construction of the marketing plan, why do so many strategies fail? What can be done to reduce the likelihood of failure?
7. Why is it important to challenge some of marketing's long-held paradigms? Discuss in detail.

2.6 REFERENCES

2019 in Brief. 2019. Migros Annual Report 2019. The Migros Group. Accessed 22 March 2021. https://report.migros.ch/2019/2019-in-kuerze/#reisen.

Becher, Jonathan. 2013. The Vanishing Distinction Between B2B and B2C. Insights from the 2013 Marketing Leadership Summit. Northwestern University Kellogg School of Management. 7 November. Accessed 25 April 2021. www.youtube.com/watch?v=zuv8MZoBQjQ.

Bjerke, May Britt and Ralph Renger. 2017. Being Smart about Writing SMART Objectives. *Evaluation and Program Planning, 61*, 125–7.

Boakye, Danquah Jeff, Ishmael Tingbani, Gabriel Ahinful, Isaac Damoah, and Venacio Tauringa. 2020. Sustainable Environmental Practices and Financial Performance: Evidence from Small and Medium-sized Enterprise in the United Kingdom. *Business Strategy and the Environment, 26* (6), 2583–602.

BPS. 2021. What is Psychology? The British Psychological Society. Accessed 2 May 2021. www.bps.org.uk/public/what-is-psychology.

BSA. 2021. Modern Sociology. The British Sociological Association. Accessed 2 May 2021. www.britsoc.co.uk/what-is-sociology/origins-of-sociology/.

Britannica. 2021. Bear Bryant: American Football Coach. Encyclopaedia Britannica. Accessed 26 April 2021. www.britannica.com/biography/Bear-Bryant

Bursztynsky, Jessica. 2022. Airbnb Beats Estimates with 70% Revenue Growth as Travel Rebounds. CNBC. 3 May. Accessed 17 June 2022. www.cnbc.com/2022/05/03/airbnb-abnb-earnings-q1-2022.html.

Clark, Gordon L., Andreas Feiner, and Michael Viehs. 2014. From the Stockholder to the Stakeholder: How Sustainability Can Drive Financial Performance. A Report from the University of Oxford and Arabesque Partners. September. Accessed 21 April 2021. www.arabesque.com/docs/sray/From_the_stockholder_to_the_stakeholder.pdf.

Collins, Jim. 1999. Turning Goals into Results: The Power of Catalytic Mechanisms. *Harvard Business Review, 77* (4), 70–82.

Council of the EU. 2020. Climate Change: Council Adopts EU Long-term Strategy for Submission to the UNFCCC. European Council. 5 March. Accessed 28 March 2021. www.consilium.europa.eu/en/press/press-releases/2020/03/05/climate-change-council-adopts-eu-long-term-strategy-for-submission-to-the-unfccc/.

Dunlap, Riley E. and Kent D. Van Liere. 1978. The "New Environmental Paradigm": A Proposed Measurement Instrument and Preliminary Results. *Journal of Environmental Education, 9*, 10–19.

Economist. 2009. Idea. Triple Bottom Line. *The Economist* (Online). 17 November.

Elkington, John. 2018. 25 Years Ago I Coined the Phrase "Triple Bottom Line." Here's Why It's Time to Rethink it." *Harvard Business Review*. 25 June. Accessed 24 April 2021.

Figge, F. and Hahn, T. 2012. Is Green and Profitable Sustainable? Assessing the Trade-off between Economic and Environmental Aspects. *International Journal of Production Economics, 140* (1), 92–102.

Friedman, Milton. 1970. The Social Responsibility of a Firm is to Increase its Profits. *The New York Times Magazine*, September *13*, 32–3.

Glusac, Elaine. 2020. The Future of Airbnb. *The New York Times*. 24 September, updated 16 November. Accessed 25 April 2021. www.nytimes.com/2020/09/24/travel/airbnb-pandemic.html.

Hax, Arnoldo C. and Nicholas S. Majluf. 1983. The Use of the Growth-Share Matrix in Strategic Planning. *Interfaces, 13* (1), 46–60.

Henderson, Bruce. 1970. The Product Portfolio. *The Boston Consulting Group*. Perspectives No. 66. Boston Consulting Group, Boston, Massachusetts.

Hoek, Marga. 2018. *The Trillion Dollar Shift: Achieving the Sustainable Development Goals: Business for Good is Good Business*. Routledge, Abingdon, UK.

Huawei. 2019. *ICT Sustainable Development Goals Benchmark*. Huawei Technologies Co., Ltd.

IPCC. 2014. *Climate Change 2014: Synthesis Report*. Contribution of Working Groups I, II, and III to the Fifth Assessment Report of the Intergovernmental Panel on Climate Change [Core Writing Team, R.K. Pachauri and L.A. Meyer (eds.)]. IPCC, Geneva, Switzerland.

Jack, Andrew. 2020. The Rise of the 'Sustainable' MBA. *The Financial Times*. 21 January. www.ft.com/content/2a73f3de-339d-11ea-a329-0bcf87a328f2.

Kim, W. Chan and Renee Mauborgne. 2004. Blue Ocean Strategy. In: *Harvard Business Review*, Oct, *82* (10), 76–84.

Kulp, Scott A. and Benjamin H. Strauss. 2019. New Elevation Data Triple Estimates of Global Vulnerability to Sea-Level Rise and Coastal Flooding. *Nature Communications, 10*, Article number 4844. https://doi.org/10.1038/s41467-019-12808-z.

Loock, Moritz and Diane M. Phillips (2020). A Firm's Financial Reputation vs. Sustainability Reputation: Do Consumers Really Care? *Sustainability, 12* (24), 1–17.

Mankins, Michael C. and Richard Steele. 2005. Turning Great Strategy into Great Performance. *Harvard Business Review,* July–August, 64–72.

Morton, Valerie. 2011. Overcome Fear of Planning by Using Smart Objectives. *Third Sector.* Issue 681, 25 October, p. 21.

Nath, Atanu, Parmita Saha, and Esmail Salehi-Sangari. 2019. Blurring the Borders Between B2B and B2C: A Model of Antecedents Behind Usage of Social Media for Travel Planning. *Journal of Business & Industrial Marketing, 34* (7), 1468–81.

Neilson, Gary L., Karla L. Martin, and Elizabeth Powers. 2008. The Secrets to Successful Strategy Execution. *Harvard Business Review,* June, *86* (6), 61–70.

Nidumolu, Ram, C.K. Prahalad, and M.R. Rangaswami. 2009. Why Sustainability is Now the Key Driver of Innovation. *Harvard Business Review. From the Magazine.* September.

Our Standards. 2021. Sun & Earth Corporation. Accessed 26 April 2021. https://sunandearth.com/our-standards/.

Our Strategy. 2021. Ronald McDonald House Charities. Accessed 24 April 2021. https://corporate.mcdonalds.com/corpmcd/our-purpose-and-impact/community-connection/rmhc.html.

Phillips, Diane M. 2013. Advice from the Front Lines of Sustainability: Take the Stairs, there is No Elevator, *Journal of Applied Management and Entrepreneurship, 18* (2), 103–15.

Porter, Michael E. and Mark R. Kramer. 2006. Strategy & Society: The Link Between Competitive Advantage and Corporate Social Responsibility. *Harvard Business Review,* December, 78–92.

Porter, Michael E. and Mark R. Kramer. 2011. Shared Value: How to Reinvent Capitalism—and Unleash a Wave of Innovation. *Harvard Business Review,* January–February, 62–77.

Purtill, James. 2021. Heatwaves May Mean Sydney is Too Hot to Live in 'Within Decades.' ABC News. 24 January. Accessed 21 April 2021. www.abc.net.au/news/science/2021-01-24/heatwaves-sydney-uninhabitable-climate-change-urban-planning/12993580.

Russon, Mary-Ann. 2021. The Cost of the Suez Canal Blockage. BBC News, Business. 29 March. Accessed 19 April 2021. www.bbc.com/news/business-56559073

Simon, Ruth. 2020. The Company of Second Chances. *The Wall Street Journal.* 25 January. Accessed 26 April 2021. www.wsj.com/articles/the-company-of-second-chances-11579928401?fbclid=IwAR0LBFcIRs2jdoNwFMvx0VZ9W9qw5gfUjmSy0ish0TzuxzHIk5T5SgwLRiw.

Tan, Emily. 2017. Burger King Just Became the First Brand Fail on Google Home. Campaign. 13 April. Accessed 30 April 2021. www.campaignlive.co.uk/article/burger-king-just-became-first-brand-fail-google-home/1430559.

The 17 Goals. 2021. Department of Economic and Social Affairs, Sustainable Development. The United Nations. Accessed 2 April 2021. https://sdgs.un.org/goals.

The History of Migros. 2021. The History of Migros. The Migros Group. Accessed 22 March 2021. www.migros.ch/de/unternehmen/geschichte.html.

Townsend, Solitaire. 2018. 88% of Consumers Want You to Help Them Make a Difference. *Forbes.* 21 November. Accessed 21 April 2021. www.forbes.com/sites/solitairetownsend/2018/11/21/consumers-want-you-to-help-them-make-a-difference/?sh=29e02d1a6954.

Van Boom, Daniel and Sean Keane. 2021. Ever Given Seized in Egypt After Blocking Suez Canal: Everything to Know. CNET. 13 April. Accessed 19 April 2021. www.cnet.com/news/ever-given-seized-in-egypt-after-blocking-suez-canal-everything-to-know/.

Webb, Bella. 2021a. Tommy Hilfiger Ramps Up Adaptive Fashion. Who's Next? *Vogue Business.* 22 March. Accessed 3 April 2021. www.voguebusiness.com/fashion/tommy-hilfiger-ramps-up-adaptive-fashion-whos-next

Webb, Bella. 2021b. L'Oréal Lifts the Lid on Sustainability Strategy. *Vogue Business*. 11 March. Accessed 9 April 2021. www.voguebusiness.com/sustainability/loreal-lifts-the-lid-on-sustainability-strategy?itm_source=manual_article_recommendation.

WeSpire. 2021. 2021: State of Employee Engagement. A Report by WeSpire. Boston, Massachusetts. Accessed 21 April 2021. www.wespire.com/state-of-employee-engagement-2021/.

Wilson, Dominic F. 2000. Why Divide Consumer and Organizational Buyer Behaviour? *European Journal of Marketing, 34* (7), 780–96.

Zinkhan, George M. and Arun Pereira. 1994. An Overview of Marketing Strategy and Planning. *International Journal of Research in Marketing, 11*, 185–218.

3 REASON-BASED STRATEGIC DECISION-MAKING

LEADERSHIP INSIGHTS 3

Photo 3.1 Christina Mallon

Source: courtesy, Christina Mallon

Christina Mallon, Head of Inclusive Design & Accessibility

Wunderman Thompson

Do not even think about walking into a client meeting without data, says Christina Mallon, a fierce advocate for people with disabilities. Mallon is the Head of Inclusive Design & Accessibility at Wunderman Thompson, one of the world's biggest advertising and brand-management agencies. She works with some of the world's most well-known brands to find creative and accessible solutions for people with disabilities. Today, she oversees the work of 28,000 people to provide clients with advertising, brand management, messaging, and social media strategies that are completely accessible for anyone with vision, hearing, motor, or cognitive disabilities.

How did she find this niche? Shortly after graduating from university and settling in New York, she started to lose control of her hands and arms, and was diagnosed with a rare form of ALS, a motor neuron disease. The diagnosis prompted her to reassess her life goals and ask, "what is my role in making the world a better place, especially for people with disabilities?" Soon, the answer to her question was glaringly simple: she could use her design and strategy experience to help brands become more accessible for people living with disabilities. Mallon quickly advanced through the ranks in the advertising world and after a few years, she landed her first position at Wunderman Thompson. As brands started to implement her strategic plans, her clients started to reap significant financial outcomes, and management started to notice.

One such client was Tommy Hilfiger. Mallon and her team were integral to the success of Tommy Adaptive, the first mainstream clothing line designed for people with disabilities. For people with limited dexterity in their hands, the line replaces buttons with magnet or Velcro closures. For people with prosthetic limbs, the clothing includes extra seams and closures. Importantly, the advertising for Tommy Adaptive speaks in an authentic way to customers. "We made sure that it was as inclusive as possible, that it wasn't just 'inspiration porn.' Instead, we just showed a bunch of people with disabilities living their everyday lives," she explained. "We had a blind director who shot it, and the cast and crew were all in the disability community. It was a big hit in the market. It even won a few Cannes Awards," she noted (learn more about the campaign here: www.youtube.com/watch?v=cYTOaAYnppM).

Mallon regularly assesses trends in the external environment. "The disability community has $8 trillion in disposable income – this is larger than the disposable income for all of China! But there are really no brands that are thinking about them. Even today, there are more clothing lines for dogs than there are for people with disabilities. Only 4% of businesses are focused on this, so there is a lot of room for companies to be first movers in their industry," she concluded. Because of the target market's willingness to use technology, synergies can be achieved and innovations can be identified. "When you look at some of the best inventions of our time – email, voice activation, the touchscreen – those were created to offer solutions for people with disabilities, but they're now used by all." Another reason why Mallon is optimistic about the future of this market concerns young people. "We know that 70% of Millennials would rather buy a brand that is more expensive but also reflects their own personal values" and inclusivity is definitely something that is appreciated by this demographic segment (see Photo 3.2).

Mallon relies heavily on both quantitative and qualitative research, and confirms the validity of her team's ideas by identifying and tracking several important KPIs. For example, when Microsoft introduced a new adaptive controller for its Xbox in mid-2018, the objective was to increase revenue. Beating every expectation, however, Microsoft saw an almost immediate 44% lift in its gaming revenues (Valentine 2018). Tommy Hilfiger saw a 300% increase in Return on Investment (ROI) that was directly attributable to the Tommy Adaptive line. Although the line itself broke even, consumer perceptions increased for the broader Tommy Hilfiger brand. Customers appreciated the campaign and the brand refresh, and ended up buying its mainstream clothing too. Indeed, global sales of the brand increased from $3.8 billion in 2017 to $4.2 billion in 2018 (Ang 2019).

Photo 3.2 Millennials appreciate businesses that foster inclusivity

Source: Unsplash.com

For students about to graduate from university, Mallon emphasizes the importance of understanding how technology and data will affect consumers and their buying habits. "As a strategist, you need to understand the data. The data is becoming more available and it is critical to be able to model out data and do predictions based on the model. Companies like Amazon have been successful because they do not do anything without data. In my own decision-making and when I am about to give my opinion to some of these global, billion-dollar companies, I always ask, 'where is the data?'" explained Mallon.

3.1 TOUGH DECISIONS

Founded in 2001, Terracycle is a small company located in Trenton, New Jersey that works under the mantra of "eliminating the idea of waste." It converts a wide assortment of post-consumer materials into a variety of consumer products, which are then sold in big box retail outlets and online. Because of its efforts at upcycling these items, Terracycle has diverted millions of items away from landfill and put them back into consumer hands as new products. The most lucrative time of year for Terracycle is back-to-school time. The company sells backpacks, totes, pencil cases, and a variety of other school supplies. It also sells products for the home, garden, and office (see Photo 3.3). Interest in Terracycle's sustainably-produced products has been facilitated by a variety of organizations that have been encouraging more sustainable consumption, as well as consumers who are seeking more sustainable solutions in their lives. Over the years, Terracycle enjoyed a slow but steady increase in sales and profit (Phillips and Phillips 2016).

Photo 3.3 Watering can made from recycled materials

Source: courtesy, Terracycle

By 2012, however, the company was having difficulty achieving the volume needed to scale its operations and was losing money on every unit sold. In addition, Terracycle was having an increasingly difficult time meeting the orders of some of its most important big box customers. It seemed like the ideal time to locate a new production facility that offered high-volume, low-cost production. CEO Tom Szaky's goal was to "make green mainstream" and he insisted that the cost of production be lowered such that it was equivalent to that of traditionally-manufactured products. Simply put, consumers should not have to pay more to get sustainable products. The most important decision criterion, therefore, was the cost of production. Decision-makers at Terracycle turned their sights to China, where they were assured that production costs would be cut in half and they could achieve the volume demanded by some of their biggest retail customers. In 2013, a portion of Terracycle's production was moved to China (Phillips and Phillips 2016).

Unfortunately, the timing was less than ideal. First, the exchange rate between the US and China shifted such that the dollar had significantly less purchasing power than it had just 6–12 months before. Second, the Chinese economy was slowing down and a variety of economic indicators suggested that this slow-down would be long-lasting. Third, the Chinese manufacturing facility was not able to consistently deliver the volumes needed to satisfy Terracycle's retail customers. Finally, the biggest issue was that labor costs in China were increasing dramatically each year, such that the predicted savings of 50% was no longer possible. Indeed, the savings in production costs were closer to 10%. This low level of savings made it impossible to meet Szaky's goal of achieving price parity with traditional mainstream products. Consequently, Szaky and the team reevaluated their decision and quickly located a US-based manufacturing facility that was capable of delivering the volumes and low costs necessary. Production was moved back to the US in mid-2014 (Phillips and Phillips 2016) (see Photo 3.4).

Photo 3.4 Terracycle Headquarters in Trenton, New Jersey

This chapter focuses on the all-important process of reason-based strategic decision-making. It pays particular attention to establishing clear decision criteria and utilizing marketing metrics and key performance indicators (KPIs). The decision to move a portion of Terracycle's manufacturing to China was done with the objective of lowering production costs so that Terracycle's sustainable products could achieve price parity with other traditionally manufactured consumer products. The decision criterion was clear: if production costs could be lowered enough (50% or more), the move would be made. However, once it was clear that the anticipated cost savings would not materialize, decision-makers shifted back to a US production facility to achieve price parity. Sound decision-making requires a set of objectives and reliable measures. This chapter is organized into two sections. First, we discuss the process of reason-based decision-making. Then, we take a deep dive into some marketing metrics that are often used to facilitate this process.

3.2 LEARNING OBJECTIVES

After studying this chapter, you will be able to do the following:

1 Distinguish between decision criteria, marketing metrics, and marketing analytics in reason-based decision-making.

2 Discuss the various costs and benefits of big data.
3 Describe how marketing metrics are utilized in marketing decision-making.
4 Identify and utilize a variety of marketing metrics.
5 Discuss the concept of systemic thinking and identify its benefits to reason-based decision-making.

3.3 THE DECISION-MAKING PROCESS

Before we go any further, it is important to recognize that the discipline of marketing has a set of principles by which it operates, not a set of laws or rules. This distinction is important because "principles" imply a flexibility to alter the decision-making process to fit the context and even alter the direction of the decision-making mid-process, if needed, because of new data or information. This may be frustrating to students of marketing strategy because there is rarely a "correct" answer in marketing. That's ok. In the end, the goal for marketing decision-making is to develop the best possible decision to address the threats and opportunities of the external environment, given the reality of the internal environment. To be effective, marketing decision-makers need to base their decisions on a careful analysis of the situation as well as the relevant data that is available. **Reason-based decision-making** starts with a purposeful set of steps designed to help solve a problem. It starts with problem identification, creates a set of decision criteria, identifies relevant data to use, analyzes the data, and develops insights. Importantly, reason-based decision-making relies on a set of marketing metrics which provide further clarification and evidence of the problem marketers are facing (see Figure 3.1).

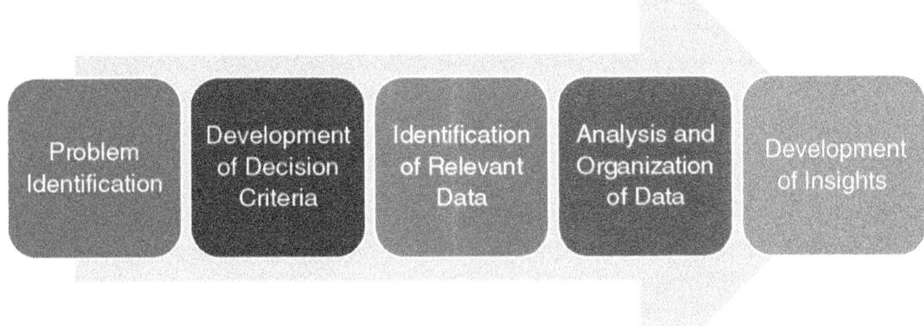

Figure 3.1 The decision-making process

What's the Problem?

The first step builds on the situation analysis that the team has already performed. Here, the marketing team must precisely focus its attention on the identification of a key problem that needs to be addressed. **Problem identification** occurs when the marketing decision-maker identifies a difference between the organization's current situation and its ideal situation. Problem identification has its genesis in careful monitoring of the external environment that will reveal opportunities that can be leveraged and threats that must be addressed. Is there a new competitive encroachment into our market? Have consumer tastes changed? Is a new regulation about to be implemented? With a careful articulation of the problem, the marketing team can shift its efforts toward solving that problem. Problem identification is an important first step because data will only give us the right answers if we ask the right questions (cf. Burnett-Lemon 2015, Chapman 1989). How might decision-makers at Costa Coffee, for example, handle problem identification if they started to see a sharp decline in coffee sales? Here, there is a clear problem because there is a difference between where Costa Coffee wants to be (steady or increasing coffee sales) and where it is (declining coffee sales). Perhaps the decline is due to the fact that a new coffee shop just opened up across the street. Maybe it is because the taste of Costa Coffee is simply not very good. Maybe another coffee shop is running a half-off promotion. Perhaps a new health report was just released that ties coffee to a multitude of health problems. Maybe a new trend is emerging for people to make their coffee at home. Each of these possibilities point to a completely different set of actions on the part of the marketing team. Therefore, once the marketing team precisely identifies the problem, the team can get to work on solving the problem.

Consider what happened during the problem identification phase with Unilever, which owns and manages such well-known global brands as Axe, Dove, Knorr, Domestos, Lifebuoy, Lipton, Hellmann's, and Ben & Jerry's. In 2010, Unilever launched its Sustainable Living Plan, a bold set of initiatives designed to improve the health of the planet and millions of people around the world. This plan was originally developed because decision-makers at Unilever identified a very real problem that hindered positive sustainable development. They noticed that many businesses, including their own, were faced with a significant roadblock: they operated as if a tradeoff needed to be made between sustainable growth and prosperity. Thus, there was a very real problem between where they wanted to be (a broad focus on uplifting communities and helping the environment, while also making a profit) and where they were (a singular focus on maximizing profit). Once decision-makers at Unilever realized that there was no contradiction between these two ideas, they were free to think creatively and develop a series of initiatives to simultaneously increase the health and well-being of people, improve the natural environment, and increase prosperity for the company and others. Unilever's plan included the following broad goals (Hoek 2018):

Photo 3.5 More than 2.5 billion people around the world consume Unilever brands each day

Source: Pixabay

- Improve the health and well-being of one billion people.
- Decouple environmental impact from growth.
- Sustainably source 100% of its raw materials.
- Become carbon positive by 2030.
- Enhance the livelihoods for millions of people, with a special focus on women.

Unilever was able to leverage its size and scale to tackle these problems; every day, over 2.5 billion people around the world use Unilever products. By 2018, progress on many initiatives was ahead of schedule, the plan itself had become a benchmark model for other organizations, and shareholder return had increased by more than 290% (Hoek 2018) (see Photo 3.5).

How will we Decide?

The next step in reason-based decision-making is the development of a clear set of decision-criteria. A **decision criterion** is a guideline or rule by which a decision will be made. In the earlier example of Terracycle, if production costs could be reduced by 50%, a portion of the company's production would move to China. With Costa Coffee, perhaps the problem is that consumers are simply dissatisfied with the taste. Here, the marketing team may develop a decision criterion such that if they can introduce a new premium variety without cannibalizing sales of their other varieties by more than 10%, they will do so. Developing a list of decision criteria will help keep the team's focus on how the decision will be made. At this point, a set of if–then statements could be created, such as:

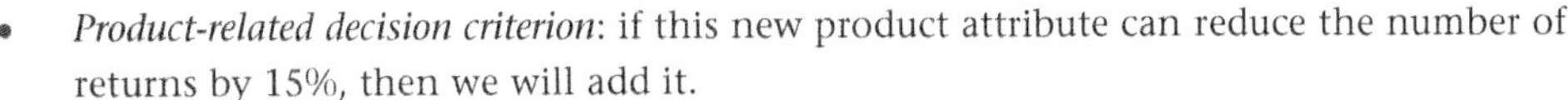

- *Product-related decision criterion*: if this new product attribute can reduce the number of returns by 15%, then we will add it.

- *Price-related decision criterion*: if the cost can be kept below €12 per unit, then we will proceed.
- *Place-related decision criterion*: if the new distributor can get us access to at least 100 stores across the country, then we will use its services.
- *Promotion-related decision criterion*: if this new ad campaign can increase visits to our website by 25%, then we will launch it.

It is important to recognize that decision criteria need to be based on somewhat "consequential" factors, such as financial results. Novice marketers sometimes make the mistake of creating decision criteria that focus on criteria that are less consequential, such as increasing awareness for the product. Sure, consumers need to be aware of the product before they buy it. However, as important as awareness is, an increase in awareness does not necessarily translate to an increase in sales. Many consumers are *aware* of Tesla cars, but does that awareness motivate them to rush out and buy one? No. Compared to our competition, does greater awareness help the organization do a better job at delivering the value proposition? Probably not. Instead, marketers need to focus on developing criteria that are more consequential in nature. Specifically, decision criteria in marketing need to be directly tied to a measurable outcome such as those listed in Table 3.1 (Kelly 1996, Miller and Lim 2020, Winer 1966).

ENDURING INSIGHTS 3.1

"However beautiful the strategy, you should occasionally look at the results." – Sir Winston Churchill, UK Prime Minister and statesman

During WWII, Churchill directed the British efforts and was pivotal in the Allied efforts against the Axis powers. Churchill and the Allies freed Europe from the grip of fascism and set the course for economic prosperity in the second half of the 20th century. Given this context, this quote, which emphasizes the importance of results-driven strategies, takes on added significance. When developing and implementing its strategy, the marketing team needs to always keep the end-goal in mind.

Table 3.1 A selection of quantitatively-based decision criteria

Decision Criteria Based on the Marketing Mix	Decision Criteria Based on Financial Considerations
Product: • number of product returns • number of complaints • product ease-of-use • cross-selling and up-selling • number of calls to the help center • satisfaction scores • attitude scores • behavioral intention scores • product trial Price: • production costs • costs for raw materials • distribution costs • disposal costs Place: • number of retail outlets • time to delivery Promotion: • number of visits to the website, time spent on the website • number of visits to the showroom • advertising recall scores • social media shares and likes • click-through rates • number of page views • client recommendations and positive word-of-mouth	• number of clients/customers • sales • market share • share of wallet • client defections • amount of time between sales • customer retention • customer lifetime value • sales to a new target market • ROI

Decisions rarely involve a simple yes/no determination. Instead, they are often much more multi-faceted, involving two or more competing decisions, each with its own set of short-term and long-term implications for costs, revenues, and investments. Consider the case study about the American convenience store chain, Wawa (see case study on p.438). The marketing team was trying to determine which customers would receive a free refillable travel coffee mug. Should they reward their heavy users, who have already demonstrated an almost-fanatical loyalty to the chain or should they reward light users, with the hope that they will become more engaged with the brand? Each group was expected to behave differently – the heavy and light users were expected to have different rates of redemption for the free mug offer, different frequency of use of the free mug, and different lengths of time that they would use the mug. In the end, the team used a decision criterion based on the expected increase in sales for each alternative: the offer of a free travel coffee mug would be provided to the group with the highest expected net increase in sales. Read the case study to find out more. In the end, the group that received the mug demonstrated an increase in sales that lasted several weeks after the promotion concluded.

BLUNDERS & INSIGHTS 3.1

This Ketchup is Not for Kids!

WHAT HAPPENED: Ketchup is a much-loved addition to food as well as an important ingredient in recipes around the world. In places like Lebanon and Poland, it is squirted on pizza; in Japan, it is used as substitute for tomato sauce in pasta dishes; in Germany, it is used as a base for curry sauce; and in Canada, people enjoy ketchup cake. Founded in 1876 in the US by the son of a German immigrant, Heinz ketchup has a 60% market share in the US and an 80% market share in Europe, mainly because of factories in the UK, Netherlands, and elsewhere (Albala 2018). When a German consumer scanned a QR code on a bottle of Heinz ketchup in 2015, however, he got a lot more than he expected. Imagine his surprise when, thinking he was about to read detailed information about the product, he instead ended up on a hardcore pornographic website.

The QR code was originally part of a Heinz promotional campaign that expired in 2014. After the contest concluded, Heinz marketers failed to update the domain rights for the QR code, and the code was acquired by a pornographic website. Ketchup has a long shelf-life and consumers often keep it around for several months. Unfortunately, any consumer who scanned the QR code from a bottle that was purchased during the promotional campaign would have been directed to the same pornographic website. Not surprisingly, the story went viral as soon as it was posted on social media and Heinz experienced significant negative backlash (Guzman 2015). Who knew ketchup could be so controversial (see Photo 3.6)?

Photo 3.6 Heinz ketchup has 80% market share in Europe

Source: Shutterstock/JJava Designs

(Continued)

DEBRIEF: As a family-friendly company and product line, Heinz should have researched the longevity of the QR code and made sure the code lasted a few years beyond the conclusion of the campaign. Importantly, data and information from consumer research would have revealed insights about consumer purchasing and consumption behaviors. Research would have definitely revealed that some consumers keep their ketchup around for a long time. In the end, Heinz apologized for the error, updated the QR code, and even sent a new custom-designed bottle of ketchup to the German consumer (Guzman 2015).

In addition to quantitative-based criteria, qualitatively-based decision criteria can be utilized by marketing decision-makers in guiding their decision-making efforts. While many efforts have been made to quantify some of these measures, some qualitative decision criteria remain difficult to quantify (see Table 3.2). Despite this, it would be a mistake to think that qualitative criteria are any less consequential than quantitative decision criteria. One of the biggest marketing blunders of all time – the New Coke debacle – can be attributed to the marketing team's lack of understanding of the depth of the sentimental attachment consumers had with the brand. In 1985, Coca-Cola announced that it was retiring its century-old formula and introducing a new formula for Coke, one that was smoother and sweeter. Customers were outraged. Consumers associated Coke with summertime picnics, important life celebrations, and their favorite sports teams; they felt betrayed that Coke would no longer be available. Petitions and signatures were gathered, telephone hotlines were overwhelmed with calls, and thousands of letters flooded into corporate headquarters. A group called the Old Cola Drinkers of America was formed and lobbied strenuously to bring the old formula back. A few months later, Coca-Cola did so (Haoues 2015). Qualitative criteria are definitely consequential.

Table 3.2 A selection of qualitatively-based decision criteria

Decision Criteria Based on Qualitative Measures
Trust
Innovative solutions to a consumer problem
Sentimental attachment to our brand
Healthier lives
Racial or gender equality
Brand credibility
Consumer education
Engagement with the brand or brand's message

What Data do we Need?

Huge piles of data can be seductive – what manager wouldn't be enticed by thousands or even millions of data points? Not so fast. **Identification of relevant data** is the next step in the decision-making process and involves the selection of the data that will have the greatest chance of helping the team make a well-informed decision. This step in the decision-making process reinforces the importance of the first step of problem identification. How, exactly, does a marketing team decide which data is relevant and which is not? The answer is: the most relevant data is that which will have the greatest likelihood of generating insights about the problem.

The ultimate purpose of any data collection effort is to provide insights (Sicular 2013). An **insight** is an interpretation of the data and information that will be useful in helping decision-makers solve the key problem of interest. An insight is much more than a research finding. It represents a deeper level of understanding about the market, consumers, competitors, and key variables. Figure 3.2 depicts the relationship between data, information, and insights. There are several considerations in making the determination about the most appropriate data to collect. These are explored in the following sections.

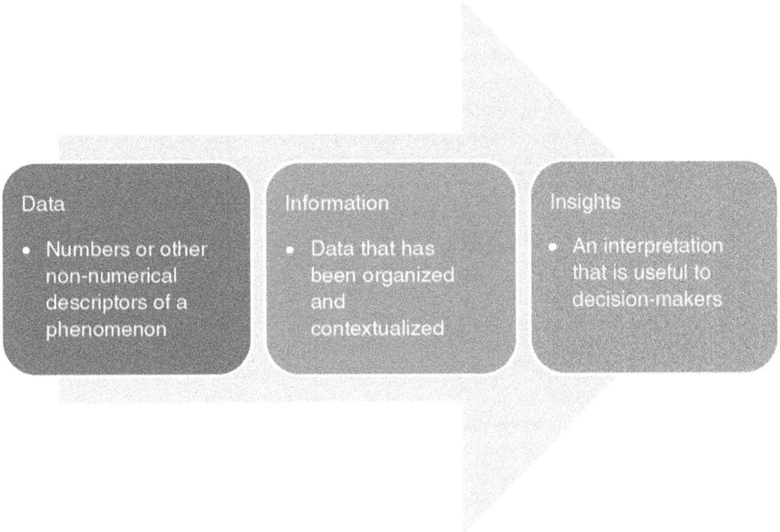

Data
- Numbers or other non-numerical descriptors of a phenomenon

Information
- Data that has been organized and contextualized

Insights
- An interpretation that is useful to decision-makers

Figure 3.2 From data to insights

17 PARTNERSHIPS FOR THE GOALS

Secondary vs. Primary Data

One consideration is whether the team can use data that has been previously gathered for another purpose (**secondary data**). Secondary data has the benefit of being relatively inexpensive and quick to obtain. It is available from a wide variety of sources. For-profit firms such as Nielsen and Mintel gather data and sell reports to organizations. Another alternative for obtaining secondary data is government agencies. For a number of reasons, including encouraging foreign direct investment (FDI) in their countries, most governments around the world provide free reports to organizations. Global non-profit organizations like the World Bank, the IPCC, and the UN also provide free reports that are useful for decision-makers (see Photo 3.7). Another method of collecting secondary data is to examine data that has

Photo 3.7 Organizations like the UN provide free reports to the public

Source: Pixabay

already been generated by the organization itself. Sales data offers the ability to create invaluable insights about the company's own customers, as do other sources of company-generated data, such as customer service inquiries, complaints, and online search behavior.

If the question facing the marketing team is very specific, it is likely that secondary data may not provide the insights the team needs to answer its problem. If this is the case, primary data will need to be gathered. **Primary data** is collected when the question facing the marketing team is so specific that it is likely that secondary data cannot provide the insights the team needs. Primary data can be generated from a variety of sources. First, the research team can generate data themselves by interacting directly with customers and asking them questions. The team can conduct interviews, focus groups, surveys, or experiments with customers. Responses are recorded and the results are analyzed and interpreted. Second, the research team has the option of gathering data from indirect contact with customers. Here, researchers can observe what consumers do in a variety of settings, such as watching how consumers examine food nutrition labels in a grocery store or watching how consumers prepare a meal at home (with their permission, of course). The biggest benefit associated with primary data is that, because it was gathered with a specific purpose, it is very well-suited to provide insights that can help the marketing team.

Qualitative vs. Quantitative

Data can be **qualitative** and use descriptors to describe the phenomenon of interest. Qualitative data is generated, for example, from in-depth interviews, projective techniques, and focus groups. The resulting data includes transcripts from interviews, stories from projective techniques, or comments from focus groups. Experts review this data and identify recurring themes. Qualitative data is often utilized in the early stages of a marketing team's efforts, as when it might need to identify initial impressions from consumers about a new product or new promotional campaign.

Data can also be **quantitative**, in which case, numbers are used to describe the phenomenon of interest. Quantitative data is generated from a myriad of sources, such as surveys or experiments, administrative activities, sales activities, or search activities. The resulting data is generally downloaded into data files, which are then subjected to sophisticated statistical analyses. Quantitative data is utilized at all stages of reason-based decision-making.

Big Data

One type of data that attracts significant attention is **big data**, which involves the generation, handling, and analysis of massive amounts of quantitative data. In assessing digital advertising effectiveness, marketers can determine, for example, the amount of time a potential customer spends on the website, how many pages were examined, and what other products the consumer reviewed. With traditional print, outdoor, or TV advertising, such precision is impossible. Today, data is automatically gathered, transformed, analyzed, and stored, often in the cloud. It is not surprising, therefore, that big data has become widely utilized in marketing. Big data has four unique characteristics (Kitchin and McArdle 2016):

- Volume – it involves enormous amounts of data.
- Velocity – it is created in real time.
- Variety – it is structured, semi-structured, and unstructured.
- Exhaustivity – it is comprehensive in, for example, tracking *all* customers in the market or *all* keystrokes on the website.

The importance of big data cannot be overstated, especially with devices that are linked with one another and that learn over time. Google, for example, executes an estimated 63,000 searches each second, which translates to 5.6 billion searches each day (Prater 2021), while on Twitter, there are over 6000 tweets per second, or 500 million each day (Smith 2020). The purpose of big data is to eventually utilize it to make smarter, faster decisions about a plethora of marketing-related actions, such as product or message personalization, customer engagement, segmentation and targeting, and more effective communications (Miller and Lim 2020), all in an effort to better deliver the value proposition. The benefits of big data to decision-making fall into four broad categories: improving comprehension, improving competitiveness, driving customization, and spurring creativity and innovation (Rejeb, Rejeb, and Keogh 2020) (see Figure 3.3).

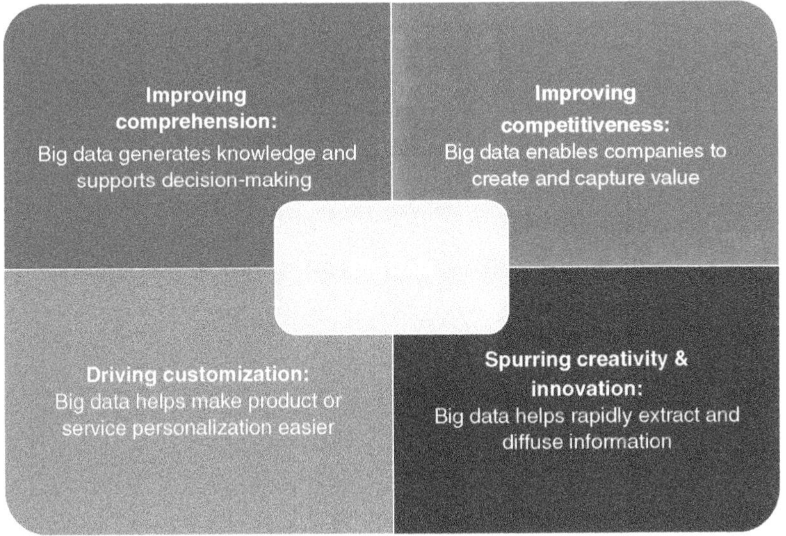

Figure 3.3 Benefits of big data

Source: Rejeb, et al. 2020

ENDURING INSIGHTS 3.2

"It is a capital mistake to theorize before one has data." – Sherlock Holmes

Known for his meticulous attention to detail, Holmes always finds a way to solve the most perplexing problems and catch the most illusive criminals. The first step, however, is to carefully gather the data and interpret it. Holmes continues to gather data throughout the entire investigative process and revisits the evidence when needed throughout the duration of his investigations.

Privacy Concerns

While big data certainly has provided benefits to organizations, a problem still remains: data security and privacy. Consumers and organizations have reason to be concerned. A 2018 data breach at Marriott Group resulted in the theft of 383 million guest records, 18.5 million encrypted passport numbers, and 9.1 million encrypted payment card numbers. As a result, the organization was fined $123 million. British Airways was fined $229 million in 2019 for a similar data breach (O'Flaherty 2019). The global Covid-19 crisis sparked a surge in ransomware attacks on organizations, as well as on critical infrastructure such as transportation, food suppliers, and utilities (Kay 2021). In 2020, attacks increased by 150% from just 1 year before (Sharton 2021) and in 2021 they increased by another 100%. Ransomware attacks are particularly effective because they insert encrypted malware onto an organization's computers and servers. Often, this allows for sensitive data to be exported and then held hostage until the organization makes a payment. Why have these attacks become so prevalent? Experts cite four factors (Kay 2021):

- Cloud computing and infrastructure make it much easier for criminals around the world to operate within a standardized environment. This allows them to scale their efforts and to do so from afar.
- Criminal ransomware organizations now sell their attack "services" to other bad actors, generating an additional revenue stream for themselves.
- Attacks are increasingly being made on critical infrastructure, which cannot tolerate long periods of downtime. These organizations are thus more likely to pay the ransoms.
- Bigger organizations, including rogue nations and terrorist organizations, are now starting to get into the ransomware game. These organizations are well-funded and benefit from the economic and political disruptions that their attacks cause.

Another factor that benefits ransomware attackers is the reluctance of the management team to publicly admit that an attack has occurred. Although only 10% ever recover all of the data that was stolen and the cost for clean-up is often 10x the ransom paid (Kay 2021), many organizations would rather quietly pay the ransom and then get back to business before customers, business partners, and other stakeholders are made aware of the attack. Not surprisingly, organizations are especially concerned about the reaction from their customers. The concerns that consumers have about the privacy of their data stems from skepticism about how the data is handled and a general lack of control over the process. Importantly, when consumers have significant concerns about their privacy, key KPIs (including attitudes and behaviors) can be negatively impacted (Okazaki, Eisend, Plangger, de Ruyter, and Grewal 2020).

Forward-thinking organizations are responding to issues of security and privacy by instituting a variety of safeguards. An important first step, however, is for the organization's leadership team to create a clear plan. This includes identifying who is responsible for decision-making, establishing methods of communication among the leadership team in the event normal communication is not possible, and updating the firm's insurance. A necessary second step is to train all employees on cybersecurity methods, with specific attention on any high-risk employees who have access to especially-sensitive data and systems. Finally, the organization should institute a variety of new protocols, such as multi-factor identification systems, back-up systems, and security systems for key business partners. This step could also include hiring cybersecurity experts to identify any areas of weakness (Sharton 2021).

Governments and other large trading blocs are also working to address the issue of privacy and security. **The General Data Protection Regulation (GDPR)** came into effect in 2018. It protects EU citizens by clearly defining how data about them can be collected and used. The regulation places particularly strong restrictions on the use of personal data and any data that can be utilized, combined, or manipulated to identify a person. The GDPR has seven core principles (see Table 3.3 and Photo 3.8).

Photo 3.8 The GDPR protects EU citizens from unauthorized collection, storage, or use of personal data

Table 3.3 Core principles of the GDPR

GDPR Principle	Meaning
Data minimization	Organizations must not collect more personal data from people than what they need.
Integrity and confidentiality (security)	Personal data must be kept secure against any unauthorized and unlawful processing. This includes safeguards against accidental loss, destruction, or damage.
Accountability	Procedures for the handling and administration of personal data must be clearly documented.
Lawfulness, fairness, and transparency	Organizations must process all personal data in a lawful, fair, and transparent manner.
Accuracy	Organizations must quickly and accurately correct any inaccuracies in the data that they have collected.
Purpose limitation	Organizations must only collect and process personal data for explicit and legitimate purposes; personal data shall not be further processed for reasons that are incompatible with their original purpose.
Storage limitation	Personal data must only be stored and archived for the period of time for which it is needed.

Source: European Parliament (2016)

Problems with Big Data

There is no doubt that big data has provided numerous benefits to marketing teams. As important as they are, however, numbers can be very misleading. Indeed, big data has four distinct problems. First, the data collection process is, by its nature, biased. When consumers are asked about their consumption attitudes or behaviors, their responses frequently do not map onto actual behaviors. Consumers often tell researchers what they want to hear or respond in a way that makes them look good. Worse yet, consumers often are untruthful in their responses. One study by a well-known global marketing research firm found that 42% of respondents lied about simple demographic information (Murphy 2021).

One of the most prevalent types of bias is **selection bias**, which occurs when data is gathered from some consumers and not others. Unfortunately, most sources of big data are from an organization's own consumers, such as customer loyalty data and sales data. However, by just gathering data about the organization's own consumers, marketers miss out on the opportunity to derive critical insights from non-consumers (Louviere, Swait, and Frischknecht 2013), especially those people who are previous consumers and those who have looked at the firm's value proposition and have decided to say "no." These individuals potentially represent a very valuable source of insights.

The second problem with big data relates to how it is interpreted. Often, the marketing team has a preconceived notion about what they expect to find and will interpret the findings through that lens. Further complicating matters, the interpretation is often conducted by analysts who are often very different from the individuals who are being studied. Indeed, interpretations are often done by individuals who have a Western cultural frame of reference, are university-educated, are White, and middle- or upper-middle class. Sometimes the interpretations are deep and insightful; sometimes they are not. This problem related to interpretation of big data can be particularly prevalent in cross-cultural applications, such as the case of an aluminum foil manufacturer that was having trouble getting traction in the Latin American market. To reach this market, the marketing team initially tried a strong advertising push, backed by price discounts. The marketing team was surprised when these efforts did not work. Researchers soon determined that the product did not present a significant value proposition to this demographic – foil was not needed for cooking or heating up food (because corn husks and banana leaves were preferred) and it was not needed for wrapping up left-overs (because families were fairly big, left-overs were rare). The aluminum foil manufacturer decided to concentrate its efforts elsewhere (Murphy 2021). Regardless of how it occurs, misinterpretation of data can lead to lost opportunities and marketing missteps.

Still another problem is referred to as **data hubris**, a belief that the numbers are the story, rather than simply part of the story. Sometimes, marketing decision-makers get so distracted by data collection efforts and the sheer abundance of data, that they lose sight of the original purpose of data collection. The problem is, up to 73% of data that is collected by organizations is not used (Barrett 2018). With so much data, it is often difficult to sort through and determine which data will be most helpful in solving the problem. Adding to this difficulty is that, once the system is established for big data collection, it is relatively easy and inexpensive for marketers to keep collecting it. By comparison, focus groups can cost upwards of $5000–$9000 per group, and other qualitative research methods like in-home visits or in-depth interviews are also expensive, difficult to arrange, and time-consuming (Murphy 2021). When the marketing team is experiencing data hubris, it will likely favor big data solutions over solutions that are based on multiple sources of data.

A fourth problem is that big data can be **dehumanizing**. Indeed, advances in data collection technology have resulted in an exponential explosion of data that is collected from our GPS systems, wearable technology, home assistant devices, online behaviors, etc. On one hand, this data is useful in providing the ability for marketers to engage in pin-point targeting of messages and offerings to consumers. This saves customers time and effort. Some critics, however, have issued a note of caution. The crux of the argument is that data is gathered according to very specific algorithms that are primarily useful for marketers, not consumers. Essentially, pre-programmed rules of data collection and manipulation are driving the interactions between consumers and the marketing team. Rather than being used to promote human welfare, some critics argue that these "instrumental" interactions are dehumanizing (Deighton 2019).

These problems – bias, interpretation, data hubris, and dehumanization – all stem from the fact that the purpose of big data is a determination of the *what* of a given phenomenon, rather than *why* it happened. Big data certainly has the ability to provide tremendous information about broad demographic trends, shifts in attitudes, purchase patterns, and other types of consumer behavior. However, it cannot provide the relevant context. Sure, the Latin American market seemed like a huge untapped potential for aluminum foil. However, differences in cultural attitudes and norms about cooking and the family meant that aluminum foil presented no discernible value proposition to these consumers. Using data collected from other sources, such as qualitative methods, provided the answer to *why* these consumers were not interested in the product (Murphy 2021). Incorporating data from different sources and using different data collection methods is likely to provide a better understanding of these *why* kinds of questions.

Systemic Thinking

The notion of a simple cause-and-effect relationship is insufficient to account for the myriad of effects that often occur in the context of the marketplace. Instead, it is more accurate to think of the impact of a single decision in terms of a *web of effects*. This type of thinking is not linear – it is multi-dimensional and forward thinking.

The Triple Bottom Line is an example of systemic thinking because it recognizes that each part of the model effects other parts of the model. Consider the example of a marketing objective that seeks to improve customer satisfaction scores by 20%. The intent is to positively impact the *people* dimension of the Triple Bottom Line with the introduction of a new customer service initiative. However, what will be the impact on other people, such as employees, who will have new tasks and greater responsibilities? Similarly, what will be the likely impact on the *prosperity* dimension? Prosperity might be simultaneously hurt by higher costs, but helped by the brand attaining a more competitive position in the marketplace. Regarding the *planet* dimension, what will be the impact on energy usage or implementation of new materials or computer systems? Each of the three dimensions needs to be carefully assessed.

Another example of systemic thinking is taking account of **externalized costs**, those indirect costs that are often not borne by the company, but are offloaded onto another entity, such as the local community, the environment, or society at large. Companies that do not pay their employees a fair or living wage are one example in which costs are externalized. Because these employees earn such low wages, they often take advantage of other social services, such as housing or food assistance programs. These programs are funded by tax receipts, so in effect, taxpayers are supplementing the company's low-wage policies. Take another example: an energy company that drills for oil in environmentally-sensitive areas. A proper accounting of externalized costs would include, for example, extra costs needed for clean up of spills, environmental degradation, habitat loss, and reduced human health. When externalized costs are properly incorporated, the price that consumers pay for a liter of gas at the pump will include these costs too. Although some critics might balk at the thought of an increase in gas prices, it is important to remember that these costs will eventually be paid by someone, somewhere. For example, farmers and fishermen will pay because of lower yields, consumers will pay because of higher prices at the grocery store, the tourism industry will pay because of fewer tourists, and workers will pay because of unhealthy and hazardous working conditions. In 2010, one of the worst environmental disasters in history occurred when an oil rig in the Gulf of Mexico blew up, killing 11 people, and eventually spilling 3.2 million barrels of oil into the pristine waters of the Gulf. All told, the actual cost to BP for clean up, legal fees, and other compensation was

estimated to be $146 billion. However, if externalized costs were incorporated, estimates would have also included an additional $5.2 trillion to the nearly 7 million local businesses who were affected and $47.66 billion for the environment (Lee, Garza-Gomez, and Lee 2018).

International business-related organizations, such as the International Monetary Fund (IMF), have called for governments and businesses to fully account for externalized costs in the fossil fuel industry. In 2015, the IMF found that $4.7 trillion (or 6.3% of global GDP) was used to subsidize fossil fuel use; in 2017, that amount increased to $5.2 trillion. Counterintuitively, if fossil fuels were fairly priced, including all externalized costs such as environmental damage and premature deaths from air pollution, the overall cost would have actually been *less than* the subsidies. That's right. Overall, if all externalized costs were incorporated into fossil fuel exploration, production, distribution, and consumption, it would cost less than the amount spent by governments on subsidizing the industry. Notably, deaths from fossil fuel-related air pollution would drop by half and CO_2 emissions would drop by 28%. Bottom line, eliminating fossil fuel subsidies would result in a net economic welfare gain of $1.3 trillion, or 1.7% of global GDP (Dickinson 2019).

The Value of Qualitative Data

As important as quantitative data is, qualitative data should also be considered and incorporated into the marketing team's decision-making. Robert McNamara perfected the use of data and statistical analyses in managerial decision-making. During a 1967 speech, he famously claimed that to "not quantify what can be quantified is only to be content with something less than the full range of reason." He was a product of his generation. At the time, leadership and management theory emphasized the importance of analyzing data and maximizing efficiency. He was a Harvard University professor, corporate leader, and the US secretary of defense during the Vietnam war. The failures in Vietnam, however, opened his eyes to a more holistic perspective on the use of data (Rosenzweig 2010).

McNamara experienced a stunning realization from the many mistakes that were made by the US in the planning and execution of the Vietnam war, which relied on what he believed to be an unbiased analysis of the data. Too late, he realized that such a hard-nosed examination of data ignored the very real qualitative motivators also at play, such as the motivations and passions of the individuals involved. In order to develop a full and nuanced understanding of the situation, McNamara acknowledged that he needed to have empathy for the enemy and that his so-called "unbiased" data could itself have built-in biases because of the way it was gathered, organized, analyzed, and interpreted. Because of these realizations, McNamara shifted his approach to work toward improving the lives of people around the world. He became the first non-family member at the helm of Ford Motors and later became the head of the World Bank. In all his work, he pushed his organizations to take a data-driven approach that was more holistically understood by layering in findings from qualitative data (Rosenzweig 2010). Today, scholars and leadership experts have confirmed the importance of embracing both qualitative and quantitative data (e.g., Joly and Lambert 2021).

Triangulation

Often, the marketing team will get a more accurate indication of the phenomenon of interest when it incorporates data from more than one method into its analyses (Adamek 1994). **Triangulation** refers to the use of multiple research methods (ideally including both quantitative and qualitative) to develop a holistic and nuanced picture of the phenomenon of interest. Consider the example of Lego Group and the precipitous drop in sales it experienced in the early 2000s. The problem was that sales were dropping – that was the *what*. The issue, however, was determining the *why*. The marketing team looked at the increased sales of video games and concluded that the reason for the sales slump was children who were more interested in video games and the instant gratification they provided. Based on this conclusion, Lego introduced a variety of Lego sets with bigger components that could be assembled more quickly to tap into the "instant gratification motivation." Sales dropped even further. Eventually, the team decided to embark on some qualitative data collection to help develop a more nuanced picture of the situation. They conducted a series of focus groups, home visits, and in-depth interviews with individuals in the target market. As a result, the team found something surprising – children in the target market were not looking for instant gratification at all. Instead, they were interested in sets that connected to characters they loved, such as Harry Potter. Lego responded with more intricate sets based on well-loved characters. Sales increased and by 2021, Lego was the world's largest toy company by sales (Murphy 2021).

BLUNDERS & INSIGHTS 3.2

Actually, Lisa is very nice

BACKGROUND: In 2014, Bank of America (BofA) collaborated with an international collegiate honor society to offer an exclusive credit card promotion to its members. The Golden Key International Honour Society forwarded its membership list to BofA so that the promotional materials could be mailed to society members. Everything was fine until one member received her BoA offer. The envelope was addressed to "Lisa Is a Slut McIntire" in Menlo Park, California. Inside, the letter read, "Lisa Is a Slut McIntire, you've earned this special offer!" News of the incident splashed across Twitter and Facebook. McIntire laughed off the incident, but needless to say, she did not sign up for a new Visa card. The reputations of both organizations, however, were tarnished. After a careful investigation by both Golden Key and BofA, two important problems related to data collection and automated processing were identified. First, Golden Key discovered that someone in the organization had entered "Is a Slut" into McIntire's data file, most likely as a prank. Second, although BofA's automated mailing system had safeguards for flagging certain key words, "slut" was not one of those words (Pearce 2014)

DEBRIEF: Two things. From Golden Key's perspective, extra security measures and periodic review of data files are necessary to ensure the continued integrity of the data. As the saying goes, "garbage in, garbage out." From BofA's perspective, relying on automated data scans for key words was clearly inadequate in identifying problem text. More robust scanning software and reviews were needed.

How Do we Make Sense of all this Data?

The next step in reason-based decision-making is **organization and analysis of the data**, where we make any corrections to the data and prepare it for analysis. As the previous example with BofA illustrates, it is crucial to ensure that the data is correct. Incomplete data files need to be fixed or eliminated, data entry mistakes need to be fixed, and any outliers should be examined carefully. An **outlier** is a datapoint that, for some reason, is very atypical compared to the rest of the data in the dataset. In order to identify outliers, analysists can calculate the means for key variables of interest and examine scatterplots. If, for example, a consumer's age, income, or attitude score is very far outside the normal range of scores, data analysts need to examine the reason for this discrepancy. The score might be correct. If it is not, however, the correct data needs to be entered. In the event that the datapoint cannot be corrected, it must be eliminated before any analyses take place.

After analysts are sure the dataset is cleaned of errors and outliers, the dataset needs to be organized into files so that it can be subjected to analysis. There are a variety of sophisticated analytical software programs that can subject the data to a variety of manipulations and statistical techniques. **Marketing metrics** are a set of calculations that can be utilized to help the marketing team quantify a phenomenon of interest and answer a marketing problem. These metrics include measures such as break-even point, market potential, and customer lifetime value. **Marketing analytics** takes a set of marketing metrics (and likely other statistical analyses) and puts the results into context. Marketing analytics often incorporates big data and sophisticated modeling techniques that churn through terabytes or even exabytes of data to identify current patterns and predict future behaviors or events in the marketplace. While marketing analytics is certainly a useful tool for strategists to employ, the focus of this discussion is the decision-making process. At this stage of the process, it is important that the research team differentiates between correlation and causation before they utilize data visualization tools to summarize the results.

Correlation vs. Causation

An important note of caution needs to be made in examining the data: just because two concepts or variables are correlated, it does not mean that one causes the other. That is, correlation does not imply causation. **Correlation** describes a situation in which two variables move together. However, just because they move together, it does not mean that one variable causes the other variable to move. One strange example found that per capita consumption of margarine has a 99% correlation with the divorce rate in the US state of Maine. Does an increase in margarine *cause* more marriages in Maine to break up? Obviously not. However, the two variables move together very reliably over time (Vigen 2015). A well-designed research study and intimate knowledge of the phenomenon of interest will reveal **causation**, which is an *actual* relationship between two variables such that one variable causes a change in the other. Because of decades of research and experience with some variables, we can be confident of several different causal relationships in marketing. For example, more positive attitudes toward an advertisement results in more positive attitudes toward the brand in that ad; stronger brand loyalty results in a willingness to pay a higher price for the product; and stronger intentions to buy the product result in a higher likelihood of actually purchasing the product.

Data Visualization

Data visualization depicts data in an organized format to help communicate important findings in order to assist decision-makers in creating insights. The results of marketing metrics or data analytics are summarized in easy-to-interpret charts and graphics. Rather than slogging through long and complicated reports, decision-makers can view the most important results in one place and in context with one another. Further, data visualization tools allow for this important information to be shared both inside and outside the organization. Data visualization is becoming an increasingly indispensable tool and is especially useful when the marketing team is utilizing big data (DeGraaf 2015). To illustrate the increasing importance of data visualization, simply look at the 2019 purchase of Tableau, the world's largest data visualization platform, by Salesforce, the world's largest customer relationship management (CRM) platform. The purchase price was $15.7 billion, *ten times* Tableau's annual revenue at the time of the acquisition (Miller and Lim 2020) (see Photo 3.9).

Photo 3.9 Data visualization helps decision-makers create insights from data and information

Source: Kaspars Grinvalds / Shutterstock

How can we develop Useful Insights?

In the next step of reason-based decision-making, the team develops a set of **insights**, or useful interpretations of the information and data. In crafting insights, the marketing team must have a deep level of understanding about the relevant context (Miller and Lim 2020). Useful insights generally are not crafted from a single research finding. Instead, they are generated from the convergence of several different research findings, such as the team's previous experience in working with this marketplace and target market, information from exercises such as developing a SWOT, examining secondary research, and conducting primary research. The nature of the competitive landscape needs to be examined, as does the market outlook. There is no magic formula for developing good insights. However, only when the marketing team examines these and other pieces of information in a systemic way can insights be generated (see Figure 3.4).

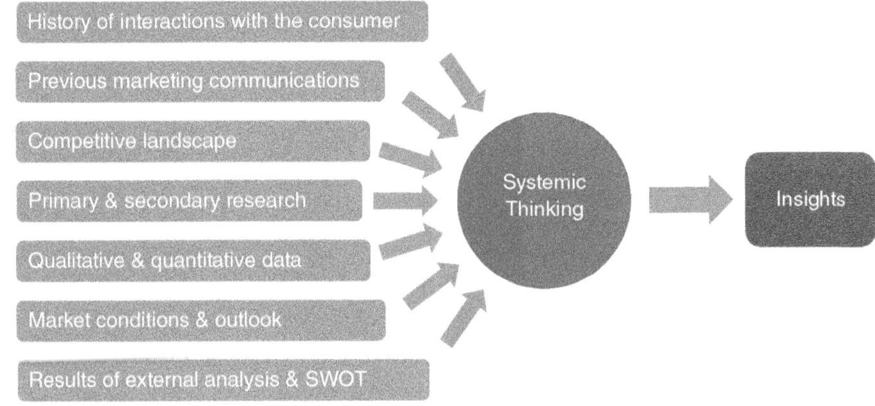

Figure 3.4 Systemic thinking and insights

In a study of chief marketing officers (CMOs) from around the world, the importance of data and insights to the development of strategy was confirmed. Indeed, the top two most important strategic priorities for these CMOs were market research/competitive insights and marketing analytics (Starita 2019). This underscores the importance of the data → information → insights relationship in the development of effective and impactful strategy. It also underscores the importance of clearly articulating the problem of interest in the early stages of the process; if marketing managers are not able to ask the right questions, they will not be able to get the right answers.

It is critical that decision-makers utilize both volume metrics and value metrics when creating insights. **Volume metrics** are those that are derived from big data and other sources that track the market and consumer behavior. They include the types of quantitative measures found in Table 3.1. **Value metrics**, by contrast, are those measures that are often derived from qualitative research and describe a phenomenon, such as the strength of customer relationships or the sentimental meaning consumers attach to our brand (Starita 2019). Measures like these are found in Table 3.2. Systemic thinking can be the difference between a mediocre strategy and a great strategy. As we've discussed, there are numerous benefits of decision-making that incorporates both qualitative and quantitative dimensions. As an example, simply look at a fascinating result from a study of individuals who won a Nobel Prize in the sciences – 80% of them were able to identify specific instances in which the arts enhanced their innovative and creative abilities (Root-Bernstein 2008).

ENDURING INSIGHTS 3.3

"We cannot solve our problems with the same thinking we used when we created them." – Albert Einstein

Perhaps the world's best-known physicist, Einstein is known for his development of the Theory of Relativity. His intellectual achievements in the first half of the 20th century have had such a profound impact on life today, that "Einstein" has become synonymous with "genius." With this quote, Einstein acknowledged the importance of expanding one's thought process beyond its traditional range.

3.4 MARKETING METRICS

Earlier in this text, we emphasized the importance of marketing objectives that were measurable. This is why. Marketing battles will be fought and won (or lost) on the foundation of data, data analytics, and the insights we derive from them. With the proliferation of big data, the number of analytical tools has also increased. Five of the most frequently utilized marketing metrics are: market potential, conversion rate, return on investment, break-even point, and customer lifetime value. Each one of these concepts is briefly described below. Refer to Appendix 2 for more detail and examples of these and other marketing metrics.

Market Potential

Market potential is an estimate of the amount of sales or profit that can be made from a given market segment. This metric helps the marketing team assess the attractiveness of a new target market and reassess its existing target market. Marketing budgets are rarely unlimited, so the marketing team needs to carefully select the target market that has the strongest potential for profits. When everything else is equal between two target markets (e.g., they are equally easy to reach, they have a similar expected longevity), the marketing team will select the market that has the highest market potential. When PEZ, Inc. was contemplating expanding into a new target market in the US, it conducted an analysis of the market potential for two very different target markets. Find out more by reading the case study on p.397.

Conversion Rate

The **conversion rate** represents the percentage of consumers who perform a desired behavior. Conversion rates can be assessed for the percentage of consumers who complete a purchase after going to our store, who add a service plan after purchasing the product, or who click through for more information after visiting our website. Therefore, the conversion rate is useful in indicating the effectiveness of different promotional channels. For example, research indicates that globally, the conversion rate for online shoppers was 2.17% in late 2020. That is, just 2.17% of individuals who visited a website completed a purchase (Chevalier 2021).

Return on Investment (ROI)

One of the most widely-used metrics in marketing, **return on investment (ROI)** is an assessment of how much profit we can expect to make from a particular investment. If the marketing team launches a new advertising campaign, opens up a new market, or invests in search engine optimization (SEO), for example, what will be the financial payoff?

Return on environment (ROE) is a concept that is similar to ROI. However, this measure takes into account the broad array of financial, social, and environmental benefits (think Triple Bottom Line) that result from an environmentally-related investment. When organizations shift to more pro-environmental operations, there are numerous financial benefits, such as lower disposal costs, greater energy savings, and higher operating efficiencies. There are also indirect prosperity-related benefits, such as longer-term increases in organizational reputation (Loock and Phillips 2020) and respect (Parletta 2019). Social benefits might include, for example, stronger communities, happier families, and healthier consumers. Finally, environmental benefits include such things as clean air, clean water, healthier habitat, and less waste. Each of these dimensions can be quantified to provide an overall ROE metric.

Break-Even Point

Often, a marketing manager will want to know the **break-even point**, the point at which the amount of revenue the organization generates equals the organization's expenses in delivering those items to consumers. After the break-even point, the organization starts to generate profit. The break-even point can be assessed from a volume perspective (how many iPhones do we need to sell to break even?) or from a sales perspective (how much revenue do we need to make before we can break even?). A recent analysis compared the environmental impact of gasoline cars (with higher per km impact, but lower production impact) with electric cars (lower per km impact, but higher production impact). Experts concluded that drivers needed to drive 21,725 km in their electric vehicles in order to break even with gasoline vehicles. After that, every km driven represents an environmental benefit. Of particular interest, however, was an assessment of the method by which the electricity was generated

Photo 3.10 The environmental break-even point in the US for an electric car is 21,725 km

Source: Pixabay

to power the electric car. This study was conducted in the US, where 23% of the electricity comes from renewables. In countries like Norway, where close to 100% of the electricity is produced by renewable energy, the break-even point occurs around 13,518 km. In countries like China or Poland, however, where almost all of the electricity is generated by coal, the break-even point is an astounding 126,655 km (Lienert 2021) (see Photo 3.10). Even in the extreme case where 100% of electricity is generated by coal, electric vehicles are still better for the environment on a per-km basis than gasoline-powered vehicles (see Table 3.4).

Table 3.4 The environmental costs of electric vs. gasoline vehicles

	Environmental Cost of Production	Environmental Operating Cost Per Year*
Electric Vehicle	8.1 million grams of CO_2	4.1 million grams of CO_2
Gasoline Vehicle	5.5 million grams of CO_2	4.6 million grams of CO_2

*Assumes typical distance driven by an owner in 1 year and electricity generated from 100% coal

Source: Lienert (2021)

Customer Lifetime Value (LTV)

This marketing metric, **customer lifetime value (LTV)**, assesses the amount of profit that a given customer is worth to the organization, over that customer's entire lifetime of interactions with the organization. This metric is based on the fundamental notion that it is more profitable to keep a customer than it is to find a new one. Simply put, the LTV metric reveals which customers are worth more and therefore may be deserving of extra attention. Customer relationship management efforts are often based on providing differential attention to those customers who demonstrate higher LTV.

3.5 SUMMARY

In marketing, reason-based decision-making starts with a clear identification of the problem at hand. This step launches the rest of the process which will eventually end with the creation of a set of insights that will help decision-makers answer the problem. Critical to this process are the generation and use of data, one of the organization's most important strategic assets (Burnett-Lemon 2015; Connolly 2013). If the data was generated from the organization's own customers, as with sales data, use of warranties, or customer inquiries, it is especially valuable and can provide a rich source of detail, history, and context regarding what makes these customers tick. Further, a detailed and rich set of data can provide predictive ability for how customers may react to a new offering. Data should therefore never be sold or left vulnerable to data breaches. When reason-based decision-making is well-executed and in alignment with the organization's overall goals and values (see Gadiesh and Gilbert 2001), it can serve as a competitive advantage for the organization because it provides the organization with decision-making capabilities more quickly, that are more in-tune with the realities of the marketplace. It's the difference between a pencil drawing vs. a full-color 3D image of the dynamic and turbulent competitive landscape and all of its possibilities. Armed with better data and more relevant and timely reason-based decision-making, the organization will be poised to out-maneuver the competition and better-deliver the value proposition to the target market. For a detailed listing of important marketing metrics, refer to Appendix 2.

QUESTIONS FOR REVIEW & DISCUSSION

1 Terracycle's decision to move some of its production to China and then move it back to the US again ended up being very costly for the organization. Using the model of reason-based decision-making, what did they do right? What may they have done wrong?

2 What do we mean when we say that decision criteria should be consequential? Create an argument for how quantitative and qualitative criteria can each be consequential.

3 Big data presents at least four important problems. Describe each problem, providing an example of each. Why do marketing decision-makers still use big data?

4 One of the steps in the reason-based decision-making process is selecting the most relevant data. How do we know which data will be the most relevant?

5 Imagine that your neighbor Alex is very much against government interference and believes that the market should determine the cost of different items, such as food and gasoline. Create an argument to convince Alex that all externalized costs should be incorporated into the price of a liter of gasoline.

6 What are the benefits of systemic thinking in reason-based decision-making? What might be some drawbacks?

3.6 REFERENCES

Adamek, James C. 1994. Fusion: Combining Data from Separate Sources. *Marketing Research, 6* (3), Summer, 48–50.

Albala, Ken. 2018. A Brief (But Global) History of Ketchup. *SmithsonianMag.com*. 24 July. Accessed 17 June 2021. www.smithsonianmag.com/arts-culture/brief-but-global-history-ketchup-180969725/.

Ang, Katerina. 2019. Tommy Hilfiger is selling better than ever. Here's its plan to win the future. *Vogue Business*, 9 April. Accessed 18 April 2020. www.voguebusiness.com/companies/tommy-hilfiger-daniel-grieder-interview-technology-sustainability.

Barrett, Jeff. 2018. Up to 73 Percent of Company Data Goes Unused for Analytics. Here's How to Put it to Work. *Inc*. 12 April. Accessed 7 July 2021. www.inc.com/jeff-barrett/misusing-data-could-be-costing-your-business-heres-how.html.

Burnett-Lemon, Jessica. 2015. The Key to Research? Ask the Right Questions: A Q&A with Sarab Kochhar. *International Association of Business Communicators*. 8 July. Accessed 12 July 2021. www.iabc.com/actionable-research-depends-on-asking-the-right-questions-sarab-kochhar-2/.

Chapman, Randall G. 1989. Problem-definition in Marketing Research Studies. *Journal of Consumer Marketing*, *6* (2), 51–9.

Chevalier, Stephanie. 2021. Global Online Shopper Conversion Rate 2018--2021. *Statista*. 7 July. Accessed 12 July 2021. www.statista.com/statistics/439576/online-shopper-conversion-rate-worldwide/

Connolly, Mark. 2013. The Importance to Brands of Owning Their Own Data. *Global CMO The Magazine*. November/December, 8–9.

DeGraaf, Justin. 2015. The Social Game: From Social Media to Analytics, a Firm Grasp on Fundamentals Makes All the Difference. *Marketing Insights*. January/February, 18–19.

Deighton, John A. 2019. Big Data. *Consumption Markets & Culture*, *22* (1), 68–73.

Dickinson, Tim. 2019. Study: US Fossil Fuel Subsidies Exceed Pentagon Spending. *RollingStone*. Politics News Section. *8* May. Accessed 9 July 2021. www.rollingstone.com/politics/politics-news/fossil-fuel-subsidies-pentagon-spending-imf-report-833035/.

European Parliament. 2016. *Regulation (EU) 2016/679 of the European Parliament and of the Council, Chapter II, Principles*. 27 April 2016.

Gadiesh, Orit and James L. Gilbert. 2001. Transforming Corner-Office Strategy into Frontline Action. *Harvard Business Review*, *79* (5), 72–9.

Guzman, Zack. 2015. Ketchup-maker Heinz: Sorry About the Porn. *CNBC.com*. 18 June. Accessed 17 June 2021. www.cnbc.com/2015/06/18/ketchup-maker-heinz-sorry-about-the-porn.html.

Haoues, Rachid. 2015. 30 Years Ago Today, Coca-Cola Made its Worst Mistake. *CBS News*. 23 April. Accessed 13 July 2021. www.cbsnews.com/news/30-years-ago-today-coca-cola-new-coke-failure/.

Hoek, Marga. 2018. *The Trillion Dollar Shift: Achieving the Sustainable Development Goals: Business for Good is Good Business*. Routledge, Abingdon, UK.

Joly, Hubert and Caroline Lambert. 2021. *The Heart of Business: Leadership Principles for the Next Era of Capitalism*. Harvard Business Review Press, Boston, Massachusetts.

Kay, Barbara. 2021. The Destructive Rise of Ransomware-as-a-Service. *Forbes.com*. 9 June. Accessed 7 July 2021. www.forbes.com/sites/servicenow/2021/06/09/the-destructive-rise-of-ransomware-as-a-service/?sh=1ca65f351e16

Kelly, Allan. 1996. Make Decisions Based on Data. *Marketing News*, *30* (22), 21 October. 4.

Kitchin, Rob and Gavin McArdle. 2016. What Makes Big Data, Big Data? Exploring the Ontological Characteristics of 26 Datasets. *Big Data & Society*. January–June, 1–10. doi: https://doi.org/10.1177/2053951716631130.

Lee, Yong-Gyo, Xavier Garza-Gomez, and Rose M. Lee. 2018. Ultimate Costs of the Disaster: Seven Years After the Deepwater Horizon Oil Spill. *Journal of Corporate Accounting & Finance*, *29* (1), 69–79.

Lienert, Paul. 2021. Analysis: When Do Electric Vehicles Become Cleaner Than Gasoline Cars? *Reuters*. *29* June. Accessed 2 July 2021. https://apple.news/AQg7f1avbQhOI2s2aFdWFrQ

Loock, Moritz and Diane M. Phillips. 2020. A Firm's Financial Reputation vs. Sustainability Reputation: Do Consumers Really Care? *Sustainability*, *12* (24), 1–17. http://dx.doi.org/10.3390/su122410519.

Louviere, Jordan, Joffre Swait, and Bart Frischknecht. 2013. Seeing Forests Instead of Trees: The Pervasiveness of Selection Bias in Market Research. *Marketing Insights*, Fall, 18–19.

Miller, Janet Driscoll and Julia Lim. 2020. *Data-first Marketing: How to Compete and Win in the Age of Analytics*. John Wiley & Sons, Inc., Hoboken, New Jersey.

Murphy, Kate. 2021. Why Companies Shouldn't Give Up on Focus Groups. *The Wall Street Journal*. 23 May.

O'Flaherty, Kate. 2019. Marriott Faces $123 Million Fine For 2018 Mega-Breach. *Forbes.com.* 9 June. Accessed 7 July 2021. www.forbes.com/sites/kateoflahertyuk/2019/07/09/marriott-faces-gdpr-fine-of-123-million/?sh=494f5beb4525.

Okazaki, Shintaro, Martin Eisend, Kirk Plangger, Ko de Ruyter, and Dhruv Grewal. 2020. Understanding the Strategic Consequences of Customer Privacy Concerns: A Meta-Analytic Review. *Journal of Retailing, 96* (4), 458–73.

Parletta, Natalie. 2019. Going Green – What's Good for the Planet is Good for Business. *Forbes.com.* 14 May. Accessed 12 July 2021. www.forbes.com/sites/natalieparletta/2019/05/14/going-green-whats-good-for-the-planet-is-good-for-business/?sh=452d0f8d3201.

Pearce, Matt. 2014. Junk Mail Misfire: Bank of America Mailer Calls Woman a "Slut." *Los Angeles Times.* World & Nation Section. 6 February. Accessed 8 July 2021. www.latimes.com/nation/nationnow/la-na-nn-bank-of-america-mailer-20140206-story.html.

Phillips, Diane M. and Jason Keith Phillips. 2016. Sustainable growth at Terracycle: Should manufacturing be moved? Case 9B16A010 and Teaching Note 8B16A010. *Ivey Publishing, Ivey Management Services,* The University of Western Ontario, London, Ontario, Canada.

Prater, Meg. 2021. 25 Google Search Statistics to Bookmark ASAP. *Hubspot.* 9 June. Accessed 14 June 2021. https://blog.hubspot.com/marketing/google-search-statistics.

Rejeb, Abderahaman, Karim Rejeb, and John G. Keogh. 2020. Potential of Big Data for Marketing: A Literature Review. *Management Research and Practice, 12* (3), 60–73.

Root-Bernstein, et al. 2008. Arts Foster Success: Comparison of Nobel Prizewinners, Royal Society, National Academy, and Sigma Xi Members. *Journal of the Psychology of Science and Technology, 1* (2), 51–63.

Rosenzweig, Phil. 2010. Robert S. McNamara and the Evolution of Modern Management. *Harvard Business Review, 88* (12), 88–93.

Sharton, Brenda R. 2021. Ransomware Attacks are Spiking. Is Your Company Prepared? *Harvard Business Review Magazine,* Security & Privacy Section. 20 May. Accessed 7 July 2021. https://hbr.org/2021/05/ransomware-attacks-are-spiking-is-your-company-prepared.

Sicular, Svetlana. 2013. Gartner's Big Data Definition Consists of Three Parts, Not to be Confused with Three "V"s. *Forbes.com.* 27 March. Accessed 11 May 2021. www.forbes.com/sites/gartnergroup/2013/03/27/gartners-big-data-definition-consists-of-three-parts-not-to-be-confused-with-three-vs/?sh=79d0b2b42f68.

Smith, Kit. 2020. 60 Incredible and Interesting Twitter Stats and Statistics. *Brandwatch.* 2 January. Accessed 14 June 2021. www.brandwatch.com/blog/twitter-stats-and-statistics/.

Starita, Laura. 2019. 4 Key Findings in the Annual Gartner CMO Spend Survey 2019–2020. *Gartner.* 3 October. Accessed 14 June 2021. www.gartner.com/en/marketing/insights/articles/4-key-findings-in-the-annual-gartner-cmo-spend-survey-2019-2020.

Valentine, Rebekah. 2018. Microsoft Gaming Revenue Up 44% Despite Quiet Q1 2019. *Games Industry Biz,* 25 October. Accessed 26 April 2020. www.gamesindustry.biz/articles/2018-10-24-microsoft-gaming-revenue-up-44-percent-despite-quiet-q1-2019.

Vigen, Tyler. 2015. *Spurious Correlations: Correlation Does Not Equal Causation.* Hachette Book Group, New York, NY.

Winer, Leon. 1966. A Profit-oriented Decision System. *Journal of Marketing, 30* (January), 38–44.

4 THE MOST IMPORTANT PERSON: PRIORITIZING THE CONSUMER EXPERIENCE

LEADERSHIP INSIGHTS 4

Photo 4.1 José Díaz Jurado fashion show

Source: courtesy, José Díaz Jurado

Meet José Díaz Jurado

Founder of José Díaz Jurado (JDJ) Couture

It was typical day at José Díaz Jurado's studio in Panama City, Panama: armed guards were outside and secret service police were patrolling the streets. The Vice President of Panama, Isabel St. Malo, was getting a dress for an upcoming event.

Although Jurado is one of the most exclusive couture designers in Panama, he came from very humble beginnings. Born in a rural province of Panama, he followed in his family's footsteps and learned how to sew and tailor clothing. At the age of 18, he followed his dream of becoming a fashion designer and moved to Panama City. There, he started working with some of the city's top designers. "I was born to be an artist," Jurado explained. His first big break came in 1997, when he made a dress for the wife of the president of Peru.

In 2013, he established his own brand, JDJ, in one of the most prominent locations in the city. "I design, cut, and assemble haute couture dresses for high-end clients. We have a constant growth of new clients because people see my designs and the word spreads. Once they see it, they also want to have one," reflected Jurado. "Ladies from high society like the First Lady, Vice President, and business executives, come here for their own designs. I have had my dresses at the Grammys, Emmys, and other international events. When the First Lady of Panama went to New York for the Grammys, she wore a dress that I made. She always buys dresses here. When the Vice President, Isabel St. Malo, had a meeting at Buckingham Palace, I made her a blue coat. I made the dress that Miss Panama used for the Miss World pageant. I made the dress for Erika Ender when she went to the Grammys. This global exposure has helped me transcend international boundaries," Jurado observed.

Photo 4.2 2021 JDJ fashion show

Source: courtesy, José Díaz Jurado

In growing his business, Jurado has faced several challenges, one of which was locating high-end materials, "I just cannot get high-quality fabrics, beading, and other high fashion materials locally." What did Jurado do? He went out and struck exclusive deals with some of the top global purveyors of fabrics and other supplies. "I have exclusive arrangements with several companies around the world, like Lanificio Cerruti fabrics, which is made in Italy. I am the only one in Panama who can carry their fabric. It gives me an edge," reported Jurado. In fact, when the Vice President was welcomed at Buckingham Palace, her blue coat was made with Cerruti fabric.

Jurado has worked hard over the years to become the designer of choice for some of the country's top entertainers, government officials, and business leaders. In creating one-of-a-kind dresses for his clients, Jurado focuses on the entire human form; he envisions the final finished product in his head before he even starts. Because of this holistic perspective, "we do the whole cycle of production here, from ideas, to cutting, to assembly, to hand beading, to finishing. That is another part of my competitive edge. I do everything," offered Jurado. "When I have a client, we need to both trust *each other* in order for everything to work." For his part, Jurado needs to know that the client will give him the creative freedom to make the perfect dress. For clients, they know that Jurado will go to great lengths for them. "If there is an urgent need for a dress for an event, we will deliver it to the airport before my client boards the flight; we will go to the theater to make sure it fits perfectly before she takes the stage. We have shown a real dedication to our clients. We will do what it takes to make it work." Because of this dedication, "they buy from other designers too, but they keep coming back to me." A big part of that trust is exclusivity. "They know that no one else will have that same dress... it is always unique to them and they can feel confident that they will enjoy what they wear. We are the only house in Panama that produces high-end couture dresses. And, because we have been here for 25 years and have satisfied all kinds of clients, we have a very loyal following."

Jurado's advice for marketing students? Never forget where you came from or the people who helped you out along the way (see Photo 4.2).

4.1 WHAT DO CONSUMERS WANT?

Headquartered in Munich, Germany, Siemens corporation posted revenue of €55.3 billion and net income of €4.2 billion in 2020. The company is the largest engineering company in Europe and employs 293,000 people worldwide (A Focused Technology Company 2020). It provides cutting-edge technology solutions to a variety of industries in four primary areas: industry, transportation, infrastructure, and healthcare. Its customers are hospitals, office complexes, telecommunications companies, transportation companies, and manufacturing facilities. In recent years, its industry division has worked to help food manufacturers deliver healthier, tastier, and more sustainable food to a growing contingent of consumers who demand these products. How does Siemens deliver value to its customers so that they, in turn, can deliver value to their end-consumers? By conducting extensive research on end-consumers to find out what they want and expect. Siemens also engages in extensive research to identify emerging trends and predict competitive reactions (Siemens 2021).

Siemens' research found, for example, that millennial consumers across Europe were especially interested in health and wellness. Further, more than 80% of these consumers would be willing to switch brands if food companies provided more transparency about their products. Because of this, researchers at Siemens characterized these consumers as more "data loyal" than "brand loyal." Importantly, these data-savvy customers generally did not believe the food company's claims; they wanted to see the data themselves. How did Siemens provide the solutions to help companies provide this information to their customers? It started with a recognition that, with processed foods, the entire global sourcing, production, and distribution process needed to be tracked. Using wireless devices that communicate with one another via the **Internet of Things (IoT)**, Siemens technology was able to shine a light into some of the dark corners of the distribution chain – the fields, the harvesting, the production process, packaging, transportation, and retail operations.

Data were gathered and stored in secure, permanent records that could not be altered. All of this data on the entire supply chain is stored in a **blockchain**, a digital ledger of transactions that is shared across the network and stored in secure, immutable files. In addition, it is available via QR codes on product packaging so customers can check it out. If any claims are made about the product being organic, cruelty-free, or carbon neutral, for example, data across the entire supply chain is immediately available to confirm those claims. This transparency is not just valuable for consumers, it is also valuable for each member of the value chain so that they can verify the claims of their business partners and, if necessary, can collaborate with one another in managing a recall, for example. Previously, the recall of a food product would take several weeks after a problem is initially identified, because of extensive paperwork and many layers of approvals. With these digital solutions from Siemens, a recall can happen as quickly as it takes to click a few keys (Siemens 2021).

In one recent project with a well-known global snack-food manufacturer, Siemens helped reconfigure the manufacturing facility to quickly and efficiently shift production to respond to changes in customer preferences for new flavors of potato crisps. Using a combination of digital tools, Siemens was able to quickly identify new flavor profiles in the marketplace, reconfigure manufacturing plants using modular equipment, and then produce and deliver new flavors of crisps to the market, such as paprika or sour cream and sweet chili. The first step was spotting new flavor preferences using **Artificial intelligence (AI)** systems, a set of systems that identify patterns, perform automated decision-making, and even learn over time. Second, once these new preferences were identified, recipes were created and then automatically transmitted to manufacturing facilities all over the world. The third step was employing modular "plug and play" equipment to retool the facilities to efficiently produce and package the new crisps. Finally, in one final check of the efficacy of the system, Siemens ran several digital simulations called "digital twins" to ensure that the process would run seamlessly. This final check was necessary because a mistake is 10x more expensive when it occurs in real-life, as opposed to a simulation (Siemens 2021) (see Photo 4.3).

Photo 4.3 Siemens conducts research on its customers' customers

Source: Shutterstock/Juergen Wallstabe

In this chapter, we will examine how the marketing team uses insights about its customers, along with time-tested models of consumer behavior, to predict how those customers will behave. The Siemens example highlights the importance of assessing B2B as well B2C consumer needs. As we have seen, Siemens provides solutions to businesses so that they, in turn, can provide value to their consumers. In the following sections, the psychological and the sociological underpinnings of consumer behavior will be examined. Next, the strategic implications of a deep understanding of consumer behavior will be discussed and the need for actionable insights will be presented.

4.2 LEARNING OBJECTIVES

After studying this chapter, you will be able to do the following:

1 Create an argument as to why the customer must be the central figure in the organization.
2 Compare and contrast the AIDA model and the five-step consumer decision-making model.

3 Carefully describe two models of attitude change: the Theory of Reasoned Action and the Elaboration Likelihood Model.
4 Discuss the differences between culture, subculture, and tribes, as well as why these concepts are referred to as social processes.
5 Construct an argument for the strategic importance of actionable insights.

4.3 THE PRIMACY OF THE CONSUMER

Small organizations like JDJ Couture place their customers at the very forefront of every decision that is made. When owner José Díaz Jurado selects exclusive fabrics, creates a design, and locates embellishments like beading for each dress, he has his client in mind. These one-of-a-kind creations have instilled a fierce loyalty among his clientele. Larger corporations like Siemens also keep their customer's needs at the forefront of each and every decision. In Siemens' case, cutting-edge technological solutions are provided to customers, who in turn, use those technologies to better deliver the value proposition to their end customers. Critical to Siemens' success, however, is the extensive research it conducts on all of those end-consumers, as well as on emerging trends. Once a new trend emerges, Siemens responds quickly and decisively. Regardless of an organization's size, its focus remains the same: delivering the value proposition to customers better than that of the competition.

ENDURING INSIGHTS 4.1

> "We see our customers as invited guests to a party, and we are the hosts. It's our job every day to make every important aspect of the customer experience a little bit better." – Jeff Bezos, founder of Amazon

Amazon's value proposition rests on its vast selection of items, low prices, intuitive interface, and easy shipping. As Amazon grew, it was able to achieve the scale needed to strengthen its grip on these distinguishing features and thus, strengthen its competitive advantage. It's not surprising that Amazon's corporate motto is: "Spend less. Smile more."

Predicting Consumer Behavior is Not Easy

One reason consumer behavior is difficult to predict is that it is often quite difficult to spot emerging trends. Take the example of the 2021 global frenzy to obtain a pair of Golden Goose sneakers. These sneakers are handmade from premium leather in Venice, Italy. They were sold around the world for about $500, but could reach $1700 per pair, rivaling prices realized by top fashion houses such as Tory Burch and Valentino. The most expensive pair incorporated ostrich feathers; the shoelaces alone were $70. What is especially puzzling about these sneakers is that some of them come with a distressed look, with plenty of scuffs and worn marks. The highly-scuffed Golden Goose Beige sneaker, for example, can be purchased for $530 per pair and comes with taped trim at the shoe's toes. University students found the ultra-expensive grunge look to be particularly appealing. However, the trend received a significant backlash from observers who accused these consumers of "mocking" poverty (Hoffower 2019). Some trends are quite difficult to predict.

Trends aside, another reason why marketers face difficulty in predicting consumer behavior is that consumers often do not do what marketers expect them to do. Marketers have known for decades that a significant intention–behavior gap exists. Consumers *claim* they will engage in a behavior far more often than they *actually* perform that behavior (c.f., Eckhardt, Belk, and Devinney 2010; Englis and Phillips 2013; Park and Lin 2020). This gap is of particular concern with environmentally-focused products and behaviors. The case of upcycled and recycled clothing is one example. In one study, the gap between consumers who intend to purchase these products and those who actually do purchase them is 35% (Park and Lin 2020). There are several reasons why consumers sometimes do not follow through on their attitudes or intentions. First, consumers may not have a clear idea of the product's value proposition, how it can fit into their lives, or how it may be better than the competition. This is sometimes especially true with products that have a pro-environmental message (Park and Lin 2020). Second, a variety of social factors may prevent consumers in following through on what they intend to do. Friends, family, and a person's social group exert strong influence on consumer behavior. As an example of the strength of social influence, simply look at the large numbers of people around the world who are hesitant to get a variety of life-saving vaccines. One of the biggest predictors of vaccine hesitancy is the social network to which a person belongs (Stahl, et al. 2016). Finally, situational factors such as a consumer's financial circumstances, time pressures, contextual features (such as a rude salesperson), or even the weather can interfere with a consumer taking an intention and turning it into a behavior.

Non-Consumers

Often, the organization can learn as much from non-consumers as it can from consumers. Maybe the product perfectly meets the needs of these non-consumers, but they have not heard of the product or the communications strategy does not resonate with them. Perhaps these individuals have already been exposed to your organization's offerings, but have decided that the competition has a stronger value proposition. Perhaps these individuals have decided to wait or to not engage in the market. Alternatively, perhaps these individuals used to find value in your product or service, but have found that your offering no longer meets their needs. Regardless of why these individuals are not buying or consuming your product, they still have the opportunity to provide tremendous insights about what your organization is doing well and not-so-well. It could also provide useful insights into how market and consumer preferences might be shifting.

Over the decades, researchers have created a collection of models that help predict, with some degree of precision, how consumers might behave. In the following sections we will explore some of these models by exploring some psychological and sociological foundations of consumer behavior.

4.4 PSYCHOLOGICAL FOUNDATIONS OF CONSUMER BEHAVIOR

Consumer behavior theory has been strongly influenced by the field of psychology. When taking a psychological perspective in understanding consumer behavior, decision-makers focus on the internal workings of the human mind; how consumers think, remember, learn, and decide. Although there are hundreds of models that are used to predict consumer behavior, four models have been particularly helpful to decision-makers: the AIDA model, the model of consumer decision-making, attitudes models, and the Elaboration Likelihood Model.

AIDA

There are several attitude models that are built upon psychological foundations of consumer behavior. During the first step, the **awareness phase**, the consumer first becomes aware of the product's existence. With consumer packaged goods (CPGs) that are new to the market, for example, this is often done with mass advertising. During the **interest phase**, consumers may want to learn a little more about it and how it might fit into their lives. For marketers, the goal is to generate curiosity about the product. During the **desire phase** of the AIDA model, consumers shift their curiosity to a yearning for the product. During this stage, marketers try to leverage the interest that consumers have and turn it into a simmering desire for the product. Consumers need to be convinced that this brand, not others, will provide them with value. During the **action phase**, consumers purchase the product, purchase another item, or disengage from the whole process. For marketers, the goal is to encourage a behavior, such as a purchase. This can be done, for example, by using a scarcity appeal (only a few left!), offering limited-time discounts, or easy-credit terms. Action can also be encouraged by letting consumers think that they are missing out or that they are among the last in their social group to get the product (everyone else has one, why don't you?). Action can also be fostered by simply having an irresistible offering that consumers have a hard time passing up. Consumers need to complete each step before moving to the next. For example, it is not possible for a consumer to desire a product before actually first becoming aware of it and then becoming interested in it.

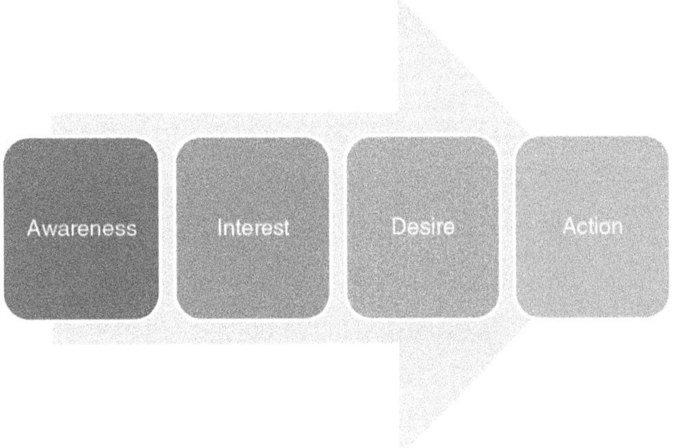

Figure 4.1 The 4-step AIDA model of consumer behavior

The AIDA model has been an especially useful tool for salespeople, who can alter their sales strategies with clients, depending on where the client is situated in the AIDA model. Similarly, advertising strategies can be tailored to fit the needs of consumers at each step (see Table 4.1).

Table 4.1 Advertising appeals for each stage of the AIDA model

Step in the AIDA Model	Advertising Appeal
Awareness	Engage in mass advertising so that consumers learn the name and some basic information about the brand.
Interest	Generate curiosity about the brand by discussing the value proposition and differentiating it from the competition.
Desire	Foster a feeling of yearning for the product by convincing consumers that this product will fulfill an unmet need.
Action	Encourage a behavior, such as a purchase.

Consumer Decision-Making Model

The consumer decision-making model and the AIDA model both propose that consumers proceed through a series of steps as they contemplate the world around them and make consumption-related decisions. With the consumer decision-making model, however, consumers start with a problem and then work through a series of steps in an attempt to solve that problem. In the **problem recognition phase** (just like our earlier discussion of the research process), consumers notice a difference between their ideal state and their actual state. For example, a consumer is about to go outside, but it is raining and the consumer has no umbrella. Ideally, the consumer would like to be warm and dry, but actually, our unfortunate consumer is about to get soaked. In the **search for alternatives phase**, consumers engage in an internal search of their memories and an external search in order to gather enough information to help them make the decision about what to do. Going back to our consumer, this person may remember that there is a shop a few blocks away that sells umbrellas and may do a quick online search to see where it might be possible to purchase a raincoat. In the **evaluation of alternatives phase**, consumers weigh the costs and benefits of each of the alternatives. Our consumer might like the convenience of an umbrella, but also think that a raincoat would be a better long-term solution. At the end of this phase, the consumer should have something akin to a mental list of pros and cons for each alternative. In the **purchase decision phase**, consumers will select the alternative that best fits their needs. It is also possible here to make a decision to not purchase something – our consumer will just have to get soaked in the rainstorm. Continuing with the example, suppose our consumer decides to purchase a low-cost umbrella at a convenience store a few blocks away. In the **post-purchase decision phase**, consumers will look back at the purchase and make a determination about whether or not they were happy. Unfortunately, after using the umbrella for a few days of rain, a sudden gust of wind rips the umbrella fabric, making it useless. Our consumer decides that investing in a more durable raincoat would have been a smarter choice and resolves to go shopping for raincoats at the next opportunity (see Figure 4.2 and Photo 4.4).

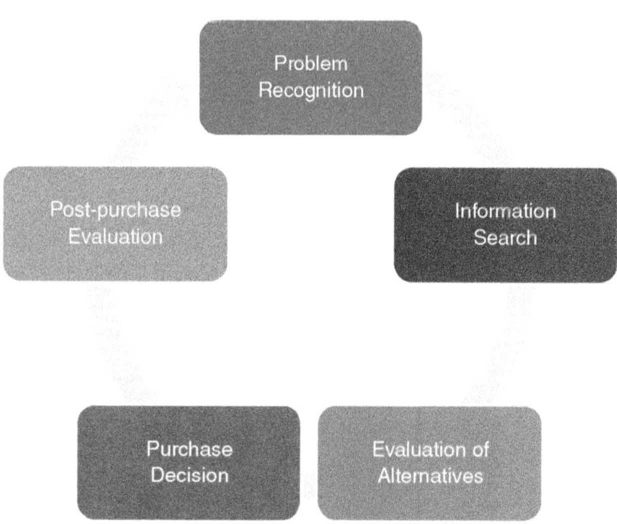

Figure 4.2 The consumer decision-making model

Photo 4.4 Problem recognition kicks off the consumer decision-making process

Source: Pixabay

There are two important things to note about this model. First, the consumer decision-making process is not something that ends with a purchase and post-purchase evaluation. Indeed, every experience consumers have will have an impact on how they view the next problem recognition and purchase decision. Second, as with the AIDA model, the consumer decision-making model provides valuable insights into what a marketer should do to influence each phase. For example, if marketers know that consumers are searching for information, it would be incumbent on them to provide information that is easy to access and understand. Essentially, since marketers know how consumers proceed through the decision-making process as well as what happens at each phase, they can create initiatives to influence *each phase* of the process.

Attitudes

Another set of models based on psychological foundations of consumer behavior is the broad category of attitudes. Attitude models have been used extensively by for-profit organizations to predict a variety of consumer behaviors, such as making purchases, making returns, signing up for extended warranties or service packages, or recommending the company to a friend or acquaintance. Attitude models have also been used extensively in the non-profit space to predict consumer behaviors toward voting, making donations, engaging in health-related behaviors like quitting smoking, and signing up for blood or organ donation. Perhaps because of their fairly good ability to predict actual behaviors, attitude models are among the most widely-utilized models of consumer behavior.

An **attitude** is a "learned predisposition to respond in a consistently favorable or unfavorable manner in relation to some object" (Fishbein and Ajzen 1975, 6). Attitudes have several important characteristics. Attitudes:

- are *learned* through previous experiences, social systems, education, and other social interactions
- have an *evaluative dimension*, which means attitudes are positive or negative
- have *intensity*, which means that some attitudes are very strongly held and others are quite weak
- have *consistency*, in that they generally align with other attitudes and beliefs (Oskamp and Schultz 2005)
- have *stability*, in that they change very little across time or contexts (Oskamp and Schultz 2005)
- help *predict behavior*. Attitude models do not provide a perfect prediction of consumer behavior, but their predictive ability often out-performs other models.

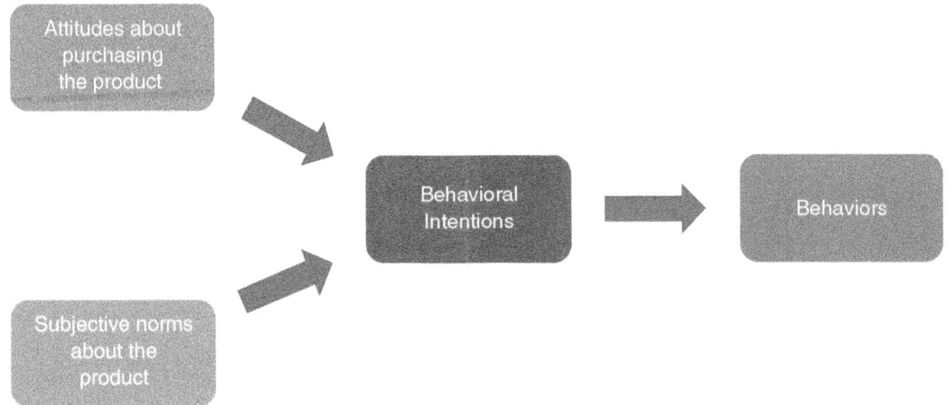

Figure 4.3 Theory of Reasoned Action

Source: adapted, in part, from Ajzen and Fishbein (1980)

There are several attitude models, but the **Theory of Reasoned Action** is perhaps the most well-used one. It has fairly good predictive ability, partially because it incorporates important psychological *and* sociological forces influencing the consumer. The Theory of Reasoned Action has several important components. First, it assesses **attitudes toward purchasing the product**, which gives an indication of a consumer's overall positive or negative inclination toward purchasing the product. Next, it assesses the social influences that consumers perceive with **subjective norms**. Subjective norms take into account what the consumer believes about how other people may react ("will my friends and family approve or not?"). Attitudes and subjective norms each independently influence the next component of the model, **behavioral intentions**, which captures the extent to which a consumer plans to purchase the product. Finally, the last component of the model is an assessment of the actual purchase behavior of the consumer (Ajzen and Fishbein 1980) (see Figure 4.3).

BLUNDERS & INSIGHTS 4.1

You Know Its Bad When *These* People Like You

BACKGROUND: German skin and body care brand Nivea was founded in 1911 and is sold in over 173 countries around the world (Caring 2021). In 2017, Nivea's Middle East division released an ad for its new "Invisible for Black and White" deodorant, which leaves no deodorant stains on black or white clothing. The ad proclaimed "White Is Purity" with a picture of a White woman with long, dark, wavy hair in white clothes. The ad included the caption, "Keep it clean, keep bright. Don't let anything ruin it." The reaction to the racist message was immediate and strong, with messages like, "fire your marketing person and anyone who approved this ad." The problem was amplified, however, when white supremacist groups started reposting the messages to their networks and encouraging others with racist attitudes to support the Nivea brand. The global uproar was palpable. In response, Nivea deleted the ad, issued an apology saying that it was "inappropriate and not reflective of our values as a company," and individually replied to thousands of seething Twitter messages (Wang 2017) (see Photo 4.5).

Photo 4.5 Nivea's ad amplified racist attitudes

Source: Pixabay

DEBRIEF: This situation was a marketing blunder in two respects. First, Nivea failed to predict the attitudes of millions of its regular customers around the world to the brand's tagline, as well as the behaviors of those customers who identify as white supremacists. Second, Nivea failed to instill safeguards that would have prevented such messaging. What makes the lack of a safeguard particularly perplexing is that, given Germany's dark history with racism, decision-makers at Nivea very likely regularly demonstrate extra caution about creating messaging with any hint of racial overtones. Even though the campaign was created far from corporate headquarters, the corporate giant should have had strict safeguards in place for all of its divisions and locations to prevent such messaging blunders.

Elaboration Likelihood Model

The **Elaboration Likelihood Model** describes two ways in which consumers may be persuaded by an advertising message to change their attitudes (Petty and Cacioppo 1986). To persuade consumers to change their attitudes, marketers must first know their customers' motivation and ability to process the information in the ad; not all consumers will be equally interested in our ads. If consumers are able and motivated, such as when they are thinking about purchasing a car or planning an overseas trip, they will *elaborate* on the message. That is, they will engage in deep, critical thinking about the message because they are likely involved in the decision and they want to make the right choice. Because of this, an advertising message should

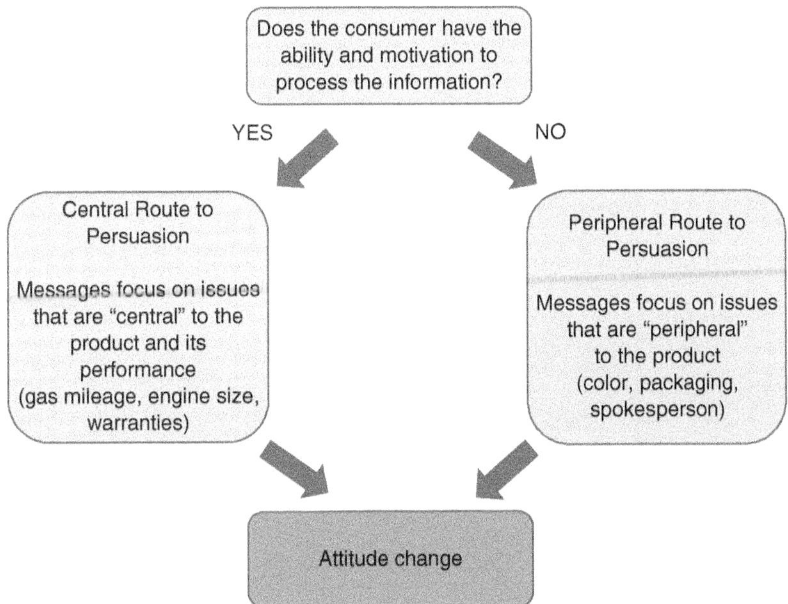

Figure 4.4 The Elaboration Likelihood Model

Source: adapted, in part, from Petty and Cacioppo (1986)

focus on messages that are *central* to the product and its performance, such as a car's gas mileage, engine size, and warranty. If, however, a consumer is not able or particularly motivated, such as may be the case when they are thinking about purchasing a t-shirt or a candy bar, they are likely not highly involved in the decision and will probably engage in shallow or cursory processing of any advertising message. Advertising messages, therefore, should focus on peripheral issues such as interesting product packaging or the celebrity spokesperson (O'Keefe 2008, Petty and Cacioppo 1986) (see Figure 4.4). The Elaboration Likelihood Model offers important direction to advertisers on messaging strategy.

These four models of consumer behavior, which are based on psychological foundations, do not come close to capturing the vast number of theories and models that researchers have developed over the decades. They are, however, some of the most widely used models in marketing strategy and practice. Next, we will discuss external influences on consumer behavior.

4.5 SOCIOLOGICAL FOUNDATIONS OF CONSUMER BEHAVIOR

As much as consumers might like to think that the decisions they make are independent of external influences, the reality is that the influence of other people can shift consumer perceptions and behaviors in profound ways. The following sections discuss the broad topics of social structures and processes.

Social Structures

Social systems are comprised of social structures, such as the educational system, political system, and economic system. We call them social structures because they were designed by people. **Social structures** are designed to achieve certain goals or outcomes in a society, such as the education of young people or the efficient functioning of an economy. Social structures also include groups of individuals that come together organically for other reasons, such as a common set of interests, family, or friendship groups. It is obvious that social structures such as these exert influence on the way consumers think about their role within a social system, as well as their goals, values, and behaviors. Many of these issues are beyond the scope of this discussion. However, one type of social structure that is particularly relevant to marketing and consumer behavior is reference groups.

Reference groups are a type of social structure comprised of one or more individuals that serve as a basis for observation, comparison, and guidance to other individuals. Consumers look to reference groups as a way to evaluate their own attitudes, beliefs, and situations (Hyman 1942). In order to exert influence, the reference group should be relevant in some way to the consumer (Park and Lessig 1977).

Formal and Informal Groups

Businesses, religious groups, sports groups, scouting groups, and other organized groups are examples of **formal reference groups.** They have structure, a hierarchy, a set of rules, and a clear set of goals. Often, individuals in formal reference groups have a shared sense of purpose and an affinity for the history of the organization. Individuals who are members of a formal reference group know that there are expectations about the way they should behave, dress, and consume. Simply take the example of individuals who work for the Vanguard Corporation, which offers a variety of financial planning and investment services. Vanguard has a strong and cohesive corporate culture that includes stories about the company's founder, John Bogle, that achieve almost mythic status. Group cohesion is strengthened with special team-building exercises, events for families, and volunteer opportunities. Employees are called crew members and are promoted from within the organization; many of them stay with Vanguard for their entire careers.

An **informal reference group** is created by individuals who come together because of a shared interest, a common goal, similar values, or friendship. These groups are drawn together, not because they have to, but because they want to. Informal groups that come together for a specific purpose or goal are called **tribes**. Examples include a group of gamers who gather together on the weekends to play Minecraft, a group of neighbors who are working together to oppose a new highway project, or a group of friends who scour online thrift stores to find great deals on luxury fashion brands. A **consumer tribe** is comprised of a group of people who gather together around their shared passion for a particular consumption experience (Cova 1997). These individuals share their love for the experience, not necessarily a specific brand. Examples of consumer tribes include skateboarding enthusiasts who regularly get together at the skatepark to try out new moves, or trap music fans who share their new beats online. Social media makes it very easy to connect and communicate with tribes of like-minded people around the world (Godin 2008). Indeed, advances in technology have allowed individuals from all over the world to connect, communicate, and collaborate with one another to achieve common goals (Friedman 2009).

Opinion leaders and **influencers** are unique in that they are viewed by their followers as having unique or desirable skills, expertise, or other characteristics. Individuals who admire these influencers are interested in their thoughts and advice about a wide variety of topics and often try to emulate their attitudes and behaviors. In 2022, footballer Cristiano Ronaldo lead the rest of the world in the number of Instagram followers with 455 million, followed by supermodel Kylie Jenner (349 million), footballer Leo Messi (338 million), actress Selena Gomez (328 million), actor Dwayne Johnson (The Rock) (322 million), and media personality Kim Kardashian (318 million) (Statista 2022).

Another highly-influential reference group is the family. Family structures have characteristics of both formal and informal groups. **Families** can be made up of many different people, some of whom are related and some who may not be related to one another – there are no formal rules about how a family should be constituted. However, once the family is constituted, there is often formal recognition by government and/or religious institutions, which results in implications for taxes, inheritances, and other rights. From a consumer behavior standpoint, families exert influence on the consumption choices and behaviors of their members. Ideally, families teach their children about important decision-making and consumption skills. A family's influence is particularly strong for young people as they mature into adulthood and start making their own consumption choices. In essence, children are consumers-in-training. The more a child participates in family purchase decisions, the more closely that young person's consumption habits will mirror that of their family. Conversely, the more a family encourages independent choices for the child, the greater the likelihood that the young person will have consumption patterns in adulthood that are different from their family's (Bravo, Fraj, and Martinez 2006). Several trends indicate that children around the world learn to make consumption-related decisions at an early age (Euromonitor 2017):

- Assuming adult roles – this is occurring at home and at school as parents increasingly struggle to achieve an ideal work–life balance. In addition, children are learning about "adult" topics such as climate change, identity, politics, and sexuality. Because they assume adult-like roles in these other domains, they often participate in the family's consumer decision-making too.
- Practicing consumption – young children use a variety of apps and games to practice shopping and making other consumption-related decisions.
- Becoming proficient online – more than ever, children connect and communicate with one another online via social networking sites. The China-based social networking site, Musical.ly, for example, is targeted at 13–20-year-old individuals, but has many users who are much younger than that. Through these connections, children learn about new products, product attributes, and brands.

ENDURING INSIGHTS 4.2

"The key to good decision making is not knowledge. It is understanding. We are swimming in the former. We are desperately lacking in the latter." – Malcolm Gladwell

An author, consultant, and frequent speaker, Gladwell distinguishes between simple knowledge of a phenomenon and deep, contextualized understanding, that takes into account history as well as shifting cultural and environmental dynamics. It is only with this deep level of understanding that decision-makers can create insights.

Influence on Consumer Behavior

Groups and individuals have influence because of the perceived power they wield. **Social power** describes the potential to influence an individual's beliefs, attitudes, behaviors, and values. When discussing social power, the types of power are always viewed from the perspective of the person upon whom the power is exerted. There are five sources of social power (see the work of French 1956, French and Raven 1959, and Raven 1993) (see Table 4.2).

Table 4.2 The five dimensions of social power

Dimension of Power	Explanation
Reward power	Influence occurs because benefits are provided for conforming to group norms. *Example*: because of your hard work and dedication to your team, the team members utilize reward power and invite you out for pizza on Friday night.
Coercive power	The opposite of reward power, behavior is influenced because of the threat of punishment. *Example*: the team exerts coercive power when it issues a warning that, unless you perform at a certain level, you will not be invited to go out with the team on Friday night.

Dimension of Power	Explanation
Legitimate power	Influence occurs because someone has a particular position of authority. *Example*: your supervisor has legitimate power to influence your behavior.
Expert power	Influence occurs because a group or individual has special experience, skills, or expertise. *Example*: doctors, lawyers, and scientists have expert power.
Referent power	Influence occurs because you admire some quality of another person or group and try to emulate their attitudes and behaviors. *Example*: celebrities and sports stars exert referent power

Source: French and Raven (1959)

It is important to note here that the dimensions of power can sometimes overlap one another. Indeed, a family could exert reward power, coercive power, and referent power; a manager could exert legitimate power, reward power, and expert power. In Photo 4.6, for example, actor Emilia Clarke is promoting Clinique products. Clarke has had many acting roles, but may be best remembered for her starring role in the *Game of Thrones* series. In the Clinique ad, Clarke exerts expert power (she undoubtedly is knowledgeable about makeup and skin care) and referent power (Clarke is widely admired for her acting abilities and has 27 million followers on Instagram).

Photo 4.6 Emilia Clarke exerts expert and referent power in this Clinique ad

Source: Advertising Archives

Social Processes

Social processes concern the constantly shifting meanings that occur as one moves between cultures, as well as within a given culture. In marketing, culture and subculture are two of the most important ways in which a social group's values and norms are created, communicated, and reinforced.

Culture

Culture describes the collection of shared understandings, meanings, norms, and customs which help guide the behavior of its members. Some dimensions of culture are fairly stable and resistant to change, while other dimensions are flexible enough to adapt to the context. All cultures change over time. Simply put, a culture is the personality of a society.

A given culture is comprised of a set of beliefs, knowledge, values, norms, and customs. **Beliefs** are the thoughts an individual has about some object, idea, or person. Beliefs may or may not be based on fact. **Knowledge** refers to factual information which is attained through education or experience. A person might not *know* the name of the main character in the TV series *Mad Men*, but *believes* it might be George (it's actually Don Draper). Cultural **values** represent a set of standards and priorities for the culture, which reflect a distinct sense of right or wrong. They guide behavior within a culture by establishing priorities. The French motto "Liberty, Equality, and Fraternity" clearly describes an important set of cultural values for the French people (see Photo 4.7). **Norms** are a set of informal rules for behavior, such as what to do when someone invites you to dinner at their house or how to behave when you are in an elevator. Norms also influence more macro-level issues, such as generally-accepted rules for dating and relationships. Cultural **customs** are long-standing norms of behavior that have been passed down through the generations and may have ties to cultural values. Examples here include a set of behaviors related to important life events like weddings, or important holidays, like the Jewish holiday of Yom Kippur.

Photo 4.7 The values of liberty, equality, and fraternity are central to French culture

Source: Pixabay

Cultural beliefs, knowledge, values, norms, and customs are not static. Cultural values change very slowly over time, but other elements of culture change more quickly as new trends, technologies, and other circumstances arise. When the Covid-19 pandemic shut down much of the global economy in 2020 and 2021, the French food culture was sorely tested. Restaurants and cafes throughout the country were shut down and, for a nation that loves its food and wine, this was particularly difficult. The solution? The Rungis International Market, just south of Paris. Rungis is the world's biggest fresh food market in the world, and in normal times, ships food to restaurants and markets throughout Europe. Ten thousand tons of food pass through the market

each night, 40,000 people work there, and the market serves 18 million French consumers each day (Capa Presse 2020). Two different developments impacted Rungis during the height of the pandemic. First, restaurants in Europe were shut down, leading to a decrease in demand for exotic items that are typically found on the menus of the most exclusive restaurants. Second, grocery stores and fresh produce markets in France stopped importing fresh food from other locations. These two factors resulted in a surge in demand for locally-sourced French ingredients. Rungis responded by finding new sources of locally-produced ingredients and then sold those items to grocery stores, food markets, butcher shops, bakeries, etc. Rungis even started a home delivery service. Sales of locally-sourced cheeses, for example, rose so dramatically that Rungis experienced some difficulty in meeting the demand. The one constant, however, was France's strong food culture. Instead of frequenting restaurants and cafes, French consumers selected ingredients at markets and grocery stores, cooked their favorite dishes at home, and then enjoyed the meal at home. "We pass the time cooking and eating," said one customer at an open-air market. What do they cook? Traditional comfort foods and hearty dishes. "We treat ourselves to good food. We eat well, despite corona," commented another. Overall, sales at Rungis increased during the pandemic (DW 2021). Joie de vivre (see Photo 4.8)!

Photo 4.8 For the French, even a global pandemic did not stop their love of food and wine

Source: Pixabay

Classification of Cultures

How is it possible to make sense of the wide variety of cultures across the globe such that marketing decision-makers can create culturally-relevant insights and strategies? Dutch researcher Geert Hofstede suggested that all cultures can be classified along six separate dimensions (Hofstede 1984, 2001):

- Individualism–collectivism – describes the extent to which individual goals are balanced against collective or group goals. Individualistic cultures such as Germany tend to prioritize an individual's goals over those of the group, whereas collectivistic cultures such as Japan prioritize interpersonal connection and sharing of responsibility.
- Masculinity–femininity – assesses the motives for behavior. Cultures that are more masculine, such as Slovakia, are more achievement-oriented and appreciate heroism, assertiveness, and material reward (Sidle 2009). By contrast, cultures that are more feminine in their orientation, such as Sweden, are more consensus-oriented and appreciate cooperation, caring, and quality of life (de Mooij and Hofstede 2002).
- Power distance – describes the extent to which a hierarchy exists in the relationships that people have with one another. Cultures with high power distance, such as Malaysia, are more likely to have a steep hierarchical structure, with power concentrated at the top. In these cultures, it is likely that a manager makes most of the decisions, with very little input from subordinates (de Mooij and Hofstede 2002). In low power distance cultures, such as Israel, flat hierarchies are the norm and power is shared (Aguinis, Joo and Gottfredson 2012).
- Uncertainty avoidance – describes the extent to which individuals in a culture feel comfortable with ambiguity, uncertainty, and risk. Individuals in high uncertainty avoidance cultures, such as Austria, are more likely to experience anxiety when they are in ambiguous situations. Individuals in these types of cultures reduce risks by enacting rules, laws, and regulations. By contrast, individuals in low uncertainty avoidance cultures, such as China, enjoy novel events and unexpected outcomes (Aguinis et al., 2012).
- Long-term orientation – relates to a culture's perspectives on time and tradition. Cultures with a long-term orientation, such as China, appreciate the fact that they may have to wait for a while to achieve their objectives. Individuals persevere. In contrast, shorter-term cultures, such as the US, tend to de-emphasize the future and focus on achieving quick results.
- Indulgence – describes the extent to which a culture emphasizes the natural human motivation to have fun and enjoy life, such as Australia. Cultures who are restrained, such as the case with many communist and former communist countries, hold back on their desire to have fun and enjoy life (Hofstede, Hofstede, and Minkov 2010).

Although Hofstede's work has been widely deployed in a variety of different cultures and settings, it is not without its critics. Hofstede developed his original set of dimensions after conducting a series of in-depth interviews at just one company: IBM. Because of this, his dimensions were created with a Western cultural perspective. Over the years, he collected data in different settings, but the static nature and Western influence of the dimensions remained. Importantly, Hofstede's model does not allow for the fact that cultural values have subtleties and contradictions, nor does it allow for the fact that cultural values shift over time (Baskerville 2003, Eckhardt 2002, McSweeney 2002). In the end, Hofstede's model can be informative as a blunt instrument to establish a broad understanding of a culture. To create a more finely-tuned, nuanced understanding of a culture, additional methods of analysis must be employed.

The Creation and Movement of Cultural Meanings

Although cultural values remain fairly constant in the short term, we have seen that other elements of culture can change to suit the needs of a new situation. The French culture's strong appreciation of food and wine stayed constant during the global Covid-19 pandemic, but individual behaviors shifted in response to the new realities of lockdowns. An important vehicle by which elements of culture shift and change over time is the cultural production system.

For many people, Coca-Cola has strong associations with summer and fun times with friends and family. How did these meanings become associated with Coca-Cola? **Cultural production** is the process by which important meanings become embedded into a product.

Decades of research suggest that the attachment of meaning to products is no accident. First, cultural producers such as artists, musicians, designers, or marketers create objects or products. Second, cultural intermediaries like advertising and fashion systems connect these objects and products to meanings that are important to consumers. Advertising for Coca-Cola often depicts consumers frolicking on the beach or enjoying a summer picnic with friends. A cold Coke is always present. The final step occurs when consumers consume the products in special ways that help connect the product meanings to the self (McCracken 1986, Venkatesh and Meamber 2006). Consumers may, for example, keep an icy bucket of cold Cokes readily available during a summer get-together or may give their children a small amount of money to buy a Coke while at the beach. Once consumption occurs, the "summertime fun" associated with the product becomes associated with the consumer: "the perfect drink for a day at the beach is a Coke" (see Photo 4.9).

Photo 4.9 Coca-Cola has strong cultural meanings

Source: Pixabay

Subcultures

Compared to a culture, **subculture** is a smaller group of individuals who share similar values, beliefs, knowledge, norms, and customs. Subcultures exhibit many of the same characteristics of the broader culture, but are much smaller in size. In marketing, subcultures are often defined in terms of shared demographic characteristics, shared life experiences, or shared consumption interests. Subcultures based on demographic characteristics, for example, include those based on age or generation (18–25-year-olds or Baby Boomers), those based on ethnic or racial heritage (Hispanic people or Indigenous people), or those based on gender or gender identity (male/female or transsexual). There are many different demographic variables that can be used to define a group of people. Subcultures can also be based on shared consumption interests, such as groups of consumers who really love certain sports or activities, or even people who have a special love for certain brands, like Apple or Harley Davidson. Marketers often find it useful to focus their efforts on subcultures because they are comprised of individuals who are similar to one another and therefore may respond in a similar way to a marketing strategy.

Technology has changed the nature of subcultures in three important respects. First, it has enabled individuals to access greater volumes of information, which exposes individuals to different content and perspectives. Because of this, subcultures develop and shift in a more fluid fashion than ever before; they develop and evolve much more quickly over time as new perspectives are incorporated and older perspectives are dropped. Second, subcultures are much more flexible and tolerant of individuals expressing their own individuality within the given subculture; every member *does not* have to have the same jacket, listen to the same music, nor use the same slang phrases. In a related vein, individuals are free to express themselves differently when they are in different circumstances; members of a subculture will likely behave differently when they're with their families vs. their friends. This is okay. Third, technology has allowed individuals to connect and form relationships with one another across vast distances, so members of a subculture do not need to be in close physical proximity to one another. In short, contemporary conceptualizations of subculture suggest that they are fluid, flexible, and far-reaching. Because of this, our understanding of subcultures has evolved to more closely resemble that of tribes, as discussed earlier in this section.

BLUNDERS & INSIGHTS 4.2

Lesson #1: Don't Promote Snacks to People Who are Fasting

BACKGROUND: In 2015, UK grocery store Tesco launched a "Ramadan Mubarak" ("Blessed Ramadan") campaign to appeal to the Muslim community. So far, so good. At the time, more than one million Muslims lived in London (Gani 2015). The problem started when red cardboard point-of-purchase displays included stacks of Pringles, an American brand of potato crisps. Promoting snacks during a time when Muslims are required to fast is fairly tone deaf. However, the real problem happened when it was discovered that the flavor on display was "smokey bacon." Pork is forbidden in the Muslim diet. When a Tesco consumer posted a picture of the display online, it stirred up a social media controversy as many Muslim consumers expressed dismay, amusement, and even anger at the display (see Photo 4.10).

Photo 4.10 Tesco botched its Ramadan promotion with Pringles

Source: Pixabay

DEBRIEF: Tesco quickly removed the display and both Pringles and Tesco expressed apologies to the community. The idea of targeting the Muslim community may have been a good one, but the execution of the in-store promotion was senseless. Even a marginal understanding of the religion would have immediately identified the promotion as a double blunder (Satran 2015).

4.5 STRATEGIC IMPLICATIONS

Regardless of whether insights are drawn from consumers using psychological or sociological foundations, they are still generated by getting to know the most important person in the organization: the consumer. Remember, consumer behavior models and data are merely tools that give decision-makers the ability to generate actionable insights. In examining Figure 4.5, think of the steps in the process as answering these questions: What? So what? Now what?

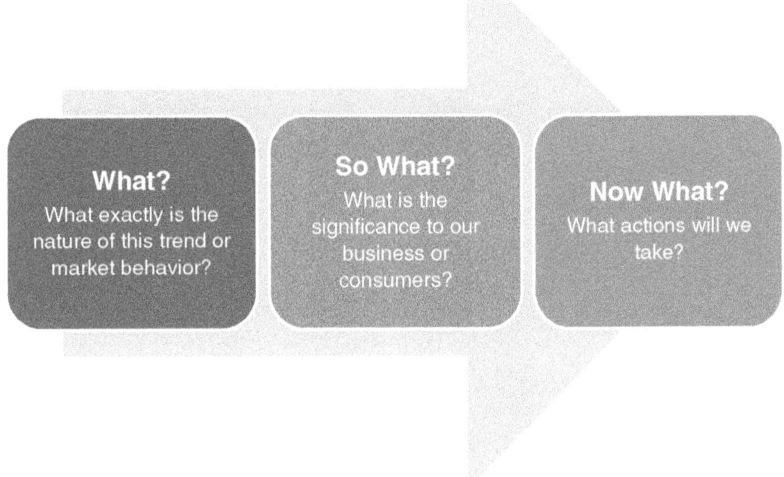

Figure 4.5 From insights to action

ENDURING INSIGHTS 4.3

"If ignorant both of your enemy and yourself, you are certain to be in peril." – Sun Tzu

Marketing decision-makers need to be fully aware of the organization's abilities to leverage knowledge about consumers to its own advantage. Fertile ground for the creation of insights exists at the intersection of knowledge about the consumer, the organization, and the context.

Experts at CPG giant Unilever focus on the "art of insights," rather than the "craft of data," and know that developing insights is a never-ending quest. The goal of the consumer insights team is to *become* the consumer. In one of its research efforts, marketing team members were outfitted with old-age simulation equipment so that they could experience first-hand what it was like to struggle to read the tiny print on packages and handle Unilever products such as heavy shampoo bottles (Van den Driest, Sthanunathan, and Weed 2016). For the marketing team to help achieve the strategic objectives of the organization and have an influence on the organization's strategic direction, it must generate better data and actionable insights.

Better Data, not More Data

The psychological and sociological models of consumer behavior discussed earlier in this chapter provide important frameworks that assist decision-makers in understanding how consumers make decisions and they identify influences on the decision-making process. As important as these models are, however, they need data. The difficulty is in finding the appropriate amount of data that is needed. Decision-makers often make the mistake of thinking that collecting more data is the solution. Unfortunately, more data does not lead to better decision-making. Better data leads to better decision-making and the first step in being able to utilize data strategically is to generate data from multiple sources, which allows the marketing team to triangulate findings and create a more holistic depiction of the phenomenon of interest. This includes quantitative and qualitative data. Online reviews, surveys, and social media are vehicles by which customers can upload thoughts, criticisms, and suggestions about the organization's product. Customers know the product, and sometimes their descriptions about what works and does not work for them will provide just the right spark of inspiration for the marketing team. Comments that consumers make about the competition's products should also be analyzed for key themes and takeaways. Key themes from these comments can be distilled using a variety of analytical software and machine learning tools. The sales team, customer service team, shipping department, and business partners are also valuable sources of data. Importantly, the marketing team should talk to anyone within the organization that has a customer-facing position, such as sales clerks, warranty fulfillment specialists, or service staff. Often these individuals have a deep knowledge of the customer experience and can identify problems before others in the organization.

The second step to using consumer data strategically is to treat it as a strategic asset. An organization should never sell or share its data. Ever. Think about it. The data and information generated by the marketing team is about something that no other competitor knows about. It represents a unique lens by which the marketing team can view its customers in context. In addition, there are two other more practical reasons why selling data can damage the organization. First, selling data represents, at best, only a minor revenue stream to the organization. Second, selling data can damage the reputation of your own organization, especially if the organization that buys the data is unscrupulous or experiences a data breach. At the very minimum, your customers will become quickly annoyed if they are suddenly becoming inundated with sales pitches from other organizations. In the early 2010s, well-meaning people who donated money to the World Wildlife Fund were dismayed when, a few months after they made their donations, they were inundated with sales promotions from other environmental organizations. WWF quickly learned its lesson and stopped selling its data. No competitor knows your customers as well as you do; customer data is a valuable competitive asset and should be treated as such.

Although *more data* does not necessarily mean *better data*, there are indeed instances in which it is necessary to collect extra data. The more "yes" responses to the questions listed below, the stronger the case for collecting more data (Hagiu and Wright 2020):

- Compared to the value provided by the original product, will the collection of additional data potentially provide more value to the customer?
- Is the marginal value of the additional data worth the time and effort?
- Will the data stay relevant for a long period of time? Is it unlikely to quickly be obsolete?
- Is the data unique, not easily copied, not easily found from other sources, and/or proprietary?
- Will any product improvements based on our findings be difficult for competitors to copy?

- Will the data from one customer help improve the customer experience for other customers?
- Can our organization turn insights into action quickly?

Actionable Insights

If insights are to be of strategic importance to the organization, they must be actionable. If the conclusion that is drawn from the data is already well-known among the marketing team ("our customers prefer vanilla over chocolate"), it's not an insight and it's not worth trying to turn it into an actionable insight. By contrast, true insights confirm the team's suspicions, surprise the team, or provide a deep level of context to the data. Actionable insights take a simple conclusion further and suggest organizational actions to help position the organization for long-term strengthening of the value proposition. Ideally, an actionable insight out-maneuvers the competition in some way. Actionable insights are more likely when the team is comprised of individuals with diverse backgrounds, talents, and experiences. Paramount to creating actionable insights is the ability to think critically and holistically. Creating actionable insights is not easy. Although 74% of organizations aspire to data-driven decision-making, only 29% admit that they are good at creating actionable insights (Hopkins 2016).

Decision-makers at Starbucks, for example, turned an interesting research finding into an actionable insight when they found that a significant proportion of its customers were concerned about the impacts of climate change and were especially concerned about single-use plastics. Starbucks is responsible for the distribution of six billion paper and plastic cups each year, so there was plenty of room for action. The organization implemented a series of initiatives to address these concerns and reassure consumers that Starbucks can be a partner in helping them achieve their sustainability goals. The four-part initiative to reduce single use plastics included the following (Stories 2022):

- Promoting reusables – implementation of reusable cup and borrow-a-cup programs. Ceramic cups are the default cups for those who consume the coffee on premisis.
- Customer incentives – for consumers who bring their own cups, Starbucks offers discounts and, during certain promotions, may make donations to environmental organizations.
- Cup innovation – Starbucks doubled the recycled content for its hot cups and eliminated plastic straws. Any virgin paper is 100% sustainably sourced and certified.
- Recycling – partnerships with organizations that promote recycling, closed-loop recycling solutions, and the expansion of community recycling programs.

The logic behind the creation of actionable insights is that decision-makers are not simply predicting the future, they are crafting the future. What are some necessary ingredients for the creation of actionable insights? Research by the insights team at Unilever has found that organizations that possess a unique set of operational and people characteristics are likely to create actionable insights and out-perform their competitors. The team studied the process of insight creation at a variety of firms in different industries, including transportation, pharmaceutical, financial services, hospitality, and CPG firms. The team's findings underscored the importance of the notion that more data is not necessarily better data. It found, for example, that the ability to synthesize data was an important ingredient for an organization's ability to create actionable insights. In fact, 67% of firms that out-performed the competition had strong data synthesis capabilities. By contrast, for those firms that under-performed the competition, only 34% had strong data synthesis capabilities. These analytical capabilities were instrumental in helping with the promotion of Unilever's line of cholesterol-lowering spreads and drinks. Data from several different sources revealed two interesting patterns: consumers needed to use the product for 3 weeks before it became a habit, and consumers were strongly influenced in their consumption behaviors for these products by their social groups. As a result of these two findings, the insights team suggested a new initiative that became known as *It Takes a Village*, a dashboard with networking capabilities and resources for an entire town to work together to lower their cholesterol (Van den Driest, et al. 2016) (see Table 4.3).

Table 4.3 Ingredients for the creation of actionable insights

People Characteristics	Proportion of Organizations that Possess this Characteristic*	Description
Data synthesis	Overperforming: 67% Underperforming: 34%	The ability to extract key findings and identify connections; the ability to integrate massive amounts of disparate structured and unstructured data.
Independence	Overperforming: 29% Underperforming: 12%	Placement of the insights function that is outside of and independent of a formal marketing department; insights leaders report directly to senior management.
Integrated planning	Overperforming: 61% Underperforming: 46%	Full involvement of insights leaders in strategic planning, as well as involvement in marketing, finance, and sales.
Collaboration	Overperforming: 69% Underperforming: 52%	Full cooperation and coordination between insights leaders and other functions and customers throughout the organization. Importantly, every individual throughout the organization should be encouraged to learn more about customers and create insights.
Experimentation	Overperforming: 40% Underperforming: 13%	The creation of a safe place such as an innovation incubator to try new things and implement new approaches. Insights leaders could also safely test new initiatives by running simulations.
Forward-looking orientation	Overperforming: 32% Underperforming: 28%	Less emphasis on using the past to predict future consumer behavior; more emphasis on *creating* the future by examining present behavior and using tools like predictive analytics.
Affinity for action	Overperforming: 79% Underperforming: 47%	A tendency to act on the findings. The insights team should provide specific recommendations for organizational actions and should hire other like-minded individuals who have a proclivity to act.

People Characteristics	Proportion of Organizations that Possess this Characteristic*	Description
Whole-brain mindset	Overperforming: 79% Underperforming: 47%	An insights team that makes full use of left-brain (analytical and methodical) and right-brain (creative and artistic) skills. Thinking must be holistic and integrative.
Business focus	Overperforming: 75% Underperforming: 50%	An insights team that understands the business implications of a recommendation (revenue, ROI, market share). The end-goal is to accelerate customer-centric business growth.
Storytelling	Overperforming: 61% Underperforming: 37%	A marketing or insights team that is skilled in conveying a story or an engaging narrative that brings the numbers to life.

*Overperforming organizations are those that outpace their competitors in revenue growth; underperforming organizations are those that lag behind their competitors in revenue growth

Source: Van den Driest, et al. (2016)

Psychologically- and sociologically-based models of consumer behavior can be used to assist marketing decision-makers to strategically position the organization to better deliver the value proposition to its customers. The questions that need to be asked are not what will trigger the next purchase, but what will lead to long-term relationships with these customers? What will create a value proposition so strong that consumers will not switch, even for a lower price (Dawar 2016)? If used in an integrative and intuitive way, these time-tested models of consumer behavior and the data itself will be sources of strategic advantage to the organization.

4.6 SUMMARY

How can marketers make sense of some of the inexplicable things consumers do, and find a way to use them to create actionable insights? When an organization puts the needs of the consumer at the forefront of every decision, it reinforces the notion that the purpose of marketing is to deliver a compelling value proposition to consumers, while making a profit and doing the right thing. Understanding the influences on consumer behavior is a critical first step in developing a deep and nuanced understanding of the consumer.

Psychological foundations of consumer behavior, such as the AIDA model, the consumer decision-making model, attitude models, and the Elaboration Likelihood Model, describe some of the internal workings of the consumer mind. Similarly, sociological foundations of consumer behavior, such as social structures and social processes, describe external influences on consumer decision-making and behavior.

Although there are times when it makes sense to collect more data, more data does not necessarily lead to better decision-making or more actionable insights. In the end, smart marketing decision-makers realize that knowledge of the consumer can be a strategic asset to the organization.

Predicting consumer behavior is difficult. Even the best models are only accurate some of the time. However, this dynamic and challenging arena is exactly what makes the job of a marketer so fascinating.

QUESTIONS FOR REVIEW & DISCUSSION

1. As discussed earlier, Siemens focused just as much on the needs of its immediate B2B consumers as it did on the needs of its end-consumers. In what ways was this approach instrumental to the success of Siemens? Identify another B2B organization that takes a similar approach and describe how it satisfies both its immediate customers and its end-customers.
2. In what way are the first two psychologically-based models of consumer behavior (AIDA and consumer decision-making) similar to the second two psychologically-based models of consumer behavior (attitude models and the Elaboration Likelihood Model)? In what ways are they different?
3. Recall the discussion of the Rungis International Market and the global Covid-19 pandemic. What dimensions of culture stayed the same and what dimensions shifted? Discuss in detail.
4. Imagine a scenario in which a new startup produces underwater pods in which plants can be grown. Initial reports indicate that the plants grow faster, require no pesticides, and have a higher nutrition content than plants grown on land. Using the Theory of Reasoned Action, provide a detailed description of how the startup might try to influence attitudes toward buying pod-grown vegetables, social norms regarding the vegetables, and intentions to purchase the vegetables.
5. With the consumer decision-making model, marketers can influence each step of the process. Imagine that a young couple is trying to decide whether or not to feed their new baby organic baby food. If you were on the marketing team of a large baby-food manufacturer, what would you do to influence *each phase* of the consumer decision-making process for this young couple? Be specific.
6. Formal and informal reference groups both exert influence on consumers. Which influence is stronger? Why?
7. What do we mean when we say that insights should not just predict the future, they should create the future?

4.7 REFERENCES

A Focused Technology Company. 2020. About Us. Siemens. Accessed 19 July 2021. https://new.siemens.com/global/en/company/about.html.

Aguinis, Herman, Harry Joo, and Ryan K. Gottfredson. 2012. Performance Management Universals: Think Globally and Act Locally. *Business Horizons*, 55 (4), 385–92.

Ajzen, Icek and Martin Fishbein. 1980. *Understanding Attitudes and Predicting Social Behavior.* Prentice Hall, Englewood Cliffs, New Jersey.

Baskerville, Rachel F. 2003. Hofstede Never Studied Culture. *Accounting, Organizations and Society, 28*, 1–14.

Bravo, Rafael, Elena Fraj, and Eva Martínez. 2006. Differences and Similarities in Measuring Family Influences on Young Adult Consumers: An Integrative Analysis. *Advances in Consumer Research – European Conference Proceedings, 7*, 104–11.

Caring Since 1911. 2021. NiveaUSA. Accessed 27 July 2021. www.niveausa.com/?

Capa Presse. 2020. A Night at Rungis, France's Fresh Produce Market. *FRANCE24*. 2 March. Accessed 7 August 2021. www.france24.com/en/20200203-you-are-here-france-a-night-at-rungis-fresh-produce-market-food-fish-meat-wholesalers.

Cova, B. 1997. Community and Consumption: Towards a Definition of the "Linking Value" of Products or Services. *European Journal of Marketing, 31* (3/4), 297–316.

Dawar, Niraj. 2016. Use Big Data to Create Value for Customers, Not Just Target Them. *Harvard Business Review*. 16 August. Accessed 22 July 2021. https://hbr.org/2016/08/use-big-data-to-create-value-for-customers-not-just-target-them.

de Mooij, Marieke and Gert Hofstede. 2002. Convergence and Divergence in Consumer Behavior: Implications for International Retailing. *Journal of Retailing, 78* (1), 61–9.

DW. 2021. France: Gourmet Food as an Antidote to Lockdown Blues. *Deutche Welle*. Focus on Europe. 4 February. Accessed 7 August 2021. www.dw.com/en/france-gourmet-food-as-an-antidote-to-lockdown-blues/av-56406860.

Eckhardt, Giana M. 2002. Review: Culture's Consequences: Comparing Values, Behaviors, Institutions and Organisations Across Nature. *Australian Journal of Management, 27* (1), 89–94.

Eckhardt, Giana M., Russell Belk, and Timothy M. Devinney. 2010. Why Don't Consumers Consume Ethically? *Journal of Consumer Behavior, 9*, 426–36.

Englis, Basil and Diane M. Phillips. 2013. Does innovativeness drive environmentally conscious consumer behavior? *Psychology & Marketing, 30* (2), 160–72.

Euromonitor Research. 2017. Top Consumer Trends: Consumers in Training. Market Research Blog. Euromonitor International. 4 April. Accessed 7 August 2021. https://blog.euromonitor.com/top-consumer-trends-consumers-training/.

Fishbein, Martin and Icek Ajzen. 1975. *Belief, Attitude, Intention and Behavior*. Addison-Wesley, Reading, Massachusetts.

French, John R.P. 1956. A Formal Theory of Social Power. *Psychological Review, 63*, 181–94.

French, John R.P. and Bertram H. Raven. 1959. The Basis of Social Power. In *Studies in Social Power*, edited by D. Cartwright. Institute for Social Research, Ann Arbor, Michigan.

Friedman, Thomas L. 2009. *Hot, Flat, and Crowded: Why We Need a Green Revolution – and How it Can Renew America*. Release 2.0: Updated and Expanded. New York, Picador.

Gani, Aisha. 2015. Muslim Population in England and Wales Nearly Doubles in 10 Years. *The Guardian*. 11 February. Accessed 9 August 2021. www.theguardian.com/world/2015/feb/11/muslim-population-england-wales-nearly-doubles-10-years.

Godin, Seth. 2008. *Tribes: We Need You to Lead Us*. Penguin Books, London, UK.

Hagiu, Andrei and Julian Wright. 2020. When Data Creates Competitive Advantage and When it Doesn't. *Harvard Business Review. The Magazine*. January–February. Accessed 10 August 2021. https://hbr.org/2020/01/when-data-creates-competitive-advantage.

Herr, Paul and Russell H. Fazio. 1993. "The Attitude-to-Behavior Process: Implications." In *Advertising Exposure, Memory and Choice*, edited by A. Mitchell, 119–40. Erlbaum, Hillsdale, New Jersey.

Hoffower, Hillary. 2019. Tech Execs in $400 Sneakers and Instagram Influencers in $6000 Louis Vuitton Windbreakers: 5 Ways Wealthy Millennials are Turning to "Uniforms" to Cement their Identity and Status. *Business Insider*. 1 July. Accessed 15 June 2021. www.businessinsider.com/what-do-rich-millennials-wear-outfits-clothes-fashion-2019-6.

Hofstede, Geert. 1984. *Culture's Consequences: International Differences in Work-Related Values*. Abridged edition. Sage, London, UK.

Hofstede, Geert H. 2001. *Culture's Consequences: Comparing Values, Behaviors, Institutions and Organizations across Nations*. 2nd edition. Sage, London, UK.

Hofstede, Geert, Gert Jan Hofstede, and Michael Minkov. 2010. *Cultures and Organizations: Software of the Mind*. McGraw-Hill, New York.

Hopkins, Brian. 2016. "Data-Driven?" Insight is the New Data. *Forrester*. 9 March. Accessed 9 August 2021. https://go.forrester.com/blogs/16-03-09-think_you_want_to_be_data_driven_insight_is_the_new_data/.

Hyman, Herbert. 1942. The Psychology of Status. *Archives of Psychology, 269*, 1–95.

McCracken, Grant. 1986. Culture and Consumption: A Theoretical Account of the Structure and Movement of the Cultural Meaning of Consumer Goods. *Journal of Consumer Research, 13* (1), 71–84.

McSweeney, Brandan. 2002. Hofstede's Model of National Cultural Differences and Their Consequences: A Triumph of Faith – a Failure of Analysis. *Human Relations, 55* (1), 89–118.

O'Keefe, Daniel J. 2008. "The Elaboration Likelihood Model." In *International Encyclopaedia of Communication*, edited by W. Donsbach, *4*, 1475–80. Wiley-Blackwell, Oxford, UK and Malden, Massachusetts.

Oskamp, Stuart and P. Wesley Schultz. 2005. *Attitudes and Opinions*. Erlbaum, Hillsdale, New Jersey.

Park, C. Whan and V. Parker Lessig. 1977. Students and Housewives: Differences in Susceptibility to Reference Group Influence. *Journal of Consumer Research, 4* (2), 102–10.

Park, Hyun Jung and Li Min Lin. 2020. Exploring Attitude-Behavior Gap in Sustainable Consumption: Comparison of Recycled and Upcycled Fashion Products. *Journal of Business Research, 117*, 623–28.

Petty, Richard E. and John T. Cacioppo. 1986. *Communication and Persuasion: Central and Peripheral Routes to Attitude Change*. New York, Springer-Verlag.

Raven, Bertram H. 1993. The Bases of Power: Origins and Recent Developments. *Journal of Social Issues, 49* (4), 227–51.

Satran, Joe. 2015. London Supermarket Tries to Sell Smokey Bacon Pringles to Muslims for Ramadan. *Huffington Post*. 6 December. Accessed 19 July 2021. www.huffpost.com/entry/ramadan-bacon-pringles-tesco-supermarket_n_7666184.

Sidle, Stuart D. 2009. Building a Committed Global Workforce: Does What Employees Want Depend on Culture? *Academy of Management Perspectives, 23* (1), 79–80.

Siemens. 2021. Food Trends: Healthier, Tastier, and More Sustainable. *Talking Digital Industries*. 20 April. Accessed 17 July 2021. https://feeds.acast.com/public/shows/talking-digital-industries.

Stahl, J.-P., R. Cohen, F. Denis, J. Gaudelus, A. Martinot, T. Lery, and H. Lepetit. 2016. The Impact of the Web and Social Networks on Vaccination: New Challenges and Opportunities Offered to Fight Against Vaccine Hesitancy. *Médecine et Maladies Infectieuses, 46*, 117–22.

Statista. 2022. Instagram Accounts with the Most Followers Worldwide 2022. *Statista Research Department*. 20 July. Accessed 18 June 2022. www.statista.com/statistics/421169/most-followers-instagram/.

Stories. 2022. Starbucks Innovates, Tests, and Learns from Store Partners to Achieve Waste Goals. Starbucks Stories & News. 15 March. Accessed 9 September 2022. https://stories.starbucks.com/stories/2022/starbucks-innovates-tests-and-learns-from-store-partners-to-achieve-waste-goals/.

Van den Driest, Frank, Stan Sthanunathan, and Keith Weed. 2016. Building an Insights Engine: How Unilever Got to Know its Customers. *Harvard Business Review*, September, 64–74.

Venkatesh, Alladi and Laurie A. Meamber. 2006. Arts and Aesthetics: Marketing and Cultural Production. *Marketing Theory, 6* (1), 11–39.

Wang, Amy B. 2017. Nivea's "White Is Purity" ad campaign didn't end well. *The Washington Post*. 5 April. Accessed 19 July 2021. www.washingtonpost.com/news/business/wp/2017/04/05/niveas-white-is-purity-ad-campaign-didnt-end-well/.

5 LEADERSHIP. WHO IS STEERING THIS SHIP?

LEADERSHIP INSIGHTS 5

Meet Carolyn S. Fraser, Founder & Principal

The PR Shoppe

Photo 5.1 Carolyn S. Fraser

Source: courtesy, Carolyn S. Fraser

If you ever find Carolyn S. Fraser sitting back, relaxing, and taking it easy, call emergency services. She's not feeling well. Fraser is the founder and principal of The PR Shoppe, a Chicago-based integrated marketing firm specializing in strategic public relations, social media, and small business consulting. Fraser has been particularly successful in helping some of the largest brands in the health and wellness, lifestyle, and beauty industries better connect to diverse audiences by utilizing influencers, music, imagery, and messages that particularly resonate with them. Fraser's formula for success is to combine the strategies of traditional communications with the tactics of new media. The result is effective, message-driven results that are tailored to her clients' needs. One of the first things you notice about Fraser is her boundless energy and enthusiasm. Fraser keeps a keen eye on emerging trends in media consumption and often preempts other PR firms in delivering value to her clients. Fraser's energy, drive, and in-depth knowledge of emerging trends have proven to be a strong foundation for her leadership success.

After working her way up the corporate ladder in several New York PR firms, Frazer moved to Chicago in 2012 to start her own firm. "I thought the firm would have a better chance in Chicago because the city was in need of top-notch PR services and the field was pretty crowded in New York," explained Fraser. The move to Chicago proved very advantageous. The PR Shoppe has grown every year since its inception and has been successful in securing top media coverage for its clients in such well-known and respected outlets as *The Wall Street Journal, Forbes, The New York Times,* and *The Los Angeles Times.*

Recently, more of Fraser's clients demanded a stronger presence in the digital and social space. To achieve that, Fraser has forged numerous influencer partnerships to increase social engagement with her clients' brands. Influencer marketing comes with its own challenges – the influencer and the message must be trusted, the execution needs to be creative, and the message must resonate with the target audience. Fraser also knows that the only way to retain clients is to produce tangible results for their brands. In the world of PR, relevant KPIs include items such as media hits, followers, and engagement. In one particularly successful project for a leading hair care brand, the client's goals were to increase its social media following, overall brand awareness, and exposure. The team created a multi-level marketing strategy, which included elements of influencer marketing, endorsement coordination, digital advertising, giveaways, and public relations. Importantly, the team partnered with a top influencer to create a "traptorial" (video tutorial + trap music) that would resonate with the target audience. In the end, the team exceeded *every one* of its KPIs. In addition, the team forged a lasting relationship with the top-rated beauty influencer; the Instagram post alone achieved more than 176,000 views and hundreds of comments, and was even featured on the Instagram page of a leading urban media company.

Fraser identified an unmet need in the Chicago market and opened her business there to better serve the needs of clients needing top-quality PR services. By developing a deep understanding of each client's needs, her team was able to create arresting campaigns that regularly met and exceeded the client's KPIs. What advice does Fraser have for young professionals? "Take calculated risks early in your career and take advantage of professional development opportunities in your field; leverage the power of social networking to make and maintain meaningful relationships; face rejection head on – it's inevitable; a strong work ethic and integrity leave long-lasting impressions."

5.1 THE COOLEST COMPANY YOU'VE NEVER HEARD ABOUT

Ray Anderson never thought he would change the world when he started to manufacture carpet in 1973. Anderson was the founder and CEO of Interface, an approximately $1 billion manufacturer of carpet targeted at the business market and headquartered near Atlanta, Georgia. Aside from ensuring that it complied with environmental regulations, the very heavily-petroleum-dependent company produced its products with little thought to any environmental ramifications. That is, until customers starting asking what the company was doing to be more sustainable. After some research, Anderson had an epiphany. He realized that his life's work in industry was causing irreparable harm to the environment, and that his children's and his grandchildren's lives would be severely impacted by the decisions he made. This made him question his and his company's ultimate purpose.

In 1999, Anderson shocked many observers when he admitted, "in the future, people like me will go to jail" (Kinkead 1999). He elaborated that the realization felt as if a spear had been thrust into his chest: "business is the biggest culprit in the decline of the biosphere; it therefore has the greatest potential to do good as it re-creates itself to be sustainable" (Anderson 2010).

Anderson realized that existing business models needed to be discarded and replaced with something completely different. Every dimension – from sourcing raw materials through disposal – needed to change (Kinkead 1999). In reconstructing his business, Anderson charted a new course for the strategic direction of the organization so that it could not just co-exist with the environment, but mutually prosper with the environment. As a result of this reformulation, the priorities and practices of everyone working at the company shifted too (Cullen 2020).

A question from a customer was the spark that ignited Anderson's epiphany and his insistence on being a part of the solution, rather than being a part of the problem. Anderson worked with engineering experts to reimagine the entire production system such that raw materials were put into a closed-loop system in which they were manufactured, used, and recycled into new carpet (more about this later) (Watson 2011). Having a marketing mindset was an essential component to Anderson's success. First, Anderson had confidence that there would be a market for newly-formulated products made of natural materials such as wool and hemp (Anderson 2010). Second, because it was a better and more sustainable product, he knew that his customers would be willing to pay a higher price for it. Third, Anderson recognized that he could work collaboratively with his business partners to help them achieve their own sustainability goals. By installing sustainably-made carpet, Interface's customers provided healthier work environments for their own employees and increased their own sustainability credentials.

The good news is the changes that were implemented not only had a positive impact on the environment, they had a positive impact on the bottom line. Using resources more efficiently and more judiciously means that the operation itself is more efficient. Diverting waste away from landfills reduces dumping fees. Recycling and reusing materials means that fewer raw materials need to be purchased. In a related vein, fewer purchases on the open market means fewer fluctuations in prices for raw materials, particularly oil. Interface's greenhouse gases (GHGs, which include CO_2, plus a variety of other heat-trapping gasses) were reduced by 82%, fossil fuel consumption was cut by 60%, and water usage was decreased by 75% (Watson 2011). The company also reduced or avoided waste to the tune of $433 million (Anderson 2010).

Photo 5.2 Carpet for the B2B market

Source: Pixabay

What is particularly impressive is that these and other accomplishments were made at the same time sales increased by 66% and profits doubled (Watson 2011) (see Photo 5.2).

Why is Anderson considered a marketing leader? A true visionary for his time, Anderson became aware of the severity of the climate crisis, identified an opportunity in the market, and did something about it. Anderson implemented these changes into his organization in the 1990s, well before any of his contemporaries were thinking about it, let alone doing anything about it. At the time, there were no models, benchmarks, or expertise for Anderson to utilize. Anderson's work, as well as his mantra of "doing well by doing good" (Kinkead 1999), resulted in numerous accolades and he is often referred to as America's Greenest CEO (Watson 2011). It is not an exaggeration to say that Ray Anderson helped drive the sustainability revolution in marketing.

Both Fraser and Anderson exemplify marketing leadership. This chapter will explore some key characteristics of marketing leadership and will then discuss how a leader thinks and what a leader does.

5.2 LEARNING OBJECTIVES

After studying this chapter, you will be able to do the following:

1 Distinguish between management, leadership, marketing leadership, and market leadership.
2 Describe the various ways in which a leader thinks and behaves differently.
3 Describe the purpose and promise of the Cradle-to-cradle product design philosophy.
4 Differentiate traditional views of economics with that of Doughnut economics.
5 Differentiate between utilitarianism, the common good, and the capabilities approach.
6 Discuss ways in which leaders communicate effectively.

5.3 WHAT IS LEADERSHIP?

Great marketing strategy requires great marketing leadership. Although the organization's effectiveness improves when different members of the organization are brought in to collaborate on strategy creation or are empowered to carry out strategy, the ultimate decision about the scope and direction of the strategy rests with the leader of that organization. This person defines the trade-offs that must be made and clearly communicates the strategy to the organization (Porter 2005). So, what exactly is leadership? Dwight D. Eisenhower, former President of the United

States and Supreme Commander of the Allied Expeditionary Force in Europe in WWII, once said that leadership is "the art of getting someone else to do something that you want done because he wants to do it" (Baier 2017). The great military leader Sun Tzu once said, "a leader leads by example, not by force" (Jackson 2014). **Leadership** can be thought of as the "art of inducing others to follow" (Byron 2010, 11). Implicit in these definitions is the notion that leadership does not happen simply because of an individual's position of authority. Instead, leadership depends on the leader's ability to persuade people. The ultimate test of leadership is followership; if someone is leading, someone else must be following. Also implicit in these definitions is the contention that leadership is not a science, with exact formulaic recommendations or rules. Instead, the success of leadership depends on a more artful and creative approach to a particular issue or problem. Finally, successful leaders model the behavior they are seeking from others; they lead by example.

What is the difference between a manager and a leader? A **manager** carries out the organizational strategy, ensures that its goals are met, and acts as a careful steward of the organization's resources and operations. Managers are not leaders. **Market leadership** is a fairly narrow concept. It simply refers to the organization in a given industry that has the highest market share. Windows by Microsoft, for example, is a market leader in operating systems around the world. In 2022, 75% of the world's computers used Windows, while just 15% used macOS operating systems (Statcounter 2022). **Marketing leadership** is the ability to identify and leverage a marketing-related opportunity that strengthens the competitive standing of the organization's value proposition. Carolyn Fraser identified a gap in the competitive landscape in Chicago for top-notch PR firms. She relocated her firm there and, compared to any other firm in the city, was able to offer a superior level of service to her target clients. Ray Anderson identified a gap in the industry's current ability to sustainably produce carpeting for businesses. Importantly, he also identified an opportunity in the marketplace for these products such that clients could partially meet their own sustainability goals by purchasing Interface carpets. In short, management is about making sure the ship stays afloat; leadership is about steering the ship in the right direction.

Several aspects of the definition of marketing leadership are particularly important. First, marketing leadership requires the person or team to be visionary in identifying opportunities in the marketplace. Perhaps there is a target market that is not having its needs met; perhaps there is a new trend or innovation on the horizon; or perhaps a new law or regulation is about to be implemented. Regardless, a marketing leader has a curiosity about these environmental developments and can imagine them as new opportunities. Second, a marketing leader is capable of identifying ways to leverage those opportunities. Some leaders are capable of utilizing the firm's existing internal capabilities, whereas others such as Anderson needed to seek out expertise in order to leverage those opportunities. Anderson hired engineers and consulted countless experts in his quest to create a new sustainable production system. Third, rather than worrying about short-term criteria like market share, a marketing leader worries more about strengthening the brand's or the product's long-term position against the competition. Finally, this conceptualization of a marketing leader keeps the customer as the central focus of the organization's efforts. The issues that matter most to customers need to be the same issues that matter most to marketing leaders.

The Chief Marketing Officer (CMO)

Generally speaking, the job of the **Chief Marketing Officer (CMO)** is to be the manager of the marketing function of the organization. The role of CMO has become more complicated in recent years with the fragmentation of markets, increasing customer expectations, and powerful channel members (Kumar 2008). As a result, many top B2C organizations, such as McDonald's and Coca-Cola, have eliminated the position of CMO and replaced it with a set of new responsibilities and titles that reflect a more strategic focus on consumers and the marketplace. These individuals now have titles such as chief experience officer, chief innovation officer, and chief growth officer. Regardless of the exact title, this person's role is to navigate the intersection of traditional marketing theory, with increasing consumer expectations and the reality of business performance. It is a difficult task, especially when this happens on a constantly-shifting foundation of new technology and innovations (Miller and Lim 2020). The person with the title of CMO or chief experience officer, for example, is not necessarily a marketing leader. However, this person becomes a true marketing leader when they identify and leverage marketing-related opportunities that strengthen the competitive standing of the organization's value proposition.

What else can the CMO do to move beyond management and toward marketing leadership? Two things. First, marketing leaders know that an important part of their responsibilities is to help create shared value for the organization. Shared value, as we discussed in an earlier chapter, is the simultaneous creation of economic value and societal/environmental value. Thus, the organization itself is not singularly focused on maximizing profit. Instead, the organization takes a long-term view and seeks to increase profit, while also increasing the well-being of society and the environment at large (Porter and Kramer 2011). Marketing leaders recognize the benefits to the shared value approach and will utilize their expertise to help the organization achieve it. Second, marketing leaders will ensure that the strategic direction of the organization incorporates marketing-related priorities such as the value proposition. Successfully influencing the organization's performance hinges on integrative, cross-functional thinking (Kumar 2008), intelligent use of the marketing mix, and the ability to assess the impact of a new strategic initiative on the organization's bottom line.

Incidentally, some organizations are particularly good at training the next generation of marketing leaders. The top three firms are global CPG and marketing powerhouses P&G, Pepsico, and Coca-Cola. These organizations put junior-level people in charge of developing and implementing mid-level marketing strategies in order to gain experience (Whitler 2016), put consumers at the center of their organizational decision-making, and recognize the critical nature of stakeholders and the external environment.

ENDURING INSIGHTS 5.1

> "Don't worry when you are not recognized, but strive to be worthy of recognition." – Abraham Lincoln, 16th president of the United States of America

Lincoln was the president during the American Civil War (1861–65) and developed a clear sense of the purpose and responsibility of leadership: his goal was to keep the country whole. After the North started to win more battles and then eventually won the war, Lincoln objected to any notion that he was a hero. Instead, he wished to be remembered as a man of goodwill and benevolence toward the South. Lincoln is generally regarded as one of the most important presidents in US history.

5.4 HOW A LEADER THINKS

This section focuses on the ways in which marketing leaders think about the world, how they interpret the organization's place within it, and their thoughts about their own roles and obligations.

Looks Internally

Compared to other people, leaders possess several innate characteristics that make them unique. One of the most important characteristics of leadership is **self-awareness**, an in-depth and realistic understanding of their own strengths, weaknesses, values, and worldview (Lowney 2003). Leaders must be able to take a critical look at their own internal strengths and weaknesses, then build on those strengths and find ways to compensate for those weaknesses (Goodwin 2018). Yvon Chouinard, founder of outdoor brand Patagonia, is a great example of someone with a clear-eyed understanding of himself. During his youth, Canadian-born Chouinard developed a deep appreciation for nature and the outdoors, which led to his life-long love of hiking and rock climbing. As a young person, Chouinard would make hand-forged climbing tools and sell them to other rock-climbing friends to earn enough money to go off grid in order to climb mountains for a few weeks or months at a time. As word of his climbing-tool-making talents spread, Chouinard built on those strengths of purpose and passion by creating a business that was designed to help individuals appreciate nature. He named the company Patagonia after a climbing trip he took to South America in 1968. Patagonia produces a variety of products for outdoor use that are made with durable materials and timeless designs. Chouinard promotes sustainable consumption as much as possible, even though it might cost the company money. The products incorporate as much organic and recycled content as possible. If a product is damaged or torn, customers can get it repaired through the company's Worn Wear program (Chouinard 2016). In 2011, Patagonia launched its "Don't Buy This Jacket" campaign, just in time for the holiday shopping season, encouraging consumers to carefully consider the environmental consequences of their consumption choices. The company explained, "it would be hypocritical for us to work for environmental change without encouraging customers to think before they buy" (Godelnik 2011). Throughout the years, Chouinard has encountered countless opportunities to use cheaper materials, cut corners on distribution and production, and use short-term marketing tactics. He has even received numerous offers to sell the company to bigger global sportswear conglomerates. In a true testament to his original commitment to use "business to inspire and implement solutions to the environmental crisis" (Chouinard 2016, xii), in late 2022, Chouinard gave away the company. In a move that is without precedent, he transferred ownership of the $3 billion company to a specially-designed trust and a nonprofit organization, who are committed to working together to address climate change (Gelles 2022) (see Photo 5.3).

Photo 5.3 Fairtrade certified Patagonia jacket

Hadrian / Shutterstock.com

One example of a company that has demonstrated a surprising lack of self-awareness is Toyota. Known as the first major automotive manufacturer to produce a hybrid car for the mass market, the Prius, Toyota invested heavily in hydrogen fuel cell technology as the next logical step in providing carbon-free transportation. However, technologies changed so quickly and significantly, that most other manufacturers embraced electric technology, leaving Toyota's early gamble with hydrogen fuel

Photo 5.4 Toyota has squandered its marketing leadership position

Source: Pixabay

cell technology a costly one. Several manufacturers have committed to eliminating gas-powered vehicles from their lineup by 2030. This leaves Toyota at a distinct disadvantage and, in response, Toyota has not only emerged as a vocal critic of electric technology, it has actively opposed a variety of government initiatives aimed at facilitating faster transitions to electric vehicles. In India, Toyota executives publicly criticized the country's target of 100% electric by 2030; in Mexico, executives sued the country over its fuel efficiency standards. In the US, Toyota's efforts have been particularly aggressive. Toyota executives actively fought against California's Clean Air Act; met with members of congress behind closed doors to push against any quick transition to electric vehicles; and donated money to members of congress who publicly questioned the science of climate change. Toyota is certainly in a tough situation. As of 2021, only 11,000 of its hydrogen powered cars had been sold worldwide. One of its biggest markets, China, is aggressively pushing automotive manufacturers to offer more electric options. Toyota has gone from an industry leader in innovation and market-leading strategies to electric car critic and pariah (Tabuchi 2021) (see Photo 5.4).

BLUNDERS & INSIGHTS 5.1

True Leaders Don't Have to Twist Arms

BACKGROUND: In 2018, Apple found itself at the center of a controversy when it was discovered that its recent software update slowed down the performance of older model iPhones. The problem was made worse when consumers had phones with batteries that happened to be nearing the end of their useful lives. Consumers concluded that Apple was pressuring them to upgrade to the newest iPhone models. Apple's CEO Tim Cook issued a half-hearted public apology' saying that "we did say what it was, but I don't think a lot of people were paying attention... maybe we should have been clearer." The company also cut the price of its battery replacements from $79 to $29 and released new features in the next update to help monitor battery health. Regardless of these moves, the US Department of Justice launched an investigation into the problem (Schoenberg, Robinson, and Gurman 2018).

DEBRIEF: As discussed in the previous section, true leaders inspire people to follow them because they want to do so. Apple has a long history of leading the way in innovations and customer experience and has a loyal following to show for it. Two points about this blunder are noteworthy. First, regardless of whether or not the slowdown was intentional, Apple squandered a significant amount of goodwill from its fiercely-loyal customers. Second, with respect to Apple's response to the controversy, an important component of leadership is effective communication. Details about software updates should have been clearly communicated. Further, a genuine apology would not have tried to place blame on consumers (see Photo 5.5).

Photo 5.5 Apple committed a blunder with its software upgrades

Source: Pixabay

Envisions a Different Future

Predicting the future is one thing. Charting a new path and seeing an alternate future to which the path might lead is quite another thing. **Ingenuity** is another characteristic of leadership. In a constantly changing world, leaders must demonstrate ingenuity by confidently innovating and adapting their thinking to new realities (Lowney 2003). Throughout history, there have been many different artists, scientists, and visionaries who have been able to envision alternate futures. In the mid-18th century, Austrian-born musical genius Wolfgang Mozart, for example, broke convention with his musical compositions that inspired other artists to try new approaches and methods. He also caused a considerable shift in how musicians were beholden to rich and powerful benefactors when he started to independently compose music (Rothstein 2006). Fifteenth century Italian artist and scientist Leonardo DaVinci created groundbreaking new methods for sculpture and painting that resulted in the creation of new art schools that attempted to build upon his methods. Indeed, DaVinci's painting of the Mona Lisa and the Last Supper are viewed as important and consequential leaps forward in artistry and technique. DaVinci's engineering and scientific inventions also demonstrate an alternate vision of the future. By combining his observations of nature with mathematical calculations and engineering principles, he created detailed plans for a variety of never-before-imagined inventions, such as an armored military vehicle (Kemp 2016) (see Photo 5.6).

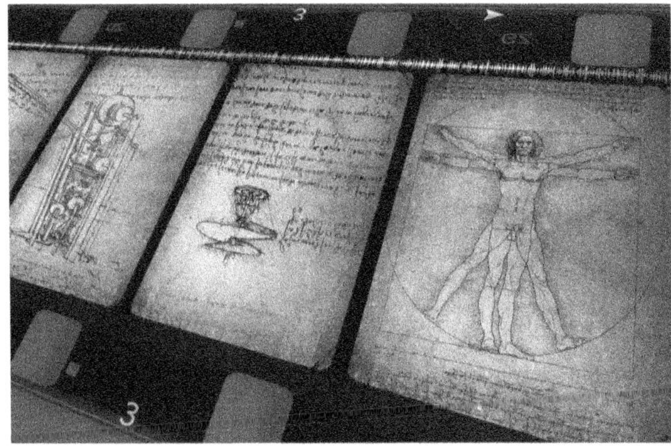

Photo 5.6 DaVinci Drawings from 1492

Source: Shutterstock/Janaka Dharmasena

Pope Francis set out to alter the path of 1.2 billion Catholics around the world when he published a call to action entitled *Laudato Si': On Care for our Common Home* in 2015. In it, he called for leaders and ordinary citizens to take urgent action on climate change. This plea came just a few months before world leaders signed the Paris Climate Accord, a pledge to lower CO_2 emissions such that global warming will be kept at no more than 2°C. One of the biggest problems in human-induced climate change, he said, was a relentless global consumer culture. Marketing and technology have facilitated this consumer culture, so leaders and individuals need to chart a new path toward a common good such that all people, especially people in developing nations, can be lifted up. Such a statement was a radical departure from stances taken by previous popes and other world leaders (Francis 2015).

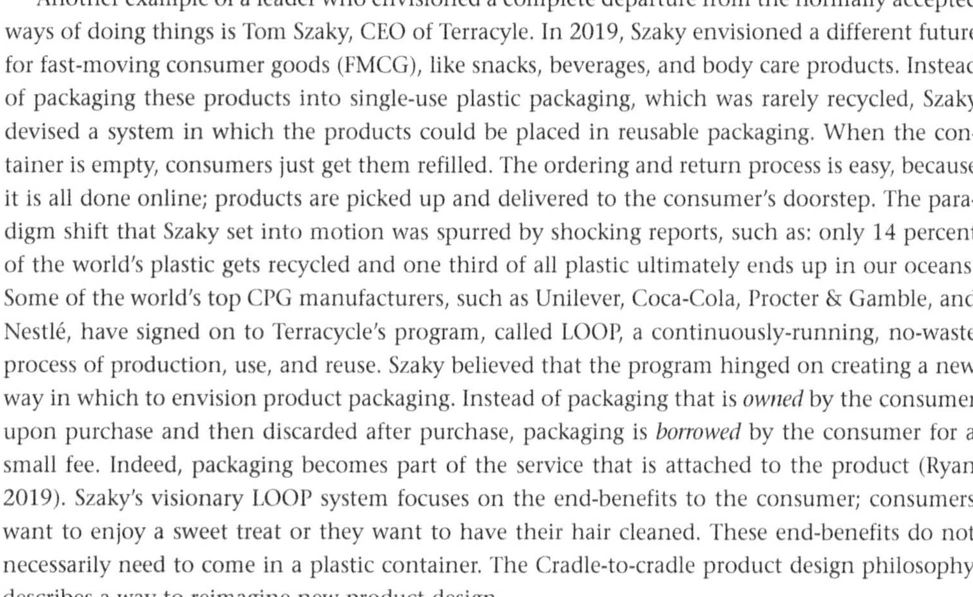

Another example of a leader who envisioned a complete departure from the normally accepted ways of doing things is Tom Szaky, CEO of Terracyle. In 2019, Szaky envisioned a different future for fast-moving consumer goods (FMCG), like snacks, beverages, and body care products. Instead of packaging these products into single-use plastic packaging, which was rarely recycled, Szaky devised a system in which the products could be placed in reusable packaging. When the container is empty, consumers just get them refilled. The ordering and return process is easy, because it is all done online; products are picked up and delivered to the consumer's doorstep. The paradigm shift that Szaky set into motion was spurred by shocking reports, such as: only 14 percent of the world's plastic gets recycled and one third of all plastic ultimately ends up in our oceans. Some of the world's top CPG manufacturers, such as Unilever, Coca-Cola, Procter & Gamble, and Nestlé, have signed on to Terracycle's program, called LOOP, a continuously-running, no-waste process of production, use, and reuse. Szaky believed that the program hinged on creating a new way in which to envision product packaging. Instead of packaging that is *owned* by the consumer upon purchase and then discarded after purchase, packaging is *borrowed* by the consumer for a small fee. Indeed, packaging becomes part of the service that is attached to the product (Ryan 2019). Szaky's visionary LOOP system focuses on the end-benefits to the consumer; consumers want to enjoy a sweet treat or they want to have their hair cleaned. These end-benefits do not necessarily need to come in a plastic container. The Cradle-to-cradle product design philosophy describes a way to reimagine new product design.

Cradle-to-Cradle

Another leap forward in ingenuity is represented by the Cradle-to-cradle product design philosophy. It rests on the contention that waste that is derived from consumption or production is simply "food" for some other process. Think about it. Landfills around the world are filled with plastic, wood, glass, metal, and other materials that, if cleaned and processed, could be used for the production of new products. These materials represent a vast, mostly untapped resource. The **Cradle-to-cradle product design philosophy** points out that, if new product designers incorporate easy-to-recycle materials into their designs, when products eventually reach the end of their lives, those products could be pulled apart, the materials could be put back into the production process, and new products could be created. After design and production, the process is called a **closed-loop production process** because its goal is a never-ending circle of raw materials, manufacturing, and consumer products, which eventually become raw materials for something else (McDonough and Braungart 2002). When Timberland introduced its Earthkeeper line of shoes in 2007, it was one of the first mainstream fashion brands to utilize Cradle-to-cradle product design and a closed-loop production process. How does it work? After purchase, consumers register the shoes with Timberland. Then, when they are eventually ready for a new pair of shoes, customers send the old ones back to Timberland, where the shoes are disassembled into their component parts: rubber soles, leather, nylon, etc. These raw materials are then used in the production of new Earthkeeper shoes. Timberland initially designed the Earthkeeper shoes using a Cradle-to-cradle philosophy; materials such as leather and rubber were selected that would be easy to use again and the shoes were assembled such that they would be durable, but easy to disassemble when needed (Schwartz 2009) (see Figure 5.1).

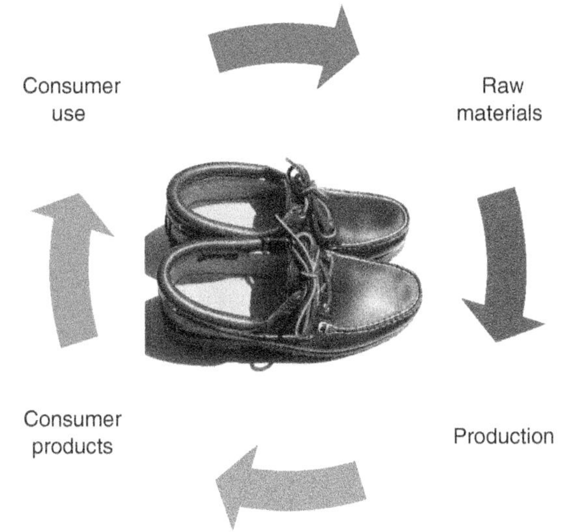

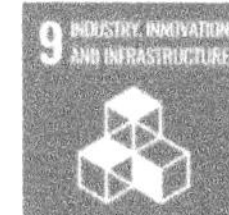

Figure 5.1 The closed loop production process

Source: Pixabay

ENDURING INSIGHTS 5.2

> "How was your day? If your answer was 'fine,' then I don't think you were leading." – Seth Godin, author and speaker

Leadership is hard and demanding work. Let's face it, looking internally, envisioning a different future, thinking systemically, and admitting fallibility is not easy. In addition, leaders need to anticipate shifts in the market and in the competitive landscape. Despite these challenges, the job of a leader is incredibly dynamic, exciting, and rewarding.

Thinks Systemically

The natural environment is an interconnected system of different influences and impacts. Disturb the web in any area, and the entire web will feel the effects. When a singular species is threatened or worse, goes extinct, every other organism that depends upon or interacts with that species is also imperiled. Simply look at the example of the increasing mismatch between newly-hatched birds and their favorite food: caterpillars. With climate change, springtime is arriving earlier than ever before. The warmth causes plants to bloom earlier and insects to hatch earlier in the spring. Unfortunately, birds build their nests and lay their eggs on the same timeline that they have for millennia. This means that when the eggs hatch and the baby birds are hungry for a meal, most of the caterpillars upon which they would have feasted are gone. The result is a widespread, worldwide collapse of bird populations (Burgess, Smith, Evans, et al. 2018). In short, the natural environment is an interconnected set of relationships.

As applied to business and marketing, **systemic thinking** occurs when decision-makers understand that the actions of the organization both impact and are impacted by a wide variety of other influences. Just like the natural environment, organizational decisions create a web of different effects, of which marketing leaders need to be cognizant. The Triple Bottom Line is one tool that assists systemic thinkers by encouraging a careful consideration of three broad dimensions of impacts: people, planet, and prosperity. Another example of systemic thinking is doughnut economics.

Doughnut Economics

The economic theory of **Doughnut economics** starts with the contention that organizations cannot continually grow; they exist within a web of connections to other organizations, governments, and entities. Continuous growth puts pressure on these other important systems that also need to thrive. One key feature of this economic model is that it questions the long-held notion that continual economic growth is necessary. Consider the analogy of a natural healthy organism that is experiencing unchecked growth in one area. That growth will eventually either encounter constraints to keep it in check, or the growth will overwhelm the organism. Continuous growth, especially within a healthy, living, thriving system, will cause big disruptions. Just as natural systems cannot support unchecked growth in one part of the system, economic systems cannot continue growing; they will either bump up against constraints or they will overwhelm and destroy the entire system. Doughnut economics represents a profound shift in mindset (Raworth 2017).

Traditional economic theories of capitalism were created in the 17th century (Nugent 2021) when economists were not faced with the realities of any of the climate or environmental guardrails that systems are facing today. At the time, there were no imminent dangers of collapsing ecosystems or tipping points that would result in sudden and severe climate emergencies. Indeed, early economists rarely took into account *any* externalized costs, including pollution, habitat collapse, or vast disparities in wealth distribution. It is not surprising then, that economists – with no experience in systemic thinking regarding the limitations of the natural world – would fail to account for those realities (Raworth 2017).

Doughnut economics suggests that, because of the need to coexist within a network of other thriving systems, the ideal space for sustainable economic growth exists somewhere between a social foundation and an economic ceiling. Economies can still thrive, but must do so within the boundaries of the social and ecological systems. It is important to remember that boundaries are not to be feared; they are the very thing that inspire some of the world's most innovative and creative people – Jimi Hendrix had six strings on his guitar and Mozart had just five octaves on his piano (today there are typically seven), yet both created ground-breaking innovations in music. Boundaries unleash ingenuity (Raworth 2017).

The economic ceiling and the social foundation provide a safe and just space for humanity that is both regenerative and distributive. A **regenerative system** turns degenerative industries that take, make, and waste upside down and instead promotes long-term functioning of the system.

Thus, lumber industries will restore the land and plant new trees; fisheries will replenish and restock after they catch their harvest; energy companies will shift away from non-renewable to renewable sources of energy. A **distributive system** is one in which resources and their benefits, such as wealth, knowledge, energy, and political power, are shared, not hoarded by a select few. A distributed system is a network of interconnected links. It is a **sharing economy** that, for example, generates and distributes energy for all citizens. This could be accomplished, for instance, by a small wind or solar array that generates energy for an individual neighborhood. A localized and networked system like this has the benefit of shorter transmission distances, which is much more efficient than transmitting electricity over long distances. A small distributive system is also easier to repair if there are any power disruptions. A distributive system encourages participation and shared responsibility. It helps everyone thrive, whether or not the system itself grows (see Figure 5.2).

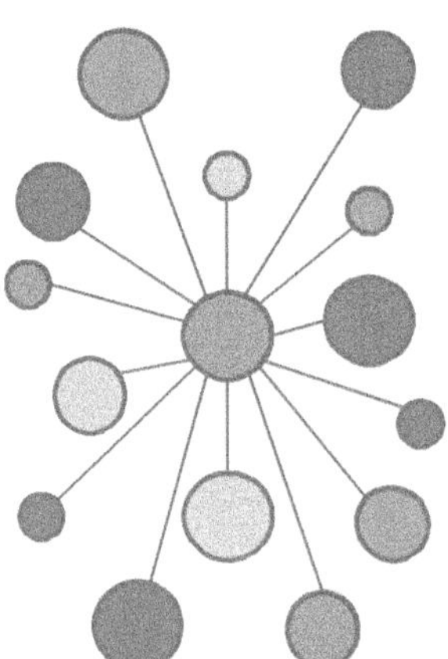

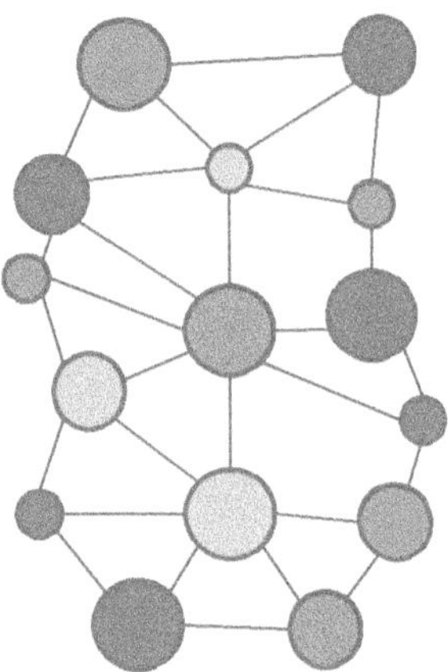

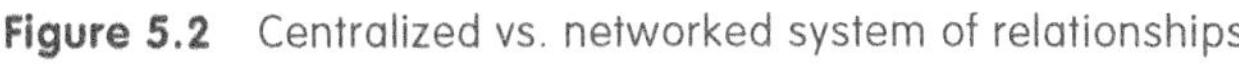

Figure 5.2 Centralized vs. networked system of relationships

Source: developed from Raworth (2017)

In examining the model, the upper limit of efficient economic functioning is the **ecological ceiling**. It represents an upper boundary for the nine life-supporting systems of planet earth, including, for example, ocean acidification, chemical pollution, and biodiversity loss. Cross one of these boundaries and further economic activity could result in long-term or irreversible damage. The **social foundation** represents the 12 basic human needs. If an economic system falls short in providing at least the minimum level of one of these needs such as health, education, or social equity, any further economic activity could damage the foundation upon which a functioning social system thrives. If this occurs, people will not have the ability to access the resources that are essential for a life of dignity and opportunity. Between the ecological ceiling and the social foundation exists a dynamic, regenerative, and distributive system (Raworth 2017).

Doughnut economics proposes that economic growth should not in itself be viewed as an indicator of success, but should instead be viewed as a means to achieve social and environmental goals. In 2020, the city of Amsterdam adopted doughnut economics as a guiding principle for the entire city. This move was quickly followed by other cities around the world, such as Copenhagen, Denmark; Dunedin, New Zealand; Nanaimo, British Columbia; and Portland, Oregon (Nugent 2021). As economies around the world rethink their financial, social, and

climate plans, many are embracing a more wholistic and connected approach. They are recognizing that continuous growth should not be a goal; instead, they are pursuing systems that promote thriving, resilience, and community-wide well-being (Nugent 2021, Raworth 2017) (see Figure 5.3).

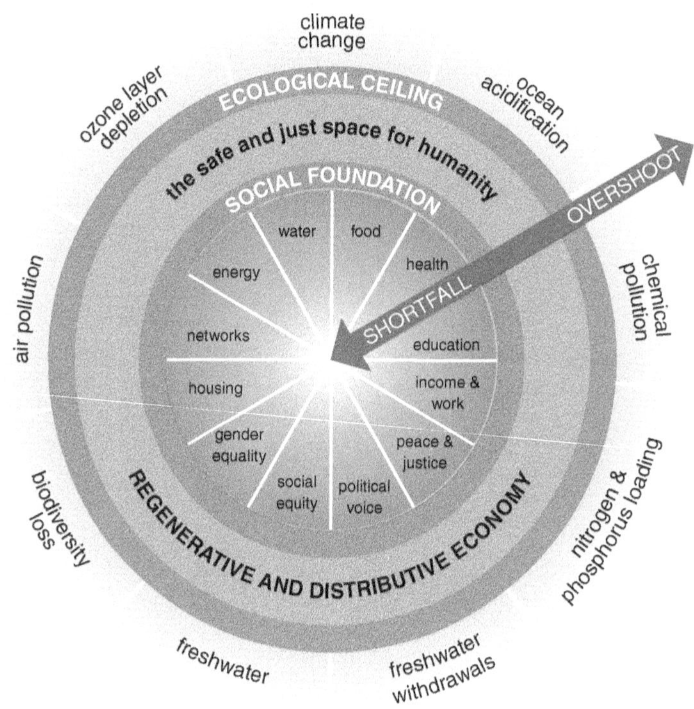

Figure 5.3 Doughnut economics

Source: Raworth (2017)

Admits Fallibility

Real leaders admit when they've done something wrong. Sometimes the unexpected happens: a natural disaster or an accident occurs and, despite the best preparations, people get hurt, the environment gets damaged, and customers become angry. Sometimes, mistakes happen because of poor planning or poor decision-making. Regardless of how it happens, stakeholders appreciate when a leader admits a mistake. Rather than place blame on the situation, or worse yet, someone else, a real leader must own up to their bad decisions. Otherwise, stakeholders will assume the worst: that the leader is disengaged, doesn't care, or is simply not qualified to hold the job (Whitehurst 2015). When British Petroleum CEO, Tony Hayward, famously complained that he wanted his "life back" while he was dealing with the aftermath of the company's 2010 explosion and oil spill in the Gulf of Mexico that resulted in 11 deaths and the biggest environmental disaster in US history, observers were understandably flummoxed. Hayward's inability to admit his failures and his frequent dodging of questions about the clean up led him to be called "the most hated man in America." After suffering widespread anger at the company's handling of the disaster, a loss of confidence, and a decline in stock price, the board of directors asked for Hayward's resignation a few months later (Macalister and Wray 2010).

Moral recovery occurs when a leader realizes that they have engaged in a behavior that has violated their own values and moral compass. It goes a step further than simply admitting a mistake. With moral recovery, the person works to remedy the situation and achieve balance again (Cullen 2020). Ray Anderson realized that his company was causing irreparable harm to the environment that made it difficult for future generations to thrive. His moral recovery took the form of concrete steps to shift his business to more sustainable operations. In addition, he was a frequent speaker and strong advocate for other businesses to make similar shifts. Another example of moral recovery occurred in 2020 with Eric Yuan, CEO of video-conferencing platform Zoom. When the world shut down because of the Covid-19 pandemic and many organizations shifted to virtual meetings and instruction, Zoom became one of the most widely-used platforms. Zoom was the most downloaded app on Apple iOS and the number of global users went from 10 million to 200 million in just a few weeks. However, it was soon plagued by instances of "Zoom bombing" where unauthorized users were able to gain access to meetings and harass meeting participants. Yuan admitted to his own and the company's failings. Yuan admitted, "I really messed up ... this kind of thing shouldn't have happened." His moral recovery occurred when he worked around-the-clock with teams of engineers who created and implemented security and encryption fixes (Tilley and McMillan 2020).

BLUNDERS & INSIGHTS 5.2

L'Oréal's Temporary Amnesia

BACKGROUND: After receiving accolades for the hiring of its first Black transgender model, L'Oréal Paris unceremoniously fired Munroe Bergdorf in 2017 after she made a heated social media post about the Black Lives Matter movement and claimed that all White people were racist. In hiring Bergdorf, L'Oréal received significant positive recognition for breaking down barriers, especially within the Black and trans communities. However, it seems as if decision-makers at L'Oréal temporarily lost sight of the corporate values that facilitated the model's hiring in the first place. In response to the firing, Bergdorf called for a boycott of L'Oréal, which received significant social media support. Three years later in 2020, Bergdorf had a one-on-one conversation with the president of L'Oréal Paris, Delphine Viguier. Shortly afterward, the company announced the creation of an advisory board focused on diversity and inclusion, on which Bergdorf would have a prominent seat (Aviles 2020).

DEBRIEF: The initial blunder committed by L'Oréal resulted in significant negative feedback for the organization from individuals who accused it of not being truthful to its espoused values. There were certainly other leadership options open to L'Oréal, other than simply retaining or firing Bergdorf. For example, they could have put the comments in their context and elaborated on what she meant by them. In the end, however, Viguier acknowledged that

(Continued)

the company's ethical standards should not be "put aside in difficult times" and rectified the problem by giving Bergdorf an important advisory role (see Figure 5.4).

In a changing world, our Ethical Principles of Integrity, Respect, Courage and Transparency serve as our compass for acting ethically day-to-day... These principles shape our culture, underpin our reputation, and allow all L'Oréal employees to build trust through our actions every day (Our Ethical Principles 2022).

Figure 5.4 L'Oréal's statement on ethical principles

Source: Our Ethical Principles (2022)

5.5 WHAT A LEADER DOES

Marketing leaders engage in a variety of different behaviors. Among them are setting goals and objectives, setting ethical standards and values, inspiring others to action, assembling the team, and doing the unexpected.

Sets Goals and Objectives

Ultimately, it is the organization's leader that sets the goals for the organization. In setting ambitious goals for the organization, leaders are being heroic, because they are reaching beyond what is comfortable for the organization (Lowney 2003). To be clear, organizational **goals** are broad and somewhat abstract statements about what the organization seeks to achieve. Marketing leaders work with their teams to create a set of marketing-related goals that are designed to strengthen the organization's competitive position and deliver the value proposition. A marketing goal, for example, might be to strengthen long-term relationships with consumers. As discussed earlier in the text, organizational **objectives** are much more specific and tangible. They provide specificity and direction to the goals. With respect to the goal of stronger long-term customer relationships, a marketing objective could be to increase customer repurchase rates from 15% to 25% in the next 12 months. Using the tools in the marketing mix – product, price, place, and promotion – the marketing team will then work to carry out those objectives. Objectives that are quantifiable are especially useful in motivating the team and in providing clear expectations (Byron 2010) (see Figure 5.5).

Figure 5.5 Goals vs. objectives

Sets Ethical Standards and Values

An important part of a leader's responsibility is setting the values and vision for the organization. Some leaders are driven by their own internal moral compass, such as Tim Cook of Apple, who is known for his strong support of LGBTQIA rights or Mark Schneider of Nestlé, who led his company to announce industry-leading initiatives on climate change. The ubiquitous nature of social media demands accountability and transparency from marketing leaders. No longer can they hide their actions from stakeholders. Indeed, many are pushed to take a stand on issues such as the environment and social justice. As more leaders take a stand on these issues, neutrality is no longer an option because those who remain on the sidelines will be "named and shamed" on social media. Because marketing is a conduit between the world outside the organization and that inside the organization, a marketing leader will ensure that the broader organizational values are carried out. Importantly, the marketing leader will ensure that, in carrying out various marketing objectives and performing marketing functions, a set of marketing values are upheld. Among other things, the value proposition must be strengthened and nurtured; consumers must be treated fairly and equitably; and all promotions about the product or service must be honest.

The example of bamboo illustrates the importance of setting clear marketing-related values and adhering to those values. Some sustainably-minded consumers have been attracted to products that are made from bamboo, a fast-growing renewable fiber that has been incorporated into products such as towels, bedsheets, and clothing. Bamboo is just as soft and durable as cotton, but grows much more quickly and requires fewer pesticides and environmentally-harmful processing. Often, consumers pay a price premium for products with bamboo content. In 2021, a report was released that found that consumers were often being deceived by product labels claiming to have bamboo content. Consumers from around the world who thought they were purchasing products made with bamboo actually were not. When researchers contacted 10 companies about the labeling errors, 6 responded immediately by changing their websites, product descriptions, or labeling. Two brands took longer, but eventually responded, and two brands never responded (GH 2021). In reviewing their actions, it is clear which brands were concerned about adhering to a set of values and which were not.

How do marketing leaders determine right from wrong? How is it possible to assess whether a given marketing action is ethical? Importantly, how is it possible to make a determination about ethics when the situation in question may involve a different culture or even time? **Values** describe the core guiding principles in a person's life. They can be thought of as desired end-states and include such things as happiness, a world at peace, and wisdom. Marketing core values are also guiding principles for the marketing team. They might include, for example, items such as innovation, quality, teamwork, and a commitment to our customers. Guided by a set of over-arching values, **ethics** describe a set of moral standards for behavior. For example, it is important to treat one another with integrity, honesty, and fairness. Ethical frameworks do not provide an answer to a problem or a how-to guide for behavior. Instead, ethical frameworks help to clarify issues and identify the parameters of the problem. Because marketing is the bridge between the external world and the internal world of the organization, it is essential that the marketing team engages in ethical decision-making.

The ethical leader will set the tone and focus for the organization and will determine how the organization perceives its role within the broader environment. Will the organization's role be one of merely extraction, where it will endeavor to pull as many resources from the environment as possible, in an effort to maximize output and minimize costs? Alternatively, will the organization's role be one of reciprocity, where it will take from the environment only what it needs while it also returns resources into that same environment? Responsible forestry stewardship, for example, is a process that selectively harvests trees and then plants new tree seedlings to replace the ones that were harvested, thus resulting in a resource that continually renews itself. Enlightened leaders will work according to principles of reciprocity, rather than extraction, to ensure that soils, water, land, and other resources needed for business to thrive will be there for the long term (Kimmerer 2013).

Three methods of ethical decision-making that are particularly relevant to marketing strategy are utilitarianism, the common good, and the capabilities approach. These frameworks provide a clarifying lens through which to view a given situation or problem.

Utilitarianism

One framework for assessing ethical questions is **utilitarianism**, which proposes that the most ethical choice is the one that benefits the greatest number of people. Utilitarianism relies on stark assessments of expected utility to help clarify which of several decisions will objectively be the best. Consider the example of a quaint neighborhood on the edge of a city. The city would like to build a new sports complex in the area, but in order to do so, it must demolish several houses along two streets to make room for the new complex. Many thousands of residents across the city and in surrounding areas are expected to enjoy the new facilities for games, concerts, and other events. In addition, they are expected to enjoy the new restaurants, shops, and bars that will be built in the area. However, the residents who live in the affected area are less than enthusiastic. More traffic and crime are likely to result, and their quaint little neighborhood will never be the same. Using the utilitarianism framework, the city should buy out the residents, demolish the homes, and build the new sports complex. After all, the number of people who will benefit exceeds the number of people who will suffer. Utilitarianism does not account for human rights, social justice, or the environment (Driver 2009). In addition, with a greater recognition of the need to be inclusive of different perspectives and life experiences, the utilitarianism perspective has become even less relevant as an informative ethical framework.

The Common Good

Another framework for assessing ethical questions is **the common good**. Here, the most ethical decision is the one that provides the greatest good to the entire group. Compared to utilitarianism, the common good takes into account economic benefits, as well as benefits that might accrue to human health and well-being, society as a whole, and the environment. For the common good to be effective, the group needs to have a shared set of beliefs and an agreement about what is right and wrong. In addition, group members need to interact with one another with honesty and integrity, and according to a set of generally-accepted rules (Reich 2018). Consider another example. This time, picture a football game in which every player behaves according to their own self-interest, instead of the common good. Rather than players supporting one another to score points and win the game, players try to outshine one another and attract the attention of fans and recruiters. Without the team working cooperatively toward a common goal (a win), the game and its outcome will be disappointing for everyone. The common good approach is especially relevant to marketers, who create compelling value propositions and use their skills to motivate consumers to buy their products, vote for their candidates, sign up for their services, or visit their destinations. Organizations that are guided by the common good understand that their own success is intertwined with that of the society in which it resides. When society prospers, businesses prosper too. Therefore, mutual benefits can be achieved when marketers and consumers work together (Kotler 2019).

The Capabilities Approach

The third ethical framework that is particularly relevant to marketing leadership is the capabilities approach, which starts with the observation that broad measures of economic health, such as a country's per capita GDP, are wildly inaccurate measures of individual well-being because they are aggregate measures that do not take into account how people are doing across a variety of dimensions, like health, political liberty, education, and race relations. The **capabilities approach** suggests that human well-being should be assessed not by what individuals actually do or have (their functionings), but by what they *can do* (their capabilities). An important aspect of this approach is the focus on the "capability" to achieve a particular goal, not necessarily the actual achievement of the goal. Because of the freedom of countries and citizens to make choices, the capability to achieve the goal is paramount. So, for example, countries should have access to free, high-quality health care so everyone is capable of accessing it. Some people will and some will not. In some countries, not everyone is capable of voting (because of strict hours, long lines, intimidation, etc.). When assessing a society for social justice or human welfare, the key question to ask is, "what is each person able to do and be?" (p. 18). It asks not about the total average well-being of the group, but about the well-being of each individual person. This is very consistent with a customer-centric approach (see Table 5.1) (Nussbaum 2011).

Table 5.1 10 capabilities necessary for human well-being

Capability	Definition
1. Life	The ability to live in a reasonable state to the end of one's life.
2. Bodily health	The ability to have good health throughout one's life. This includes nourishment, shelter, and reproductive health.
3. Bodily integrity	The ability to move around freely, to be safe against all kinds of assault, including sexual assault. To also have the ability to achieve sexual satisfaction and make reproductive choices.
4. Senses, imagination, and thought	The ability to participate in an informed and cultivated way in what it means to be truly human. This is informed by adequate education, and includes creative expression, political and artistic speech, and freedom to exercise one's religion.
5. Emotions	The ability to experience and express a wide range of emotions and not have them hampered by fear or anxiety.
6. Practical reason	The ability to critically evaluate one's life and plan one's life goals.
7. Affiliation	The ability to (a) live with and for others, to demonstrate empathy, and to interact with others and (b) have self-respect and be treated with dignity and as a person of worth.
8. Other species	The ability to live in connection with the natural world.
9. Play	The ability to engage in play and enjoy recreation.
10. Control over one's environment	The ability to (a) from a political perspective – to effectively participate in self-governance, including protections for free speech and freedom of association and (b) from a material perspective – to hold property and have property rights (land and goods), attain employment, not be subject to unwarranted search or seizure, be treated equally and with dignity at work.

Source: Nussbaum (2011)

Consider the UN's 17 SDGs and the common dilemma that marketing decision-makers must sometimes make about prioritizing one SDG over another. Although all 17 SDGs work synergistically, due to resource constraints, it is sometimes necessary to prioritize one over another, as when a decision-maker must decide whether to build a new water treatment facility (SDG6), a new school (SDG4), or a new renewable energy generation facility (SDG7). When faced with a question about which course of action to take, the capabilities approach recommends the best choice is the one that maintains or strengthens as many of the 10 capabilities as possible.

Stays True to Values

Does it really matter what leadership does? Yes. A true leader must be true and authentic (Watson 2011). Even in a leader's private life, adhering to a set of ethical standards is essential. In fact, when leaders engage in ethically questionable behavior with respect to the environment, the organization's reputation can suffer (Loock and Phillips 2020). Establishing a set of ethical standards is one thing. Staying true to them is another. An important component of leadership is that it must be authentic. **Authenticity** is not a static trait; instead, it is a "the lifelong process of learning about yourself ... and becoming your own person." An important part of this definition is that it is flexible and open to continuous improvement (Iberra 2021). An authentic and strategic leader takes into account the demands of the situation and the values of the organization to develop a flexible and meaningful strategy.

Olympic gymnast Simone Biles, for example, ended her partnership with Nike in order to partner with athleisure brand Athleta because it resonated more closely with her values. Nike, which had $9.3 billion in endorsement deals in 2020, actively pursued a partnership with Biles, America's most decorated gymnast. However, Nike came under fire after it was revealed that women athletes are often penalized for getting pregnant during an endorsement contract. Track star Allyson Felix, for example, was offered 70% less after a difficult pregnancy, which ended in a caesarian section in 2019 (Isidore 2021). Felix, incidentally, went on to win her 11th Olympic medal in Tokyo in 2021, making her America's most decorated track and field champion (Cacciola 2021). Several high-profile athletes have found a better connection with Athleta, which has a long history of empowering women and girls (Isidore 2021) (see Photo 5.7).

Photo 5.7 Athleta empowers women and girls

Source: courtesy, Athleta, Inc.

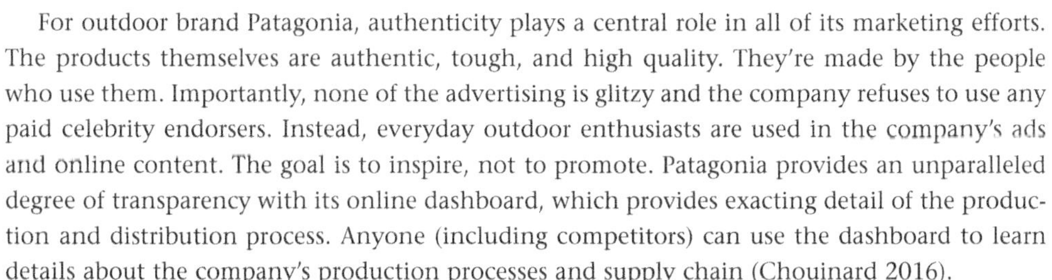
For outdoor brand Patagonia, authenticity plays a central role in all of its marketing efforts. The products themselves are authentic, tough, and high quality. They're made by the people who use them. Importantly, none of the advertising is glitzy and the company refuses to use any paid celebrity endorsers. Instead, everyday outdoor enthusiasts are used in the company's ads and online content. The goal is to inspire, not to promote. Patagonia provides an unparalleled degree of transparency with its online dashboard, which provides exacting detail of the production and distribution process. Anyone (including competitors) can use the dashboard to learn details about the company's production processes and supply chain (Chouinard 2016).

Inspires Others to Action

A person or a team cannot be a leader unless there are others to lead. Therefore, motivating others to action is another critical leadership quality. Here, a leader must leverage the appropriate type of motivation and effectively communicate with the group.

Intrinsic vs. Extrinsic Motivation

Intrinsic motivation occurs when an individual is inspired to behave because of some sort of internal drive. Perhaps the leader's message really resonates with the person or perhaps the person gets some sort of satisfaction or enjoyment as a result of performing the behavior. Intrinsic motivation is long-lasting. There is an old saying that "if you love your job, you will never work a day in your life." That's intrinsic motivation. Alternatively, **extrinsic motivation** occurs when individuals perform the behavior because they get some kind of reward, such as a payment or special recognition. As fun and interesting as a job may be, most individuals work at their jobs because they are paid to do so. Although both are practical, it is not surprising that leaders prefer their followers to be intrinsically motivated more than extrinsically motivated.

Admittedly, extrinsic motivation does help, as when a person's compensation is directly tied to important KPIs. Some experts have called for executive compensation to be tied to an organization's sustainability performance. Numerous metrics exist, making it easy to track progress toward a variety of different goals (Burchman and Sullivan 2017), such as improvements in CO_2 emissions, factory working conditions, recycled content, or the amount of waste diverted from landfills.

Effective Communication

Another way in which leaders can inspire others to action is through effective communication. First, marketing leaders need to communicate the team's strategy to both internal and external stakeholders. Internal communication should go beyond informing the team about what is happening and why. Here, it is essential to engage subordinates so that everyone feels as if they are a part of a collective effort. Importantly, individuals working within the organization and on the team have different perspectives and insights, so their input is valuable. A second important component of inspiring others to action is to demonstrate a genuine concern for your team, such that the leader engages with others, such as employees, customers, and business partners, with a positive and caring attitude (Lowney 2003). The most effective marketing leaders are receptive, open, and willing to engage in two-way communication that is honest and transparent. Third, the marketing leader must be able to tell a good story. Describing the "how and why" of a given strategy with vivid descriptions will help energize the team and might even turn them into evangelists for the project. At Interface, for example, Ray Anderson told the compelling story of how we went from a plunderer to a protector of the environment. This resulted in an almost fanatical following of dedicated employeess who helped carry out his vision (Watson 2011). As Interface employees started seeing some of the sustainability initiatives implemented as well as their positive effects, they were further energized and galvanized in shifting the organization to more sustainable operations. These employees worked with tireless dedication and passion to bring Anderson's ideas to fruition (Winston 2009).

After interacting with and communicating with one another over time, the team will eventually develop its own culture. The **team culture** is akin to the team's personality and encompasses a standard set of behaviors it deems appropriate. In the end, effective leadership communication within the team encompasses four key dimensions (Groysberg and Slind 2012) (see Figure 5.6):

- Intimacy – describes how leaders relate to employees.
- Interactivity – describes how leaders use communication channels.
- Inclusion – describes how leaders develop organizational content.
- Intentionality – describes how leaders convey strategy.

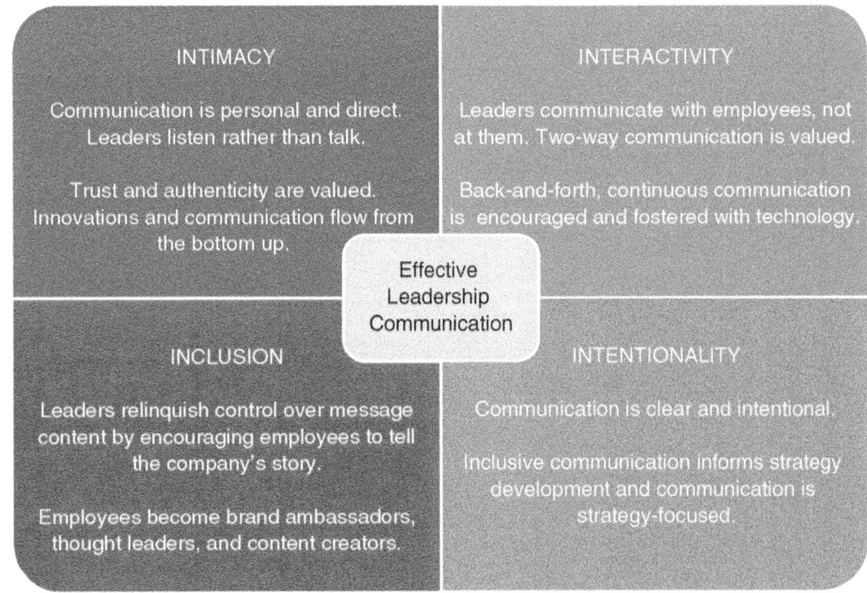

Figure 5.6 The four dimensions of effective leadership communication

Source: adapted from Groysberg and Slind (2012)

ENDURING INSIGHTS 5.3

"People will forget what you said, people will forget what you did, but people will never forget how you made them feel." – Maya Angelou, poet

This quote illustrates how the mind and the heart react to different communications. Some messages are logical or rational in nature; they are designed to convey information, such as facts and statistics. Other messages are emotional in nature; they are designed to engender feelings. Emotions are often long-lasting and commonly result in strong, long-lasting memories.

Assembles the Team

Successfully selecting team members is another indicator of a good leader. These individuals must embrace the team's vision and strategy, and be willing to provide their input without fear of negative consequences. Indeed, team members should feel free to offer opinions and challenge one another. More importantly, they must represent a diverse range of perspectives.

Abraham Lincoln, President of the United States during that country's Civil War, had a keen sense of purpose during the war: keep the individual states together as a single country and end slavery. To do this, he surrounded himself with a "team of rivals," three individuals who were his biggest political rivals. In addition, he appointed his philosophical and political rivals to top posts throughout the administration. Because most of these key team members were better educated and more experienced in the political arena, these appointments took everyone by surprise, especially the rivals themselves. However, a combination of political genius and personal qualities enabled Lincoln to gain the trust of these individuals and form genuine friendships with these men. What did Lincoln do to win them over and assemble such an effective team? He clearly communicated his objectives and worked with them until the entire team agreed on a common vision. Among other things, he shared the credit of his own successes with others, he sometimes assumed responsibility for the failures of his subordinates, and he and the team members learned from their mistakes. He was also very quick to repair injured feelings that, if left unaddressed, could have escalated into distance and hostility. Lincoln also possessed some personal characteristics that facilitated team cohesiveness and effectiveness. For example, he had a gift for storytelling, he was aware of his own limitations, and he was generally an upbeat and calming influence. Together with Lincoln, this team of rivals changed the course of American history by successfully winning the Civil War to keep the country together and end slavery (Goodwin 2005).

Individuals with diverse backgrounds and perspectives can work effectively when they have an effective leader, as well as clear and common objectives. It took an extreme amount of self-confidence for Lincoln to assemble these men onto his team, because they could have easily eclipsed him and pursued their own individual agendas. Instead, Lincoln took control of the situation with his fierce ambition, exceptional political acumen, and emotional strength. The team successfully navigated the war and ensuing economic and social upheaval. Within a decade, the country was growing and prospering (Goodwin 2005) (see Photo 5.8).

Photo 5.8 Abraham Lincoln, one of America's greatest leaders

Source: Pixabay

Does the Unexpected

Most marketing strategy textbooks encourage reason-based decisions. In fact, Chapter 3 of this book is all about the importance of defensible decision-making. However, there are times when marketing leaders defy all expectations with their actions. They use their own intuition and insights to chart a new course. Sometimes, things turn out quite well. Take the example of Hubert Joly, the French executive who was hired to resurrect the failing electronics retailer Best Buy.

With operations mainly in Canada, the US, and Mexico, at one time, Best Buy was the largest chain of consumer electronics stores in the world. When Joly stepped to the helm in 2012, all external indicators suggested dark clouds on the horizon. Consumers were purchasing their products online and suppliers like Apple and Samsung were opening up their own brick-and-mortar shops. Most leaders would have shuttered stores, sold off real estate, laid off workers, and aggressively negotiated with suppliers for better terms. Joly's insightful and deft orchestration of the Best Buy turn-around was impressive in many respects, but he engaged in two distinct courses of action that were especially expectation-defying. First, Joly had his suppliers open up small, branded boutique-style shops within Best Buy stores. This move returned those suppliers who had opened up their own brick-and-mortar shops back to the status of partner, instead of competitor. Second, he empowered front-line employees, which "unleashed the human magic" of their creativity and ingenuity. Employees felt as if they were part of the team and were valued partners in bringing the company back from the brink. Business partners and employees all worked cooperatively toward a common purpose. By 2019, share prices had increased tenfold (Joly and Lambert 2021) (see Photo 5.9).

Photo 5.9 Hubert Joly of Best Buy orchestrated a remarkable turnaround by doing the unexpected

Source: Nolichuckyjake / Shutterstock.com

Muhammad Yunus also defied expectations in 1983 when he opened a microcredit bank in Bangladesh called Grameen Bank (The Nobel Prize 2022). The goal was singular in focus: to help poor people. To do this, the bank provided loans for sometimes as little as $50 or $100 to allow people to purchase necessary supplies, tools, or other materials to help them establish small businesses. Women were able to purchase supplies in order to start making baskets to sell at local markets; farmers bought a few chickens to start producing and selling eggs. Most observers thought that Yunus's idea was terrible. They predicted that he would never see a return on his money. However, by 2006, Yunus's embrace of the unexpected paid off when the bank was awarded the Nobel Peace Prize for its efforts to address poverty. Grameen Bank was serving 40 million people, a quarter of the population of Bangladesh. Repayment rates on loans were 99% and women owned 97% of the shares of the bank (Beard 2012) (see Photo 5.10).

Photo 5.10 Microcredit loans enabled people in Bangladesh to improve their economic situation

Source: Pixabay

5.6 SUMMARY

This chapter examines the basic characteristics of leadership, as well as how leaders think and what leaders do. Marketing leaders identify opportunities in the external environment that can be leveraged to better deliver the value proposition to the target market. Ideally, these opportunities will provide the organization with a competitive advantage in the marketplace. Carolyn Fraser at the PR Shoppe and Ray Anderson at Interface are both examples of marketing leaders.

Compared to other people, leaders simply see the world and think about it differently. They take an honest and critical internal assessment of their own strengths and weaknesses, they possess an ingenuity that allows them to imagine an alternate future, they think systemically, and they are self-aware enough to admit when they've made a mistake. During this discussion, two examples of innovative new perspectives were presented. The first was the Cradle-to-cradle product design philosophy, which proposed that products could be designed so that the process of manufacturing, using, and recycling products could be reconceptualized as a circular, zero-waste system. The second model was Doughnut economics, which challenged the centuries-long perspective that economies need to always strive for continuous growth. Indeed, Doughnut economics proposes that economies can thrive over the long term and provide benefits shared by all people if they operate within the boundaries of a social foundation and an ecological ceiling.

Compared to other people, leaders also do things differently. This discussion relied heavily on establishing the organization's values, setting goals and objectives, and considering ethics. The ethical frameworks of utilitarianism, the common good, and the capabilities approach were introduced. These tools may help the leader not just steer the ship, but ensure that it is being steered in the right direction. When inspiring others to action, marketing leaders need to be able to tap into intrinsic motivation and effectively communicate with the team. In assembling the team, marketing leaders should select individuals with different backgrounds and perspectives, perhaps even assembling a team of rivals. Unfortunately, there is no magical formula for great leadership. Often, it depends on the situation, the person, and individual followers. What worked in one situation may not work in other situations. As discussed in the last section of the chapter, sometimes the best course of action is to defy all expectations.

QUESTIONS FOR REVIEW & DISCUSSION

1. Describe the concepts of management, leadership, marketing leadership, and market leadership. Give an example of each.
2. Describe the Cradle-to-cradle product design philosophy. Ideally, what is the model supposed to do? How is this design philosophy different from a closed-loop production system? Sketch out a closed-loop system and provide an example, providing detail for each part.
3. What do we mean when we say that leaders need to envision a different future? Provide a detailed example of a marketing leader who has envisioned a different future. What exactly did this person do that was so different? What were the results?
4. In what way does Doughnut economics represent a radical departure from traditional ways of thinking about economics? What is meant by the concepts of regenerative and distributive systems? Provide an example of each. Why should an economic system operate within the boundaries of the social foundation and the ecological ceiling?
5. What is moral recovery? Why is it an important component of effective leadership? Provide a detailed example.
6. Broadly speaking, what is the purpose of an ethical framework? Describe the utilitarianism, common good, and capabilities approach frameworks.
7. What is the difference between intrinsic and extrinsic motivation? Which one would a leader prefer for the team? Why?
8. Describe the four dimensions of effective leadership communication. Think about the last time you were in a group and there was a leader – a class project, a sports team, student club: to what extent did the leader utilize each of these dimensions? Describe in detail. In the end, how well did the group perform in achieving its objectives?

5.7 REFERENCES

Anderson, Ray C. 2010. The 40th Anniversary of Earth Day (A Special Report): Voices – Business as the Cause, Business as the Solution. *The Wall Street Journal*. Eastern Edition, New York. 17 April. R8.

Aviles, Gwen. 2020. Munroe Bergdorf rehired at L'Oréal, 3 Years After Being Fired Over White Supremacy Comments. *NBCNews*. 9 June. Accessed 23 July 2021. www.nbcnews.com/feature/nbc-out/munroe-bergdorf-rehired-l-or-al-3-years-after-being-n1228376.

Baier, Bret. 2017. Seven Business Leadership Lessons from Dwight Eisenhower. *Forbes.com*, 31 January. Accessed 14 September 2022. https://www.forbes.com/sites/forbesleadershipforum/2017/01/31/seven-business-leadership-lessons-from-dwight-eisenhower/?sh=4c48e2443b18.

Beard, Alison. 2012. Life's Work. *Harvard Business Review*, *90* (12), December, 136. https://hbr.org/2012/12/muhammad-yunus.

Burchman, Seymour and Barry Sullivan. 2017. It's Time to Tie Executive Compensation to Sustainability. *Harvard Business Review*, 17 August. Harvard Business School Publishing, 2–5.

Burgess, Malcolm D., Ken W. Smith, Karl L. Evans, et al. 2018. Tritrophic phenological match–mismatch in space and time. *Nature Ecology & Evolution, 2* (6), 970–75. https://doi.org/10.1038/s41559-018-0543-1

Byron, William J. 2010. *Next Generation Leadership: A Toolkit for Those in Their Teens, Twenties, & Thirties, Who Want to be Successful Leaders.* University of Scranton Press, Scranton, Pennsylvania.

Cacciola, Scott. 2021. From Athens to Tokyo, Allyson Felix's Journey to the Olympic Record Books. *The New York Times.* 7 August. Accessed 6 September 2021. www.nytimes.com/2021/08/07/sports/olympics/allyson-felix-olympic-medals.html.

Chouinard, Yvon. 2016. Let My People Go Surfing: The Education of a Reluctant Businessman. 2nd edition. *Including 10 More Years of Business Unusual.* Penguin Random House LLC, New York.

Cullen, John G. 2020. Moral Recovery and Ethical Leadership. *Journal of Business Ethics*, October, 1–13. DOI: 10.1007/s10551-020-04658-3.

Driver, Julia. 2009. *The History of Utilitarianism. Stanford Encyclopedia of Philosophy.* Stanford Center for the Study of Language and Information. Accessed 28 August 2021. https://plato.stanford.edu/entries/utilitarianism-history/.

Francis, Pope. 2015. *Laudato Si': On Care for our Common Home.* Encyclical Letter. Our Sunday Visitor, Inc. Huntington, Indiana.

Gelles, David. 2022. Billionare No More: Patagonia Founder Gives Away the Company. *The New York Times*, 14 September. Accessed 14 September 2022. https://www.nytimes.com/2022/09/14/climate/patagonia-climate-philanthropy-chouinard.html.

GH Editors. 2021. The Truth About Bamboo Sheets and Plant-Based Fabrics. *Good Housekeeping.* 24 June. Accessed 26 August 2021. www.goodhousekeeping.com/home/a35604410/bamboo-eucalyptus-fabric-false-labeling/.

Godelnik, Raz. 2011. Patagonia's Black Friday Message: Don't Buy This Jacket. *TriplePundit: The Business of Doing Better.* 30 November. Accessed 18 June 2022. www.triplepundit.com/story/2011/patagonias-black-friday-message-dont-buy-jacket/71076

Goodwin, Doris Kearns. 2005. *Team of Rivals: The Political Genius of Abraham Lincoln.* Simon & Schuster, New York.

Goodwin, Doris Kearns. 2018. *Leadership: In Turbulent Times.* Simon & Schuster, New York.

Groysberg, Boris and Michael Slind. 2012. Leadership is a Conversation. *Harvard Business Review, The Magazine.* June. Accessed 6 September 2021. https://hbr.org/2012/06/leadership-is-a-conversation.

Iberra, Hermina. 2021. Yes, Good Leaders are Authentic Leaders – But Here's What That Actually Means. *Ideas.Ted.Com.* 16 February. Accessed 8 March 2021. https://ideas.ted.com/yes-good-leaders-are-authentic-leaders-but-heres-what-that-actually-means/?utm_source=recommendation&utm_medium=email&utm_campaign=explore&utm_term=ideas-blog-2.

Isidore, Chris. 2021. Simone Biles Drops Nike and Signs with Athleta. *CNN Business.* 23 April. Accessed 6 September 2021. www.cnn.com/2021/04/23/business/simone-biles-nike-gap-athleta/index.html.

Jackson, Eric. 2014. Sun Tzu's 31 Best Pieces of Leadership Advice. *Forbes.* 23 May. Accessed 22 August 2021. www.forbes.com/sites/ericjackson/2014/05/23/sun-tzus-33-best-pieces-of-leadership-advice/?sh=524eb0fa5e5e.

Joly, Hubert and Caroline Lambert. 2021. *The Heart of Business: Leadership Principles for the Next Era of Capitalism.* Harvard Business Review Press, Boston, Massachusetts.

Kemp, Martin. 2016. Why Leonardo da Vinci Was a Genius. *The Conversation.* 9 February. Accessed 25 August 2021. https://theconversation.com/why-leonardo-da-vinci-was-a-genius-54207.

Kimmerer, Robin Wall. 2013. *Braiding Sweetgrass: Indigenous Wisdom, Scientific Knowledge, and the Teachings of Plants*. 1st edition. Milkweed Editions, Minneapolis, Minnesota.

Kinkead, Gwen. 1999. In the Future, People Like Me will Go to Jail. *Fortune*, 00158259, *139* (10).

Kotler, Philip. 2019. *Advancing the Common Good: Strategies for Businesses, Governments, and Nonprofits*. Praeger, Santa Barbara, California.

Kumar, Nirmalya. 2008. The CEO's Marketing Manifesto. *Marketing Management. November/ December. 17* (6), 24–9.

Loock, Moritz and Diane M. Phillips (2020). A Firm's Financial Reputation vs. Sustainability Reputation: Do Consumers Really Care? *Sustainability*, *12* (24), 1–17. http://dx.doi.org/10.3390/su122410519.

Lowney, Chris. 2003. *Heroic Leadership: Best Practices from a 450-year-old Company that Changed the World*. Loyola Press, Chicago, Illinois.

Macalister, Terry and Richard Wray. 2010. Tony Hayward to Quit BP. *The Guardian. 26* July. Accessed 26 August 2021. www.theguardian.com/business/2010/jul/26/tony-hayward-to-quit-bp.

McDonough, William and Michael Braungart. 2002. *Cradle to Cradle: Remaking the Way We Make Things*. North Point Press, a division of Farrar, Straus, and Giroux, New York.

Miller, Janet Driscoll and Julia Lim. 2020. *Data-first Marketing: How to Compete and Win in the Age of Analytics*. John Wiley & Sons, Inc., Hoboken, New Jersey.

Nugent, Ciara. 2021. Amsterdam is Embracing a Radical New Economic Theory to Help Save the Environment. Could it Also Replace Capitalism? *Time*. 22 January. Accessed 8 September 2021. https://time.com/5930093/amsterdam-doughnut-economics/.

Nussbaum, Martha C. 2011. *Creating Capabilities: The Human Development Approach*. The Belknap Press of Harvard University Press, Cambridge, Massachusetts.

Our Ethical Principles. 2022. Our Compass for Acting Ethically. L'Oréal Group. Accessed 18 June 2022. www.loreal.com/en/group/governance-and-ethics/our-ethical-principles/.

Porter, Michael. 2005. CEO as Strategist: Become the Guardian of All Trade-offs. *Leadership Excellence*, a publication of Executive Excellence Publishing, 11.

Porter, Michael E. and Mark R. Kramer. 2011. Shared Value: How to Reinvent Capitalism—and Unleash a Wave of Innovation. *Harvard Business Review*. January–February, 62–77.

Raworth, Kate. 2017. *Doughnut Economics: 7 Ways to Think Like a 21st Century Economist*. Chelsea Green Publishing. White River Junction, Vermont.

Reich, Robert. 2018. *The Common Good*. Knoft, New York.

Rothstein, Edward. 2006. Mozart: In Search of the Roots of Genius. *Smithsonian Magazine*. February. Accessed 25 August 2021. www.smithsonianmag.com/arts-culture/mozart-in-search-of-the-roots-of-genius-109425513/.

Ryan, Kevin J. 2019. The Containers for Your Most Basic Household Products Are About to Look a Lot Different, Thanks to This Company. *Inc. The Future of Work Section*. 27 March. Accessed 26 August 2021. www.inc.com/kevin-j-ryan/terracycle-loop-reuse-recycle-plastic-containers.html.

Schoenberg, Tom, Matt Robinson, and Mark Gurman. 2018. Apple is Responding to Government Probe into iPhone Slowdowns. *Bloomberg.com*. 1 January. N.PAG.

Schwartz, Ariel. 2009. The Earthkeepers 2.0 Boot: Timberland's Attempt at Closing the Loop. *FastCompany*. 8 July. Accessed 28 August 2021. www.fastcompany.com/1305648/earthkeepers-20-boot-timberlands-attempt-closing-loop.

Statcounter. 2022. *Desktop Operating System Market Share Worldwide*, April 2022. *Statcounter GlobalStats*. April. Accessed 18 June 2022. https://gs.statcounter.com/os-market-share/desktop/worldwide/#monthly-202204-202204-bar.

Tabuchi, Hiroko. 2021. Toyota Led on Clean Cars. Now Critics Say It Works to Delay Them. *The New York Times – International Edition*. 27 July.

The Nobel Prize. 2022. Grameen Bank – Facts. NobelPrize.org. Nobel Prize Outreach AB 2022. Accessed 14 September 2022. https://www.nobelprize.org/prizes/peace/2006/grameen/facts/.

Tilley, Aaron and Robert McMillan. 2020. Zoom CEO: 'I Really Messed Up' on Security as Coronavirus Drove Video Tool's Appeal. *Wall Street Journal* (Online). 4 April.

Watson, McClain. 2011. Doing Well by Doing Good: Ray C. Anderson as Evangelist for Corporate Sustainability. *Business Communication Quarterly*. March, *74* (1), 63–7. DOI: 10.1177/1080569910395567.

Whitehurst, Jim. 2015. Be a Leader Who Can Admit Mistakes. *Harvard Business Review Digital Articles*. 2 June. 2–4.

Whitler, Kimberly A. 2016. Survey Reveals the Companies that Develop the Best C-Level Marketing Leaders, *Forbes.com*. 21 August. Accessed 14 September 2022. https://www.forbes.com/sites/kimberlywhitler/2016/08/21/best-companies-for-developing-c-level-marketing-leaders/?sh=6290458b4c31.

Winston, Andrew. 2009. Energize Employees with Green Strategy. *Harvard Business Review*. September, *87* (9), 24.

6 ESTABLISHING AND STRENGTHENING A STRATEGIC COMPETITIVE ADVANTAGE

LEADERSHIP INSIGHTS 6

Photo 6.1 Leland Foster Laury

Source: courtesy, Leland Foster Laury

Meet Leland Foster Laury, Senior Account Executive

Brian Communications

Question: How do you get reporters from CNN to call you back?

Answer: Know what they need before they do.

Leland Foster Laury has spent his career working with corporate clients to get their stories published in some of the most well-respected news outlets in the world. He credits this success to the time and energy he spends forging strong relationships with reporters. Few people in PR do the background and prep work that Laury does. First, he identifies several key reporters at well-respected publications. Then, in order to learn more about the kinds of stories they find interesting, he follows them on social media and reads the stories they've published. He also connects with them by sending personal congratulatory messages when they've published a particularly compelling article. Taking what he already knows about the kinds of stories each reporter likes, he pitches his clients' stories to them. Second, Laury works to make the reporter's job of writing a story as easy as possible. He provides carefully-crafted summaries that they can simply incorporate into their stories. Importantly, he stays cognizant of their deadlines and is quick to respond if they have questions or require any additional information. Finally, Laury's creativity and ingenuity also help him attract the news media. He stages press conferences, fairs, and other events, often with big crowds, local politicians, company executives, and chances to shoot visually-appealing video. In short, he provides his target reporters with plenty of newsworthy content. Over time, Laury's hard work has given him and his agency a strong strategic competitive advantage over other firms (see Photo 6.2).

Laury has two important takeaways from his years of experience. First, it is important for a PR team to manage client expectations. Regardless of how hard Laury works, sometimes stories will not get picked up. Clients need to know this ahead of time. Second, "relationships are so important! I follow all the reporters that I pitch stories to. I know what they write and what they think is newsworthy. It's part of the relationship," he offered. The time and effort that Laury spends on building these relationships has certainly paid off because Laury is able to get stories picked up that few other PR people can – this gives him a strategic competitive advantage among his peers and makes him an asset to his clients. "I love what I do – it's all about the chase. It's very fast paced and you have to learn to manage the stress, but I love to get my clients coverage," he reflected.

Photo 6.2 Successful PR starts with knowing what reporters want

Source: iStockPhoto

If Laury had to give some advice to students today, it would be the following: "It took me a long time to realize this, but … it's not all about you. The sooner you realize that, the better. My clients know I have a genuine interest in them and realize that we are all in the fight for getting that story. I'm very passionate. They trust me and want to work with me."

6.1 THIS COMPANY HAS BEEN INNOVATING 630+ YEARS

The Antinori Family of Florence, Italy has been making and selling wine since at least the year 1385, when a family member officially joined the Florentine Wine Guild. Twenty-six generations later, the Antinori family still lives in its 15th century palace in Florence's city center and runs some of its operations from there (Gibson 2017; Virbila 2014). On the ground floor, a tiny door with the word "vino" can still be found that harkens back to the old days. In centuries past, busy Florentine citizens would knock on the door and hand over a few coins. In return, a cellar worker would fill up a cup of wine – an early precursor to today's drive-through windows (Frank 2016). Over the centuries, the Antinori Family continued to produce and sell wine, despite wars, famine, plagues, and political upheavals.

The year 1966 was a turning point in the history of the world's oldest wine dynasty. A manufacturing error resulted in a chemical being added to a batch of wine, and numerous customers got sick. After an extensive investigation, the longtime general manager accepted responsibility for manufacturing standards that were far too lax, and retired. Later that year, after several days of unusually heavy rain, Florence experienced a devastating flood. Throughout the city, thousands of priceless items of Renaissance artwork and manuscripts were threatened and some were not able to be saved. Water poured into the Antinori basement and destroyed several hundred bottles of old wine. It was during this turbulent time that Piero Antinori took his father's place at the helm of the family business, determined to reassure his business partners, expand the business, and thus position it for many more generations of success (Frank 2016).

Piero Antinori has embraced his family's long and distinguished history as a key asset to his business. In Italy and throughout the global wine industry, the Antinori name is synonymous with high-quality Tuscan wines, especially the highly-prized Chianti Classico. The family is fully aware of its unique historical position, as well as its obligation to future generations. Piero Antinori uses this history, however, as a strong foundation upon which to build his strategic competitive advantage: innovation. After taking the reins of the company, Piero Antinori pioneered and implemented several cutting-edge innovations in winemaking and sustainability that make the Antinori name distinct among its peers. One category of innovations involves new techniques for pruning, harvesting, processing, and bottling which greatly improved the quality of the wines. These innovations were first implemented with Antinori-owned properties, then were rolled out to business partners in Europe and abroad. Later, many of these innovations were adopted industry-wide.

Another category of innovations relates to sustainability. For example, Antinori uses drip irrigation, which reduces the amount of water that is wasted through run off or evaporation. On most of the estates, organic practices are utilized, although only a few estates have gone through the rigorous process of obtaining official organic certification. One of the most stunning examples of the company's embrace of sustainability is the design and construction of the new company headquarters

Photo 6.3 Walkway near the entrance of Antinori Headquarters

Source: Shutterstock/Antonio Gravante

in 2012, just south of Florence. The stunning 50,000-square-metre Antinori Estates Headquarters is built mostly underground, into the folds of a rolling Tuscan hillside. The roof is almost entirely covered with trellised vines. Inside, strategically-placed openings bring in abundant light and air. Built of sustainably sourced materials, the entire two-level structure incorporates numerous sustainable features (Gibson 2017) (see Photo 6.3).

Arguably, one of the most innovative decisions was the selection of the heir apparent to the dynasty: Piero's oldest daughter, Albiera Antinori, who took over as president of the company in 2017. The first woman in the history of the dynasty, Albiera quickly made several bold decisions. Under her leadership, the company started utilizing social media, implemented direct online sales, expanded into China, and increased Antinori's footprint in North America. Always looking toward the future, Albiera Antinori is willing to try new innovations and explore new markets. For example, with the company's emphasis on sustainable agriculture, she worked with several experts to develop relevant industry-wide certification standards that capture not just organic agriculture, but an entire sustainable agricultural system. Over the generations, Antinori-led innovations have strengthened the company's value proposition; Albiera Antinori is confident that innovation will continue to be the source of the company's strategic competitive advantage for the next 26 generations (Gibson 2017)!

This chapter is about establishing and strengthening a strategic competitive advantage in the marketplace. To start, the importance of conducting an assessment of the competition, as well as an honest assessment of the organization's own capabilities, will be discussed. Next, four categories of competitive marketing moves will be examined. Finally, the discussion will turn to sustainability as a source of strategic competitive advantage for the organization.

6.2 LEARNING OBJECTIVES

After studying this chapter, you will be able to do the following:

1. Describe the concepts of barriers to entry and first mover advantage.
2. Discuss why it is essential for the organization to understand the competition and itself before it can successfully engage in any competitive moves.
3. Describe and differentiate between the three traditional bases for achieving a strategic competitive advantage: innovation, low cost, and customer intimacy.
4. Compare and contrast military strategy and marketing strategy.
5. Demonstrate an understanding of each of the four broad competitive marketing moves.
6. Construct an argument for why sustainability should be considered a source of strategic competitive advantage for the organization.

6.3 KNOW THE COMPETITION

No one goes into a competitive arena without knowing something about the competition. In professional sports, for example, coaches will spend hours reviewing video of the competitor's games and will convey a set of insights to the team. Military conflicts are rarely successful without a precise understanding of the opponent. The same is true with marketing. In order to establish and strengthen a firm's strategic competitive advantage, the marketing team needs to study the competition.

ENDURING INSIGHTS 6.1

"From one thing, know ten thousand things."– Miyamoto Mushashi, 17th century master Japanese samurai

Mushashi was a master swordsman, as well as a philosopher and strategist. He understood that simply mastering the techniques of fighting and swordsmanship would only go so far in giving him what he needed to be successful. He also studied metallurgy in order to understand how to make the strongest sword; he studied human anatomy to understand his opponents' physical vulnerabilities; he studied psychology in order to discern areas of mental weakness; and he studied geometry and physics to understand the concepts of force and leverage. As in any battle, understanding one dimension of the competition must generate inquiries into other dimensions.

A **strategic competitive advantage** is a characteristic (or set of characteristics) of the organization that, relative to the competition, provides it with the ability to better deliver the value proposition to its customers. At least two aspects of this definition are particularly important. First, it is long-term in focus. Sure, most competitors can out-perform the competition for a short period of time by, for example, dropping prices or launching an eye-catching promotional campaign. However, how long-lasting are these tactics? Any firm can temporarily drop its prices, but can it sustain such low margins over the long term? Any strategic competitive advantage should be built not on a fleeting tactic, but on robust organizational characteristics that can be strengthened over the long term. The second aspect of the definition is that the strategic competitive advantage must be built on something that is important to the consumer. Consumer research will reveal what is important to consumers and where they may be willing to make trade offs with regard to their products and services. It will also reveal where they are not willing to compromise. Swedish car manufacturer, Volvo, has positioned itself as a car company that manufactures safe and reliable cars for the family. They're not especially sporty and certainly not the lowest price car on the market. However, with the target market of consumers who are not willing to compromise on safety, Volvo has a strategic competitive advantage (see Photo 6.4).

Photo 6.4 Volvo has a strategic competitive advantage in the "safety" market

Source: Pixabay

Barriers to Entry and First Mover Advantage

When marketing decision-makers develop their strategies, they need to be designed to strengthen the long-term competitive position of the product, brand, or organization (Porter and Kramer 2006). Two very broad concepts related to a firm's competitive actions are creating a barrier to entry and leveraging a first mover advantage. A **barrier to entry** is an impediment of some kind that makes it difficult for competitors to enter the market. Very low prices, for example, represent a barrier to entry because competitors will recognize that there are few profits to be made in this market and will thus stay away. Another barrier to entry could be expensive business set-up costs, such as licenses or permits. A legal patent, which allows the producer to exclusively produce the product for a number of years, could be another barrier and thus dissuade the competition from entering. Small, upstart pharmaceutical companies face significant barriers to entry because of the significant costs involved in setting up laboratories, hiring researchers, and conducting research. In addition, in the interest of public safety, there are also often long lists of legal and regulatory requirements for pharmaceutical companies. If it is possible to do so, it is to the organization's advantage to erect barriers to entry.

Photo 6.5 Apple Watch reaped advantages from being a first mover

Source: Pixabay

Another concept related to competitive action is the **first mover advantage**, which suggests that there are distinct competitive advantages for the organization that is the first to enter a new market. One advantage is that the organization gets to "write the rules of the game" in the market. It establishes standards by which the product is delivered to customers, how it is priced, how it is advertised or promoted, and expectations for customer service, warranties, and returns. Another advantage to being a first mover is the fact that the organization is now viewed as the benchmark against which all future market entrants will be compared. Consider the Apple Watch. Although wearable technology, wristwatches, and fitness trackers have been around for decades, Apple Watch was the first to seamlessly integrate all of these together into a user-friendly, attractive, wearable device (see Photo 6.5). There are distinct competitive advantages to erecting barriers to entry and to being a first mover in the marketplace.

Traditional Bases for Competitive Advantage

There are three bases upon which an organization can establish and strengthen a strategic competitive advantage: innovation, low cost, and customer intimacy. In most cases, organizations can achieve a competitive advantage by focusing on one or two of these bases; it is highly unusual for an organization to achieve all three.

Innovation

A competitive advantage can be attained by companies with the capacity to continually innovate and improve. Organizations that have invested heavily in research and development are able to introduce a continuous stream of new, sometimes ground-breaking innovations. In 2021, the top three most innovative global organizations were Moderna, Pfizer, and Shopify. Each of them was able to leverage their innovation and expertise to address the crisis brought on by the global Covid-19 pandemic. The first two were pharmaceutical giants that leveraged their strong investments in technology and research to create life-saving vaccines. Moderna created a vaccine that could be stored at normal refrigerator temperatures, making it easy to transport and deliver. Pfizer formed a strategic alliance with German biotechnology company BioNTech to create and deliver a similar vaccine. Although the Pfizer/BioNTech vaccine needed to be stored at much lower temperatures, it was able to achieve an advantage in distribution because of more efficient production and supply chain structures. The last company making it to the "top three" list of innovative companies was Shopify, which had the technological architecture to enable it to assist thousands of companies around the world to convert their brick-and-mortar operations to online e-commerce sites. Shopify made it possible to seamlessly handle currency conversions, confusing shipping procedures, and translations between a multitude of different languages. The process was made even more seamless with Shopify's app, an easy mobile payment option, and an innovative plug-in that allowed for shopping via TikTok (FastCompany 2021).

Organizations that rely on innovation to achieve a competitive advantage are often viewed as benchmark organizations for their technology, research, and product quality. Often, technological constraints that previously restricted an organization's effectiveness are eliminated by new innovations (Porter and Van der Linde 1995). Distribution constraints, for example, are often experienced in the pharmaceutical industry where drugs need to be kept refrigerated. This is especially challenging in getting vaccines to lesser developed countries around the world. New innovations in the future, however, might eliminate this as a constraint. In the case of Antinori Estates, a variety of new innovations have kept it especially competitive for the last few decades. One innovation, for example, has been particularly effective in eliminating a key constraint concerning the blending of different varieties to produce an optimal tasting wine each year. Some wines, such as the Super Tuscan wines, are a blend of six different varieties. Each year, a variety of weather-related factors influence the taste of wines. Previously, expert tasters made decisions about the ideal proportion of each variety. However, human error sometimes results in less-than-perfect-tasting blends. Antinori wines are now computer analyzed each year to recommend the precise blend of each varietal to produce a blended wine with the ideal flavor, level of tannins, and other characteristics (see case study on p.422).

Low-Cost Structure

At the heart of a low-cost strategy is operational excellence. Organizations can achieve low cost in a variety of different ways, such as utilizing propriety processes, implementing operational efficiencies, or even **scaling** production, such that the firm increases the volume of production to reduce the product's per-unit cost. A low-cost structure allows for the organization to achieve attractive margins that competitors may not be able to achieve. It also allows the organization to better withstand price competition in the marketplace. It is important to note here that a low-cost strategy does not necessarily mean a low-price strategy. Low costs can be passed along to consumers with lower prices, but it is not necessary to do so.

Ryanair holds a commanding share of Europe's low-cost, short-haul flights. It initially offered a limited number of destinations for Europeans who were content to put up with the cramped, no-frills experience to get great deals on flights around the continent. Passengers put up with paying for their own in-flight meals, tightly-packed seats that do not recline, and even advertising on seatbacks and overhead compartments. In order to speed up cleaning, the seatbacks do not even have pockets. As Ryanair expanded to new cities, it was able to achieve scale and pass the savings along to consumers. Ryanair's ultra-efficient operations have led some experts to conclude that low-cost is the future of European aviation (Georgiadis 2021) (see Photo 6.6).

Photo 6.6 Ryanair employs a low-cost strategy to achieve its competitive advantage

Source: Pixabay

Customer Intimacy

As we learned in the chapter opener with Leland Laury and his success in public relations, customer intimacy can be an important source of strategic competitive advantage. **Customer intimacy** occurs when the organization develops a deep understanding and connection with its customers. Extensive, continuous research should reveal what makes the customer tick, as well as consumer thoughts, emotions, attitudes, goals, motivations, and dreams. How does the consumer view the product and the company, and importantly, how does this product play a role in the consumer's life? Only after a continuous system of learning and dialogue has been established with customers can the organization hope to forge long-term relationships with them.

Different cars have different personalities, and the Mini, made by BMW, has its own distinct personality too: young, adventurous, and friendly. Advertising has reinforced these characteristics over the years, with particular emphasis on the "friendly" part. The car's slogan is, "Mini: the car that comes with friends included." A variety of options are available to loyal Mini customers to get together and share their enthusiasm for the brand. Thousands of informal groups around the world regularly get together to hang out and talk about their Minis. In one of the biggest annual get-togethers, Mini drivers from around the world converge on a mountain top in Tennessee, USA that happens to have the ominous name, "the dragon." Local authorities shut down the road for the weekend, and dedicated Mini drivers take on the exciting twists and turns of the road as it climbs up the stunning mountainside. Of course, the marketing team at BMW is intimately involved in many of these gatherings so it can interact with customers and find out what is on their minds. It was through some of these discussions with customers that BMW realized how important a manual transmission was to the driving experience and rededicated its efforts to offer the option with every model (see Photo 6.7).

Photo 6.7 BMW utilized a customer intimacy strategy to achieve its competitive advantage

Source: Pixabay

BLUNDERS & INSIGHTS 6.1

Budweiser Blows $2.5 Million on a Bet?

In an effort to position itself as the beer of choice in one of America's biggest cities, Budweiser made what it thought was a safe bet: if the Philadelphia Eagles football team won the 2018 Super Bowl, Budweiser would supply free beer for the entire city. They tweeted to one of the star players, "Win it all and the party is on us. Deal?" At the beginning of the season, the Eagles were longshots to win the championship game, plus they were plagued by injuries and even lost their star quarterback to an injury late in the season. At this point, Budweiser's marketing team probably thought it had made a pretty safe bet. Very few people, even the most crazed Philadelphia fans, ever thought it was possible, but by the end of the season, the Eagles were scheduled to play the New England Patriots in the Super Bowl. The Patriots had already won five Super Bowl Championships and were the heavy favorites. Right before the game, the Eagles player who had started it all tweeted, "one game away? Bet still on?" to which Budweiser responded, "we haven't forgotten." In the end, The Eagles won the game for the first time in franchise history with a score of 41–33. Budweiser honored its promise at the team's victory parade 2 weeks later. Budweiser reps handed out free tokens for one free can of Bud Light, redeemable at any one of 36 taverns and bars in the city. Representatives checked IDs and stamped the hands of those who received a can. In addition, for anyone who could not make it to the parade, the company offered a limited-time

(Continued)

voucher for a free six-pack. Experts estimated that free beer for as many as 700,000 Eagles fans at the parade (Avril 2018) cost Budweiser $1.28 million (Burgess 2018). In addition, the cost of the free six-packs, as well as advertising and other support, likely left Budweiser with a total price tag of close to $2.5 million.

DEBRIEF: Marketing managers need to have some flexibility in making changes to their strategies to meet the changing needs of the marketplace. However, was it a smart strategic move for Budweiser to spend this much of its marketing budget on free beer for Philly fans? Probably not. Although it received a significant amount of publicity, it is very unlikely that the event gave Budweiser a competitive edge or helped it to better deliver its value proposition, the key defining characteristics of a strategic competitive advantage.

6.4 KNOW THYSELF

Remember that a strategic competitive advantage occurs when an organization finds a better way to deliver the value proposition to its customers. In establishing and strengthening its competitive advantage, one of the first things an organization does is create a set of objectives it hopes to achieve. In creating SMART objectives, one element is especially important here: the "A" asks whether the objective is "achievable." That is, does the organization possess the internal capabilities to carry out the objective? In addition to the fairly straightforward questions of adequate talent, time, budget, and motivation, organizational decision-makers must come to a consensus about the somewhat more complex questions about how it will define the scope of the competition, assess its tolerance for risk, evaluate its current strategic alliances, and utilize competitive intelligence.

Scope of the Competition

One of the first steps in examining the organization's own capabilities is to determine the **scope of the competition**, how narrowly or broadly the firm should define its competition. In defining the scope of the competition, first ask consumers what they think. As discussed earlier in this text, when an organization is myopic and defines its competitive landscape narrowly, only direct competitors are seen as having the potential to influence the organization's own performance. However, when an organization defines its competitive landscape broadly, not only direct competitors but also indirect competitors are considered. Any mismatch in how organizational decision-makers and consumers define the scope of the competition can be a problem. Why? Threats can often come from indirect competitors who offer new and unique offerings to consumers. If the marketing team is too narrowly focused, it might not identify a competitive threat until it is too late.

Tolerance for Risk

Following through on insights and creating a set of objectives requires an acceptance of some amount of risk. In marketing, **risk** is the probability or threat of loss, damage, or another negative external event that can harm the organization or its ability to perform. In order to mitigate those risks, the marketing team will engage in **risk management**, a set of processes and procedures that identify risk and establish steps to reduce risk occurrence and risk impact. A variety of external forces could exert a negative impact on the organization, such as changes in consumer tastes, the introduction of new technology, competitive action, shifts in social trends and norms, macroeconomic forces (such as changes in trade policies or interest rates), governmental actions and laws, and climate change. It is the job of the marketing team to ensure that its internal capabilities – the team's talent, motivation, budget, time, and procedures – compensate for those risks (see Figure 6.1).

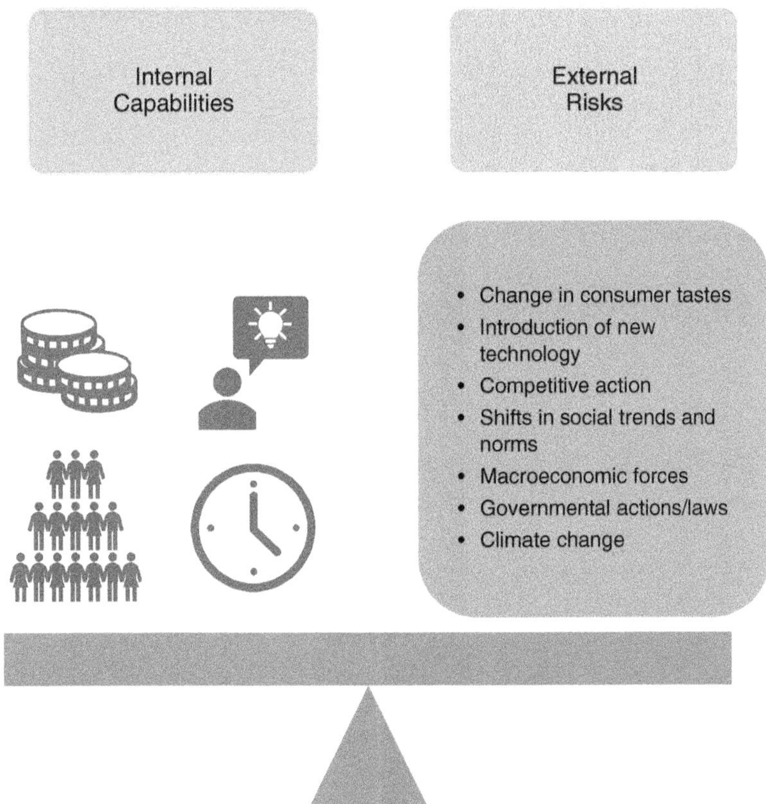

Figure 6.1 External risks must be balanced by internal capabilities

ENDURING INSIGHTS 6.2

"You miss 100 percent of the shots you don't take."– Wayne Gretzky

Gretzky is a former Canadian ice hockey player who is often described as the greatest hockey player of all time ("the Great One"), leading the league in lifetime goals and assists. Gretzky claimed that understanding the competition was the key to his success because he skated to where the puck *would be,* not where it was. Then, Gretzky never hesitated to take the shot (Stubbs 2017). Successful marketers know that to get big wins, they need to understand the competitive landscape.

In the coming decades, the threats of climate change represent important safety, operational, and financial risks. Rising seas and wildfires cause severe damage to infrastructure and operations (Bloomberg 2019, Layne 2019) and are already lowering property values around the world (Layne 2019). From a marketing perspective, the effects of climate change have impacted each one of the four dimensions of the marketing mix. Access to raw materials and components for *products* has been disrupted; *prices* for these items have been absorbed by organizations or passed along to consumers; distribution channels and supply chains (*place*) have experienced disruptions and delays; and because consumers are becoming increasingly aware of climate change, *promotional* efforts increasingly touch on the subject.

Because of the effects of climate change, a multitude of new regulations around the world have been passed and many more are being considered. These regulations represent another risk for the organization to consider. One concept that has been gaining traction is **ecocide**, human-caused destruction of a natural system, species, or life forms. If international law adopts ecocide as a guiding principle, it will rise to the level of other crimes of international importance, such as genocide, war crimes, and crimes against humanity. Anyone accused of ecocide, including CEOs of companies that pollute the environment and world leaders who promote environmental destruction, would be brought before The International Criminal Court (ICC), which adjudicates crimes that are considered the most serious to the international community (Godin 2021).

With any new initiative, the marketing team should have a common understanding of its **risk tolerance**, the amount of risk the team is willing to accept in order to achieve its objectives. Most everyday activities involve some degree of risk: driving a car, eating sushi, or going for a swim. Individuals have an internal gauge of risk tolerance and often conclude that the rewards for performing these activities generally outweigh the risks involved. The marketing team's degree of risk tolerance is based on a careful assessment of risks and rewards, and guides them as they pursue their marketing strategies.

Strategic Alliances

In looking at the organization's internal capabilities, the marketing team must also take a discerning look at the organization's existing strategic alliances and determine whether new alliances need to be forged. If the organization falls short in its internal capabilities, it is sometimes more efficient to partner with another firm than it is to build that capability from within. A **strategic alliance** is a mutually beneficial arrangement between two or more organizations for the purposes of achieving organizational objectives, such as launching a promotional campaign, developing a new product, or targeting a new market. Often, a strategic alliance is forged in order to achieve a short-term purpose. Why would an organization wish to forge a strategic alliance? An alliance can result in a variety of benefits, including the following:

- *Sharing expertise* – one partner may have more experience and talent with a given market, production process, or distribution system.
- *Sharing resources* – one partner may have access to critical resources, such as raw materials, that the other partner does not have.
- *Providing access to key markets* – one partner may already be doing business in a market into which the other partner wishes to expand.
- *Expanding production* – one partner may have excess capacity in production that it could provide to the other partner.

Strategic alliances can often be quite beneficial to both parties, such as the long-running partnership between Coca-Cola and the World Wildlife Federation (WWF), which was originally forged in 2007. The partnership was designed to improve the health of seven of the planet's biggest river systems (Bonini 2021). From Coca-Cola's perspective, the partnership allowed it to tap into WWF's expertise and global goodwill. WWF is well-respected around the world for its work and is often called upon to offer its expertise on wildlife issues. From WWF's perspective, the partnership allowed it to access some of Coca-Cola's marketing and distribution expertise, as well as a portion of its comparably vast budget. Sometimes, strategic alliances need to come to an end. Outdoor clothing and equipment manufacturer Patagonia is a privately-held company with an estimated $1 billion in annual revenue. Over the years, Patagonia has turned down strategic alliances with companies that do not share in Patagonia's mission of social and environmental justice. In 2021, Patagonia announced it would sever its partnerships with several dozen corporate clients for whom it produced custom jackets and vests. Previously, larger corporations would order custom-made Patagonia jackets with their corporate logo. The jackets were then provided to the company's employees as "thank you" gifts or incentives. Patagonia became concerned that these custom garments were being disposed of at a high rate when employees changed jobs or left the company. Further, donated items with company logos are difficult to sell or repurpose. Patagonia continues to sell its own branded items (see Photo 6.8) (Segran 2021).

Photo 6.8 Patagonia no longer sells jackets or vests with corporate logos

Competitive Intelligence

Data collection is time-consuming and expensive. The process of conducting data analytics and generating insights helps organizations become more attuned to consumer needs and aware of potential competitive moves. **Competitive intelligence** is the process of collecting data, analyzing and organizing it into information, and generating insights about consumers, the marketplace, or environmental forces for the purpose of providing the organization with a competitive advantage. Competitive intelligence is about developing a deep understanding of the competitive landscape so that, compared to the competition, the organization can more effectively and efficiently deliver the value proposition. Two points about competitive intelligence:

- First – competitive intelligence is *not corporate espionage*, which gathers data and information by subterfuge, theft, or other illegal or unethical means. Corporate espionage is illegal.
- Second – competitive intelligence *creates insights*, which may be useful to decision-makers to deploy *competitive moves*.

In 2016, consumers around the world started to become aware of the problem of microbeads in products such as body wash, scrubs, and toothpaste. The problem was that the scrubbing ingredients in these products were tiny plastic beads, the size of a grain of sand. When the beads got washed down the drain, they ended up in waterways, damaging the environment and sickening marine life. Through their ongoing competitive intelligence operations, however, consumer product giants Johnson & Johnson and Procter & Gamble, were able to quickly identify the wave of disapproval and outrage that was starting to well up from concerned consumers around the world. The companies quickly shifted to more environmentally-friendly abrasives (Shoe 2018), such as salt and sugar, in their product formulations. Being first movers in getting these more eco-friendly alternatives on the shelves reassured their customers and strengthened their reputations as trusted brands. In addition, as the EU, the US, and other areas of the world started to enact microbead bans (Shoe 2018), these two organizations were several steps ahead of the competition in complying with these strict regulations.

ENDURING INSIGHTS 6.3

"All warfare is based on deception. Hence, when we are able to attack, we must seem unable; when using our forces, we must appear inactive; when we are near, we must make the enemy believe we are far away; when far away, we must make him believe we are near."– Sun Tzu

The decisions that marketing decision-makers must make are certainly not as consequential as the decisions that generals must make during wartime. However, the sentiment captured by this quote is still relevant to competitive action. Marketers must avoid giving the competition any indication about planned competitive moves.

6.5 COMPETITIVE MARKETING MOVES

Experts recommend identifying the competition's **strategic center of gravity** – the point where it would be severely weakened if it were to lose control. Think about it as a unique capability or market that the competition controls (Cohen 1986). Marketers need to identify and concentrate their efforts on this strategic center of gravity, as well as stay vigilant for any shifts that may occur over time. Early on, Apple's strategic center of gravity was its intuitive user interface. Artists, writers, and other individuals working in creative pursuits used Apple computers in their work. However, over time, the strategic center of gravity shifted. Today, Apple- and Mac-branded computers are not only intuitive, they are also powerful. Further, as consumers have integrated other devices into their lives, Apple opened up a second strategic center of gravity: the ease with which these devices can be seamlessly integrated with one another. As another example, Antinori Estates and many firms headquartered in Asian countries operate according to a long-term perspective. Decision makers with a long-term orientation resist temptations for short-term marginal gains and are motivated to invest in the organization in order to improve the long-standing competitive position of the firm and to maximize profits over the long term. Firms that have a long-term orientation utilize this strategic center of gravity as a competitive advantage over firms that typically operate according to a short-term perspective (German, Donahue, and Schnaars 1991).

Strategic thinking is a complex mental process that sifts through and organizes often disparate pieces of information to identify patterns and solve problems. Strategic thinking is essential in understanding the dynamics of the situation, thinking systemically, carefully preparing, and precisely implementing the marketing plan (Cohen 1986, German et al. 1991, Porter and Kramer 2006). Strategic thinking is a skill, and like any skill, decision-makers need to practice strategic thinking. Further, the marketing team needs to engage in strategic thinking on a continual basis; it should become adept at taking an insight and imagining how that insight could be put to good use. In determining an appropriate competitive action, strategic thinking also involves the following:

1 Ensuring that the decision-making is mission-driven. Remember that marketing is designed to support the overall mission and vision of the organization.
2 Staying focused; do not get distracted and waste time on peripheral issues. Importantly, be sure to focus on strategic, not tactical issues.
3 Being willing to say "no." If a market opportunity does not strengthen the competitive position of the organization or better deliver the value proposition, create another strategy that will.
4 Being vigilant against any complacency that comes with a strong marketplace position. There is always room to strengthen the organization's long-term competitive position.
5 Being willing to fail. Without risk, there is no reward.

Figure 6.2 Military strategy vs. marketing strategy

In 1981, Philip Kotler, one of marketing's most influential theorists, predicted that successful marketing in the future will rely on competition-centered strategies, many of which are built on principles of military strategy (Kotler and Singh 1981). A simple look will reveal that many concepts taken from military strategy can easily be applied to marketing strategy. Just like military strategy, marketing strategy starts with the formulation of objectives, which then lead to the development of strategy and tactics. Indeed, the three-step planning sequence is the same: objectives → strategy → tactics. Just like the military, the marketing team identifies its own strategic competitive advantage and then concentrates its strengths against the competition's weakness. Just as military forces divide and conquer their opponents, marketing strategists segment the market in order to out-maneuver the competition in delivering a better value proposition to those customers. Just as the military maneuvers and deploys forces and supplies, marketing teams allocate time, talent, and materials in carrying out their strategies. Just as military forces sometimes split up into smaller companies, platoons, and squads, marketing teams often create short-term task forces to carry out specific tasks. Just as the military utilizes carefully-crafted messaging to demoralize the opponent and win over the local population, marketing strategists also employ carefully-crafted messaging to win over consumers (see Figure 6.2).

The following sections will introduce four broad strategic moves that are available to the marketing decision-maker: defensive, offensive, flanking, and guerrilla.

Defensive Moves

Defensive moves strengthen the firm's competitive position and lessen the risk of being successfully attacked. Defensive moves are often used by industry leaders to solidify their positions in the marketplace (German, et al. 1991). In the global telecommunications industry, for example, cellular service providers routinely go head-to-head in fierce battles for often incremental gains in market share. In doing so, they attempt to strengthen their own position, while weakening the opponent.

Strengthen your Existing Position

This competitive move is deployed when the organization already has an exceptionally strong position in the marketplace. Before deploying this competitive move, the marketing team needs to take a critical assessment of the organization and determine how it can be made stronger (Reis and Trout 1986). This competitive move is based on the notion that it is easier to keep a customer than to wrestle one away from the competition. The firm can fortify its position by establishing a barrier to exit, improving brand equity, or enhancing the customer experience such that consumers will have no reason to look to other competitors to have their needs fulfilled. Loyalty programs, customer service, and continued high quality help strengthen an organization's position and keep it "on the high ground" – a position of strength. In marketing, online gaming giant Epic Games, which hosts *Fortnite*, has solidified its position in the digital metaverse by offering more than just exciting and engaging gaming experiences. Epic now offers in-game concerts, movie trailers, and other streaming content (FastCompany 2021). The result is that Epic Games has strengthened its position against its competitors, giving gamers less reason to switch.

Mobilize Positions

The goal of this competitive marketing move is to disorient the competition, thus making it more difficult for it to launch an attack. It is based on the notion that it is difficult to hit a moving target. Organizations that mobilize their positions frequently move around resources, introduce new products, and launch new promotional campaigns (Kotler and Singh 1981). As a competitive option, mobilizing positions involves *new* markets and *new* product offerings; because of this, its moves are often unexpected. Entrepreneurial, innovation-driven companies that rely on innovation as a strategic competitive advantage may be especially effective in using this marketing move. SpaceX has been particularly effective in being at the forefront of industry-led, as opposed to government-led, missions to space for a variety of purposes. The company reuses rockets, keeping costs down, and has had an admirable record of safety. In 2021, it added over 1000 satellites to its Starlink constellation of communications satellites and made its fourth trip to the International Space Station, bringing fresh supplies and crew members (FastCompany 2021) (see Photo 6.9).

Photo 6.9 One of many SpaceX communications satellites

Source: Pixabay

ENDURING INSIGHTS 6.4

"Never interrupt your enemy when he is making a mistake." – Napoleon Bonaparte

Keeping a keen eye on the competition is imperative because it reveals important clues about what they are about to do. Smart marketers who make evidence-based decisions can easily identify when a competitor is pursuing a less-than-lucrative market or is using a less-than-effective messaging strategy. Smart marketers can then sit back and enjoy the show.

Offensive Moves

Often used by second-tier competitors in the marketplace, **offensive moves** are designed to leverage a firm's existing strengths. If successfully employed, the firm is strengthened and the competitor is weakened (German, et al. 1991). An important part of the success of offensive moves is identifying the competitor's Achilles Heel, or its weakest point, to attack (Reis and Trout 1986).

Frontal Attack

This marketing move engages the competitor with a head-on frontal assault and is not for the faint-hearted. To be successful, the organization must amass substantial resources and be willing to get hurt in the process. This is an "all-hands-on-deck" moment not just for the marketing team, but also for other parts of the organization that need to be mobilized, including distribution, accounting, finance, customer service, IT, and manufacturing. Such an aggressive move is especially effective when the opponent is experiencing a setback or weakness of some sort. In this moment where the competition's attention is diverted elsewhere, the organization has the chance to target the competitor's customers and convince them to switch. Frontal attacks are expensive, time-consuming, and very risky. In addition, an angered competitor can easily launch a counterattack. In the summer of 2021, upstart Wizz Air launched a frontal attack against the strongly entrenched low-cost Irish carrier Ryanair. As a result of travel restrictions during the Covid-19 pandemic, one expert estimated that the volume of low-cost, short-haul airline seats in Europe would contract by 20%. As air travel slowly started to pick up again and carriers tried to establish themselves in this new, smaller market, Ryanair was poised to start claiming back some of its own lost business as well as grow and strengthen its competitive position across Europe. At the same time, Wizz Air, a Hungarian carrier, took advantage of the uncertainty of the situation and launched a frontal attack against Ryanair. It purchased 130 new planes and aggressively booked slots at airport gates through Europe, especially Western Europe, where Ryanair had a long-standing presence (Georgiadis 2021).

Counterattack

This competitive move is a counterpunch against a competitor's attack. In marketing, a successful counterattack can occur in two different ways. First, the organization can engage in a frontal counterattack and hit the competition where it is strongest. Here, the organization would go toe-to-toe against the competitor's offerings on pricing, product upgrades, distribution, or promotion. Just like any frontal attack, however, this can be expensive, time-consuming, and risky. Second, the organization has the option of finding the competition's weakest point and hitting there. The success of this type of counterattack hinges on a deep knowledge of the competition in order to find that weak point. Founded in 2005, YouTube became the go-to resource for video content of all varieties. Whatever your interest, videocasters and influencers have a seemingly endless supply of explainer videos, demonstrations, talk shows, and creative expressions. In fact, YouTube launched the careers of a variety of highly-compensated influencers around the world. Then along came TikTok in 2016, targeted at young people who consume the majority of their content on their phones and often don't have the attention spans to watch a long ("boring") video. Young audiences were captivated by TikTok's endless array of bite-sized videos, and the app's easy editing and uploading interface made it easy for users to create their own 15–60 second videos. By September 2021, TikTok had racked up 1 billion active monthly users.

Enter YouTube Shorts. Not content to cede such a massive portion of its audience and advertising revenue to TikTok, YouTube staged a counterattack with its own short video platform. The launch was supported by a $100 million fund to incentivize users to create compelling short videos. By June 2022, YouTube Shorts reported 1.5 billion active monthly users, easily surpassing TikTok (Tedder 2022).

Flanking Moves

Flanking moves are often employed by third-tier competitors in the marketplace (German, et al. 1991) and rely heavily on marketing intelligence. **Flanking moves** start with identifying an underserved segment in the marketplace, then successfully meeting the needs of individuals in that target market. These smaller, often underserved, market niches can be quite lucrative. When engaging in a flanking move, surprise is important, as is a narrow focus on the competitor's area of weakness (Reis and Trout 1986).

Flank Attack

A straight flank attack depends on catching your competitor by surprise by targeting a new geographic area or market segment. This competitive move is especially effective if consumer needs are not being met and the marketing team has a value proposition that would be particularly appealing to this new market. From military history, straight flanking is the "most effective and economic form of strategy" (Kotler and Singh 1981, p. 36). In 2021, British toy store chain Hamley's launched a flanking move against Toys "R" Us to claim a piece of the lucrative Indian market, where one out of every five babies in the world are born each year. Hamley's was founded in 1760 and, for many, the Hamley's flagship store in London is a must-see destination for its hands-on, immersive retail experience. Despite the presence of Toys "R" Us in India, by 2021, India accounted for just 1% of the $90 billion global toy industry, so there was significant room for growth. The Indian market had 378 million children, with plenty of parents and grandparents who were willing to spend money on them (Sanjai and Kay 2021). Toys "R" Us was just a toy store, but Hamley's was an *experience*. By 2021, Hamley's had opened more than 100 stores in 36 cities, each one offering a unique hands-on experience in which children can explore and play. Toys "R" Us had seven stores (see Photo 6.10).

Photo 6.10 Hamley's stores offer something unique to the Indian consumer – an immersive, hands-on experience.

Source: Pixabay

Encirclement

The encirclement strategy is a form of flanking because it is an indirect assault on the competition, by way of identifying a consumer need that is not being met. Unlike straight flanking, however, encirclement creates several areas of attack, such that the competitor needs to simultaneously defend its front, back, and sides. The goal is to cause the competitor to disperse resources and dilute its ability to hold onto several market segments simultaneously. If successful, an encirclement move will result in the competitor having a more diluted and more fluid front that "can be pierced at a number of points and enveloped into new segments" (Kotler and Singh 1981, p. 36). In 2020, Canadian athleisure brand Lululemon engaged in an encirclement move against other athleisure brands, most notably Athleta. Lululemon purchased Mirror, a company that produces digital, wall-mounted screens. In addition to selling more Lululemon-branded clothing, it hoped to strengthen relationships with customers by offering streaming events and free nutrition and fitness classes; users could even interact with one another and their instructors through the Mirror. The Mirror even connected consumers to events at local Lululemon stores, breaking down the divide between the brick-and-mortar and online environments (FastCompany 2021). The encirclement strategy launched by Lululemon has significantly strengthened Lululemon's customer intimacy and has ensured that other lifestyle/athleisure brands need to compete not just with clothing, but in at least two other fronts: nutrition and fitness.

Leapfrog

The leapfrog competitive move completely bypasses the competition in order to attack easier markets. There are two forms of the leapfrog (or bypass) move. First, the organization can diversify its offerings with completely new and unrelated products, often relying on new innovations or technology. Second, it can expand into a completely new market (Kotler and Singh 1981). Joby Aviation has spent at least a decade in prototype development and testing, but by 2024, it hopes to start offering its first commercial, ride-sharing air taxi service. Yes, *flying taxis*. Joby has offices in the US and Germany, and has received funding from Toyota and Uber. It has completed more than 1000 test flights and received airworthiness approval from the US Air Force. If these accomplishments are not impressive enough, Joby air taxis promise vertical takeoffs and landings, and run on 100% electric power (FastCompany 2021). As this example demonstrates, leapfrog moves are not simply incremental improvements.

BLUNDERS & INSIGHTS 6.2

Tesco Tries to Share the Blame

BACKGROUND: In 2013, British supermarket chain Tesco was found to be selling burgers and ready-to-eat meals that had a mixture of beef and horse meat to unsuspecting consumers. When the report was made public, consumers were understandably outraged. Tesco responded with a two-page response in newspapers across the country, as well as a public relations campaign by the company president. In its messaging, Tesco strongly implied that all grocery stores had horse meat in their burgers and that the issue was something that affected "the whole food industry." Consumers became even more angry. The UK's Advertising Standards Authority (ASA) banned the campaign and the whole fiasco erased £300 million in value from Tesco (Heilpern 2016).

DEBRIEF: Tesco's efforts to divert attention away from its own operational failures and ensnare several other competitors in the controversy can be interpreted as a flank attack. At first glance, it seems as if this may have been a reasonable strategy. However, the accusations were not based on fact. The problem of horse meat was primarily limited to Tesco and a few other small stores. Other national grocery stores, however, reacted swiftly and aggressively to Tesco's accusation that their meat was tainted. Public officials got involved and ASA put a stop to any further messaging from Tesco. In the end, Tesco's flank attack backfired.

Guerrilla Attack

Often used by small and entrepreneurial firms in the industry (German, et al., 1991), **guerilla attacks** rely on deception to launch a series of quick and unexpected attacks on bigger firms in the industry. The goal of this competitive move is to harass and demoralize the competitor in order to secure concessions (Kotler and Singh 1981). The organization weakens the bigger competitor with pricks instead of knock-out blows by using a variety of tactics, such as implementing selective and steep price cuts, hiring away key personnel, finding ways to disrupt the competitor's supply chain, or launching selective and intense promotions. Ideally, these actions should be taken against the opponent's weak positions, which are harder to defend (perhaps because it is located far from headquarters) and make it easier for the organization to find a means of retreat if necessary. Conventional military wisdom suggests that continual guerilla attacks can weaken a stronger opponent. Red Bull is very adept at using guerilla attacks against the soft drink market, including industry giants Coca-Cola and Pepsi. In order to capture a greater share of the attention of its target market (young adult men), Red Bull often engages in surprise stunts, such as turning a bus shelter into a vending machine or "airdropping" crates of Red Bull on university campuses around the world. In 2012, Red Bull launched an incredibly high-risk guerilla attack. Red Bull, an Austrian-owned company, rocketed fellow Austrian extreme sports dare-devil Felix Baumgartner 39,000 meters in the air and live-streamed his descent back to earth. Eight million viewers watched the event live on YouTube and millions more watched it on live television broadcasts or on later replays. Baumgartner reached a speed of 1342 km/h and is the first person to travel faster than the speed of sound without a vehicle (Welch 2012). For the entire 8-minute descent, viewers saw the Red Bull logo plastered on the sleeves of flight engineers, inside the control room, and on Baumgartner's spacesuit. The entire event captured the attention and imagination of countless millions of people around the world. Red Bull does not have the marketing budget of the other big players in the beverage industry, but these surprise guerilla attacks keep it solidly in the minds of consumers as an irreverent and edgy brand.

6.6 SUSTAINABILITY AS A SOURCE OF COMPETITIVE ADVANTAGE

As organizations, customers, and other stakeholders are increasingly dealing with the effects of climate change, there are new challenges as well as opportunities for organizations. Marketing decision-makers need to discard old, outdated ideas about the need to make a trade off between sustainability and organizational competitiveness (Porter and Van der Linde 1995). At the beginning of this chapter, three sources of competitive advantage were identified: innovation, low-cost, and customer intimacy. In the coming decades, another source of competitive advantage will be sustainability. Many of the concepts that are used to describe an organization's long-term competitive advantage can also be applied to an organization that transitions to more sustainable operations.

Sustainability-Related Barriers to Entry and First Mover Advantages

Recall that a barrier to entry is an impediment that the organization erects to make it difficult for competitors to enter the market. The investment needed for organizations to become more sustainable is significant and for some, represents a barrier to entry. In becoming more sustainable, organizations must set goals, measure progress toward them, and then report on those goals. In addition, new skills need to be learned, new processes need to be implemented, and some reluctant employees may need to be convinced. Clearly, although the investments pay off in the long-run, these initial costs do represent a barrier to organizations who are considering a shift to more sustainable operations. One sustainability-related barrier is the publication of annual sustainability reports, which help prove an organization's sustainability credentials. These reports require a significant investment in time and talent to compile, as well as a set of established goals, benchmarks, and KPIs on which the organization reports. Another barrier to entry into the realm of sustainability operations is that of third-party certifications, which lend legitimacy to an organization's sustainability claims. One such organization is the Marine Stewardship Council (MSC). Headquartered in London, the MSC is a non-profit organization that sets standards for sustainable fishing. Filet-o-fish sandwiches at all McDonald's restaurants in Brazil, Canada, the US, and Europe are MSC certified (Press release 2018). Similarly, the Forest Stewardship Council (FSC), is a non-profit organization headquartered in Bonn, Germany that sets standards for responsible forest management. More than 98% of the wood used in IKEA products is either FSC certified or recycled (About 2021). The MSC and the FSC are global in their reach and influence. While a certification from either one of these organizations provides consumers and other stakeholders with greater confidence in the sustainability claims made by companies, it also represents a barrier to entry.

With respect to the concept of the first mover advantage, we know that there are distinct competitive advantages for the organization that is the first to enter the sustainability space. One advantage is that an organization's reputation improves when it is a first mover in the sustainability space. Stakeholders perceive first movers to be more genuine in their commitment to sustainability, rather than simply another organization that is following the rest of the pack (Loock and Phillips 2020). Another advantage to being a first mover in sustainability is that the organization gets to establish the standards for the industry. When this occurs, it becomes the benchmark against which all other organizations are compared. Outdoor clothing and equipment manufacturer Patagonia stands out as a benchmark organization in sustainability. It was not only the first in its industry, but was the first organization across most industries to operate under a sustainability philosophy. Patagonia can trace its origins to the 1960s, but it was officially incorporated in 1973 (Chouinard 2016). What makes its contributions remarkable is that this occurred before the IPCC issued any of its reports or made its ground-breaking statement on sustainable development. It occurred before any visible signs of climate change were available to any laypersons and before scientists started to seriously consider the issue.

Sustainability as Another Source of Competitive Advantage

We know that the value proposition is the set of solutions that the organization offers to its customers that they cannot get from the competition. The concept of shared value suggests that when the organization operates from a sustainable perspective, it can deliver shared value through the generation of profits, as well as benefits to society and the environment (Porter and Kramer 2006). This perspective is very much in alignment with the Triple Bottom Line, which calls for decision-makers to consider the consequences of their decisions on *people*, the *planet*, and the company's *prosperity*.

Sustainability works in concert with the other three avenues by which an organization can establish and strengthen its strategic competitive advantage. Specifically, sustainability can spur innovation and lower costs, and strengthen customer intimacy. Organizations that operate in a sustainable manner become open to seeing new methods and new processes they may have never considered, thus making them more *innovative*. Sustainable organizations operate more efficiently (Porter and Van der Linde 1995), by making more efficient use of natural resources and materials, thus *lowering costs*. Sustainable organizations also provide sustainable solutions to consumers who are seeking them, thus increasing *customer intimacy* (see Figure 6.3).

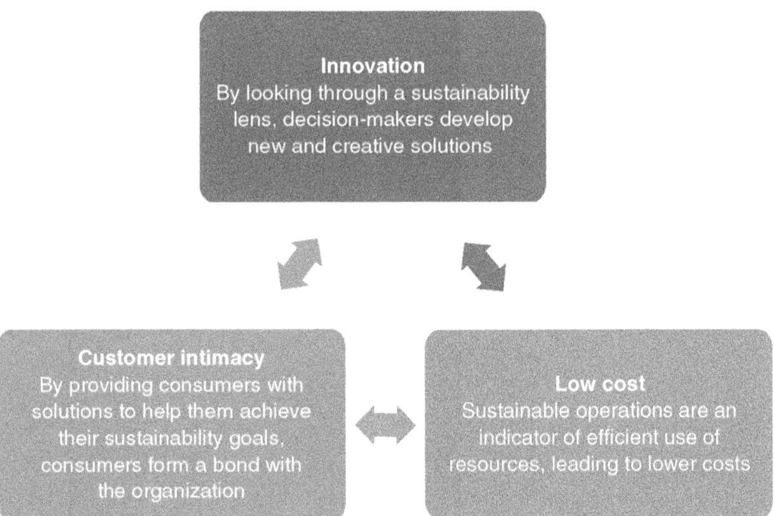

Figure 6.3 Sustainability works in concert with the other sources of competitive advantage

It may be argued, however, that sustainability is so critical to the long-term competitive position of the company, it warrants its own recognition as a source of competitive advantage. Recall that a strategic competitive advantage is a characteristic or set of characteristics of the organization that, relative to the competition, provides it with the ability to better deliver the value proposition to its customers. It must be long-term in focus and must be built on something that is important to the consumer.

Does a sustainability philosophy allow for the ability to better deliver the value proposition? Yes. Consumers who rely on products to make their lives happier, healthier, or more fulfilling can certainly have their needs and wants fulfilled by products and services that were sustainably

produced. Indeed, organizations that are operated more sustainably will likely have lower costs, which can then be passed along to consumers. They will also likely be more innovative, giving them the ability to create new and innovative solutions to consumer problems. Amazon delivers packages to over 100 countries around the world and has implemented a variety of sustainability measures throughout the company. Because of its size and scale of operations, even small, incremental improvements result in big differences, such as massive reductions in CO_2 emissions and increases in the amount of material recycled. Amazon employees, however, saw room for improvement, formed a climate justice group, and pushed the company to do even more (Amazon 2019), thus making it possible for Amazon to do an even better job at delivering the value proposition.

Does a sustainability philosophy represent a long-term focus for the organization? Certainly. To start, acknowledging that the climate crisis will impact organizational operations indicates that decision-makers are preparing for an uncertain future. Visionary leaders are able to spot trends in the marketplace and the external environment that they can use to leverage their existing strengths for long-term benefit. In an effort to capture a commanding share of the electric sports utility truck market and become a first mover in this arena, in 2021, Ford Motors announced an $11.4 billion investment in a new electric car manufacturing plant and two lithium-ion battery manufacturing facilities. This investment was in addition to the $30 billion it had already pledged to completely integrate EV electric technology throughout its fleet (Wayland 2021). Ford's investment is certainly long-term in focus.

Is a sustainability philosophy important to consumers? Of course. As consumers increasingly see news reports of climate catastrophes around the world and have personal experiences with those events, climate change will be pushed to the forefront of their consciousness. According to the Pew Research Center, 72% of consumers in the most economically-developed countries are concerned that climate change will impact them personally at some point in their lifetimes and 80% are willing to make changes in how they live and work, in order to reduce the effects of climate change. Generally speaking, across the 17 countries studied, younger people, women, and those on the political left are more concerned about climate change (Bell, Poushter, Fagan, and Huang 2021). However, although they are willing to do their part, consumers would like big companies and brands to do their part too by, for example, providing better labeling on what items can be recycled or composted. By offering more sustainable solutions to consumers, organizations can help them achieve their own sustainability goals. In 2019, German shoe manufacturer Adidas crafted a short-term partnership with Parley for Oceans to produce 7000 limited edition sneakers made from plastic waste recovered from the ocean. The sneakers sold out so quickly, the partnership was extended to manufacture five million more pairs (Parletta 2019). So, is sustainability important to consumers? You bet.

The four sources of long-term, sustainable competitive advantage for an organization are: innovation, low-cost, customer intimacy, and sustainability (see Figure 6.4).

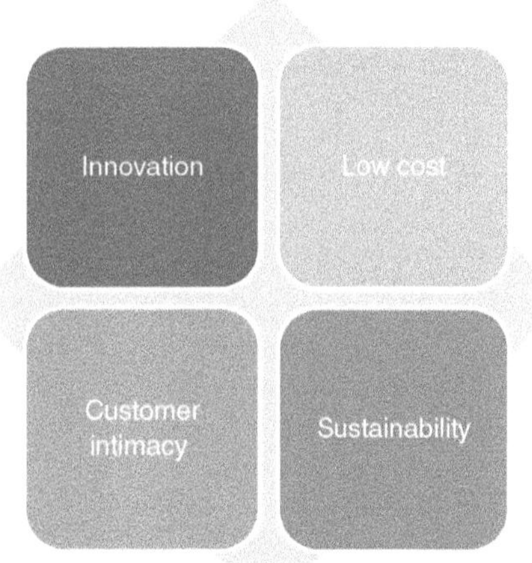

Figure 6.4 The four sources of competitive advantage

6.7 SUMMARY

When an organization establishes a strategic competitive advantage, it is able to better deliver the value proposition to its customers. However, establishing a competitive advantage does not necessarily mean that it will be long-lasting. Unfortunately, with shifting consumer trends, new technologies, changes in the external environment, and competitive moves, a strategic competitive advantage can be fleeting. Therefore, organizations must not just establish a competitive advantage, but continue to strengthen their own *capabilities* to deliver the value proposition over the long term. This involves developing a deep understanding of the competition as well as a keen self-reflection regarding the organization's own capabilities. Then, by employing strategic thinking, decision-makers can identify where the organization's own capabilities can be used to out-maneuver the competition. This process is dynamic and forward thinking.

The process of getting to know the competition involves understanding the concepts of barriers to entry and the advantages of being a first mover. Traditional bases for establishing a strategic competitive advantage are innovation, low cost, and customer intimacy. Several examples were provided and it was found that, although Budweiser's promotion to provide free beer in Philadelphia may have received significant media attention, from the standpoint of delivering the value proposition or strengthening its own competitive standing, it was not a good strategic move. During the process of getting to know itself, the organization needs to take a critical look in the mirror in order to assess how it might stand up against the competition. Here, the organization needs to determine the scope of the competition, assess its tolerance for risk, examine its strategic alliances, and engage in competitive intelligence. After the marketing team has developed an understanding of the competition and itself, it should have a clear idea about how it will fare against the competition, an essential precondition before determining the organization's next competitive move.

The marketing team has several choices in determining which competitive move would be most appropriate and impactful: defensive moves, offensive moves, flanking moves, or a guerilla attack. Each of these strategic moves was discussed and examples were provided. For example, grocery giant Tesco's flank attack against other UK retailers ended up backfiring and costing the company significant money and goodwill.

Finally, an argument was made for adding one more source of competitive advantage: sustainability. Although principles of sustainability work in concert with the existing three sources of competitive advantage, sustainability is so important to the long-term viability of the organization, that it rises to the level of being its own, distinct source of competitive advantage.

QUESTIONS FOR REVIEW & DISCUSSION

1 Why is it necessary for an organization to know the competition and know itself before it can launch a competitive move?

2 What is a barrier to entry? What are its benefits to the organization? What kind of barrier to entry might exist for a new startup company that wants to manufacture and sell ice cream? How about a startup that manufactures airplane guidance systems?

3 In many developed countries, the number of university-aged students is stagnant or even dropping. Therefore, universities are increasingly competing more aggressively for students. How might a university work to *strengthen its existing position*? How might it *mobilize positions*? Be creative.

(Continued)

4 Why might an organization want to forge a strategic alliance? What downsides might there be to strategic alliances? Provide an example of a strategic alliance that did not work out as intended. What went wrong?

5 As more automotive manufacturers are making stronger commitments to producing electric cars, it is likely that they will rely on innovation as a source of competitive advantage. What might an auto manufacturer do if it wanted to produce electric cars, but focus on *customer intimacy* as its source of competitive advantage? Be creative.

6 Consider this scenario. The tiny island nation of Malta competes with Spain for tourists who are looking for sunny skies, warm weather, and beautiful beaches. Tourism Malta just launched a €30 million multi-media advertising campaign in the UK to encourage British citizens to spend their holidays there. What type of competitive move is Malta launching against Spain? Explain.

7 Construct a detailed argument for why sustainability should be considered a source of strategic competitive advantage for the organization.

REFERENCES

About. 2021. Being Forest Positive. *IKEA.com*. Accessed 27 September 2021. https://about.ikea.com/en/sustainability/responsible-sourcing/being-forest-positive.

Amazon Employees for Climate Justice. 2019. Open Letter to Jeff Bezos and the Amazon Board of Directors. *Medium*. 10 April. Accessed 17 September 2021. https://amazonemployees4climatejustice.medium.com/public-letter-to-jeff-bezos-and-the-amazon-board-of-directors-82a8405f5e38.

Avril. Tom. 2018. Eagles Parade Attendance: Close to 700,000, Experts Say. *The Philadelphia Inquirer. Sports Section*. 8 February. Accessed 23 September 2021. www.inquirer.com/philly/super-bowl-lii/eagles-parade-attendance-crowd-estimate-philadelphia-super-bowl-20180208.html.

Bell, James, Jacob Poushter, Moira Fagan, and Christine Huang. 2021. In Response to Climate Change, Citizens in Advanced Economies are Willing to Alter How They Live and Work. *Pew Research Center*, 14 September. Accessed 19 June 2022. www.pewresearch.org/global/2021/09/14/in-response-to-climate-change-citizens-in-advanced-economies-are-willing-to-alter-how-they-live-and-work/.

Bloomberg. 2019. Pentagon Warns Bases Imperiled by Climate Change in Dire Report. *Fortune.com*. 18 January. p. N.PAG-N.

Bonini, Sheila. 2021. The Coca-Cola and WWF Partnership: Working Toward a Resilient Future. *WorldWildlife.org*. 23 August. Accessed 25 September 2021. www.worldwildlife.org/blogs/sustainability-works/posts/the-coca-cola-and-wwf-partnership-working-toward-a-resilient-future.

Burgess, Omar. 2018. Bud Light Could Owe Over a Million People Beer if the Eagles Win the Super Bowl. *Complex*. 4 February. Accessed 23 September 2021. www.complex.com/sports/2018/02/bud-light-could-owe-over-a-million-people-beer-if-eagles-win-super-bowl.

Chouinard, Yvon. 2016. *Let My People Go Surfing: The Education of a Reluctant Businessman*. Penguin Books, New York.

Cohen, William A. 1986. War in the Marketplace. *Business Horizons*, March–April. 10–20.

Corporate. 2021. What's Actually in our Filet-O-Fish™ Sandwich? *McDonalds.com*. 2 March. Accessed 27 September 2021. https://corporate.mcdonalds.com/corpmcd/en-us/our-stories/article/OurStories.sustain-filet-o-fish.html.

FastCompany. 2021. The World's Most Innovative Companies: 2021. *FastCompany & Inc*. Accessed 20 September 2021. www.fastcompany.com/90603436/the-worlds-most-innovative-companies-2021.

Frank, Mitch. 2016. The Family Trust. *Wine Spectator*. 30 April. Accessed 22 March 2020. https://top100.winespectator.com/article/the-family-trust/.

Georgiadis, Philip. 2021. Wizz Challenges King of Europe's Skies in Battle for Budget Carrier Crown. *Financial Times*. Asian Edition, Edition 1. London. 10 July.

German, Myna, Donald A. Donahue, Jr., and Steven P. Schnaars. 1991. A Chink in Marketing's Armor: Strategy Above Tactics. *Business Horizons*, March–April, 74–8.

Gibson, Amber. 2017. Albiera Antinori Talks Wine, Family, and Business. *Forbes*. 17 July. Accessed 15 September 2021. www.forbes.com/sites/ambergibson/2017/07/17/albiera-antinori/#dc5d01e1856e.

Godin, Melissa. 2021. Lawyers Are Working to Put "Ecocide" on Par with War Crimes. Could an International Law Hold Major Polluters to Account? *Time. Science and Climate Change Section*. 19 February. Accessed 25 September 2021. https://time.com/5940759/ecocide-law-environment-destruction-icc/.

Heilpern, Will. 2016. 18 False Advertising Scandals that Cost Brands Millions. *Business Insider*. 31 March. Accessed 26 September 2021. www.businessinsider.com/false-advertising-scandals-2016-3.

Kotler, Philip and Ravi Singh. 1981. Marketing Warfare in the 1980s. *Journal of Business Strategy*, *1* (3), 30–41.

Layne, Rachel. 2019. In New England, Home Prices Fall as Seas Rise. *CBS News. Moneywatch*. 24 January. Accessed 17 September 2021. www.cbsnews.com/news/climate-change-in-new-england-home-prices-fall-as-seas-rise/.

Loock, Moritz and Diane M. Phillips. 2020. A Firm's Financial Reputation vs. Sustainability Reputation: Do Consumers Really Care? *Sustainability*, *12* (24), 1–17. http://dx.doi.org/10.3390/su122410519.

Parletta, Natalie. 2019. Going Green – What's Good for the Planet is Good for Business. *Forbes.com*. 14 May. Accessed 12 July 2021. www.forbes.com/sites/natalieparletta/2019/05/14/going-green-whats-good-for-the-planet-is-good-for-business/?sh=452d0f8d3201.

Porter, Michael E. and Claas van der Linde. 1995. Toward a New Conception of the Environment-Competitiveness Relationship. *Journal of Economic Perspectives*, *9* (4), 97–118.

Porter, Michael E. and Mark R. Kramer. 2006. Strategy & Society: The Link Between Competitive Advantage and Corporate Social Responsibility. *Harvard Business Review*, December, 78–92.

Press release. 2018. McDonald's Uses Scale for Good to Advance Fish Sustainability. The Marine Stewardship Council. 7 June. Accessed 21 December 2022.https://www.msc.org/en-us/media-center/news-media/press-release/mcdonalds-scale-for-good-advance-fish-sustainability

Ries, Al and Jack Trout. 1986. Marketing Warfare. *Journal of Consumer Marketing*, *3* (4), 77–82.

Sanjai, P.R. and Chris Kay. 2021. Mukesh Ambani Comes to Struggling Hamleys' Aid, Plans to Quadruple Outlets. *Bloomberg*. 13 April. Accessed 26 September 2021. www.business-standard.com/article/companies/mukesh-ambani-comes-to-struggling-hamleys-aid-plans-to-quadruple-outlets-121041300138_1.html.

Segran, Elizabeth. 2021. Pour One Out for the Tech Bro Uniform: Patagonia Ditches Corporate Logos on its Vests. *FastCompany*. 19 April. Accessed 25 September 2021. www.fastcompany.com/90626274/pour-one-out-for-the-tech-bro-uniform-patagonia-ditches-corporate-logos-on-its-vests.

Shoe, Des. 2018. The U.K. Has Banned Microbeads. Why? *The New York Times*. 9 January. Accessed 25 September 2021. www.nytimes.com/2018/01/09/world/europe/microbeads-ban-uk.html.

Stubbs, Dave. 2017. Wayne Gretzky: 100 Greatest NHL Players. NHL.com. 1 January. Accessed 25 September 2021. www.nhl.com/news/wayne-gretzky-100-greatest-nhl-hockey-players/c-285574558?tid=283865022.

Tedder, Michael. 2022. YouTube Tells TikTok to Eat its Shorts: YouTube Says its Short Form Content is a Hit. *TheStreet*. 16 June. Accessed 19 June 2022. www.thestreet.com/investing/youtube-is-taking-the-fight-to-tik-tok-google.

Virbila, S. Irene. 2014. More than 600 Years of Chianti History in Piero Antinori's New Book. *Los Angeles Times*. 8 September. Accessed 22 March 2020. www.latimes.com/food/dailydish/la-dd-antinori-chianti-book-20140908-story.html.

Wayland, Michael. 2021. Ford and SK Innovation to Spend $11 Billion, Create 11,000 Jobs on New U.S. EV and Battery Plants. *CNBC*. 27 September. Accessed 27 September 2021. www.cnbc.com/2021/09/27/ford-battery-supplier-to-spend-11point4-billion-to-build-new-us-plants.html.

Welch, William M. 2012. Skydiver's Space Jump Pays Off for Red Bull. *USA Today*. 15 October. Accessed 26 September 2021. www.usatoday.com/story/money/business/2012/10/15/red-bull-skydiver/1635235/.

7 TARGET MARKETS: IDENTIFYING AND TARGETING THOSE INDIVIDUALS MOST LIKELY TO RESPOND TO THE MARKETING STRATEGY

LEADERSHIP INSIGHTS 7

Photo 7.1 Erin Hannon

Source: courtesy, Erin Hannon

Meet Erin Hannon, Director of Retail Sales

E & J Gallo

Family-owned since 1933, E & J Gallo is the world's largest family-owned winery and has an impressive array of more than 120 brands in its portfolio, including Barefoot, Apothic, and DaVinci. Erin Hannon has worked for Gallo since 2002, where she has had a number of different roles. Prior to her current position, she was the director of recruiting, where she employed highly-qualified, hard-working college graduates for entry-level sales positions. Because the recruiting process is so expensive and time-consuming, Hannon launched an initiative to increase the likelihood that individuals will accept the job offers they receive. An important realization happened when she recognized that "parents were my audience too; Millennials and Gen Zs listen to their parents." In effect, the recruiting team had two distinct target markets: students and parents.

The team started by acknowledging that Gallo's family-oriented, fun-loving, entrepreneurial culture made it a great place to work, and their carefully-planned recruiting efforts were designed to find individuals who would feel comfortable in such a culture. They needed to create a similarly well-planned program to engage parents. Hannon explained, "we go to campuses and meet students. If we like what we see, we invite students for a first-round interview. If they pass that interview, they go to a second-round interview by a director-level person at our company. There are not too many directors at our company, so this is a big deal. Then, if they pass that, they go to a two-day recruiting conference, where all of the finalists in a given region come to learn even more. There, they go through another interview and even do a sales pitch in front of all of us. The Vice President of our company even comes to meet the candidates. It's intense."

At the same time, parents are sent an information packet that includes a personalized letter from Hannon saying, "Congratulations, we just wanted you to know a few things about us, such as how selective we are in our recruiting process. Less than 1% of all of the students we meet get invited to the conference." The packet includes several business cards from regional recruiters, a list of Gallo's brands, and a QR code that links to a series of videos from Gallo family members. Parents are informed about the history of Gallo, its strong culture of family and tradition, and the fact that it is, and will remain, a family-owned company. Finally, information is provided about the company, trends in the wine and spirits industry, why the industry is a great career choice, and why Gallo is the best company in the industry to start their son's or daughter's career.

Included in the packet is a request for the parents to call their son or daughter and ask them a set of questions. This part of the strategy is designed to encourage an informed discussion between the students and their parents. Full roll out of the new targeting strategy occurred in spring 2019 and Hannon's team received positive feedback almost immediately. "There was overwhelming support. Parents thought the effort was great. They can't believe how many brands we sell; they never knew those brands were ours," explained Hannon.

The next step is the actual offer of employment. Candidates and their parents are invited to visit the facilities where they can meet people, see the office, and tour the warehouse. Once a candidate accepts, the parents are sent packages to congratulate them. They get a bottle of champagne with a customized label and some Gallo swag. "We really try to engage the parents from pre-offer, through the actual offer, all the way to post-offer," said Hannon. The efforts have paid off. The first recruiting season saw an acceptance rate of 85%, a 7% increase from the previous year. Hannon reflected upon her team's success, "Gallo is a great place to work; it is no surprise that the average length of time that an employee stays with the company is 19 years. Even if we can get an additional two or three candidates because of this two-pronged targeting strategy, we can save a ton of money over their entire tenure with the company and, of course, secure great talent."

Hannon's advice for new graduates? "Some young people see it as a badge of honor to just jump from one company to the next every few years. If you choose wisely, you can still develop your skills by having different and challenging jobs all within the same company."

7.1 "OFF THE WALL" TARGETING OF OUTCASTS AND MISFITS

Vans sneakers made their first splash into the market in 1966 when they were adopted by the southern California skateboard culture as a critical part of the skate "uniform." From the start, the shoes were targeted toward individuals who typically existed at the fringes of society – these consumers were young, irreverent, unconventional, and anti-establishment. For them, skateboarding was an entire lifestyle. It determined who they hung out with, their food and fashion choices, and the music they preferred, especially indie bands. Vans came in unique styles with bold patterns, which appealed to skateboarders with an the irreverent, youth-oriented brand message. Vans were even featured in the 1982 American coming-of-age movie, *Fast Times at Ridgemont High* (Roderick 2016). From a practical standpoint, fans liked the way the shoes fit and the way the soles adhered to the skateboard. Fans of the brand felt a strong connection to the brand's values and mystique; they drew inspiration from the brand, just as the Vans' marketing team drew inspiration from the skateboard culture. To capture its unique position in the minds of its consumers, Vans uses the slogan, "Off the Wall" (see Photo 7.2).

Photo 7.2 The Vans brand connects seamlessly with the values of skateboarders

Source: Pixabay

The brand strategy at Vans takes a long-term perspective with its target market, which has been part of the reason for its success and credibility as an iconic brand for misfits and outcasts around the world. From its earliest days, Vans worked to solidify an important position in the minds of consumers: elite skateboarding and the Vans brand are inextricably linked. To solidify this positioning, Vans sponsors up-and-coming skateboarding celebrities and has constructed numerous skateparks around the world where it invites users to hone their skills and have fun. At some of the more elite parks, Vans hosts competitions, bringing in world-class skateboarders. More recently, the company has established retail pop-up outlets around the world called "House of Vans." Shoppers get to peruse shoes, as well as Vans apparel and accessories. Importantly, these pop-ups are immersive experiences, showcasing the brand and its links to creative expression in music and fashion. The experience itself is disruptive but relevant, with more emphasis on "the glue" that brings people together than on the products themselves (Roderick 2016).

The Vans marketing team works closely with its fans to ensure that the brand stays relevant and "the glue" continues to stick. It solicits feedback from customers on colors and designs, which are then incorporated into new shoes (Roderick 2016). The company also encourages creative, fashion-forward consumers to design their own one-of-a-kind shoes online (Bachelor and Whiting 2004) and forges short-term collaborations with other brands within the skateboarding universe, such as makeup company Urban Decay.

In 2018, Vans launched an effort to expand and strengthen its connections with the young female target market. The goal was to break down gender stereotypes and empower female creative forces through skateboarding. To do this, Vans hosted 100 pop-up clinics around the world, in places ranging from St. Petersburg to Bangalore to São Paulo, to teach young women and girls how to skateboard. They were introduced to some of the stars of skateboarding and were invited to give the sport a try. For some of its biggest markets like India, Vans brought in nationally well-known female skateboarding stars to give hands-on advice. These influencers drew huge crowds and helped connect the brand to that country's youth culture (Glenday 2018).

By 2021, Vans could be found in 97 countries (Press Release 2021) and was estimated to generate more than $3 billion in annual revenue (Roderick 2016). Going forward, Vans promises to continue to promote creative self-expression with young people across cultures by tapping into extreme sports, indie music, artistic expression, and street culture. The goal is to strengthen the deep connectivity it has with its target market and continue to generate "brand heat" (Press Release 2021).

This chapter starts with the recognition that not everyone is going to be interested in our brand, nor would the marketing team want this to happen. In 2022, there were 8 billion people on this planet (Worldometers 2021), each one with a unique history, perspective, and set of needs, wants, and motivations. Even the biggest global organizations have limited resources and would not be able to effectively meet the needs and wants of all of these consumers. Therefore, the marketing team needs to identify smaller groups of individuals who, ideally, will be interested in the company's value proposition. In order to identify these consumers, marketers must engage in the process of market segmentation, targeting, and positioning.

7.2 LEARNING OBJECTIVES

After studying this chapter, you will be able to do the following:

1 Describe the IPAT model and how it can be adapted for regenerative systems.
2 Describe the three-step process of segmentation, targeting, and positioning.
3 Distinguish between the four methods of segmentation and describe the benefits of a layered segmentation strategy.

4 Explain the concept of positioning and why repositioning is often difficult.
5 Create an argument for why it makes sense to discard the four key assumptions from traditional marketing thought when it comes to the sustainability market.

7.3 A CROWDED WORLD & IPAT

The effects of an increasing global population have many experts worried. More people means increased pressure on supplies of clean water, arable land, and a host of other necessities. According to estimates from the UN, the world's population is growing to staggering heights. It took from the beginning of time until just after the year 1800 for the world's population to reach one billion people. By 1928, we had added another billion. Just 32 years later, another billion were added. In looking at Figure 7.1, it is clear that the time it takes to add each additional one billion people to the population is getting shorter and shorter. The world's political and business leaders have a moral imperative to provide these individuals with easy access to the resources they need, as well as ensure that those resources are not depleted for future generations. In addition to the tremendous strain on resources, these additional human beings will exert additional pressure on the climate; by their mere existence, more CO_2 will enter the atmosphere, and the warming of the planet will accelerate, ushering in additional strains on the entire system (c.f., Friedman 2009).

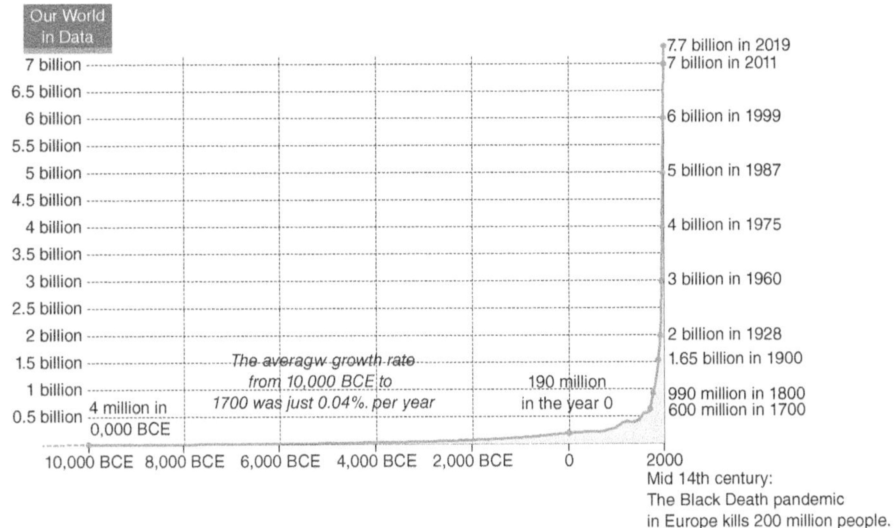

Figure 7.1 Our world's population growth

Source: Roser, Ritchie, and Ortiz-Ospina (2013)

Scientists have concluded that 1950 marked the start of the latest epoch in planetary history: **the Anthropocene Epoch**. This epoch is characterized by the collective impact the human species is having on the health of the planet. Together, humans are exerting damaging and sometimes irreversible impacts on the planet's oceans, atmosphere, surface, and systems of nutrient cycling (Rafferty 2020) (see Figure 7.2 and Photo 7.3).

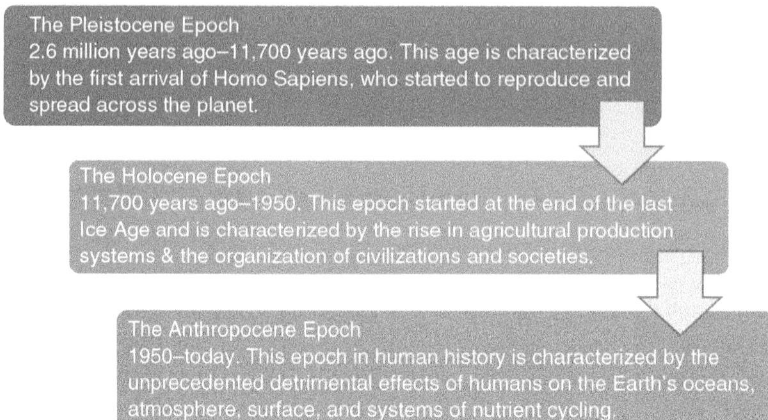

Figure 7.2 The human epochs

Source: adapted, in part, from Rafferty (2020)

Photo 7.3 Cave paintings from the end of the Pleistocene epoch

Source: Pixabay

As early as the 1960s, economists developed models to describe the increased negative impacts on the environment that accompanied increases in population. One model describing this impact has become widely used and cited: the **IPAT model**. The model has four essential components (Ehrlich and Ehrlich 1972):

I = Impact, a measure of adverse environmental influences

P = Population, the number of humans on the planet

A = Affluence, measured by a country's GDP/person

T = Technology, a measure of how efficiently scarce resources are used

Figure 7.3 The IPAT model

Source: Ehrlich and Ehrlich (1972)

As originally conceived, the IPAT model vividly depicts the increased harm on the environment that occurs with the increase in *population*. Indeed, the authors refer to this effect as the "population bomb." In addition, the model says that a society's increased *affluence* will act as a multiplier in the detrimental impact it will have on the environment; with increased affluence is increased consumption of a variety of resources, such as consumer products, energy, land, and water. Further, increased consumption is directly related to increases in a country's **carbon footprint**, a measure of the greenhouse gasses that are emitted (especially CO_2) by a country's or another entity's level of economic activity and consumption. When applied to individual consumers, a carbon footprint is a reflection of that individual's consumption and lifestyle choices. In 2020, per capita CO_2 emissions dipped as a result of the economic downturn spurred by the global Covid-19 pandemic. Despite this downturn, Australia and the US were still responsible for the world's highest carbon emissions per person at about 15 metric tons per person (see Figure 7.4). The final component of the model, *technology*, is also a multiplier on impact because it represents the efficient, exploitive extraction of fossil fuels and other non-renewable resources.

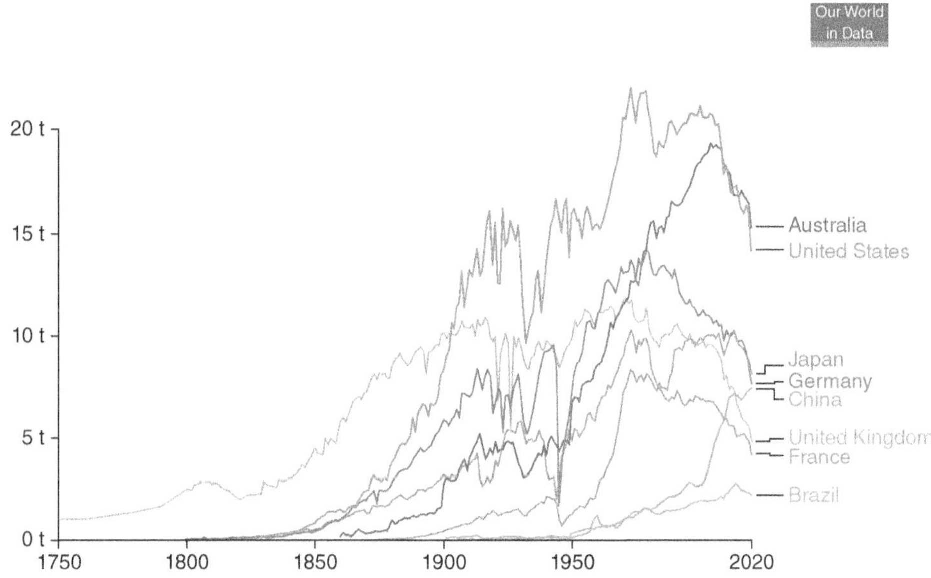

Figure 7.4 CO_2 emissions per capita in selected countries around the world

Source: Ritchie and Roser (2020)

In examining the IPAT model and its implications for climate and environmental impact, it is easy to conclude that the situation is hopeless. However, recent innovations in technology and new conceptualizations of economic systems indicate that the IPAT model may offer a more

hopeful, rather than hopeless, perspective on humanity's future. Rather than conceiving of the model's elements as only capable of destructive effects, they can instead be viewed as **regenerative systems**, such that they repair and strengthen damaged systems, making them healthier and more capable of performing at peak capacity again. Using a regenerative conceptualization has the potential to recharge aquifers, restore coral reefs, repair soils, and rebuild communities. How does it work? Starting with *technology*, new innovations allow for a shift toward renewable energy. Innovation can also be a springboard for creative solutions like carbon-absorbing cement, carbon-negative plastics, and carbon-negative building materials, all of which help limit and lower CO_2 in the atmosphere. Technological advancements also enable better measurement and control of systems. Moving to *affluence*, governments and businesses need to shift toward policies and operations that promote successful and thriving economies that are based on regenerative, rather than exploitive, principles (Newman 2020). Doughnut economics, for example, provides significant promise in this respect. This economic model proposes that a safe and just economic system will provide a social foundation such that all individuals have equitable access to the basics of food, housing, and energy, as well as at least a minimum standard in dimensions such as healthcare, education, and social equity. At the same time, the regenerative economic system cannot overshoot any ecological limits such as chemical pollution, ocean acidification, or climate change (Raworth 2017). Finally, when thinking about *population*, every person now existing within a regenerative system is driven by efforts to recharge, restore, repair, and rebuild, so the population component of the model drives more positive change. As the world's governments and economies move toward regenerative systems, IPAT can become a tool to describe the positive impacts, rather than negative impacts, on the natural environment (Newman 2020).

7.4 SEGMENTATION PROCESS

Some marketers might be quite excited by the prospect of a market made up of billions of customers. Marketing novices often think that if they simply get the word out about their brand to as many people as possible, consumers will be so delighted that they will purchase the product. This rarely happens. Given the fact that 90% of new products fail, despite significant investments in time and money, it is up to the marketing team to locate a target market that is likely to respond favorably to the company's offering (Christensen, Cook, and Hall 2005). Why does this make sense? First, consumers are bombarded with hundreds, if not thousands, of advertising messages each day. Think about it. Every brand image or logo that passes across a consumer's field of vision, every advertisement, every sign, every wrapper or package, every brand message that shows up in social media – these all contribute to the multitude of messages that a consumer encounters every day. There is no reason to add our brand to this clutter unless there is a reasonably good chance that consumers will see it and be interested in it. Second, it is a waste of the consumer's attention and goodwill to place a marketing communications message in front of them when they will likely never have any interest in the product or need to use it. Third, simply put, there likely is not enough money in the marketing budget to advertise everywhere to everyone. **The segmentation process,** describes the three-step process by which a target market is identified and selected through segmentation, targeting, and positioning (see Figure 7.5).

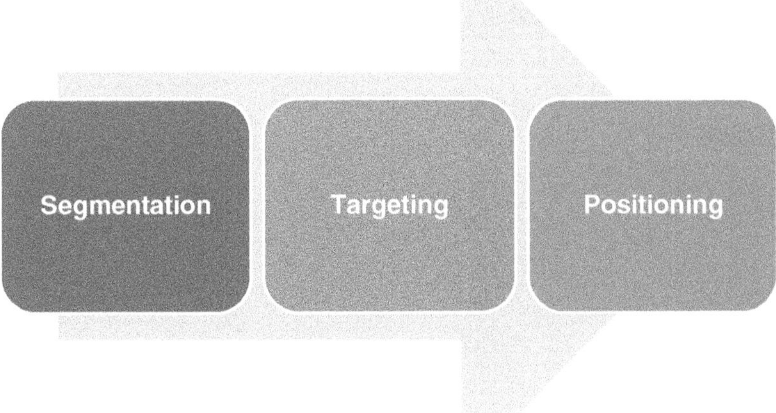

Figure 7.5 The three-step segmentation process

ENDURING INSIGHTS 7.1

> "Learn from Napoleon, warfare's greatest master: speed and adaptability come from flexible organization. Break your forces into independent groups that can operate and make decisions on their own. Make your forces elusive and unstoppable by infusing them with the spirit of the campaign, giving them a mission to accomplish, and then letting them run." – Robert Greene, author

Napoleon was a master at strategy and recognized the benefits of effective segmentation. Not only did it weaken the enemy by disrupting lines of supply, communication, and coordination, it also provided critical benefits to his own operations. From Napoleon's perspective, fighting an entire army with one strategy was not effective or efficient. Instead, smaller, quicker, and more flexible units could more effectively address the specific challenges of smaller enemy segments. The same is true with marketing.

Identifying Consumers: Segmentation

The first step in the three-step segmentation, targeting, and positioning process (STP) is **segmentation**, where the entire market is broken up into smaller groups using criteria that *make sense* for the product. Beauty and haircare products, for example, often offer different formulations for different skin colors, skin types, and hair textures. In this case, it makes sense to use ethnicity as a segmentation criterion (see case study on p.478). For automobiles, it makes sense to segment by income and by family size. At the end of the segmentation step, the marketing team should have a collection of segments, or *potential* target markets. If done correctly, the individuals within these potential target markets will be very similar to one another and will likely have a

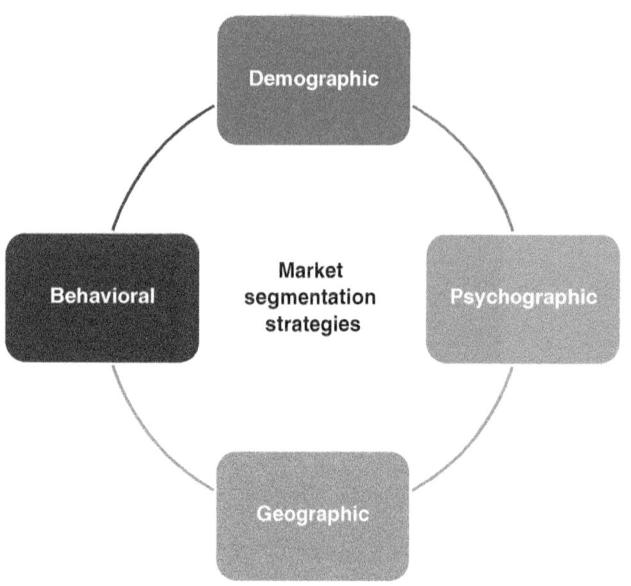

Figure 7.6 Market segmentation strategies

similar reaction to any efforts by the marketing team. There are four main criteria by which the marketing team can segment the market: demographic, psychographic, geographic, and behavioral (see Figure 7.6).

Demographic Criteria

When using **demographic criteria**, the market is broken up according to demographic characteristics like age, gender, income, education, family size, or ethnicity. Colleges and universities often segment the market by age. Later, they may select one segment of younger individuals who are 18–20 years old and another comprised of adult learners who have been working for a few years. Using demographic criteria during the segmentation step provides two distinct benefits to marketing teams. First, compared to other segmentation strategies, demographics are fairly easy to assess. Second, demographics are particularly useful later in the process when the marketing team is developing its communications strategy. This is because media buying decisions are often made using demographics; radio, TV, online, print, outdoor, and mobile ads are purchased (at least partially) on the basis of demographics.

Demographic criteria have been utilized in efforts to reach those consumers often forgotten by the business community: **Bottom of the Pyramid** consumers, who make up about two-thirds of the planet's population and live in extreme poverty. It is generally accepted that extreme poverty is defined as someone surviving on less than $2/day, with extremely limited access to food, clean water, sanitation, education, and healthcare (Prahalad and Hart 2002). It is estimated that 4 billion people on the planet live on less than $1500/year (Simanis and Duke 2014). Because there are so many people in this segment, a low-price, low-margin, high-volume strategy presents tremendous opportunities for profit. The challenge for the world's multinational companies, however, is to find ways to address the needs of these individuals, while doing so in culturally-appropriate and environmentally-sensitive ways. SC Johnson, an American company producing cleaning products and other household chemicals, has been successful in tapping into Bottom of the Pyramid markets around the world. In Ghana, for example, malaria is a constant problem, causing sickness and deaths in thousands of people each year. To help control the mosquito problem in Ghana, SC Johnson employed a direct sales force that gave presentations in villages and community centers to explain the necessity of controlling these disease-carrying insects. To increase trial, insect repellent was bundled with other cleaning products consumers were already buying. To encourage repurchase, the product was redesigned so that it only needed simple refill pods, thus dramatically reducing the price (Simanis and Duke 2014). Unilever, the global food, personal care, and home care giant, has become particularly adept at leveraging its scale to meet the needs of the Bottom of the Pyramid segment. Unilever taps the creative ingenuity of its research and development (R&D) team to develop small, single-use product packaging and products that meet the needs of these consumers. For example, Unilever reformulated its laundry detergent to create a single-use laundry sachet that requires less water and is easy to rinse out of clothes (see Photo 7.4).

Photo 7.4 Single-use packets of soup mix and soap hanging in an Indian market

Source: Pixabay

Just like other consumers with more financial means, Bottom of the Pyramid consumers engage in some consumption that is aspirational in nature. That is, they acquire and display products to help signal their social status to others. These products might include articles of clothing or other items that are visible to others (Gupta and Srivastav 2016). The UN's first SDG focuses on the eradication of poverty and tremendous strides have been made around the world in achieving this goal.

Psychographic Criteria

Psychographic characteristics are used to break up the market according to criteria such as consumer attitudes, interests, or lifestyles. Let's face it, sometimes, consumers are really *into* a particular topic. Some people love outdoor winter sports like snowboarding and skiing. Some people love music and are particularly passionate about their favorite band. Some people are really into their favorite football team or player. Others can't seem to get enough of watching and posting videos on TikTok. Regardless of the topic, marketers sometimes find it useful to segment the market by psychographic criteria.

One consumer segment that has been created from psychographic criteria is the **Lifestyles of Health and Sustainability (LOHAS).** It is comprised of individuals who are motivated by a connection to the natural environment and are inspired to live a healthy and sustainable lifestyle. When making consumption decisions, LOHAS consumers take into account their own personal benefits, but also consider the more macro-level impacts on the community and the planet (Picha and Navratil 2019). What is particularly interesting about LOHAS consumers is the fact that they don't just *talk* about their deeply-held concern for the natural environment, they *act* on those concerns. These consumers might, for example, purchase organic food, frequent second-hand shops, visit farmers' markets, and use organic cleaning products and soaps. One study found, for example, that animal welfare was becoming an increasingly important concern among European shoppers (see Table 7.1). New consumer products, however, seem to be lagging behind the concerns that are expressed by these LOHAS consumers. For example, just 7% of new product labels in European markets make claims about the ethical treatment of animals (see Table 7.2 and Photo 7.5).

Table 7.1 Proportion of European consumers who are concerned about animal welfare

	Poland	France	Germany	Italy	Spain
Proportion of consumers who are concerned about how food companies treat animals	55%	67%	68%	74%	75%

Source: Mintel Group (2019)

Table 7.2 Proportion of new consumer products with animal welfare or vegan claims

	Labels Regarding the Ethical Treatment of Animals	Labels Claiming to Contain No Animal Ingredients (Vegan)
Middle East & Africa	7%	3%
Latin America	3%	1%
North America	13%	2%
Europe	7%	5%
Asia Pacific	6%	2%

Source: Mintel Group (2019)

Photo 7.5 LOHAS consumers turn their sustainable values into action

Source: Pixabay

Geographic Criteria

Geographic criteria are another means by which the marketing team could break up the market into segments. Geographic criteria rely on physical location and break up the market according to regions, countries, states, cities, neighborhoods, or postal codes. Restaurants, for example, would be likely to use geographic segmentation because they attract diners from the local community or tourists to the area (see Photo 7.6). Global food companies utilize geographic segmentation because they know that different regions of the world prefer different combinations of spices and flavorings. Outdoor clothing manufacturers also use geographic segmentation as a basis for creating segments of consumers who live in different climates. Canada Goose, for example, is a company that makes expensive, high-end outdoor winter clothing that is especially well-known for its durability. Although Canada Goose is the brand of choice for extreme explorers who trek to places like Mt. Everest and the South Pole, the brand is primarily targeted at individuals who live in very cold weather climates.

Photo 7.6 Many brick-and-mortar operations rely on geographic segmentation

Source: Pixabay

Behavioral Criteria

The last traditional method of segmentation, **behavioral criteria**, utilizes the consumer's purchase and consumption behavior to segment the market. Here, there are a variety of options that the marketing team could use to break up the market. One possibility is *purchase volume*, where segments could be created for light, medium, and heavy users. Another possibility for segmenting by behavioral criteria is based on the consumer's *user status*. Some possibilities include: customer prospects, new customers, long-time customers, and former customers. Once these segments are created, marketers can get to work creating strategies to communicate with these individuals and

Photo 7.7 Segmenting by consumer need helped Carhartt identify two distinct segments

Source: courtesy, Carhartt. Photo Credit: Elliot Ross

finding ways to fulfill their needs and expectations. For example, former customers were once familiar with your organization and pleased with its value proposition. What happened? In what way did we let them down? Importantly, can we convince them to come back?

Still another way to segment the market according to behavioral criteria is to focus on *consumer needs*. Here, the marketing team needs to first determine what problem the product solves for consumers. Essentially, how does this product make the consumer's life happier, more efficient, healthier, more productive, or more fulfilling? Remember that consumers don't *need* a product, they need the *benefits* that the product provides. Kodak, the former giant of film and photography, made a critical miscalculation by failing to realize the importance of consumer needs when it ignored the digital photography revolution. In short, consumers didn't *need* film, they needed solutions to help them capture and share high-quality images (Christensen, Cook, and Hall 2005). Airbnb, by contrast, understands that vacationing families need a safe, unique, and comfortable place to relax and reconnect with family. They don't need a hotel to do so. When marketers segment the market by consumer needs, they ideally identify two to three unique needs. Carhartt, for example, has concluded that consumers use their iconic clothing to fulfill two unique needs. The first segment is comprised of a group of consumers who buy the well-made clothing because of its superior performance, comfort, and protection. These people generally work in the trades or construction, are on their feet for a long time, and need the clothing to protect them against injury (see Photo 7.7). The second segment of consumers is comprised of consumers who wear the clothing as a fashion statement. Indeed, Carhartt clothing is a favorite for hip-hop and trap music artists and fans. Segmenting by consumer needs has allowed the marketing team at Carhartt to create innovative communications strategies that resonate with the needs of these two very different consumer segments.

Layered Criteria

As discussed, there are four main criteria by which the marketing team can segment the market: demographic, psychographic, geographic, and behavioral. However, it is often beneficial to combine segmentation criteria to create more precise representations of groups of individuals. **Layered criteria** occurs when several different types of criteria are used to segment the market. There are countless ways to layer criteria in creating customer segments. Several are listed below.

Geographic + Demographic

Geodemographic criteria combine geographic and demographic criteria. This method is based on the assumption that people who live or work near one another are alike in their demographics too. From a somewhat narrow perspective, in order to afford the costs of housing in a particular neighborhood, people who live there very likely have similar incomes, educational levels, and occupations. From a more macro-level perspective, people who live in broader geographic regions are likely to be similar to one another on some selected demographic characteristics, such as ethnicity. Organizations that utilize geodemographic segmentation recognize that geographic and demographic characteristics are often related to one another.

Geographic + Psychographic

It should come as no surprise that people living in a given geographical area are also similar from a psychographic perspective. These individuals likely come from similar backgrounds, have similar occupations, and have some broad shared interests. It makes sense; these individuals likely send their children to the same schools, cheer for the same sports teams, engage in similar leisure activities, and frequent the same collection of shops. Management consulting firm Claritas uses a tool called PRIZM to create customer segments based on geographics and psychographics. It is based on the notion that people who live near one another also share psychographic similarities.

Psychographic + Demographic

One segmentation tool that has been used quite successfully is the **VALS™ Framework**, which combines psychographic and demographic criteria to create eight separate segments of consumers. Using psychographic criteria, the framework identifies a consumer's primary motivation for consumption: adherence to ideals, achievement, or self-expression. Using demographic criteria, the framework identifies a consumer's access to resources, which might enhance or constrain the consumer's primary motivation. The "experiencer" segment, for example, has substantial resources and is motivated by self-expression. These individuals are very aware of new trends and fashions, often go against the mainstream, and are very sociable and spontaneous (Strategic Business Insights 2021). The VALS™ Framework has been used successfully since the 1970s to assist countless marketers in developing a deeper understanding of customer segments.

Geographic + Psychographic + Demographic

Marketers often use a variety of segmentation criteria, and one London radio station has found that three criteria are needed to create the segments it needs to sell advertising time on its station. The station started with research indicating that approximately 40% of the churchgoers (psychographic) in inner London (geographic) are from the African-Caribbean community (demographic). Therefore, if a potential advertiser wanted to reach the churchgoing, African-Caribbean community living in London with a radio spot, the sales staff at the radio station would direct them to either Premier Christian Radio or Premier Gospel, where the prices vary, based on the length of the ad and whether or not the ad will be broadcast London-wide or nationwide (see Table 7.3).

Table 7.3 Media pricing using layered criteria

Spot Length	London-wide	Nationwide
10 seconds	£15.00	£25.00
20 seconds	£22.50	£37.50
30 seconds	£30.00	£50.00
40 seconds	£37.50	£62.50
50 seconds	£49.50	£82.50
60 seconds	£60.00	£100.00

Source: Premier (2019)

Although this discussion has focused on B2C situations, segmentation is also necessary in the B2B space. The segmentation step of the STP process for B2B contexts starts with understanding of the needs and characteristics of potential customers/clients. Organizations can be segmented by:

- demographic criteria – including the size of the organization (for example, sales, number of employees, market capitalization), types of technologies used by the organization, types of distribution channels, and the industry in which the organization operates
- geographic criteria – including where the customer is located, where *their* customers are located, and the number of different locations in which the customer operates
- behavioral criteria – including purchase volume, user status, and customer needs
- layered criteria – a combination of any of the above

Selecting the Ideal Group of Consumers: Targeting

At the conclusion of the segmentation step in the STP process, the result should be a set of several clearly-defined segments of individuals who will likely have a similar response to the organization's value proposition. Next, the marketing team needs to select the ideal segment to pursue. **Targeting** involves the selection of one or two segments that the marketing team believes is most likely to respond in a favorable way to our offering. There are several criteria for selecting the target market.

Criteria for Selecting the Target Market

Selecting the optimal target market (or small group of target markets) starts with having a deep understanding of the consumer through insights. In addition, the organization needs to conduct an assessment of its own internal capabilities and external opportunities. There is no simple formula for selecting the target market, but answering these questions will provide a basis by which a decision can be made. Key questions to ask are:

- How well will the new market segment fit with our existing target markets? Is it possible to take advantage of any synergies?
- How easy will it be for our organization to satisfy the needs of this target?

- Does this market segment have a potential for long-term growth?
- From a competitive standpoint, will it be a good move to serve this target market?
- Is the target market big enough to produce a profit?
- Is the target market easy to reach?

Selecting Niche Markets

Niche markets are target markets that are created from very narrowly defined segments. Just like any other target market, the niche market is likely to have been developed by layering several types of segmentation criteria. The resulting target market has very specific needs. Consider fashion retailer H&M's 2021 promotion for sustainably-minded, Gen Z gamers, a decidedly narrow, but potentially very lucrative target market. H&M's clothing line featured animal-friendly clothing items that were all PETA-approved. Notably, to effectively connect with this target, key items in the fashion line, messaging, and the H&M logo were featured in Nintendo's Animal Crossing game (Mintel 2021).

Creating New Markets

Behavioral segmentation strategies that focus on consumer needs, perhaps layered with other segmentation criteria, may help the marketing team identify potential Blue Ocean segments. As discussed previously in this text, Blue Ocean Strategies identify new markets where there is very little or no competition. These individuals may no longer be customers or perhaps they never were customers of the organization. Blue Ocean Strategies focus attention away from existing markets that are often crowded with competitors and in which fierce competition occurs for incremental gains in market share. There are distinct benefits for moving into Blue Oceans to create new markets, the most important of which is that the organization is free to meet the needs of new consumers with little or no competitive pressure (Kim and Mauborgne 2004).

Market Retreat

Sometimes new technologies are introduced that make it necessary for existing companies in the industry to radically adapt. Unfortunately, many are incapable of doing so. When this is the case, the organization has the option of engaging in a **market retreat**, which is the deliberate act of ceding control to the firm with the new dominant technology in order to identify a smaller sub-segment of the existing market that still sees value in the old technology. A market retreat strategy avoids a head-to-head battle in which there is very little chance of winning; market retreats should be proactive and deliberate. When quartz movement watches were first introduced in 1969, most manufacturers switched to this new, more efficient technology. Some watchmakers, however, realized that there was still a significant segment of consumers who preferred the traditional mechanical movement. The segment was smaller, but because some individuals were willing to pay a premium for these mechanically-driven watches, margins were very attractive (Adner and Snow 2010).

Once the marketing team selects the segment, it is referred to as a **target market**. The **target market** is the group of individuals that the marketing team will pursue. It is made up of individuals that have similar need and wants, and will likely respond in a similar fashion to marketing efforts.

BLUNDERS & INSIGHTS 7.1

Selecting the Wrong Target Market

BACKGROUND: In 2014, Monsanto was ranked the third most hated company in the world by global research firm Nielsen. This reputation was based on its expanded use in the 1980s of a new technology in agriculture called genetic modification (Schwartz 2016). **Genetically modified organisms (GMOs)** are agricultural products that are produced by inserting the DNA strands of one plant or animal into the DNA of another plant or animal. This process is not able to be done in nature; it is done in a laboratory. The target market for these GMO products was global food-manufacturing firms, who in turn sold to the mass market of consumers. A problem arose when consumers and consumer advocates started to worry about the safety of genetically modified crops and had particular concerns about potential long-term health impacts on humans and the environment (Phillips and Hallman 2013). Monsanto also engaged in aggressive tactics to sell its genetically modified products around the world. Farmers were subjected to strong-arm tactics, lawsuits, and empty promises about the product's capabilities. In an effort to achieve its long-term goal of eliminating the competition, Monsanto started buying independent seed companies in the 1990s and by 2016 it dominated 23% of the global market. It is not surprising that Monsanto had such a bad reputation (Schwartz 2016).

At the same time it was engaging in these questionable practices, Monsanto also had another dedicated division that continued its non-GMO R&D work. Using traditional methods of plant breeding, this division developed tomatoes with extra antioxidants, tastier peppers, and the "Ever Summer" melon, a somewhat sweet winter melon, with a firm skin to withstand shipping over long distances. Because of the strong backlash over its GMO products, Monsanto refrained from putting its brand name on its non-GMO products in grocery stores (Schwartz 2016). Could Monsanto have done a better job at selecting target markets to pursue for its GMO and non-GMO products?

DEBRIEF: Most definitely. The marketing team at Monsanto demonstrated very little understanding of its target markets. Early in the development of its GMO products, the Monsanto team should have anticipated the reluctance that consumers had about the health and safety of the food. Non-GMO products with distinct benefits like higher antioxidants should have been targeted directly to end-consumers. These non-GMO products could have been branded with the Monsanto name, thus helping to build a strong position for the company as one that was focused on health and wellness. Unfortunately, once a company has an established position in the minds of consumers, it is often quite difficult to change.

Differentiating Your Product from the Competition: Positioning

At the end of the targeting phase of the STP process, the marketing team should have one or two target markets that it wishes to pursue. The next step is **positioning**, which is the process of creating a distinct set of meanings in the minds of consumers that sets the product apart from the competition. Positioning is all about the mental real estate your product occupies in the minds of consumers. Importantly, positioning is actualized in the organization's marketing strategy – product, price, place, and promotion will all be designed to work in concert with one another to solidify the positioning in the minds of consumers. Several positioning tools that marketers utilize are positioning maps, positioning statements, consumer personas, repositioning, and Blue Ocean positioning.

ENDURING INSIGHTS 7.2

> "Strategy is about setting yourself apart from the competition. It's not a matter of being better at what you do – it's a matter of being different at what you do." – Michael Porter, strategist and professor

From the perspective of the target market, the organization's value proposition needs to be compelling, interesting, and *different*. Otherwise, the brand will not capture the consumer's attention, interest, desire, or action.

Positioning Maps

A **positioning map** provides a two- or three-dimensional representation of the position of the organization's products and those of its competition. Positioning maps are an important tool because they illustrate what consumers in the target market believe about the marketplace. To create a positioning map, first ask consumers in the target market to identify their two (or three) most important criteria for selecting a brand in this category. Consider the airline industry. Business travelers, for example, might be most interested in price and service. Next, ask customers in the target market to rate the airlines on these criteria, using a 1–10 scale. Finally, plot the data on a two-dimensional grid (see Figure 7.7).

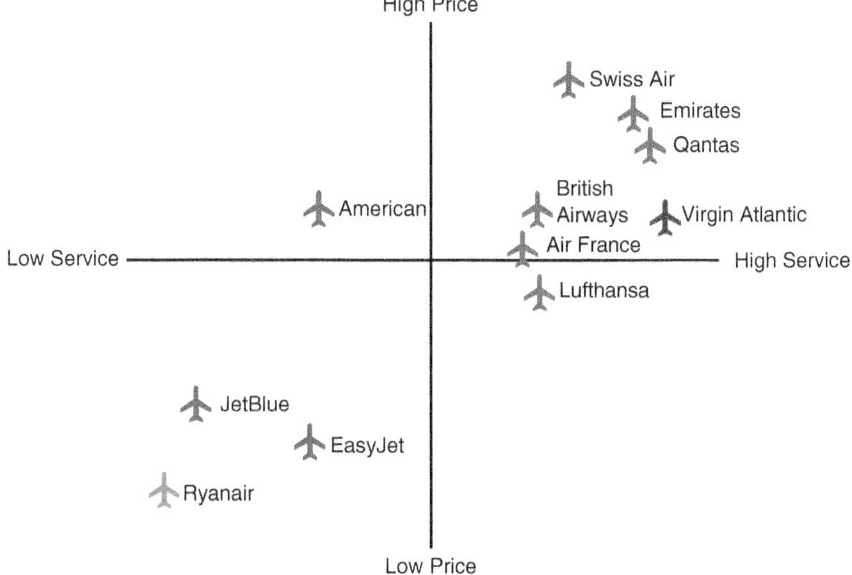

Figure 7.7 Positioning map of several selected airlines

Often, managers are surprised by the results of a positioning map because what *they think* about the brand or product is often different from *what consumers think*. What insights can a marketer derive from a positioning map? Among other things, a marketer might be able to:

1. identify new market opportunities or Blue Oceans
2. identify when a change in the communications strategy is needed – this might occur when a brand actually performs well on one of the dimensions, but the target market is not aware of this, so it is not reflected on the positioning map
3. confirm when the brand is in a position of intense competition with a collection of other brands that, to the consumer, are easily substitutable.

Positioning Statement

A **positioning statement** is a brief description of what the product or service will do for the target market and how it will solve a problem these might have. Because positioning is always done relative to the competition, the positioning statement should offer an explicit statement of how the brand does a better job than the competition at solving the consumer's problem. Positioning statements are used internally to provide inspiration and guidance to the marketing team as it develops its marketing strategy. In crafting a positioning statement, the following template can be used (Stayman 2015):

> For [insert target market], the [insert brand] is the [insert point of differentiation] among all [insert frame of reference] because [insert reason to believe].
>
> Example:
> For budget-conscious business travelers within Europe, Lufthansa offers reliable service, business-focused amenities, and more on-time arrivals than any other carrier. We can do this because we have access to more gates in more cities than anyone else (see Photo 7.8).

Photo 7.8 Lufthansa offers relatively high service at reasonable prices

Source: Pixabay

Customer Personas

Customer personas are another internal tool that the marketing team utilizes to focus and clarify its efforts. A **customer persona** is a fictional character created by the marketing team that represents the demographic, psychographic, geographic, behavioral, and layered characteristics of the target market. Customer personas are often posted in a prominent location, such as on the wall of the marketing team offices. When discussing strategy, the marketing team will often refer to the consumer persona and ask questions like, "what would Christine say about that?" This ever-present reminder and personalization of the target market helps the team keep the needs of the target market at the forefront of its decision-making (see Figure 7.8).

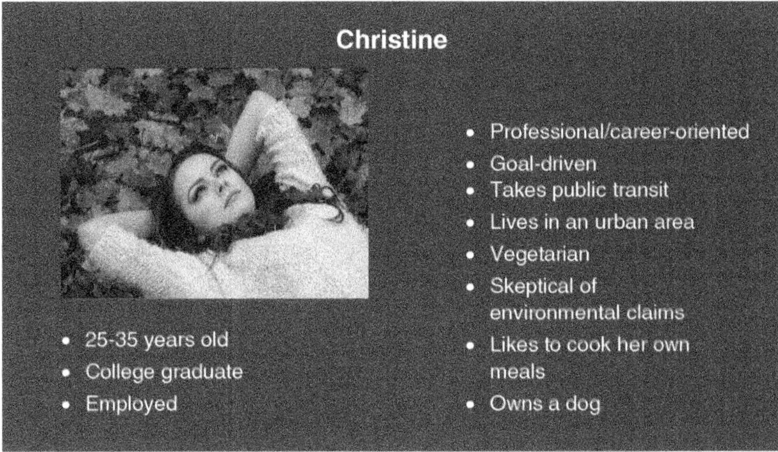

Figure 7.8 Customer persona

Repositioning

After the STP process is complete and the marketing team coalesces around a coherent positioning strategy for the product or brand, the marketing strategy is created. Changes to the product and its attributes are made, a pricing strategy is developed, a distribution strategy is implemented, and a promotional strategy is enacted. Importantly, each element of the marketing mix is developed in such a way that it resonates with the needs and concerns of the target market. All of this work requires significant investments in time, talent, money, and other resources. However, there are some instances when repositioning needs to occur. **Repositioning** happens when the organization works to shift the brand or product's existing position to a new position.

A variety of circumstances might prompt a decision to reposition the product, but they all start with an acknowledgment that the target market's existing positioning of the brand is not ideal. First, new innovations or new technologies could change the way consumers consume, shop, search for information, etc. It could also impact the way the organization delivers the value proposition. A very compelling B2B example comes from Veolia Environmental Services, a French multi-national organization that specializes in residential recycling and waste management. After incorporating new technologies into its operations, it was able to utilize cutting-edge technology to more accurately sort and separate materials that it picked up from homeowners. This technology helped consumers have more confidence that their items would be effectively and efficiently recycled. With this new technology and an effective messaging strategy, Veolia was repositioned from a simple waste hauler to a partner in helping homeowners achieve their sustainability objectives (Allchin 2011).

A second compelling reason for repositioning is that over time, markets shift, which necessitates a shift for brands in order to be able to continue to meet the needs of the target market. In the early days of Starbucks, founder and CEO Howard Schultz positioned the brand as a place where people would linger and enjoy a good-quality coffee. He believed that Starbucks could become a "third place" for coffee lovers to linger: home, work, and the local Starbucks. With global expansion and a distinct shift in consumer purchasing and "lingering" habits, the concept of the third place was no longer relevant by 2008. The company was losing money and closing hundreds of stores. In 2010, Starbucks engaged in a repositioning shift to greater convenience, while still maintaining an "unequivocal, absolute commitment to quality" (Ignatius 2010, p. 111). A similar situation happened with iconic brand Kodak. As mentioned earlier, consumers wanted the ability to store and share their photos. They did not necessarily need film to do that. However, it turns out that some consumers did seek the unique qualities that film provided. In 2017, Kodak refocused its efforts on pursuing individuals who sought film as a medium for their creative pursuits, while it simultaneously leveraged an increased interest in "retro" analog technology (Keinan, Eckhardt, and Beverland 2018).

A third reason for repositioning is that, despite the marketing team's best efforts, bad things sometimes happen and it sometimes makes sense for the brand positioning to shift away from negative brand associations. In 2016, several Samsung Galaxy Note 7 phones caught fire because of poorly-designed battery casings. Airlines stopped allowing customers to turn on or charge their phones during flights and the US Consumer Product Safety Commission issued a recall. After a quick but thorough investigation, Samsung took full responsibility and recalled 2.5 million phones, costing it £4.3 billion (BBC 2017). After the recall, Samsung engaged in a repositioning strategy to make the brand younger, hotter, and more urban. The brand's new position was strengthened with a partnership forged with South Korean K-pop band BTS. Among other things, Galaxy phone consumers could download an augmented reality experience of the band's global art project, Connect. The experience included videos of band members explaining the specific art installations and why they were important additions to the collection (McIntyre 2020). In 2022, the partnership collaborated on a sustainability-related campaign to bring attention to the problem of plastic in the world's oceans. The campaign was coordinated with the release of Samsung's new Galaxy line of smartphones and tablets made from repurposed ocean fishing nets (Kaufman 2022) (watch the video here: https://www.billboard.com/music/pop/bts-samsung-galaxy-for-the-planet-sustainability-initiative-1235029516/).

Blue Ocean Positioning

If a completely new Blue Ocean segment is identified (see Kim and Mauborgne 2004), the marketing team needs to turn its attention to creating a new value proposition and positioning its product to deliver that value proposition. In developing a new and relevant value proposition, it is useful to distinguish between differentiation and positioning. Differentiation is what sets your organization's offering apart from that of the competition. Because market creation happens in a completely new space where there is no existing competition, the marketing team is not engaging in differentiation (Kim and Mauborgne 2015). Instead, it is engaging in **Blue Ocean positioning,** a unique opportunity with a new segment and new market in which a timely, relevant, innovative, and effective value proposition is created. Blue Ocean positioning has the potential to set new standards for product performance and consumer expectations.

A Note on Stereotyping

Before completing the discussion of STP, a note of caution is warranted. Because there are vast individual differences within each target market, there are distinct dangers in drawing conclusions about an entire group of people. Any broad generalizations about demographic or other segments run the risk of stereotyping, with all of its ethically-questionable implications. Further, extra caution needs to be taken with any marketing communications that try to paint consumers with broad generalizations. The goal of STP is to separate individuals into segments such that, with respect to our product, the differences *within* a segment are likely to be smaller than the differences *between* segments.

7.5 DIFFERENT TARGET MARKETS REQUIRE DIFFERENT STRATEGIES

Now that one or two target markets have been identified and the marketing team has a clear idea of how the brand is positioned with respect to the competition, it is time to engage the four elements of the marketing mix – product, price, place, and promotion – to deliver the value proposition. The marketing team must create a different strategy for each individual target market. Individuals in different segments have different lives, experiences, and problems that need to be solved. Therefore, different strategies need to be deployed to effectively reach these target markets. Consider the plethora of secure, cloud-based platforms that healthcare professionals turned to during the Covid-19 pandemic. These telemedicine platforms facilitated quick communication, diagnosis, and in some cases, treatment of patients. At least three separate target markets would be relevant for these diagnostic telemedicine platforms: emergency first responders, emergency room staff, and nursing home or doctor's office staff. Because each of the three target markets have different concerns and requirements for the platform, three separate strategies would need to be created. For example, after stabilizing patients in the field, first responders often have difficulty in communicating effectively and efficiently with hospital staff when they are en route to the hospital. For the first responder target market, there would be particular interest in a platform that allows them to send instant alerts to hospital staff, who are waiting and prepping for the ambulance to arrive. Using a secure network, first responders would benefit from the ability to send pictures, videos, and preliminary assessments of patients and their status. As a part of the development of its marketing strategy for this target market, these product attributes would be highlighted (see Photo 7.9). Bottom line, different target markets require different marketing strategies.

Photo 7.9 Emergency first responders are one target market for diagnostic telemedicine platforms

Source: Pixabay

BLUNDERS & INSIGHTS 7.2

Sending an Unwanted Email? Get Ready for Hefty Fines

BACKGROUND: In 2017, Flybe, the UK-based European airline, got slapped with a £70,000 fine. That same year, Honda Motor Europe was hit with a £13,000 fine. Both were targeting *their own* customers. What happened? After a thorough investigation, it was discovered that both organizations violated the privacy of their customers. There are several UK and EU regulations designed to protect customer privacy, but perhaps the most far-reaching regulation is the General Data Protection Regulation (GDPR), an EU law on data protection and privacy that went into full effect in 2018. The GDPR requires companies to institute robust privacy procedures for the use and sharing of consumers' personal data. Marketers need to be especially concerned about data permission, data access, storage, and use of data (Information Commissioner's Office (ICO) 2017).

Flybe sent an email to 3.3 million individuals with the subject line, "Are your details correct?" The email encouraged people to update out-of-date personal information and marketing preferences. As an incentive, the email also offered these individuals an opportunity to enter a prize drawing. Investigators found that each one of these 3.3 million individuals had previously opted out or unsubscribed from marketing emails. As one regulator explained, "sending emails to determine whether people want to receive marketing without the right consent, is still marketing, and it is against the law." Honda made a similar mistake when it sent out approximately 300,000 emails to clarify customers' choices for marketing communications. Although all of these individuals were existing customers, Honda could not provide evidence that it had obtained permission from these customers for such communications (ICO 2017).

DEBRIEF: Although both Flybe and Honda issued apologies, existing privacy laws and the GDPR are clear that no individuals, even customers, should receive unsolicited emails, texts, calls, or other communications. These violations occurred before the GDPR went into full effect in 2018. However, these actions by Flybe and Honda were done as they were preparing for the GDPR to be implemented. As one official noted, "business must understand that they can't break one law to get ready for another." In Flybe's case, the offense was more egregious because these consumers had all already opted out of all email communications (ICO 2017). When marketers communicate with their target markets, it is imperative to comply with existing – as well as soon to be implemented – regulations.

7.6 THE SUSTAINABILITY MARKET

More than 99% of scientists agree that climate change is happening and that it is caused by human activity (Lynas, Houlton, and Perry 2021). A variety of stakeholders, especially consumers, are demanding more sustainable options from businesses. Organizational and marketing leadership is starting to recognize the benefits of a sustainability approach. However, in order to successfully meet the needs of consumers, marketing decision-makers need to first discard some out-of-date assumptions about how markets work.

Crushing Traditional Market Assumptions

According to traditional economic thought, the marketplace operates dispassionately, according to principles of supply and demand. Consumers make calculations about expected utility and purchase the products that provide them with the highest levels of utility for a given price. These basic assumptions about how markets work are no longer relevant in today's world.

Assumption #1: the sanctity of markets.

This assumption is based on the notion that if markets are permitted to work with perfect efficiency (that is, they are left unrestricted and unregulated), over time, they will sort out disparities in supply, demand, and wealth. Unfortunately, many forces in the natural environment cannot be sorted out by market activity because damage inflicted upon the environment cannot be distilled down to a simple price, as in the price of a product. How can one put a price on vital natural resources like air, water, habitat, or species that are depleted or damaged? This assumption has four dimensions:

(a) Markets have great difficulty in valuing environmental resources – how can one put a price on the extinction of a species or the destruction of an ancient forest?
(b) Markets do not consider thresholds – natural systems are generally fairly resilient for a while. After a certain point, however, each additional unit of damage makes it much more difficult for the system to recover or for the few remaining resources to increase in price enough to encourage preservation.
(c) Markets do not take irreversible processes into account – natural systems often do not behave in a linear fashion over time. At some point, a tipping point occurs in which the system collapses, beyond which repair or rehabilitation is not possible.
(d) Markets cannot predict future demand for vital species and other resources – scientists and other researchers (in medicine, for example) may have yet to discover new innovations or cures for a variety of diseases or medical conditions (Belz and Peattie 2012).

Assumption #2: the sovereignty of consumers.

The notion that the "customer is king or queen," free to consume with reckless abandon, is hopelessly myopic. The problem is that freedom to consume is no longer a right, when the act of such consumption causes real damage to others, the environment, and future generations. This is particularly relevant to the consumption patterns of consumers in developed countries and the impact it has on individuals living in lesser-developed countries (Belz and Peattie 2012).

Assumption #3: the satisfaction of needs.

A basic assumption underlying traditional marketing thought is that when consumers satisfy their needs and wants with consumer products, their standards of living and the quality of their lives will improve. However, this is not the case. Abundant research confirms that after consumption reaches a certain level of satisfying basic needs, any additional consumption has very little impact on an individual's life satisfaction (Belz and Peattie 2012).

Assumption #4: the peripheral nature of nature.

In traditional marketing textbooks, decision-makers are cautioned to consider a variety of external influences, including the economic environment, political/legal environment, social environment, technological environment, and competitive environment. The natural environment, however, influences *every* action that consumers and organizations undertake – nature is certainly not "peripheral." Therefore, decision-makers must also consider the natural environment as not separate from the organization's operations, but as another critical external influence. This failure to do so blinds decision-makers to the impacts of climate and other ecological disruptions, which can cause substantial impacts on economic, technological, social, competitive, and political/legal systems (Belz and Peattie 2012) (see Photo 7.10).

Photo 7.10 The sustainability market requires a crushing of existing assumptions about the way markets work

Source: Pixabay

ENDURING INSIGHTS 7.3

"The archer who misses his mark does not blame the target. He stops, corrects himself, and shoots again." – Confucius, Chinese philosopher

With the critical re-evaluation of traditional assumptions about how markets work and rapidly changing trends in the market, it is no wonder that marketers sometimes miss the mark in effectively connecting with their target markets. However, carefully-derived insights should prove effective in recalibrating their efforts.

Sustainable Market Trends

Market growth for sustainable products has increased dramatically in recent years. A recent study revealed that in more than 90% of CPG categories, sales of sustainability-related products grew faster than their traditional counterparts. On average, that growth was 5.6 times faster than traditional products (Whelan and Kronthal-Sacco 2019). These trends are somewhat uneven across the planet. Austrians (42%) and Italians (41%) lead the world with the greatest proportion of consumers who have made significant changes to their purchasing behaviors or have completely changed their lives to be more sustainable. This is followed by Spanish (35%), German (35%), and American (22%) consumers. Globally, 60% of consumers cite sustainability as an important criterion for their decision-making. Importantly, 34% are willing to pay more for sustainable products and are willing, on average, to pay a 25% premium for them (Businesswire 2021).

LOHAS consumers are especially skeptical. They believe that a sustainable economy is incompatible with marketing, advertising, sales promotion, impulse purchases, and low prices (Picha and Navratil 2019). Despite the challenges in reaching out to knowledgeable and skeptical consumers, some organizations have been successful in navigating shifting market trends. Unilever's "sustainable living" brands are delivering 70% of the company's turnover growth. Unilever strengthened its commitment to aligning its values with those of consumers, by purchasing several sustainable brands, including Seventh Generation, Sundial Brands, and Pukka Herbs (Whelan and Kronthal-Sacco 2019). As sustainability issues are becoming more relevant to consumers, organizations need to ensure that, in serving these markets, sustainability is a core part of the value proposition. Organizations need to innovate and transform in order to deliver on the value proposition. Otherwise, the organization risks being left behind. As marketers progress through the three steps of STP in their pursuit of the sustainability market, they will be well-advised to take into account the short-term, near-term, and long-term shifts that are expected to occur (see Table 7.4).

Table 7.4 Short-, near-, and long-term shifts in the sustainability market

Short-term shifts (now–2 years)	
Shorter-term focus. Goals for 20+ years in the future will not motivate immediate change. Instead, organizations need to encourage immediate shifts in behaviors to immediately reduce carbon emissions.	**Understandable metrics.** Third-party certifications and easy-to-understand measures of climate impact will help consumers make more evidence-based decisions.
Offsets only as a last resort. Carbon offsets, such as planting trees to offset emissions, should only be used to achieve emissions reductions after all other efforts have been employed.	**Renewable Energy.** As the planet shifts away from fossil fuels towards renewable energy, disruptions need to be minimized and prices need to be kept low.
Near-term shifts (2–5 years)	
Lifecycle assessment. Consumers will demand information on a product's climate impact over its entire lifecycle (from production, through use, through disposal).	**Misleading Language.** Consumers will have little patience for misleading language about the product's or the organization's sustainability performance. They will demand clear and transparent communications.

(Continued)

Table 7.4 (Continued)

Adopt a Regenerative Mindset. Organizations need to select materials and ingredients that are recycled and reused, as they shift towards cradle-to-cradle operations.	**Focus on Food Waste.** The food and beverage industry will need to provide innovative solutions to reduce packaging, encourage packaging reuse, extend product shelf-life to reduce food waste.
Long-term shifts (5+ years)	
Deforestation and Biodiversity. Consumers will no longer be content to know that brands are no longer destroying the natural environment; they will want to see proof that their favorite brands are rehabilitating these places.	**Stronger Sense of Story.** Organizations will need to create a compelling reason why sustainably-produced products are worth more than their traditional counterparts.
Climate Resilience. Organizations will need to find a way to thrive in a world with increasing food insecurity, water shortages, crop failures, and political instability.	**Coping with Heat.** As more consumers experience the impacts of climate change (floods, fires, heatwaves), they will increasingly demand that organizations make significant changes to their operations.

Source: Young (2022)

7.7 SUMMARY

This chapter starts out with two very different examples of the benefits of the STP process. In the first, marketers at E&J Gallo found that after they identified and targeted two separate markets in their recruiting efforts (new graduates and their parents), the proportion of individuals who accepted offers of employment increased significantly. In a different vein, marketers at Vans have found success in their efforts to connect their own corporate values to those of their primary target market: young, artistic, and irreverent skateboarders. For decades, these shared values have been the foundation of a strong connection (or "glue") between the brand and its customers.

The problem of an increasing global population was presented and the concept of the Anthropocene epoch was introduced. Next, the original IPAT model was introduced as a tool for assessing the harmful environmental impact from the confluence of three forces: an increasing global population, a shift toward greater levels of consumption, and more harmful fossil fuel-based technologies. However, as economies and businesses start to operate according to regenerative principles, the IPAT can be adapted so that it offers a more hopeful, rather than hopeless, perspective on humanity's future.

Rather than target all consumers in a given marketplace, we found that the process of STP was far preferable. In the first part of the process, segmentation breaks up the market into smaller segments that make sense for the product or offering. The four traditional methods of market segmentation were discussed and the benefits of a layered segmentation approach was introduced. In the second step, targeting involves selecting one or two segments that will be most likely to respond to the organization's value proposition. Several criteria for selection were discussed. Finally, positioning is the process of creating a distinct set of meanings in the minds of consumers that set the product apart from the competition. Several positioning tools were introduced and the necessity to sometimes reposition the brand was discussed.

The chapter wrapped up with a discussion of encouraging trends in the sustainability market. In order to successfully meet the needs and desires of the sustainability market, four key assumptions about how markets traditionally work need to be cast aside. As marketers develop strategies to pursue the sustainability market, they need to be aware of short-term, near-term, and long-term trends.

QUESTIONS FOR REVIEW & DISCUSSION

1 In what way can the IPAT model be adapted for regenerative economic systems? What do we mean when we say that the IPAT model may offer a more hopeful, rather than hopeless, perspective on humanity's future?
2 Imagine that you are working on a marketing strategy team project with several other students who are non-marketing majors. They think the best path forward is to target *all* of the consumers in a given marketplace. Construct an argument for why it makes better sense to utilize the STP approach.
3 List the four traditional methods of market segmentation. For each one, provide an example of a brand that likely used this method of segmentation. Describe layered segmentation and discuss why it might offer benefits over a single method of segmentation. Give an example.
4 When might it be necessary to reposition a brand? Why is it sometimes quite difficult to accomplish this? Provide a detailed example of a brand that has been successfully repositioned.
5 Earlier in this chapter, it was mentioned that universities often have at least two distinct target markets: younger students (around 18–20 years old) and older students. Why is it necessary to have a different marketing strategy for each target market? For *each* of these target markets, create a value proposition that would likely appeal to that target market's unique needs and wants.
6 What is meant by the "sanctity of markets" and why is it such an important cornerstone of our understanding of how markets work? When operating within the sustainability market, why must we reject this notion?

7.8 REFERENCES

Adner, Ron and Daniel C. Snow. 2010. Bold Retreat: A New Strategy for Old Technologies. *Harvard Business Review, 88* (3), 77–81.

Allchin, Josie. 2011. Repositioning Rubbish: How a B2B Brand Won a Marketing Week Award. *Marketing Week*, 7 September. Accessed 14 November 2021. www.marketingweek.com/repositioning-rubbish-how-a-b2b-brand-won-a-marketing-week-award/.

Bachelor, Beth and Rick Whiting. 2004. Closer Connections. *InformationWeek*. Issue 1004. 6 September. 20–22.

Belz, Frank-Martin and Ken Peattie. 2012. *Sustainability Marketing: A Global Perspective*, second edition. John Wiley & Sons, Ltd., Chichester, UK. 119–24.

BBC. 2017. Samsung Confirms Battery Faults as Cause of Note 7 Fires. *BBC News*. 23 January. Accessed 14 November 2021. www.bbc.com/news/business-38714461.

Businesswire. 2021. Recent Study Reveals More than a Third of Consumers are Willing to Pay More for Sustainability as Demand Grows for Environmentally-Friendly Alternatives. *Businesswire: A Berkshire Hathaway Company*. 14 October. Accessed 25 November 2021. www.businesswire.com/news/home/20211014005090/en/Recent-Study-Reveals-More-Than-a-Third-of-Global-Consumers-Are-Willing-to-Pay-More-for-Sustainability-as-Demand-Grows-for-Environmentally-Friendly-Alternatives.

Christensen, Clayton M., Scott Cook, and Taddy Hall. 2005. Marketing Malpractice: The Cause and the Cure. *Harvard Business Review*. December. 74–83.

Ehrlich, Paul R. and Anne H. Ehrlich. 1972. *Population, Resources, Environment: Issues in Human Ecology*, second edition. Freeman, San Francisco, California.

Friedman, Thomas L. 2009. *Hot, Flat, and Crowded 2.0: Why We Need a Green Revolution – and How it Can Renew America*. Picador/Farrar, Straus, and Giroux, New York.

Glenday, John. 2018. Vans Gets its Skates on for Global Brand Campaign. *The Drum*. 2 March. www.thedrum.com/news/2018/03/02/vans-gets-its-skates-global-brand-campaign.

Gupta, Shruti and Pratish Srivastav. 2016. An Exploratory Investigation of Aspirational Consumption at the Bottom of the Pyramid. *Journal of International Consumer Marketing, 28* (1), 2–15.

ICO. 2017. ICO Warns UK Firms to Respect Customers' Data Wishes as it Fines Flybe and Honda. *Information Commissioner's Office*. 27 March 2017. Accessed 24 November 2021. https://ico.org.uk/about-the-ico/news-and-events/news-and-blogs/2017/03/ico-warns-uk-firms-to-respect-customers-data-wishes-as-it-fines-flybe-and-honda/.

Ignatius, Adi. 2010. "We had to Own the Mistakes": Starbucks CEO Howard Schultz on the Challenges of Leading a Turnaround at a Company He Made a Household Name. *Harvard Business Review, 88* (7–8), 108–15.

Kaufman, Gil. 2022. BTS Pay Homage to Bob Dylan in Samsung "Galaxy for the Planet" Ad. *Billboard*. 10 February. Accessed 19 June 2022. www.billboard.com/music/pop/bts-samsung-galaxy-for-the-planet-sustainability-initiative-1235029516/.

Kienan, Anat, Giana M. Eckhardt, and Michael B. Beverland. 2018. Kodak: The Rebirth of an Iconic Brand. *Harvard Business School Publishing*. 5 December. Case #9-519-051.

Kim, W. Chan and Renée Mauborgne. 2004. Blue Ocean Strategy. *Harvard Business Review, 82* (10), 76–84.

Kim, W. Chan and Renée Mauborgne. 2015. Red Ocean Traps: The Mental Models that Undermine Market-Creating Strategies. *Harvard Business Review, 93* (3), 68–73.

Lynas, Mark, Benjamin Z. Houlton, and Simon Perry. 2021. Greater than 99% Consensus on Human Caused Climate Change in the Peer-Reviewed Scientific Literature. *Environmental Research Letters, 16* (11), *114005*, 1–7.

McIntyre, Hugh. 2020. BTS Officially Launch Partnership with Samsung. *Forbes*. 20 February. Accessed 19 June 2022. www.forbes.com/sites/hughmcintyre/2020/02/20/bts–officially–launch–partnership–with–samsung/?sh=e5435ca3e0a3.

Mintel Group. 2019. *Veganism Meets Home Care*. 22 July. Mintel Group, Ltd. London.

Mintel Group. 2021. *H&M Reveals Virtual All Vegan Fashion Collection*. 11 April. Mintel Group, Ltd. London.

Newman, Peter. 2020. *Hope in a time of Civicide: Regenerative Development and IPAT. Sustainable Earth, 3* (1), 1–11.

Phillips, Diane M. and William K. Hallman. 2013. Consumer Risk Perceptions and Marketing Strategy: The Case of Genetically Modified Food. *Psychology & Marketing, 30* (9), 739–48.

Picha, Kamil and Josef Navratil. 2019. The Factors Lifestyle of Health and Sustainability Influencing Pro-environmental Buying Behaviour. *Journal of Cleaner Production, 234*, 233–41.

Prahalad, C.K. and Stuart L. Hart. 2002. The Fortune at the Bottom of the Pyramid. *Strategy + Business, 26* (1), 2–14.

Premier. 2019. Radio Advertising Rate Card. Accessed 1 November 2021. www.premier.org.uk/wp-content/uploads/2021/03/Rate-Card-Radio-Revised-Jan-19.pdf.

Press Release. 2021. Vans Appoints Kristin Harrer as Global Chief Marketing Officer. *Vans, a VF Corporation.* 21 April. Accessed 2 October 2021. www.vfc.com/news/press-release/1759/vans-appoints-kristin-harrer-as-global-chief-marketing.

Rafferty, John. 2020. Anthropocene Epoch. *Encyclopedia Britannica.* Accessed 11 November 2021. www.britannica.com/science/Anthropocene-Epoch

Raworth, Kate. 2017. *Doughnut Economics: 7 Ways to Think Like a 21st Century Economist.* Chelsea Green Publishing, White River Junction, Vermont.

Ritchie, Hanna and Max Roser. 2020. CO_2 and Greenhouse Gas Emissions. Published online at *OurWorldInData.org.* Accessed 12 November 2021. Retrieved from: https://ourworldindata.org/co2-and-other-greenhouse-gas-emissions (Online Resource).

Roderick, Leonie. 2016. Vans: 'We're Not Just a Shoe Company.' *Marketing Week* (Online), London. 22 March.

Roser, Max, Hannah Ritchie, and Esteban Ortiz-Ospina. 2013. World Population Growth. Published online at *OurWorldInData.org.* Accessed 12 November 2021. Retrieved from: https://ourworldindata.org/world-population-growth (Online Resource).

Schwartz, Ariel. 2016. This is the Most Surprising Thing Monsanto is Working On, and it's Already Changing the Way You Eat. *Business Insider.* 27 July. www.businessinsider.com/most-surprising-thing-monsanto-working-on-2016-7.

Simanis, Erik and Duncan Duke. 2014. Profits at the Bottom of the Pyramid. *Harvard Business Review.* October. Accessed 8 November 2021. https://hbr.org/2014/10/profits-at-the-bottom-of-the-pyramid.

Strategic Business Insights. 2021. US Framework and VALS™ Types. Strategic Business Insights. Accessed 8 November 2021. www.strategicbusinessinsights.com/vals/ustypes.shtml.

Stayman, Doug. 2015. How to Write Market Positioning Statements. *eCornell. #IMPACT. Inspiring People Across the World Through Lifelong Learning.* Accessed 14 November 2021. https://ecornell-impact.cornell.edu/how-to-write-market-positioning-statements/.

Whelan, Tensie and Randi Kronthal-Sacco. 2019. Research: Actually, Consumers Do Buy Sustainable Products. *Harvard Business Review.* 19 June. 2–4.

Worldometers. 2021. Current World Population. Accessed 25 November 2021. www.worldometers.info/world-population/.

Young, Elysha. 2022. *Consumer Trend: Climate Complexity.* 19 November 2021. Mintel Group, Ltd. London.

8 PRODUCT STRATEGIES: CREATING THE VALUE PROPOSITION

LEADERSHIP INSIGHTS 8

Photo 8.1 Ed Harris

Source: courtesy, Ed Harris

Meet Ed Harris, President & CEO

Discover Lancaster

Ed Harris' career has taken a lot of twists and turns over the years. Immediately after graduating from university in 2001, he started working for a startup sportswear company called And1, which was then acquired by Converse. Over the years, he has worked for some of the most well-known brands in the world: Converse, Timberland, Under Armour, and Ebay. In 2020, as the world was in the midst of its first Covid-19 shutdown, Harris took a job in the most unlikely field: tourism. Harris believed he could apply some of the lessons he had learned about branding, global expansion, and market growth to marketing one of most unusual and diverse destinations in the world. He certainly had his work cut out for him.

Today, Harris and his team at Discover Lancaster work to promote, build, and grow the $3 billion tourism industry in Lancaster, Pennsylvania. Lancaster is located about 1 hour west of Philadelphia, on the East Coast of the US and is well-known for its conservative Amish community. The Amish are descended from German and Swiss people seeking religious freedom and first arrived in Lancaster around 1720. Also called "Pennsylvania Dutch," they value humility, hard work, community, and a separation from the modern world, including modern conveniences like cars and electricity. At 30,000 strong, most Amish people live with their families on farms and make their living in farming, as well as other trades such as carpentry or masonry. Although the Amish community exerts a strong influence on the culture of the area, Lancaster also has a thriving food and art culture, business community, and city life. Approximately 9 million tourists visit each year, spending approximately $253 each. One out of every 15 jobs in the area is dependent on tourism (Tourism Economics 2019). Marketing a destination in the middle of a global pandemic is certainly a formidable task.

To meet this challenge, Harris and his team engaged in detailed market development and product development strategies. They started with research that indicated that, more than ever, tourists were seeking authenticity. Tired of working from home and feeling the itch to travel, but still worried about the dangers of the pandemic, families were drawn to the appeal of fresh air, a simpler lifestyle, family bonds, authentic craftsmanship, and hearty home-style cooking. As such, the team engaged in a *market development strategy* not just by broadening the target market to individual families, but by encouraging intergenerational and multi-family trips to take part in the Lancaster experience. With its wide-open spaces, messaging focused on the numerous opportunities for outdoor experiences like horseback riding, water activities, buggy rides, farm tours, and camping. Importantly, messaging emphasized that these places could accommodate big groups and outdoor dining where families could reconnect after long separations and make lasting memories.

The team also engaged in a concerted *product development strategy* by emphasizing new characteristics of the product – personal wellness and slower living – in its messaging to its existing target market. The team's goal was to portray Lancaster as a haven for those who were seeking a chance to unplug and rejuvenate. Attributes such as spa treatments, hiking trails, biking trips, water activities, and yoga were highlighted. Visitors could also disconnect by reading a book, catching a nap, taking a swim, wandering around the city, or by simply enjoying the view. Whether it involved a simple day trip, a family vacation, or even a remote work getaway, Lancaster was promoted as a welcoming place to relax and unwind.

By late 2021, tourist numbers were impressive. Hotel bookings reached 95% occupancy, web traffic was up 25% over pre-pandemic levels, and tourism revenue was the highest it had been in 4 years. For Harris, one of the most appealing things about his job is the variety that the tourism industry provides: "every season there is a new trip to promote. Every marketer wants to stretch themselves creatively, and I get to do that here," reflected Harris.

Harris' advice for marketing students? "Ask for advice and be humble enough to take it. You might think you know it all. You don't."

8.1 KFC KNOWS IT'S NOT *JUST* ABOUT THE CHICKEN

Fried chicken powerhouse KFC is a division of Yum! Brands, which controls fast food giants Taco Bell, KFC, Pizza Hut, and The Habit Burger. KFC has had an impressive amount of success in global markets, with considerable expansion in India, Latin America, the South Pacific, and Russia in recent years. By 2019, KFC had 23,000 stores and McDonald's had 38,000 stores worldwide. However, KFC was growing much faster than its competitor. It had a presence in 140 countries and increased its footprint by 71% between 2013 and 2019. As a comparison, McDonald's increased its footprint by just 8% during the same time period. As it grows, KFC's scale provides numerous advantages, such as taking advantage of many operational synergies and trying out new innovations like plant-based menu options. In many of its international locations, KFC has a first mover advantage. Looking forward, the global fried chicken market is expected to grow by 5.47% compound annual growth rate (CAGR) through 2025, which bodes well for KFC. However, other chicken chains, including Popeye's, are also aggressively expanding globally (Kelso 2019).

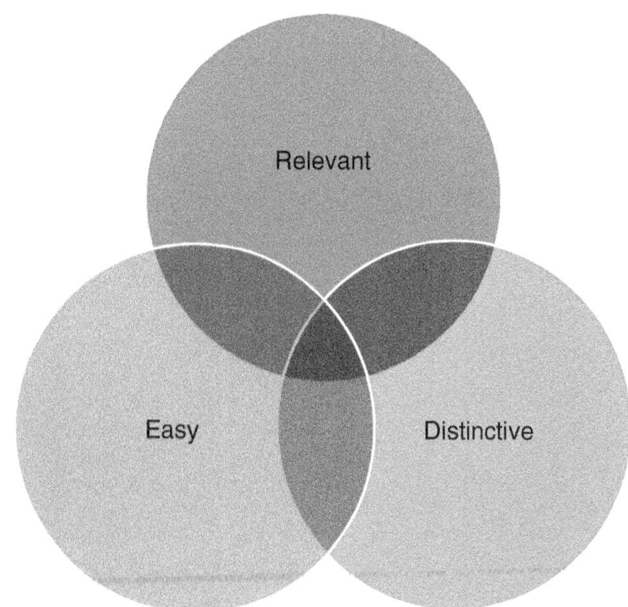

Figure 8.1 The RED Marketing model suggests that brands should be relevant, easy, and distinctive

Source: Creed and Muench (2021)

To continue its record of success, marketing decision-makers at KFC plan to rely heavily on the organization's three-part product strategy called **RED Marketing**, which suggests that, for a product to successfully connect with customers, it should be relevant, easy, and distinctive. The strategy is based on the contention that, from the target market's perspective, products are not simply a collection of attributes that provide utility to the consumer. Instead, products are a collection of attributes that deliver the value proposition. The first dimension in RED Marketing is *relevance* and ensures that in some way, the product embodies cultural, functional, or social relevance to the target market. Apple has made itself relevant by taking a strong stand on privacy, a top-of-mind issue for many consumers. The second dimension is *easy*, which recommends that the product be easy to notice and easy to access in a crowded marketplace. Amazon, for example, makes online purchases incredibly frictionless. The third dimension is *distinctiveness*, which suggests that the brand should be unique, ownable, and consistent. KFC's spokesperson, the Colonel, was dusted off after many years of not being utilized and leveraged to become the personification of KFC. The Colonel is certainly unique; no one else has a mascot quite like him. He is also ownable, meaning that no other brand could legitimately copy the Colonel. Finally, he is consistent; regardless of where in the world you visit a KFC, the same Colonel is there to greet you (Creed and Muench 2021) (see Figure 8.1).

KFC's marketing team believes that the relevance dimension is the key lever for successful global expansion. They believe that the more relevant the brand is in a particular community, the more it will flourish. For example, KFC has research indicating that sustainability and employee working conditions are increasingly important to consumers. In response, it instituted a series of new policies on worker rights and animal rights, and has introduced several plant-based items to the menu (Kelso 2019). KFC has learned that relevance, however, can shift over time. In 1994, when Apartheid ended in South Africa, the nation started to see itself as a "rainbow" nation – a new flag was adopted, Nelson Mandela became president, and the country had high hopes of ushering in a new era of complete acceptance of everyone, regardless of skin color. KFC had 1000 stores in South Africa and made plentiful use of the rainbow's ideals in connecting with customers. By 2015, however, disillusionment was starting to set in with young South Africans. University tuition prices were increasing dramatically and many of the promises from 1994 remained unfulfilled (Clark 2019). By 2019, anthropologists and sociologists recognized that the "rainbow nation" was no longer relevant. Instead, young people were more motivated by a "born-free" message – living in a world that has never seen Apartheid and charting their own path (Clark 2019, Creed and Muench 2021). KFC responded by adapting its advertising to convey this new, more relevant, message (Creed and Muench 2021) (see Photo 8.2).

Photo 8.2 KFC in San Juan, Puerto Rico

Source: Pixabay

This chapter on product kicks off the discussion of the marketing strategy – the use of the four critical components of the marketing mix to deliver the value proposition. Although each one of these components – product, price, place, and promotion – will be discussed in separate chapters, it is important to remember that the components are interdependent. The marketing literature is filled with product and brand strategy models. RED Marketing is just one. Changing goals, shifting trends, and the realities of the competitive landscape will determine which models are most relevant for a given situation.

8.2 LEARNING OBJECTIVES

After studying this chapter, you will be able to do the following:

1 Create an argument for why a product is much more than just a collection of attributes.
2 Describe at least two methods by which the marketing team can create product objectives.
3 Differentiate between design thinking and design for the environment.
4 Describe the process by which a new market can be entered, as well as the specific case in which a new non-domestic market can be entered.
5 Describe why brand equity is such an important concept for brand management.

8.3 WHAT IS A PRODUCT?

A product can be anything that delivers the value proposition to the consumer: an idea, a tangible product, a service, a person, a destination, or an experience. A **product** is a collection of attributes, benefits, beliefs, emotions, and cultural meanings that deliver the value proposition. A **product attribute** is a characteristic or feature of the product. Think about it as something you might read on an ingredient label, something a political candidate might promise, something you might observe when you visit a destination, or something you might hear about from a salesperson. A **product benefit** is the consequence or outcome of the attribute (see Table 8.1).

Table 8.1 Product attributes vs. product benefits

Product Attributes	Product Benefits
B2C contexts:	
100% wool content in a new sweater	Warmth, comfort
Electric engine in a new car	Zero CO_2 emissions, quiet ride
Free breakfast at a hotel	Less hassle, more value for the money
Cash back rewards for a credit card	Easy rewards/money for purchases
Solar panels on the roof of a new house	Lower energy costs
Promises of tax breaks from a political candidate	Lower taxes
B2B contexts:	
On-site training for your staff with the installation of new computer equipment	A staff that is well trained and competent with the new computer software and hardware
An upgraded service plan for the new factory equipment	Easy and fast service, limited production downtime
An integrated pest-management plan as a part of a groundskeeping contract	Fewer pesticides, healthier work environment and corporate campus
Organic and vegetarian food options in the company cafeteria	Happier and healthier employees

8.4 NEW PRODUCT DEVELOPMENT

This chapter will explore the nature of products, new product development, and the product planning process, where objectives, strategies, and tactics are created. First, however, it is informative to develop a foundational understanding of how products perform in the marketplace. In this section, the Product Life Cycle will be introduced. Then, several concepts related to new product development will be introduced, including design thinking, design for the environment, sustainability-related products, and life cycle assessment.

Product Life Cycle

Just like all living things, products have a "life" – they are developed and introduced into the market, where they eventually grow, mature, and decline. **The Product Life Cycle** describes this process (see Figure 8.2) and suggests a variety of strategic moves that can be made by the marketing team at each one of the stages of the life cycle (Levitt 1965):

- *Introduction stage* – this is a period of high risk because of the high rate of new product failures. Marketers must create demand in the market.
- *Growth stage* – competitors start to enter because demand and sales are starting to accelerate. Marketers must expand distribution and convince consumers to prefer *their* brand over that of the competition.
- *Maturity stage* – the product is distributed widely and competition is fierce. Marketers typically differentiate their product with small changes or improvements in product attributes or service. Differentiation may also occur through advertising, packaging, or a unique appeal to niche segments. Price competition intensifies.
- *Decline stage* – demand declines, margins shrink, and competitors start to exit the market. Marketers concentrate their resources and may try to hasten their competitors' exit from the market.

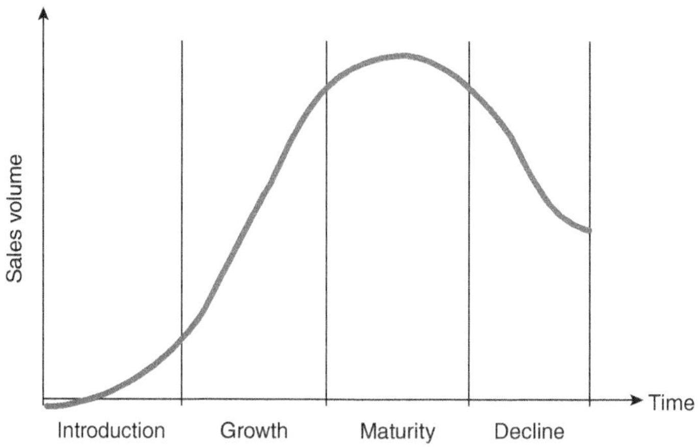

Figure 8.2 The traditional Product Life Cycle

Source: iStock

Levitt's conceptualization of the Product Life Cycle has informed countless strategic decisions over the years. However, more contemporary representations of what happens to products in the marketplace acknowledge the importance of a consumer-centric focus and the possibility that products sometimes have a second life. These representations expand the concept as one in which the product not only is a collection of attributes that deliver the value proposition, but it is also a collection of important cultural meanings and emotions.

BLUNDERS & INSIGHTS 8.1

Are HP Computers Racist?

BACKGROUND: In 2009, when two workers at an electronics store, "Black Desi" and "White Wanda," were checking out the facial recognition tracking feature on a new HP computer, they discovered something very strange. The tracking feature worked perfectly when White Wanda was in the frame, by following her movements and zooming in and out when she got closer to the camera or moved away. However, when Black Desi moved into the frame, the tracking feature stopped working (check out the video here: www.youtube.com/watch?v=t4DT3tQqgRM&t=8s). The video is presented humorously and the two friends claimed that they only wanted to share this quirky finding with their friends and family. Soon, however, other customers started reporting similar problems. The story was quickly picked up by a variety of global news organizations and spread around the world. As of 2022, it garnered more than 3 million views. HP's initial response to the accusation was that the camera had insufficient "foreground lighting" to pick up Desi's face and then provided tips on how to improve the lighting (Simon 2009). Other critics, however, did not believe that foreground lighting was the only problem.

DEBRIEF: Perhaps the lighting could have been improved and HP should have tested its facial recognition feature on non-White faces. It is more likely, however, that the biggest problem is that product designers at HP failed to realize that the technical features and benefits of a product are only a *part* of the product's value proposition. A product is also a collection of various beliefs, emotions, and cultural meanings. Unfortunately, as facial recognition software is being utilized more frequently around the world, it does not appear as if the technology has improved. As compared to the accuracy for White faces, the programs have a 10–100 times greater likelihood of misidentifying Black, Asian, and elderly faces (Singer and Metz 2019).

Design Thinking

Design thinking is a process by which the organization endeavors to solve problems by attempting to optimize the positive impact on people. Design thinking has been applied to a variety of organizational problems, from customer service call centers, to shipping procedures, to warranty fulfillment. Design thinking can be thought of as an umbrella term for a process that keeps the needs of individuals top-of-mind in the creation of a solution. One type of design thinking involves creating new products to solve customer problems. To start, members of the new product development team are recruited from many different parts of the organization to bring a variety of perspectives and skill sets to bear on the problem. As the team works on developing a consumer-centric product, they engage in an iterative process; new solutions are deployed, measured, adapted, and deployed again. Using design thinking for new product development creates solutions to consumer needs that are technologically elegant and offer a strategic advantage to the organization (Brown 2008).

The main reason design thinking for new products is so effective is that it addresses several internal biases that typically hamper innovation, such as offering incremental solutions or innovating based on the organization's capabilities, rather than on consumer needs. Most successful new products offer superior customer solutions, with lower risks and costs for the consumer. The process starts with a deep dive into the consumer's life. The three-step process is as follows (Liedtka 2018):

- *Step 1 – Customer discovery*: the goal of this step is to understand the problem from the customer's point of view. It involves three sub-steps. First, *immersion* involves going deep into the customer experience in order to get a sense of how the customer lives and works. The target customer's history and important sociocultural influences are identified. Second, *sensemaking* requires a distillation of how this problem influences the customer's life. How pervasive is this problem and what other aspects of the consumer's life could potentially improve if this problem were solved? Finally, *alignment* occurs when the marketing team tries to forge a customer–organization connection by trying to find an alignment between the customer's problem and what the organization could potentially do to solve that problem. At the end of this step in the design thinking process, the marketing team will be able to articulate what, in an ideal world, it could do to solve the customer's problem.
- *Step 2 – Idea generation*: the goal of this step of the design thinking process is to create a set of ideas that could be actualized to help solve the customer's problem. The first sub-step is *emergence* and involves brainstorming and testing any pre-conceived assumptions about how the organization could address the problem. This step is iterative in nature; each idea builds on the previous one. The second sub-step is *articulation*, the creation of a detailed product concept. At the conclusion of the idea generation step, the team will know exactly what it needs to do to solve the customer's problem.
- *Step 3 – The testing experience*: the goal of this step is to check the viability of the product concept. It involves two sub-steps. First, *pre-experience* involves the generation of flexible artifacts, which are very rough prototypes that can easily be altered. Second, *learning in action* involves developing the actual prototype and testing it with the target market. Feedback is gathered and the final "go" or "no go" decision is made.

At the conclusion of step 3, the process starts again with customer discovery (see Figure 8.3).

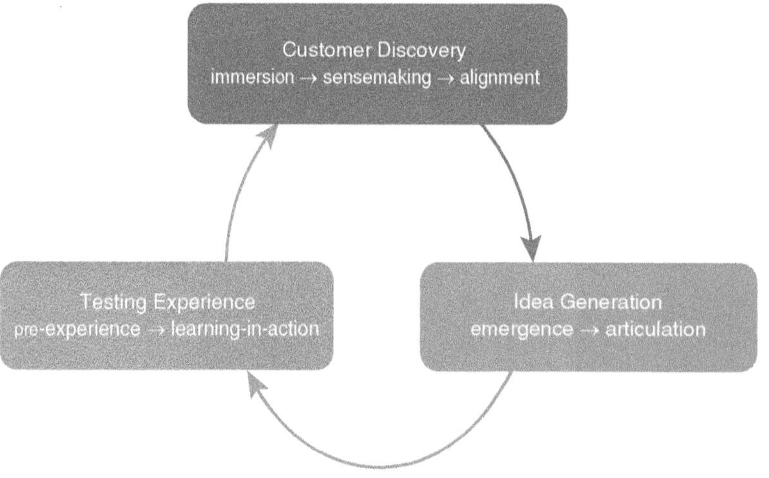

Figure 8.3 Design Thinking

Source: adapted from Liedtka (2018)

Design for the Environment

Design for the Environment (DfE) represents a set of processes and procedures for new product design that ensures that environmental considerations are emphasized at each step of the product's life: from selecting the raw materials, to manufacturing and distribution processes, to product use and reuse. The point is to bake environmental considerations into each step of the new product development process (Allenby 1994). It requires the R&D team to anticipate how the product will be distributed, used, and discarded by consumers. The design team could, for example, design components that are easy to dissemble so they can later be replaced or recycled. The team could include components with a high percentage of recycled content or that are free of harmful chemicals. Further, the design team could select components that were made not from composite plastics (a combination of several types of plastics that are almost impossible to recycle), but from single-type plastics, such as PET, which are easy-to-recycle.

Herman Miller is a US-based manufacturer of high-end office furniture and was founded on principles of artistic design, exceptional functionality, and environmental sustainability. In 2001, Herman Miller became a very early adopter of DfE processes, which it has used to help design a variety of new products, including its award-winning Mirra Chair. Not only is this ergonomically-designed chair incredibly comfortable, over 94% of the chair can be recycled, 50% of it is built with recycled materials (including 28.5% post-consumer recycled content), and the chair can easily be disassembled at the end of its life for recycling (Herman Miller 2020) (see Photo 8.3).

Photo 8.3 The Herman Miller Mirra® 2 Chair

Source: courtesy, Herman Miller

Sustainability-Related Products

Greenwashing is a frequently-used marketing communications technique that overemphasizes a product's sustainability credentials. Greenwashing is deceptive; it misleads consumers into thinking that the product or the organization is sustainable when it is not. One study found that greenwashing was rampant, especially in the online environment. In examining several hundred "seemingly dubious" online stores, EU authorities concluded that 42% were likely false and deceptive under EU law. Moreover, greater than 50% of the online stores failed to provide consumers with adequate information about the environmental attributes of the product (Abnett 2021). With the proliferation of greenwashing, it is no wonder that consumers are skeptical. Table 8.2 describes some commonly-used greenwashing terms.

Table 8.2 Misleading terms often found on sustainability-related products

Misleading Term	Problem	Preferred Term
Recyclable	Labels that claim a product is recyclable often fail to mention that many local and municipal recycling systems do not offer recycling for that particular type of material. If a consumer cannot recycle the item with curbside recycling, the item ends up in a landfill.	*XX% post-consumer recycled content* indicates that the material was already used by a consumer, has been added back into the manufacturing process, and has found a second life as a new product. *XX% pre-consumer recycled content* means that the materials have been gathered up from manufacturing waste and, instead of going to a landfill, have been put back into the manufacturing system.
Eco-friendly, natural, or green	These vague terms provide no guidance or standard of comparison.	*Organic*, *Fairtrade*, and other certifications indicate that the product or ingredient has been raised, processed, and certified according to strict standards.
Net zero or carbon neutral	These terms are often associated with new projects or initiatives, such as building a new manufacturing facility or launching a new product line. Unfortunately, they allow for some amount of CO_2 and other greenhouse gas emissions, as long as those emissions are compensated for with other carbon-reduction projects, such as planting trees.	While it is not the perfect solution, *carbon negative* indicates that the amount of greenhouse gasses emitted by an initiative will be *more than* compensated for by projects such as planting trees. A far preferable solution, however, is to institute severe cutbacks on total CO_2 emissions. This can be measured and tracked over time with a *carbon footprint*.

Photo 8.4 H2 Green Steel will be produced without fossil fuels

Source: Pixabay

The case of "Green Steel" illustrates the importance of using precise terms when describing a sustainability-related product or service. Headquartered in Sweden, H2 Green Steel made international headlines in 2021 when it announced that it would start producing fossil-free, high-quality steel in 2030. According to some estimates, 75% of the energy for steel production comes from coal, giving the steel industry the dubious distinction of being the largest industrial consumer of coal. Steel production is responsible for more CO_2 emissions than the combined emissions of cement and chemical production. At first, observers were skeptical of H2 Green Steel's ambitious claims. After all, just the name of the company should be reason enough to raise some suspicions. However, a careful investigation of its product claims indicates that H2 Green Steel's products are very likely legitimate. First, the steel will be produced using a "fossil-free manufacturing process" that uses hydrogen energy. In most cases, hydrogen comes from fossil fuels, specifically, natural gas. However, H2 Green Steel plans to use hydrogen that has been created by electrolysis, which occurs when an electric current in water splits H_2O molecules into hydrogen and oxygen. It also plans to use electricity that is generated from wind and solar sources. Second, Green Steel has partnered with several European manufacturers of furniture, automobiles, appliances, and other industrial products. These organizations plan to use the steel to help meet their own sustainability goals. Production will begin in 2024; by 2030, the company expects to produce 5 million tons of steel per year (Frangoul 2021) (see Photo 8.4).

Life Cycle Assessment

Also called the Life Cycle Analysis, the **Life Cycle Assessment (LCA)** is a decision-making tool that assesses the environmental impact at each step of the product's life, from extraction of raw materials all the way through to the end of the product's life. The LCA allows the marketing team to better identify where environmental impacts occur so that they can better address them. It involves four phases, as outlined in Figure 8.4 (Belz and Peattie 2012). Global food giant Nestlé has been at the forefront of utilizing LCA to assess the environmental impact of its products. When its Nespresso division launched the Citiz espresso machine, decision-makers conducted an LCA. The Citiz was designed to allow users to make a hot, fresh cup of espresso at home, using single-use pods. The machine was elegantly designed and provided a high-quality cup of espresso. Unlike the competition, who supplied pods that were made of plastic and almost impossible to recycle, these Nespresso pods were made of aluminum and were 100% recyclable (see Photo 8.5).

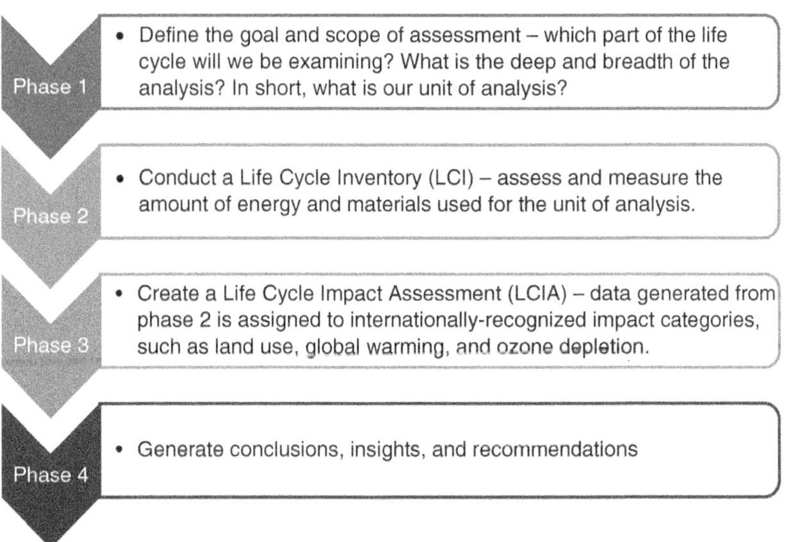

Figure 8.4 The Life Cycle Assessment process

Source: adapted from Belz and Peattie (2012)

Photo 8.5 The Nespresso Citiz coffee maker by Nestlé

Source: iStockphoto

In phase 1, Nestlé defined the scope as greenhouse gas emissions that were specifically related to the production of the machine and coffee pods, from sourcing and production of raw materials, through consumer in-home use and recycling of the pods. Nestlé selected to not investigate the impacts that occurred during product or pod disposal. In phase 2, the organization measured a variety of impacts, including water usage, amount of energy used, type of energy utilized, and materials used. In phase 3, these measurements were distilled down and converted into estimates for impacts on greenhouse gas emissions, specifically CO_2 emissions. Finally, in phase 4, the final report was created and recommendations for actionable steps were provided (see Table 8.3). After receiving the final report in phase 4, Nestlé decision-makers could easily identify areas that needed their immediate attention. Because 33% of all CO_2 emissions could be attributed there, Nestlé's first initiatives focused on helping local growers and processors find better ways to reduce the impact of cultivation and processing. Nestlé installed drip-irrigation systems for growers and modernized their roasting machines to enable better quality roasting of the coffee beans, with much lower CO_2 emissions. Nestlé decision-makers were shocked to discover that 21% of all CO_2 emissions could be attributed to in-home use. Upon closer investigation, product designers found that they could reduce that proportion significantly. In the second edition of the Citiz machine, designers added two new features to reduce the machine's electricity consumption: an automatic shut-off feature and an insulated water tank.

Table 8.3 Results from Nestlé's Life Cycle Assessment

Life Cycle Assessment for the Citiz Machine	Percentage of CO_2 Emissions*
Cultivation and processing – the growing, harvesting, cleaning, and roasting of coffee beans.	33%
Pods and packaging – the production of aluminum, production of coffee pods, and packaging	24%
Distribution via land and sea – the movement of raw materials through the supply chain and the movement of the finished product through the distribution channel to the consumer	8%
Machine production – the manufacturing of the Citiz machine	8%
Consumer in-home use – the amount and type of electricity used to power the machine and keep the water tank hot	21%
Pod disposal – the processes involved in recycling or disposing of the espresso pods	6%

*These numbers are estimates and should be used for discussion and illustration purposes only.

8.5 PRODUCT-RELATED OBJECTIVES AND STRATEGY

For each dimension of the marketing mix, the team must create a set of objectives, strategies, and tactics (see Figure 8.5).

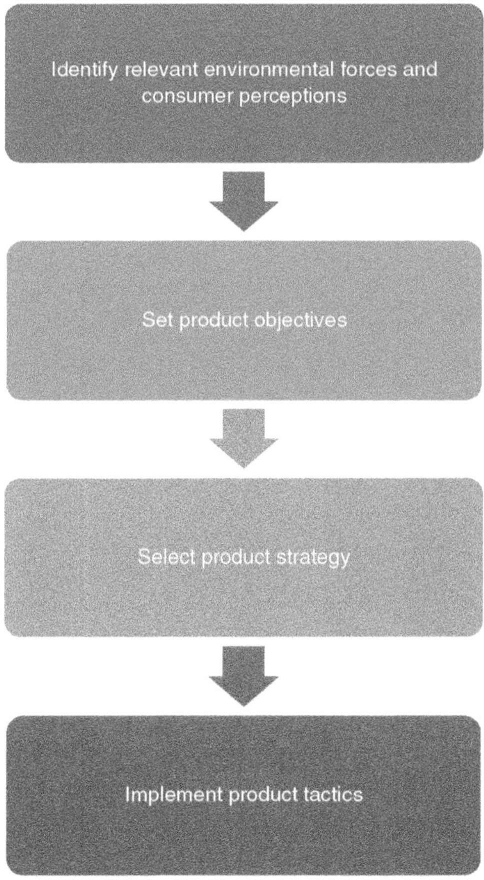

Figure 8.5 Product-related objectives, strategy, and tactics

Before the marketing team can launch a set of product strategies, it must first create a coherent set of **product-related objectives**: the overall goals that need to be achieved for the product. Product objectives need to be competitive in nature; they should address the essential question of how the product can help the organization achieve a competitive advantage in the marketplace. An indispensable tool for helping the marketing team identify a strategic direction for its product or product line is the **Ansoff Growth Matrix** (or the Product/Market Growth Matrix), which suggests four possible product-related growth objectives (see Figure 8.6). This two-dimensional matrix places products (existing or new) on one dimension and markets (existing or new) on the other dimension, resulting in four possible product-related objectives. The first option represents the lowest risk for the marketing team: **market penetration**. If the marketing team selects this product objective, it will attempt to sell more of an existing product to an existing market. The goal is to have customers buy more frequently or in greater quantities.

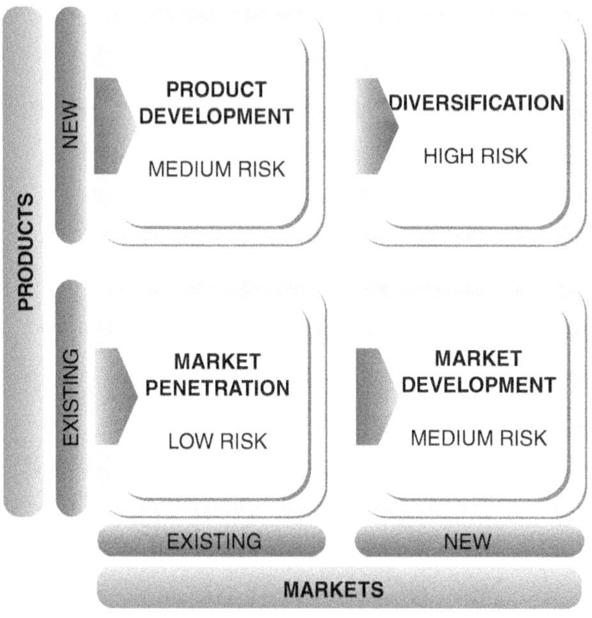

Figure 8.6 The Ansoff Growth Matrix

Source: Shutterstock

The next two objectives represent moderate risk to the organization. **Product development** is an objective in which a new product is introduced to an existing market, while **market development** involves the introduction of an existing product into a new market. According to the matrix, the last option represents the highest level of risk: **diversification**. Here, a new product is introduced to a new market. Although there are many other product-related objectives that the team could create, the Ansoff Growth Matrix offers four possibilities that specifically focus on product and market growth (Ansoff 1957).

Another possibility for generating objectives is to consider the product from the perspective of the problem that the product is designed to address in the consumer's life. In this case, there are two possibilities. Both of these perspectives necessitate a clear and comprehensive understanding of how the product fits into the consumer's life; in what way does this product make the consumer's life better, healthier, happier, more efficient, or more fulfilling? The first possibility for a product-related objective using this perspective is to address the same problem for the consumer, but use different products to do so. Here, the goal is to provide greater interest and variety for the consumer. The second possibility is for the organization to use the same product to address different problems for different customers. Here, the goal is to more fully utilize the existing product (see Figure 8.7) (Christensen, Cook, and Hall 2005). Regardless of where the marketing team finds inspiration for the creation of its product-related objectives, in order to provide the most precise guidance for the marketing team, the product-related objectives should follow the SMART format (specific, measurable, attainable, realistic, and time-bound).

After product objectives, the next step is to develop a **product strategy**, which involves a keen consideration of internal and external forces on the consumer, competitors, and the company's own operations to identify new ways to create and deliver the value proposition to the target market, or even to a new target market. Successful product strategy needs to be based on an organizational structure that is flexible and fast enough to respond to challenges as well as opportunities in the market. In addition, product strategists look internally to see what can be changed, adapted, or scaled to better deliver the value proposition. For example, the organization might forge a partnership with a new stakeholder because there is a recognition that the new partner has capabilities that the company cannot easily develop on its own.

Product management involves a set of deliberate actions that are taken to manage the organization's portfolio of products. Many of the decisions here are tactical in nature and concern specific decisions about product branding, packaging, product lines, and the product mix. Understanding the difference between product lines and the product mix is an important first step in product management. A **product line** is a group of related products that exist under one brand name. An example would be Pepsi and the various products in this product line, including

Pepsi, Diet Pepsi, Caffeine-free Pepsi, and Pepsi Wild Cherry. Every product in a product line has the same brand name and fulfills a similar need or want for the consumer, in this case, a cold, fizzy, cola-tasting drink. In examining car service Uber, it is clear that the organization excels in product strategy by having a very well-developed product line. Uber has been very aggressive about offering a strong value proposition to riders with its basic UberX service, but has also added other services such as UberXL for bigger cars, UberSUV for those individuals who prefer the ride of a sports utility vehicle, UberBLACK for luxury vehicles, UberPOOL for riders who would like to save some money by carpooling, and UberWAV for individuals who need a wheelchair-accessible vehicle. Uber has also expanded its footprint into other areas of the transportation sector: UberTAXI allows users to use the Uber app to hail a taxi, the UberFreight service ships freight for businesses, and UberEats delivers hot, fresh food to consumers (see Photo 8.6).

Same problem/ different products	Different problems/ same product
Creates new products to solve existing consumer problems; provides interest/variety. Example: Starbucks offers a wide variety of hot and cold coffees and seasonal flavors. They all address the same problem: the need for an interesting/creative caffeine delivery system	Leverages a well-known and respected brand name to solve different problems for different consumers. Example: Marriott hotels offer amenities for business travelers (conference rooms, business services), families (complementary breakfasts, pools), and extended-stay guests (in-room kitchen facilities, laundry services).

Figure 8.7 Consumer-focused product-related objectives

Source: adapted, in part, from Christensen, et al. 2005

Photo 8.6 Uber's product strategy has found many new ways to deliver value to customers

Source: Pixabay

A **product mix** is an organization's collection of product lines. French cosmetics company L'Oréal, for example, has four distinct product lines. The first is active cosmetics that are designed by dermatologists and researchers to address specific skincare needs like acne or dry skin. This product line includes brands such as CeraVe, La Roche Posay, Vichy, and SkinCeuticals. The second line is consumer products, which seeks to "democratize" beauty by offering top-performing and sustainable products at a reasonable price. Brands include Maybelline, Garnier, and Dark and Lovely. The third is L'Oréal Luxe, which is a line of skincare and beauty products that are micro-targeted to very narrowly-defined target markets that seek very specific benefits from their products. Brands include Lancôme, Kiehl's, Ralph Lauren, Diesel, Giorgio Armani, and Urban Decay. L'Oréal's fourth product line is focused on professionals who work in skincare and beauty, such as stylists, spa technicians, and make-up artists. Brands include Matrix, Redken, and Pureology (Our Global Brands Portfolio 2022).

The following sections will discuss several product-management strategies and tools, including new product innovation, branding, and market entry strategies.

New Product Innovation

New product innovation is necessary to consistently deliver the value proposition and to keep the competition at bay. Staying still is not an option.

ENDURING INSIGHTS 8.1

> "In the long history of humankind, those who learned to collaborate and improvise most effectively have prevailed." – Charles Darwin

Darwin, an English naturalist and biologist, is best known for his 1859 book entitled, *On the Origin of Species*, where he introduced his theory of evolution, which states that only the strongest and most able to adapt will survive. These principles can be applied to marketing strategy too – organizations that are able to collaborate and adapt to the changing dynamics of the market will have a competitive advantage over those that do not.

Types of Innovations

Not every new innovation is created equal. The degree to which a new product is innovative depends on the extent to which the consumer must learn and enact new consumption-related behaviors. A **continuous innovation** is simply a modification to an existing product and does not require extensive learning from the consumer. Think about the new updates for your phone or computer. It might take a few minutes to review some new features, but the updates are generally quite intuitive and easy to navigate. A **dynamically continuous innovation** is a pronounced modification to an existing product and requires a modest amount of learning. One example is a new category of kitchen appliances that changes the way consumers cook and prepare food, such as Suvie, a counter-top appliance that can both refrigerate and cook a meal. Another example would be AI-based holographic personal assistants. To qualify as a **discontinuous innovation**, the product must create major changes in the way people live. Consumers must engage in extensive learning and behavior change. The advent of driverless cars will most certainly require a significant amount of new learning and behavior as "drivers" learn about new programming and safety features.

BLUNDERS & INSIGHTS 8.2

It's Just a Cup of Coffee, Right?

BACKGROUND: In the late 1980s, two coffee aficionados began their quest to create a coffee maker that would reliably make a great-tasting, single cup of coffee. Research indicated that a significant market existed for such a product. The result was a coffeemaker and coffee pods that brewed an on-demand hot cup of coffee in a variety of flavors. Although the pods ("k-cups") were somewhat expensive, the Keurig coffeemaker gave consumers a choice of different flavors, while saving time, water, and coffee. Problems started to arise, however, when consumers found that the k-cups were difficult, if not impossible, to recycle (Evans 2015). One estimate found that if all the world's discarded k-cups for just 1 year were lined up, it would be enough to wrap around the planet ten times. For years, the company spoke about its commitment to a more sustainable k-cup design that could be recycled, and its original inventor has been very public in voicing his regret about the invention (Evans 2015). With complaints about product quality, concerns about environmental impact, and additional competition, Keurig's control of the market dropped to 23% by 2018, down from 40% in 2013. By 2018, through a series of acquisitions and mergers, Keurig settled under the umbrella of European investment fund JAB Holding (Lombardo and Turner 2018). After the reorganization, Keurig instituted a series of changes to the ubiquitous k-cup. First, it switched the plastic in the k-cup to #5 polypropelyne, which made it much more likely to be accepted at municipal recycling facilities. In fact, 90% of k-cups could be recycled this way. Second, it added labeling and instructions on how to recycle the k-cups. For transparency, consumers were urged to check with their local recycling authorities to confirm that the k-cups could be recycled (Keurig 2021).

DEBRIEF: Keurig machines offer a compelling value proposition: a quick, easy, and convenient cup of coffee in a variety of flavors. Unfortunately, for some consumers, difficult-to-recycle k-cups add a negative dimension to that pleasure of consumption. For years, product managers at Keurig missed an important opportunity to address the issue; even after the reorganization, the solution is still imperfect.

Diffusion of Innovations

Product adoption is the process by which an individual consumer or business customer begins to buy and use a new good, service, or idea. **Diffusion** is the process by which the use of a product or innovation spreads throughout a population. The **Diffusion of Innovation model** describes a process by which a new innovation is adopted by the target market over time. The way in which a new innovation is spread throughout a social system is strongly dependent upon the concept of **social contagion**, a theory in psychology that describes the spread of perceptions, attitudes, emotions, and behaviors throughout a social system. Social contagion is strongly influenced by the strength of ties that individuals have with one another, as well as the extent to which individuals feel compelled to go along with the forces in their social networks. With respect to Diffusion of Innovation, consumers are divided into five different categories, depending on when they adopt a new innovation (Rogers 1995) (see Figure 8.8):

- **Innovators** make up 2.5% of the target market's population. These consumers are comfortable with risk and uncertainty; they are daring, venturesome, and often cosmopolitan. These consumers are the gatekeepers for a new innovation's entry and acceptance into a market.
- **Early Adopters** comprise 13.5% of the target market's population and are somewhat more socially integrated into their social networks, where they often behave as opinion leaders within their groups. Early adopters are respected within their social network and, to maintain that status, make careful decisions and recommendations.
- **Early Majority** consumers are 34% of the population. These individuals frequently interact with their social networks, but are unlikely to take on a leadership role. They are very deliberate in their decision-making.
- **Late Majority** make up 34% of the population and are quite cautious and somewhat distrustful. Although they may be convinced of the benefits of a new innovation, they will likely not adopt until they experience social pressure to do so.
- **Laggards** are the last consumers to adopt an innovation and comprise 16% of the target market population. These individuals are very traditional, cautious, and somewhat suspicious of innovations and change.

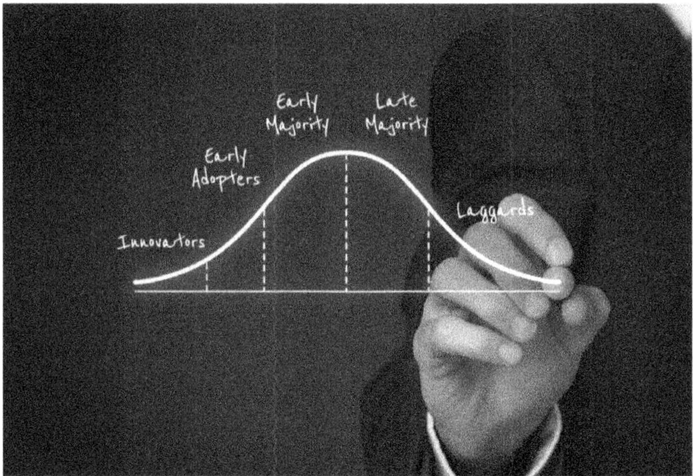

Figure 8.8 The Diffusion of Innovations model

Source: Jirsak/Shutterstock

ENDURING INSIGHTS 8.2

> "It is all very well to have a great many good ideas but if you can't say them so that any child of five can understand them, you might just as well not have them." – Eleanor Roosevelt

Roosevelt was the former first lady of the United States and became the country's first delegate to the United Nations. This quote underscores the importance of effective communication in social contagion. If the message does not clearly and simply describe how the new innovation can play a role in the consumer's life, the marketing team will certainly have an uphill battle in getting the innovation to diffuse throughout the population.

For dynamically continuous and discontinuous innovations, where consumers are required to learn new behaviors, an interesting thing happens when the adoption curve transitions from increasing at an increasing rate, to increasing at a decreasing rate. Here, visionaries (innovators and early adopters) have already adopted the product, but the more pragmatic early majority has not yet done so. Some experts have referred to this as **crossing the chasm** while others call it a tipping point. Why is this point so critical? Once the rate of adoption is able to successfully cross the chasm, the product has a much better chance at success because it has moved into the mainstream market and is gaining market share. In essence, the product has turned from a fad into a trend. In order to successfully cross the chasm, marketers should be forward thinking in their approach to product development and market entry such that, by the time the product is on the precipice of the chasm, the marketing strategy can be altered as follows (Moore 2014):

- *Product-related strategy*: develop the "whole product," with a complete set of features, options for service, warranties, and any other add-ons. Any defects should be eliminated and any concerns about product quality should be addressed.
- *Price-related strategy*: price the product relative to the competition, rather than using other pricing strategies, such as value-based, skimming, or penetration strategies.
- *Promotion-related strategy*: position the product to appeal to the skeptical pragmatists who make up the early majority. Appeal to the desire of these consumers to see proof of concept as well as proof that other consumers have successfully adopted the product. Third-party certifications and transparent communications will assist in these efforts.
- *Place-related strategy*: distribute the product widely through the right channels to make it easy for consumers in the mainstream market to access the product. Optimally, promotional efforts will create enough excitement and demand that channels will be compelled to carry it.

Branding and Brand Management

A **brand** is a combination of symbols and meanings associated with the organization's value proposition. It includes a unique name, symbol, or mark that identifies the product so that consumers know exactly what they are getting when they purchase the product. In effect, a brand is a promise to consumers – if you consume this brand, you will receive a set of benefits. Consumers will know that, regardless of where in the world they may happen to be, if they go to KFC, the experience will be the same: hot and tasty chicken, clean dining room, and friendly service. The same is true with other brands. From the consumer's perspective, well-known and respected brands reduce uncertainty by communicating exactly what a consumer should expect from consuming the brand. **Brand equity** is the value of the brand, over and above that of a generic version of the product. Brand equity is the reason why consumers pay more for a Coca-Cola, as opposed to a no-name fizzy cola drink; it's the reason why consumers pay more for a pair of Nike shoes, as opposed to a no-name pair of running shoes. What does the Coca-Cola consumer get that a generic cola drinker does not get from consumption? The consumer of Coca-Cola can trust that the drink will be sweet, fizzy, refreshing, and satisfying. It will taste the same, regardless of where in the world it is consumed. Consumers of Nike shoes can be confident in the performance and fit of their Nikes. Brands with high brand equity can charge higher prices, and often enjoy a high level of customer loyalty and market share. In 2021, the most valuable global brands were Amazon, Apple, and Google (see Table 8.4).

Table 8.4 The top 10 most valuable global brands

2021 Rank	Brand	Brand Value in $ millions (USD)	% Increase from 2020
1	Amazon	638,852	64
2	Apple	611,997	74
3	Google	457,998	42
4	Microsoft	410,271	26
5	Tencent	240,931	60
6	Facebook	226,744	54
7	Alibaba	196,912	29
8	Visa	191,285	2
9	McDonald's	154,921	20
10	MasterCard	112,876	4

Source: courtesy, Kantar BrandZ

An **iconic brand** is one that connects the meanings associated with the brand to important cultural values and a person's cultural identity. One example of an iconic brand is Lego, the ubiquitous plastic building blocks. In 2021, Lego was worth $9.082 billion, up from $5.362 billion in 2015 (Tighe 2022). Headquartered in Denmark, Lego is the world's most popular toymaker. In 2021, Lego's impressive sales results caught even the most cynical observers by surprise. Revenues surged by 46% and net profit hit an astounding 140% increase from the previous year. These earnings were 10 times that of its next closest competitor, Hasbro. From 2017 through 2021, Lego grew at twice the pace of the rest of the toy market. One reason for these results can be attributed to the boredom many consumers experienced as a result of the Covid-19 lockdowns. However, the growth can also be credited to Lego's long-term strategy to make its product accessible to more consumers with investments in new product lines (such as digital building sets) and the opening of brick-and-mortar stores, several of which offer very hands-on immersive experiences (Milne 2021). The most successful iconic brands revolve around an existing tension between the consumer's experience and the prevailing cultural message (Holt 2003). In our fast-paced, high- achievement world, Lego says its ok to play. No other construction toy or puzzle quite stacks up (see Photo 8.7).

Photo 8.7 The Lego brand has strong brand equity

Source: Pixabay

ENDURING INSIGHTS 8.3

"It's become my brand in a way, you know, speaking the truth even though it was not politically correct." – Christine Lagarde

The managing director of the International Monetary Fund and later, the president of the European Central Bank, Lagarde was the first woman to hold these positions. This quote indicates that Lagarde understands her brand as a blunt, tough, and honest leader. The "promise" of this brand is that she can always be counted on to be forthright. Forbes ranks Lagarde as the third most powerful woman in the world (Forbes and McGrath 2021).

Building Brand Identity

An important part of the brand is the **brand identity**, which constitutes the more "tangible" elements of the brand, such as the brand logo, name, symbols, shape colors, font, unique descriptions, or anything else unique and identifying. One part of the brand identity is a **Unique Selling Proposition (USP)**, a product benefit that is different from what the competition can provide. Before selecting these elements, brand managers need to understand how consumers will interpret them (Zaichkowsky 2010). There are five criteria for creating a distinctive and relevant brand identity (see Table 8.5).

Table 8.5 Five criteria for a compelling brand identity

Creating the Brand Identity	Examples
1. Brand names should be unique in sound, spelling, pronunciation, and meaning.	When marketers selected the name Exxon for the global oil giant, they made sure that, across the 50 most frequently-spoken global languages, the name had no pre-existing meanings.
2. The font should be congruent with the image the brand wishes to convey.	Script fonts are interpreted as feminine and elegant; bold fonts are interpreted as strong.
3. The selection of colors should be consistent throughout all of the marketing communications, but should also be congruent with the brand meanings.	Colors are interpreted differently in different cultures. For example, red is generally associated with hunger, but also excitement and passion. In China, brides wear red wedding dresses.
4. If relevant to the brand message, utilize unique shapes for the products or packaging.	Examples include the Pringles potato crisp can or the distinctively-curved Coca-Cola bottle.
5. Create USPs that clearly offer a product benefit that is important to the consumer and different from what the competition can offer.	Apple products offer the benefit of easily syncing with other Apple products. No other competitor offers a process that is as quick and intuitive.

Source: adapted from Zaichkowsky (2010)

Having a strong and compelling brand identity delivers at least two distinct benefits to the organization. First, the organization can charge a higher price for the brand because consumers perceive it to be of greater value. Second, consumers are less likely to engage in detailed comparisons between alternative brands; the promise of the brand is enough (Zaichkowsky 2010). A unique form of brand identity is the organization's identity. Here, the organization is the brand. An **organizational brand identity** is about an underlying truth and authenticity. It reveals a genuine set of values by which the organization is driven. Organizational brand identity is constant over the long term. It provides the reason for the company's existence, its truth, and its values. From the target audience's perspective (employees, customers, other stakeholders), it should be believable and relevant. For organizations that have a strong and compelling organizational brand identity, the quality and performance of their products – perhaps hardworking, durable, trustworthy, authentic – is evidence of the company's value system. If carefully managed, brand identity can be a strategic lever for growth (Kapferer 2002).

One way for a product or organizational brand to demonstrate its authenticity is by providing proof of its claims with independent third-party certifications. There are a multitude of different third-party certifications that will provide independent, unbiased assessments of a brand's claims. Layering these independent third-party certifications on brands adds credibility and value. One example is organic certification, a promise that the product was produced and processed without synthetic pesticides, herbicides, or fungicides. In addition, no GMOs were used (see Photo 8.8). As another example, Marine Stewardship Council (MSC) certification ensures that wild seafood was caught in a humane way and did not use methods that harmed other sea life, such as corals or turtles (see Photo 8.9). Third party certifications add value to the brand, in part, because consumers can be confident in the brand's claims.

Photo 8.8 The EU's organic certification logo

Source: Shutterstock/Photo_Pix

Photo 8.9 The MSC certification logo

Source: Shutterstock

Brand Management

The purpose of **brand management** is to increase brand equity. It needs to take into account the needs of the target market, predictions about how markets may shift or how trends may change over time, and the competition. While managing its brands, the marketing team will enact a series of strategies and tactics focused specifically on brand recognition, brand loyalty, and brand building. These items work to further enhance and strengthen the brand's equity.

Brand recognition is the process of selecting the symbols, colors, logos, and other factors that clearly identify your organization's brand as unique from all others. Think about the unique sound that accompanies the appearance of the Netflix logo when you open a streaming device, the shape of the Nike swoosh symbol, or the selection of bright colors that comprise the Google logo. Marketers carefully select these items such that the brand is immediately recognizable to consumers. Brand logos and other identifying markers change over time to ensure that they remain relevant and recognizable with the target market. Importantly, marketers must ensure that the identifying markers they select are protected and trademarked so they cannot be imitated (see Photo 8.10).

Photo 8.10 The unique color combination in Google's logo is an important part of its brand recognition

Source: Pixabay

Brand loyalty is the consumer's preference for purchasing one brand over another. It is important to distinguish two different types of loyalty: purchase loyalty and attitudinal loyalty. **Purchase loyalty** describes the repeated purchase of the same brand. Often, this is done out of habit, as when a consumer stops at the same coffee shop each afternoon for a shot of caffeine. **Attitudinal loyalty** describes a preference for the brand that is based on the consumer perception that the brand offers unique value. For whatever reason, consumers just like the brand. The marketing implications of the differences between these two types of loyalty are significant. Purchase loyalty leads to higher levels of market share, while attitudinal loyalty leads to a higher willingness of consumers to pay more money for the brand (Chaudhuri and Holbrook 2001). This is valuable information that the marketing team can utilize to create insights to further strengthen and grow brand equity.

Brand building is one more brand-management issue for the team to consider as it works to enhance brand equity. Brand building involves strengthening the brand competitively over the long term by expanding and growing the brand. The Ansoff Matrix discussed earlier in this chapter provides four separate avenues for expansion and growth for products and can be used for brands too (refer again to Figure 8.6). With brand building, the focus is long-term and the goal is to make the brand a stronger force against the competition.

Market Entry Strategies

If the objectives call for it, the brand may need to expand into new markets where it will likely encounter a host of soon-to-be competitors. **Barriers to entry** are obstacles that have been set up by the market's existing competitors or are a natural consequence of how the market operates. Regardless of how they were erected, however, barriers to entry make it very difficult for new entrants. There are seven different types of barriers to entry (see Table 8.6).

Table 8.6 Barriers to market entry

Barrier to Market Entry	Description	Consequence
1. Supply-side economies of scale	These economies of scale result from large-scale production that reduces the per-unit cost of manufacturing the product.	New market entrants must enter the market ready to either engage in large-scale production or accept smaller margins.
2. Demand-side benefits of scale	Existing competitors benefit from the fact that they are well-known and respected in the market by customers and other stakeholders.	New market entrants need to work to convince customers to switch to a new and unknown provider.
3. Customer switching costs	Customers will be reluctant to switch to a new entrant's offerings because of the high costs involved in refitting new products and/or learning new skills.	New market entrants need to convince potential customers that the benefits of switching outweigh the costs.
4. Capital requirements	Huge capital investments are often required to construct facilities, establish distribution and warehousing systems, and secure financial capital and credit.	New market entrants must carefully assess the new market's capital requirements, find creative ways to secure new capital, or even reduce the capital requirement.
5. Incumbency advantages	Regardless of size, the existing incumbents often have cost and/or quality advantages from their experience within the marketplace.	New entrants can attempt to bypass such advantages with creative use of the elements of the marketing mix.
6. Unequal access to distribution channels	Well-established distribution channels often have little capacity or incentive to make room for new entrants.	New entrants must break into the existing distribution channels or create their own, such as direct-to-consumer options.
7. Restrictive government policies	Governments can make market entry very difficult for new entrants with complicated and expensive licensing and certification requirements.	New entrants must hire experts to help the organization navigate these complicated and expensive processes.

Source: adapted, in part, from Porter (2008)

Special care must be taken in selecting the product's market entry strategy. Too often, organizations contemplating market entry rush to market too quickly. Consequently, they falter and then lose out to the second or third market entrants. Often, this occurs because the strategic commitments that are made by the too-anxious first organization make it very difficult to pivot to a new strategy – these organizations have already committed to a distribution system or production process, for example, and are not nimble or flexible enough to address any shifts in market dynamics (Gans, Scott, and Stern 2018). Perhaps the most important lesson when contemplating the possibility of entering a new market with a strong and firmly-entrenched incumbent is to not wage a frontal assault. The incumbent can quickly and decisively counterattack, causing significant losses. Instead, there are three possibilities that can be used to successfully gain a foothold (Bryce and Dyer 2007):

- *Leverage existing assets* – to overcome barriers to entry, organizations can rely on their own strengths or they can form a partnership with another organization that has a particular strength the firm is lacking. For example, a company might utilize shelf space it already controls to introduce a new product to the market, as when a retailer provides shelf space for its own store brand. An organization might also utilize any idle production capacity to produce a new product.
- *Reconfigure value chains* – organizations can alter or adapt the distribution channel to more effectively deliver value to consumers. For example, the organization could distribute its product through different types of retailers or establish a direct-to-consumer salesforce. Netflix is infamous for reconfiguring the entertainment value chain.
- *Establish niches* – organizations can identify and target a smaller niche segment of consumers within the overall market. For example, Red Bull never tried to go head-to-head with the two giants in the industry, Pepsi and Coca-Cola. Instead, it targeted a different group of consumers: people who wanted a quick caffeine buzz. Red Bull sold the product in tall, thin cans so that more product could be stacked on store shelves. It also promoted the product in bars where it could be consumed straight or mixed with alcohol.

The marketing team does not need to select just one of these strategies. Indeed, it can deploy these strategies sequentially or simultaneously. In fact, the combination of several of these strategies may be quite powerful (Bryce and Dyer 2007).

ENDURING INSIGHTS 8.4

> "Avoid a frontal attack on a long-established position; instead, seek to turn it by flank movement, so that a more penetrable side is exposed to the thrust of truth." – B.H. Liddell Hart, WWI British soldier and military historian

This quote illustrates the importance of identifying a weak space in the market that can be leveraged by the new market entrant to gain a foothold. Importantly, this quote suggests that it might be especially advantageous to *distract* the attention of the incumbent in order to expose an undefended space in the market.

When entering new markets that happen to reside outside a domestic market or common market, there are four different options for the marketing team. As we proceed through the list of options, the level of commitment to the market and risk increase. The first two options require a very limited commitment of financial capital, whereas the last two options require significant capital investment (see Figure 8.9). Following are the four options (Pan and Tse 2000):

- *Export* – the market can be entered by exporting to the target market. An export merchant will receive the delivery of products and arrange for delivery to retail outlets or directly to consumers.
- *Contractual agreements* – the market is entered by forging a contractual agreement with a stakeholder. One type of contractual agreement, a license, conveys the rights to a proprietary process, the brand identity, operations, and other brand or product-specific materials and procedures.
- *Joint ventures* – the market is entered by forging a partnership with another entity that already has a presence in the new market. The new entrant invests its own expertise, financial capital, and even personnel in the effort.
- *Direct investment* – the market is entered by the new entrant committing a very significant investment in the new market. The new entrant is likely to acquire or build office space as well as production facilities, distribution channels, or warehouse space.

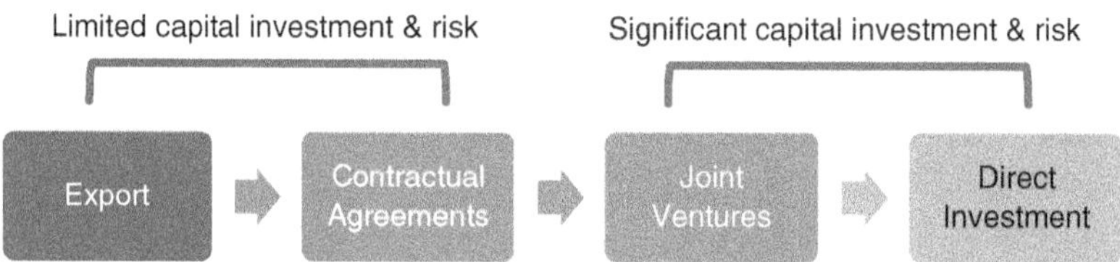

Figure 8.9 Market entry strategies for markets residing outside a domestic market or a common market

Source: Pan and Tse (2000)

8.6 PRODUCT TACTICS

After establishing the organization's product-related objectives and strategies, the marketing team next needs to implement a variety of product-related tactics. **Product tactics** involve a variety of small-scale, focused decisions that help to achieve the organization's product strategies. Tactics might involve a wide variety of decisions, such as decisions about the product's packaging or warranties, as well as those about specific ingredients or raw materials to be used in the product. Global food manufacturers, for example, will regularly adjust product ingredients to stay current with shifts in consumer tastes and preferences. Tactical decisions must be flexible enough to respond to competitive moves.

8.7 SUMMARY

This chapter started with two examples of how product strategies were utilized in two very different contexts: tourism and fast food. In both examples, product strategies were utilized to differentiate the product in the minds of consumers and deliver a value proposition that was relevant to the target market. Just as the overall marketing strategy starts with objectives, and then moves to strategy and tactics, the product strategy follows a similar path: objectives → strategy → tactics. To first create a foundational understanding of products, several key concepts relating to how products behave in the marketplace and new product development were explored. Perhaps the most important was the definition itself: a product is a collection of attributes, benefits, beliefs, emotions, and cultural meanings that deliver the value proposition. During the process of new product development, two concepts were introduced, design thinking and design for the environment. As concerns about the environment and sustainability increase, organizations will come under increasing scrutiny and pressure to adopt more sustainable operations and provide more sustainable products so that consumers can achieve their own sustainability goals. At the same time, they need to be especially careful not to engage in greenwashing. Often, third-party certifications help add additional value by adding credibility to an organization's sustainability claims. It is only with this foundational understanding that meaningful objectives can be created.

Product objectives are created using a variety of methods. The product/market growth matrix advocated by Ansoff and the consumer-focused product-related method were identified as two starting points for the creation of product objectives. Moving on to product strategy, we discussed several product-management concepts and emphasized the importance of effectively integrating all elements of the marketing mix to deliver the value proposition. An important consideration in product strategy is brand management, the purpose of which is to enhance and strengthen brand equity over time. It requires a deep and comprehensive understanding of the target market, predictions about how markets may shift or how trends may change over time, and an assessment of the competitive landscape. This can be accomplished by several different means, including a focus on brand recognition, brand loyalty, and brand building.

QUESTIONS FOR REVIEW & DISCUSSION

1 Why is it important for marketers to differentiate between product attributes and benefits? Imagine that you are thinking about taking a trip abroad with some friends and you have decided to visit the Fijian Islands. List five product attributes and the accompanying five benefits. Would a Fijian resort be more likely to promote its attributes or benefits in its promotional material? Why?

2 Sometimes, because of resource limitations, a marketing team needs to make the difficult decision to prioritize one SDG over another. Provide at least two examples of a product-related strategy that would result in two SDGs potentially being in conflict with one another. What would Nussbaum's capabilities approach suggest as an answer?

3 In what way does design thinking provide a customer-centric method of designing new products? Why is the model configured in a circle?

4 Why is it so important to start with a careful articulation of product objectives? For each of the two methods for generating objectives, create at least three different product-related objectives using the SMART format.

(Continued)

5 Explain how barriers to entry can hurt the ability for a new entrant to successfully enter the market. Which one might be the easiest for a new entrant to overcome? Which might be the most difficult? Explain in detail.
6 Why do we say that a brand is a promise? How do we determine when this promise is fulfilled?
7 In discussing market entry strategies, why do we say that it is important to not wage a frontal assault? Identify a company that has successfully entered a new market by adhering to this advice. Describe what happened. Did the company leverage existing assets, reconfigure value chains, and/or establish a niche? Describe in detail.

8.8 REFERENCES

Abnett, Kate. 2021. "Greenwashing" is Rampant in Online Stores, Authorities Find. *Reuters. Environment Section.* 28 January. Accessed 4 December 2021. www.reuters.com/article/us-eu-environment-greenwashing/greenwashing-is-rampant-in-online-stores-consumer-authorities-find-idUSKBN29X1Y6.

Allenby, Braden R. 1994. Integrating Environment and Technology: Design for Environment. *The Greening of Industrial Ecosystems,* Washington, DC: National Academy Press. 137–48.

Ansoff, H. Igor. 1957. Strategies for Diversification. *Harvard Business Review, 35* (5), Sept/Oct, 113–24.

Belz, Frank-Martin and Ken Peattie. 2012. *Sustainability Marketing: A Global Perspective,* 2nd edition. John Wiley & Sons, Ltd., Chichester, UK. 66–7.

Brown, Tim. 2008. Design Thinking. *Harvard Business Review, 86* (6), 84–92.

Bryce, David J. and Jeffrey H. Dyer. 2007. Strategies to Crack Well-Guarded Markets. *Harvard Business Review, 85* (5), 84–92.

Chaudhuri, Arjun and Morris B. Holbrook. 2001. The Chain of Effects from Brand Trust and Brand Affect to Brand Performance: The Role of Brand Loyalty. *Journal of Marketing, 65* (2), 81–93.

Christensen, Clayton M., Scott Cook, and Taddy Hall. 2005. Marketing Malpractice: The Cause and the Cure. *Harvard Business Review.* December. 74–83.

Clark, Christopher. 2019. South Africa Elections: "Born Frees" Call for Change: Young Generation Born After the End of Apartheid in 1994 Wants "Real Equality" in the Country. *Aljazeera.* 7 May. Accessed 1 December 2021. www.aljazeera.com/news/2019/5/7/south-africa-elections-born-frees-call-for-change.

Creed, Greg and Ken Muench. 2021. *RED Marketing: The Three Ingredients of Leading Brands.* HarperCollins Leadership, an imprint of HarperCollins, LLC, New York.

Evans, Pete. 2015. K-cup Creator John Sylvan Regrets Inventing Keurig Coffee Pod System. *CBC News.* 5 March. Accessed 9 December 2021. www.cbc.ca/news/business/k-cup-creator-john-sylvan-regrets-inventing-keurig-coffee-pod-system-1.2982660

Forbes, Moira and Maggie McGrath. 2021. The World's Most Powerful Women: 2021. *Forbes Media, LLC.* 7 December. Accessed 11 December 2021. www.forbes.com/power-women/#6f261cec5e25.

Frangoul, Anmar. 2021. Sweden Will Soon be Home to a Major Steel Factory Powered by the "World's Largest Green Hydrogen Plant." *CNBC.* Sustainability Energy Section. 25 February. Accessed 4 December 2021. www.cnbc.com/2021/02/25/steel-factory-to-be-powered-by-worlds-largest-green-hydrogen-plant.html.

Gans, Joshua, Erin L. Scott, and Scott Stern. 2018. Strategy for Start-ups. *Harvard Business Review, 96* (3), 44–51.

Herman Miller. 2020. Environmental Product Summary, EMEA: Mirra® 2 Chair. *Herman Miller*. June. Accessed 3 December 2021. www.hermanmiller.com/content/dam/hermanmiller/documents/environmental/eps/emea/mirra_2_chairs_eps_en-gb.pdf.

Holt, Douglas B. 2003. What Becomes an Icon Most? *Harvard Business Review, 81* (3), 43–49.

Kapferer, Jean-Noël. 2002. Corporate Brand and Organizational Identity. *Corporate and Organizational Identities*. Routledge, London. 175–93.

Kelso, Alicia. 2019. KFC is on Pace to At Least Double its Global Footprint. *Forbes.com*. 5 December. Accessed 28 November 2021. www.forbes.com/sites/aliciakelso/2019/12/05/kfc-is-on-pace-to-least-double-its-global-footprint/?sh=331cdf2553a7.

Keurig. 2021. Recycling is a Big Deal at Keurig. Keurig. Accessed 10 December 2021. www.keurig.com/recyclable.

Levitt, Theodore. 1965. EXPLOIT the Product Life Cycle. *Harvard Business Review, 43* (6), 81–94.

Liedtka, Jeanne. 2018. Why Design Thinking Works. *Harvard Business Review. The Magazine*. September/October. Accessed 1 December 2021. https://hbr.org/2018/09/why-design-thinking-works.

Lombardo, Cara and Zeke Turner. 2018. Keurig to Acquire Dr Pepper Snapple in Largest Soft-Drink Deal Ever. *Wall Street Journal*. Business Section. 29 January. Accessed 9 December 2021. www.wsj.com/articles/dr-pepper-snapple-to-merge-with-keurig-green-mountain-1517231161.

Milne, Richard. 2021. Lego Sales and Profits Surge to Record Highs. *Financial Times*. 28 September. Accessed 11 December 2021. www.ft.com/content/d2e845f1-1484-4745-8e3e-4995ee85f772.

Moore, Geoffrey A. 2014. *Crossing the Chasm: Marketing and Selling Disruptive Products to Mainstream Customers*, 3rd edition. HarperCollins Publishers, New York.

Our Global Brands Portfolio. 2022. Our 4 Divisions. *L'Oréal Groupe*. Accessed 19 June 2022. www.loreal.com/en/our-global-brands-portfolio/.

Pan, Yigang and David K. Tse. 2000. The Hierarchical Model of Market Entry Modes. *Journal of International Business Studies, 4th Quarter, 31* (4), 535–54.

Porter, Michael E. 2008. The Five Competitive Forces that Shape Strategy. *Harvard Business Review, 86* (1), 79–93.

Rogers, Everett M. 1995. *Diffusion of Innovations*, 4th edition. The Free Press of New York, a division of Simon & Schuster., Inc., New York.

Simon, Mallory. 2009. HP Looking into Claim Webcams Can't See Black People. *CNN*. 23 December. Accessed 29 November 2021. www.cnn.com/2009/TECH/12/22/hp.webcams/index.html.

Singer, Natasha and Cade Metz. 2019. Many Facial-Recognition Systems are Biased, Says U.S. Study. *The New York Times*, 19 December. Accessed 28 November 2021. www.nytimes.com/2019/12/19/technology/facial-recognition-bias.html.

Tighe, D. 2022. Global Brand Value of LEGO from 2015 to 2021. *Statista*. 10 March. Accessed 21 September 2022. https://www.statista.com/statistics/985451/lego-brand-value-worldwide/#:~:text=This%20statistic%20presents%20the%20brand,billion%20U.S.%20dollars%20in%202015.

Tourism Economics. 2019. *The Economic Impact of Tourism in Lancaster County*. A report by Tourism Economics: An Oxford Economics Company. June. Philadelphia, USA. Accessed 28 November 2021. https://s3.us-east-1.amazonaws.com/lancaster-2019/images/files/TE-LancasterEconImpact2018full.pdf?mtime=20200112174704&focal=none.

Zaichkowsky, Judith Lynne. 2010. Strategies for Distinctive Brands. *Brand Management, 17* (8), 548–60.

9 PRICING STRATEGIES: SIGNALING THE VALUE PROPOSITION

LEADERSHIP INSIGHTS 9

Photo 9.1 Shawn Dragann

Source: courtesy, Shawn Dragann

Meet Shawn Dragann, CEO

Idea Evolver

Idea Evolver utilizes search engine market research and search experience optimization to provide insights to some of the world's most well-known consumer brands. After doing a deep-dive into consumer online search data, Dragann and his team uncover what consumers are thinking about when they search for information about a product.

One recent client was Tiffany & Co. Founded in 1837 in New York, the Tiffany brand is strongly associated with exclusivity and luxury. "When you're working for a company like that, because value is their model, everything has to exude that luxury vibe. All of their messaging, the way their website looks, their colors, and any celebrity that would be associated with the brand. Jay-Z and Beyoncé are two of their spokespeople – they're incredibly successful. So, the question is, for everything you do, how do you exude this image of success and luxury? When you do it right, you create enough demand in the marketplace, and you are able to use a value-based pricing model." Dragann and his team provided Tiffany with key insights into the brand's mystique. "Take a piece of jewelry to be appraised and they will tell you all about the quality of the diamond and the purity of the precious metal … they will tell you exactly what it's worth. But if it has the name Tiffany on it, it is worth so much more," explains Dragann. Shortly after working with Idea Evolver, Tiffany was acquired by French global luxury giant LVMH for a whopping €16 billion (Jucca 2021) (see Photo 9.2).

Photo 9.2 A gift from Tiffany

Source: Pixabay

Just like Tiffany, Idea Evolver utilizes a value-based pricing strategy for the work it does for its clients. In its Consumer Insights and Media division, the team utilizes online search data and patterns to create managerially-relevant insights for its clients. The team recently worked with French food giant Danone, which had just acquired the WhiteWave brand for €10.93 billion. WhiteWave brought several healthy food brands to Danone, including Silk, So Delicious, Horizon Organic, Earthbound Farm, and Alpro. In 2016, global sales for these brands were €3.67 billion (Watrous 2017). Danone noticed that for several years, a growing segment of consumers were becoming interested in non-dairy alternatives such as almond milk and soy milk. Danone partnered with Idea Evolver to explore this trend. Before the rest of the industry was even aware of it, Idea Evolver identified an important shift. "We started to see a shift toward oat milk. We showed those stacked trends over time and how oat milk was continuing to gain popularity against almond milk." The team concluded that almond milk had opened the door to all of the other non-dairy milks. They provided this insight to Danone and said, "you were on-trend with almond milk … but where are you going to be with the next trend?" Danone introduced an oat milk product, beating the competition to market by 6 months and gaining a significant first mover advantage (see Figure 9.1).

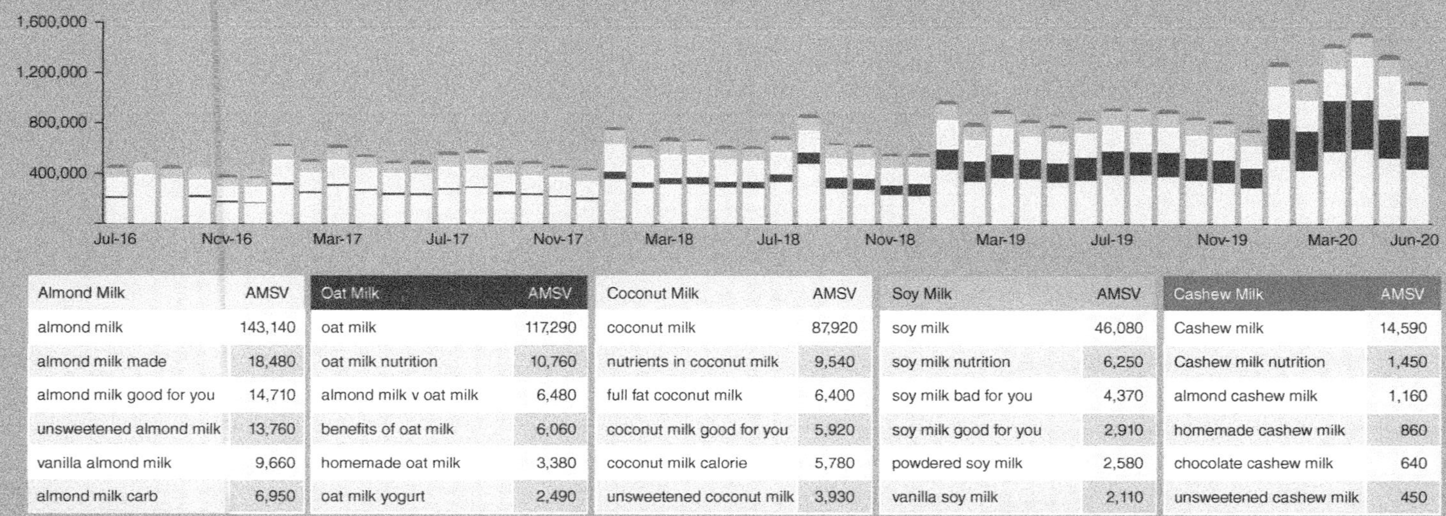

Almond Milk	AMSV
almond milk	143,140
almond milk made	18,480
almond milk good for you	14,710
unsweetened almond milk	13,760
vanilla almond milk	9,660
almond milk carb	6,950

Oat Milk	AMSV
oat milk	117,290
oat milk nutrition	10,760
almond milk v oat milk	6,480
benefits of oat milk	6,060
homemade oat milk	3,380
oat milk yogurt	2,490

Coconut Milk	AMSV
coconut milk	87,920
nutrients in coconut milk	9,540
full fat coconut milk	6,400
coconut milk good for you	5,920
coconut milk calorie	5,780
unsweetened coconut milk	3,930

Soy Milk	AMSV
soy milk	46,080
soy milk nutrition	6,250
soy milk bad for you	4,370
soy milk good for you	2,910
powdered soy milk	2,580
vanilla soy milk	2,110

Cashew Milk	AMSV
Cashew milk	14,590
Cashew milk nutrition	1,450
almond cashew milk	1,160
homemade cashew milk	860
chocolate cashew milk	640
unsweetened cashew milk	450

Figure 9.1 Search results for different types of non-dairy milk

Source: courtesy, Idea Evolver

With this and every other insight the team provides to its clients, Idea Evolver is months ahead of important consumer trends. The result is that the client beats its competitors to market with a new and innovative product that consumers are already curious about. The ability to be first to market provides numerous first mover advantages, including the ability to capture a commanding share of the market before the competition even is aware of what is happening.

Dragann is confident that his pricing strategy is a perfect fit for the insights the team provides. "We deliver insights to clients which then inform the product they will make or which spokesperson they will select. This then drives incredible value for their brands. They see a lot of ROI from that. They're willing to pay because it's worth so much to them. They don't care if they're paying a lot ... that's what it's worth to them. If they don't pay us to provide these insights, they can't pay anyone else."

9.1 IS CRYPTO THE FUTURE?

Cryptocurrencies are digital assets that are organized, distributed, and traded on a vast, decentralized network of computers. Just like other currencies such as the pound or the euro, cryptocurrencies can be used to purchase just about anything. However, because of its distributed structure, trading in crypto is faster and may actually be safer than traditional systems that rely on big banks, governments, and financial institutions for financial transactions. The trading of cryptocurrency is secured by blockchain technology. In fact, "crypto" refers to the technology that encrypts the transfer of these assets to (theoretically) keep them safe from hacking. Experts suggest that the global recession of 2008–2009, which was sparked by the failure of American financial institutions, would not have happened with cryptocurrencies. Because they do not have to be routed through banks, global financial transactions in cryptocurrencies are easier, cheaper, and more efficient. Further, because there are only a limited number of currency units – for example, there are only 21 Bitcoins that will ever be made available to investors – the price tends to increase over time (Frankenfield 2022).

Because their transaction fees are much lower than traditional credit card companies, an increasing number of organizations accept payment using cryptocurrencies, such as Mastercard, Microsoft, Starbucks, Tesla, Amazon, Visa, Paypal, Sotheby's, Coca-Cola, Expedia, and Lush (Walsh 2021). Although there are a variety of cryptocurrencies, such as Ethereum and Ripple, Bitcoin is the most popular, with about 41% market share in the cryptocurrency market. Markets and countries around the world have a patchwork of different regulations regarding the trading of crypto, as well as its use in paying for products and services. The EU, for example, instituted a series of regulations and safeguards for cryptocurrencies in 2021. As of December 2021, the market capitalization for Bitcoin was $862.1 billion (Frankenfield 2022).

There are some downsides to cryptocurrencies. Although cryptocurrency trading is made secure because of blockchain technology, which provides several layers of protection, hacks have occurred with other crypto repositories such as exchanges and wallets. Another downside is the market for cryptocurrencies can experience dramatic swings because of a few especially-important influencers. A tweet from Elon Musk, for example, can result in wild fluctuations in the crypto market. Finally, there are very real environmental concerns associated with the massive energy needs of the servers required for crypto mining transactions and trading (Frankenfield 2022).

How pervasive is cryptocurrency? Sixty-six percent of UK consumers are familiar with cryptocurrencies. Of those who are aware, 29 percent have invested in them. Fifty-one percent of crypto investors have made their purchases since 2019, making them a fairly new and growing phenomenon. Importantly, 55% of crypto investors are planning to increase their investments. Who is buying? Seventy-two percent of global high net worth individuals have invested in crypto (Tattersall 2021). Cash and credit are unlikely to go away any time soon. However, as global consumers and businesses become increasingly familiar with cryptocurrencies, they will likely acquire more mainstream acceptance and use (see Photo 9.3).

Photo 9.3 Indications are that cryptocurrencies are here to stay

Source: Pixabay

This chapter is concerned with pricing, the one element of the marketing mix that is easiest to adjust and the one element that generates revenue for the organization. All of the strategic decisions that occur around the issue of pricing revolve around the idea of assessing and signaling the value proposition – what exactly is the value proposition *worth* to consumers?

9.2 LEARNING OBJECTIVES

After studying this chapter, you will be able to do the following:

1 Identify and describe the various economic forces that influence a product's price.
2 Identify and describe several consumer perceptions that influence a product's price.
3 Explain the importance of the pricing planning process and sketch the four steps involved in the process.
4 Identify and describe the four categories of pricing strategies.
5 Differentiate between the various types of competitive pricing strategies.
6 Describe the unique challenge of creating a pricing strategy for a new product, as well as the four options for new product pricing.

9.3 THE IMPORTANCE OF PRICING

Pricing is the one element of the marketing mix that generates income for the organization, so it is not surprising that a significant amount of time and effort is devoted to pricing decisions. The pricing planning process starts with a delineation of various economic forces and an identification of consumer perceptions that are relevant to pricing. Next, marketing decision-makers create pricing objectives, strategies, and tactics (see Figure 9.2).

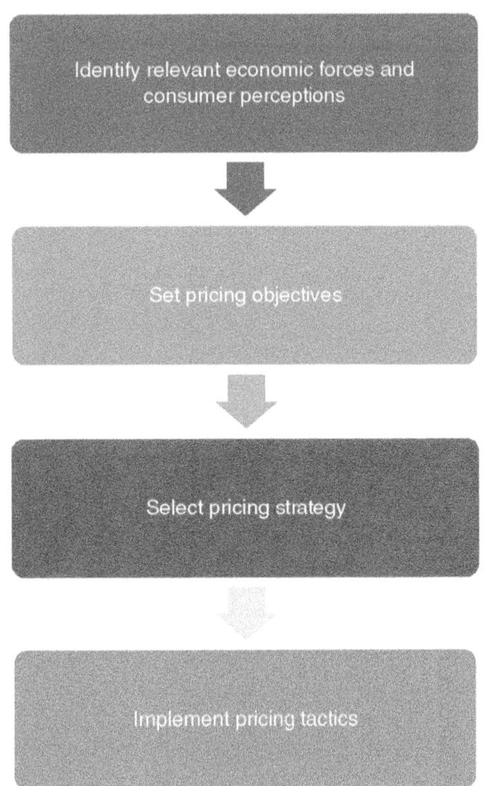

Figure 9.2 The pricing planning process

9.4 ECONOMIC PRINCIPLES & FORCES

The first step in the pricing planning process is an identification of the relevant economic principles and forces that influence the marketing team's pricing decision.

Cost vs. Price

A product's **cost** represents the total expenses related to bringing the product to market. It includes all of the variable and fixed costs associated with sourcing the raw materials, as well as manufacturing, distribution, and promotion. The **price** of the product is the amount of resources that the customer exchanges for the product or service, usually expressed in euros, pounds, dollars, Bitcoin, etc. The difference between the price and the cost of the product is the product's **margin**. The margin is the amount of profit that is made from the sale of each product.

Elasticity

To understand how the market may react to pricing changes, marketing decision-makers need to have a clear understanding of elasticity:

Elasticity = percentage change in quantity demanded / percentage change in price

In most instances, marketers would prefer the demand of their product to be **inelastic**. Inelastic demand indicates that increases in price result in very little change in demand for the product. This would happen in situations in which there are very few substitute products or services available or the product is very exclusive or hard to get. Examples include very special purchases, such as tickets to the World Cup (there is no easy substitute), as well as everyday purchases, such as gasoline for personal vehicles (the shift to electric cars or public transportation is often not easy), specific drugs that are needed for certain medical conditions, and utilities (there are only so many ways to cut back on electricity usage).

Photo 9.4 Rather than purchasing luxury brands, consumers can rent them

Source: Pixabay

Demand for products can also be **elastic**. This occurs when small changes in the price of the product will result in relatively large changes in the demand for the product. When the product has several substitutes, demand is more likely to be elastic. Examples of products that have elastic demand are most of the products consumers use on an everyday basis. Many food products are elastic; if the price of chicken doubles, for example, consumers can switch to pork, fish, or vegetarian options. Demand for clothing is also elastic; if the price increases, consumers can cut back on their spending or engage in other means to obtain the product, like thrift stores or rental companies. Demand for some specialty products like champagne (see case study on p.502) and designer clothing is also elastic. In response to increases in prices, consumers find other ways to satisfy their consumption needs. Instead of champagne, for example, consumers might switch to prosecco, a lower-priced sparkling wine. The high prices associated with designer clothing, for example, prompted a variety of new organizations to offer rental options. With Girl Meets Dress in the UK and Borrower Boutique in Ireland, women can rent luxury branded clothing for special occasions. With Elite Rent in Switzerland, anyone can experience what it feels like to be James Bond by renting an Aston Martin, or a variety of other luxury brand cars (see Photo 9.4).

Some products are so desirable, however, that the demand for these items follows a different pattern. Norwegian-American economist Thorstein Veblen studied the process of **conspicuous consumption**, the tendency of some individuals to purchase certain products or brands as a way to gain social recognition. Here, a higher price results in higher demand for the product. These types of products are called **Veblen goods** (Veblen [1899] 2007). Think of Cristal champagne or a Chanel handbag. There are no easy substitutes and consumers might be somewhat suspicious of a low price. Legal services and specialty services like Lasik surgery or plastic surgery are other examples of Veblen goods; no one wants to go to the discount eye surgeon or lawyer. For these consumers, dropping a lot of money on these kinds of purchases is a part of the experience. Thus, a higher price is not just an indication of higher quality, it is an added reason to purchase the product.

Purchasing Power Parity

Purchasing power parity (PPP) is measured in international dollars (the same value as the US dollar) and estimates the purchasing power that is required for a similar "basket of goods" in different countries, while smoothing out the effects of different exchange rates, interest rates, and trade policies. It takes into account economic activity and the standard of living in different countries. When examining the ability of target consumers to pay for an organization's products or services, knowledge about PPP provides important information to the marketing team about its pricing strategy.

ENDURING INSIGHTS 9.1

"The generation that destroys the environment is not the generation that pays the price." – Wangari Maathai, social and environmental activist

In 2004, Maathi became the first African woman to win the Nobel Peace Prize. She observed that, although people in developing nations are least likely to contribute to climate change, they are some of the most likely to experience its effects. Her work brought the issue of social justice to the forefront in many discussions of sustainable development.

Economies of Scale

Achieving economies of scale is another important economic influence in the development of the marketing team's pricing strategy. A firm achieves **economies of scale** when an increase in production volume results in a decrease in the per unit cost of production. Thus, when the marketing team is developing its projections for market potential and expected sales, special care must be taken to incorporate any economies of scale that would decrease the per-unit cost of the product.

Externalized Costs

Still another issue of concern for the marketing team is that of **externalized costs**, or negative externalities. These occur when some of the indirect costs associated with the production and delivery of the product are off-loaded to a third party. Take the example of a shoe company that sources the rubber for its shoes from the Amazon Rain Forest. To get access to rubber plantations, there are very real detrimental effects to the environment and the local culture, such as pollution of a local river, disruption of local wildlife habitats, and upheavals to a local village. These detrimental effects are the externalized costs – they are not borne by the company; they are paid for by someone else. The marketing team needs to carefully identify and account for all costs, including externalized costs.

The creation of the French sneaker brand VEJA was a reaction to the issue of externalized costs. At 25 years old, the company's two founders realized that in many instances of globalized production and distribution, damage was being inflicted on local cultures, workers, and the environment. When thinking about the biggest global names in sportswear, 70% of the price consumers paid for sneakers was due to advertising and communication; only 30% was for the materials and production. Bottom line, local cultures, workers, and the environment were paying the price for the world's consumers to wear some of the most well-known global brands. VEJA's founders decided to eliminate advertising in order to spend the money on materials and production, but still offer the product to consumers at a competitive price. Decision-makers at VEJA set up manufacturing in Brazil, where they were able to source organic and sustainable raw materials, many of which were also Fair Trade Certified. For all of its financial needs, VEJA switched to banks that were transparent and did not have accounts in global tax havens; for all of its energy needs, VEJA switched to renewable energy. Each of these strategic decisions resulted in increased costs. However, the prices that consumers pay are commensurate with other sneaker brands. VEJA not only seeks to eliminate its impact, it seeks to have a positive social and environmental impact through greater economic and social justice (Project 2022). VEJA became a certified B Corporation™ in 2018 (bcorporation.net 2022) (see Photo 9.5).

Photo 9.5 VEJA does not externalize its costs

Source: courtesy, VEJA

BLUNDERS & INSIGHTS 9.1

No, Poverty is Not a Game

BACKGROUND: German grocery store giant Aldi launched a "tone deaf" campaign in the UK that left many observers baffled. In an attempt to demonstrate Aldi's low prices, the company challenged a popular influencer to provide a week's worth of nourishing meals (breakfast, lunch, and dinner) for herself and her family of four for £25. Although the goal of the campaign was to show

(Continued)

the affordability of Aldi, consumers and critics interpreted the campaign as insensitive and patronizing to people experiencing real struggles to feed their families. Critics argued that there are far too many people in the UK and throughout the world who are experiencing food poverty and food insecurity. The campaign "turned real struggles into hashtags." Aldi UK apologized.

DEBRIEF: The biggest problem was that the campaign and the influencer lacked authenticity; it was perceived as contrived and performative (Hickman 2020). In addition, it is surprising that the marketing team, in preparation for the campaign rollout, did not identify any concerns during its pretests of the concept. To demonstrate how their low prices help people on a budget, Aldi UK could have engaged in a variety of other promotions, such as testimonials or slice-of-life depictions.

Tragedy of the Commons

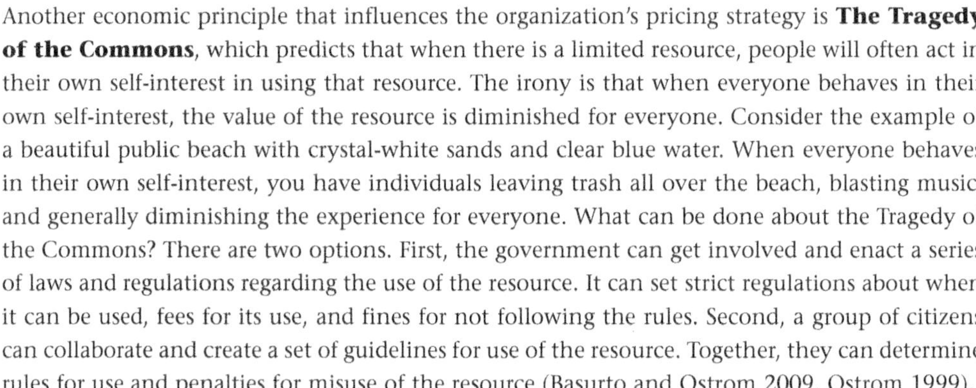

Another economic principle that influences the organization's pricing strategy is **The Tragedy of the Commons**, which predicts that when there is a limited resource, people will often act in their own self-interest in using that resource. The irony is that when everyone behaves in their own self-interest, the value of the resource is diminished for everyone. Consider the example of a beautiful public beach with crystal-white sands and clear blue water. When everyone behaves in their own self-interest, you have individuals leaving trash all over the beach, blasting music, and generally diminishing the experience for everyone. What can be done about the Tragedy of the Commons? There are two options. First, the government can get involved and enact a series of laws and regulations regarding the use of the resource. It can set strict regulations about when it can be used, fees for its use, and fines for not following the rules. Second, a group of citizens can collaborate and create a set of guidelines for use of the resource. Together, they can determine rules for use and penalties for misuse of the resource (Basurto and Ostrom 2009, Ostrom 1999).

How does the Tragedy of the Commons relate to the marketing team's decisions about pricing? The tendency for individuals to act in their own self-interest means that resources that are necessary for prosperity and even basic survival are at risk of being depleted. At the very least, the long-term sustainable viability of these resources is at risk. When this happens, other sources must be located, resulting in dramatic increases in costs.

Inflation

Another issue to consider is the inflation rate at home and abroad. As the world started to recover from the economic effects of the global Covid-19 pandemic, many economies experienced inflation, making everything more expensive. Inflation is an increase in the cost of goods and services over time. It makes almost everything more expensive (Fernando 2022). In the US, inflation went from 2.3% to 8.6%. Most of the world's economically developed countries experienced at least a two-fold increase in inflation, including Israel (where the inflation rate increased from 0.13% to 3.36%), Italy (from 0.29% to 5.67%), and Switzerland (from 0.13% to 2.06%). Turkey, which was struggling to contain its economy before the pandemic, experienced an eye-popping inflation rate of 54.8%. Why did this happen? Experts suggest that most countries experienced a relatively similar pattern: relatively low rates of inflation before the pandemic, followed by economic contraction during the pandemic (Desilver 2022). As economies started to kick into gear again, demand for goods and services surged, causing prices to increase.

Costs for commodity prices also increased, causing down-stream increases in consumer products. In addition, because prices increased, workers starting demanding higher wages, also putting upward pressure on inflation (Fernando 2022).

Regulatory Restrictions

Another external influence that impacts the economics of the pricing decision is the existence of regulatory restrictions on pricing. Many countries and trading blocs have regulations that protect small competitors and disadvantaged consumers. These laws often protect against competitors that collude on prices and firms that deceive consumers. Generally, the overall purpose of these laws is to ensure that free and fair trade is not impeded. Pricing strategies should never result in reduced competition or in financial injury to consumers (Tellis 1986).

9.5 CUSTOMER PERCEPTIONS OF PRICE AND VALUE

Why do people pay so much for diamonds, gold, and precious antiques? Part of the answer is due to the fact that these items are in rare supply and, in some instances, irreplaceable. However, consumer perceptions are also a necessary condition for a consumer's willingness to pay a given price. That is, just because an item is rare does not mean that the price will be high. Consider an important family heirloom; it might be very valuable to the family, but few people outside the family would be interested. Experts acknowledge that consumer demand is strongly influenced by both economic forces and consumer perceptions of value. This line of inquiry into consumer perceptions and pricing strategy is referred to as **behavioral pricing**. Behavioral pricing acknowledges the important psychological and behavioral motivations in a consumer's perceptions of price (Kienzler and Kowalkowski 2017, Somervouri 2014) (see Photo 9.6).

Photo 9.6 Experts agree that The Mona Lisa is priceless

Source: Pixabay

ENDURING INSIGHTS 9.2

"Perhaps the reason price is all your customers care about is because you haven't given them anything else to care about." – Seth Godin, best-selling author and speaker

The importance of creating a value proposition cannot be overstated. However, the organization must also communicate the value proposition to the target market in a way that clearly resonates with their lives. In the minds of consumers, it must be clear how this product or service will make their lives happier, healthier, safer, or more efficient.

Consumer beliefs and attitudes about renewable energy presents a fascinating example of how incorrect perceptions can hurt consumers in the wallet and impede progress toward addressing climate change. A strong majority of consumers believe that renewable energy has a positive effect on the environment. Indeed, 70% believe that solar generation and 65% believe that wind generation has a positive effect on the environment. However, only 36% believe that solar energy is less expensive and just 35% believe that wind energy is less expensive than energy derived from fossil fuels (Kennedy and Spencer 2021). The facts, however, speak for themselves. The renewable energy sector has experienced such a tremendous drop in prices in recent years, that renewable energy is often far less expensive than energy derived from fossil fuels. Much of this progress can be attributed to continued technological advancements as well as economies of scale. Industry experts have estimated that globally, 42% of coal-fired utility plants are unprofitable. Further, it is less expensive to build a new renewable energy facility than it is to keep many fossil fuel facilities running. Since 2009, the consumer price for solar energy has dropped 88%, while the price for wind energy has dropped 69%. On the current trajectory – that is, without any technological breakthroughs (which is unlikely) – experts predict that the costs associated with renewable energy generation will drop 80% by 2050. Most of these savings will be passed along to consumers (Mahajan 2018).

Reference Price

When contemplating an upcoming purchase, consumers have a **reference price**, which they consider to be a reasonable price to pay for the product. Further, they will consider purchasing a product if it falls within what they consider an acceptable range of prices around that reference price (Rao and Sieben 1992). Consumers use price information to evaluate the product's quality and to evaluate the monetary sacrifice associated with buying the product. At the higher end of the price range, consumers are more concerned about the monetary sacrifice required for purchase. They might wonder, for example, if the high price is worth it. By contrast, at the lower end of the price range, consumers are more concerned about the product's quality. Here, consumers are likely to worry that the product will not perform as expected (Monroe 2003) (see Figure 9.3).

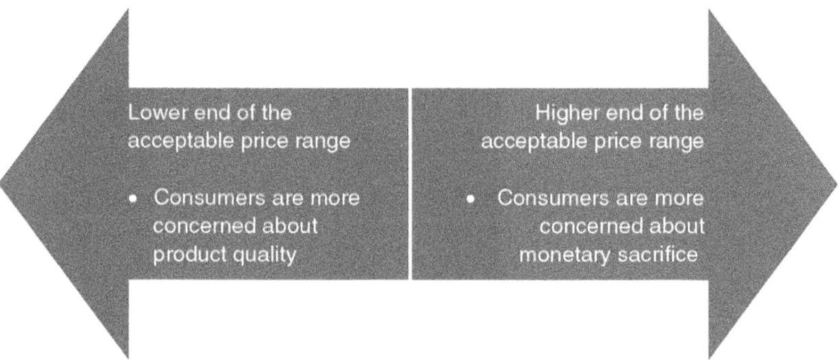

Figure 9.3 Consumers concerns at the high end and low end of the acceptable range

Source: adapted from Monroe (2003)

Perceptions of Scarcity

Claims of "limited time only" and "time's running out" are common across a variety of industries. When a market is in a situation of **scarcity**, or limited supply, many consumers have a fear of missing out (FOMO). These perceptions of scarcity may be heightened in online environments. Amazon, for example, will often claim to have only a few items left in stock. Other online retailers provide information about how many other customers are currently viewing a particular item. These claims are designed to encourage consumers to purchase the product now, rather than wait. In situations of scarcity, how do consumers in the target market interpret the price of the product? The answer is, it depends. Building on previous research (e.g., Monroe 2003), evidence suggests that the extent to which consumers perceive value from the offering depends on whether or not the consumer is motivated to process information about the product. Generally speaking, a consumer will be motivated to process information if the product is self-relevant or if there is risk associated with the decision (e.g., the price is very high or there is a very real chance of making a wrong choice). If consumers are highly motivated to process price-related information, they will interpret a high price as a signal that the product is high in quality. For these consumers, *value* will be achieved by a high-priced, high-quality product. Imagine a couple who are romantically involved and one partner wishes to purchase a diamond ring for the other partner. This consumer is obviously very motivated by the decision and will likely be most content and happy with the purchase of a high-priced, high-quality ring. Such a purchase demonstrates this person's own good taste, as well as love and commitment for the partner. Conversely, if consumers are not motivated to process price-related information, they will interpret a low price as a signal that they will need to make only a very small monetary sacrifice. For them, *value* is achieved by a low-priced product that did not require a huge monetary outlay (Suri, Kohli, and Monroe 2007). In this case, consider a consumer who is shopping online for a new winter coat. This person comes across a fantastic bargain on a well-known brand name because the manufacturer wants to liquidate its stock to make room for next season's product line. Our lucky consumer would be most content and happy by simply knowing that the purchase did not require a huge monetary outlay and might even overlook the fact that the style is one season out of date. This fascinating finding underscores the importance of remembering that value means different things to different consumers (see Figure 9.4).

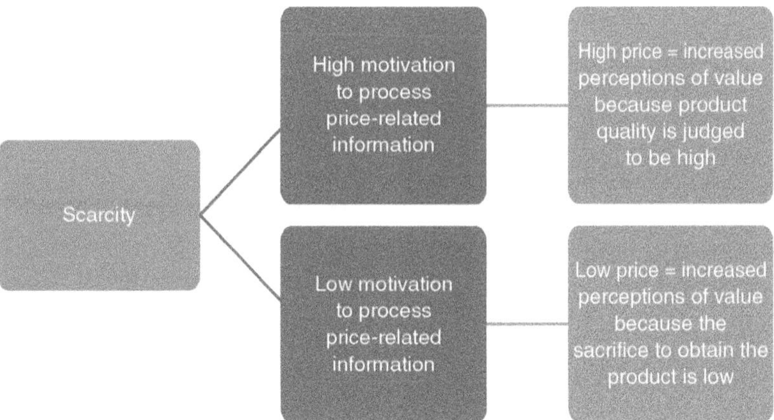

Figure 9.4 Perceptions of value in a situation of scarcity

Source: adapted from Suri, et al. (2007)

Perceptions of Quality

In making their purchase decisions, many consumers are guided by the old saying, "you get what you pay for." Indeed, consumers often use price to infer quality (see Tellis 1986 for a discussion). Price and quality have a somewhat complicated relationship with one another in the minds of consumers. Consumers who simultaneously consider price and quality generally fall into one of five different categories that fall along a continuum that ranges from those consumers who almost always buy products based on price (bargain hunters) to those who almost always buy based on quality (quality conscious consumers) (Ding, Ross, and Rao 2010). (See Figure 9.5).

Figure 9.5 Consumer perceptions of price vs. quality

Source: Ding, et al. (2010)

Opportunity Costs

When consumers commit to purchase one product, there are other products that they are not purchasing. A consumer's **opportunity costs** are the potential benefits that could have been obtained by purchasing the other alternative. By purchasing a fruit smoothie after class, for example, a consumer gets a tasty and refreshing treat, but foregoes the opportunity of having a cup of coffee with some (perhaps) much-needed caffeine to help them get through the rest of the afternoon. Consumers think about opportunity costs as they make their purchase decisions.

9.6 PRICING OBJECTIVES

After examining economic forces and consumer perceptions that will influence its efforts, the marketing team needs to determine its pricing objectives. **Pricing objectives** are the strategic pricing-related goals that the organization wishes to achieve as it seeks to deliver the value proposition. Pricing objectives tell us what the firm wishes to accomplish with regard to price. Many firms pursue multiple pricing objectives and adjust them over time. There are several types of objectives for the marketing team to consider that each have important implications for the price of the offering (see Table 9.1). After the objectives are set, the pricing strategies are a means by which those objectives are accomplished.

Table 9.1 Price-related objectives

Pricing Objective	Explanation
Market share	Perhaps the marketing team wishes to stake a claim to a certain portion of the market in a given time period. In this case, the team should assess the number and strength of the competitors in the market, as well as its own size and strength. In an industry populated by just a few big players, a 30% market share might be far too conservative, whereas in a densely packed market, a 10% market share might be wildly optimistic.
Profit	Perhaps the most widely-used pricing objective, the marketing team could quite reasonably want to set a pricing objective to achieve a certain level of profit in a given time period. For example, the team wants to achieve €10 million in profit by end-of-year 2024.
Sales volume	The team might establish an objective related to achieving a specific sales goal, such as 10,000 units sold by the second quarter of 2025. A pricing objective focusing on sales volume could be useful in situations where an organization seeks to gain a foothold in a new market.
Competitive effect	The team might want to weaken the competition or perhaps leverage an opportunity to strengthen its brand's relative position in the market. For example, the organization will provide greater value to its consumers by bundling two products, offering a discount for volume purchases, or offering add-ons like loyalty points. The point is that the value of the product, relative to the competition, increases.
Consumer perceptions	The team might establish a pricing objective that influences consumer perceptions. For example, setting the price relatively high will likely influence consumers to believe that the quality is also high.

BLUNDERS & INSIGHTS 9.2

The Rise and Fall of Peloton

BACKGROUND: Peloton sells high-end exercise equipment for at-home use and in 2022, it was available in the US, the UK, and Germany. The equipment starts at about $1500 for a simple treadmill or bike; prices for some of the more complex equipment range all the way up to $5000. In addition, Peloton charges a monthly subscription price starting at $39 in order to access thousands of workout routines and programs. At the start of the Covid-19 pandemic in 2020, Peloton experienced a tremendous uptick in sales of its equipment, which prompted it to expand quickly. It spent $420 million to acquire a competitive exercise equipment manufacturer and $400 million for a new production facility (Thomas 2022).

As people started going back to in-person work and gyms in 2022, interest in at-home fitness equipment dropped precipitously. By mid-2022, gym usage was almost back to pre-pandemic levels (Heilweil 2022). Global economic and geo-political concerns also slowed down interest in the bikes. As sales dropped, the company was too over-extended to easily recover. By early 2022, $40 billion (80%) in market capitalization had been erased in just 1 year. To help achieve better financial footing, Peloton announced that it would start charging customers $250 for delivery and setup (Thomas 2022). It also laid off 2800 employees, shuttered plans for the $400 million production facility, and announced that its founder and CEO would immediately step down (Heilweil 2022) (see Photo 9.7).

Photo 9.7 Peloton sales dropped when people started going back to gyms

Source: iStockphoto

DEBRIEF: The company created wildly optimistic revenue projections, upon which it based its plans for expansion. At the time, efforts to further scale production and reduce per-unit costs seemed like reasonable strategic moves. However, Peloton's heavy capital investment impeded the company's ability to be flexible enough to act quickly when consumers changed their behavior and sales dropped precipitously.

9.7 PRICING STRATEGIES

A pricing strategy is an evidence-based decision that aims to achieve a pricing objective within a given planning period. In actuality, organizations may deploy several different pricing strategies. In order to be most effective, each pricing strategy must take into account price elasticity for the product or service (Rao and Bass 1985), as well as other economic forces and consumer perceptions, so that the marketing team will be able to reasonably predict the effect on sales. There are four broad categories of pricing strategies: competitive effect strategies, product-line pricing strategies, consumer-focused pricing strategies, and new product pricing strategies.

Competitive Effect Pricing Strategies

The purpose of **competitive effect pricing strategies** is to increase the firm's value proposition relative to the competition. This can be accomplished in a variety of ways.

Cost-Plus Pricing

Perhaps the easiest pricing strategy for a firm to implement, **cost-plus pricing**, simply adds a fixed percentage to the total fixed and variable costs associated with producing the product and delivering it to the consumer. Often, between 20% and 50% will be added to the cost of a product to arrive at its final price; this is the product's margin. Items such as cosmetics and perfume often have margins as high as 80%.

Price Leadership

When the organization is fairly powerful in the market, a **price leadership strategy** should be considered. Price leaders have higher prices than other competitors, and often have higher market share. When price leaders raise or lower prices, competitors often follow with pricing adjustments of their own. This strategy works particularly well when the organization has low costs, price changes are easy to detect, and overall demand in the market is fairly inelastic (Noble and Gruca 1999). With 27.4% of the global athletic footwear market (Sabanoglu 2021), Nike exerts enough power over its next closest competitors, Adidas and UnderArmour, to be a price leader.

Competitive Parity Pricing

Also referred to as a "going rate pricing strategy," a **competitive parity pricing strategy** sets the price of the offering such that it is on par with the competition. Often, weaker competitors in the market utilize this pricing strategy. Otherwise, a superior quality product would command a higher price, while a low-cost structure would allow the organization to set a lower price. Setting the price on par with the competition implies that neither of these scenarios is the case (Noble and Gruca 1999). Small-scale or single-proprietor operations, such as an auto mechanic shop or a bakery, will often set their prices to be on par with the competition.

Low-Price Strategy

If an organization has the advantage of a low-cost structure, it can deploy a **low-price strategy**. Everday Low Prices (EDLP), for example, is a common pricing strategy at big box retailers and large online retailers. This strategy is particularly effective when the overall market for the product demonstrates high elasticity (Noble and Gruca 1999). Because of its size and scale, German grocery giant Aldi pursues a low-price strategy that its competitors have a hard time matching. Aldi claims to offer "top quality, bottom prices" at its stores (see Photo 9.8).

Photo 9.8 Aldi pursues a low-price strategy

Source: Pixabay

Dynamic Pricing

Dynamic pricing adjusts the product, based on shifts in demand, remaining inventory, stage of market diffusion, and competitive actions (Rao and Bass 1985). This pricing strategy is regularly utilized by marketers. Many Airbnb properties, for example, are more expensive in the summer and on holiday weekends. Similarly, Uber charges higher rates during peak hours and on holidays. In addition, when there are fewer drivers on the road, prices increase (to reflect a reduced supply of drivers, but to also encourage more off-duty drivers to pick up their keys and start picking up passengers). Airlines and hotels often provide deeply discounted last-minute rates in an effort to recoup some of their fixed costs (see Photo 9.9). Sports fans have become accustomed to dynamic pricing in sports, as teams regularly use dynamic pricing to fill seats in stadiums or arenas. Sophisticated software programs adjust the ticket prices for seats in real-time, based on the number of seats still remaining unsold, as well as the weather and the amount of time still remaining before the game starts (see case study on p.415).

Photo 9.9 Airbnb utilizes dynamic pricing

Source: Pixabay

Differential Pricing

A **differential pricing strategy** involves charging different target markets different prices for the same product. One type of differential pricing is peak load or surge pricing, which sets the price higher during busy times and lower during less busy times. This is done to spread out demand and utilize capacity that would otherwise remain idle. Restaurants and movie theaters often offer discounts to customers who visit during off-peak hours. Another type of differential pricing is geographic pricing – charging consumers in different locations a different price. This is often based on what consumers in this market are willing to pay, but differential pricing based on geographics also happens if a particular market has higher demand, if it has a higher number of competitors, if it is subject to higher taxes, or if the cost to deliver to the market is higher. Compared to the rest of the US, Hawaii has much higher prices for most products. This is partially because Hawaii is a popular tourist destination with large numbers of people willing to pay high prices. It is also due to the fact that shipping costs are much higher than other states that are connected by railroads and highways.

Secondary Market Pricing

When an organization introduces a new version of the product to market, but still has an existing product available for sale, **secondary market pricing** is an option to consider. When using this strategy, the organization will sell the older version of the product to the secondary market at a lower price than it sells the newer version of the product in its primary market. Software updates and technological upgrades often make products seem out of date within a very short period of time. In this case, it is reasonable for the organization to recoup some of its costs by selling the slightly out-of-date version to a different market at a lower price (Tellis 1986). Western-based companies have come under fire for sending severely out-of-date and expired items to developing countries in recent years. At the height of the global Covid-19 pandemic, Europe sent Nigeria up to 1 million vaccine doses that were so close to their expiration date that, by the time they arrived and were able to be administered, they needed to be discarded (Merelli 2021).

Loss Leader Pricing

The marketing team will employ a **loss leader strategy** when it drops the price below cost in order to encourage consumers to purchase other products. Grocery stores and electronics stores often hold seasonal sales in which several items are heavily advertised as having exceptionally low prices. These sales generate excitement and foot traffic to the store, with the belief that consumers will buy the advertised item, as well as other items. The organization thus makes up for its loss with the margin it makes on the sales of other items.

Predatory Pricing

A **predatory pricing strategy** involves a deep cut in prices in a particular market. Existing competitors in the market will then respond by dropping their prices. Over a sustained period of time, margins will be so slim that the competitor will exit the market. The Organization of the Petroleum Exporting Countries (OPEC) nations regularly adjust their output to keep the price of oil low and inflict damage on renewable energy sources, such as wind and solar energy. Predatory pricing is not recommended and, in many countries, the practice is illegal. Violations are met with harsh penalties.

Price Wars

A price war is a strategy of last resort and should only be deployed with extreme caution. **Price wars** occur when each competitor systematically drops its price to retaliate against the competitor's price drop. They do this to compete for sales or market share, but to also inflict damage on the competitor. Over time, retaliatory price cuts by each side result in a full-blown price war. Experts caution against engaging in a price war, because they are impossible to sustain over the long term. In the end, each competitor loses. Despite the fact that price wars often inflict economically devastating damage on participants, examples of price wars abound. In 2021, German grocery giant Aldi engaged in a banana price war with the UK's Tesco chain, bringing the price down to 13p per banana at each store. Unfortunately, increases in supply chain costs resulted in significant losses for both retail chains, as well as to business partners and farmers (Wood 2021).

If a price war does occur, it is sometimes necessary to launch a response, especially when a competitor is attacking the organization's core business or premier brand. To have a chance at succeeding in a price war, the organization should have a low-cost structure, a large enough target market of price-sensitive consumers, deep pockets to withstand a prolonged war, the possibility of achieving economies of scale because of greater volume of sales, or the possibility of causing damage to an especially fierce competitor. In this case, there are several price-related and non-price-related responses that the marketing team could deploy (see Table 9.2). In the end, however, price wars should be avoided. In addition to the obvious financial hit that the firm will suffer, there are several other reasons why price wars result in long-term damage to the organization. First, price wars teach consumers that they should buy based on price, not value. The marketing team spends significant time and effort creating and communicating its value proposition in order to convince consumers that the price they pay is worth it. Price wars destroy those hard-fought gains in value perceptions. Second, it will be difficult for the organization to raise prices in the future. Consumers will be conditioned to wait till the next price drop. Third, consumers might conclude that a drop in price means that there is also a drop in quality. Finally, some of the organization's most important stakeholders and business partners might suffer damage because of decreased margins throughout the supply chain (Rao, Bergen, and Davis 2000).

Table 9.2 Price-related and non-price-related responses to a price war

Price-related Responses	Non-price-related Responses
Change customers' choices – reframe the price war in the minds of consumers (rather than product A price vs. product B price, reframe the choice to include loyalty points, volume discounts, bundling, etc.).	*Reveal your strategic intentions and capabilities* – explain the rationale for your pricing strategy (for example, everyday low prices or price matching) in order to communicate that the organization would prefer to compete on non-price criteria. The organization can also reveal that it has a very low-cost structure and can therefore sustain a long price war.
Modify only certain prices – selectively reduce prices on some products, not others.	*Compete on quality* – emphasize the quality of the organization's offering, as well as any added attributes (such as extra service or guarantees). Emphasize the potential risks to consumers of selecting a low-price option (do you really want to have your Lasik eye surgery at the low-cost clinic?).
Create and introduce a flanking brand – to take the brunt of competitive price cuts, add another product to the line that has a low price and will go toe-to-toe with the competitor's brand.	*Appeal to stakeholders* – seek assistance from business partners and others who might also be harmed by a prolonged price war.
Selectively cut prices in some channels – but not others.	

Source: adapted from Rao, et al. (2000).

Product Line Pricing

When the marketing team needs to make a decision about the pricing strategy for an entire product line, it has a few **product line pricing strategies** to consider. Here, the organization has a set of related products that it utilizes in a coordinated way to achieve its pricing objective. Accounting for consumer perceptions and purchasing patterns is especially important when utilizing these pricing strategies.

Bundling Strategy

A bundling pricing strategy occurs when two or more items are combined into one lower price for the consumer. Examples include lower prices for season tickets or lower prices for a bundle of options on a new car. Bundling works best when the products are not easily substitutable (leather seats and an upgraded sound system in the car) and when the products are perishable (seats in a stadium during a concert). This strategy is generally beneficial to consumers, who get a better overall price than they would have if they had purchased the items individually. It is also beneficial to sellers because they sell more products or services (Tellis 1986).

The business model at Netflix is an example of bundling. Established industry giants like Disney and Universal produce new content and then release new movies to theaters one at a time. There are typically several times of the year that are particularly popular, such as the summer, but movie studios generally prefer to spread out the release of their movies. By contrast, Netflix releases new movies on its streaming service as a part of a bundle of other movies and shows. This strategy benefits smaller independent filmmakers, who might not get much attention if their films had been released straight to the theater. In addition, Netflix benefits because it does not have to engage in the often-flawed process of predicting how much theater-goers might be interested in each individual movie that is released. Instead, Netflix simply needs to determine how much a bundle of movies and shows is worth to its consumers (Smith and Telang 2019).

Unbundling Strategy

After the global economic meltdown of 2008–2009, the trend of unbundling started to become more common as consumers tried to trim costs. An **unbundling pricing strategy** occurs when the organization splits apart a bundle of options into its component parts, each with an individual price. Unbundling provides an added advantage to consumers who do not want to pay for some of the items that were previously bundled together. An example of unbundling is the shift in the music industry from selling entire albums to selling individual songs on iTunes or other music sites (see Photo 9.10).

Photo 9.10 The music industry utilizes an unbundling pricing strategy

Source: Pixabay

Complementary Product Pricing

A **complementary pricing strategy** is utilized when two products "go together." The main product is priced at a relatively low cost, while the complementary product is sold at an expensive price (Noble and Gruca 1999). For example, Gillette razors are fairly inexpensive, but purchasing replacement blades is quite expensive. Similarly, desktop printers are fairly inexpensive, whereas print cartridges for the printer are very expensive. This pricing strategy works well for the firm when there are high switching costs for the consumer (Tellis 1986).

Consumer-Focused Pricing Strategies

Consumer-focused pricing strategies take into account consumer needs and perceptions. Often, they include the consumer as an active participant in the process of determining the optimal price for the product or service.

Participative Pricing

Participative pricing occurs when both the seller and the buyer participate in setting the final price for the product or service. This can occur in a formal environment, such as auctions, or negotiating to buy a house or a car. Participative pricing can also occur in informal environments, such as when one haggles over a price with a street vendor or at a flea market. In some parts of the world, participative pricing is the norm, even in stores. One type of participative pricing is "name your own price," which allows individuals to pay what they wish for a product or service.

An interesting pattern of results happens for consumers who engage in participative pricing. Compared to those consumers who are in a fixed price environment, consumers who are in a participative environment and who have high confidence in their own ability to negotiate a good price will have higher intentions to purchase the product (see Figure 9.6). Why does this happen? Because these individuals have shifted their mindsets toward the completion of the sale, rather than on the evaluation of the product (Chandran and Morwitz 2005).

Figure 9.6 Participative pricing and higher confidence can lead to stronger intentions to purchase

Source: adapted, in part, from Chandran and Morwitz (2005)

Value-Based Pricing

Also called perceived value pricing, the **value-based pricing strategy** looks first to how much the offering is *worth* to the consumer, then sets the price for the product or service accordingly. Managers who deploy a value-based pricing strategy have a keen understanding of consumer needs and what the firm's offering means to them. This strategy is appropriate for both B2C and

B2B settings (Liozu, Hinterhuber, Boland, and Perelli 2012). As discussed in the chapter opener, the management team at Idea Evolver effectively utilizes a value-based pricing strategy because the insights it provides to its clients cannot be found anywhere else (a B2B setting). Tiffany also utilizes a value-based pricing strategy, because there is value in the meanings and sentiments that are communicated with any gift that comes in the little blue box (a B2C scenario).

Subscription Pricing

Designed to strengthen the relationship between the organization and the consumer, a **subscription pricing strategy** requires consumers to pay a monthly fee for continued use of the product or access to certain features. As discussed earlier, Peloton requires users to pay a $39 monthly fee for access to workout routines and programs. Much of the draw for the 2.5 million subscribers (Thomas 2022) is the fitness experts who star in these programs, many of whom have become important athletic and fitness influencers on social media. An important benefit to subscription pricing is that consumers stay connected and engaged with the company; they learn about new releases and upgrades before the rest of the market.

ENDURING INSIGHTS 9.3

"In for a penny, in for a pound." – Daphne Caruana Galizia, investigative reporter and advocate for a free press

This well-known saying really has very little to do with money or pricing. However, it uses these terms as metaphors to express a person's intention to follow through on a project once it has been started, regardless of the amount of time, effort, or money it takes to do so. Galizia was an outspoken critic of some highly-placed individuals in the Maltese government. She was a fierce advocate of the free press, especially after threats were made against her life. In 2017, she was murdered near her home by a car bomb.

New Product Pricing Strategies

When introducing a new product to market, extra care must be taken. **New product pricing strategies** are a critical determinant in the likelihood of long-term success for the product. As they say, "first impressions count," and a new product's price, along with the other elements of the marketing mix, makes an important first impression on a new market where consumers likely have very little knowledge or experience with the product.

Skimming

The first new product pricing strategy is a **skimming strategy**. When entering a new market, the price is set relatively high and then systematically discounted over time. This strategy has the benefit of discriminating between those consumers who are not price sensitive and are thus willing to pay more to get the product early, and those who are more price sensitive and are willing to wait so that they can pay a cheaper price. This strategy works best when the organization is the first to market and has some time before the next market entrant arrives. It also works well when products are highly differentiated and there are no close substitutions (Noble and Gruca 1999). When a new technological advance is first introduced to the market, a skimming strategy is often utilized. Apple follows this strategy when it introduces each version of its iPhone to the market; in the first few weeks of introduction, the price is high. Then, the price slowly drops over time.

Penetration

A **penetration pricing strategy** sets the price just above the product's per unit cost. The goal is to achieve high levels of sales and expand market share. This strategy works particularly well when consumers are price sensitive and there is a threat of a competitor entering the market (Tellis 1986). When an organization uses a low price to penetrate the market, competitors will see very little opportunity for profit and will be discouraged from entering the market. If done effectively, an added benefit to penetration pricing is that once the product gains market share, it becomes the industry standard, against which all competitors are compared (Noble and Gruca 1999). In an extreme example of penetration pricing, consider Hulu. When it first appeared in 2007, Hulu's streaming content was free. Viewers were quite happy to watch a few ads in exchange for free access to their favorite shows. In 2016, after customers became accustomed to this relationship and Hulu had a sizable portion of the market, Hulu started charging a subscription price of $7.99 per month (Frej 2016).

Experience Curve Pricing

The **experience curve pricing strategy** is built upon the well-known finding that as an organization becomes more experienced in a market and is able to scale production, its per unit costs decrease. The initial price is set fairly high. Then, as costs decrease, the marketing team lowers the product's price even more, while still maintaining an acceptable margin. This strategy puts pressure on competitors who need to match the price and therefore suffer a decrease in their margins. The strategy works particularly well for an organization that has more experience in the market (or in a similar market) than its competitors and when consumers are price sensitive (so appreciate a drop in prices) (Tellis 1986). Many car manufacturers are likely anticipating the use of experience curve pricing with their electric vehicle (EV) product lines. As acceptance of EVs becomes more widespread, production volumes will accelerate and per-unit costs will decrease, allowing for lower prices but consistent margins (see Photo 9.11).

Photo 9.11 With increased production, EV manufacturers will achieve lower per-unit costs

Source: Pixabay

Scarcity Pricing

Sometimes, the introduction of a new product is so highly anticipated, it becomes the hottest, most-sought-after item on the market. The release of the latest PlayStation or game are examples. Established economic theory (and simple logic) would suggest that if an organization is experiencing a situation of product scarcity, it could do one of two things: increase prices (to decrease demand) or increase supply. However, researchers have suggested that there may be a better way to optimize profits. For organizations that are planning to introduce a new product to market in an environment of scarcity, a **scarcity pricing strategy** will optimize overall profits by keeping the price high until it achieves a broad level of acceptance in the market. Harkening back to the Diffusion of Innovation curve, innovators are willing to pay a high price because they want to be first to obtain the product. In addition, for early adopters and the early majority, a scarcity strategy is a signal that the product's quality is high, so they are willing to pay a high price for it. Once the product reaches the early majority and late majority, the price can start to drop. The scarcity pricing strategy is especially effective with new specialty products and is not effective with commodity products (Stock and Balachander 2005) (see Figure 9.7).

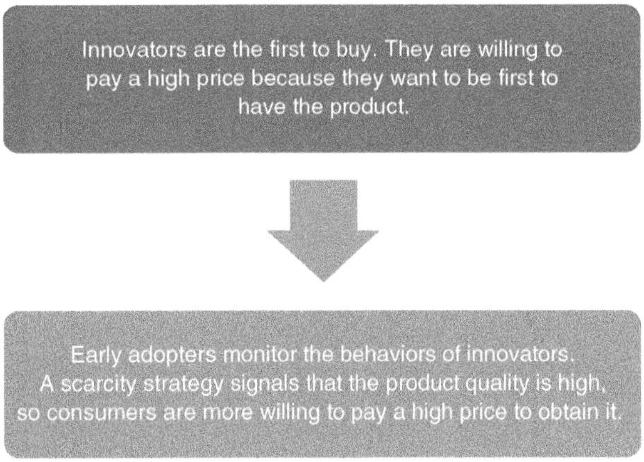

Innovators are the first to buy. They are willing to pay a high price because they want to be first to have the product.

Early adopters monitor the behaviors of innovators. A scarcity strategy signals that the product quality is high, so consumers are more willing to pay a high price to obtain it.

Figure 9.7 Scarcity pricing strategy

Source: Stock and Balachander 2005

BLUNDERS & INSIGHTS 9.2

Money Drop Gone Wrong

BACKGROUND: In December 2020, after months of strict lockdowns and a 12.2% contraction of the economy, The Safety Warehouse in Auckland, New Zealand launched a promotion designed to "give back" to the local community, which was experiencing a significant amount of economic distress. The Safety Warehouse is a deep discount retailer offering name-brand clothing and household products. The company would drop $100,000 NZD into a crowd of people. "We are the people's company & proud of it, so we're dropping $100,000 in value from the sky in Aotea Square. Yes, ACTUAL MONEY will be flying from the sky," the company declared on social media. Enthusiastic locals and other citizens spent hours traveling to the location and before long, a very large crowd was gathered at the drop site. As soon as the "money" started to fall from the sky, it became clear that something was very wrong. Instead of actual cash, fake bills and vouchers were falling. Individuals could bring the vouchers and fake bills to the store for discounts on products. Understandably, people were outraged. Some threw rocks at event organizers and broke car windows. Dozens of people were injured and riot police were called in. Fearing for their own safety, organizers fled the scene (Ayling 2020).

DEBRIEF: From the outset, the idea of a money drop was poorly conceived. The Covid-19 pandemic was in full swing and life-saving vaccines had not yet been approved for human use.

(Continued)

New Zealand fared better than many countries, but strict lockdowns were causing high unemployment and economic hardships. Dropping money on desperate people made a mockery of their hardship. Worse yet, the company was not truthful. They claimed they would drop "$100,000 *in value*" on the crowd. Although a small amount of actual money was indeed dropped, vouchers made up the majority of what fell from the sky that day. It is no surprise that people felt manipulated and deceived.

In summary, the marketing team has a wide variety of pricing strategies from which to select as it attempts to carry out its pricing objectives (see Figure 9.8).

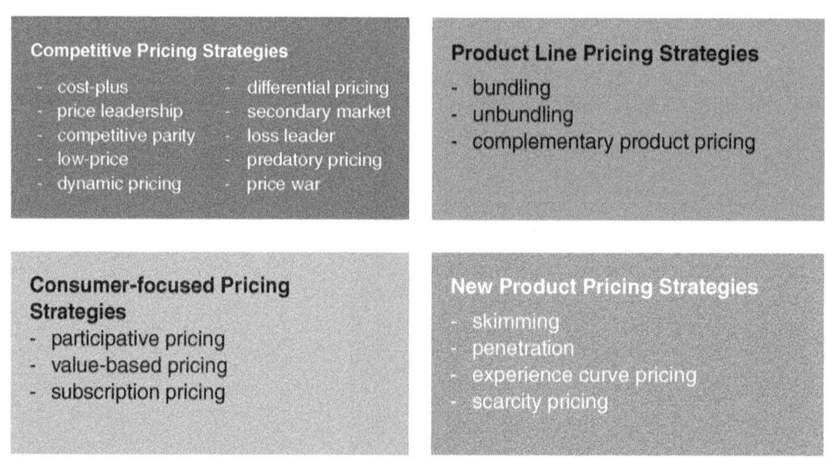

Figure 9.8 The four types of pricing strategies

9.8 PRICING TACTICS

After establishing the organization's pricing objectives and selecting the pricing strategies, the marketing team next needs to implement a variety of pricing tactics. **Pricing tactics** involve a variety of small-scale, focused decisions that help to achieve the organization's pricing strategies. Tactics might involve a wide variety of decisions, such as ending each price with a "9," as in £5.99. Marketers have long used this tactic because there is some evidence to suggest that consumers view the price as less expensive than, for example, £6.00. Other tactical choices would involve the timing of implementation of the pricing strategy; many retailers have big sales in the spring to clear out inventory and sustain sales. Tactical decisions need to be flexible because they also depend on competitive reactions, changes in consumer perceptions, and other market and economic realities. Many data-driven consulting firms provide advice to organizations regarding tactical pricing decisions. Competera, for example, is a UK-based consulting firm with offices in Singapore and the US. Using deep learning algorithms, it claims to increase revenues for its clients by up to 9% by helping marketers determine the optimal prices for products and product lines (competera.net 2022).

9.9 SUMMARY

The purpose of the pricing planning process is to assess the value proposition and then communicate important information about that value proposition to customers and other stakeholders. Done correctly, the pricing planning process results in a clear signaling of what the value proposition is *worth* to consumers.

Several economic forces that influence a product's price were identified, including an assessment of costs and price, the elasticity of demand, purchasing power parity, economies of scale, externalized costs, the Tragedy of the Commons, inflation, and regulatory restrictions. During this discussion, VEJA was introduced as an example of a company that does not externalize its costs. Aldi's tone-deaf campaign was discussed to underscore the need to understand the context within which a price-related promotion is deployed. By identifying these economic forces, the marketing team is better able to understand the context within which it will enact the pricing planning process. Consumer perceptions of the product and its price also were also identified, including the consumer's reference price, perceptions of scarcity, and price-quality perceptions. By understanding consumer perceptions related to price, the marketing team will be better able to predict how consumers in the target market might react to the pricing strategy.

After setting its pricing objectives, the marketing team must then select from among a wide variety of pricing strategies. These strategies fall into four broad categories: competitive pricing strategies, product line pricing strategies, consumer-focused pricing strategies, and new product pricing strategies. Each one of these categories was discussed in detail, strategies were presented, and examples were provided. Depending on its objectives, the marketing team could utilize one or several different strategies. In the end, marketing managers utilize price – in coordination with the other marketing mix elements – as an effective tool to deliver value to customers.

QUESTIONS FOR REVIEW & DISCUSSION

1. Explain the importance of the pricing planning process and sketch the four steps involved in the process. Why do we say that the most important first step in the pricing planning process is setting a pricing objective?
2. In what way would a consumer's perceptions be relevant to the marketing team's decision about the product's price?
3. What happens when a firm does not take into account its externalized costs? Critics claim that when a firm takes externalized costs into account, the price of the product is likely to increase and the consumer will suffer. Do you agree or disagree? Why? Support your answer with evidence from the chapter and elsewhere.
4. Examine competitive pricing strategies and consumer-focused pricing strategies in Figure 9.8. Which of these strategies is used by your own college or university? Does it use more than one? Provide a detailed rationale for your answer.
5. As tempting as it might be to respond to a competitor's price cut, it is rarely the best choice to do so. Imagine that you are starting a new job and your new boss is about to launch the company into a price war with the biggest competitor in the market. Create a convincing argument for why your boss should avoid the temptation of participating in a price war.
6. There are four new product pricing strategies. For each one, provide an example of a product that has utilized the strategy (remember: a product can include a tangible product, a service, idea, person, or destination). Be creative!

9.10 REFERENCES

Ayling, Louise. 2020. Wild Scenes as an Angry Mob in New Zealand Turns Violent After Flocking to a $70,000 "Cash Drop" Only to Discover the Money is FAKE. *The Daily Mail Australia*. 6 December. Accessed 21 February 2022.

Basurto, Xavier and Elinor Ostrom. 2009. Beyond the Tragedy of the Commons. *Economics and Policy of Energy and the Environment, 52* (1), 35–60.

bcorporation.net. 2022. VEJA. Accessed 10 February 2022. www.bcorporation.net/en-us/find-a-b-corp/search?query=veja.

Chandran, Sucharita and Vicki G. Morwitz. 2005. Effects of Participative Pricing on Cognitions and Actions: A Goal Theoretic Perspective. *Journal of Consumer Research, 32* (2), 249–59.

competera.net. 2022.

Desilver, Drew. 2022. In the U.S. and Around the World, Inflation is Higher and Getting Higher. *Pew Research Center*. 15 June. Accessed 20 June 2022. www.pewresearch.org/fact-tank/2022/06/15/in-the-u-s-and-around-the-world-inflation-is-high-and-getting-higher/.

Ding, Min, William T. Ross, Jr., and Vithala R. Rao. 2010. Price as an Indicator of Quality: Implications for Utility and Demand Functions. *Journal of Retailing, 86* (1), 69–84.

Fernando, Jason. 2022. Guide to Inflation. *Investopedia.com*. 12 June. Accessed 20 June 2022. www.investopedia.com/terms/i/inflation.asp.

Frankenfield, Jake. 2022. Cryptocurrency. *Investopedia*. 11 January. Accessed 7 February 2022. www.investopedia.com/terms/c/cryptocurrency.asp

Frej, Willa. 2016. You Can No Longer Stream Hulu for Free. *Huffington Post*. 8 August 2016. Accessed 24 February 2022. www.huffpost.com/entry/stream-hulu-free_n_57a89976e4b03ba68012faa9.

Heilweil, Rebecca. 2022. Peloton's Problems Aren't Just Peloton's. *Vox Recode*. Vox Media, LLC. 9 February. Accessed 11 February 2022. www.vox.com/recode/22925513/peloton-recall-gyms-nordictrack-mirror.

Hickman, Arvind. 2020. Aldi's 'Food Poverty' Influencer Campaign 'Tone Deaf' and 'Lacking Authenticity.' *PRWeek. News*. 5 February. Accessed 10 February 2022. www.prweek.com/article/1672984/aldis-food-poverty-influencer-campaign-tone-deaf-lacking-authenticity.

Jucca, Lisa. 2021. Tiffany Shine Contradicts LVMH Deal Tantrum. *Reuters*. 27 July. Accessed 7 January 2022. www.reuters.com/breakingviews/tiffany-shine-contradicts-lvmh-deal-tantrum-2021-07-27/.

Kennedy, Brian and Alison Spencer. 2021. Most Americans Support Expanding Solar and Wind Energy, But Republican Support Has Dropped. *Pew Research Center*. Energy Section. 8 June. Accessed 23 February 2022. www.pewresearch.org/fact-tank/2021/06/08/most-americans-support-expanding-solar-and-wind-energy-but-republican-support-has-dropped/.

Kienzler, Mario and Christian Kowalkowski. 2017. Pricing Strategy: A Review of 22 Years of Marketing Research. *Journal of Business Research, 78* (101), 101–10.

Liozu, Stephan M., Andreas Hinterhuber, Richard Boland, and Sheri Perelli. 2012. The Conceptualization of Value-Based Pricing in Industrial Firms. *Journal of Revenue and Pricing Management, 11*, 12–34.

Mahajan, Megan. 2018. Plunging Prices Mean Building New Renewable Energy is Cheaper Than Running Existing Coal. *Forbes*. 3 December. Accessed 12 February 2022. www.forbes.com/sites/energyinnovation/2018/12/03/plunging-prices-mean-building-new-renewable-energy-is-cheaper-than-running-existing-coal/?fbclid=IwAR2AWbr9n6N0OjtCVfwN8gO05pGjqbUASg4NMwihI0eRF7ANTMboTzxYLA8&sh=ac8900731f31.

Merelli, Annalisa. 2021. Europe Sent Nigeria Up to 1 Million Near-Expired Doses of Covid-19 Vaccine. *Quartz Africa*. 10 December. Accessed 23 February 2022. https://qz.com/africa/2100629/europe-donated-near-expired-doses-of-vaccine-to-african-countries/.

Monroe, Kent B. 2003. *Pricing: Making Profitable Decisions*, 3rd edition. Irwin Professional Publishing, Burr Ridge, Illinois.

Noble, Peter M. and Thomas S. Gruca. 1999. Industrial Pricing: Theory and Managerial Practice. *Marketing Science, 18* (3), 435–54.

Ostrom, Elinor. 1999. Coping with Tragedies of the Commons. *Annual Review of Political Science, 2* (1), 493–535.

Project. 2022. The VEJA Founders Tell You About Their Vision and the Brand's History. Accessed 10 February 2022. https://project.veja-store.com/en/intro/.

Rao, Akshay R., Mark E. Bergen, and Scott Davis. 2000. How to Fight a Price War. *Harvard Business Review, 78* (2), 107–16.

Rao, Akshay R. and Wanda A. Sieben. 1992. The Effect of Prior Knowledge on Price Acceptability and the Type of Information Examined. *Journal of Consumer Research, 19* (2), 256–70.

Rao, Ram C. and Frank M. Bass. 1985. Competition, Strategy, and Price Dynamics: A Theoretical and Empirical Investigation. *Journal of Marketing Research, 22* (3), 283–96.

Sabanoglu, Tugba. 2021. Forecast of Nike's Global Market Share in Athletic Footwear from 2011 to 2025. *Statista*. 4 February. Accessed 23 February 2022. www.statista.com/statistics/216821/forecast-for-nikes-global-market-share-in-athletic-footwear-until-2017/.

Smith, Michael D. and Rahul Telang. 2019. Netflix and the Economics of Bundling. *Harvard Business Review*. 25 February. Accessed 24 February 2022. https://hbr.org/2019/02/netflix-and-the-economics-of-bundling.

Somervouri, Outi. 2014. Profiling Behavioral Pricing Research in Marketing. *Journal of Product and Brand Management, 23* (6), 462–74.

Stock, Axel and Subramian Balachander. 2005. The Making of a "Hot Product": A Signaling Explanation of Marketers' Scarcity Strategy. *Management Science, 51* (8), 1181–92.

Suri, Rajneesh, Chiranjeev Kohli, and Kent B. Monroe. 2007. The Effects of Perceived Scarcity on Consumers' Processing of Price Information. *Journal of the Academy of Marketing Science, 35*, 89–100.

Tattersall, Michael. 2021. 66% of UK Consumers are Now Aware of Cryptocurrencies. *Business Insider*. 10 December. Accessed 7 January 2022. www.businessinsider.com/growing-uk-crypto-consumer-awareness-will-draw-more-wealth-managers-2021-12.

Tellis, Gerard J. 1986. Beyond the Many Faces of Price: An Integration of Pricing Strategies. *Journal of Marketing, 50* (4), 146–60.

Thomas, Lauren. 2022. Peloton to Halt Production of its Bikes, Treadmills as Demand Wanes. *CNBC*. Retail Section. 20 January. Accessed 11 February 2022. www.cnbc.com/2022/01/20/peloton-to-pause-production-of-its-bikes-treadmills-as-demand-wanes.html.

Veblen, Thorstein. [1899] 2007. *The Theory of the Leisure Class*. Oxford University Press, Oxford, UK.

Walsh, David. 2021. *Paying with Bitcoin: These are the Major Companies that Accept Crypto as Payment*. 12 April. Accessed 8 February 2021. www.euronews.com/next/2021/12/04/paying-with-cryptocurrencies-these-are-the-major-companies-that-accept-cryptos-as-payment.

Watrous, Monica. 2017. Danone Seals the Deal with WhiteWave. *Food Business News*. 14 April. Accessed 7 January 2022. www.foodbusinessnews.net/articles/9197-danone-seals-the-deal-with-whitewave.

Wood, Zoe. 2021. Banana Price War in UK Supermarkets is Hurting Farmers, Growers Warn. *The Guardian*. 30 October. Accessed 22 February 2022. www.theguardian.com/business/2021/oct/30/banana-price-war-uk-supermarkets-hurting-farmers-growers-warn.

10 PLACE STRATEGIES: DELIVERING THE VALUE PROPOSITION

LEADERSHIP INSIGHTS 10

Photo 10.1 Brittany Ford

Source: courtesy, Brittany Ford

Meet Brittany Ford, Regulatory Compliance Executive

BDP International

Brittany Ford is the Regulatory Compliance Officer with the Belgium office of BDP International, one of the largest, privately-held supply chain management companies in the world. "Every single country does things differently, so we need to adapt our strategy for every single country," she offered.

To optimize the efficiency of their supply chain strategies, companies come to BDP for expert help in navigating a variety of issues, such as tariffs, regulations, safety protocols, and licenses. What sets BDP apart from the competition is its flexibility and individualized customer solutions. BDP has particular expertise in helping customers who are entering new markets. Customers "need help working with governments and government agencies. We help them address these problems," said Ford. When the US imposed a series of severe tariffs on the EU and China in 2018–19, Ford's job became increasingly complicated. "If you were previously importing anything from China, you needed to source from different locations because the duty rate was so astronomical, it didn't make sense from any perspective to import from there. The EU and China retaliated by imposing higher rates on US products. The EU, for example, put a higher tariff on US whiskey. It's all integrated," explained Ford, "we help customers find alternatives." Global shipping is a complicated process indeed.

Brexit presented a different set of challenges. In October 2019, the UK formally left the EU. BDP's internal client research found that a full 41% were unable to predict Brexit's financial impact on their companies. When asked to identify the person responsible for handling Brexit-related implications for their company, 38% of company representatives said it was the responsibility of logistics, 25% said supply chain, and 24% said compliance. In fact, *all* functional areas were needed in order to navigate the new reality. With decades of expertise in global shipping, BDP was well equipped to prepare its customers for the reality of a post-UK European Union.

The team found that it needed to provide different services to big companies vs. smaller companies. "For the big companies, who are used to shipping all around the world, this is not a major problem for them. But there are a lot of companies who just operate intra-Europe and they don't know what to do. That's why they come to BDP because they need our help to make export declarations, set up their own internal structures, and complete the necessary registrations and permits. There were new procedures for everything. We provided step-by-step advice for everything," explained Ford.

BDP positioned itself as a resource for information and expertise, and ensured that this positioning was in place well before the UK's actual exit, giving their customers sufficient time to adapt. Even after Brexit, the team continued to assist with new registrations, declarations, safety protocols, duties and taxes, proper classifications and values, and licenses. The team also developed a set of recommendations for companies to adapt their accounting and invoicing systems for the increased costs of extra fees, delays, and procedures.

8 DECENT WORK AND ECONOMIC GROWTH

If Ford could give her 20-year-old self some advice, it would be this: "never expect something to just come to you. You need to go after it yourself. When you advocate for yourself, that's when things start happening."

10.1 "LOGISTICS" SHOULD GET A GOLD MEDAL

The job of hosting a successful Olympic event has brought host cities to their knees. Despite having about 10 years to plan for the event, most host cities severely underestimate the amount of time and resources needed not only to construct the venues where the events will take place, but to efficiently and effectively move approximately 30,000 athletes, support staff, and press around the venue. These numbers do not take into account the throngs of spectators who attend the events. In addition, about 30 million items – furniture, equipment, supplies – need to be shipped from around the world to help support the event.

The International Olympic Committee (IOC)'s Operational Requirement Contract provides such exacting detail, that the 300-page document leaves nothing to doubt about what the host city is required to provide to support this logistical marvel. For example:

- *Accommodations* – regulations require 41,000 rooms be made available for the Summer Olympics and 24,000 for the Winter Olympics (this does not include spectators). These specifications include proximity of the rooms to the sporting venues, food, services, medical care, and security. Even the quality of the accommodation is specified: those traveling with the IOC get 4–5 star accommodations, whereas marketing affiliates get 3 star accommodations, and it is acceptable to provide the media with 2.5 star accommodations. The requirements even specify the size of the rooms, size of the beds, the number of athletes per bathroom (no more than four), and schedules for cleaning and changing towels (IOC 2018).
- *Food & Beverage* – the IOC requires 24/7 free access to hot and cold food options within the Olympic village for sit-down and "grab and go" meals. Food and beverage options need to include options for a wide variety of dietary needs, taking into account a variety of cultural and religious sensibilities (IOC 2018). There are tremendous logistical challenges in delivering and preparing the volume of food needed for the most elite athletes in the world. Athletes are often hungry – the average female Olympian consumes 5000 calories/day and the average male Olympian consumes 7000 calories/day (Belluz 2018). In addition, the demand has substantial spikes during the day because athletes are usually hungrier at specific times (breakfast, lunch, and dinner). During the Rio Summer Games, chefs used 210,000 kilograms of raw ingredients to make and serve 60,000 meals for the 18,000 athletes, coaches, and staff *each day* (Wade 2016) (see Photo 10.2).

The logistical challenges of the Olympics are daunting in normal years. During a global pandemic, the challenges are almost Herculean. After the Tokyo Summer Olympics were rescheduled and moved back 1 year to 2021, international spectators were prohibited. For domestic spectators, Olympians, and staff, strict rules were implemented for masking and social distancing. One of the biggest challenges was getting the teams to the games. Prices skyrocketed and

Photo 10.2 The Olympic Games is a logistical feat in itself

Source: iStock

international flights were cancelled and rerouted. High transmission rates in some countries resulted in travel bans into and out of those countries, making the arrangements even more complicated. The Sri Lankan team, for example, had to endure many hours of connecting flights going in opposite directions before arriving in Tokyo. With commercial flights into and out of the country severely curtailed, Fiji's Olympic team hitched a ride on a seafood cargo plane in order to make it to Tokyo (Nicholas 2021).

During the Beijing Winter Olympics in 2022, pandemic-related restrictions were even more stringent. China had a "zero Covid" policy, which presented challenges to athletes before they even arrived. Beijing required all flights into the country be booked through a small set of hubs like Hong Kong, Paris, or Singapore. Everyone arriving needed to provide certification of two negative PCR tests from a small set of approved testing centers within 96 hours of departure. Then, upon arrival, athletes, staff, and the media were required to stay within a "bubble" and were prevented from leaving it for any reason. The bubble contained hotels, competitive venues, the Olympic village for the athletes, and media centers. Local volunteers and workers also stayed within the bubble and were tested on a daily basis (Keh 2022).

The level of detailed planning necessary for a normal Olympic event is mind-boggling; the effort and coordination involved during a global pandemic is a recipe for a splitting headache. If the supply chain is well-planned and running smoothly, few people notice. It is only when there are problems that everyone notices, as the world witnessed when supply chain disruptions during the global Covid-19 pandemic resulted in shortages of a variety of products. This chapter is devoted to the "place" part of the marketing mix. Because it is the part of the marketing mix that is most difficult for competitors to duplicate, decisions that are made regarding the place dimension of the marketing mix have a unique ability in helping the firm achieve a strategic competitive advantage.

10.2 LEARNING OBJECTIVES

After studying this chapter, you will be able to do the following:

1 Differentiate between the purpose and functions of the supply chain, distribution channel, and logistics.
2 Explain how the supply chain can be a source of strategic competitive advantage.
3 Describe the various supply chain objectives an organization could pursue.
4 Describe the seven broad categories of supply chain strategies that a marketing manager must consider.
5 Create an argument for making the supply chain more sustainable.

10.3 THE CRITICAL ROLE OF THE SUPPLY CHAIN

The **supply chain** describes the entire set of processes and steps involved in getting a product into the hands of consumers. The supply chain performs two primary functions: (1) *a physical function* that converts raw materials into products and moves them to locations for easy customer access and (2) *a mediation function* that ensures that the right products reach the right consumers at the right time and the right place (Fisher 1997). Supply chains accomplish a lot.

They are responsible for the sourcing of raw materials, movement of materials, production, storage, and retailing. They also cover all of the planning, actions, functions, and movement of the raw materials and product. They are involved in negotiations with other members of the supply chain, sales projections, people, data sharing, customer service, and other functions, such as those performed at BDP, like invoicing, registrations, declarations, safety protocols, duties, and taxes. The overall goal of the supply chain is to help the organization achieve a competitive advantage by delivering the value proposition earlier, cheaper, safer, or more efficiently.

Supply chains vary in the number of intermediaries. **Intermediaries** are wholesalers, retailers, shippers, and distributors that often take control or ownership of the product as it moves along the way to the next intermediary and on to the consumer. With each intermediary, costs are added. Some supply chains have no intermediaries, as when a farmer sells products from the farm directly to consumers at a farm stand. Other supply chains have a large number of intermediaries. Think about the global supply chain for clothing, for example. Cotton is sourced in one part of the world, it is shipped to a facility where it is cleaned and spun into thread, another entity weaves it into cloth, another dies the fabric, another cuts it and assembles it into jeans, the jeans are then shipped to a wholesaler, distributor, and then a retailer. In very customer-centric operations, the supply chain is referred to as **the value chain**, because value is added at each step along the way in getting the finished product into the hands of the consumer (see Figure 10.1).

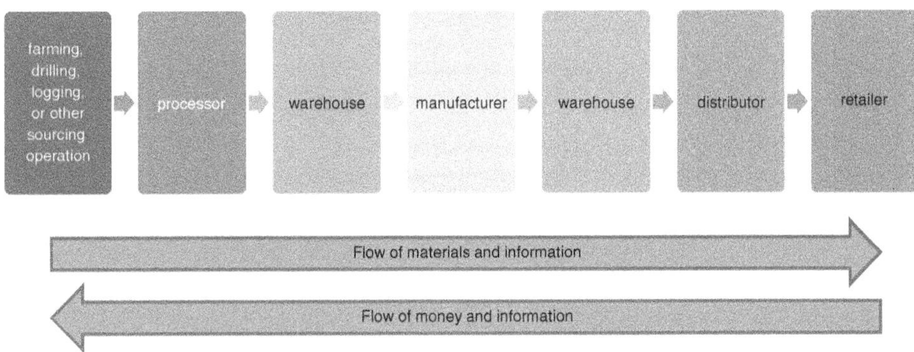

Figure 10.1 A supply chain should add value at each step

The supply chain is best able to deliver value to consumers when it has three characteristics, referred to as the **Triple A framework**: it must be *agile* enough to react to sudden changes in supply and demand, be *adaptable* to shifts in the market structure or organizational strategy, and must *align* the interests of all of the supply chain stakeholders so that organizational objectives can be achieved. Supply chains that achieve all three of these characteristics are in the best position to deliver the value proposition (Lee 2004).

Planning for sudden shocks to the normally-efficient supply chain is essential. Natural disasters happen, as do accidents and other disruptions, such as the war in Ukraine which erupted in 2022. Marketers need to be prepared for these shocks by building a "Plan B" into the planning. If, for example, a fire happens at a facility, what is the backup plan to still deliver the product when and where it is needed? The marketing team can make its supply chain more *agile* by enabling the supply chain to respond quickly and cost-efficiently to sudden changes in supply and demand. If needed, the system should be enabled to bypass distribution hubs or ship less

Photo 10.3 7-Eleven stores are aligned with their supply chain partners

Source: Shutterstock/Tupungato

than full cargo loads. Collaboration with other supply chain partners is essential. As much as possible, it is also essential to ensure that processes and products (or product components) are interchangeable so they can be easily substitutable. An agile supply chain can be used to differentiate the organization from its competitor. Fast fashion giants H&M and Zara are differentiated from their competitors by their lightning-quick identification of a new fashion trend, production, and delivery of that new trend to store shelves (Lee 2004).

Alignment is achieved when the organization and its supply chain partners work toward a common goal. If, for example, the overall objective is to increase customer convenience, every intermediary will work toward that end. It is important to realize here that another objective, such as customer relationships, will motivate a different strategy on the part of the supply chain partners. Aligned objectives mean that incentives for performance need to be aligned too (Lee 2004). The world's biggest convenience store chain, 7-Eleven, aligns its interests with its supply chain partners to deliver high-quality, fresh food to its customers. The Japanese-owned company has over 77,700 stores located in 18 regions and countries around the world (Press Release 2022). In its home market of Japan, 7-Eleven has 290 dedicated manufacturing plants and 293 separate distribution centers producing fast food for its stores. Delivery trucks pick up and deliver a variety of supplies and fresh food to stores 11 times each day (freshly-made fast food is delivered three times per day). The product assortment is altered to reflect demand at different times of the day; breakfast sandwiches, for example, arrive before the sun is up. To facilitate quick and efficient delivery, drivers are not required to wait for store managers to review each delivery. This alignment of interests results in quicker delivery, less traffic disruption, and fresh supplies of high-quality food (Chopra 2005) (see Photo 10.3).

Finally, the supply chain must be structured to be *adaptable*, in order to respond to shifts in the structures of the market, supply and demand, or organizational objectives. For example, a shift in demand might result in a production facility no longer located close to a center of demand. The marketing team can construct an adaptable supply chain if it is first able to identify shifts before they occur. Flexible product designs and standardized processes make it easier to be prepared for shifts, as can preemptive relocation of factories or distribution centers (Lee 2004). During the Covid-19 pandemic, countless organizations adapted their supply chains to deliver needed medical supplies and equipment. The alcohol industry responded to the surge in demand for hand sanitizer by quickly adapting its operations. Specifically, makers of distilled spirits found that much of the equipment and supply chain could be easily adapted to produce hand sanitizer. This extra source of revenue was especially welcome as some experts estimated that sales at bars and restaurants had dropped 64% during the first few months of the pandemic (Browning 2020) (see Figure 10.2).

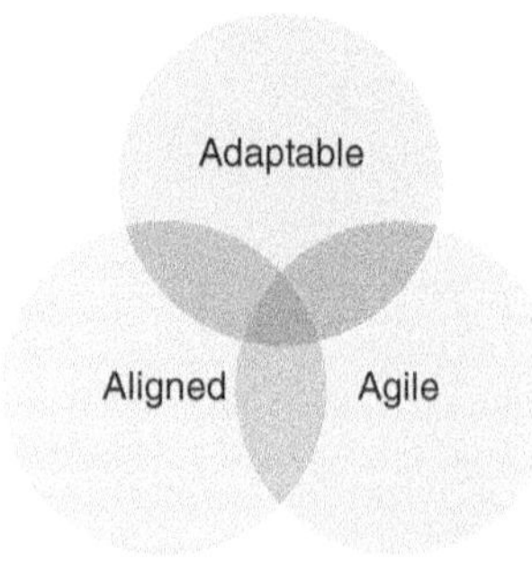

Figure 10.2 Three dimensions necessary for an efficient and effective supply chain

Source: Lee (2004)

Logistics

Logistics is a part of the supply chain. It is more narrowly-focused on coordinating and managing the physical movement and storage of materials, information, and product on its way to its final destination. The goal of logistics is to get materials into the hands of the right entity – including the right consumers – at the right time and price. Large global organizations and operations like the Olympics often have very complex logistical systems. This is especially the case when an organization sources its materials or ingredients from different parts of the world and sells to a variety of consumers around the world. Some organizations hire experts to perform their logistical functions, rather than doing it themselves. **Third Party Logistics (3PL) providers** like BDP are independent organizations that are completely integrated into the organization's own operations and carry out the logistics functions for the organization.

Channels of Distribution

The distribution channel is also a part of the supply chain. It includes all of the activities performed by intermediaries involved in delivering the finished product to the consumer. The important part here is that the distribution channel covers the movement and storage in just that portion of the supply chain that exists between the organization and the consumer.

To clarify the differences between these concepts, think about the iconic chocolate bunny manufactured by Swiss chocolate-maker Lindt. The supply chain describes the *entire* process involved in getting all of the raw materials from different suppliers around the world (sugar, cocoa butter, chocolate, gold foil, red ribbon) to facilities where these ingredients are processed and packaged. It also includes all of the steps involved in getting the bunnies delivered to warehouses, distributors, and retailers where consumers can buy them, as well as invoicing, data sharing, customer service, and other functions. The distribution channel is concerned with just that part of the supply chain that exists between the bunny and the consumer; it is not concerned with what happens before all of these raw materials are formed into the final product. Finally, logistics covers the coordination and management function involved with the physical movement and storage of the raw materials and finished product (see Photo 10.4).

Photo 10.4 The Lindt chocolate bunny

ENDURING INSIGHTS 10.1

"My logisticians are a humorless lot ... they know if my campaign fails, they are the first ones I will slay." – Alexander the Great, military leader of ancient Greece

Known for his shrewd strategic skills, Alexander the Great recognized the importance of the supply chain and specifically, logistics, to the success of an operation. The same is true in marketing. The most well-conceived strategies will fail without a successful logistical operation.

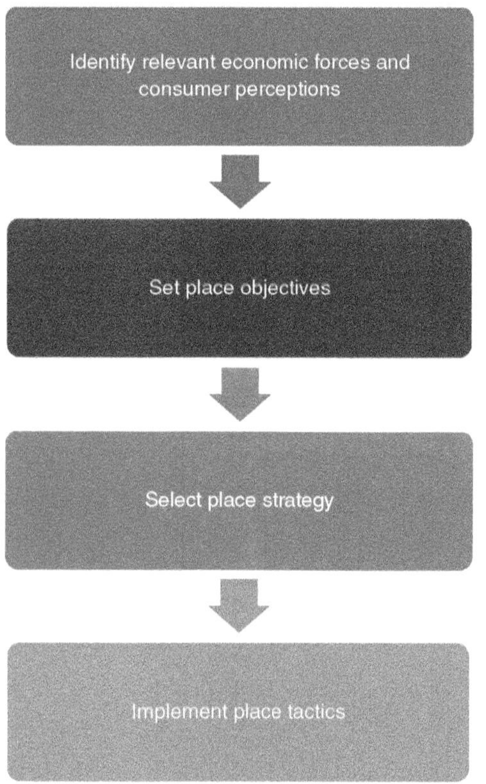

Figure 10.3 The supply chain planning process

The supply chain planning process starts with an identification of the relevant economic factors and consumer perspectives that influence the supply chain. Then, the marketing team must create a set of supply chain objectives, strategies, and tactics (see Figure 10.3).

10.4 RELEVANT ECONOMIC FACTORS

A well-functioning supply chain is relatively immune to small day-to-day economic events. Instead, long-term shifts in economic and consumer trends are much more likely to influence the supply chain, as are big events such as natural disasters, a global pandemic, or military conflicts. Indeed, these types of events could very well send supply chains into chaos. However, if the supply chain is structured so that it is agile, adaptable, and aligned, it will be able to better weather these events (Chopra 2005). There are a variety of economic factors that influence the supply chain.

Interconnectedness of Operations

One of the most important issues for the marketing decision-maker to assess is the **interconnectedness of operations**, the extent to which its own supply chain and that of its partners is interconnected with the global economy. A deeply interconnected system may result in additional risk if there are disturbances somewhere in that system. A disturbance in one section of the supply chain is often felt throughout the entire system. Shortages of component parts, such as computer chips, cause significant delays in the manufacturing of numerous other products. At the height of the Covid-19 pandemic, the world experienced severe supply chain disruptions. The price of moving goods from China to ports around the world increased tenfold. In response to the computer chip shortage, Toyota slashed production by 40% in August 2021. Around the world, manufacturing slowed because of shortages in metal, glass, and plastic. Adding to the problem were labor shortages and closures of global shipping ports (Goodman and Bradsher 2021).

Socioeconomic Trends

Marketing decision-makers also need to assess **socioeconomic trends**, the broad human-focused trends that could impact the economy and the organization's ability to successfully deliver the value proposition to its customers. Experts have identified five key socioeconomic trends in Europe (JLL 2019) (see also Figure 10.4):

1 *Strong urbanization* – a greater proportion of European citizens are moving to cities. In 2019, 74.5% of Europeans lived in cities and by 2029, that proportion is expected to grow to 76%. Among other things, this trend will result in the need for additional housing, as well as services, amenities, and improvements to infrastructure to help people move around.

2 *Overall ageing* – taken as a whole, the median age of Europeans is expected to increase from 43.1 in 2018, to 45.4 by 2030, and 46.5 by 2040. This is mainly due to increased longevity and declining birth rates across the region. Northern Italy has an especially large population of older residents, particularly in the cities of Genoa, Bologna, Milan, and Turin. This ageing population will desire different kinds of products and services than their younger counterparts.

3 *Youthful cities* – despite an overall ageing population, about a third of the populations in European cities will continue to be made up of younger people under the age of 30. These individuals will likely create a robust demand for products related to youthful and young family lifestyles, such as bars, restaurants, athletic spaces, parks, and schools.

4 *Declining household sizes* – although the overall population in Europe is increasing, the number of distinct households is also increasing, leading to a smaller number of people per household. There seem to be several smaller trends that are driving this trend. Compared to 2009, the average age of first marriage today is increasing (29.4 years vs. 27.2), the average age that a woman becomes a mother is increasing (30.7 years vs. 29.7), and the proportion of households with no children is on the rise (71% vs. 68%).

5 *Growing university enrollment* – for the past decade, an increasing proportion of students are enrolling in university education across Europe, partially because of somewhat dreary job prospects for young people. The three cities with the highest number of university students are London, Paris, and Warsaw.

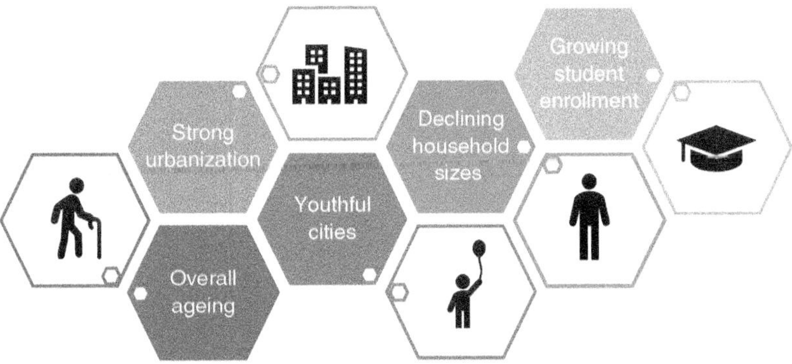

Figure 10.4 Five key European trends

Source: adapted, in part, from JLL (2019)

Relevant Regulations

The marketing team also must identify regulations that are relevant to supply chain operations. Countries and trading blocs around the world have a wide variety of supply chain-related regulations that are generally designed to accomplish one of three objectives. The first type is designed to protect the health and safety of the citizens in the country or trading bloc. These regulations cover the types of food, medicine, extracts, and associated waste that can be shipped within the country or trading bloc. They also cover handling, labeling, and proper disposal of these items. The second broad type of regulations covers the dark side of marketing and includes items such as counterfeit products and illegal goods like drugs, weapons, and endangered species. The EU's Wildlife Trade Regulations, for example, prohibit the importation of a wide variety of items, such as alligator and crocodile products, items made from snake and lizard skins and leathers, turtle and tortoise shells, and elephant ivory and skin products. Violations are met with stiff fines and confiscation (Enforcement Group 2022). The third broad category of place-related regulations are tariffs or quotas designed to reduce the volume of products being shipped into a country or trading bloc. This category might also include economic sanctions against a country or trading bloc. For both, the goal is to either protect domestic producers or inflict economic hardship on foreign producers. After Russia's attack on Ukraine in February 2022, leaders of the G7 (UK, US, Germany, Italy, France, Japan, and Canada) and the EU joined forces with other countries around the world (more than 30 in all) to impose a series of economic sanctions on Russia (White House 2022).

Increasingly, supply chain regulations are addressing the global climate crisis. In 2022, a French law required all automotive company ads to include statements encouraging consumers to take more environmentally-friendly modes of transportation. Statements such as "for day-to-day use, take public transportation" and "for short trips, opt for walking or cycling" must be included in all automobile ads. This measure is a part of the overall effort to reduce CO_2 emissions from transportation, which makes up about 25% of the EU's total carbon footprint. Violations will be met with a stiff fine of €50,000 (Hernandez 2022).

The decade of the 2020s started out with a variety of new climate legislation. As a brief sampling, Canada passed the Canadian Net-Zero Emissions Accountability Act, which requires the country to achieve net-zero emissions by 2050 at the latest. The Act also includes strict oversight as well as several benchmarks to track progress (Grantham 2021). In 2021, the European Climate Law went into effect, which seeks to make the EU climate neutral by 2050; EU institutions and member countries are required to take the necessary measures to achieve this goal (LOC 2021). New Zealand passed a law which required financial institutions doing business in the country to report on plans to manage climate-related risks and opportunities (Reuters 2021). This patchwork of laws around the world is a strong motivator for organizations to shift toward more sustainable operations, shipping, and products. Manufacturers benefit from supply chain efficiencies and economies of scale when they produce all of their products according to the strictest environmental standards, rather than producing different versions of their products for different regions or countries.

Growth and Momentum

An assessment of a city's, region's, or country's growth and growth rate provide valuable information to the marketing decision-maker, especially for long-term investments such as supply chain operations. When examining a variety of socioeconomic factors, commercial property metrics, and business activity, the top three most dynamic cities in the world are Hyderabad, Bengaluru, and Ho Chi Minh City. Because of their infrastructure as well as their youthful and skilled workforce, these cities are poised to continue to experience above-average growth over the next decade, despite an expected slowdown in the global economy (JLL 2020).

10.5 THE CONSUMER CONNECTION

Because delivery of the value proposition is the overarching goal of the supply chain, the marketing team needs to carefully identify any relevant place-related consumer perceptions and concerns.

Level of Customer Involvement

Consumer involvement is the perceived personal relevance of the product to the consumer. It is based on the consumer's needs, values, and interests (Zaichkowsky 1985). The marketing team needs to understand the nature of the product and the role it plays in the lives of consumers. Is this product essential to the consumer's self-worth, self-concept, or self-definition? Are there any health, safety, or financial risks involved with the decision or consumption of the product? If so, involvement will be higher and consumers may be less willing to accept any delays in delivery or damage to the product. They may also expect greater service levels, such as special handling or warranties.

Another consideration is not just the existing level of consumer involvement, but the opportunity for the organization to potentially forge stronger ties with consumers and encourage greater levels of involvement with the product, brand, or organization. If there is indeed such an opportunity, the supply chain could be designed to facilitate that goal.

Customer Expectations

With respect to the supply chain, **customer expectations** are the pre-conceived notions about how, where, and when the product will be delivered. Do customers expect the ability to get expedited deliveries? Guarantees of delivery times? Extra services such as help with invoicing, duties, and taxes? When supply chain managers ship their products from Asia to the East Coast of the US or Europe through the Panama Canal, they are better able to meet the expectations of their retail customers for quick delivery. In addition, as customers of the Panama Canal, these managers have expectations that they will receive a variety of services themselves, such as assistance with tariffs, taxes, and duties (see case study on p.453). Having a clear assessment of customer expectations will help direct the marketing team in its decisions about how to construct and operate the supply chain.

The Concept of Terroir

The **concept of terroir** describes the location-specific natural and human components of a product that make it unique. Often, a product's terroir is highly sought-after; consumers place greater value on some products simply because they come from a particular place. Take the example of champagne (see case study on p.502), or other specialized products like Italian truffles, Cuban cigars, or Irish whiskey. Sure, consumers can get sparkling wine, truffles, cigars, and whiskey from other locations, but they are especially tasty and sought-after when they come from a specific place. Terroir has two primary dimensions. The first is soil composition, weather, topography, and climate. Distinct minerals, clay, and microorganisms in the soil, as well as the number of sunny days, the amount and timing of rain, the amount of humidity in the air, the coolness of the nights, and the angle of the sun all imbue food and beverage products with a unique taste, composition, and texture. The second component of terroir encompasses a region's unique social and cultural characteristics – the people, history, and shared values of the place. This human element of terroir includes the work ethic of the people, their shared values, language, and philosophy, as well as a shared set of skills and methods that were likely passed down through many generations (Charters, Spielmann, and Babin 2017). Terroir is impossible for a competitor to copy and serves as a barrier to market entry. As a part of the brand's value proposition, terroir can be a foundation for the organization's sustainable competitive advantage (Charters, et al. 2017) (see Figure 10.5).

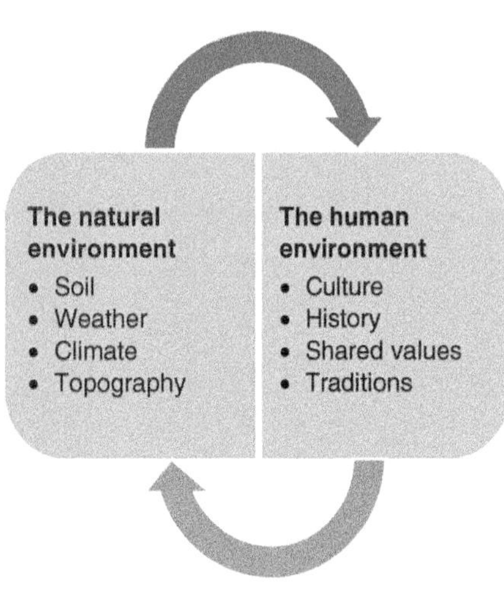

Figure 10.5 The two-dimensional nature of terroir

Source: adapted, in part, from Charters, et al. (2017)

BLUNDERS & INSIGHTS 10.1

Stranded in Paradise

WHAT HAPPENED: Founded in 1841, the UK's Thomas Cook Travel Agency started out offering short day trips around the country. The small company grew quickly and by the 1850s, it offered its first international trips (Borden 2019). The agency offered something new and compelling: package tours that allowed people to travel relatively stress-free with the agency making all of the bookings for hotels, transportation, excursions, and food. As the world started to rebuild after WWII, interest in international travel became more realistic for the world's middle class. Through the 1990s, the company expanded quickly and aggressively. At the same time, it added more debt with the addition of brick-and-mortar stores located in some of the world's most exclusive "high street" locations (Ludden 2019). After a merger with a German travel organization, Thomas Cook debuted its own airline division in 2003 (Borden 2019).

By the 2010s, however, the travel industry had changed dramatically. Younger travelers were not interested in buying package holidays and were instead making many of their own travel arrangements using budget airlines and Airbnb. At the same time, Thomas Cook had crushing debt payments related to its aggressive expansion efforts a few years earlier. By

2011, its debt reached £930 million (Borden 2019). By September 2019, after Thomas Cook failed to get a last-minute emergency loan, it immediately ceased operations, leaving 150,000 travelers stranded around the world and 21,000 people out of work (Borden 2019). Because all of its assets were seized, it could not even send its own planes to pick up stranded travelers (see Photo 10.5).

Photo 10.5 Thomas Cook airplane

Source: Pixabay

DEBRIEF: In its last year, the company boasted 22 million customers, 550 agency shops, 40,000 hotel rooms, and a fleet of 105 airplanes (Borden 2019). Regardless of how hard they worked, Thomas Cook employees could not convince travelers to pay for its full-service travel packages. In the end, the per employee contribution to the bottom line was a paltry £188 per year. In an effort to bring home stranded travelers from around the world, the UK's Civil Aviation Authority engaged in what was called the "largest repatriation in peacetime history" (Ludden 2019). Between Thomas Cook's crushing debt load and its failure to quickly respond to dramatic shifts in consumer travel and planning behaviors, this once iconic brand is no more.

10.6 SUPPLY CHAIN OBJECTIVES

There are a variety of place-related objectives that can guide the marketing team's supply chain efforts (see Table 10.1). Like any objective, supply chain objectives should follow the SMART format and each objective will necessitate its own set of strategic decisions.

Table 10.1 Several supply chain objectives

Objective	Explanation and Strategic Implications
Enhance customer convenience	Customer convenience can be enhanced by ensuring that the product is widely available and accessible any time the customer might need it or want it. Convenience can also be enhanced by frequent deliveries, efficient invoicing/returns, or deliveries on demand.
Influence consumer perceptions	Supply chains have a significant influence on consumer perceptions and have the capability of playing an important role in the organization's positioning strategy. Brands that are offered at high-end luxury retailers, for example, benefit from a "halo effect" and are also perceived as high quality. The same is true for low-end retailers.
Strengthen customer relationships	The marketing team may wish to build or strengthen long-term customer relationships. The supply chain can facilitate this effort by tracking previous purchases and interactions with the customer, presenting consumers with targeted offerings, and fostering information sharing and follow-up with customers.
Support supply chain partners	Supply chain decisions are strongly influenced by the needs of business partners and intermediaries. The supply chain can support other supply chain stakeholders by sharing data, information, and resources. The supply chain could be designed to facilitate joint use of data and software resources (such as invoicing or inventory management systems), hardware resources (such as trucks or pallets), or human resources (such as drivers or warehouse workers).
Strike a competitive effect	Supply chain decisions should be designed with an eye toward the competition. If the supply chain can out-maneuver the competition by facilitating any of the above objectives – customer convenience, customer perceptions, customer relationships, or supply chain partners – it can strike a blow against the competition. In addition, in some instances, the supply chain can be designed and implemented to provide the organization exclusive access to an essential raw material or to a target market. Scale can also result in better supply chain efficiency and performance.

ENDURING INSIGHTS 10.2

> "Any customer can have a car painted any color that he wants so long as it is black." – Henry Ford, founder of Ford Motor Company

Henry Ford introduced the assembly line to manufacturing, which drastically lowered the per unit cost of automobiles, making them affordable for middle-class consumers. In an effort to cut costs, he simplified his supply chain so that, for several years, Ford only produced one type of car: the Model T. Customers had no ability to select features or options, including the color of the car.

10.7 SUPPLY CHAIN STRATEGIES

Supply chain strategies are designed to help achieve the supply chain objectives. Several strategic decisions need to be made by the marketing team.

Number of Channel Intermediaries

One of the first strategic decisions that needs to be made is the total number of intermediaries in the supply chain. The decision must be made by first considering the needs of the product (does it need refrigeration, special handling?) and the organization's own skills and capabilities (do we have the expertise needed?). Next, the marketing team must balance the need for greater control over the handling of the product with the need to bring in another intermediary who might be more skilled, offer faster/more efficient handling and delivery, or provide less expensive handling and delivery (see Table 10.2).

Table 10.2 Balancing risks and benefits of intermediaries

	Benefits	Risks
Few Intermediaries	• Greater control • Fewer costs	• Organization may not have the ability for specialized/expert handling • Risk is concentrated with the organization • Fewer operational efficiencies
More intermediaries	• Specialized/expert handling • Risk is distributed along the entire supply chain • Operational efficiencies due to each intermediary's ability to perform a single function	• Higher costs • Less control

Disintermediation is the phenomenon of reducing the number of intermediaries in the supply chain. In the most extreme case, all intermediaries are eliminated and the organization deals directly with the consumer. The trend of disintermediation has transformed the travel industry. With a variety of search tools and apps that are now available, as well as a greater level of experience and confidence, many tourists now make their own arrangements. A more recent shift away from online travel agents (OTAs) like Expedia and Agoda has effectively eliminated the last remaining intermediary in the travel industry. Management consulting firm Deloitte found that 54% of travelers booked their hotel stays directly with hotels, rather than through OTAs (just 17%). Similarly, 69% of travelers booked their flights directly with an airline, rather than through OTAs (just 18%). Why? Travelers found that by going direct to hotels and airlines, they got better deals, more flexible options in rescheduling or canceling, and more rewards such as loyalty points (Caputo, Jackson, Murali, and Rauch 2021).

Distribution Intensity

Another issue facing the marketing decision-maker is determining the ideal intensity of distribution. Consumer perceptions and expectations should be considered when making the decision about intensity. As the name implies, an **intensive distribution strategy** means that the company's products can be easily found in a variety of channels. Coca-Cola has an intensive strategy; Coke products can be found almost everywhere around the world: in convenience stores, restaurants, grocery stores, and vending machines. Customers thirsty for a Coke can easily find one. An **exclusive distribution strategy** is one in which the product is only found in a few outlets. High-end luxury brands like Chanel utilize exclusive distribution. Its stores are located in a very limited number of urban centers such as Avenue des Champs-Élysées in Paris. A **selective distribution strategy** is a balance between the two extremes. The product is found in some locations and is not very difficult to find.

Vertical vs. Horizontal Integration

Another strategic decision is the extent to which the organization will have direct control or ownership over the intermediaries in the supply chain. **Vertical integration** occurs when an organization owns two or more links in the supply chain. Vertical integration can be a strategic advantage because it can create synergies that reduce overall costs and increase efficiencies. **Backward vertical integration** occurs when the organization acquires an intermediary that exists somewhere in the supply chain between the organization and the source of raw materials. For example, Tiffany & Co. is not just a designer and retailer of high-end luxury jewelry, it also owns several diamond-polishing operations around the world. This allows it to have added control and transparency within the supply chain in order to ensure that its diamonds are not sourced from conflict zones. In fact, Tiffany's polishers engrave a tiny ID number on each of its diamonds over 0.18 carats to ensure added transparency and traceability. Tiffany & Co. cites its backward vertical integration strategy as one of its strategic strengths (Cumenal 2017).

Forward vertical integration happens when the organization owns one or more intermediaries that are located in the supply chain between the organization and the retailer (i.e., somewhere in the distribution channel). The organization might, for example, acquire a wholesaler, distributor, or retailer. By having a more direct connection to the consumer, the organization is able to exert greater control of its relationship with the consumer. In addition, the organization can leverage operational efficiencies and cost-saving measures. One example of forward vertical integration is the increasing prevalence of farm-to-table connections between farmers and restaurants. In a typical supply chain, a farmer will sell products to a wholesaler, who might sell to a distributor, who will sell to a restaurant. These extra steps in the supply chain mean that the product quality is diminished by extra transit and storage time. A farm-to-table structure has farmers selling direct to restaurants. This structure works particularly well with small, family farmers who can make one to two deliveries per week to a small set of restaurants. Farmers benefit because they get higher prices for their products; restaurants benefit because they get fresher products and forge stronger relationships with farmers who are often able to deliver special orders or fulfill special requests from the restaurants.

Tesla's supply chain is unique because it is vertically integrated in both directions, backward and forward. Indeed, it produces its own batteries and other components for the cars, it manufactures the cars, and it sells the cars through its own retail stores (see Photo 10.6).

In addition to vertical integration, the marketing team must also consider horizontal integration as an avenue by which it might exert direct control or ownership over the entire supply chain. With **horizontal integration**, the organization controls or owns several entities in the supply chain that are at the same level. The goal is to reduce costs through greater efficiencies and synergies. Italian food manufacturer Ferrero has three primary brands: Tik Tac, Kinder, and Ferrero. Ferrero would be engaging in horizontal integration if, for example, it owned several different packaging facilities, each with different specializations (e.g., plastics, cardboard, plastic wrappers) for its many products.

Photo 10.6 Tesla is both backward and forward integrated

Source: Shutterstock/Alex Millauer

Just-in-Time

A **just-in-time (JIT) inventory system** is a method by which raw materials arrive at the processing facility at the precise time they are needed, not before. The system was introduced in the 1950s by Toyota to reduce the costs and risks associated with carrying large inventories. As a car made its way down the assembly line, the appropriate part arrived just in time for the worker to install it. Organizations that utilize JIT systems rely heavily on their supply chain partners to schedule deliveries at the precise time the component parts are needed. All of this changed during the Covid-19 pandemic. Supply chains were disrupted and were unable to deliver items to manufacturers using JIT. Because many manufacturing facilities had little or no inventory, manufacturing shut down completely. When the marketing team believes that external forces may produce shocks to the system, it is preferable for them to establish a **just-in-case system**, where resiliency is built into the supply chain with, for example, larger inventories, interchangeable parts, and diversified production (Jiang, Rigobon, and Rigobon 2022).

Retail Strategies

Whether it is an online or brick-and-mortar operation, **retail** is the last stop along the supply chain. Retail is unique in that it is the vehicle by which the consumer is able to obtain the product.

Product Assortment Strategies

When the marketing team is establishing its retail strategy, one consideration is the type of product assortment it will offer to consumers. If the retailer uses a **blockbuster strategy**, it will provide a narrow selection of highly sought-after products that have a proven track record of sales. The rationale for this strategy is that the retailer has limited floor space and should therefore offer products that will return the highest revenue possible per square meter. These products are typically priced low and achieve high sales volume. The retailer might also consider pursuing a **long tail strategy**, where it would offer a selection of high-margin, niche products that a smaller number of consumers might seek. A small number of consumers will be drawn to the retailer and will pay a high price because these products are not available anywhere else. Although retailers can often be successful when they employ a long tail strategy, experts suggest that over the long term, the blockbuster strategy is more lucrative for both online and brick-and-mortar operations. The most successful retailers offer blockbuster products, but add a small selection of niche products to appeal to their variety-seeking consumers. Importantly, in order to maintain attractive margins, the costs of manufacturing and delivering these niche products must be kept as low as possible (Elberse 2008).

Level-of-Service Retailing Strategies

When determining the level-of-service retail strategy, the team needs to balance the cost with the benefits of extra levels of service. In addition, the team needs to determine what consumers expect from a service experience and, as much as possible, try to exceed those expectations. At one end of the service continuum are self-service operations like vending machines or other operations that allow consumers to select items and self-pay. In these situations, the items are fairly low priced and are fairly standardized with few varieties from which to select. A self-service retail strategy works particularly well when consumers are knowledgeable, have few choices, and have little need for the guidance of a salesperson. In 2022, Whole Foods, introduced a new self-service grocery store concept. Whole Foods is owned by Amazon and operates over 500 stores in the US, Canada, and the UK. At the concept store, customers "sign in" when they enter the store by either scanning a QR code on their Amazon app or by scanning their handprint. From there, thousands of sensors and cameras positioned around the store and suspended from the ceiling track each item consumers select and place in their carts. When they're done, consumers simply walk out with their purchases and their Amazon accounts are charged (Kang 2022).

At the other end of the service continuum is full-service operations. With these operations, consumers expect and receive customized services. Examples include high-end retailers who will perform custom tailoring and high-end shops that visit customers at their homes to show a variety of dresses, jewelry, or furnishings. Consider the Hotel Arts Barcelona in Barcelona, Spain, where no client request is too outlandish. At the Hotel Arts, discretion is an important part of the experience, because the clientele often includes members of royal families, presidents, prime ministers, and other highly-placed government officials, icons of fashion, music, or sports, and other millionaires and billionaires. The hotel offers a chef and waitstaff that will visit the suite and prepare meals. It also offers private massages, yoga, and meditation sessions for its clients. The hotel will even deliver a live elephant to the ballroom for the increasing number of Indian weddings it hosts!

Experiential Retail Strategy

The marketing team also must determine the extent to which the retail experience will be immersive and experiential. Rather than viewing the retail space as simply a setting where products are sitting on shelves, marketers who pursue an **experiential retail strategy** attempt to engage with consumers while they are in their establishments. A combination of the store layout, displays, lighting, music, and sales staff encourages consumers to linger and explore the offerings. At LUSH, Inc. retail stores, consumers can pick up and sample the wide variety of soaps, bath bombs, lotions, and other items on display. Salespeople are friendly and will even mix custom-made creations for consumers. Shopping at an IKEA store is also very experiential, with dozens of small rooms through which consumers can wander and see how the products will look when they're used together in different rooms.

Nike takes the concept of experiential retailing several steps further with its Nike Live concept, which combines premium personal service with a highly-localized approach to the store design, offerings, and experience. Open on a members-only basis, customers are invited to try out products, design customized shoes and apparel, and receive customized coaching and workouts. All of this is made possible with strong predictive analytics (Press Release 2019). For any retail setting, technology enhances the ability for the experience to be immersive and experiential. Virtual Reality (VR) and Artificial Intelligence (AI) take the concept of experiential to the extreme. Consumers can simply slip on a VR headset to make countless alternative worlds come alive as they explore and "use" products (see Photo 10.7).

Photo 10.7 VR technology facilitates experiential retail

Source: Pixabay

Demand-Based Strategies

Another option is to use **demand-based strategies**, which first assess the nature of consumer demand and then fit the supply chain strategy to meet that demand. Here, the first task is to determine whether the product fulfils a functional or innovative need for the consumer.

Strategy for Functional Products

Products that fulfil a functional need satisfy basic needs, such as food or fuel. These products have low margins, and the demand is long-term and stable. Remember that there are two functions of the supply chain: a physical function and a mediational function. With functional products, the physical function of the supply chain predominates and the focus is on efficiently converting raw materials into products and moving goods to locations where consumers can easily access them. An important goal is driving down production, storage, and transportation costs. To achieve that, the team needs to create a process whereby the organization efficiently meets demand at a low cost. Problems sometimes occur when organizations over-use price promotions, which can result in unpredictable demand as consumers and retailers stock up or wait for sales. These demand spikes add to cost, which severely undercuts the effectiveness of the price promotion. A note of caution is warranted here. This demand-based strategy works because consumers pay a low price for a product that is both good quality and very reliable (Campbell's soup is a good example) – the implicit agreement between the seller and the consumer is that this will continue (Fisher 1997) (see Photo 10.8).

Photo 10.8 Functional products require a focus on the physical function of the supply chain

Source: Shutterstock/Keith Homan

Strategy for Innovative Products

Products that are innovative give consumers an additional reason to buy the product over and above the pure function of the product. These products are purchased because of fashion, technology, or new approaches/concepts. They are characterized by short-term volatile demand, fast turn-around, higher margins, and a short product life cycle. Beats wireless headphones are an example of a fashion-forward electronic product that falls into the broad category of innovative products (see Photo 10.9). For these products, the demand-based supply chain strategy focuses on efforts that facilitate the mediation function of the supply chain to ensure that consumers get the products they desire. Extra costs can be incurred with a mismatch in supply and demand, resulting in either deep discounts (for oversupply) or lost sales (for undersupply). Therefore, one goal for the team is monitoring the market and being ready and flexible enough to respond quickly. In a related vein, the marketing team should create a process of market response, whereby the firm is nimble and flexible enough to respond to unpredictable demand which might result in stockouts, markdowns, and obsolete inventory (Fisher 1997).

Photo 10.9 Innovative products like Beats require a focus on the mediation function of the supply chain

Source: Pixabay

A Note on Dealing with Uncertain Demand

Although volatile demand can occur in many different circumstances and with many different products, it occurs more frequently with innovative products. When there is volatility in demand, the efficiency and effectiveness of the supply chain suffers. How can the marketing team manage uncertainty? There are four options (Fisher 1997):

1 *Accept uncertainty* – simply acknowledge the fact that uncertain demand is something that is inherent in innovative products. Risks and rewards go hand-in-hand, so greater risks associated with these products mean that there are also likely greater rewards.
2 *Reduce uncertainty* – utilize data analytics to better predict shifts in demand. In addition, the marketing team could also attempt to flatten overall demand spikes by, for example, creating products that share the same component parts.
3 *Avoid uncertainty* – invest in supply chain efficiencies and flexibility to give the organization better abilities to meet fluctuations in demand.
4 *Hedge against uncertainty* – although it will increase costs, create buffers by increasing inventory or expanding capacity.

Competitor-Focused Supply Chain Strategies

Depending on the competitiveness of the market, the needs and expectations of customers, and the likely reaction from competitors, the supply chain can be used strategically to strike a blow at the competition in a variety of ways.

Postpone and Speculate

Strategically limit inventory or delay deliveries. This gives the organization the advantage of reducing the risks of accumulating obsolete or out-of-date materials (Heskett 1977). It might also encourage the competition to over-order or under-order, thus increasing its costs.

Consolidate Services

Encourage B2B customers to take advantage of several coordinated services such as simultaneous refrigeration, long-haul shipping and sorting of the product. The organization could consolidate products into a single shipment, resulting in lower rates for the customer and economies of scale for the shipper (Heskett 1977). 7-Eleven's system of fresh food deliveries with a streamlined billing/inventory system gives it an advantage over other competitors.

Differentiate Distribution

Differentiate the services offered by the organization from those offered by competitors. This could be personalized services, specialized handling, and shipping of high-value types of items, such as high-end electronic equipment (Heskett 1977). BDP differentiates itself from the competition by offering personalized services to its clients.

BLUNDERS & INSIGHTS 10.2

Fool Me Twice: Airbnb Commits a Double Blunder

At the beginning of the global Covid-19 pandemic in March 2020, Airbnb bookings plummeted and cancellations surged. In Europe, bookings dropped by 80% in just 1 week as travelers cancelled plans and stayed at home. Airbnb responded by offering travelers easy, no-fee cancellations. Property owners ("hosts") were given no forewarning about the new policy and were understandably outraged at the loss of revenue because they were also feeling a very significant financial pinch. To make amends, Airbnb offered hosts an undisclosed financial compensation. The next blunder occurred when bookings started to slowly pick up again in July 2020. Airbnb launched a promotional campaign asking travelers to consider making a small donation to their hosts to show extra appreciation for what they endured because of the pandemic. This time, travelers were outraged. One Twitter user asked, "why would I donate to my host? I can't even afford one house!" (Horowitz-Rozen 2020).

DEBRIEF: To start, the properties are the "product" that consumers are "buying" when they book a stay at a host's house. Most Airbnb hosts work hard to keep their properties in beautiful condition and provide their guests with a comfortable stay. To ensure a continued array of desirable products to offer travelers, hosts needed to stay engaged. Both of Airbnb's blunders suggest that Airbnb did not seem to understand the nature of its own supply chain nor the importance of communication and engagement with supply chain partners.

Supply Chain KPIs

An important KPI for determining the effectiveness of a supply chain strategy is the **inventory turnover rate**. This figure reveals how fast the organization is selling its inventory. A high turnover rate suggests strong sales. It could also indicate insufficient inventory, which increases the risk of stockouts. A low turnover rate suggests weak sales or potentially too much inventory, which might necessitate a drop in prices. Inventory turnover rates are most informative when they are compared over time or across products in the organization's product lineup. Inventory turnover is calculated by dividing cost of goods sold (COGS) by the average value of the inventory:

Inventory turnover = COGS / average value of inventory

Return on capital employed (ROCE) is an assessment of how efficiently the organization is using its capital to generate profits. Since the supply chain represents a significant investment for the organization, ROCE is often assessed during decisions regarding the supply chain. ROCE can be used to help determine which of two different supply chain scenarios would be most profitable to the organization. It can also be used to assess how well a capital investment met the organization's objectives. ROCE is calculated by dividing EBIT (earnings before interest and taxes) by the total value of the capital employed:

ROCE = EBIT / capital employed

10.8 THE SUSTAINABLE SUPPLY CHAIN

Creating a sustainable supply chain has been an important challenge in recent years, as consumers and businesses are increasingly facing the stark reality of the effects of climate change and environmental degradation.

Empowerment Along the Supply Chain

Intermediaries along the supply chain and consumers are increasingly becoming more empowered to demand that global supply chains work to improve environmental, economic, and social justice. Other stakeholders, such as the media, governments, and NGOs, are also pushing for improvements. In the South Pacific, for example, eight tiny island nations, including Tuvalu and Kiribati, formed a cooperative partnership to force fishing operations from the US, Japan, Taiwan, China, and the EU to start paying for fishing licenses and engaging in sustainable fishing practices. Before this measure went into effect, these supply chain giants paid no fees for fishing directly off the coasts of these countries and faced no consequences for overfishing and depleting important fishing stocks (Pala 2021). Speaking of fish, a recent meta-investigation of 44 research reports, more than 9000 seafood samples, and 30 countries revealed that 36% of seafood was mislabeled. Indeed, 55% of the fish in the UK and Canada was labeled incorrectly. Inexpensive fish often had labels incorrectly identifying it as a higher-quality fish species. In addition, a wide variety of endangered and vulnerable species were mislabeled as common fish varieties. Armed with this information, NGOs and sustainable fisheries are pushing for stricter global standards (Leahy 2021).

Much of this movement toward sustainable supply chains is being driven by global brands. German athletic giant Adidas forged a partnership with the environmental organization Parley for the Oceans to reduce its environmental footprint and create products that turn marine plastic into sportswear. Experts predict that if nothing is done to stop the dumping of plastic in the oceans, there will soon be more plastic in our oceans than fish. Adidas makes over 400 million pairs of shoes each year and sources the materials for those shoes from a variety of different places. With this new initiative, plastic waste is recovered from beaches, melted, and turned into thread, which is then used in a variety of clothing and shoes. By 2019, Adidas produced 11 million pairs of shoes from recycled ocean plastic and removed more than 2800 tons of plastic from the world's oceans. This NGO partnership demonstrates the power of brands to combine their supply chain influence with their production and branding expertise to address important environmental issues (Morgan 2020) (see Photo 10.10).

Photo 10.10 Adidas has partnered with Parlay for the Oceans

Source: Pixabay

Transparency and Traceability

With respect to the supply chain, **transparency** refers to the openness of an organization's operations to outside review and scrutiny. Transparency is both a philosophy (we have nothing to hide and we are eager to share information about our supply chain with others) and a practice (we take concrete steps to provide information to stakeholders). Given the increasing levels of concern from consumers and business partners, it is not surprising that transparency is becoming more important to marketing decision-makers. **Traceability** is a method by which an organization can achieve transparency. It refers to strict standards and methods of tracking each ingredient or raw material as it proceeds throughout the supply chain. This can be accomplished with bar codes, QR codes, or other devices/tags that are attached to the item. Some can be smaller than a grain of sand (New 2010). Traceability can assist the marketing team to preemptively prevent supply chain disruptions as well as make quick corrections if problems arise.

Transparency and traceability are very important to consumers, who would otherwise have very little proof of an organization's sustainability claims; an ethically-produced pair of jeans looks just like one that was produced unethically, just as cruelty-free shampoo works just as well as non-cruelty-free shampoo. Traceability technology can allow for real-time data and even video of where a particular raw material is in the supply chain, such as cotton shipments in Malaysia or fabric-dying operations in India. The Siemens Corporation provides technology that traces items along the entire supply chain. Traceability and transparency are relevant throughout the supply chain and produce several key benefits: they (1) ensure that inferior components/ingredients are not added, (2) ensure environmental harm is mitigated, (3) ensure that no counterfeit components/ingredients infiltrate the supply chain, (4) provide invaluable information on how to improve over time, (5) allow the organization to align its accounting and costing functions to the supply chain (New 2010), and (6) allow business partners and other stakeholders to confirm that other entities along the supply chain are operating as expected. If done well, transparency and traceability can work together to increase the value proposition that is delivered to the consumer.

For several years, Tiffany & Co. had been receiving an increasing number of inquiries from stakeholders about the sourcing of its diamonds. **Conflict diamonds (or blood diamonds)** are mined from areas where there are wars, insurrections, and severe human rights violations. Many of these operations use slave labor and the profits from those operations often are used to fund further conflicts. Unlike many of its competitors, Tiffany buys directly from mining operators; its size gives it significant power in the supply chain. Its chief sustainability officer reports directly to the CEO and has spearheaded efforts to reduce GHG emissions to net zero by 2050. As discussed earlier, Tiffany uses a laser to micro-inscribe its diamonds with an ID code, which allows them to be traced through the entire supply chain. It also trains its sales staff to talk about the sourcing of diamonds and how Tiffany's supply chain differentiates it from its competitors (Cumenal 2017).

ENDURING INSIGHTS 10.3

> "Looking at the world through a sustainability lens not only helps us 'future proof' our supply chain, it also fuels innovation and drives brand growth." – Paul Polman, Dutch business executive and sustainability influencer

A former top executive at consumer product giants Unilever, Nestlé, and P&G, Polman implemented greater transparency, as well as several traceability initiatives in order to achieve a competitive advantage and strengthen the value proposition of a wide variety of brands.

Reverse Logistics

As discussed earlier in this text, the Cradle-to-cradle concept of product design and production promotes the idea that when a product comes to the end of its useful life, it can be used again to produce something new. Worn-out, broken, and used products can be gathered and used as raw materials for new products. **Reverse logistics** describes the process of moving and storing these materials so that they make it back into the production stream. For many years, China accepted materials from around the world to be recycled into new products. However, even China could not keep up, and in 2018 it closed its doors to shipments of materials destined to be recycled. After the shutdown, the rest of the world was forced to create its own reverse logistics systems and to do so in a way that was cost-competitive with virgin plastic. At the time, some countries already had fairly sophisticated systems in place, which helped tremendously. In Europe, for example, about 35–40% of plastic is recycled, compared to only about 10% in the US. Because of the mountains of materials piling up, increased pressure is being placed on product manufacturers to do something. Some manufacturers have redesigned their packaging to be more easily recycled and others have incorporated recycled content into their products, thus strengthening the market for recycled plastic. Unfortunately, these well-meaning manufacturers are facing a tough up-hill battle; the World Economic Forum predicts that global plastic production will double by 2039 (Joyce 2019).

Prove It!

To satisfy the concerns of key stakeholders, the marketing team has several options it can use to prove its sustainability credentials. First, the organization can create a code of conduct for all of its supply chain partners. The code of conduct should articulate clear penalties for violation of the codes. Second, the organization should conduct audits of its own operations, as well as the operations of its suppliers. Third-party experts are often hired to perform audits. Third, the organization's chief sustainability officer should report directly to the CEO of the organization. This allows for quick and direct reporting, without the chance of information getting diluted before it reaches the C-suite (C-suite refers to the company's upper-level management team which includes individuals such as the CEO, CFO and CMO). The CEO then has the ability to quickly and decisively fix problems that are identified. In addition, for key stakeholders like employees and customers, this direct reporting relationship demonstrates the importance that the organization places on sustainability. Finally, the organization can obtain third-party certifications, which provide an unbiased stamp of approval for the organization's operations (third-party certifications will be discussed in Chapter 13).

10.9 SUPPLY CHAIN TACTICS

Supply chain tactics are the small-scale, place-related decisions and actions that are designed to help achieve the supply chain strategy. In the tactical phase of the supply chain planning process, the organization will make a variety of decisions that fall into four broad categories. The first category concerns the timing of shipments and deliveries. Decisions include how often deliveries are made, what time of day they are made, and under what circumstances shipments may need to be slowed down or accelerated. Second, the marketing team will make decisions regarding the physical location of intermediaries, warehouses, and other supply chain partners. Decisions here also include considerations such as the physical layout of warehouses and optimal delivery routes. The third broad category of tactical decisions concern the content of the deliveries. The marketing team will make decisions about a variety of issues, such as the assortment of items in shipments and full or less-than-full shipments. Finally, decisions need to be made about facilitating functions, such as the choice of inventory management software, data collection and reporting, taxes and tariff collection procedures, etc.

10.10 SUMMARY

This chapter is about the supply chain, the element of the marketing mix that delivers the value proposition to the consumer. It is unique in that it is the point at which the organization and consumer "meet." It is also unique in that it is the one part of the marketing mix that is most difficult for competitors to copy.

The supply chain is the umbrella term for every function and system that brings the value proposition to the consumer. As with other dimensions of the marketing mix, the supply chain planning process starts with a careful review of the external environment, especially economic conditions and consumer perceptions, then moves on to a determination about objectives, strategy, and tactics. There are a variety of supply chain objectives, including enhancing customer convenience, influencing consumer perceptions, strengthening customer relationships, supporting supply chain partners, and striking a competitive effect. Each objective will result in a unique set of strategies.

The marketing team must next determine how it will attempt to achieve its objectives, by assessing a wide variety of supply chain strategies. It needs to make several decisions regarding the number of channel intermediaries, distribution intensity, and horizontal vs. vertical integration. In addition, the marketing team must make a determination about retail, demand-based, and competitor-focused strategies.

The supply chain represents tremendous opportunities for the organization to be more sustainable. By incorporating transparency and traceability into its operations, the organization can prove its sustainability credentials to stakeholders. Importantly, sustainability adds to the organization's value proposition.

QUESTIONS FOR REVIEW & DISCUSSION

1. What are the primary differences between the supply chain, distribution channel, and logistics? Think about ice cream manufacturer Ben & Jerry's. Briefly describe what might occur in its supply chain, distribution channel, and logistics operations, making sure to clearly differentiate what happens in each of these. How might Ben & Jerry's incorporate traceability into its operations? What might be some benefits of doing so?
2. What are the two main functions of the supply chain? When the organization is selling a product in which terroir is an important part of the value proposition, which function of the supply chain is most relevant? Why?
3. Describe the various supply chain objectives an organization could utilize. In what way could each of these objectives strike a competitive effect? What are some other ways to strike a competitive effect? What do we mean when we say that each supply chain objective will have its own strategy?
4. There is often a tradeoff in balancing the risks and benefits of having a small number vs. a large number of intermediaries. A large, complex organization like a university has many intermediaries. Imagine that you and some other students would like to approach the administration with a proposal to lower its costs by reducing the number of intermediaries in the university's supply chain. Construct an argument for why the university should do this. Be specific. How do you think the administration might react to this suggestion from your group?
5. Reevaluate Blunders & Insights 10.1 about Thomas Cook, Inc. using the Triple A supply chain framework. In what way could Thomas Cook have altered its supply chain to be more agile? More adaptable? More aligned? Be specific.
6. This chapter claims that the supply chain presents an opportunity for the organization to achieve a competitive advantage. If the supply chain is sustainable, however, is it still possible for it to achieve an advantage over the competition? How? Discuss.

10.11 REFERENCES

Belluz, Julia. 2018. How Many Calories Olympians Eat: Performance Nutrition is Now a Critical Part of Athletes' Strategy to Win. Vox. 18 February. Accessed 23 September 2022. https://www.vox.com/2018/2/13/17003696/what-olympic-athletes-eat.

Borden, Taylor. 2019. Thomas Cook Bankruptcy: How the Iconic Travel Brand Went from Transporting Anti-Liquor Protesters in the 1800s to Collapsing and Stranding 600,000 Passengers in 2019. *Business Insider*. 24 September. Accessed 27 February 2022. www.businessinsider.com/thomas-cook-news-bankruptcy-travel-origins-company-history-2019-9.

Browning, Kellen. 2020. Distilleries Raced to Make Hand Sanitizer for the Pandemic. No Longer. *The New York Times*, Business Section, 4 August. Accessed 9 March 2022. www.nytimes.com/2020/08/04/business/distilleries-hand-sanitizer-pandemic.html.

Caputo, Peter, Anthony J. Jackson, Ramya Murali, and Maggie Rauch. 2021. Keen but Cautious: US Leisure Travel in the Second Summer of COVID-19. *Deloitte Insights*. Accessed 11 March 2022. www2.deloitte.com/us/en/insights/focus/transportation/summer-travel-plans-survey-2021.html.

Charters, S., Spielmann, N. and B.J. Babin. 2017. The Nature and Value of Terroir Products. *European Journal of Marketing, 51* (4), 748–71.

Chopra, Sunil. 2005. *Seven-Eleven Japan Co.*, Case # KEL026, Kellogg School of Management, Northwestern University, United States.

Cumenal, Frederic. 2017. Tiffany's CEO on Creating a Sustainable Supply Chain: The Jewelry Company Has Long Led the Industry in Working to Address Environmental and Human Rights Concerns. *Harvard Business Review, 95* (2), 41–6.

Elberse, Anita. 2008. Should You Invest in the Long Tail? *Harvard Business Review, 86* (7/8), 88–96.

Enforcement Group. 2022. *The Wildlife Souvenirs Guide*. The European Commission, CITES. Accessed 11 March 2022. https://ec.europa.eu/environment/cites/info_souvenirs_en.htm.

Fisher, Marshall L. 1997. What is the Right Supply Chain for Your Product? A Simple Framework Can Help You Figure Out the Answer. *Harvard Business Review, 75* (2), 105–16.

Goodman, Peter S. and Keith Bradsher. 2021. The World is Still Short of Everything. Get Used to it. *International New York Times*, 31 August; *International Herald Tribune*.

Grantham. 2021. Canadian Net-Zero Emissions Accountability Act. The Grantham Research Institute. Accessed 2 March 2022. https://climate-laws.org/geographies/canada/laws/canadian-net-zero-emissions-accountability-act.

Hernandez, Joe. 2022. Car Ads in France Will Soon Have to Encourage More Environmentally Friendly Travel. *National Public Radio*. 4 January. Accessed 1 March 2022. www.npr.org/2022/01/04/1070297325/france-car-ads-climate.

Heskett, James L. 1977. Logistics – Essential to Strategy: Management Cannot Measure the Importance of Logistics in Terms of Cost Alone. *Harvard Business Review, 55* (6), 85–96.

Horowitz-Rozen, Shani. 2020. How Airbnb Angered Both Sides of its Marketplace During the Pandemic. *The Marker*. 17 August. Accessed 12 March 2022. https://marker.medium.com/airbnbs-misunderstanding-of-audiences-emotional-connection-resulted-in-a-double-backlash-fec773cfa22a.

IOC. 2018. *Host City Contract: Operational Requirements*. June. The International Olympic Committee.

Jiang, Bomin, Daniel Rigobon, and Roberto Rigobon. 2022. From Just-in-Time to Just-in-Case, to Just-in-*Worst*-Case: Simple Models of a Global Supply Chain Under Uncertain Aggregate Shocks. *IMF Economic Review, 70*, 141–84.

JLL. 2019. *European City Dynamics*. A report by EMEA Living Division. Jones Lang Lasalle IP, Inc.

JLL. 2020. *Creating a Resilient and Responsible City: City Momentum Index 2020*. A report by JLL Global Research Division. Jones Lang Lasalle IP, Inc.

Joyce, Christopher. 2019. U.S. Recycling Industry is Struggling to Figure Out a Future Without China. *NPR*. All Things Considered. 20 August. Accessed 12 March 2022. www.npr.org/2019/08/20/750864036/u-s-recycling-industry-is-struggling-to-figure-out-a-future-without-china.

Kang, Cecilia. 2022. Here Comes the Full Amazonification of Whole Foods. *The New York Times*. Technology section. 28 February. Accessed 5 March 2022. www.nytimes.com/2022/02/28/technology/whole-foods-amazon-automation.html.

Keh, Andrew. 2022. At the "Logistics Games," Just Arriving is a Victory. *The New York Times*. 31 January. Accessed 26 February 2022. www.nytimes.com/2022/01/31/sports/olympics/beijing-covid-tests-travel.html.

Leahy, Stephen. 2021. Revealed: Seafood Fraud Happening on a Vast Global Scale. *The Guardian*, Environment Section, 15 March. Accessed 12 March 2022. www.theguardian.com/environment/2021/mar/15/revealed-seafood-happening-on-a-vast-global-scale.

Lee, Hau L. 2004. The Triple-A Supply Chain. *Harvard Business Review, 82* (10), 102–12.

LOC. 2021. European Union: European Climate Law on Achieving Climate Neutrality by 2050 Enters into Force. An article by *The Library of Congress*. Accessed 2 March 2022. www.loc.gov/item/global-legal-monitor/2021-08-31/european-union-european-climate-law-on-achieving-climate-neutrality-by-2050-enters-into-force/.

Ludden, James. 2019. Thomas Cook Files for Bankruptcy After Bailout Talks Fail. *Bloomberg.com*, 22 September. N.PAG.

Morgan, Clancy. 2020. How Adidas is Turning Plastic Ocean Waste into Sneakers and Sportswear. *Business Insider*, Tech Section. 27 October. Accessed 12 March 2022. www.businessinsider.com/adidas-sneakers-plastic-bottles-ocean-waste-recycle-pollution-2019-8.

New, Steve. 2010. The Transparent Supply Chain: Let Your Customers Know Everything about Where Your Products Come From – Before They Discover it First. *Harvard Business Review, 88* (10), 76–82.

Nicholas, Katrina. 2021. Getting Athletes to Pandemic Olympics is Logistics Nightmare. *Bloomberg*. 4 July. Accessed 26 February 2022. www.bloomberg.com/news/articles/2021-07-04/getting-athletes-to-pandemic-olympics-is-a-logistical-nightmare.

Pala, Christopher. 2021. The Mice that Roared: How Eight Tiny Countries Took On Foreign Fishing Fleets. *The Guardian, World News Section, Pacific Plunder Series*, 15 June. Accessed. 12 March 2022. www.theguardian.com/world/2021/jun/16/the-mice-that-roared-how-eight-tiny-countries-took-on-foreign-fishing-fleets.

Press Release. 2019. Nike Live Launches in Long Beach and Tokyo. *Nike News*. 31 October. Accessed 5 March 2022. https://news.nike.com/news/nike-live-launches-in-long-beach-and-tokyo.

Press Release. 2022. 7-Eleven Opens 77,711th Store. *7-Eleven, Inc*. 21 January. Accessed 9 March 2022. https://corp.7-eleven.com/corp-press-releases/01-21-2022-7-eleven-opens-77-711th-store.

Reuters. 2021. New Zealand Passes Climate Change Disclosure Laws for Financial Firms in World First. Reuters. 21 October. Accessed 2 March 2022. www.reuters.com/business/sustainable-business/
new-zealand-passes-climate-change-disclosure-laws-financial-firms-world-first-2021-10-21/#:~:text=SYDNEY%2C%20Oct%2021%20(Reuters),business%2C%20officials%20said%20on%20Thursday.

Wade, Stephen. 2016. The Chefs in Rio's Olympic Village are Preparing an Insane Amount of Food. *Business Insider*. 10 May. Accessed 28 February 2022. www.businessinsider.com/ap-rio-olympic-spread-anything-from-halal-to-kosher-to-kimchi-2016-5.

White House. 2022. FACT SHEET: United States, European Union, and G7 to Announce Further Economic Costs on Russia. *The White House*, Briefing Room. Accessed 11 March 2022. www.whitehouse.gov/briefing-room/statements-releases/2022/03/11/fact-sheet-united-states-european-union-and-g7-to-announce-further-economic-costs-on-russia/.

Zaichkowsky, Judith Lynne. 1985. Measuring the Involvement Construct. *Journal of Consumer Research, 12* (3), 341–52.

11 PROMOTIONAL STRATEGIES: ADVOCATING THE VALUE PROPOSITION

LEADERSHIP INSIGHTS 11

Photo 11.1 Orlando Acevedo

Source: courtesy, Orlando Acevedo

Meet Orlando Acevedo, Program Operations Manager

TechnoServe, Mozambique

When Orlando Acevedo moved to Mozambique for a 2-year stint with the Peace Corps, he had no idea that this decision would change the trajectory of his life, nor indeed, the lives of thousands of other people. Several years after leaving the Peace Corps, with an MBA in hand, Acevedo returned to Mozambique to work full time to improve the lives of people living in Africa. Today, Acevedo and his team at TechnoServe implement a variety of promotional strategies to bring top-quality products from local farmers to customers willing to pay for them.

The $10.5 million funding for the Mozambique project, the largest in all of Africa, comes from French company TotalEnergies, which produces fuel derived from biomass, hydrogen, and natural gas, and has 100,000 employees worldwide (Our identity 2021). TechnoServe is the nonprofit organization that implements the economic development project for TotalEnergies. TechnoServe was founded in 1968 and works in 40 countries across Africa, Latin America, and Asia. Over the years, it has assisted thousands of businesses in carrying out projects in developing countries and has improved the economic livelihood of millions of people. Its goal is to initiate self-sustaining economic impact (Our History 2021).

In Mozambique, Acevedo and his team work with locals to transform the agricultural value chain to produce and deliver high-quality, high-priced products. "We're trying to couple production with a ready market. We're constructing the value chain from scratch. We work with farmers who already have an enterprising mindset and find ways to communicate with them so they can actualize their potential. It's part of our long-term marketing strategy," Acevedo explained.

One of Acevedo's biggest challenges is related to communication and reframing perceptions. First, the team reinforces the message that farms need to be run as businesses. Farmers are required to attend business and marketing classes so that they can develop skills to run their farms as commercial enterprises and to be customer-centric when determining what products the farm will produce. With this new mindset, farmers created a new market for themselves: food service operations at big multi-national businesses, restaurants, and hotels throughout Mozambique. Rather than chaotic open-air markets, these food service operations offered a more reliable demand and higher prices. Importantly, as farmers got to know their corporate clients better, they were able to produce and deliver special requests for them.

Acevedo also worked to reframe perceptions about the fact that his client makes most of its profits from fossil fuels. "I think about this all the time. The question really is, how do you make sure that the wealth you're generating isn't just going to the people who already have it? That's where TechnoServe comes in. How do you redistribute that wealth that's coming in? I see it as an opportunity. It's a way of using funds from the private sector to do good. The big driver of the economies in places like sub-Saharan Africa is extractive operations. There are a lot of bad practices going on in those industries. How do we transform that dynamic so that some real good can come out of it?" By reframing the dialogue about the relationship between TechnoServe and TotalEnergies, the team has a more balanced perspective of its own role.

What would Orlando Acevedo like to tell his 21-year-old self? "Do not get caught up in the pressure to conform your career goals and personal path to what others think may be best for you. Everyone has a different path in life, and most people are still figuring theirs out in one way or another, even as middle-aged adults. Follow what feels right, and don't let your convictions get drowned out by the opinions of others."

11.1 WHAT DOES A DIAMOND RING REALLY MEAN?

A diamond ring is often given by one person to another as a symbol of commitment and undying love. In 1939, only 10% of American brides received a diamond, but that proportion had increased to 80% by 1990 (Statista 2011). This same pattern was repeated across Asia and other parts of the world. In 1967, almost no Japanese brides received a diamond, but by 1987, more than 70% of them received one. In China, an overwhelming majority of brides are given a diamond ring when they become engaged to be married. How did the diamond ring become synonymous with love and commitment? It was a result of a carefully-choreographed, decades-long promotional effort led by DeBeers, one of the biggest and most influential players in the diamond industry (Klein and Posner 2021).

Starting in the 1950s, the London-based DeBeers corporation engaged in a promotional campaign to ensure that demand stayed high, prices stayed high, and the meaning of a diamond became inextricably linked to love. An important part of the plan was to first control the supply chain to limit the global supply of diamonds. DeBeers purchased several competitors and created its own strategic stockpile of diamonds. After several decades of operating as a monopoly and enjoying high prices, the courts broke up the monopoly and forced DeBeers to pay a stiff fine. Today, three companies control the market: DeBeers, Alrosa, and Rio Tinto. Together, their control of much of the world's diamond supply continues to keep prices high (Klein and Posner 2021).

The second critical part of the DeBeers strategy was more specifically focused on promotion and incorporated three components. First, to stimulate demand, DeBeers launched the slogan, "a diamond is forever" – a diamond is supposed to represent the couple's everlasting love. Importantly, because it is "forever," once a diamond is purchased, it is rarely re-sold, which keeps the supply of diamonds limited and the prices high. Second, DeBeers linked the purchase of a diamond to a reflection of the purchaser's professional success. In the US, customers were advised to spend 2 months' salary and in Japan, they were advised to invest 3 months' salary on the purchase of the diamond ring. The bigger and flashier the ring, the more successful the purchaser. Third, DeBeers sought to educate consumers about a diamond's "4 Cs," those characteristics of a diamond that make it unique: color, cut, clarity, carat weight. Of course, these characteristics matched up perfectly with the types of diamonds that DeBeers was mining and selling. By carefully crafting a 3-part promotional strategy, DeBeers was able to shift consumer perceptions and demand (Klein and Posner 2021) (see Photo 11.2).

Photo 11.2 "A diamond is forever" was a critical part of the DeBeers promotional strategy

Source: Advertising Archives

DeBeers launched an additional promotional effort to help it solidify the position that diamonds hold as the ultimate expression of love and commitment. In the 1960s, laboratories started to produce diamonds that were structurally identical to diamonds that are mined. These lab-made diamonds were increasingly entering the market and only experts could tell the difference between a mined diamond and a lab-made diamond. To ensure that lab-made diamonds would not be viewed as a substitute for mined diamonds, DeBeers launched its own line of lab-made diamonds and priced them extremely

low as an indicator of how much the lab-made diamonds are worth. It certainly appears as if DeBeers was well aware of the concept of Veblen goods, those products for which demand increases when the price increases (designer handbags, champagne, lawyers)! In addition, it launched a promotional campaign claiming that even though lab-made diamonds were "not real," they were a nice alternative for someone who cannot afford an authentic diamond. Manufacturers of lab-made diamonds responded to DeBeers by calling their diamonds "dirt diamonds" and questioned the ethics of mining operations in areas with political and military conflict, calling them "blood diamonds" (Klein and Posner 2021).

DeBeers was masterful in its ability to successfully position mined diamonds as a necessary part of a couple's commitment to one another. Further, it solidified the notion that the more expensive the diamond, the better. The DeBeers example illustrates how diamonds are promoted, but also highlights how promotional decisions are intertwined with decisions about the product, price, and place. This chapter is about promotion, the most well-known part of the marketing mix and the element that advocates for the value proposition.

11.2 LEARNING OBJECTIVES

After studying this chapter, you will be able to do the following:

1. Describe the four external and three consumer-related influences on the promotional planning process.
2. Create relevant and SMART promotional objectives.
3. Describe the components of the AIDA model and how it influences the selection of different dimensions of the promotional mix.
4. Discuss how marketing mix decisions evolve as a product moves along the product life cycle.
5. Describe several decisions that must be considered as the marketing team develops its promotional strategy.
6. Create an argument for why sales and market share are the most important KPIs, but why marketers should also assess other KPIs.

11.3 THE POWER OF PROMOTION

Communication involves the sharing or exchange of information or ideas between two entities. Communication can be one-way, where one entity imparts information or ideas on another, as when a news reporter provides information about a natural disaster to a large audience. It can also be two-way, in which the information and ideas flow back-and-forth between two entities, as when a salesperson has a conversation with a customer. Effective communication is more likely to occur if the two entities share a **common frame of reference**, a shared understanding based on education, common experiences, or cultural sensitivities. Messages are first **encoded**, or structured in such a way that they will be easily understood by the message recipient. The message is then conveyed through a **communications channel**, or the vehicle that delivers the message (a text, phone call, TV ad, or face-to-face conversation, for example). The next step occurs when the message recipient **decodes** the message by attaching meaning to the message. This is where the recipient creates an understanding of what was communicated. After decoding, the recipient responds in some way. A **response** could be in the form of a comment, question, or other behavior like a sale. This response is then communicated back to the sender through a communications channel in the form of **feedback**, which lets the message sender know how well the recipient received the message. At the same time all of this is happening, **noise** works to interrupt the process and distract both the sender and the recipient. Noise could be anything that disrupts the efficient working of the communications process, such as a distracting sound, image, person, or event (see Figure 11.1).

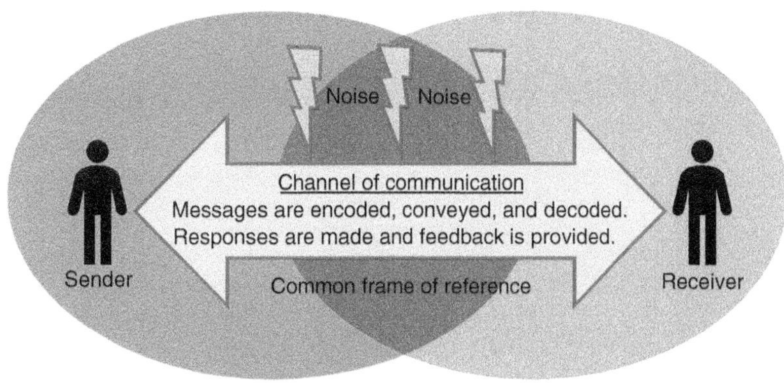

Figure 11.1 The communications model

Promotion is a type of communication that advocates for a particular company, brand, or product. Promotion is the set of processes that the organization uses to communicate an important message to its target market and other stakeholders. In marketing strategy, the communications channel is referred to as the **media vehicle** and specifies the exact TV show, radio station, magazine, mobile app, etc. by which the message will be conveyed. In most instances, the sender is the organization and the receiver is the consumer. Promotion is especially critical to the success of the marketing strategy because it is the one tool in the marketing mix that conveys important meaning to stakeholders. An organization can have the most well-designed product or service that will ideally meet the needs of its target market. However, as legendary showman P.T. Barnum once said, "without promotion, something terrible happens ... nothing!"

ENDURING INSIGHTS 11.1

"The pen is mightier than the sword." – Edward Bulwer-Lytton, 19th century British novelist and playwright

Words matter. By winning over the hearts and minds of a group of people, a carefully-crafted message can inspire people to action and even initiate political and social movements. This quote underscores the critical importance of words and ideas as a means of influence.

11.4 PROMOTIONAL PLANNING

As with the other elements of the marketing mix, the first step in promotional planning is to scan the external environment and clearly articulate the relevant environmental influences and consumer perceptions that could influence the promotional efforts. Then, the marketing team creates promotional objectives, strategy, and tactics. When done correctly, the promotion element of the marketing mix works synergistically with the other three elements to help the team achieve its overall marketing objectives (see Figure 11.2).

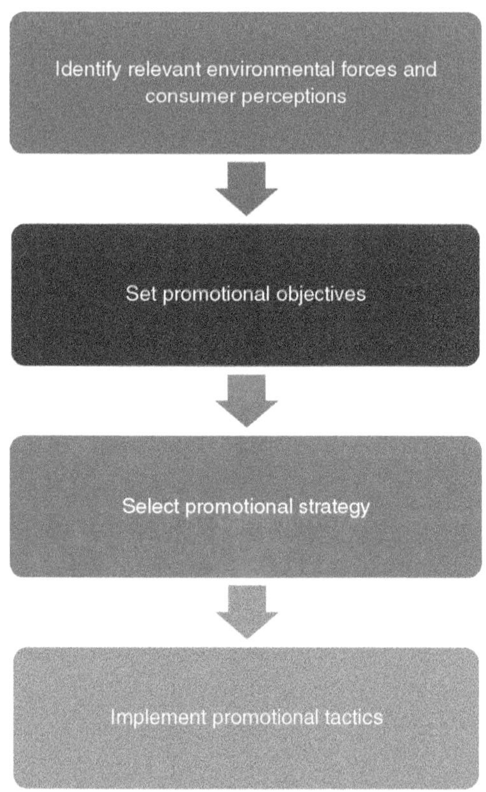

Figure 11.2 The promotion planning process

Environmental Influences

A wide variety of external influences can impact promotional planning, including regulations, uncertainty, competitive moves, and technological norms.

Regulations

A wide variety of regulations have been enacted by different governments, trading blocs, and regulatory bodies regarding promotional messages. Most are designed to ensure that promotions are truthful, non-discriminatory, and non-offensive. The goal is to facilitate honest communication, protection of consumers, and fair business. The EU has very strict rules, for example, about comparative advertising. The message cannot exaggerate or mislead; it can only compare product features that are "material, relevant, verifiable, and representative features" of the product (Directive 2006/114/EC 2006). In the UK, regulations fall into two broad categories: those that are concerned with broadcast media (TV, radio) and those concerned with non-broadcast media (print, online, direct marketing, and sales promotions). To enforce these regulations, the government has established the Advertising Standards Authority (ASA), which has the authority to enact penalties, such as removing ads and prosecuting offenders (GOV.UK. 2022). In France, alcoholic beverage companies are subject to especially strong advertising restrictions (see case study p.502).

Uncertainty

Another concern for the marketing decision-maker is the extent to which the promotional process will be occurring against a backdrop of economic, political, or social uncertainty, any of which will result in more noise interfering with the effective communication of the message. Because uncertainty creates greater noise, there is an increased chance for disruptions in the communication process. Economic uncertainty could be caused by increasing interest rates, unemployment rates, and rising prices for housing, energy, and other essentials. Changes in the political landscape from the priorities of one political party to another, for example, could also be a source of uncertainty as new initiatives are funded and implemented. Shifts in the social landscape can also create abundant noise. During the summer of 2020, for instance, Black Lives Matter protests erupted across the world in a recognition of the poor treatment that many people of color have endured. In 2019, young people around the world participated in protests for more definitive action on climate change. Inspired by Swedish teenager Greta Thunberg, the Fridays for

Photo 11.3 Global "Fridays for Future" protests for climate justice

Source: Pixabay

Future protests saw record-breaking crowds demanding that governments commit to net zero CO_2 emissions by 2030. In total, several million protesters in hundreds of cities around the world were showing up each Friday (Neuman and Chappell 2019) (see Photo 11.3).

Competitive Moves

The extent of competitive rivalry in the industry will also influence the promotional process. According to the Five Forces model, when there is intense rivalry in an industry, the competition will fight it out using a variety of means, including promotional efforts (Porter 2008). Vodafone and Airtel are fierce competitors in the global cellular services industry, with Vodafone attempting to gain ground through price discounts and Airtel focusing on higher speed. As a result, consumers reap the benefits of lower prices, better coverage, and faster speeds. In the entertainment industry, DC Comics and Marvel have engaged in a long-term competition for the attention and mindshare of consumers who are loyal to their superheroes. Marvel's Fantastic Four and other characters (Spiderman, the Hulk, and Iron Man) compete with DC's Justice League and its characters (Batman, Superman, Wonder Woman) across several different platforms: movies, games, merchandising, and streaming content. Both accuse the other of introducing characters that are surprisingly similar to their own. For example, Marvel's Deadpool is very similar to DC's Deathstroke; Marvel's Hawkeye is very similar to DC's Green Arrow; and Marvel's Wasp is very similar to DC's Bumblebee. Each universe heavily promotes its characters in an attempt to attract the attention and loyalty of fans (see Photo 11.4)

Photo 11.4 Marvel and DC Comics have a strong competitive rivalry

Source: Pixabay

Perhaps the most well-known brand rivalry is between the two brands that sparked the "cola war," the long-standing feud between Coke and Pepsi for control of the soft drink market. Each company has a presence in more than 200 countries around the globe and frequently launches campaigns promoting their brand as part of a lifestyle or as a perfect accompaniment for a variety of celebrations and occasions. Both brands have had increasing competition over the last decade from healthier drinks like waters, sports drinks, and teas. Unfortunately for Pepsi, Coke seems to be winning the cola war (see Figure 11.3).

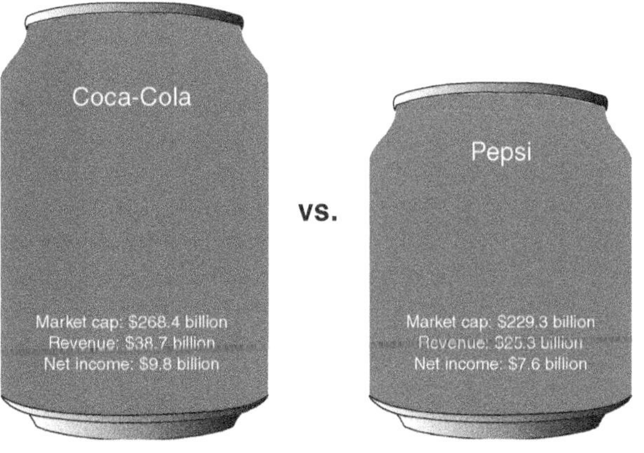

Figure 11.3 Coca-Cola and Pepsi have a very intense brand rivalry

Source: Maverick (2022)

Technological Norms

Another factor that influences the success of the promotional effort is the extent to which the target market has access to and is proficient in the use of technology. New technological advances are enabling marketers to connect with consumers in novel and previously-unimagined ways. For example, virtual reality (VR) technology allows consumers to "interact" with products in 3-D environments to check out new furnishings for their homes, test drive a new car, or visit an island paradise. In addition, in-store and mobile interfaces are increasingly utilizing artificial intelligence and machine learning to "learn" and adapt to consumer search patterns and questions. While all of these technological advancements are impressive, promotions delivered through the use of these technologies will have little effect if consumers are not proficient with them or if they do not have access to them.

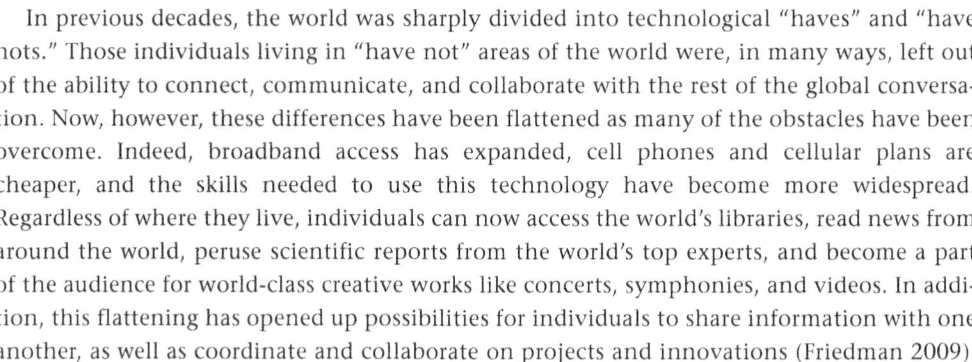

In previous decades, the world was sharply divided into technological "haves" and "have nots." Those individuals living in "have not" areas of the world were, in many ways, left out of the ability to connect, communicate, and collaborate with the rest of the global conversation. Now, however, these differences have been flattened as many of the obstacles have been overcome. Indeed, broadband access has expanded, cell phones and cellular plans are cheaper, and the skills needed to use this technology have become more widespread. Regardless of where they live, individuals can now access the world's libraries, read news from around the world, peruse scientific reports from the world's top experts, and become a part of the audience for world-class creative works like concerts, symphonies, and videos. In addition, this flattening has opened up possibilities for individuals to share information with one another, as well as coordinate and collaborate on projects and innovations (Friedman 2009).

Consumer Perceptions

With the extensive research the marketing team has already undertaken about its target market, it should have a very clear sense of what messages will resonate most effectively with its audience. A variety of issues related to consumer perceptions influence the extent to which a promotion will be effective, including cultural norms, current events, and consumer empowerment.

Cultural Norms

Cultural norms are the informal societal rules and expectations for how someone should interpret a message or event. Norms have a strong influence on behavior. Cultural norms are learned and provide a standard by which members can evaluate events, information, the behaviors of others, and promotional strategies. Take the example of Australian cultural norms. Generally speaking, Australians are perceived to be friendly, humorous, and laid-back in their approach to life. They work hard, but make an effort to enjoy time with family and friends. In addition, they are also very egalitarian in their approach to gender roles and, perhaps because of the connection to their Aboriginal history, they are multi-cultural in their approach. Because of the somewhat casual norms in Australia, don't be offended if you hear a few swear words when you talk to an Aussie (see Figure 11.4). Because cultural norms act as a filter through which consumers interpret the world, cultural norms often result in very different frames of reference and therefore different interpretations of promotional strategies.

Consumer Perceptions of Current Events

Current events also influence the ability for the promotion to occur within a common frame of reference, to minimize noise, and to effectively encode and decode the message. In short, if consumers are occupied by other more immediate concerns, effective communication is unlikely to occur. Some current events are happy occasions, such as holidays or sporting events. The World Cup final is played every 4 years and during the months-long tournament of 32 nations, millions of people around the world are concerned with little else as they keep up with their favorite teams and players. In 2018, 1.1 billion people around the world tuned in to the final match between France and Croatia (Richter 2022).

Figure 11.4 Australian cultural norms

Other current events command far more attention and concern. Immediately following Russia's invasion of Ukraine in February 2022, for example, consumers around the world focused their attention on the war and even the most inspiring promotional efforts were ineffective. At the time, consumer sentiment was enjoying an uptick because of the easing of Covid-19 restrictions across Europe. However, after the attack, consumer sentiment dropped precipitously to its lowest level since the height of the Covid-19 pandemic in 2020 to 19.6% below its long-term average (EC 2022) (see Figure 11.5). In Germany, which is especially dependent on Russia for its energy needs, consumer sentiment was decidedly negative because of concerns about a slowing economy and higher energy prices (DW 2022). These concerns and sentiment were even more pronounced for some consumers with a direct connection to the war and, not surprisingly, were reflected in changes in consumer perceptions and behavior. In Poland, which shares a border with Ukraine, 68% of consumers reported that they helped Ukrainians in some way (either financially or materially), 57% avoided buying Russian products, 11% stocked up on cash, and 8% planned or considered moving to a safer place abroad (Statista 2022). During especially stressful times such as these, a strong majority (72.2%) of CMOs believe that the role of marketing increases in importance (Moorman and Shkil 2021) because it is even more challenging to effectively communicate with the target market.

The Empowered Consumer

Consumers have increasingly been able to have an influence on a variety of marketing mix-related decisions, such as the selection of product attributes, the choice to pay-what-you-want, the method and timing of delivery, and personalized promotions. **Consumer empowerment** is a perception that consumers have about their own ability to control their own consumption choices. Does more empowerment lead to better decisions? Not necessarily. Empowered consumers can certainly make less-than-optimal decisions. However, greater consumer empowerment does influence the extent to which a consumer is satisfied with the decision-making

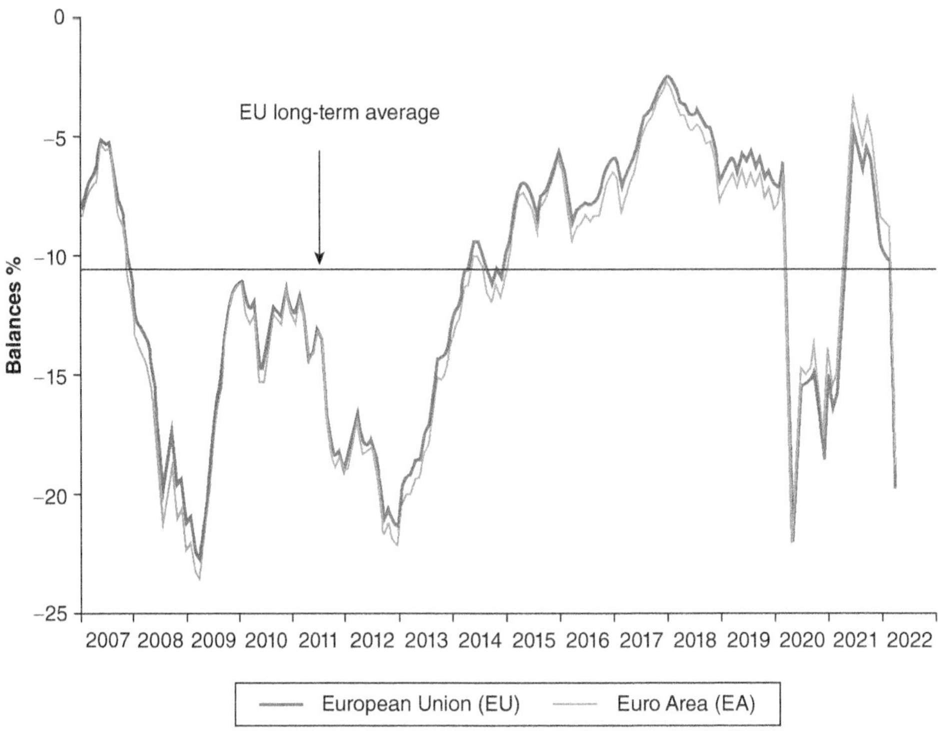

Figure 11.5 European consumer sentiment

Source: EC (2022)

process (Wathieu, et al. 2002). Empowerment and promotion have several points of intersection. For example, depicting empowered women in advertisements improves advertising recall, especially for women. The most empowering ads are the most likely to be recalled. In addition, when ads celebrate women for their accomplishments rather than their looks, women were 80% more likely to share, like, comment, and subscribe (Wojcicki 2016).

Online reviews forge another connection between promotion and consumer empowerment. Consumers who post online reviews are not just doing so because they like to share their experiences with other consumers, but they are also aware that marketing decision-makers carefully monitor those reviews. Online reviews are actually even more influential than some realize. In addition to providing other consumers with first-hand feedback and putting marketers "on notice" about product or service quality issues, the reviews often highlight product attributes that other consumers many not have considered before. Indeed, even if other consumers already have a set of product attributes under consideration, the product attributes that are highlighted in online reviews often supersede those pre-existing attributes and become more influential to the consumer's purchase decision (Liu and Karahanna 2017). Which consumers are more likely to check online reviews? The product category and the consumer's location seem to exert significant influence on a consumer's likelihood of checking online reviews (see Table 11.1) (Dsouza 2022).

Table 11.1 Consumers in different parts of the world demonstrate different patterns of checking online review before purchase

Product Category	Highest Percentage of Consumers who Check Reviews	Lowest Percentage of Consumers who Check Reviews
Household products	Singapore (43%), Indonesia (43%), and India (43%)	France (17%), Denmark (18%), and Italy (27%)
Clothes	Indonesia (50%), India (48%), and China (41%)	Denmark (14%), Australia (19%), and UK (19%)
Cinema/TV shows	India (38%), China (35%), and Indonesia (31%)	Germany (11%), Denmark (14%), and Sweden (15%)
Airlines	UAE (30%), Mexico (24%) and Singapore (24%)	Poland (10%), US (10%), and UK (10%)
Financial and investment products	India (32%), Indonesia (28%), and Hong Kong (24%)	Italy (9%), Denmark (9%), and US (10%)

Source: Dsouza (2022)

BLUNDERS & INSIGHTS 11.1

Say What?

BACKGROUND: With South Africa's long history of racial injustice, it would seem reasonable to think that marketing campaigns would be especially careful in their messaging. Think again. In 2020, Unilever shampoo brand TRESemmé collaborated with the South African retail pharmacy chain Clicks to launch an ad campaign claiming that Black hair was "frizzy and dull," but White hair was "normal." The ad was accompanied by photos showing both types of hair. Not surprisingly, this did not go over well. Clicks closed down its chain of stores after protests turned violent at about 425 of its 720 stores; outraged protesters intimidated employees and knocked over store shelves. A few days later, the chain got a restraining order to stop the violence. Other retail chains throughout the country quickly removed the product from store shelves. Social media lit up with #ClicksRacism comments about the ad's "dehumanizing" message. Unilever responded with an apology expressing its "remorse to all South Africans, Black women in particular, for the racist TRESemmé SA image." To demonstrate its remorse, Unilever removed TRESemmé products from all store shelves throughout the country for 10 days. It also announced that it would provide scholarships for Black and female students who were orphaned by the HIV and AIDS epidemics, and would donate a variety of supplies and products to people living in poor, rural settlements (McSweeney 2020).

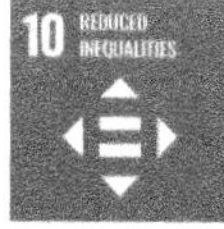

DEBRIEF: Where to start? After decades of racial oppression and mistreatment, it is not surprising that people were outraged. One of the first lessons in effective communication is having a common frame of reference. In this case, it was not necessary for the design team to be entirely comprised of Black individuals. A non-White person on the team would have helped, but all that was really needed was any person with at least a minimum level of understanding of the lived experience of South Africans. Clearly, the team that designed this ad was completely lacking in any common frame of reference.

11.5 PROMOTIONAL OBJECTIVES

The second step in promotional planning is to create a list of **promotional objectives**: the overall promotional-related goals the marketing team wishes to achieve. Promotional objectives should be crafted with an eye toward the competition; how is the organization's value proposition better than that of the competition? In the second year of the global Covid-19 pandemic, the marketing function for most organizations moved from crisis mode to something closer to normal operations as they started the long journey to economic recovery. Marketing decision-makers shifted their priorities such that market penetration (where more products are sold to existing markets) was viewed as the most important promotional objective (56.8%). Diversification, where new products are sold to new markets, was viewed by marketing decision-makers as least important (8.7%). Two objectives that saw the biggest increase from the previous 12 months were improving marketing ROI (105.6% increase) and acquiring new customers (48.6% increase). In a disappointing turn, the proportion of marketing decision-makers who viewed sustainability as an important focus dropped from 73% pre-pandemic to 55% in 2021. Why? Many decision-makers (47%) believed the costs were too high and 43% reported that their more immediate concern was the pandemic (Moorman and Shkil 2021). The marketing team has a wide variety of promotional objectives from which to select (see Table 11.2).

Table 11.2 Potential promotional objectives

Promotional Objective Category	Description
Acquiring new customers	Increasing the number of customers in the target or expanding to a new target market.
Improving marketing ROI	Creating more effective promotions.
Persuading consumers	Convincing consumers to believe, feel, or do something about the product or brand. DeBeers, for example, persuaded consumers that a diamond was necessary to demonstrate love and commitment.
Educating consumers	Informing consumers about a new feature or benefit that comes from using the product. Education can shift the demand curve to the right. DeBeers educated consumers about how to select a diamond based on the 4 Cs.
Strengthening customer relationships	Forging a stronger bond with consumers in order to encourage a long-term relationship with them.
Positioning the product	Carving out the "mental real estate" in the consumer's mind about how the product is different from the competition.
Repositioning the product	Shifting the existing position of the product to a new, more competitively beneficial location in the minds of consumers.
Reminding consumers	Telling consumers again why the organization's value proposition is relevant to them.
Striking a competitive effect	Weakening the competition's ability to deliver its value proposition.
Penetrating an existing market	Selling more product to an existing target market by, for example, encouraging customers to buy in greater volumes or to buy more often.

Promotional Objective Category	Description
Developing a new market	Introducing an existing product to a new target market.
Engaging in product development	Creating a new product and introducing it to an existing target market.
Engaging in diversification	Creating a new product and introducing it to a new target market.

ENDURING INSIGHTS 11.2

"The meek may one day inherit the earth, but not the headlines." – Indira Gandhi, former Prime Minister of India

In an age when there were few women leaders, Gandhi rose to power in the late 1960s. She believed in Indian self-determination and was very rarely willing to compromise her position. While in office, she solidified her political power, often imposing harsh penalties on those who opposed her. This quote underscores Gandhi's belief that she needed to be strong and uncompromising. With respect to marketing strategy and promotion, this quote suggests that, compared to a weak message, a strong and consistent message will be more likely to capture attention.

11.6 PROMOTIONAL STRATEGY

After the promotional objectives are established, the marketing team creates the **promotional strategy**, which is designed to help fulfill the promotional objectives. The marketing team must consider a wide variety of decisions related to its promotional strategy, but its first consideration involves the promotional tools it will utilize.

The Promotional Toolkit

Just as marketers have the marketing mix, they also have the **promotional mix**, which is the communications-related toolkit for achieving the promotional objectives. The promotional mix is comprised of five key elements: advertising, sales promotion, personal selling, publicity, and direct marketing. Each of these tools can be deployed in B2B and B2C settings (see Figure 11.6).

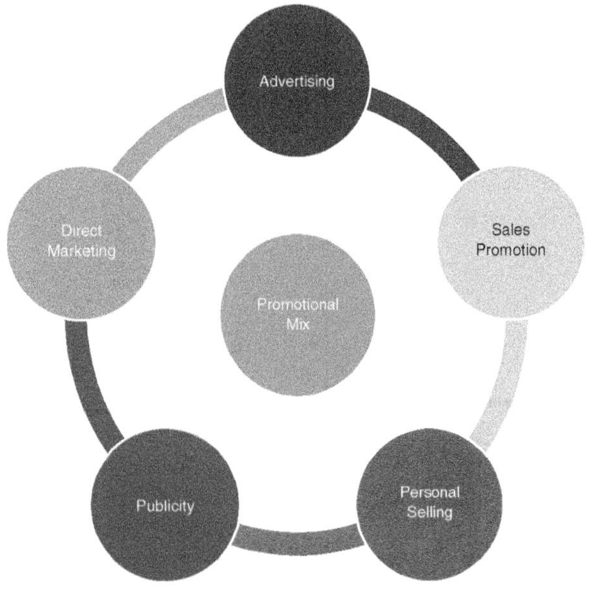

Figure 11.6 The promotional mix

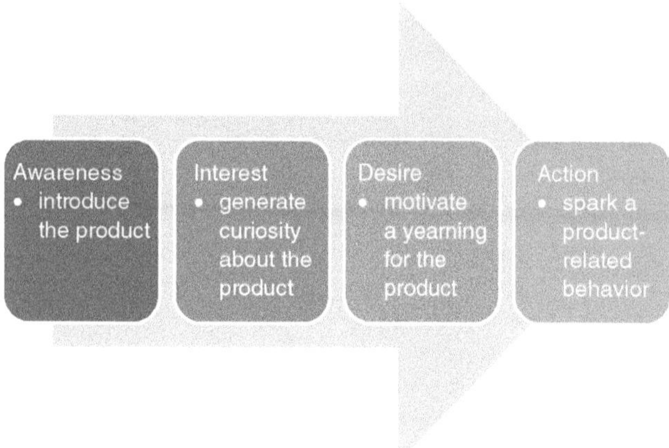

Figure 11.7 The AIDA model

When exposed to a promotional message, the consumer will move through a series of steps to an eventual behavior, such as a request for more information, a click-through, or a purchase. The model is referred to as the **AIDA model**: awareness, interest, desire, and action. The promotional toolkit and the AIDA model work together; marketing decision-makers first determine where the consumer is located along the AIDA model, then deploy the appropriate promotional tools (see Figure 11.7 as was discussed in Chapter 4).

Advertising

Advertising is a promotional tool that targets a mass audience and clearly identifies the organization or brand. Advertising consists of one-way communication from the organization to the consumer, as when an organization places an online ad, mobile ad, magazine ad, or TV ad. Because it is paid for by the organization, advertising may be interpreted by consumers with some skepticism. Consumers decode the message and then provide feedback with a wide variety of behaviors such as click-throughs, visits to the company website, further inquiries, or sales. Advertising can be effective at any point along the AIDA model. The many different types of advertising can be broken down by category:

- *Broadcast advertising* includes any promotional message that is sent over TV and radio waves. A benefit of broadcast advertising is that it can tell a story and, in the case of TV, these ads can demonstrate a product's performance or unique attributes. Unique sounds such as music or, for example, the sound of a beer pouring into a glass, add extra depth to the communication. On the downside, broadcast advertising can be very expensive.
- *Digital advertising* includes any ad on a streaming service or mobile ad, such as a video, static ad, or banner ad. It includes ads that are delivered over cable systems, Wifi, or cellular systems. The benefit of these ads is their diverse and flexible nature. Some ads that are delivered via streaming systems are indistinguishable from TV ads; in fact, many ads that appear on broadcast TV often reappear on streaming services such as YouTube. At the more flexible end of the continuum, marketers can quickly create and post videos on platforms such as Tik Tok or use GPS-enabled devices to deliver mobile ads to consumers in real-time. For example, just as a consumer is walking by, marketers can push an ad for a shoe store, accompanied by a "½ off" sales promotion. Feedback occurs in a variety of forms, such as shares, likes, reposts, or sales. On the downside, because they are so pervasive in the daily lives of consumers, very few digital ads are successful at capturing consumer attention.
- *Print advertising* includes magazine and newspaper ads. The benefits of print advertising include the ability to carefully depict and explain the product and its benefits. This may be especially true in B2B scenarios, where a detailed description of the product may be necessary for the consumer to make a decision. A negative, however, is that there are often long production lead times (especially with magazines) and limited engagement from readers. Recent evidence, however, indicates that compared to digital ads, consumers are better able to remember print ads (Venkatraman, Dimoka, Vo, and Pavlou 2021).

- *Outdoor advertising* includes bus shelters and billboards, as well as advertising that might be seen on public transit, store signs, company-owned vehicles, and sports arenas. Outdoor ads are designed to educate, remind, and generate excitement, and are used in the early stages of the AIDA model. Indeed, most sporting arenas have advertising posters prominently displayed throughout the stadium. The benefits of outdoor are that the brand's message reaches consumers in a variety of different situations and venues. The drawbacks are that outdoor contributes to advertising clutter and thus makes it more difficult for a single advertiser to cut through and grab the attention of the consumer (see Photo 11.5).

Photo 11.5 Like most arenas, Wembley Stadium in London is filled with outdoor advertising

Source: Pixabay

- *In-store advertising* includes in-store displays and point-of-purchase materials. They often have splashy signage and some even have integrated digital components that, for example, display ads or play music as customers approach them. These displays can be quite effective in grabbing the attention of consumers because they are located exactly where the consumer is making the final decision about which product to purchase.
- *Sponsorships and partnerships* are another form of advertising. Organizations can sponsor activities and events, such as sporting events or concerts, by covering a significant portion of the costs in exchange for connecting with people attending the events. Sponsors get to display their logos at these events as well as have exclusive access to the events. Budweiser, for example, is a frequent sponsor of music festivals, where it has exclusive rights to sell its beer. Brands can also sponsor individual athletes and celebrities. The goal with sponsorships and partnerships is to connect the brand to the excitement of the event or celebrity. Ideally, sponsorships are mutually-beneficial because each entity benefits from the other partner's brand equity. Just as with outdoor ads, sponsorships and partnerships generally are most relevant in the early stages of the AIDA model. After two decades with Nike, Roger Federer signed a 10-year contract with Japanese clothing retailer Uniqlo, which is known for its well-designed basic clothing as well as its high-tech line called Lifewear. Federer assists in the design process for some of the items that are especially relevant to athletes, using fabrics that wick away sweat and others that conserve warmth (Binlot 2018). Uniqlo is Asia's biggest clothing retailer (Matsukawa and Furukawa 2021) and Federer is one of the most well-known tennis stars of all time – a perfect match (see Photo 11.6).

Photo 11.6 Uniqlo is Asia's biggest clothing retailer

Source: Shutterstock/Ned Snowman

The boundaries between these advertising categories are often blurred. Digital billboards, for example, are a combination of digital and outdoor and are increasingly common. Is a digital ad really 100% digital if it appears as one is reading *The Financial Times*? How exactly shall we categorize advertising that takes place in an *indoor* arena? One consequence of this blurring of the lines is that advertisers are no longer limited to the confines of traditional advertising, like the 30-second TV ad or the quarter-page print ad. Instead, advertising creatives can develop more nuanced stories and inspiring content for consumers (Wojcicki 2016). Regardless of the blurred lines, however, the overall objective of advertising strategies is to effectively deliver a message to the target audience.

Sales Promotion

Another promotional tool is **sales promotions**, which are short-term monetary or volume incentives that encourage purchases. These can be in the form of a percentage off sale, volume discounts, buy two/get one free, or other deals. Sales promotions can be directed at supply chain intermediaries or consumers; the feedback is a sale. Sales promotions are especially effective in generating action in the AIDA model. They encourage consumers to stock up and to buy now, rather than wait. An associated benefit is that when consumers stock up, they are effectively out of the market for a period of time because they are consuming your organization's products, rather than those of the competition. One negative to this promotional tool is that it can condition consumers to wait for price breaks and deals.

Personal Selling

Organizations can also utilize **personal selling** as a way to promote the product with the target market. Personal selling involves one-on-one communication between a sales person and a customer. It is typically utilized when the product is complicated or consumers need the help of a trained expert in helping them navigate their way through the purchase, as in a B2B situation where a purchasing agent is buying a new piece of manufacturing or office equipment. Personal selling is effective at each point along the AIDA model; the sales person can introduce a new product to a consumer, describe it in detail, answer targeted questions, and then facilitate an order. When assessing costs on a per customer basis, personal selling is very expensive.

Publicity

Publicity or public relations is an effort to deliver a message to a target market through the news media. If the organization does something that is newsworthy, reporters may be interested enough to share the story with their viewers or readers. Viewers and readers consume the information and then provide feedback by reposting or sharing the news story, or searching for more information. To measure the effectiveness of the PR effort, marketers pay particular attention to **earned media**, an important KPI which assesses the monetary value of the media coverage that was not directly paid for by the organization. For example, when the Sydney Opera House launched its "Come on In" campaign, it saw a tremendous spike in earned media as local news networks picked up the story and people shared and commented about the campaign to their own social networks (see case study on p.494). Publicity is especially effective in the early stages of the AIDA model, when the organization is generating awareness and interest. Most organizations carefully control their publicity efforts with targeted press releases that discuss the company's activities and accomplishments. One important benefit to publicity is that it is free – the airtime or the space the story occupies is not paid for by the organization. The other benefit is that there is an increased level of credibility associated with the story because it has been curated by the news organization and its reporters. On the downside, the organization has very little control over what is said by reporters.

Direct Marketing

As the name implies, **direct marketing** is a direct, non-personal, one-way communication that originates with the organization and targets the potential customer. It can be done via text, mobile messaging, email, or actual mail. Consumers decode the message and then provide feedback with behaviors such as click-throughs, sales, or further inquiries. The biggest benefit of direct marketing is its flexibility in delivering a variety of messages and its ability to precisely and personally target the message. A downside is that it is difficult to get high levels of engagement with direct marketing.

There are two additional things we need to know about the promotional mix. First, each element of the promotional mix has its own purpose, as well as its benefits and drawbacks. In addition, different elements in the promotional mix are more appropriate at different stages of the AIDA model. **Integrated marketing communications (IMC)** occurs when the elements of the promotional toolkit work together to speak with "one voice" to the target audience. Consumers come into contact with brands via **touchpoints**, those encounters that occur between the brand and consumer via a salesperson, website, advertisement, retail store experience, etc. Marketing teams strive to achieve IMC because they want to ensure that regardless of the touchpoint, each communication will have a similar look, feel, and meaning. Second, the promotional strategy needs to also be unique, ownable, consistent, and distinctive. Consumers need to be able to easily recognize and connect the message to the brand, without confusing it with that of the competition. KFC spends $100 million on various promotional vehicles in the UK each year and found out the hard way what happens when its ads are not easily distinguished from the competition. In 2020, KFC launched a campaign that promoted KFC as an easy way for the family to have a quick, good-quality meal. Unfortunately, McDonald's was running a similar campaign and KFC found that 60% of UK consumers misattributed its ads to McDonald's. In effect, this was a $60 million give-away to McDonald's (Creed and Muench 2021).

Encouraging Engagement

Marketers often want to ensure that their promotions are interesting, fun, and perhaps even interactive for the consumer. Ads that are quirky or reference an "inside joke" help consumers engage, as does promotional messaging that is particularly relevant to the consumer, the context, or current events. Interactive promotions, such as those that encourage quizzes or games, are particularly engaging. The "Come on In" campaign at the Sydney Opera House used social media to encourage tourists who were there on the property taking selfies to come on in and check out the inside of the venue. It was incredibly successful, in part, because it was so engaging (see case study on p.494). Personal selling has the highest potential for engagement. Sales promotions can be very engaging, especially if consumers are encouraged to play games, post pictures, or collect rewards. Advertising can also be engaging, especially digital advertising, which provides the opportunity for consumers to interact with the ad by, for example, looking for hidden messages, answering questions, or scanning codes. The benefits of higher levels of engagement are apparent in sustainability-focused campaigns too. In one study about consumer attitudes toward organizational sustainability efforts, ads that promoted stronger

engagement resulted in consumers having more positive evaluations of the company and higher purchase intentions. Consumers were also more likely to believe that the company was engaging in the effort for altruistic reasons rather than for self-serving reasons (Lee, Kim, and Kim 2021).

Facilitating Memory Effects

Consumer memory plays an important role in marketing. When the marketing team is deliberating its promotional strategy, one of its considerations should be the expected effect on the consumer's memory. One well-known memory effect in advertising is that there are distinct memory benefits when at least two different types of advertising are used to deliver the message to the consumer. The **dual encoding effect** finds that if a message is perceived by the consumer's senses via two different sensory channels – such as visually (with a TV ad that portrays the product) and aurally (with a musical jingle) – the information is encoded into the consumer's memory in two different locations. Later, the information is more likely to be retrieved because it was stored in two different locations in the consumer's memory. In addition, compared to watching the TV ad, just hearing the jingle is often as effective in getting consumers to recall the ad's content (Stewart and Punj 1998). Because this effect is so well-known, some of the world's most successful brands have very distinctive sounds or musical jingles that accompany their promotions.

Another memory-related consideration relates to the brands the consumer can organically retrieve from memory when thinking about an upcoming purchase. The more effectively the brands are encoded in memory, the more likely those brands will be brought to mind for consumers when they are considering a purchase. The **evoked set** is the entire selection of brands that the consumer brings to mind when considering an upcoming consumption decision. The **consideration set** is a smaller subset of the evoked set. It is the collection of brands that is under serious consideration by the consumer. The consideration set takes into account the consumer's own situation, such as time and financial constraints. If a brand is not located in the consumer's consideration set, it will rarely be purchased (see Figure 11.8).

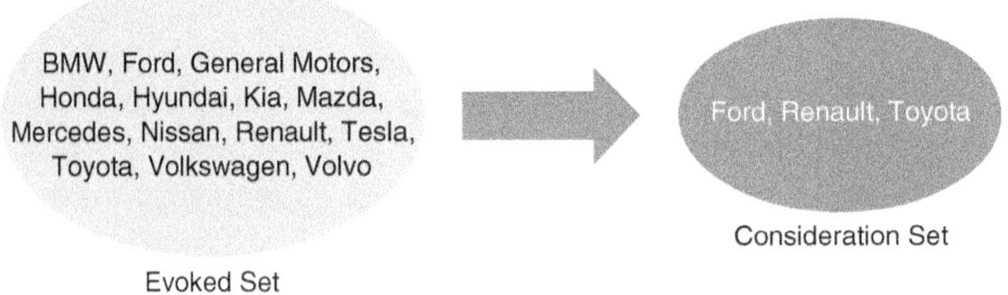

Figure 11.8 Promotion can facilitate important memory effects by placing the brand in the consideration set or evoked set

Selecting a Push vs. Pull Strategy

Another important decision is whether the team will engage in a push strategy, a pull strategy, or a combination of the two. Think of the push vs. pull decision as one that hinges on how the team would like the product to move through the distribution channel, that part of the supply chain that delivers the product into the hands of the consumer. **A push strategy** is utilized when the focus of the promotional effort is on the channel intermediaries. When using a push strategy, one of the most effective tools is sales promotion. Incentives like price or volume discounts are given to intermediaries to encourage them to stock up and push the product from the warehouse to the distributor, to the retailer, and to the consumer. Channel members could, for example, be given deep discounts for higher-volume purchases. **A pull strategy** is employed when the focus of the promotional effort is on the consumer to create such strong consumer demand for the product, that it will be eventually pulled through the distribution channel by the force of consumers. Because consumers are demanding the product, the entire distribution channel will work together to ensure that it is readily available to them. When using a pull strategy, one of the most effective tools is advertising. Many organizations use a combination of push and pull strategies; they promote the product to channel intermediaries with discounts and they promote the product directly to the consumer. Fast-moving consumer goods (FMCG) often utilize push and pull strategies. Pepsico, for example, is the parent company for several brands, including its iconic Pepsi, as well as 7 Up, Mountain Dew, and Doritos. Pepsico utilizes hefty sales promotions directed at its channel intermediaries to encourage them to keep its products in stock throughout the supply chain. Pepsico also spends heavily on promoting its brands to end-consumers with advertising, encouraging them to maintain a high demand for the product. Part of this pull effort involves introducing a steady stream of new flavors and products to keep excitement in the brand high (see Photo 11.7).

Photo 11.7 Pepsico engages in push and pull strategies

Source: Pixabay

Determining the Level of Focus

In determining the level of focus, should the message focus on the product, product line, brand, or organization? In most instances, the marketing team focuses its efforts on the product, brand, or product line because it has significant expertise in these areas as well as experience in crafting messages that resonate with the target audience.

Sometimes, however, it is necessary to communicate an important message about the organization itself. Millennials and younger consumers prefer to associate with companies that are purpose-driven, so organizations need to communicate their values to consumers and other stakeholders. Organizational-level behaviors, including the behaviors of the CEO, are often watched carefully, especially when these individuals behave badly. Simply look at the news and it is easy to find examples of CEOs who are in the midst of some kind of controversy. With respect to sustainability, stakeholders believe that a CEO's actions should fit the values espoused by the organization. Indeed, the CEO's actions have a strong and significant influence on the firm's reputation (Loock and Phillips 2020). In short, organizational values and purpose matter to consumers.

Communications efforts about values and purpose need to be planned and enacted very carefully, otherwise the communication may be perceived as disingenuous. One needs to look no further that the furor that faced Pepsi when it attempted to promote its commitment to social justice and the Black Lives Matter movement with a preposterous ad featuring American model Kendall Jenner giving a Pepsi to a policeman during a heated protest. The policeman drinks the Pepsi and the crowd suddenly rejoices. How can an organization promote its strongly held values without risking accusations of being disingenuous? First, the marketing team needs to work collaboratively with the corporate-level communications team. Efforts need to be coordinated and the messaging needs to be consistent. Further, the messaging needs to be consistent with what has been communicated in the past about the product, brand, or product line. Gillette learned this lesson in 2019 when it launched a promotion to address the problem of toxic masculinity. While the messaging itself was admirable, it was inconsistent with decades of promotions supporting macho stereotypes and claims that Gillette was "the best a man can get." For Gillette, the new message was not authentic. Second, any organizational-level promotions need to be constructed first, followed by brand, product, or product line-level promotions. This allows for the organizational-level promotion to set the tone before any other promotions are deployed (Knowles, Hunsaker, Grove, and James 2022).

Who Will Deliver the Message?

The next consideration for the marketing team is to identify which entity will be best to deliver the promotional message to the target market.

Voice of the Organization

Messages to the target audience are most regularly delivered from the perspective of the organization. When confronting some of the biggest global issues of our time, consumers want businesses to not just take a stand, they want them to take definitive action. However, an important caveat is that the organization must be authentic in its statements and actions because they often undergo a deeper level of scrutiny from outside observers. Amazon, for example, released an ad in 2020 at the height of the Covid-19 pandemic thanking its workers for their heroic dedication to keeping the global economy moving. However, after workers went on strike to protest lax safety protocols and forced overtime, Amazon's commitment to their safety and health was rightfully questioned (Alemany 2020). Regardless of the topic, sometimes it is most effective for the company to speak with authority about the product or topic. In Photo 11.8, for example, Colgate has developed a new breakthrough toothpaste formula that offers the consumer superior protection. Because Colgate is a trusted brand, messages delivered from the organization are trusted and believed.

Photo 11.8 The Colgate message is delivered by the organization

Source: Advertising Archives

Customer Generated Content

Messages to a target audience can also be conveyed by other consumers through a variety of means, such as reviews, social media, or customer generated content. **Customer generated content (CGC)** has received significant attention in recent years. It can be defined as content, such as a comment, review, podcast, photo, post, or video about the brand or organization that is created by consumers. The important thing is that the person creating the content is not an official representative of the company. If the organization is seeking to enhance engagement, CGC can facilitate this. Few organizations have embraced CGC as much as Doritos, owned by the Frito Lay Company. Doritos has a dedicated website called The Legions of Creators with a variety of tools to help consumers generate unique and creative advertising content. The website posts challenges to its users and offers prize money for any content that is selected. From Doritos' perspective, the marketing team gets a steady stream of creative and off-the-wall content. They also establish and strengthen strong relationships with consumers. For their part, consumers get access to cutting-edge creation and editing tools, the chance to see their creative ideas achieve widespread distribution, and the chance to receive payment and recognition for their work (see Photo 11.9).

Photo 11.9 Doritos encourages CGC with its Legion of Creators website

Source: Shutterstock/Keith Homan

Every Member of the Organization

In a truly customer-centric organization, everyone needs to advocate for the company and its value proposition. Consumers, business partners, employees, and other stakeholders need to be viewed as if they are all integral members of the marketing team. When every member of the organization is viewed as an essential channel of communication, the impact is amplified and the conversation is prolonged (Bonchek and France 2017).

BLUNDERS & INSIGHTS 11.2

Calling All Karens!

BACKGROUND: In recent years, the name "Karen" came to be associated in some countries with an entitled White woman who displays racist or obnoxious behaviors. Karens often complain and ask to speak to a manager at restaurants or stores. The chief marketing officer at Domino's Pizza claimed the company wanted to give Karens a break and help them take the name Karen back. The ad stated, "Calling all (Nice) Karens," and featured a smirking White woman with short blonde hair. The ad was posted on Facebook in New Zealand and Australia; it encouraged all customers named Karen to explain why they are "nice Karens" in 250 words or less. Winners would receive a free pizza (Staff 2020, Watts 2020).

Domino's marketing team was surprised when customer reaction in New Zealand was far different from that in Australia. In New Zealand, the giveaway was met with backlash as customers and individuals claimed the ad was tone-deaf and valued privilege. Twitter and

(Continued)

Facebook users claimed Domino's should not be awarding an already privileged population with additional privilege and perks. Instead, Domino's should have donated pizzas to communities or minorities in need. The company removed the ad and quickly apologized, explaining how it was trying to foster inclusivity and had simply "tried to bring a smile to customers' faces" (Staff 2020, Watts 2020). The ad was interpreted very differently in Australia. There, customers found the ad to be funny and light-hearted. By the end of the campaign, Domino's provided free pizzas to a lot of Australian Karens and received very few complaints (Staff 2020).

DEBRIEF: This blunder underscores the importance of understanding cultural norms. Although the country was ruled by a colonial government for more than a century, New Zealand has a special and unique relationship with its native population. The Maori culture is respected and revered as an important facet of the overall culture. Economic redress has been made for past transgressions, Maori have representation in government, and the entire country takes pride in its mixed culture; Maori tattoos are common among all citizens and the country fully embraces its rugby team and its traditional "haka" dance performed before each match (Staff 2018). When the Domino's ad appeared, New Zealanders, already very cognizant of issues of race and privilege, reacted negatively.

Stage in the Product Life Cycle

Still another strategic decision the marketing team must make is the selection of the appropriate strategy, given the location of the product along the product life cycle. Depending on the stage of the product life cycle, the promotional objectives will be different, as will the elements of the promotional toolkit (see Table 11.3).

Table 11.3 Marketing mix strategy based on the product life cycle

	Introduction	Growth	Maturity	Decline
Promotion	Educate and inform to acquire new customers. *Promotional mix:* targeted advertising, personal selling, and publicity	Position the product in the minds of consumers and persuade consumers to try the product. *Promotional mix:* personal selling, advertising, direct marketing	Remind consumers about the product and encourage engagement. *Promotional mix:* advertising, sales promotion, direct marketing	Reposition the product or pull back on promotional efforts to reduce costs. *Promotional mix:* minimal use of promotional tools
Price	Either set the price high to recoup R&D expenses or set the price low to achieve market penetration	Maintain the price or lower the price as competitors start to enter the market	Engage in periodic price promotions and/or lower the price	Maintain or increase the price – some consumers will still demand it, regardless of the price
Product	Offer a limited number of product attributes	Increase the number of product attributes to help with product differentiation and positioning	Maintain or increase the number of product attributes	Offer a limited number of product attributes
Place	Offer exclusive or limited distribution	Increase distribution	Maximize distribution to the mass market	Offer exclusive or limited distribution

11.6 KPIs

The last step of the AIDA model is action, the consumer behavior that the marketing team hopes to motivate. In this section, a variety of relevant KPIs based on consumer actions will be described (see Table 11.4).

Table 11.4 Commonly used KPIs in promotion strategy

KPI	Description
Sales	The total sales or change in sales as a result of the promotional effort
Market Share	The total market share or change in market share as a result of the promotional effort
ROI	The return that the organization receives from the promotional effort: (increase in sales – cost of campaign)/cost of campaign
Unaided Recall	The rate at which consumers can remember an ad without any hints or reminders ("Which ads do you remember seeing last night?")
Aided Recall	The rate at which consumers can remember an ad, with the help of hints or reminders ("Do you remember seeing any car ads last night?")
Recognition	The rate at which consumers can remember an ad, with the help of a description of the ad ("Do you remember seeing an ad for the new Jeep Grand Cherokee last night?")
Unique visitors	The number of individuals who visit the website or the retail store for the first time
Click-through rate	The percentage of consumers who see an ad and then tap or click through to find out more
Conversion rate	The percentage of consumers who buy the product or service after being exposed to the promotional message
Earned media	The monetary value of the media coverage that was not directly paid for by the organization.

In the digital arena, there are many ways in which the marketing team can assess its efforts to successfully engage consumers. Some of these measures are more effective, however, than others. For example, previous research has found that there is a very weak relationship between click-throughs and promotional effectiveness. Similarly, the numbers of likes and followers does not seem to have much influence on engagement. Further complicating matters is the problem of fraudulent accounts, hackers, and bots visiting websites. These visits distort any measures of page views or the time spent on a page. Understandably, marketers want to assess the number of actual humans visiting their sites. Overall, traditional measures of effectiveness like attitudinal changes, sales, or market share increases are just as important as ever. However, there are also some social media-specific and mobile-specific measurements that can be utilized (Fulgoni 2016) (see Table 11.5).

Table 11.5 Digital media metrics that assess consumer engagement

Category	Metric
Overall digital media metrics	Attitudes toward the website, motivations for using it, overall opinion of the site, trust in the site, length of time consumer spends on the site, the viewability of the site (does it get through ad-blockers?)
Social media-specific metrics	The number of shares, the number of postings, the positivity/negativity of posts
Mobile-specific metrics	Amount of time spent on the brand's app/site vs. that of the competitor, the amount of time spent on the brand's app/site that occurs via a mobile browser vs. the brand's mobile app (higher engagement occurs when consumers use an organization's mobile app)

Source: Fulgoni (2016)

ENDURING INSIGHTS 11.3

> "Strategy without tactics is the slowest route to victory. Tactics without strategy is the noise before defeat." – Sun Tzu, ancient Chinese military strategist

Novice marketers often make the mistake of focusing a disproportionate amount of effort on tactical decisions – a popular spokesperson, a compelling slogan, or a cool feature on an app. However, sound strategy needs to be developed first before any tactical decisions can be made. Otherwise, as Sun Tzu said, tactics without strategy is just noise.

11.7 PROMOTIONAL TACTICS

After the promotional objectives are established and the promotional strategy is created, the next step for the marketing team is to make a series of decisions regarding promotional tactics. One of the first decisions is the **promotional schedule**, which describes when and how often the promotional tool will be deployed. How often and on what schedule will the ad appear, will the sales promotion be deployed, will the salesperson call, etc.? Another decision is the selection of specific **media vehicles** that will be used. What specific TV or radio program, magazine, newspaper, digital media, or outdoor location will be the best choice in reaching our target market? Still another decision involves the **executional elements** that will be deployed. Many of these decisions are handled by the advertising agency, but they include a variety of decisions, including music, colors, fonts, imagery, text copy, dialogue, or the celebrity spokesperson. It is here that the creativity of the marketing team comes into play. Consumers remember well-executed ads much more than well-placed or well-targeted ads (Bonchek and France 2017, Scott 2016). Another tactical decision is the **promotional appeal** that will be utilized, which is the method the message will use to attract attention, interest, and desire. Promotions can utilize a variety of appeals, such as humor, sex, fear, emotions, scarcity, and rational arguments. UK retailer John Lewis Waitrose employs a variety of tactics in its yearly Christmas ads (promotional schedule). Its 2020, 2.5-minute TV ad was supported by print, outdoor, and digital (media vehicles). The ad was a mini drama in which a young girl befriends a baby dragon, which is computer generated. The dragon gets into quite a bit of trouble in his day-to-day life because every time he gets excited, fire springs forth from him and he sets fire to things (executional elements). In the end, the girl finds a very important job for the little dragon and the whole town is both happy and relieved (promotional appeal) (the video can be seen here: www.youtube.com/results?search_query=john+lewis+waitrose+2020) (see Photo 11.10).

Photo 11.10 Each year, John Lewis Waitrose ads are highly anticipated

Source: Advertising Archives

11.8 SUMMARY

When people think about marketing, they think about promotion. Promotion is a unique type of communication that advocates for the organization's value proposition. There are four external and three consumer-related influences on promotional efforts. Some of these influences are particularly problematic to effective communication because they have the potential to alter the frame of reference and create noise, which disrupts effective decoding and feedback. Although sales and market share are often viewed as the most important objectives, there are a variety of other objectives that may also be important for the marketing team to achieve. Just as the marketing team utilizes the marketing mix to deliver the value proposition, it also utilizes the promotional mix to convey important meaning to consumers about the organization, product, product line, and brand. Each element of the promotional mix – advertising, sales promotion, personal selling, publicity, and direct marketing – should operate in coordination with one another in conveying the organization's value proposition. Integrated marketing communications (IMC) is achieved when every promotional element is coordinated with the others and speaks with one voice.

In discussing the five elements of the promotional mix, the AIDA model was introduced as a way to understand how consumers perceive promotional efforts. We concluded that different promotional elements were especially effective at different stages of the AIDA model. We also demonstrated that the use of promotion, as well as the other elements of the marketing mix, evolve as the product moves along the product life cycle.

In addition to decisions regarding the product life cycle, as the marketing team is developing its promotional strategy, it must make a series of decisions regarding the extent to which it will encourage customer engagement, how its efforts might facilitate memory effects, whether it will engage in a push or a pull strategy (or both), where its level of focus will be, and who will be charged with delivering the message. As with any dimension of marketing strategy, appropriate KPIs must be identified and utilized to assess the extent to which the promotional objectives were achieved. Finally, a variety of tactical decisions must be made.

QUESTIONS FOR REVIEW & DISCUSSION

1. In Executive Insight 11, Orlando Acevedo found that he and his team faced a conflict in knowing that they were doing good work, but the work was funded by a fossil fuel company. Use Nussbaum's capabilities approach to suggest a strategy by which he could come to terms with this conflict.
2. Congratulations! You and your partner are planning to open up a new environmentally-themed coffee shop in your town. For each external and consumer-related influence on the promotional planning process, discuss how your coffee shop will address these issues.
3. During times of political, economic, and social unrest, 72.2% of CMOs said that the role of marketing increases in importance (Moorman and Shkil 2021). Do you agree or disagree? What, in particular, makes the marketer's job particularly challenging in these situations?
4. Imagine that you work for an international travel agency and you are trying to encourage tourists from your country to embark on a trip to Argentina. Create three SMART promotion-related objectives using three separate promotional objective categories (refer to Table 11.2). Be creative!
5. Describe the concept of integrated marketing communications (IMC) and why a marketing team may wish to achieve it. Identify two different organizations, one in a B2B setting and one in a B2C setting. Investigate how they communicate with their target market. To what extent does each one achieve IMC? Be specific.
6. In thinking about the various promotional strategy considerations, why is facilitating memory effects important? What does this have to do with sales or market share?
7. Imagine that you are the marketing manager of a company that specializes in manufacturing lawn care tools like mowers, clippers, and trimmers. Your subordinates want to measure recall and recognition for the ad campaign that just ran. Without being too critical, what exactly would you say to explain to them that sales and market share are the most important KPIs?

11.9 REFERENCES

Alemany, Christine. 2020. Marketing in the Age of Resistance. *Harvard Business Review Digital Articles*. 3 September. 2–6.

Binlot, Ann. 2018. Roger Federer On Why He Ditched Nike for a $300 Million Uniqlo Deal. *Forbes.com*. 28 August. Accessed 22 June 2022. www.forbes.com/sites/abinlot/2018/08/28/roger-federer-on-why-he-ditched-nike-for-a-300-million-uniqlo-deal/?sh=2d538c764db4.

Bonchek, Mark and Cara France. 2017. What Creativity in Marketing Looks Like Today. *Harvard Business Review Digital Magazine*. 22 March. Accessed 3 April 2022. https://hbr.org/2017/03/what-creativity-in-marketing-looks-like-today.

Creed, Greg and Ken Muench. 2021. *RED Marketing: The Three Ingredients of Leading Brands*. HarperCollins Leadership, an imprint of HarperCollins, LLC, New York.

Directive 2006/114/EC. 2006. Directive 2006/114/EC of the European Parliament and of the Council Concerning Misleading and Comparative Advertising (Codified Version). 12 December. Accessed 25 March 2022. https://eur-lex.europa.eu/legal-content/EN/TXT/?uri=celex%3A32006L0114.

Dsouza, Rishad. 2022. Global: To What Extent Do Online Reviews Affect Purchase Decisions Across Various Sectors? *YouGov PLC*. 2 February. Accessed 2 April 2022. https://today.yougov.com/topics/technology/articles-reports/2022/02/02/global-what-extent-do-online-reviews-affect-purcha.

DW. 2022. Germany: Consumer Mood Slumps Amid Ukraine War. *Deutsche Welle*. News. Accessed 30 March 2022. www.dw.com/en/germany-consumer-mood-slumps-amid-ukraine-war/a-61286916.

EC. 2022. Flash Consumer Confidence Indicator for EU and Euro Area. *The European Commission*. 23 March. Accessed 30 March 2022. https://ec.europa.eu/info/business-economy-euro/indicators-statistics/economic-databases/business-and-consumer-surveys/latest-business-and-consumer-surveys_en.

Friedman, Thomas L. 2009. *Hot, Flat, and Crowded: Why We Need a Green Revolution – and How it Can Renew America*. Release 2.0 – Updated and Expanded. Picador/Farrar, Straus, and Giroux. New York.

Fulgoni, Gian M. 2016. In the Digital World, Not Everything That Can Be Measured Matters. *Journal of Advertising Research*, *56* (1), 9–13.

GOV.UK. 2022. Marketing and Advertising: The Law. Advertising Codes of Practice. GOV.UK. Accessed 25 March 2022. www.gov.uk/marketing-advertising-law/advertising-codes-of-practice.

Klein, Ezra and Joe Posner. 2021. *Diamonds. Explained*. A Netflix Original Documentary Series. Vox Productions.

Knowles, Jonathan, B. Tom Hunsaker, Hannah Grove, and Alison James. 2022. What is the Purpose of Your Purpose? Your Why May Not Be What You Think It Is. *Harvard Business Review*, *100* (2), 36–43.

Lee, Sun Young, Yeuseung Kim, and Young Kim. 2021. Engaging Consumers with Corporate Social Responsibility Campaigns: The Roles of Interactivity, Psychological Empowerment, and Identification. *Journal of Business Research*, *134*, 507–17.

Liu, Qianqian Ben and Elena Karahanna. 2017. The Dark Side of Reviews: The Swaying Effects of Online Product Reviews on Attribute Preference Construction. *MIS Quarterly*, *41* (2), 427–48.

Loock, Moritz and Diane M. Phillips (2020). A Firm's Financial Reputation vs. Sustainability Reputation: Do Consumers Really Care? *Sustainability*, *12* (24). 1–17. http://dx.doi.org/10.3390/su122410519.

Matsukawa, Bumpei and Keiichi Furukawa. 2021. Uniqlo Outstrips Zara as Most Valuable Clothier at $103bn. *NikkeiAsia*. 17 February. 22 June 2022. https://asia.nikkei.com/Business/Retail/Uniqlo-outstrips-Zara-as-most-valuable-clothier-at-103bn.

Maverick, J.B. 2022. Coke vs. Pepsi: Who Controls the Market Share? Coca Cola and Pepsi Control the Global Non-Alcoholic Beverage Industry. *Investopedia. Company Profiles*. 29 March. Accessed 30 March 2022. www.investopedia.com/ask/answers/060415/how-much-global-beverage-industry-controlled-coca-cola-and-pepsi.asp.

McSweeney, Eoin. 2020. South Africa Retailers Remove TRESemmé from Shelves over 'Racist' Ad. *CNN*. 11 September. Accessed 23 March 2022. www.cnn.com/2020/09/11/africa/tresemme-clicks-ad-south-africa/index.html.

Moorman, Christine and Brittney Shkil. 2021. How Covid-19 Changed Marketing. *CMS Wire*. 12 May. Accessed 17 March 2022. www.cmswire.com/digital-marketing/how-covid-19-changed-marketing/.

Neuman, Scott and Bill Chappell. 2019. Young People Lead Millions to Protest Global Inaction on Climate Change. *NPR*. Environment section. 20 September. Accessed 30 March 2022. www.npr.org/2019/09/20/762629200/mass-protests-in-australia-kick-off-global-climate-strike-ahead-of-u-n-summit.

Our History. 2021. About us. TechnoServe. Accessed 23 July 2021. www.technoserve.org/about-us/our-history/.

Our Identity. 2021. TotalEnergies, A Broad Energy Company. Accessed 23 July 2021. https://totalenergies.com/group/identity.

Porter, Michael E. 2008. The Five Competitive Forces that Shape Strategy. *Harvard Business Review*, 86 (January), 79–93.

Richter, Felix. 2022. Super Bowl Pales in Comparison to the Biggest Game in Soccer. *Statista*. Super Bowl. 11 February. Accessed 30 March 2022. www.statista.com/chart/16875/super-bowl-viewership-vs-world-cup-final/#:~:text=According%20to%20FIFA%2C%20the%202018,in%20over%20its%2090%20minutes.

Scott, Samuel. 2016. How Google Analytics Ruined Marketing. *TechCrunch*. 7 August. Accessed 4 April 2022. https://techcrunch.com/2016/08/07/how-google-analytics-ruined-marketing/?guccounter=1.

Staff. 2018. The Kiwi Model: Australia and New Zealand. Why the Maori Do Better Than Aboriginals. *The Economist*, *429* (9120). 1 December. 54 (US).

Staff. 2020. Domino's New Zealand Drops "Free Pizza for Karen" Offer After Backlash. *BBC News*. 31 July . Accessed 23 March 2022. www.bbc.com/news/world-asia-53589897.

Statista. 2011. Share of Brides Who Received a Diamond Engagement Ring in the United States from 1939 to 1990. *Statista*. Accessed 18 March 2022. www.statista.com/statistics/238115/share-of-brides-in-the-us-with-a-diamond-engagement-ring/.

Statista. 2022. Consumer Behavior in Poland After the Russian Invasion of Ukraine in 2022. *Statista*. Retail & Trade section. Accessed 30 March 2022. www.statista.com/statistics/1298265/poland-consumer-behavior-after-the-russian-invasion-of-ukraine/.

Stewart, David W. and Girish Punj. 1998. The Effects of Using a Nonverbal (Musical) Cue on Recall and Playback of Television Advertising: Implications for Advertising Models. *Journal of Business Research*, *42* (1), 39–51.

Venkatraman, Vinod, Angelika Dimoka, Khoi Vo, and Paul A. Pavlou. 2021. Relative Effectiveness of Print and Digital Advertising: A Memory Perspective. *Journal of Marketing Research*, *58* (5), 827–44.

Wathieu, Luc, Lyle Brenner, Ziv Carmon, Amitava Chattopahyay, Klaus Wetenbroch, Aimee Drolet, John Gourville, A.V. Muthukrishnan, Nathan Novemsky, Rebecca K. Ratner, and George Wu. 2002. Consumer Control and Empowerment: A Primer. *Marketing Letters*, *13* (3), 297–305.

Watts, Marina. 2020. Domino's Pizza Drops "Calling All Karens" Free Pizza Giveaway After Backlash. *Newsweek*. 29 July. Accessed 23 March 2022. www.newsweek.com/dominos-pizza-drops-calling-all-karens-free-pizza-giveaway-after-backlash-1521362.

Wojcicki, Susan. 2016. Want Your Ads to Engage Women? Empower Them. *AdWeek*. 15499553, 25 April, *57* (15).

12 CUSTOMER RELATIONSHIP MANAGEMENT: DEVELOPING AND GROWING CUSTOMER RELATIONSHIPS

LEADERSHIP INSIGHTS 12

Photo 12.1 Matt Gibson

Source: courtesy, Matt Gibson

Meet Matt Gibson, VP of Marketing

CertainTeed

Matt Gibson is one of the few people who can get really fired up about roofing shingles, insulation, and siding. Gibson is the VP of Marketing for CertainTeed, a $4 billion brand and a subsidiary of French company Saint-Gobain®. CertainTeed manufactures premium-quality building materials.

Gibson's 43-person team is especially effective and efficient at taking a customer-centered approach to finding out what is on the minds of customers and using those insights to further build and manage customer relationships. They speak directly with their customers over time and learn about their unique needs and challenges. This detailed information is referred to as the **voice of the customer** (VOC). "We focus heavily on really getting to know our customers, so we gather VOC, develop customer insights, and then deliver the best product to them. We continually try to understand the customer experience. Everything is tied to KPIs and accountability," offered Gibson (see Figure 12.1).

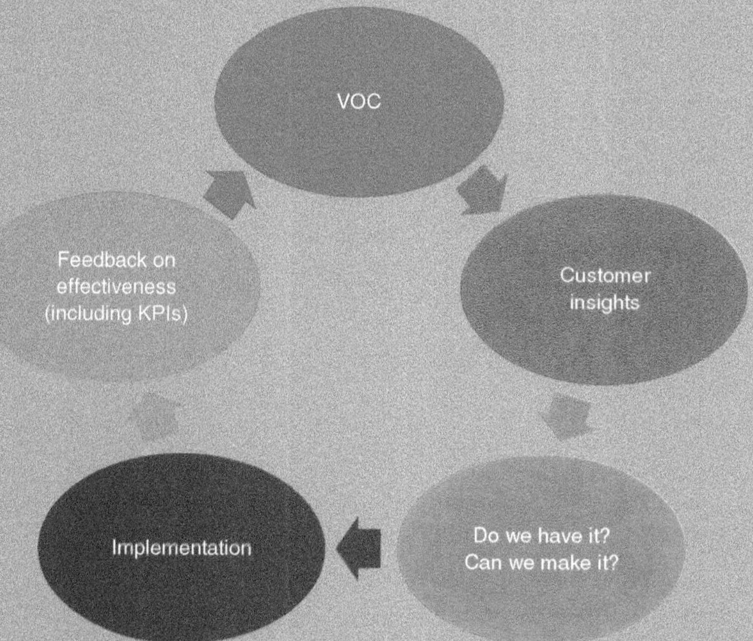

Figure 12.1 The Circular System of Customer Relationship Management at CertainTeed

Source: Matt Gibson

Two big initiatives were developed as a result of this customer-centric approach. The first initiative was launched from the insight that residential customers were having difficulty visualizing what their house would look like after a home improvement project. "We created a visualization tool where anyone can go online, upload a picture of their house, and then try out a variety of different designs and colors," explained Gibson. Another initiative grew out of commercial customers starting to demand more sustainable solutions for their new offices and office renovations. In this market, architects and building owners are key influencers and the marketing team at CertainTeed knew that it needed to involve them in any efforts to promote more sustainable building materials to their commercial clients. The result was an innovative new Customer Insights Center which opened on CertainTeed's corporate campus so that corporate clients, architects, and building owners could examine the materials firsthand. Significantly, the Customer Insights Center is housed in a remodeled 19th century barn that is located on the property, highlighting the fact that CertainTeed's products are not just sustainable and innovative, but they can easily be deployed in a variety of projects.

Gibson has several different goals for the Center. First, its interactive, hands-on nature dispels any misconceptions that influencers may have about the durability or attractiveness of sustainable products. Second, the Center highlights the one-of-a-kind, innovative, premium products that are only available from CertainTeed. Third, it helps answer questions as to how CertainTeed can help a particular company meet its own sustainability goals. Finally, the Center further builds and strengthens the relationships that the company has with its customers. Customers can meet with experts one-on-one and have their questions answered. They can also get expert advice on materials, installation, and after-installation care. According to Gibson, "our value add is the expertise we bring to the project."

If Gibson could give his 20-year-old self some advice, it would be this: "as my career evolved and I began to see my career path ahead of me, I would always be focused on what was next. When will I be a director? When will I get on the leadership team? When will I be a vice president? Be patient and enjoy what you are doing while you are doing it."

12.1 K-POP: DELIVERING WHAT FANS WANT

The $5 billion global South Korean pop music genre and industry (K-pop) is masterful at understanding what fans want and then giving it to them. Fans believe that their voices are heard, understood, and even amplified by the bands' lyrics, melodies, and complicated dance moves. Because of this, fans forge strong relationships with their favorite bands, often making the band's next album release an almost guaranteed success (Klein and Posner 2021).

The most important first step in customer relationship management is creating a deep knowledge of customers. Korean entertainment companies engage in extensive research about the global youth culture and emerging trends. Although K-pop fans come from a broad spectrum of demographic backgrounds, most are socially progressive; they appreciate the mixing of music genres and creative dance moves, as well as messages of multiculturalism. When the K-Pop band BTS donated $1 million to the Black Lives Matter movement, fans responded with a fundraising effort of their own and matched the $1 million donation. Fans seem to especially appreciate stars who are gender non-conforming. Indeed, many boy band K-pop stars wear make-up and elaborate hairstyles (Bruner 2020). In short, K-pop music and K-pop fans are an important barometer of youth culture.

Through an extensive screening process that sometimes takes several years, entertainment companies hold auditions to identify talented young stars. The companies select members based on their looks and talent, as well as their ability to work well together. Each band has at least five members and each person selected for the band must be unique in some way. For example: the singer, the rapper, the dancer, the youngest one. In addition, each band member must be drug, alcohol, and scandal free. Often, these auditions are aired in a reality show format on Korean TV so that by the time the group members are selected, they already have a built-in fan base (Klein and Posner 2021).

To strengthen the connection between bands and their fans, and to demonstrate the commitment that the stars have for their fans, K-pop stars are prohibited from talking about their own personal relationships. Further, to appeal to the biggest possible audiences, bands often have several members who can sing and speak either Mandarin or English. Continuous training ensures that the band stays innovative with new genres, dance routines, and messages that are relevant to a global youth audience. It's all about experimentalism. To keep things fresh, songs mix different genres, switching, for example, from bubble-gum pop to rap. An important dimension of a band's appeal is its music videos, with their bold colors, coordinated clothing, exciting dance moves, and stunning sets. Importantly, although the songs are optimistic, the lyrics often address difficult-to-hear cultural truths about topics like drugs, sex, and destructive behaviors (Klein and Posner 2021).

Photo 12.2 BTS fans line up to connect with their favorite group

Source: Shutterstock/Dutchmen Photography

How do audiences respond? With unabashed enthusiasm and passion. BTS, one of the most successful bands, burst onto the global music scene in 2017. Its fans are called the ARMY, and the band quickly gained such a following that it embarked on its first world tour in 2018 to sold-out audiences. At about that time, observers started to make some not-so-subtle references to another famous boy band that took over the world in the early 1960s – the Beatles. Incidentally, BTS is the first band since the Beatles to have three number one albums topping the Billboard charts in 1 year. The ARMY has an "ethos of inclusion," positivity, and acceptance of individual differences. The connection between BTS and the ARMY is palpable. BTS frequently uses socially-conscious lyrics that speak with empathy toward the struggles of young people with a message of love and self-acceptance (Cruz 2019). BTS won Billboard's award for "top social artist" for 5 years in a row from 2017–21 (see Photo 12.2).

The Korean entertainment industry has been criticized for being too heavy-handed and scripted in its formulaic approach. However, one cannot deny its success in creating a scalable formula to connect with fans. The success of these efforts has hinged on several strategies – a deep knowledge of its customers, the careful and deliberate selection of band members, relevant messaging, and continued innovation – all of which work together to maintain and strengthen relationships with fans.

This chapter is about customer relationship management. As CertainTeed and K-pop demonstrate, it all starts with a customer-centric approach. Both of these organizations reframed their focus from seeking to deliver products and services, to one that identifies, nurtures, and grows customer relationships. Because the customer is the organization's most important asset, marketing decision-makers deploying principles of customer relationship management focus their work on nurturing and growing this asset.

12.2 LEARNING OBJECTIVES

After studying this chapter, you will be able to do the following:

1 Differentiate between two important concepts that are essential to a customer-centric approach: satisfaction and loyalty.
2 Create an argument for why products and services *do not* matter, but customers *do* matter to the organization.

3 Describe the seven criteria necessary for relationship establishment and growth.
4 Explain why trust is so important to growing and strengthening relationships and describe how trust can be quantified.
5 Draw the four-step IDIC model and carefully describe each step.
6 Describe the four ways in which the strength of the customer relationship can be quantified.

12.3 STICKY CUSTOMERS

One of the biggest challenges for marketers is to deploy strategies that encourage customers to stick with the organization over the long term. The overall goal is to create a value proposition so powerful that, even if the price increases, consumers will prefer our offering over that of the competition (Dawar 2016). This section briefly describes two important concepts that are central to the marketing team's understanding of how to get consumers to stick with us: satisfaction and loyalty. Fundamentally, the push for customer relationships is based on two important principles. First, it is far easier to keep customers than it is to recruit new customers. **The Pareto Principle**, also referred to as the 80/20 Rule, states that 80% of a company's profits come from 20% of its customers. So, while marketers generally do not like to *ever* lose a customer, they *really* don't want to lose a customer who is responsible for an out-sized proportion of the company's profits. The second fundamental principle is that of **customer-centricity**. That is, the focus of the entire organization is on the customer's needs and wants, not on the organization's products or services. Japan's Ono Pharmaceuticals was founded in 1717. From the company's earliest days of providing herbal mixtures and holistic remedies to its consumers out of a single apothecary in Osaka, its purpose has been "dedicated to the fight against disease and pain." In the more than 300 years it has been in business, Ono's products changed dramatically as it expanded globally. What has not changed is Ono's customer-centric philosophy: first focus on the customer's problems, then create the appropriate product (History 2022).

Customer Satisfaction

In the 1980s, when marketers first started recognizing the importance of taking a customer-centric approach, they relied quite heavily on the concept of customer satisfaction. The contention was that if customers could be kept satisfied, they would keep coming back. **Customer satisfaction** is the extent to which a customer is content or pleased with a consumption experience. Consumers assess their degree of satisfaction by comparing their expectations about how the product will likely perform with the actual performance of the product. If product performance is greater than or equal to expectations, consumers are satisfied. Conversely, if product performance is lower than expectations, consumers are dissatisfied (see Oliver 1980). This conceptualization of customer satisfaction, however, leaves little room for the role of emotions in the consumption experience.

A more realistic conceptualization of the satisfaction response takes into account a consumer's emotional experiences during consumption (Oliver 1993, Oliver 1997). Simply look at just about any consumption experience – consumers form expectations about how the product will perform as well as expectations about their own emotional reactions to the consumption experience. For example, when wearing a new jacket for the first time, consumers might expect that it will be warm and repel water (functional expectations). At the same time, they might expect to feel happy because the jacket is especially stylish and friends are sure to admire it (emotional expectations). Research indicates that during consumption, satisfaction is influenced by both functional and emotional expectations and experiences (Phillips and Baumgartner 2002) (see Figure 12.2).

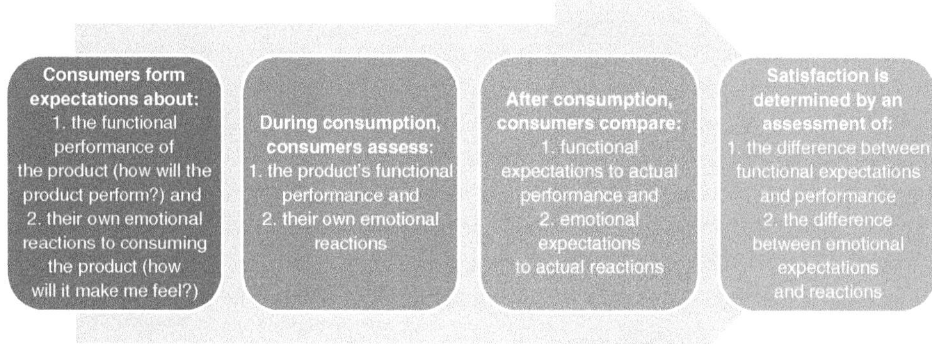

Figure 12.2 The satisfaction response

Source: Phillips and Baumgartner (2002)

Customer Loyalty

Brand loyalty is a strong commitment that a consumer has toward continuing to purchase a specific brand and is another measure of the likelihood that consumers will stick with the organization. There are two types of brand loyalty. First, **purchase loyalty** measures the extent to which a consumer is likely to engage in repeat purchases. It is easily measured by assessing purchasing rates and patterns over time. These consumers might not have any particular affinity for the brand and might instead just purchase out of habit or convenience. **Attitudinal loyalty** measures the extent to which the consumer prefers or has a commitment to the brand. Not surprisingly, purchase loyalty and attitudinal loyalty are strongly correlated with one another; consumers generally purchase brands they like. However, differentiating between these two types of loyalty is important, because each one has different implications for marketing strategy. Purchase loyalty often results in higher market share for the organization. Thus, if the marketing team's objectives are related to an increase in market share, it might try to facilitate purchase loyalty and encourage higher frequency purchases or greater volume purchases. Attitudinal loyalty, by contrast, often results in the customer's willingness to pay a higher price. Rather than purchase a less expensive competitive brand, consumers with attitudinal loyalty believe that their brand offers such an important value proposition that they are willing to pay a higher price for it. If the marketing

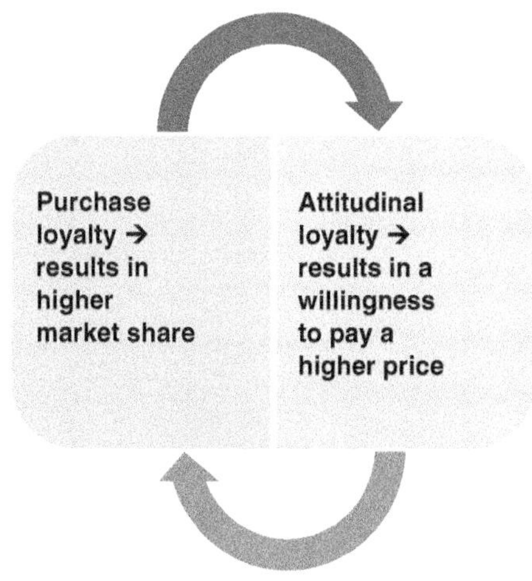

Figure 12.3 Purchase loyalty vs. attitudinal loyalty

Source: Chaudhuri and Holbrook (2001)

team's objectives relate to increasing the price or margins for the brand, it might work to improve the brand's attitudinal loyalty (Chaudhuri and Holbrook 2001) (see Figure 12.3).

The marketing team's goal, however, should not be to simply make customers satisfied or loyal. Instead, a more systematic approach needs to be implemented to forge and manage long-term customer relationships. The complicated process of managing customer relationships will be discussed next.

ENDURING INSIGHTS 12.1

"Don't find customers for your product. Find products for your customers." – Seth Godin, marketing strategist, author, and speaker

This quote illustrates the strategy that Ono Pharmaceuticals has taken and underscores the importance of the customer to the organization. Over time, companies create new and better products, but one thing that successful companies have in common is they are extremely astute in identifying customer needs and responding to those needs over time.

12.4 FORGING AND MANAGING CUSTOMER RELATIONSHIPS

Customer relationships are mutually beneficial connections between a customer and an organization. Are there benefits to forging relationships with customers? Most definitely. According to a recent report (Rioux 2020):

- companies that increase their customer retention rates by just 5% can increase their profits by 25–95%
- the cost of acquiring new customers has increased by 50% in recent years
- compared to selling to a new customer, the probability of selling to an existing customer can be as much as 14 times higher.

Customers might have positive affinity toward brands, be satisfied with their brands, or even feel a loyalty toward brands. A customer relationship, however, is different from these concepts. All human relationships like friendships or romantic relationships are characterized by several distinct criteria. These same criteria can be applied to the customer–organization relationship (see Table 12.1).

Table 12.1 Seven criteria necessary for relationship establishment and growth

Criterion	Explanation
Mutuality	Both entities in the relationship must be aware of the other and participate in the relationship
Interaction	The two entities must exchange information with one another
Iterative	Interactions must build on one another over time, so that there is a history/context to each interaction
Ongoing benefits	Both parties must continue to receive benefits from the relationship
Change in behavior	Both entities must alter their behavior as the relationship evolves
Uniqueness	Because each entity has unique needs and wants, the nature of the relationship will be different for each connection
Trust	Each entity must believe that the other is working with their best interests in mind

Source: Peppers and Rogers (2011)

Customer relationship management (CRM) is a deliberate, strategic process by which the organization attempts to increase the overall value of its customer base by sustaining and strengthening customer relationships. When organizations are committed to forging and managing long-term customer relationships, some of the more traditional marketing objectives, such as market share and profit maximization, will take a back seat to marketing objectives that focus on the strength and longevity of the customer relationship. In the following sections, several CRM concepts will be presented, a new model for CRM will be introduced, and new KPIs will be discussed.

Leading the Effort

One of the most important first steps in moving to a CRM approach is selecting someone to lead the effort, such as a **chief customer officer (CCO)**. This person's role is different from that of the chief marketing officer because the CCO's primary responsibility is to create insights that will increase the value of the organization's most important asset: its customer base. The CCO should orchestrate a paradigm shift in the entire organization's mindset toward putting the customer first in all of its decision-making. Ideally, the CCO will have budgetary and decision-making authority, will report directly to the CEO, and will be evaluated on how much the value of the organizations' customer base increases over time (Joyner 2012).

Foundational Principles

The most important principle to a CRM approach is a shift in perspective to one that prioritizes the customer, rather than sales, market share, profit, or other objectives. Indeed, an organization that embraces CRM is one in which the entire organization exists to deliver value to customers.

Customer equity is the total monetary value of all current and future relationships with an organization's customers (Peppers and Rogers 2011). By assessing the value of the organization's customer base, organizational leadership has an important tool in determining whether or not this most important asset of the company – its customer base – is increasing or decreasing in value over time. Another foundational principle in CRM is **share of customer**, a measure of the proportion of sales in a given category that are made to your brand. This is also often referred to as share of wallet. For example, of all the money a given customer spends per week on fast food, how much of that is spent at McDonald's? Organizations that do not embrace CRM often focus on **share of market**, the proportion of the entire target market that purchases your brand. Using a share of customer approach provides the marketing team with a tool to assess how important the brand is to the customer's life.

Few brands have such a loyal and dedicated group of customers as those of American motorcycle brand Harley-Davidson. For many dedicated HOGs (members of the Harley-Davidson Owner's Group), the brand is a core part of their identity; they spend their spare time riding their bikes and hanging out with other enthusiasts. Many of them even emblazon the brand on their bodies by getting Harley-Davidson tattoos. Indeed, it would be any marketer's dream to have a group of such passionate customers! Unfortunately, around its 100th anniversary in 2003, decision-makers at Harley-Davidson turned their attention away from the brand's most important customers – the core group of consumers who loved big, noisy bikes – and instead launched an effort to sell smaller, cheaper bikes to new target markets. These new target markets were not interested. In addition, by focusing on new markets, attention was diverted away from the brand's most profitable motorcycles and additional complexity was added to manufacturing processes. Even worse, existing customers grew frustrated at having to wait for new updates to their models. Soon, the CEO was forced to resign. Fortunately, Harley-Davidson underwent a course-correction by refocusing its efforts on its core customers in three different segments after flagging sales and a realization that it is between four to six times more expensive to attract new customers than it is to make your existing customers happy. Together, those customers make up about 70% of the organization's customers. The goal was to refocus the organization's efforts on these core customers and create a sense of exclusivity for the brand. Decision-makers at Harley-Davidson created different marketing strategies for each segment, complete with a preferred model that was consistently promoted to them. In the end, Harley-Davidson is fortunate that it had such a passionate group of customers. Otherwise, many would have readily left for another brand. As one upper-level executive said, "Love the customers who love you – adore your core" (Light 2020) (see Figure 12.4 and Photo 12.3).

Photo 12.3 Harley-Davidson has an especially strong relationship with its customers

Source: Pixabay

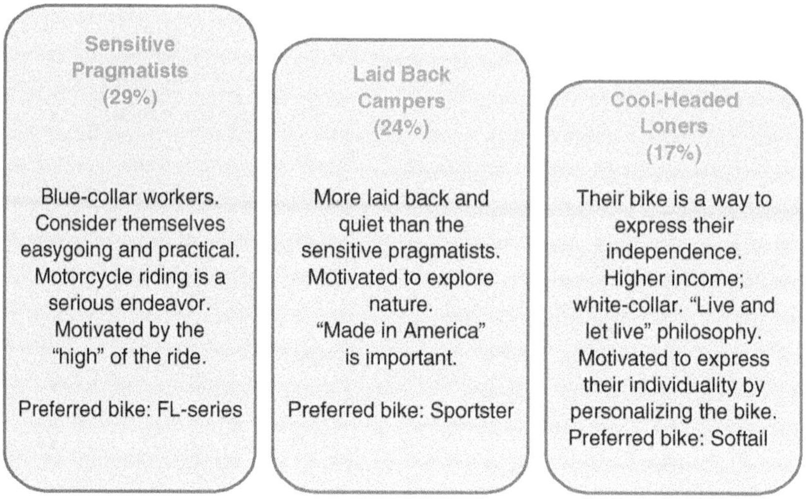

Sensitive Pragmatists (29%)

Blue-collar workers. Consider themselves easygoing and practical. Motorcycle riding is a serious endeavor. Motivated by the "high" of the ride.

Preferred bike: FL-series

Laid Back Campers (24%)

More laid back and quiet than the sensitive pragmatists. Motivated to explore nature. "Made in America" is important.

Preferred bike: Sportster

Cool-Headed Loners (17%)

Their bike is a way to express their independence. Higher income; white-collar. "Live and let live" philosophy. Motivated to express their individuality by personalizing the bike.
Preferred bike: Softail

Figure 12.4 Harley-Davidson's top three consumer segments

Source: Light (2020)

Not every organization can have a group of passionate customers like those of Harley-Davidson. However, they can utilize tools to help them build and strengthen customer relationships. The most influential CRM company in the world is Salesforce, a global company with operations in the Americas, EMEA (Europe, Middle East, and Africa), and the Asia Pacific region. Salesforce operates in the B2B space, specializing in helping businesses achieve their CRM objectives. In 2022, the company reported revenues of $26.5 billion, up 25% from 2021, in part, because Salesforce helped businesses forge and strengthen their relationships with customers during the global Covid-19 pandemic (Salesforce Announces 2022). Its interactive platform, Customer 360, helped businesses better understand the full customer experience and thus drive growth during a time of great uncertainty and global economic contraction. Customer 360 integrates disparate data and information from a variety of sources, and provides a variety of features and tools to create insights and forecasts. When other businesses were being shuttered, Salesforce was able to provide the tools necessary for their clients to facilitate customer relationships and grow their businesses (see Photo 12.4).

Photo 12.4 Salesforce is the #1 CRM company in the world

Source: iStock

Trust

Relationships are built on trust, especially from the customer's standpoint. Consumers **trust** an organization when they believe that the organization will be reliable, be truthful, and behave in their interests. Trust is built on two pillars. The first is **character**, or the extent to which this individual or organization has integrity and is motivated by good or honorable intentions. A person or organization with character will be trustworthy and honest. The second pillar of trust is **competence**, or the extent to which the customer or organization has the relevant skills, capabilities, or track record. A person or organization with competence will have the skills and talent to get the job done (Covey and Merrill 2006). Trust is a significant driver of profit, so marketing decision-makers often attempt to quantitatively assess the organization's perceived trustworthiness. Trust is enhanced by three factors. The first is **credibility**, or the extent to which the entity is truthful and possesses the appropriate credentials. The second is **reliability**, or the extent to which, over time, the entity is dependable and predictable. The third factor that enhances trustworthiness is **intimacy**, or the extent to which the entity expresses empathy and discretion in its interactions with the customer. Trust can be damaged by any perceptions of **self-orientation**, or the extent to which the organization looks out for its own, rather than the consumer's, self-interest. Combining these concepts, marketing decision-makers can create a quantitative measure for trust (Green 2011) (see Figure 12.5).

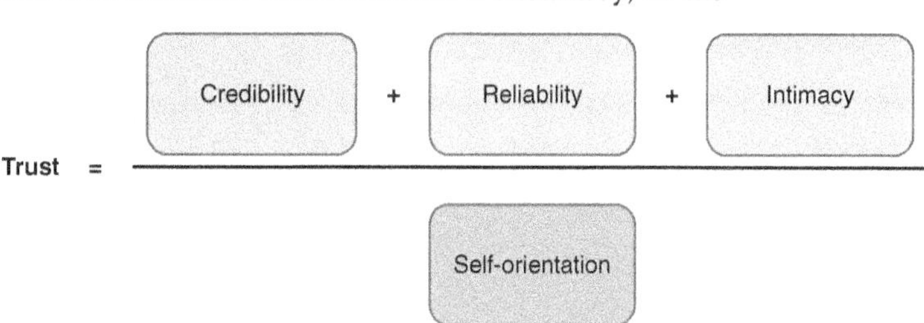

Figure 12.5 The trust equation

Source: Green (2011)

Several common misconceptions about trust exist that sometimes distract marketing decision-makers from the overall purpose of establishing a long-term, mutually-beneficial relationship with consumers (Green 2011) (see Table 12.2).

Table 12.2 Trust: myths vs. facts

Myth #1: intimate customer relationships require time and proximity	Fact #1: customers form relationships when they perceive a sense of safety in their interactions (e.g., "my data will be kept safe and confidential"). This is not dependent on proximity and does not require a significant commitment of time
Myth #2: trust takes time	Fact #2: trust is not necessarily time-bound. Although the reliability component does take some time to assess, consumers can derive a sense of trust by quickly assessing the organization's credibility, intimacy, and self-interest
Myth #3: more customized contact is better	Fact #3: within the correct context, customized contact is welcome. However, if the organization seems to have "too much" knowledge of the customer, the effect could be unsettling for the customer
Myth #4: people generally trust companies	Fact #4: today's consumers have a healthy dose of skepticism and belief that businesses are driven by a profit motive
Myth #5: people like to be asked for their opinions	Fact #5: this is only true when the consumer perceives that the organization uses customer feedback to improve the customer experience

Source: Green (2011)

As we can see from the equation, trust can be severely eroded when customers perceive that organizations are acting in their own self interests. In 2015, for example, consumer trust in

Photo 12.5 VW's breach of consumer trust was very costly

Volkswagen (VW) was severely damaged when it was found that the carmaker had installed what was dubbed a "defeat device" in its diesel-powered cars that could cheat CO_2 emissions testing equipment. Customers had purchased the vehicles, in part, because they believed that the cars were more environmentally-friendly than the competition. VW eventually admitted that it had sold about 11 million cars worldwide that contained these devices. Several high-ranking officials at VW resigned or were forced to leave and the company initially set aside £4.8 billion to cover the costs of recalls and refitting. In the end, VW's new CEO admitted that the company had "totally screwed up" and had "broken the trust of our customers and public" (Hotten 2015). By 2021, the scandal was far from over. VW had paid £25 billion in legal costs, recalls, and buy-backs, and was facing several class-action lawsuits from customers around the world (Davies 2021) (see Photo 12.5)

Trust and Sustainability

In an environment with plenty of misinformation, being a trusted resource for information about climate change and sustainability presents a tremendous opportunity for organizations to strengthen their relationships with consumers. Ray Anderson, founder and CEO of carpet company Interface, made headlines when he admitted that "in the future, people like me will go to jail." Anderson's statement sent shockwaves through the corporate boardrooms of many manufacturing companies like his that were heavily reliant on fossil fuels. Anderson made this statement in 1999 and was one of the first corporate leaders to make such an admission. At the time, his company was posting $1 billion in annual revenue and had more than two dozen manufacturing plants around the world. Anderson observed that because heavy industries like his voraciously consumed natural resources, their continued operations represented a collective form of suicide. He urged companies to start working together and was convinced that there was money to be made in doing so (Kinkead 1999). From a customer relationship perspective, at the very minimum, it is quite difficult to forge and maintain a relationship with an organization whose actions are causing such environmental damage that it poses tangible risks to the health and welfare of you and your family.

As they are seeing more evidence of the devastating effects of climate change, individuals around the world are becoming more concerned about the climate emergency. In a 2021 survey of citizens in 21 nations, China had the highest proportion of citizens who were concerned about the climate (92%), followed by Brazil (91%), and Italy (90%) (Ipsos 2021) (see Figure 12.6).

Because so many people around the world are concerned, many are seeking advice about what they can do to help the planet avoid the worst effects of climate change. Many are searching for entities they can trust to provide them unbiased information about measures that can be taken. Generally speaking, technology (34%) and pharmaceutical firms (31%) are trusted sources of information. During the Covid-19 pandemic, companies in both of these industries helped consumers answer questions and better navigate pandemic restrictions. Around the world, there is far less trust in the government (50%), the media (43%), and social media (39%) (Ipsos 2021) (see Figure 12.7).

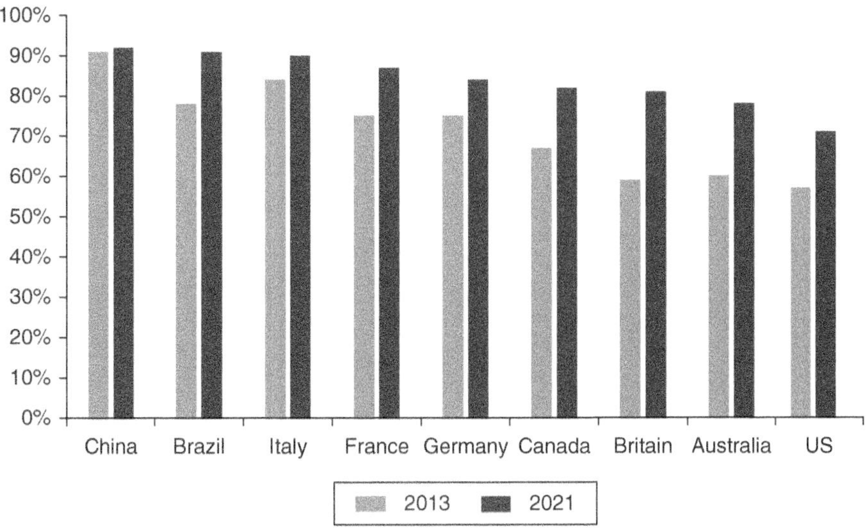

Figure 12.6 Increasing concern for the climate around the world

Source: Ipsos (2021)

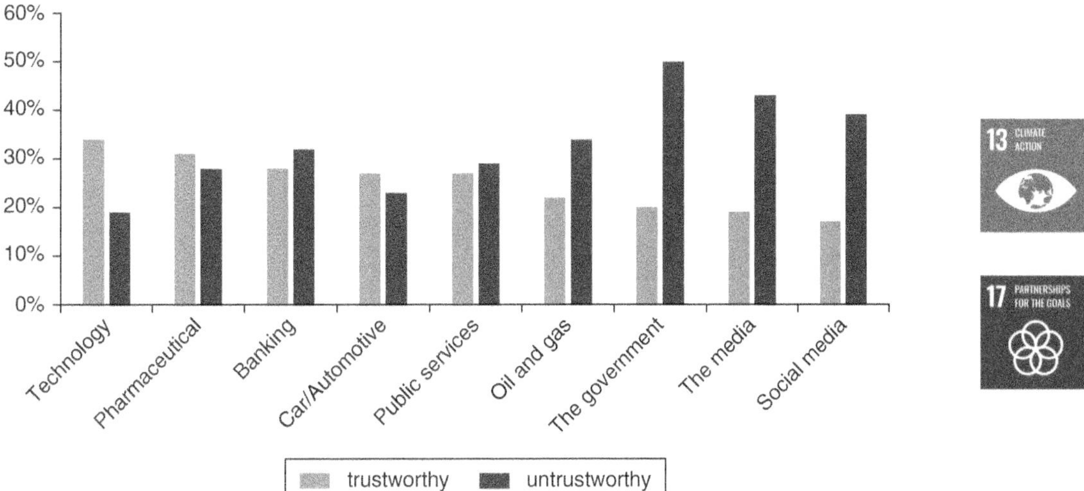

13 CLIMATE ACTION

17 PARTNERSHIPS FOR THE GOALS

Figure 12.7 Rates of trustworthiness vs. untrustworthiness for a variety of institutions

Source: Ipsos (2021)

What are some drivers of trust? Consumers around the world identified several key factors, but two stood out above the rest. First, the organization must be reliable and keep its promises (43%). Second, the organization must be open and transparent (42%) (Ipsos 2021) (see Figure 12.8).

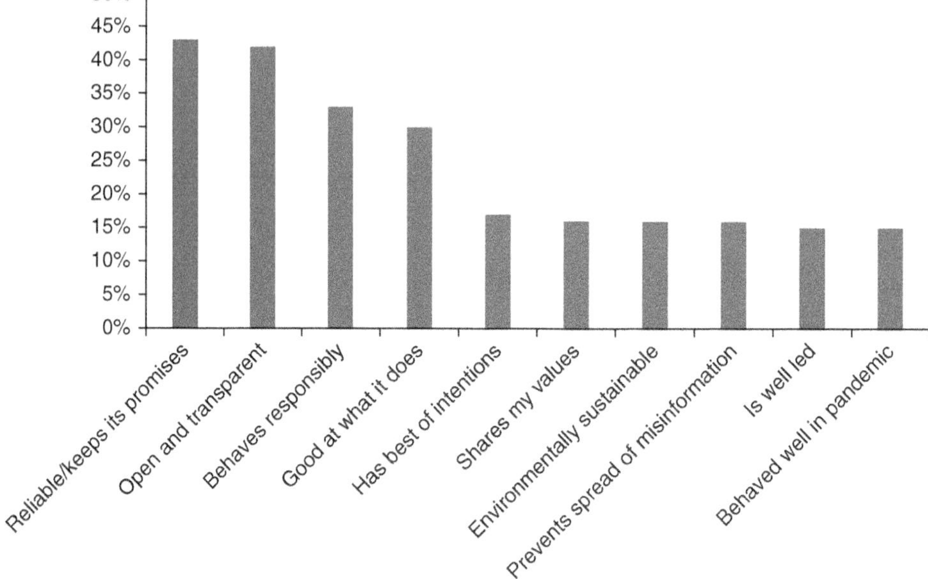

Figure 12.8 Drivers of trust

Source: Ipsos (2021)

Taken together, these figures reveal a significant opportunity for organizations to position themselves as a trusted resource to consumers on the issue of climate change. The more a customer trusts the organization, the more likely that person will be to accept recommendations and advice from the organization. As the relationship builds, the organization moves from being an organization that makes products or provides services, to one that is a trusted source of information or even a partner in the effort. In 1973, outdoor clothing manufacturer Patagonia was founded on a strong set of sustainability principles, from which it has never wavered. Because of its long history of activism, information sharing, and innovative product design and marketing, Patagonia has often been at the forefront of various industry-wide sustainability initiatives and its leaders are often invited to participate in a variety of global sustainability-related initiatives and discussions. Patagonia was one of the first companies to become B-corps certified. Patagonia's long-term solid reputation makes it a trusted resource for others seeking to be more sustainable (Chouinard 2016).

CRM and Shared Value

Strong customer relationships may be particularly advantageous in helping to enhance the creation of shared value. As discussed earlier in this text, shared value occurs when companies simultaneously create economic value, social value, and environmental value. Shared value isn't a form of charity from the business, but instead is a way for them to tangibly address a social or environmental need while making a profit (Porter and Kramer 2011). Strong customer relationships can assist an organization's efforts to create shared value because the organization's motivated and engaged customers will be willing to try new products and initiatives, thus amplifying the effect. The benefits of shared value creation are greatly enhanced by motivated users who trust the company and share in its vision.

One example of value creation is technology and commerce giant Alibaba and its popular map service, Auto-Navi. Alibaba added a feature to entice users to travel to economically depressed areas. By highlighting key points of interest in rural areas, travelers were enticed to visit "hidden gem" areas that may have otherwise been overlooked, bringing tourist dollars that boosted local economies. This feature provided direct value to Alibaba's app, while at the same time created opportunities for economic growth in remote villages that otherwise would have remained undiscovered. Alibaba leveraged technology to add value to the company, while also directly benefiting the world around them.

Leveraging Relationships

There are a variety of distinct benefits to the organization from nurturing strong relationships with its customers, including an increased willingness of customers to give the company a second chance, the ability to establish learning relationships, strengthening diversity efforts, and the possibility of leveraging the relationship to locate new Blue Oceans.

Second Chances

Mistakes happen. Sometimes products break, service providers mess up, or the offering does not live up to expectations. An often under-appreciated aspect of strong customer relationships is the willingness of customers to give the organization a second chance when mistakes happen. Just as an individual would not break up with their partner because of a pair of dirty socks left on the floor one day (hopefully not!), a long-term customer would not break a relationship with an organization over a small mishap. In fact, mistakes are often an opportunity for the organization to correct the mistake and strengthen the relationship even further. Indeed, the **recovery paradox** predicts that if an organization quickly and effectively fixes a customer's problem, the customer will be even more committed to the organization than before the unfortunate event. Two important caveats are that the failure must not be too severe and the organization must exert significant effort to fix the problem (McCollough 2009).

ENDURING INSIGHTS 12.2

"It's not whether you get knocked down, its whether you get up." – Vince Lombardi, American football coach

During his many years of coaching in the 1950s and 1960s, Lombardi was just as effective in his coaching abilities as he was in his ability to inspire people. Because of his influence, each year, the winner of the National Football League's championship game is awarded the Lombardi trophy in his honor.

Learning Relationships

Just as friends or partners learn more about one another as the relationship progresses and deepens, organizations and customers learn more about one another with each interaction too. A **learning relationship** is a collaborative set of communications between the organization and the consumer, for the purpose of facilitating the organization's ability to deliver the value proposition to the consumer. This communication must be two-way and iterative. That is, each communication builds on the last one. When a learning relationship is in place, the marketing team will have knowledge of that consumer that *no other competitor* has and can then utilize that information to better deliver the value proposition. There are two distinct benefits to learning relationships. First, customers learn more about their own preferences from each interaction with the organization. This knowledge allows customers to shop and consume more efficiently and effectively. Second, organizations learn more about their own strengths and weaknesses from each interaction with a given customer. This knowledge enables the marketing team to develop and implement more effective, efficient, and targeted strategies (Peppers and Rogers 2011).

Diversity, Equity, and Inclusion (DEI)

Strong relationships can also result in more effective efforts at diversity, equity, and inclusion (DEI). In general, an organization's **DEI efforts** are designed to create a workplace environment where everyone, regardless of race, socioeconomic status, gender, gender identity, age, physical ability, or ethnicity, is welcome, has the support they need, and can thrive. When there is strong trust within the organization, there are also two very distinct DEI-related advantages. The first, more immediate effect is that DEI initiatives are likely to be more easily and effectively implemented within the organization. Following that, because DEI considerations are baked into the organizational culture, the marketing team can then move forward and forge relationships with all types of consumers, regardless of their realities and lived experiences (see Figure 12.9).

Figure 12.9 Downstream DEI benefits of a CRM approach

Locating Blue Oceans

As discussed earlier in this text, if marketing strategists are able to locate Blue Oceans in which to operate, there are distinct benefits to the organization. Blue Oceans are new markets in which there is very little, if any, existing competition. Strong customer relationships will potentially reveal a set of unmet needs that your organization has not yet considered, which may help the organization locate new, untapped markets. The organization must develop a deep understanding of the customer's overall set of needs, their problems, and how the organization's product plays a role in their lives. It is also imperative to strike up conversations with former customers with whom the organization has had relationships. These conversations might reveal gaps or pain points that prevented your company from fulfilling their needs. Some problems may be difficult for a consumer to articulate or explain. Consider how frustrating it used to be to get a taxi home from a club on a Saturday night. Before rideshare services like Uber entered the market, if consumers were asked for their opinions about the problem, they might have suggested more taxis on the road. These suggestions would have merely skimmed the surface of the problem. Instead, developing a deep knowledge of consumer needs revealed that more taxis were not necessarily the solution. Consumers wanted a safe, convenient, and easy way to get from point A to point B. Enter Uber, which was founded in 2009. It offered an innovative, cheap, and easy solution to consumers who were frustrated at waiting for taxis or public transit. Uber jumped into a Blue Ocean by providing a solution to a specific and somewhat complex problem (Kim and Mauborgne 2015).

BLUNDERS & INSIGHTS 12.1

Doctor Disconnect

Photo 12.6 Doctors Without Borders engages in important, life-saving work around the world

Source: Pixabay

BACKGROUND: Doctors Without Borders (Médecins Sans Frontières) has a workforce of 65,000 people and does tremendous work in some of the most remote and desperately poor parts of the world. In 1999, it won the Nobel Peace Prize (Aizenman 2020) for its ongoing humanitarian work in providing medical attention and help to people in conflict zones and regions affected by endemic diseases (McVeigh 2020). In 2019, the Canadian division of Doctors Without Borders ran a £307,000 TV fundraising campaign which included images of crying Black children being treated by all-White medical teams. These images played out to the haunting tune of 'Everybody Hurts' by R.E.M. Prior to the release, several staff members expressed deep reservations about the ad, claiming that the images and presentation were exploitive and breached medical ethics guidelines. Despite these reservations, the ad was released (McVeigh 2020) (see Photo 12.6).

The ad triggered an organizational crisis at Doctors Without Borders. Critics claimed that it reinforced a racist "White savior complex" stereotype and severely damaged the trust that staff members had in the organization's leadership (McVeigh 2020). Some doctors of color complained that instances of racism were common at the organization and over 1000 staff members signed a statement calling for a change in its almost all-White leadership team (Aizenman 2020). Several people resigned in protest over the ad and the organization's toxic environment. Members of the organization called for an independent, far-reaching investigation into racism, sexism, and abuse of power. In a review of the ad, 68% either "disliked or hated it." The ad ran in Canada for 3 weeks before it was pulled. The organization never released an official apology (McVeigh 2020).

DEBRIEF: The leadership team seemed to have a profound disconnect in its perceptions about its own internal staff as well as those patients it was seeking to help. Perhaps some of this disconnect can be attributed to the days of colonialism in which affluent European countries went about spreading their culture throughout Africa, with little regard for local cultural norms or traditions. Importantly, the leadership team's insistence on running the ad, despite strong objections from the staff, was a distinct violation of trust. This hands-off, top-down approach is the antithesis of a relationship approach. Happily, improvements have occurred,

(Continued)

especially at the leadership level. The proportion of leaders who come from the global south, instead of North America and Europe, has increased from 24% to 46% (Aizenman 2020). In a recent survey of its Canadian staff, 70% reported that the work environment was inclusive, up from 59% from the previous year (McVeigh, 2020).

Managing Customer Relationships

In building and strengthening customer relationships, the marketing team must embark on a four-step process. The overall goal of this four-step model is to strengthen the trust consumers have with regard to the organization. Importantly, the model describes several mechanics of managing customer relationships, all based on mutuality and behavior change, especially on the part of the organization. The first two steps, identify and differentiate, occur behind-the-scenes and are not visible to the consumer. These steps involve significant efforts in sorting and analyzing data to create deep insights about customers. The second two steps in the model, interact and customize, are visible to consumers. These steps involve the actions that the organization implements to actualize its CRM insights (see Figure 12.10).

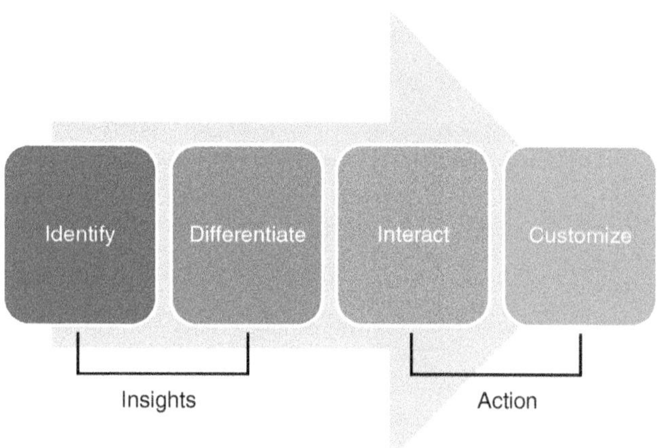

Figure 12.10 The IDIC Model for managing customer relationships

Source: Peppers and Rogers (2011)

Identify

The first step is to identify consumers. Remember that relationships are not forged with target markets, they are forged with individual customers, one at a time. In addition, relationships are based on mutuality, which means that both entities need to be aware of one another. Therefore, whether the customer visits our brick-and-mortar store, our website, or our mobile app, in the **identify** step, we need to know the *exact identity* of this customer. Importantly, the sales person or customer service representative must be able to access information about all of the customer's previous purchases and interactions with the organization (Peppers and Rogers 2011). Technology can be utilized to enable the identification of consumers, regardless of touchpoint.

Retailers often make mistakes in this step of the process, such as asking a customer for an original receipt in order to return an item. This violates the principle of identification and severely damages the successful completion of any of the other three steps in the model (Peppers and Rogers 2011).

Differentiate

Are all customers created equal? Certainly not. The second step in managing customer relationships is to engage in differentiation of customers into groups. The **differentiate** step is based on the notion that some customers are simply worth more than other customers. In addition, customers derive different value out of their interactions with the organization. First, the marketing team should differentiate by the value the customer brings to the organization. This is referred to as **value of the customer**. Since an organization's resources are often limited, long-term customers and those that are responsible for an above-average proportion of the company's profit should receive extra attention (Peppers and Rogers 2011). For example, financial services firms regularly provide their high net worth investors with their own customer service phone number. When these customers call the customer service line, the customer's entire history of interactions is on the screen when the customer service representative answers the phone, often on the first ring. Customer service representatives are empowered to solve the problem quickly and efficiently, without getting a manager's approval.

Second, customers need to be differentiated by what their connection to the organization means to them. This is referred to as **value to the customer** and represents the extent to which the organization's offering plays an important role in the customer's life (Peppers and Rogers 2011). From a B2B perspective, does your customer rely on your organization as the sole provider for a critical component of its processes? From a B2C perspective, is your service or product critical to this person's health, wellness, or future plans? Questions like these form the foundation for differentiating by the value of your offering to the consumer.

The marketing team might find it useful to utilize two additional concepts during the differentiation phase of the IDIC. One group of primary interest is the organization's **most valuable customers (MVCs)**. These individuals return the highest amount of profit to the organization and generally yield the highest margins. In addition, they are likely to connect with the organization via loyalty programs and respond to its promotional appeals. The second group of interest is a group of customers called the **most growable customers (MGCs)**. These customers have the highest potential to become MVCs through cross-selling, keeping them engaged for a longer period of time, or perhaps encouraging them to change their behavior so that the organization's margins increase (Peppers and Rogers 2011).

Customer data is an important tool for the marketing team. At the discretion of the team, it might be beneficial to provide investors with customer data and information, including the customer base's growth rate, depth, and breadth. After all, the customer base is a critical component of the success of any investor's investment (Over Time 2020). The marketing team, however, must not only be extremely careful with protecting its own customer data, but it must also ensure that its business partners are similarly careful with customer data. One area of concern is the increasing number of organizations that use payment apps like PayPal, Venmo, or Cash App for their transactions. It is estimated that by 2025, the annual total global value of transactions on these apps will be worth more than $9.4 trillion, up from $5.1 trillion in 2020. The vast majority of these transactions will take place in the Far East and China (61%), followed by North America (11%) and Europe (6%) (De Best 2022). What most people don't know is that these apps collect vast quantities of data on customer location, social media feeds, and payment histories, including the identity of the person or organization receiving the payment. Further, these apps are able to access the user's list of friends, risking the privacy of these individuals too. Although some of these apps provide an "opt out" feature that applies to some of the data collected, a surprising amount of data is impossible for any users to block (Morse 2021). Detailed, individualized customer data contains information that no one else knows about the customer that enables the organization to forge and strengthen its customer relationships. It must be protected at all costs.

Interact

The next step in managing customer relationships involves interacting with customers in a way that is respectful of their time and attention, but that gathers additional data on their needs and wants. There are few more infuriating experiences than having to explain an issue or problem multiple times to several different customer service representatives. By the time the organization progresses to the interaction stage of the customer relationship management process, each customer has already been identified and differentiated. Each previous encounter with the organization has already been carefully logged and the organization knows the value *of* the consumer and its value *to* the consumer. Now, in the **interact** step, each subsequent conversation or interaction with the customer should occur within the context of all previous interactions. In essence, the marketing team must treat each interaction as the next step in an ongoing dialogue with the customer (Peppers and Rogers 2011).

During the global Covid-19 pandemic, supply chain disruptions were common and consumers became frustrated at not being able to get the products they needed. An organization practicing efficient CRM during this time would have already identified who its customers were, then helped them navigate this frustrating time by, for example, offering seamless shopping, easy returns, or notification of incoming stock.

The interaction step is about so much more than simply asking customers a series of questions and keeping track of the answers. For example, one way to interact with customers is to include them in the process of co-creation of creative content. The organization can learn quite a bit about consumers during such a process (Bonchek and France 2017). Another creative way to interact with customers is to create a series of explainer videos that are placed on the company website or YouTube channel. These videos clearly and succinctly describe a customer problem and how the organization's product or service can solve that problem. Between 63 and 81% of all customers investigate products online before buying them. If the videos are professionally produced with a compelling message and visuals, the video can increase conversion rates by 80%. They also increase trust in the brand and are crucial throughout the purchase, use, and eventual disposal of the product. After purchase, 93% of consumers prefer explainer videos when seeking further product information or instructions (Balliett 2022). Crucially, analytics can help determine which customers watch the videos, as well as which ones stop and rewatch certain parts of the video, thus providing invaluable information about the customer's level of understanding and interest in the product.

Efforts at interaction can be facilitated with mobile apps and channels that are designed to facilitate CRM. There are several benefits to using mobile apps and channels. Perhaps most importantly, they allow for more personal, relevant, and timely interactions with customers. In addition, since they are active and monitored 24/7, these channels allow for a quick response from the organization. If, for example, consumers in one part of the world are experiencing a problem, we don't have to wait till the office headquarters opens to hear about it.

ENDURING INSIGHTS 12.3

"You can't just ask customers what they want and then try to give that to them. By the time you get it built, they'll want something new." – Steve Jobs, co-founder and former CEO of Apple, Inc.

An important benefit to interacting with and developing a learning relationship with customers is that the organization will often be able to identify trends in the marketplace and concurrent shifts in consumer perceptions that can result in innovative ideas for new products and services that can ideally meet the needs of consumers.

Customize

The last step in the IDIC model is **customize**. Here, the marketing team implements targeted solutions for its customers that are based on the value *of* the customer, as well as the value *to* the customer. These solutions could involve, for example, tailored features or add-ons, or even something as simple as invoicing changes to better coordinate billing with the customer's internal accounting processes. In the B2C space, it could include extra product features or customized fitting. The overall goal is one-to-one marketing, where each individual customer gets a specific, tailored solution to their problem. Music streaming service Spotify has completely altered the music industry landscape, in part, because of its ability to provide customized music suggestions to users, based on their previous selections. In 2021, so many customers around the world listened in, that Spotify paid $7 billion in royalties to artists and music rights holders, up 18.5% from the previous year. That year, the most frequently streamed artists were Bad Bunny, Taylor Swift, BTS, Drake, and Justin Bieber. Spotify accounts for almost 25% of the music industry's global revenue (Savage 2022) and much of this success can be attributed to its customized suggestions.

In order to provide its customers with a beer that perfectly fits their tastes, Denmark-based Carlsberg launched the Beer Fingerprinting Project. The goal is to utilize a variety of predictive analytics, taste profiles, and Microsoft AI technology to create customized beers to appeal to customers' individual tastes. To be sure, Carlsberg intends to leverage its size to produce some of the more popular blends at scale, but the Fingerprinting Project shortens the development process of a new beer by one third because it starts with what they already know consumers prefer. The blending and fermentation of the yeast, hops, and other flavors becomes a much more exacting science. In addition, the technology eliminates any errors or taste biases that can be introduced by human brewers (Ray 2018). When Carlsberg beer produces some of the more popular beer recipes at scale, it is engaging in **mass customization**, which occurs when the organization incorporates consumer insights to create products or services that meet the individual needs of consumers, but accomplishes this by taking advantage of mass production to lower per-unit costs. Mass customization does not mean that every single customer gets a completely different, unique product or service. Instead, each customer gets a product or service that will ideally address their needs (Peppers and Rogers 2011) (see Photo 12.7).

Photo 12.7 The future of beer: individually-brewed blends that appeal to individual tastes?

Source: Pixabay

An additional benefit to customization is that it acts as a barrier to entry to other organizations entering the market. Even if a competitor comes along and is able to also offer a customized product, the customer who has already forged a relationship with the first company will be unlikely to devote the time and effort to bring another company up to speed (Peppers, Rogers, and Dorf 1999). In the future, will customers expect to have 24/7 access to organizations, just in case they might want a customized solution? Trends seem to indicate that consumer expectations are shifting in that direction. Nike, for example, has sensors embedded in its workout clothing that provide real-time data on individual conditioning. Customized recommendations are then sent back to customers about how they can improve their workouts. In addition, based on the data, the company provides curated offerings for new products to consumers. This is where strong relationships amplify the effect of this 24/7 connection. When an organization ceases to be just a manufacturer of goods and becomes a partner in helping consumers find solutions, consumers are more willing to listen (Siggelkow and Terwiesch 2019).

The CRM Toolkit

There are four tools that facilitate the successful implementation of a CRM strategy: digital channels, social networks, anthropomorphized agents, and utilization of big data (see Figure 12.11). They can be deployed at each step in the IDIC model (Steinhoff and Palmatier 2021) (see Table 12.3).

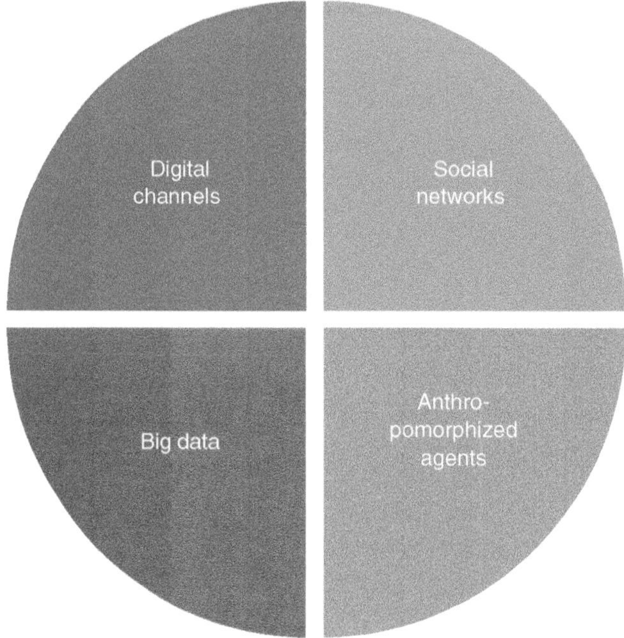

Figure 12.11 CRM communication tools

Source: Steinhoff and Palmatier (2021)

Table 12.3 The 4-part CRM toolkit

CRM Tool	Description
Digital channels	Digital channels enable digital touchpoints through mobile and e-commerce. Pre-existing time and place constraints are removed, consumers can shop at their own convenience, and the organization can respond immediately if needed. *Upsides*: lower cost to serve customers and higher profits because digital channels can promote scheduled purchases (e.g., once a month), enable cross-selling, and encourage utilization of service options. Mobile apps and digital channels also increase the number of touchpoints and allow for consumers to shop at their own convenience. *Downsides*: a chance that brick-and-mortar sales may be cannibalized. However, recent evidence indicates that online and brick-and-mortar options provide synergies for the consumer shopping and purchase experience. A consumer might, for example, do research and select the product online, but pick it up at a retail establishment. Indeed, when online sales increase, sales at brick-and-mortar establishments also increase (CNN 2020).

CRM Tool	Description
Social networks	Social networks encourage 2-way communication and simulate the social aspect of communication that happens in human relationships [see Table 12.1 for a list of relationship criteria]. *Upside*: customers might be more likely to strengthen their commitment to the relationship if they also have connections to a group of like-minded consumers (e.g., the HOGs of Harley-Davidson). *Downsides*: social networks can promote the spread of negative information and promote negative groupthink. In addition, it could make customers aware that some customers are treated better than others.
Anthropomorphized agents	Anthropomorphized agents are human-like online interfaces such as a cartoon characters, avatars, or holograms, with which consumers can interact. *Upsides*: the organization can encourage a human-like connection with customers and reduce the need for human agents, thus reducing cost. Naturalistic language and machine learning can provide relevant answers to customer inquiries. *Downside*: a genuine interaction between a customer and a live human can never be really replicated and can possibly lead to customer frustration.
Big data	Detailed customer data is the currency of successful relationships and necessary ingredient for organizational success. *Upsides*: used strategically, it can provide personalized communications and promotions to customers. This is especially beneficial when customers are able to control their privacy settings. With the help of GPS technology, these promotions can be location-specific and be deployed in real-time. *Downside*: if customers are providing their data to companies, they expect that it will be used judiciously and to their benefit. Organizations must implement strict privacy and data security measures, as well as provide transparency to customers on how their data will be utilized.

Source: Steinhoff and Palmatier (2021)

12.5 MEASURING THE STRENGTH OF RELATIONSHIPS

How happy are customers in their relationships with your organization? What is our ROI for our CRM efforts? If the marketing team is going to be tasked with the job of increasing the value of the organization's customer base, several measures are particularly useful in determining the extent to which that goal can be achieved (see Photo 12.8).

Net Promotor Score

The **net promotor score (NPS)** is a measure of the extent to which customers are not just satisfied with their experiences with the organization, but are willing to advocate for it. This score is assessed using a question like "on a scale of 1 to 10, how likely would you be to recommend our company to a friend?" Advocates are those who score 9 or 10, while detractors are those who score 6 and below. To get the NPS, simply subtract the percentage of customers who are detractors from the percentage of customers who are advocates. Perhaps the biggest benefit of the NPS is that it is very easy to assess. In 2021, NPS was used by two thirds of Fortune 1000 companies. Customer service operations and other customer-facing teams often link team bonuses to improvements in NPS (Reichheld, Darnell, and Burns 2021).

Unfortunately, NPS sometimes does not live up to its promise (Joyner 2012). It is often misused by managers who are more concerned about the score than they are about what the score represents. By linking the NPS to bonuses, there are strong incentives to manipulate scores. Managers may also promote scores to investors, potentially setting up unrealistic expectations (Reichheld, et al. 2021). In addition, there are vast cross-cultural differences in how well the NPS captures the strength of the customer–organization relationship. In Asian countries, for example, customers may be very pleased with the brand and customer experience, but would be very reluctant to recommend the company or brand, for fear of ruining their friendships. Thus, customers in these parts of the world are very unlikely to ever record a 9 or 10 on the scale (Seth, Scott, Svihel, and Murphy-Shigematsu 2016).

Photo 12.8 Are we in a mutually-beneficial relationship?

Source: Pixabay

Earned Growth Rate

An alternative to NPS is a concept called **earned growth rate**, which is the growth in revenue that can be attributed to returning customers and their referrals. The marketing team can identify these new customer referrals by asking how they found out about the company. Warby Parker, for example, sells prescription eyeglasses online and earns 90% of its new customers from referrals. When an organization focuses on earned growth rate, it is acknowledging the enormous expenses related to replacing a customer who has been lost through defection. Further, over time, *earned* customers are much more profitable than *bought* customers, who are obtained through advertising or sales promotions. Take the example of a bank that increases the number of consumer loans this year by 15% over last year. If 88% of those loans can be attributed to existing customers and their referrals, the earned growth rate would be: 0.88 × 0.15 = 0.132, or 13.2%. Earned growth rate provides a data-driven connection between a successful customer experience and repeat purchases, word-of-mouth, and other relevant KPIs (Reichheld, et al. 2021) (see Photo 12.9).

Photo 12.9 For Warby Parker, 90% of its new customers are earned

Source: Pixabay

Lifetime Value

Customer lifetime value (LTV) measures the total net present value of an individual customer over that customer's lifetime of interactions with the organization. Simply estimate how long an individual customer is likely to remain a customer of the organization (using a timeframe such as weeks, months, or days) and take the sum of all of the profit that the organization hopes to generate from that customer over that timeframe. It is very likely that customers will increase their commitment to the organization and generate more profit over time. LTV clearly demonstrates that long-term customers often provide significant value to the organization over time. LTV is often calculated on a per-customer basis, but can also be summed to create an overall metric for the entire customer base. Because of this, it can often be utilized as a KPI for the CCO or any customer relationship-related initiatives (see Figure 12.12).

$$LTV = \sum_{t=1}^{n} (\text{profit in time } t)$$

Where:

n = the amount of time the individual remains a customer of the organization

Figure 12.12 Customer LTV

Source: Peppers and Rogers (2011)

Return on Customer (ROC)

Return on customer (ROC) is based on the notion that, as with any asset, the organization should nurture and grow the value of the customer base over time; it is better to sacrifice short-term gains in order to achieve longer-term value. Consider the analogy of a farmer who can achieve a short-term increase in profit by delaying measures like leaving some fields in fallow or rotating crops. Smart farmers, however, would never do this because they know they need to invest in the land in order to keep the land rich and productive over time. It's the same thing with customers. Organizations need to invest in customers in order to keep them productive over time. Return on customer (ROC) incorporates the amount of profit a customer represents for the current period, as well as any changes to the customer's lifetime value over the period. ROC is analogous to ROI; it is a per-customer metric that represents the increase or decrease in the customer's value that is a result of the organization's investment in that customer (see Figure 12.13) (Peppers and Rogers 2006).

$$ROC = \frac{\text{Profit from customer in current period} + \text{Change in customer's value in period}}{\text{Customer's value at beginning of the period}}$$

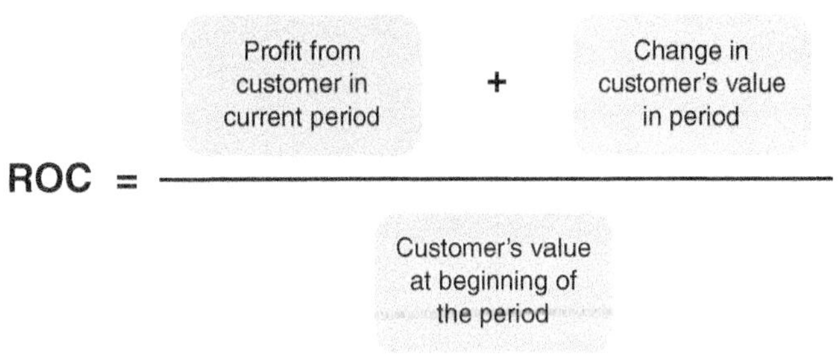

Figure 12.13 Return on customer

Source: Peppers and Rogers (2006)

ROC is not just a metric, however. It is also a philosophy by which an organization can nurture and grow its most important asset. Using this perspective, organizations will invest in their customers because they will see a return on those investments. Perhaps a financial services organization will hire professional investment advisors that it makes available to its clients or perhaps an automobile service station will invest in high-capacity Wifi for its customer waiting area. Regardless of the investment, if done correctly, an ROC perspective will allow the marketing decision-maker to confirm that the investment paid off. Trust is a critical component of an ROC perspective. Indeed, ROC and trust can be viewed from both sides of the customer value proposition. From the customer's perspective, the more customers trust the organization to behave in their interests, the more value those customers will get out of any exchange with the organization, both now and in the future. From the organization's perspective, the more it invests in the customer, the more value the customer is likely to return to the organization, both now and in the future (Peppers and Rogers 2006).

BLUNDERS & INSIGHTS 12.2

Boaty McBoatface Proves You Should Always Listen To Your Customers

BACKGROUND: Back in 2016, the UK's National Oceanography Center (NOC) was ready to launch a state-of-the-art Arctic research vessel that was designed to gather data about climate change and its impact on the world's oceans. Before its launch, the organization invited the public to suggest a name for the new ship. The clear winner was a surprise for everyone: *Boaty McBoatface*. Not only did the name have a clear majority of the votes, but it was trending on Twitter and garnering significant global media attention, putting additional pressure on the council to christen the ship with the cheeky name. Cooler heads prevailed, however, and the ship was named the *Sir David Attenborough*, in honor of the life-long environmentalist and broadcaster. The public was disappointed and several petitions were launched to encourage the council to use *Boaty McBoatface*. In the end, in a nod to the overwhelming number of citizens who voted for it, the ship retained its name, but a small bubble-shaped yellow research submarine was christened *Boaty McBoatface*. On its maiden voyage, *Boaty* dove to 4000 meters below the Antarctic and brought back important data about climate change in the area (Kennedy 2019).

DEBRIEF: If consumers are asked for their input and they expend some time and effort responding, organizations are well-advised to use that input. Otherwise, customers are likely to become very angry. The same is true with the case of *Boaty McBoatface*. By the name being retained, citizens throughout the UK can be assured that their voices are heard and appreciated. The NOC turned what could have been a blunder into a success. Today, *Boaty* plays a prominent role in the NOC's efforts to educate young people about climate change. The much-admired *Boaty* has been made into a cartoon character and is prominently featured on the organization's website, as well as its educational materials (see Photo 12.10).

Photo 12.10 *Boaty McBoatface* helps educate young people about climate change

Source: The National Oceanography Centre

12.6 SUMMARY

This chapter opened with a discussion of two organizations: CertainTeed and K-pop. The common thread that connects these vastly different organizations is that each one takes a very customer-centric approach to learning about customers, innovating, and forging relationships. The primary focus of this chapter is customer relationship management. To first provide a foundation to the discussion, the concepts of satisfaction and loyalty were introduced. As a part of this discussion, we recognized that a paradigm shift needs to occur in order to prioritize customers over products and services. This extends to the marketing team creating customer-centric objectives that focus on the strength and longevity of the relationship.

To start the CRM discussion, seven criteria were introduced that are essential for establishing and strengthening relationships. One of the criteria, trust, was explored in more depth with several examples, a formula to quantify trust, and a discussion of the controversial ad campaign that was launched by Doctors Without Borders. Next, the IDIC model was introduced to provide a step-by-step guide for enacting a CRM strategy, during which customer insights are turned into action. Finally, new metrics were introduced to help quantify the strength of customer relationships: the NPS, earned growth rate, LTV, and ROC. When the organization prioritizes customers and relationships, these metrics are essential in determining the extent to which the organization is achieving its objectives.

QUESTIONS FOR REVIEW & DISCUSSION

1. What is the difference between satisfaction and loyalty? Would a marketing decision-maker prefer to have high levels of purchase loyalty or attitudinal loyalty? Why? In what way are satisfaction and loyalty different from customer relationship management?
2. The 2010 BP Oil Spill killed 11 people and dumped about 4.9 million barrels of oil into the Gulf of Mexico before the leak was stopped. Using Table 12.1, which of the seven relationship criteria were violated by BP in its actions before, during, and after the spill? Discuss.
3. The chapter makes the point that marketing objectives change when the organization shifts to a customer-centric approach. In what way might they change? Be specific. Using a customer-centric approach, create two SMART objectives for forging stronger relationships with customers. Be creative!
4. To illustrate the importance of both pillars of trust to relationships, describe examples of situations in which a person or organization has (1) character but not competence, (2) competence but not character, and (3) both competence and character.
5. Imagine the following scenario: your two best friends are the co-owners of a successful flower shop and suddenly, the national environmental ministry declares that it is illegal to sell flowers! What would you say to your friends to convince them that they shouldn't worry? What would you suggest they do next?
6. During the differentiation phase of the IDIC, a mid-sized regional bakery differentiated its customers by two different criteria: value *of* the customer and value *to* the customer. After this differentiation decision takes place, how might the bakery behave differently toward those consumers who are: (1) high vs. low in value *of* the customer, and (2) high vs. low in value *to* the customer? Be creative!

12.7 REFERENCES

Aizenman, Nurith. 2020. Doctors Without Borders Responds to Charges of "Racism" From its Staff. *NPR*. 15 July. Accessed 19 April 2022. www.npr.org/sections/goatsandsoda/2020/07/15/864544382/doctors-without-borders-responds-to-charges-of-racism-from-its-staff

Balliett, Amy. 2022. Want to Deliver a Great Customer Experience? Make an Explainer Video for Your Website. *Inc*. 26 February. Accessed 17 April 2022. https://apple.news/AsntkhLZjSkGa_frclntF0A.

Bonchek, Mark and Cara France. 2017. What Creativity in Marketing Looks Like Today. *Harvard Business Review Digital Magazine*. 22 March. Accessed 3 April 2022. https://hbr.org/2017/03/what-creativity-in-marketing-looks-like-today.

Bruner, Raisa. 2020. How K-Pop Fans Actually Work as a Force for Political Activism in 2020. *Time*. 25 July. Accessed 14 April 2022. https://time.com/5866955/k-pop-political/.

Chaudhuri, Arjun and Morris B. Holbrook. 2001. The Chain of Effects from Brand Trust and Brand Affect to Brand Performance: The Role of Brand Loyalty. *Journal of Marketing, 65* (2), 81–93.

CNN Business. 2020. The "Retail Apocalypse, Explained." CNN. Accessed 23 December 2022. https://www.cnn.com/videos/business/2020/02/28/retail-apocalypse-explainer-orig.cnn-business

Chouinard, Yvon. 2016. *Let My People Go Surfing: The Education of a Reluctant Businessman*. 2nd edition. Penguin Books, New York.

Covey, M.R. and Rebecca R. Merrill. 2006. *The Speed of Trust: The One Thing That Changes Everything*. Free Press, New York.

Cruz, Lenika. 2019. I Wasn't a Fan of BTS. And Then I Was. *The Atlantic*. 18 July. Accessed 14 April 2022. www.theatlantic.com/entertainment/archive/2019/07/bts-paved-the-way-army-fandom/592543/.

Davies, Rob. 2021. Dieselgate: British Car Buyers' Claim Against VW Reaches High Court: 91,000 Seek Compensation After Finding Their Cars Emit More Air Pollutant Than the Company Said. *The Guardian*. 5 December. Accessed 30 April 2022. www.theguardian.com/business/2021/dec/05/dieselgate-british-car-buyers-claim-vw-reaches-high-court.

Dawar, Niraj. 2016. Use Big Data to Create Value for Customers, Not Just Target Them. *Harvard Business Review*. 16 August. Accessed 22 July 2021. https://hbr.org/2016/08/use-big-data-to-create-value-for-customers-not-just-target-them.

De Best, Raynor. 2022. Global Mobile Wallet Market Size in 2020 with Forecasts to 2025, by Region. *Statista*. 5 April. Accessed 28 September 2022. https://www.statista.com/statistics/1227576/mobile-wallet-transactions-worldwide/.

Green, Charles H. 2011. The Trust Equation: Generating Customer Trust, in *Managing Customer Relationships: A Strategic Framework*. 2nd edition. by Don Peppers and Martha Rogers. John Wiley & Sons, Inc., Hoboken, New Jersey, 82–9.

History. 2022. A History of 300 Years. Ono Pharmaceutical Co., Ltd. Accessed 22 April 2022. www.ono-pharma.com/company/history.

Hotten, Russell. 2015. Volkswagen: The Scandal Explained. *BBC News. Business Section*. 10 December. Accessed 30 April 2022. www.bbc.com/news/business-34324772.

Ipsos. 2021. *Ipsos Global Trustworthiness Monitor: Is Trust in Crisis?* A Report by Institut de Publique Sondage d'Opinion Secteur. Paris, France.

Joyner, April. 2012. Make Room for a New Face on Your Top Team: The Rise of the Chief Customer Officer. *Inc. Magazine*. April. 102–103.

Kennedy, Merrit. 2019. Boaty McBoatface, Internet Adored Sub, Makes Deep-Sea Discovery on Climate Change. *NPR*. 18 June. Accessed 21 April 2022. www.npr.org/2019/06/18/733759839/boaty-mcboatface-internet-adored-sub-makes-deep-sea-discovery-on-climate-change.

Kim, W. Chan and Renee Mauborgne. 2015. Red Ocean Traps: The Mental Models that Undermine Market-Creating Strategies. *Harvard Business Review, 93* (3), 68–73.

Kinkead, Gwen. 1999. In the Future, People Like Me Will Go to Jail. *Fortune. 00158259, 139* (10), 24 May. 90–5.

Klein, Ezra and Joe Posner. 2021. K-Pop. *Explained: A Netflix Original Documentary Series.* Vox Productions.

Light, Larry. 2020. Harley-Davidson: In a Post-Corona World, Keep Your Customers Close. *Forbes.* 26 May. Accessed 21 April 2022. www.forbes.com/sites/larrylight/2020/05/26/harley-davidson-in-a-post-corona-world-keep-your-customers-close/?sh=498368a7487d.

McCollough, Michael A. 2009. The Recovery Paradox: The Effect of Recovery Performance and Service Failure Severity on Post-Recovery Customer Satisfaction. *Academy of Marketing Studies Journal, 13* (1), 89–104.

McVeigh, Karen. 2020. MSF Ran 'White Saviour' TV Ad Despite Staff Warnings Over Racism. *The Guardian.* September 10. Accessed 19 April 2022. www.theguardian.com/global-development/2020/sep/10/msf-ran-white-saviour-tv-ad-despite-staff-warnings-over-racism

Morse, Jack. 2021. Payment Apps Collect and Share Your Data. Here's How to Lock Them Down. *Mashable.* 9 June. Accessed 28 September 2022. https://mashable.com/article/venmo-cash-app-paypal-data-privacy.

Oliver, Richard L. 1980. A Cognitive Model of the Antecedents and Consequences of Satisfaction Decisions. *Journal of Marketing Research, 17* (4), 460–69.

Oliver, Richard L. 1993. Cognitive, Affective, and Attribute Bases of the Satisfaction Response. *Journal of Consumer Research, 20* (3), 418–30.

Oliver, Richard L. 1997. *Satisfaction: A Behavioral Perspective on the Consumer.* The McGraw-Hill Companies, Inc., New York.

"Over Time, The Market Will Demand This Information." 2020. A Conversation with Vanguard Chairman Emeritus Jack Brennan. 2021. *Harvard Business Review, 98* (1), 56–7.

Peppers, Don and Martha Rogers. 2006. Return on Investment by Itself is Not Good Enough. *Journal of Direct, Data, and Digital Marketing Practice, 7* (4), 318–31.

Peppers, Don and Martha Rogers. 2011. *Managing Customer Relationships: A Strategic Framework.* 2nd edition, John Wiley & Sons, Inc., Hoboken, New Jersey.

Peppers, Don, Martha Rogers, and Bob Dorf. 1999. Is Your Company Ready for One-To-One Marketing? *Harvard Business Review, 77* (1), 151–60.

Phillips, Diane M. and Hans Baumgartner. 2002. The Role of Consumption Emotions in the Satisfaction Response. *Journal of Consumer Psychology, 12* (3), 243–52.

Porter, Michael E. and Mark R. Kramer. 2011. Shared Value: How to Reinvent Capitalism—and Unleash a Wave of Innovation. *Harvard Business Review.* January–February, 62–77.

Ray, Susanna. 2018. Can AI Help Brewers Predict How Varieties Will Taste? Carlsberg Says "Probably." *Microsoft Transform.* 16 July. Accessed 22 April 2022. https://news.microsoft.com/transform/can-ai-help-brewers-predict-how-new-beer-varieties-will-taste-carlsberg-says-probably/?utm_source=t.co&utm_medium=referral.

Reichheld, Fred, Darci Darnell, and Maureen Burns. 2021. Net Promoter 3.0: A Better System for Understanding the Real Value of Happy Customers. *Harvard Business Review, 99* (6), 80–89.

Rioux, Patricia. 2020. The Value of Investing in Loyal Customers. *Forbes.* 29 January. Accessed 22 April 2022. www.forbes.com/sites/forbesagencycouncil/2020/01/29/the-value-of-investing-in-loyal-customers/?sh=3000a7a821f6.

Salesforce Announces Record Fourth Quarter and Full Year Fiscal 2022 Results. 2022. *BusinessWire, A Berkshire Hathaway Company.* 1 March. Accessed 17 April 2022. www.

businesswire.com/news/home/20220301005835/en/Salesforce-Announces-Record-Fourth-Quarter-and-Full-Year-Fiscal-2022-Results.

Savage, Mark. 2022. Spotify Paid 130 Artists More Than $5M Last Year. *BBC*. Entertainment & Arts Section. 24 March. Accessed 22 April 2022. www.bbc.com/news/entertainment-arts-60864619.

Seth, Sanjay, Don Scott, Chad Svihel, and Stephen Murphy-Shigematsu. 2016. Solving the Mystery of Consistent Negative/Low Net Promotor Score (NPS) in Cross-Cultural Marketing Research. *Asia Marketing Journal, 17* (4), 43–61.

Siggelkow, Nicolaj and Christian Terwiesch. 2019. The Age of Continuous Connection: New Technologies Have Made 24/7 Customer Relationships Possible. It's Time to Change Your Business Model Accordingly. *Harvard Business Review, 97* (3), 64.

Steinhoff, Lena and Robert W. Palmatier. 2021. Commentary: Opportunities and Challenges of Technology in Relationship Marketing. *Australasian Marketing Journal, 29* (2), 111–117.

13 FACILITATING SUCCESSFUL STRATEGY EXECUTION

LEADERSHIP INSIGHTS 13

Photo 13.1 Ricardo Carrero

Source: courtesy, Ricardo Carrero

Meet Ricardo Carrero, Warranty Specialist

BMW

In 2005, Ricardo Carrero's first job as an account executive with advertising powerhouse J. Walter Thompson in Puerto Rico seemed like a dream. Most marketing graduates would indeed be envious – working with the world's top brands at one of the world's top ad agencies. Ricardo Carrero is not like most people. Just a few years later, Carrero left his position and entered a technical college to become an auto mechanic. Friends, family, and former professors were stunned. Why the switch? Carrero had always dreamed of becoming a top-level manager in the auto industry and knew that if he wanted that dream to happen, he needed to start at the bottom and work his way up. After all, "how can you trust a general who has never been a soldier?" he asked.

BMW has designed two programs to enhance the consumer's post-purchase experience. The first is the Genius Program and consists of a team of specialists who are experts in every feature of every new car. One week after purchase, the Genius team makes an appointment with the new owner to meet at the dealership, home, or work – wherever is most convenient. The logic behind this approach is simple: "You've already had a chance to check it out, try the features, drive it around. You probably have a lot of questions. The Genius goes through a checklist and answers all of your questions and points out features you may not have even known about. This solves a lot of issues customers have with a brand-new car," explained Carrero. "It's all about strengthening the goodwill between the owners and the manufacturer. BMW is a brand with a lot of heritage, pedigree, and history. Our job is to exceed expectations," he reflected.

BMW's other customer experience program is the Classic Program. Any owner that has a car more than 20 years old will visit a specialized dealership for all of their service needs. Because interest in classic and vintage cars has exploded recently, an increasing number of these specialized classic dealerships are popping up all over the world. Carrero pays particular attention to these classic car enthusiasts because they are "the most vociferous advocates for your brand. They may not directly provide you with sales because they bought their cars more than 20 years ago, but they sell the product for you. They talk it up. They're fanatical about the brand," said Carrero. One example of this deep connection happens every year on a twisty stretch of road in Tennessee called "the tail of the dragon." The course is a challenging and fun drive and most other car manufacturers host a week-long event there where enthusiasts are invited to drive up and down the road, hang out with one another, and take part in other activities. BMW's Classic Program is no exception. Recently, a British BMW owner had his car shipped from England so he could try out the course. Unfortunately, an engine part broke and it was impossible to get a replacement part locally. That's when the other enthusiasts went into action. People who didn't know him heard of his story, found a way to get him the part he needed, and fixed it for free so he could continue the trip. "We know that we have to keep these fans of the brand happy. If you abandon them, there will be hell to pay. BMW does not lose sight of this," reflected Carrero. With both of these programs, the organizational structure was established, key KPIs are routinely monitored, and course corrections are enabled.

It is no surprise that Carrero's advice to the next generation of students focuses on the importance of developing skills that make them indispensable: "there will be a day in your career when you need to stop working for your employer and make your employer work for you" (see Photo 13.2).

Photo 13.2 Owners of classic BMWs are the brand's most enthusiastic advocates

Source: Pixabay`

13.1 THE NOT-SO-SWEET STORY OF CHOCOLATE

Around the world, chocolate is viewed as a treat and an indulgence; a welcome gift and a nice addition to holiday celebrations. Consumption of chocolate is uneven around the world, with the average person consuming 0.9kg per year. The average European consumes 5kg of chocolate each year. Germans hold the record, with per capita annual consumption at 11kg, followed by the Swiss at 9.7kg. Overall, the value of the European chocolate market is estimated to be €46 billion. Consistent with its heavy consumption of chocolate, Germany is also the world's biggest exporter of chocolate, with 17% global market share, followed by Belgium (11%), and Italy (7.3%) (CBI 2021).

Many aspects of the global chocolate supply chain cast a distinctly less-than-sweet taste over the entire industry. Although many problems originate from place-related issues, each dimension of the marketing mix is impacted. It all starts on the west coast of Africa; tiny Côte d'Ivoire produces 45% of the global cocoa bean harvest (Barry Callebaut 2021). Tens of thousands of farmers living on small plots of land raise a few cocoa trees and harvest the cocoa pods by hand. Each pod contains about 40 beans, which must be cleaned, dried, and packed before they are sent to a variety of intermediaries and cooperatives. It takes 7 years for a cocoa tree to mature to the point where it is capable of producing pods. This is a long-term commitment for farmers who cannot easily switch to more lucrative crops. In addition, the low price that farmers get for the beans means that they have a strong incentive to illegally plant trees in nearby national parks. Although forbidden by law, the practice is often ignored by local governments. On average, a typical farmer

can expect to make the equivalent of €22 per month. Critically, farmers have very little power in the supply chain, with no bargaining power for higher prices for cocoa beans or for better working conditions. Indeed, the price of cocoa is set by the global commodities market in London and New York (Schillinger 2019). The biggest brands in the consumer chocolate market are Nestlé, Mondelez, Mars, Hershey, Lindt & Sprüngli, and Ferrero (CBI 2021). As news about the plight of cocoa farmers has slowly hit the public consciousness, some companies have responded. Unfortunately, the changes have been very slow (see Photo 13.3).

Photo 13.3 Toblerone is one of the many Mondelez brands of chocolate

Source: Pixabay

Headquartered in Zurich, Switzerland, Barry Callebaut is the world's largest cocoa and chocolate company. It has a strong presence in the consumer market as well as the business market, where it sells to restaurants, bakeries, and other CPG food companies. Because of its size, Barry Callebaut has the advantage of scale and has made especially impressive strides in addressing the problems in the global chocolate supply chain. From its 61 factories around the world, the company sells 2.1 million tonnes of chocolate to 143 countries each year. As a leader in the industry, it has implemented three critical changes, which have been replicated by others in the industry. First, Barry Callebaut implemented a cost-plus pricing model, which passes on increased costs of production to consumers. This effort helps establish a floor below which prices for farmers cannot fall. Second, the company incorporated a variety of traceability measures to track the movement of the product through the supply chain. Results are shared with internal and external stakeholders. This series of measures ensures transparency and allows for quick identification and course corrections for any problems involving worker treatment, worker health and safety, or environmental harm. Barry Callebaut's third change is its increased commitment to sustainability; its goal is to make sustainable chocolate the industry norm. To achieve this, it has instituted a wide variety of initiatives in four key areas: farmer economics, supply chain workers (especially women and children), CO_2 reduction, and sustainable sourcing of ingredients. Each one has its own set of indicators and benchmarks, facilitating the process of continuous monitoring, reporting, and, if needed, course corrections. By 2021, 100% of its gourmet brands were sustainably sourced. Further, sales were up more than 3.4% over pre-pandemic levels. The Americas had the biggest bounce, with a 9.4% increase over pre-pandemic levels, followed by the Asia Pacific region with a 9.0% increase (Barry Callebaut 2021).

The focus of this chapter is on facilitating the successful implementation of the marketing strategy. How does the marketing team ensure that it has achieved what it set out to do? How can it prepare for the next move? Because climate change is uncharted territory for many organizations, there are extra challenges to be considered. All of these issues, however, require coordinated, creative, and systemic solutions. This chapter is organized into three sections: organizing for strategic success, monitoring and reporting, and course corrections.

13.2 LEARNING OBJECTIVES

After studying this chapter, you will be able to do the following:

1 Sketch out the three-step process for facilitating successful strategy execution, being sure to provide a brief checklist of what occurs at each of the three steps.
2 Argue for why organizing for success is the most critical first step in facilitating the marketing strategy's successful execution.
3 Compare and contrast the Global Reporting Initiative (GRI), the Sustainable Development Goals (SDGs), and the Greenhouse Gas (GHG) protocol.
4 Explain the benefits of obtaining third-party certifications.
5 Describe the three-step process for initiating a course correction and the role that leadership plays in course corrections.

13.3 ORGANIZING FOR STRATEGIC SUCCESS

When preparing to implement the marketing strategy, there are three broad steps that must be taken. First, an effective organizational structure for strategy execution must be established. This includes ensuring the budget will be sufficient to meet the needs of the strategy, but it also includes establishing structures and frameworks that allow for flexibility and transparency. It is essential that these structures are in place so that, if needed, the marketing team will be able to quickly identify any deviations from the plan and will be able to quickly and efficiently adjust or adapt as the situation changes. The second broad step involves monitoring and reporting on the progress of the strategy. Here, the marketing team can select among several methods for monitoring and reporting, several of which are specifically related to sustainability objectives. The last step of the process of facilitating implementation involves course corrections. If indeed there are deviations from the plan, the marketing team needs to act swiftly, decisively, and holistically (see Figure 13.1).

Figure 13.1 The three steps for strategy implementation

How can the marketing team increase the likelihood of success for its carefully-designed strategic plans? An important first step is for the team to recognize that strategy is fluid; although it serves as a guide to the team's efforts, it must be flexible enough to shift, if conditions are warranted. Only about 63% of organizations are successful in the implementation of their strategies. The biggest reasons for failure are poor communication (26% of failures), inadequate or unavailable resources (20%), unclear accountability for strategy execution (11%), and organizational culture and silos that prevent effective execution (10%). Strategy-to-performance gaps can be significantly closed by following seven rules (Mankins and Steele 2005) (see Table 13.1).

Table 13.1 Seven rules to close strategy-to-performance gaps

Rule #1: keep it simple and make it concrete	Rather than using lofty, visionary language, use clear language to describe to lower levels of the organization what needs to be done and why. Help everyone see the connection between their performance and the strategy.
Rule #2: debate assumptions, not forecasts	Instead of overly optimistic estimates, ensure that short- and long-term projections are based on real data, market performance, and competitive strength/performance.
Rule #3: use a rigorous framework and speak a common language	Agree on a common set of assumptions about the state of the competitive environment and the target market. Develop a common framework and language for negotiations, implementation, and monitoring.
Rule #4: discuss resource deployments early	Early in the planning process, ensure that team members are aware of the level and timing of resource allocations to the different implementation teams.
Rule #5: clearly identify priorities	Prioritize key steps and benchmarks for initiatives, clearly identifying where value is created. Then, communicate these priorities to everyone.
Rule #6: continuously monitor performance	Enable real-time monitoring to provide up-to-the-moment feedback to assess actual performance against planned progress and resource deployment
Rule #7: reward and develop execution capabilities	Select and develop the team's skills in analytics, decision-making, critical thinking, etc. These talents will pay off in the long run with more effective planning and execution.

Source: Mankins and Steele (2005)

In the first step of facilitating strategy execution, the organization needs to establish an enabling organizational structure. Think of this preparation as analogous to "priming the pump." This expression comes from the fact that old-time water pumps needed to first be filled with water before they would work (Goodwin 2018). The idea is that, in order for the strategy to be successful, careful organizational steps must be taken and resources need to be invested ahead of time.

ENDURING INSIGHTS 13.1

"I was taught that the way of progress was neither swift nor easy." – Marie Curie, Polish scientist known for her research on radiation

Winner of two Nobel Prizes (physics in 1903 and chemistry in 1911), Curie conducted groundbreaking work on isolating radioactive isotopes, which led to her discovery of Polonium, named in honor of her native Poland. As the first female head of the Physics Department at the Sorbonne, Curie dedicated her life's work to exploring this new area of physics and finding therapeutic uses for radiation (Biographical 2022). In designing her experiments and implementing her research stream, Curie demonstrated the critical nature of careful organization.

Set an Appropriate Budget

How much money and other resources should be allocated to implement the marketing strategy? There are three methods for determining how much money the marketing team should allocate to achieving its objectives. Each one can be modified or adapted to the particular needs of the organization or context.

Percentage of Sales

The first method for determining the marketing budget is the **percentage of sales method**, which sets the budget for the next period based on the sales from the last period. For example, the marketing team will allocate 10% of the last period's sales for the next period's marketing budget. Although this method is very common, there are at least three fundamental problems with the percentage of sales method. First, because it is dependent on sales, this method has the potential to provide wildly different budgets for each period. Second, it has the potential to deprive the effort of resources precisely when it may need it most. If sales take a plunge in one period, the budget for the next period will experience a similar precipitous drop, thus setting up a downward spiral in subsequent periods. The third problem with this method of budget allocation is the simple fact that its logic is backwards. Marketing budgets influence sales, not the reverse.

Competitive Parity

The **competitive parity method** of budget allocation bases the organization's budget on what the competition is spending. Essentially, "what is our competitor's overall marketing spend? Let's match it." Although it is often difficult to determine exactly what the competition is spending on its marketing budget, it is not impossible to infer, based on observations of its activities. The biggest problem with this method of budget allocation is that the marketing team does not know the competition's objectives or the nature of its internal costs and constraints. Therefore, a budget that is ideally suited to the competition's needs may not be well suited at all for our organization's needs.

Objective and Task

The last broad method for allocating funds is the **objective and task method**. When the marketing team uses this method, it sets its objectives, determines how much money it will take to achieve those objectives, and then allocates the amount of money needed. The objective and task method is the most logical and strategic of the budget allocation methods because it provides the marketing team with exactly the amount of money needed to get the job done.

Prepare the Human Element

Entire books have been written about how to design and manage successful teams. From a strategic standpoint, however, it is essential that team members have the appropriate skills, especially analytic and digital skills. According to a 2020 report from the World Economic Forum, by 2025, 50% of all employees will need skill retraining in order to stay relevant and 40% of them will need such significant retraining that it will require up to 6 months of effort. Workers will likely acquire these new skills on the job (94%), via internal training (39%), online training platforms (16%), and external consultants (11%). During the global Covid-19 pandemic, individual workers sought out opportunities to improve their skills. Online government training programs around the world saw a ninefold increase in enrollments, and employers who offered their own training programs reported a fivefold increase in enrollments. The most important skills that need to be developed and polished are related to critical problem solving and systemic thinking (see Figure 13.2) (Whiting 2020).

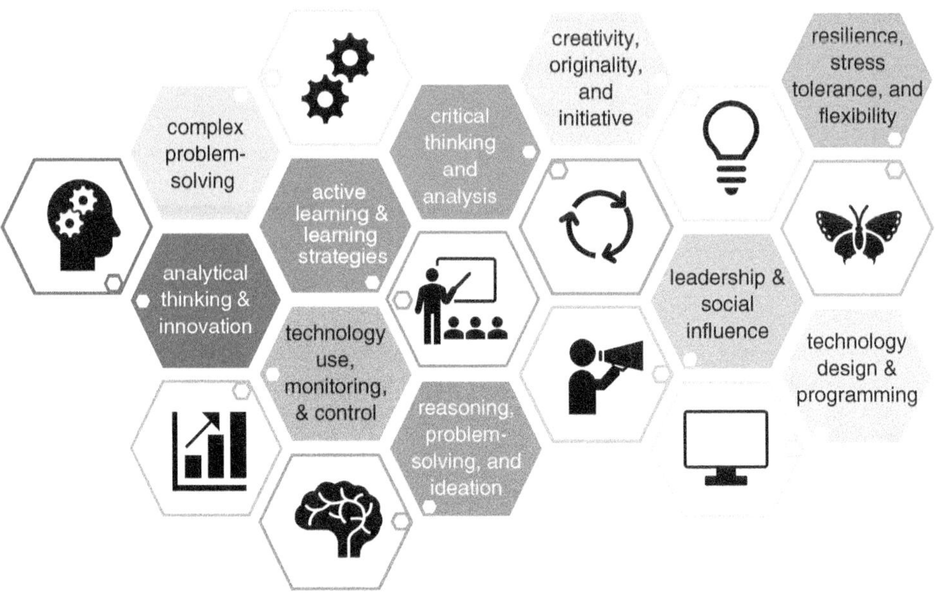

Figure 13.2 Team member skills required to help organizations succeed

Source: Whiting (2020)

Establish the Technological Infrastructure

In preparing to implement the strategy, the marketing manager must also ensure that the team has the necessary **technological infrastructure**, which includes all of the software and hardware components that will be needed to support the effort. This would include all of the necessary communications and networking systems, system architecture, development tools, application software, and bandwidth. Essentially, do we have the necessary digital assets to successfully deploy the strategy and carry it to completion?

Establish an Environmental, Social, and Governance (ESG) Framework

By establishing a framework that enables the marketing strategy to be carried out, the likelihood for success is enhanced. The **environmental, social, and governance (ESG) framework** promotes the simultaneous achievement of environmental, social, and governance goals. The ESG framework allows the marketing team to track performance across these three dimensions and immediately recognize any deviations from the plan. These three dimensions enable the organization to anticipate problems, increase its profitability, and increase its own reputation or that of its brand. In essence, ESG is a proxy for good management and sound financial performance (Weybrecht 2011):

- *Environmental* – does the organization act as a steward for the natural environment? Do its actions harm biodiversity, habitats, water or air quality, or the climate?
- *Social* – does the organization effectively manage its relationships with a variety of key stakeholders, such as employees, suppliers, customers, and business partners? Does it

promote human rights (women, LGBTQIA+, indigenous groups, and other groups that have been historically marginalized) and well-being?
- *Governance* – does the organization have effective processes and procedures related to executive pay, leadership, shareholder rights, and other internal controls?

Remember that marketing strategies are designed to support overall organizational objectives. Because of this, any framework that provides a greater level of predictability and control over the implementation of the strategy is beneficial. The ESG framework is an especially appropriate framework because it broadens the marketing team's perspective to consider the implications of its strategy – what might be the environmental, sociocultural, or governance implications? At the same time, the ESG framework also erects some limited constraints on how far the marketing team needs to consider implications. While it might be a fascinating exercise to consider all of the far-reaching and distant parties that might be impacted by the strategy, it is much more fruitful to consider the more direct and immediate impacts of the strategy. Bottom line, marketing decision-makers want to avoid the problem of **analysis paralysis**, where so much effort is spent creating a comprehensive and complete analysis, that it prevents any meaningful action from taking place. In connecting ESG to marketing strategy, the marketing team will need to consider questions that are more precisely related to consumers, the value proposition, and branding. As the marketing strategy fulfills its objectives within the ESG framework, it will indeed be supporting the organizational objectives (see Table 13.2).

Table 13.2 Marketing strategy considerations within an ESG framework

Environmental	Social	Governance
• Will the production, use, or disposal of the product harm the natural environment? Will our service harm the natural environment? • Are the product components and packaging made from recycled material? Are they recyclable? Was the product designed using a closed-loop system? • Is the product energy efficient? Does it encourage energy and resource efficiency? Does our service utilize energy efficient options? • Does our product or service promote a message of sustainability or encourage sustainable consumer behavior?	• Does our product or service help to elevate individuals who have traditionally been marginalized? • Does our product or service promote healthy behaviors and lifestyles? • Are individuals who work for our business partners treated fairly? Do they receive fair pay and working conditions? • Does our brand promote or enhance equity and social justice?	• Do senior-level decision-makers behave in a way that enhances, rather than detracts from, the brand's value? • Does the organization have a chief customer officer (CCO)? • Does the organization utilize customer relationship management (CRM) procedures? • Have we aligned with business partners that enhance our own brand's value? • Do employees have input on decision-making?

In 2022, the EU implemented sweeping new requirements on ESG reporting. Already a requirement for companies throughout the union, the new requirement applies to roughly 28,000 subsidiaries of companies that are headquartered outside the EU who must now measure and report on their environment, social, and governance performance. The push from EU lawmakers is designed to not only make the EU the global benchmark for such reporting, but to also encourage businesses to shift their operations and capital toward issues of social justice and environmental improvement (Schwartzkopff and Ainger 2022).

Clear Bottlenecks

Organizational bottlenecks are obstacles to effective decision-making and implementation. They are often long-standing issues or conflicts that need to be resolved and clarified. Importantly, they can result in stalled implementation, missed opportunities, and the loss of competitive ground. Recognizing and eliminating these bottlenecks can better position the team for success when it comes time for strategy execution. There are four bottlenecks of particular note (Rogers and Blenko 2006):

- *Global vs. local* – this bottleneck occurs because of difficulty in finding the ideal balance between the efficiencies of a global approach that allows for scaled operations and a local approach that more precisely addresses the needs of individual consumers. Until the organization can commit to a strategy, the result is a reduction in operational efficiency.
- *Center vs. business unit* – the difficulty here is caused by confusion about where decision-making authority should be located. Often, as an organization grows and becomes more complex, senior-level managers who are accustomed to making a wide variety of decisions find it difficult to delegate decision-making authority to others who are closer to the action.
- *Function vs. function* – this problem often arises when cross-functional teams are brought together for a particular purpose, but no one has clarified which members of the team have decision-making authority. Because not all decisions are of equal importance, clarification needs to be made on who provides input, who can overrule others, and who can approve or shut down the project.
- *Inside vs. outside partners* – this bottleneck appears when decisions need to be made between two different divisions of the organization or between partners at two different organizations.

The key to eliminating these bottlenecks is clarity in decision-making roles and responsibilities. First, decision-making needs to be done at the "appropriate" level of authority. Upper-level marketing managers should not be burdened with day-to-day decisions and mid-level individuals should not be given too much authority. Second, marketing managers must identify significant sources of value creation and then ensure that resources and decision-making authority are aligned with them (Rogers and Blenko 2006). In the end, by clarifying these issues, the marketing team will be more efficient and effective in its decisions about the strategy and its execution (see Figure 13.3).

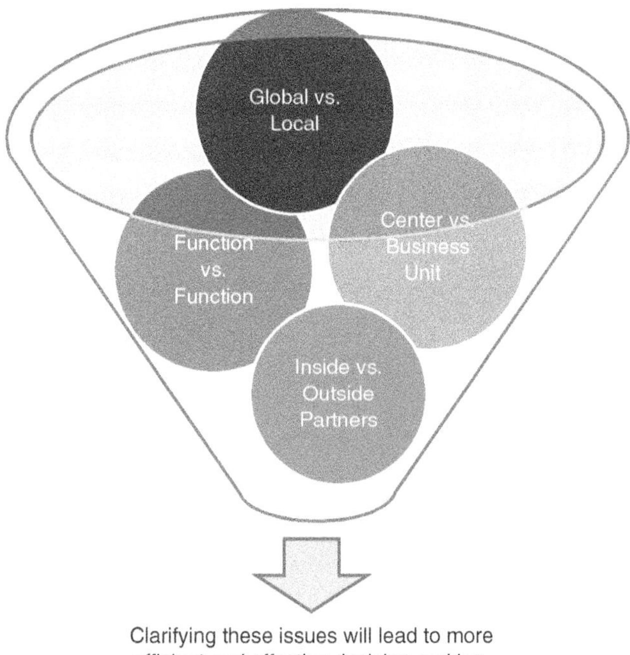

Figure 13.3 Bottlenecks to effective strategic decision-making

Source: Rogers and Blenko (2006)

Ensure Transparency

Today's consumers and business partners expect greater levels of transparency from organizations. They want to know how products are made, how and where the products' ingredients or component parts were sourced, and how the workers were treated. **Transparency** is the process and philosophy of being open, honest, and candid about the organization's operations. Mistakes happen. When an organization is transparent, it will admit responsibility for mistakes and describe its plans for fixing them. Is transparency worth it? Absolutely. Transparency leads to trust; consumers are much more likely to be loyal to an organization they can trust. These greater levels of trust also extend to employees and business partners, who demonstrate increased advocacy and commitment to the organization. How can the organization create a culture of transparency (Kappel 2019)?

1 *Solidify your values* – do not assume that everyone is clear about the organization's core mission and values; be very clear when creating them and then communicate them to stakeholders.
2 *Share information with your employees* – do not let rumors gain traction; be straight with team members and other employees about what's working and not working well.
3 *Don't mask your prices* – do not create complicated pricing structures and policies; be upfront about your pricing.

4 *Get to the point* – there is no need for flowery language; be clear and concise in your communications and reporting.
5 *Be candid about your experiences* – do not paint an overly-positive image of the company or the leadership team; be straightforward about mistakes that have been made.

After the organizational structure is established to facilitate successful strategy execution, the marketing team will next move to monitoring and reporting (see Figure 13.4).

Organizing for success checklist:

- ✓ Set an appropriate budget
- ✓ Prepare the human element
- ✓ Establish the technological infrastructure
- ✓ Establish an ESG framework
- ✓ Clear bottlenecks
- ✓ Ensure transparency

Figure 13.4 Organizing for success checklist

BLUNDERS & INSIGHTS 13.1

No, Our Beer Does not Cause the Coronavirus

BACKGROUND: In the summer of 2020, the global coronavirus pandemic was wreaking havoc on communities and economies around the world. This was not the best time for Mexican beer manufacturer Corona. Conspiracy theorists incorrectly suggested that the beer could cause the virus and the half-baked story started to gain some traction in chats and blogs. Although online searches for "beer virus" and "Corona beer virus" surged and memes abounded, the marketing team at Corona decided to not directly address the controversy. Instead, it continued with its planned launch of a new summer-themed seltzer product (Gandel 2020) (see Photo 13.4).

Photo 13.4 Corona beer sales significantly increased, despite online misinformation

Source: Pixabay

DEBRIEF: The marketing team believed that customers were smart and understood that "there's no linkage between the virus and our beer/business." By late summer and early fall of 2020, Corona sales had increased 13% and shares of Constellation Brands, the owner of Corona, were up 14% (Gandel 2020). The marketing team rightfully concluded that not every scandal, especially a manufactured scandal, deserves a response. In fact, sometimes a response can backfire on the organization and prolong the discussion, giving it more life.

13.4 MONITORING & REPORTING

As the marketing strategy is executed, the marketing team must measure and track progress to ensure that key benchmarks are being achieved using a series of KPIs, such as market share, sales, or market penetration. Organizations with a **culture of performance** regularly assess organizational-level KPIs such as market share, sales, etc. as well as team-level KPIs, such as the number of customer complaints or customer satisfaction scores. Throughout this textbook, many different marketing KPIs have been described. The organization's selection and prioritization of KPIs has critical implications for how well the strategy will be executed as well as how well the marketing team will perform. People adjust their behavior based on the metrics with which they are assessed (Ariely 2010). Take the example of a marketing manager whose annual performance review (and bonus) is evaluated on increasing sales. Not surprisingly, this person will make a variety of decisions designed to increase sales, such as lowering prices or increasing advertising and sales promotions. Importantly, this person will enact a variety of behaviors that are quite different from those of the person who is evaluated based on increasing customer lifetime value, who might work to increase the quality of the product and customer service experience. Marketing teams at more enlightened organizations know that to encourage long-term, sustainable performance, a broad set of KPIs must be utilized to encourage a wide variety of behaviors that, over the long term, will generate value. The following section will highlight a variety of KPIs that can be monitored and tracked over time.

Activate the Global Reporting Initiative (GRI)

The **Global Reporting Initiative (GRI)** formalizes ESG initiatives by applying standards for measuring each ESG dimension. The purpose of GRI is to provide a common set of standards against which organizations can assess their performance. Then, organizations can be compared against one another as well as tracked over time. The GRI framework establishes quantitative, universal standards that can be broadly applied, as well as sector-specific and topic standards. Depending on their own unique needs and priorities, organizations will select their own standards to adopt and monitor (see Figure 13.5).

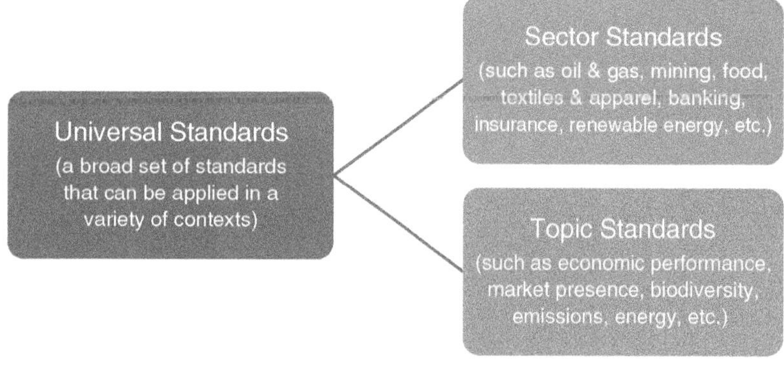

Figure 13.5 The GRI provides a variety of ESG reporting standards

According to a report by global consulting firm KPMG, 80% of the top global companies issue sustainability reports and about three-quarters of them use GRI standards or guidelines as a framework when they create them. A majority of global companies (56%) acknowledge that climate change represents a financial risk and 76% have put their own climate targets in place. As part of their reporting, a significant majority of global companies (72%) connect their efforts to the UN's SDGs. The most frequently addressed SDGs are economic growth (SDG8), climate change (SDG13), and responsible consumption (SDG12). The least frequently mentioned SDGs relate to ending hunger (SDG2), protecting life below water (SDG14), and protecting life on land (SDG15). Of the world's biggest economies, Japan and Germany lead the way with the largest proportion of organizations connecting their efforts to SDGs (see Figure 13.6). In examining the efforts of global industries, 80% of companies in the automotive industry connect their efforts to the SDGs, followed by 78% of companies in the oil and gas industry doing so (see Figure 13.7) (KPMG 2020).

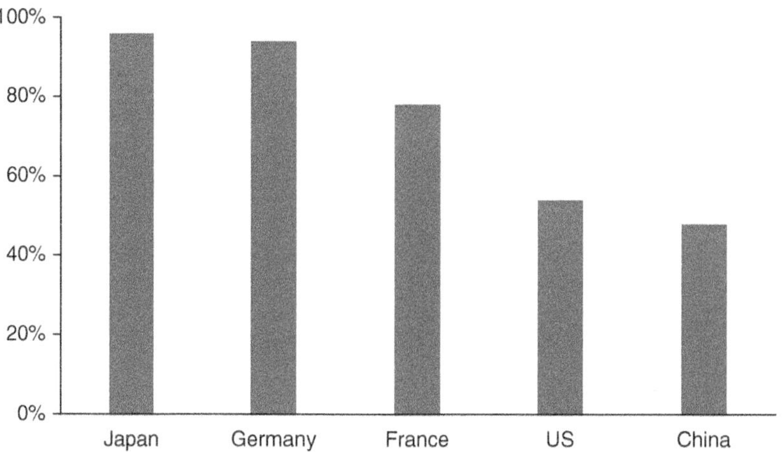

Figure 13.6 Countries where organizations are most active in connecting their efforts to SDGs

Source: adapted, in part, from KPMG (2020)

Track SDGs

We have learned throughout this book that traditional measures of performance like maximizing GDP and shareholder value are being replaced by more holistic perspectives that fully take into account the multiplicity of dimensions inherent in personal, economic, societal, and environmental well-being. The UN's goal is for the 17 SDGs to be fulfilled by 2030. There have been a variety of different tools that have been developed to help track progress toward fulfillment of these goals, but one of the more innovative tools is the SDG Dashboard, developed at Saint Joseph's University in Philadelphia, for the purpose of helping colleges and universities track their progress on five key dimensions:

- *teaching* – classroom and online instruction, as well as student advising and mentoring on sustainability topics
- *research* – academic inquiry and peer-reviewed publications on issues relating to sustainability

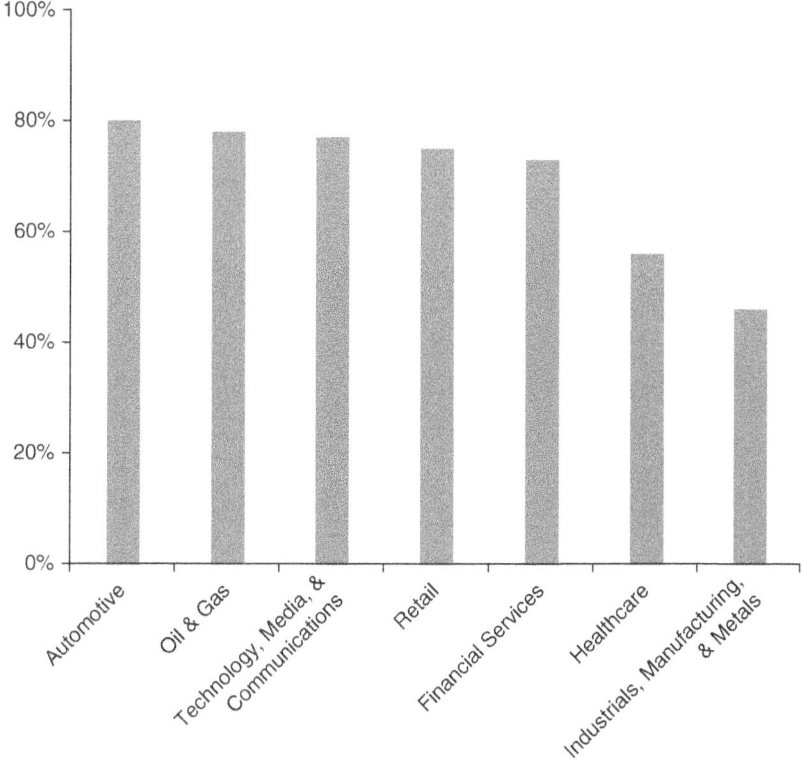

Figure 13.7 Industries that are most active in connecting their efforts to SDGs

Source: adapted, in part, from KPMG (2020)

- *dialogue* – guest speakers, expert testimony, media appearances, seminars, and discussions on sustainability-related topics
- *organizational practices* – the university's own sustainability practices
- *partnerships* – relationships with business partners, NGOs, governmental agencies, and other stakeholders that promote sustainability.

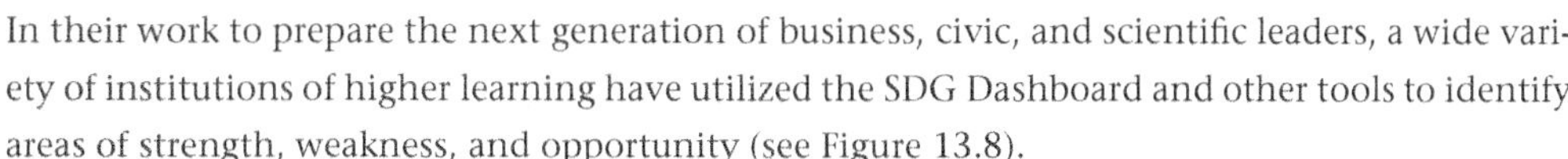

In their work to prepare the next generation of business, civic, and scientific leaders, a wide variety of institutions of higher learning have utilized the SDG Dashboard and other tools to identify areas of strength, weakness, and opportunity (see Figure 13.8).

Initiate a Greenhouse Gas (GHG) Protocol

Most of the discussions regarding organizational responses to climate change focus on reducing CO_2 emissions. However, there are other greenhouse gases that are also very damaging to the climate, including methane (CH_4) and nitrox oxide (N_2O). The **GHG protocol** is a system that categorizes all greenhouse gas emissions into different levels, or scopes, to help delineate direct and indirect sources of emissions. The scopes improve transparency and help focus climate policies and organizational goals. Importantly, the GHG protocol also ensures that two organizations do not double count GHG emissions (WRI & WBCSD 2004). The three levels/scopes follow:

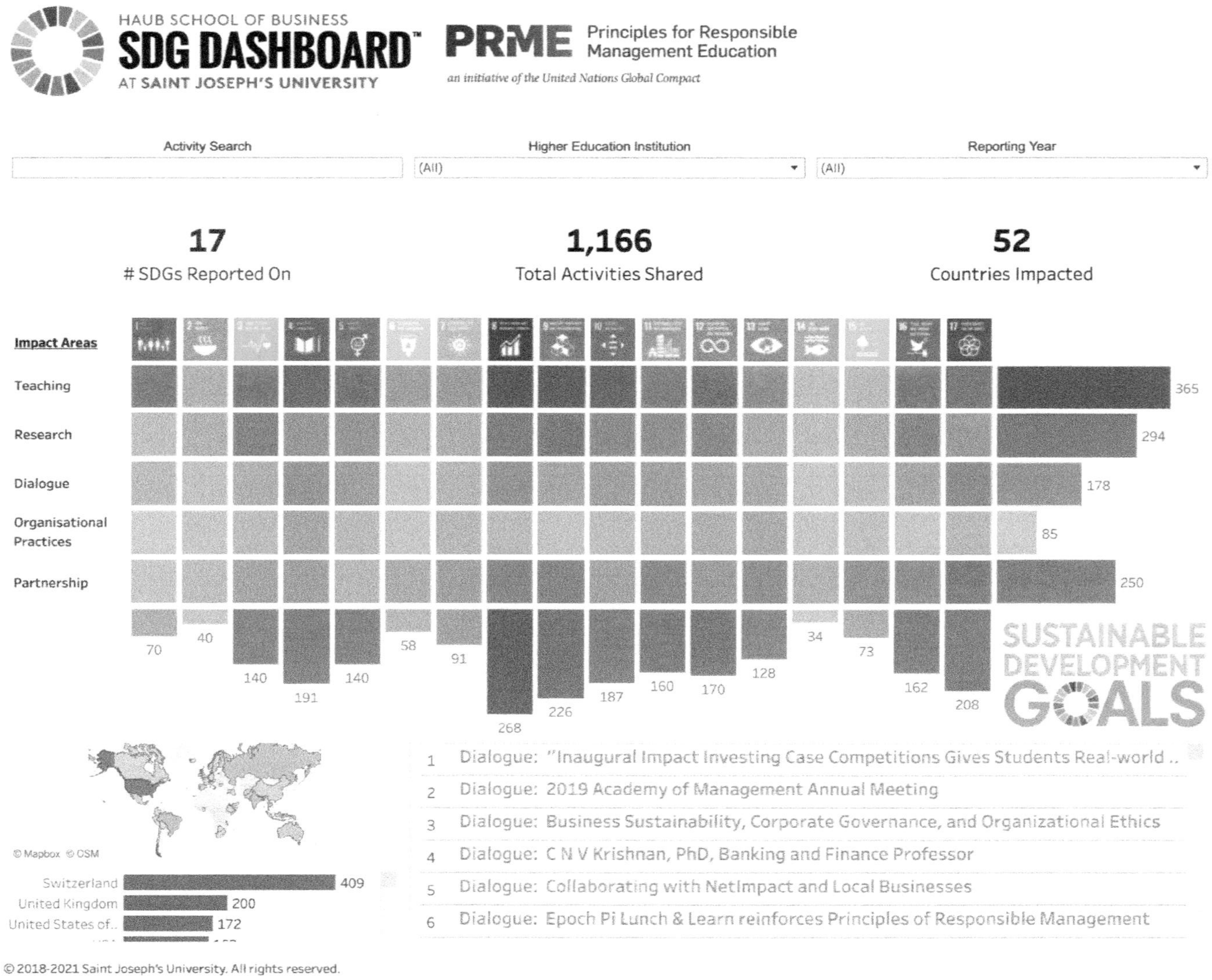

HAUB SCHOOL OF BUSINESS
SDG DASHBOARD™
AT SAINT JOSEPH'S UNIVERSITY

PRME Principles for Responsible Management Education
an initiative of the United Nations Global Compact

Activity Search | Higher Education Institution (All) | Reporting Year (All)

17 # SDGs Reported On

1,166 Total Activities Shared

52 Countries Impacted

Impact Areas
Teaching 365
Research 294
Dialogue 178
Organisational Practices 85
Partnership 250

SDG totals: 1: 70 | 2: 40 | 3: 140 | 4: 191 | 5: 140 | 6: 58 | 7: 91 | 8: 268 | 9: 226 | 10: 187 | 11: 160 | 12: 170 | 13: 128 | 14: 34 | 15: 73 | 16: 162 | 17: 208

SUSTAINABLE DEVELOPMENT GOALS

© Mapbox © OSM

Switzerland 409
United Kingdom 200
United States of.. 172

1 Dialogue: "Inaugural Impact Investing Case Competitions Gives Students Real-world ..
2 Dialogue: 2019 Academy of Management Annual Meeting
3 Dialogue: Business Sustainability, Corporate Governance, and Organizational Ethics
4 Dialogue: C N V Krishnan, PhD, Banking and Finance Professor
5 Dialogue: Collaborating with NetImpact and Local Businesses
6 Dialogue: Epoch Pi Lunch & Learn reinforces Principles of Responsible Management

Figure 13.8 Tools such as the SDG Dashboard can be used to track progress

Source: Saint Joseph's University

- *Scope 1 emissions* include those that are the direct result of the organization's operations and any organizations that are directly under the organization's control. They include, for example, emissions from manufacturing facilities, furnaces, boilers, and vehicles.
- *Scope 2 emissions* are those that are emitted as a result of energy that is purchased from utilities. The level of these emissions will vary, depending on how the energy is generated, the distance the energy needs to travel, and energy efficiency measures.
- *Scope 3 emissions* include all other indirect emissions that occur as a consequence of the organization's operations. Generally speaking, they are someone else's scope 1 emissions, as well as emissions related to the consumption of the organization's products and services.

Take the example of a small university. Scope 1 emissions would include all of the emissions that are a direct result of its operations, including HVAC systems that heat and cool the classroom buildings, offices, labs, student center, library, residence halls, and recreational facilities. It would also include emissions related to maintenance and lawncare, university-owned vehicles, and on-campus dining and housing facilities. Scope 2 emissions include the emissions related to the energy the university purchases to keep its operations running. The university needs electricity to power its computer mainframes, lights, projectors, computers, and other equipment on campus. If the university has solar panels installed on several buildings or energy-efficient lighting, for example, its electricity needs and Scope 2 emissions will be lowered. Finally, Scope 3 emissions include all other GHGs that are emitted as a result of the university's operations. Examples here are vast, but include the gas that students use in their vehicles to get to campus, emissions related to the production of books that are required by professors, and emissions related to the production of food that is consumed in on-campus dining facilities (see Photo 13.5).

Photo 13.5 Outdoor seating with solar panels

Source: iStock

From a strategic standpoint, why might it be advantageous to delineate these different scopes? There are at least four important reasons (WRI & WBCSD 2004):

- identify future climate-related risks and opportunities
- participate in voluntary and mandatory reporting programs
- publicly demonstrate the organization's commitment to climate action
- obtain external recognition for the organization's efforts from key stakeholders.

Scope 3 emissions often represent the largest proportion of an organization's emissions. When IKEA conducted a GHG protocol assessment, it found that 66% of its emissions were attributable to customers driving to their stores. This prompted IKEA to work with local governments around the world to expand public transportation options for customers wishing to visit their stores. When delivery company DHL Nordic Express conducted a GHG protocol assessment, its decision-makers were surprised to find that 98% of its emissions were Scope 3. After a closer look, it became clear that this was due to the fact that DHL outsources much of its delivery services to third-party operators. This realization prompted DHL to work with its third-party operators to use more fuel-efficient vehicles and reduce vehicle distances traveled (WRI & WBCSD 2004).

ENDURING INSIGHTS 13.2

> "You have to be fast on your feet and adaptive or else a strategy is useless." – Charles de Gaulle, former president of France

De Gaulle is best known for leading France during WWII and his fierce defense of France as a strong, sovereign global power. This quote reinforces the fact that strategy and its implementation are not static. Having a real-time assessment of the market and the competitive landscape will reveal whether and when course corrections need to be made.

Obtain Third-Party Certifications

Sometimes when the organization needs a greater level of expertise, it seeks out third-party certifications. There are at least three benefits to third-party certifications. First, because they are independent, their findings are viewed by stakeholders as more credible than an organization's own claims. Essentially, these certifications are viewed as an unbiased stamp of approval. Second, in a related vein, certifying agencies are not afraid of speaking "truth to power" when they provide their findings to the organization. Certifying organizations are under no pressure to worry about a client's internal company politics. Third, the organization that conducts the third-party certification often provides a fresh perspective to the organization. Because it likely has significant experience in conducting assessments for a variety of organizations, it might be able to suggest improvements in the organization's processes that were not previously considered. In the following section, a small sampling of certifications is briefly reviewed.

Fairtrade Certification

Fairtrade International was founded in 1998; **Fairtrade Certification** helps workers in developing countries leverage their collective power to get higher wages, better working conditions, and more environmentally-sustainable practices. Because workers receive higher wages, the money creates a cycle of increasing health and well-being in communities. For example, families can afford to connect to the electrical grid, improve their homes, and send their children to school. The Fairtrade organization conducts a rigorous certification process of a variety of products such as tea, coffee, chocolate, and bananas. Once certified, these products appear on store shelves with the Fairtrade Certification logo so consumers can distinguish them from other products (Who We Are 2022) (see Photo 13.6).

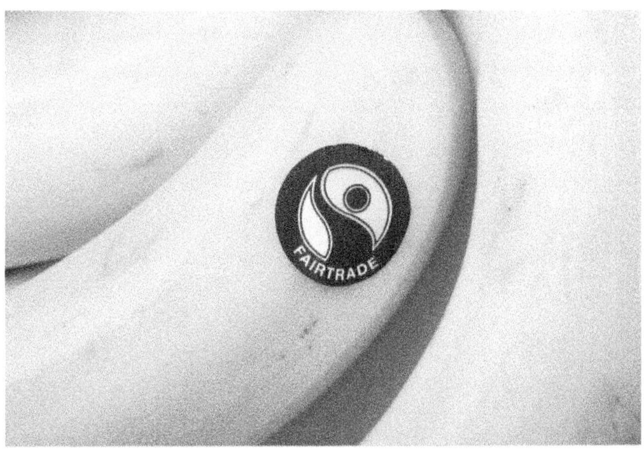

Photo 13.6 Fairtrade label on bananas

Source: Thinglass / Shutterstock.com

International Standards Organization (ISO) 14001 Certification

The **International Standards Organization (ISO)** was founded in 1947 in Geneva, Switzerland to provide sets of performance standards for organizations. Having a set of common standards helps organizations because they can make comparisons and identify areas for improvement. ISO provides a wide variety of standards. For example, ISO 9000 is a family of standards that relate to quality management, the ISO 22000 family deals with food safety, and the ISO 27000 family of standards concerns information security management. The 14000 family of standards helps organizations with a set of practical tools for managing their environmental responsibilities. The **ISO 14001 certification** is a signal to both internal and external stakeholders that the organization has exceptional structures and processes in place to assess and improve its environmental performance. In all, there are more than 300,000 certifications in 171 countries around the world that have obtained this certification. (ISO 14000 Family 2022). Firestone Building Products, headquartered in Brussels, produces roofing and building products for commercial and residential construction. With its ISO 14001 certification, Firestone gains extra credibility in helping its customers achieve their own sustainability goals (Environmental Expert 2021) (see Photo 13.7).

Photo 13.7 The ISO 14000 standards certify environmental management structures and systems

Source: Olivier Le Moal / Shutterstock

Photo 13.8

Source: courtesy, B Lab Company

B Corp™ Certification

B Corp™ Certification is an important signal to customers and business partners about the organization's sustainability values and practices. It is a holistic approach that builds on the three dimensions of the ESG framework: environmental, social, and governance. The certification examines five key dimensions of the organization's performance: the environment, customers, governance, workers, and the community. B Corp™ Certification is a signal to stakeholders that the organization has reached the highest levels of ethical and sustainable performance. Now, there are over 6000 companies, in 86 countries and 159 industries who have obtained certification (Make Business 2022) (see Photo 13.8).

LEED Certification

Office buildings, schools, recreation centers, laboratories, retail stores, and other buildings can achieve **LEED Certification**, which stands for Leadership in Energy and Environmental Design. Standards are built on ESG principles and include measurements for assessing building energy systems, waste management, transportation, CO_2 emissions, building materials, and other factors that influence the well-being of people who live, work, or study in these buildings. When buildings and other built environments are constructed using green building materials and standards, there are significant long-term monetary savings, because the building is more energy efficient. It might, for example, take advantage of natural light or allow for natural air flow. Green buildings are also much healthier for people who are not, for example, exposed to dangerous fumes or unhealthy air. Individuals have fewer sick days and are more productive when they are in these buildings. Green buildings also promote psychological well-being because they are designed and built with the human element in mind. Over 100,000 buildings worldwide have been LEED Certified (Mission and Vision 2022) (see Photo 13.8).

During the monitoring and reporting phase of marketing strategy execution, the marketing team will engage in a variety of efforts to monitor its progress. If the organization is already operating according to ESG principles, it has several frameworks that are especially useful during monitoring and reporting (see Figure 13.9). Regardless of which framework is used, it is critically important to consider how the data and the report will be used. Engaging in monitoring and reporting is very resource-intensive and far too many reports are not utilized to enact meaningful change and improvement. Bottom line, the report should be developed with purpose. Next, the marketing team needs to prepare for any necessary course corrections (see Photo 13.9).

Monitoring & reporting checklist:

- ✓ Activate the Global Reporting Initiative (GRI)
- ✓ Track SDGs
- ✓ Initiate a Greenhouse Gas (GHG) protocol
- ✓ Obtain third-party certifications

Figure 13.9 Monitoring & reporting checklist

13.5 COURSE CORRECTIONS

Strategy execution involves coordinating the efforts of the organization to implement the strategic plan. Rather than rigidly sticking to a prescribed strategic plan, the most effective teams identify and execute creative solutions to problems that arise during execution – they actively seize opportunities and avoid pitfalls during the course of execution. Research indicates that, despite advanced skills training and access to a variety of strategic planning tools, up to three-quarters of large organizations struggle with the execution and implementation of their strategic plans. Why? There are a variety of misconceptions related to strategy execution (see Table 13.3) (Sull, Homkes, and Sull 2015).

Table 13.3 The myths and realities of strategy execution

Myth	Reality
#1: Execution equals alignment – decision-makers believe that failures in strategy execution must be attributed to a breakdown in "chain of command" reporting, budgets, or processes that link strategy to action.	The reality is that these processes often work fairly well. Instead, a fundamental problem exists in the management team being unable to consistently rely on colleagues in other functions and units. In fact, only 9% of decision-makers report that they can rely on these colleagues "all of the time" and only half can rely on them "most of the time." Thus, top-down processes seem to work well, but horizontal processes that help coordinate communication and performance often need improvement.

(Continued)

Table 13.3 (Continued)

Myth	Reality
#2: Execution means sticking to the plan – because enormous resources have been devoted to its development, decision-makers often believe that any deviations from the marketing strategy should be met with extreme skepticism.	In reality, marketplace failures are more often attributable to the organization's lack of agility, not whether or not the plan is followed. Twenty-nine percent of organizations are too slow to leverage opportunities or mitigate emerging threats. To remedy this, decision-makers must be able to reallocate resources (human and monetary) as needed. In addition, if necessary, decision-makers must also be able to "cut their losses" and kill the plan.
#3: Communication equals understanding – decision-makers often believe that frequent communication will result in better comprehension of the strategic plan.	The reality is that fewer than one third of middle-level managers understand the strategy well enough to understand its priorities, how its parts are coordinated, or interconnections to other organizational initiatives. Better communication, not more frequent communication, leads to better understanding.
#4: A performance culture drives execution – decision-makers often believe that when strategies fail, it must be because the organization is not set up to promote high levels of performance.	In reality, organizations that have a culture that promotes performance still often fail in strategy execution. Why? Often, critical dimensions are left out of performance reviews. Specifically, in addition to meeting targets and goals, individuals need to be rewarded and promoted for their agility, teamwork, and ambition.
#5: Execution should be driven from the top – far too many decision-makers believe that the CEO should call the shots on any strategy-related decision.	The reality is that when the C-suite gets involved in the day-to-day execution of the strategy, performance might improve for a short period of time, but it will suffer in the long run because mid-level decision-makers will not develop their executional skills. Strategy should be guided from the top, but executed from the middle.

Source: Sull, et al. (2015)

Marketing strategy must be flexible enough to allow for changes and course corrections if needed. As an analogy, think about a chess game. If you ask a player to predict the next move, chances are you will not get a direct answer. That's because it depends on what happened with the previous move. If one player just captured the queen, the next move for the opponent would be much different than if a pawn was captured. The point is, the game of chess is a living, dynamic thing. The same is true with marketing strategy. It needs to provide a firm foundation and structure for the effort, but it must also be flexible enough to bend and change as the circumstances change. How should the marketing team handle problems when they do arise? The first step involves problem recognition and information gathering. Not every problem requires a response; some are simply more relevant to the organization and its ability to generate value. Leaders must first calculate the risks of getting involved and develop an understanding of the facts, causes, and conditions of the situation. The outcome of this step should be a set of insights into how to handle the situation. The second step involves creating a structure and gathering the resources to handle the problem. To be successful during this step, leaders must be flexible as the situation unfolds and possibly even escalates. They must be ready for any reversals or intrusions that may unravel the strategic plan. Importantly, leaders must cultivate support among those who are most directly impacted by the situation. Getting buy-in from these stakeholders will create a team of allies who will work together toward a solution. The third and final step to handling the problem is execution and requires a single-minded focus on the issue until it is resolved.

During this step in the process, rather than allow the media to control the conversation, it is necessary to frame the narrative with both internal and external audiences who will be seeking information. Hold press conferences and make experts available for comment. It is also necessary to create several contingent strategies that could be deployed if the situation changes. Again, flexibility is necessary in the event of sudden or unexpected developments. Finally, when it is time to implement the decision, move decisively (Goodwin 2018) (see Figure 13.10).

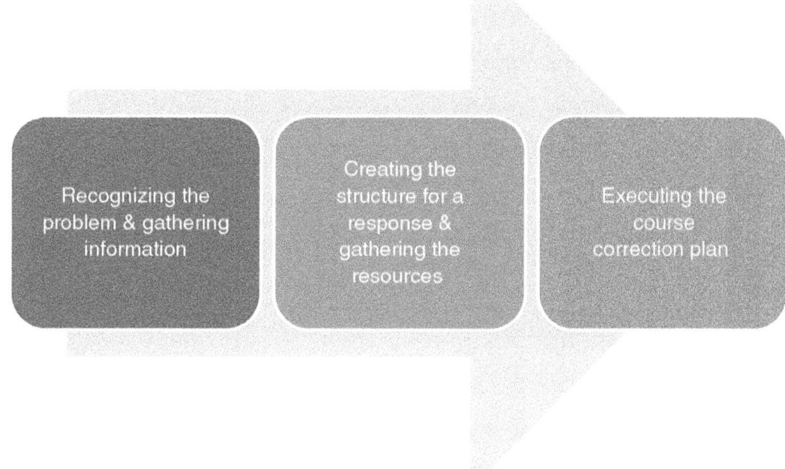

Figure 13.10 The three-step course correction process

Source: adapted, in part, from Goodwin (2018)

As an example of the three-step course correction process, consider the decision that was made by McDonald's CEO Chris Kempczinski in reaction to Russia's invasion of Ukraine in 2022. Within the first few days of the invasion at the end of February 2022, McDonald's ceased operations within Russia, as did many other Western businesses. At this time, the rest of the world was still hopeful that the conflict would be over quickly. For the next few weeks, the McDonald's team explored its options and gathered resources to help devise a response, given the long-standing friendly relationship the organization had forged with its host country. The first McDonald's restaurant in Russia opened in Moscow in 1990. The opening was incredibly symbolic; it was the end of the Cold War and the beginning of a new era of understanding and cooperation. As a symbol of Western culture, freedom, and democratic values, McDonald's was more sought-after and admired than many other brands in Russia. The CEO's decision was not an easy one. Providing food to millions of consumers and employing 62,000 people throughout the country was certainly a worthy pursuit, as was the company's presence as a continuing symbol of freedom. In addition, McDonald's invested billions of dollars in building restaurants and developing its supply chain in Russia. In the end, however, the unprovoked attack and the atrocities in Ukraine presented too much of a conflict with the company's values. On 17 May 2022, the CEO announced the company's bold and decisive plan. McDonald's would put all 850 of its restaurants in the country up for sale, with an expected write-off of approximately \$1.2–1.4 billion. "This was not an easy decision, nor will it be simple to execute given the size of our business and the current challenges of operating in Russia," Kempczinski said, "but the end state is clear" (Hirsch 2022) (see Photo 13.10).

Photo 13.9 Restaurant near Moscow.

Source: FotograFFF / Shutterstock.com

Lead the way

Because the CEO sets the vision and tone for the organization, this person's actions are integral to the successful implementation of the marketing strategy. Sometimes, the CEO needs to speak out about a sociocultural issue. When CEOs take a strong public stance on a topic that is in alignment with the sentiment and culture of the organization, employees strengthen their commitment to the organization and the CEO's ideology. Conversely, when CEOs take a public stance on a topic that runs counter to employee sentiment, employees pull back on their commitment to the organization and the CEO's ideology (Wowak, Busenbark, and Hambrick 2022).

BLUNDERS & INSIGHTS 13.2

Mouse Misstep

BACKGROUND: In 2022, Disney's upper-level management team stayed neutral on a new anti-LGBTQIA+ law that was about to take effect in Florida, only to find themselves embroiled in a mess of employee and customer outrage. When the CEO responded with an internal letter to employees and a statement to shareholders about the futility of making such public statements on current sociopolitical issues, employees and other stakeholders became even more angry. Later, Disney reversed course and issued strong and decisive statements in support of LGBTQIA+ rights. Unfortunately, many critics viewed Disney's belated overtures as too little and too late (Frankel 2022) (see Photo 13.10).

Photo 13.10 Disney engaged in a course correction in 2022

Source: Pixabay

DEBRIEF: It is no longer advisable for CEOs to stay neutral on some of the biggest issues facing humanity (Loock and Phillips 2020), and when an issue arises, the response must be quick and definitive (Frankel 2022). Luckily, decision-makers at Disney realized their error and quickly made a course correction.

Course corrections can be directed *from the top*; they can also be directed *at the top* of the organization. In the early 2000s, companies implemented quality improvements and CEO-level compensation was tied to the amount of improvement realized. More recently, a parallel situation has been underway with sustainability performance. CEOs and the other top-level executives are increasingly having their compensation tied to progress toward sustainability goals. Fortunately, because there is such a strong business case for sustainability initiatives, there are plenty of sustainability metrics from which to select. The KPIs selected should be tailored to the priorities of the organization, such as Coca-Cola's commitment to clean water around the world or the commitment that clothing retailers have toward improving worker conditions in factories in the developing world. CEO compensation plans should also have a "do not harm" clause, such that compensation is cut for any actions on the part of the CEO that cause harm to the environment. A select number of American, Canadian, and German firms have implemented CEO compensation plans that are linked to sustainability performance (Burchman and Sullivan 2017). Even tradition-bound oil companies are shifting their priorities because of increasing pressure, particularly from shareholders. Director-level pay at global oil giant Royal Dutch Shell used to be linked to gas production. By 2021, a significant portion of the compensation for top-level executives was tied to performance on a variety of sustainability-related KPIs (Staff 2021).

ENDURING INSIGHTS 13.3

"We all want progress, but if you're on the wrong road, progress means doing an about-turn and walking back to the right road; in that case, the man who turns back soonest is the most progressive." – C. S. Lewis, 20th century British author

Lewis is perhaps best known as the author of *The Chronicles of Narnia.* This quote illustrates the importance of careful monitoring so that, if necessary, fatal flaws in the marketing strategy, its execution, or other external factors can be immediately identified. If they occur, it is far better to "cut your losses" early and move on.

Create Holistic Solutions

The marketing strategist's job of creating and delivering value has become even more difficult in today's fast-paced world. Plans need to be created and implemented with speed and precision, a combination that is not always easy to achieve. However, when contemplating a course correction, the first critical step is to ensure that the team looks beyond just the hard facts of the data and understands the context of the situation. What motivates our consumers and our competitors? What role does our product or service play in their lives? What worries them most about the future? How committed are our team members to the strategy? Stark quantitative measures without the color of context are simply inadequate for providing a strong foundation for building an effective course correction (Rosenweig 2010).

In addition to having a deep understanding of the context, it is critical for marketing decision-makers to understand each of the interrelated components of the entire strategic landscape in order to identify a holistic course correction that takes into account the multitude of moving parts and competing influences. Sorting these complexities into three broad categories is an important first step in creating a better understanding of these many complexities (Collis 2021):

- *Industry attractiveness* – regardless of how the organization creates value, the industry will only be attractive over the long term if its structure allows for reasonable returns. By assessing the likely long-term attractiveness of several industries, the marketing team will know whether it should stay the course or shift its focus. It will also be able to predict any shifts in focus by other industry stakeholders.
- *Competitive positioning* – always a mainstay of marketing strategy, the team needs to identify its unique value proposition as well as where it is positioned in the market with respect to the competition. Importantly, how quickly and in what way are these positions shifting?
- *Competitive interaction* – to assess the long-term viability of the value proposition, the marketing team must predict how competitors may behave in a variety of scenarios.

Thus far, this discussion has been proceeding under the assumption that course corrections involve improving something that has gone wrong. Sometimes, however, during the course of strategy implementation, new markets or opportunities present themselves that could prove even more lucrative than the original strategy. When leveraging new opportunities in the competitive landscape, it is important to first identify the nature of the new value proposition that the organization hopes to deliver. Importantly, if a shift is made to deliver the value proposition in a new and improved manner, the marketing team must ensure that the organization's capabilities and competitive positioning will be enhanced over the long term (Collis 2021).

Utilize the Law

What happens if, during the execution phase, a competitor responds with an underhanded move, such as stealing your idea? Often, events happen which require the marketing team to seek assistance from regulatory agencies or the courts. Unfortunately, once a problem reaches this point, the eventual solution takes a long time and is not assured. The theft of intellectual property by some Chinese companies has long been the source of frustration for innovative organizations throughout the world. China remains the worst offender in producing counterfeit and pirated products, accounting for more than 83% of the items seized by global authorities in 2020. It is difficult for organizations to hold these individuals accountable for the thefts, but it is sometimes possible for governments to impose punitive tariffs or launch investigations with global or regional trading blocs (Swanson 2022).

As the climate crisis accelerates and action stalls, it is not surprising that individuals and groups are becoming frustrated at the lack of meaningful progress. One of the more innovative moves from a legal standpoint has been the filing of multiple lawsuits by young people, claiming that their futures will be fundamentally altered for the worse because of climate change. One non-profit group called Our Children's Trust launched a lawsuit called Juliana v. the United States. The lawsuit was filed on behalf of a group of 21 American children who sued the US government for not taking more meaningful action on slowing down CO_2 emissions and climate change. The plaintiffs claimed that children and future generations have a fundamental right to a clean and livable environment, and that it is the duty of the government to protect that right. Critically, they claimed that the US government has violated that duty by enabling climate change to happen. The efforts of Our Children's Trust have gained international attention and have prompted a series of similar lawsuits worldwide (Fayeulle 2022).

The topic of **climate litigation** has become an increasingly hot topic in recent years. It represents efforts to hold governments and organizations legally responsible for their contributions to climate change. These efforts also assert that governments and organizations have insufficiently prepared for the inevitable effects of climate change. The number of lawsuits filed around the world has increased dramatically in the past few years, driven by definitive proof of climate change, as well as the youth climate movement which has injected fresh momentum into the area. In addition, advancements in scientific reporting and other tools like the GHG protocol have enabled plaintiffs to more precisely pinpoint the sources of emissions. Between 2015 and 2021, more than 1000 lawsuits were filed around the world. Recent wins in the Netherlands, Germany, and Ireland suggest that the courts agree with the core argument that governments and organizations have an obligation to provide a livable world to current and future generations (Schiermeier 2021) (see Figure 13.11).

Course correction checklist:

- ✓ Lead the way
- ✓ Create holistic solutions
- ✓ Utilize the law

Figure 13.11 Course correction checklist

Marketing strategy is not so much the initial grand design, as it is the interrelated network of decisions that are made and deployed along the way. Course corrections are themselves strategic because they involve cross-functional effort, require systemic coordination (Collis 2021), consider competitive implications, and are forward thinking.

13.6 SUMMARY

This chapter was about the execution of the marketing strategy, which starts with the recognition that the strategy is a fluid and dynamic entity that provides structure and direction to the initiative, but is also flexible and dynamic enough to respond to shifts in the market or competitive landscape. The first step in facilitating the successful execution of the marketing strategy is to organize for success. Here, the goal is to ensure that the organizational structure allows for a successful outcome. Organizing starts with setting an appropriate budget. Then, team members need to have up-to-date skills, especially in critical problem solving and systemic thinking. Implementing a sophisticated technological infrastructure is also critical to facilitate all of our digital efforts. Establishing an ESG framework will allow the organization to ensure that, as the strategy execution proceeds, a holistic set of environmental, social, and governance issues will be considered. Setting up an ESG framework is an especially important early step because during the next step of the process, several methods for monitoring are built on such a framework. Next, bottlenecks to effective execution need to be clarified and cleared. In order to do this, the team must ensure that decision-making occurs at the appropriate level of authority and that resources are aligned with centers of value creation. The last item in setting up the organization is ensuring transparency, which is essential for creating and building trust with consumers and other stakeholders.

The second step in facilitating successful execution involves careful monitoring of KPIs. Tools such as the GRI, various SDG assessment tools, the GHG protocol, and even third-party certifications can be employed here. It is interesting to note that several monitoring tools are built on an ESG framework. Finally, the last step is to engage in course corrections. Here, if the marketing team detects any deviation from the strategy, it can address any deficiencies as well as leverage any opportunities for even greater success. When engaging in a course correction, it is often necessary for the CEO to lead the way as the spokesperson and figurehead of the organization. A holistic solution must be created which accounts for a wide variety of influences and, if needed, regulatory or legal solutions must be utilized.

QUESTIONS FOR REVIEW & DISCUSSION

1. Imagine that you are on the marketing team for a small organization that is about to launch a new wearable fitness device. Some members of your team want to immediately launch the product and start tracking important KPIs. Explain to them why it is so important to first ensure that you are organized for success.
2. Why is it likely that an organization will find that its Scope 3 emissions are significantly higher than its Scope 1 or Scope 2 emissions? Since the organization has such little control over them, what is the purpose of assessing Scope 3 emissions?
3. In what ways is the Global Reporting Initiative (GRI) different from and in what ways is it similar to the Greenhouse Gas (GHG) protocol? What is the purpose of each?
4. Congratulations! You just got a job as the Director of Marketing for The Armani Group, a corporation that runs some of the most exclusive restaurants in London. You've been reviewing some customer research reports over the last few days and you've found that there seems to be significant interest in sustainability. Create an argument for the CEO for why it makes sense to look for third-party certifications on some of the products/ingredients you buy and serve at the restaurant.
5. Examine Figure 13.8 in detail. First, in looking at the 17 SDGs, where might there be some opportunities for colleges and universities to do more work? What, specifically, could your college or university do to address these gaps? Second, in looking at the five dimensions, where are there opportunities? Again, what specifically could your college or university do to address these gaps? Be creative.
6. Course corrections should be carefully considered and planned. Refer to the case of the chocolate industry at the beginning of this chapter. Using Figure 13.10, describe a three-step process for initiating a course correction in this situation. In what way does leadership play a role?

13.7 REFERENCES

Ariely, Dan. 2010. You Are What You Measure. *Harvard Business Review, 88* (6), 38.

Barry Callebaut. 2021. *Roadshow Presentation: 9-Month Key Sales Figures 2020/21*. Barry Callebaut, LLC. Accessed 23 March 2022. chrome-extension://efaidnbmnnnibpcajpcglclefindmkaj/https://www.barry-callebaut.com/sites/default/files/2021-07/Barry%20Callebaut%209-Month%20Key%20Sales%20Figures%20Roadshow%20Presentation.pdf.

Biographical. 2022. Marie Curie. The Nobel Prize. 17 May 2022. www.nobelprize.org/prizes/physics/1903/marie-curie/biographical/.

Burchman, Seymour and Barry Sullivan. 2017. It's Time to Tie Executive Compensation to Sustainability. *Harvard Business Review*. Harvard Business School Publishing. 17 August. 2–5.

CBI. 2021. *What is the Demand for Cocoa on the European Market?* Centre for the Promotion of Imports from Developing Countries (CBI). A Report from the Ministry of Foreign Affairs, the Netherlands. 25 November. Accessed 23 March. www.cbi.eu/market-information/cocoa/trade-statistics#:~:text=The%20world's%20average%20chocolate%20consumption,of%2011%20kilogrammes%20per%20year.

Collis, David J. 2021. Why Do So Many Strategies Fail? Leaders Focus on the Parts, Rather than the Whole. *Harvard Business Review, 99* (4), 82–93.

Environmental Expert. 2021. ISO 14001 Certification Companies. *XPRT Media*. Accessed 22 June 2022. www.environmental-expert.com/companies/keyword-iso-14001-certification-5774.

Fayeulle, Eric. 2022. Youth-led Climate Change Lawsuits are Increasing Across the Country. *ABC News*. 22 April. Accessed 20 May 2022. https://abcnews.go.com/US/youth-led-climate-change-lawsuits-increasing-country/story?id=84172785.

Frankel, Todd C. 2022. How Disney Fell Flat in Fight Over LGBTQ Talk in Florida's Schools. *The Washington Post*. 1 April. Accessed 19 April 2022. www.washingtonpost.com/business/2022/04/01/disney-dont-say-gay-bill/.

Gandel, Stephen. 2020. No, Corona's Beer Did Not Suffer from the Coronavirus. *CBS News. Money Watch*. 25 December. Accessed 23 May 2022. www.cbsnews.com/news/no-coronas-beer-sales-did-not-suffer-from-the-coronavirus/.

Goodwin, Doris Kearns. 2018. *Leadership: In Turbulent Times*. Simon & Schuster. New York.

Hirsch, Lauren. 2022. After 32-Year Run, McDonald's to Take Arches from Russia. *New York Times*, 17 May 2022, p. B6(L).

ISO 14000 Family. 2022. ISO 14000 Family: Environmental Management. The International Standards Organization. Accessed 23 May 2022. www.iso.org/iso-14001-environmental-management.html.

Kappel, Mike. 2019. Transparency in Business: 5 Ways to Build Trust. *Forbes*. 3 April. Accessed 23 May 2022. www.forbes.com/sites/mikekappel/2019/04/03/transparency-in-business-5-ways-to-build-trust/?sh=4f5a5ffa6149.

KPMG. 2020. *The Time Has Come: The KPMG Survey of Sustainability Reporting 2020. KPMG IMPACT.* December 2020. KPMG International Limited.

Loock, Moritz and Diane M. Phillips. 2020. A Firm's Financial Reputation vs. Sustainability Reputation: Do Consumers Really Care? *Sustainability, 12* (24), 1–17.

Mankins, Michael C. and Richard Steele. 2005. Turning Great Strategy into Great Performance. *Harvard Business Review, 83* (7). 65–72.

Make Business a Force for Good. 2022. B Corporation. Accessed 23 May 2022. www.bcorporation.net/en-us/.

Mission and Vision. 2022. US Green Building Council. Accessed 23 May 2022. www.usgbc.org/about/mission-vision.

Rogers, Paul and Marcia Blenko. 2006. Who Has the D? How Clear Decision Roles Enhance Organizational Performance. *Harvard Business Review, 84* (1), 52–61.

Rosenzweig, Phil. 2010. Robert S. McNamara and the Evolution of Modern Management. *Harvard Business Review, 88* (12), 88–93.

Schiermeier, Quirin. 2021. Climate Science is Supporting Lawsuits that could Help Save the World. *Nature, 597* (September), 169–71.

Schillinger, Ted. 2019. *Bitter Chocolate*. The Rotten Series, Netflix. Season 2. Zero Point Zero Productions.

Schwartzkopff, Frances and John Ainger. 2022. Europe Moves Closer to Enforcing ESG Rules on Foreign Firms. *Bloomberg*. Markets Section. 22 March. Accessed 8 May 2022. www.bloomberg.com/news/articles/2022-03-22/europe-moves-closer-to-enforcing-its-esg-rules-on-foreign-firms.

Staff. 2021. Shell to Link Executive Pay More Closely to Group's Climate Performance. *Reuters*. Commodities News Section. 29 March. Accessed 23 May 2022. www.reuters.com/article/us-climate-change-shell-pay/shell-to-link-executive-pay-more-closely-to-groups-climate-performance-idUSKBN2BL12J.

Sull, Donald, Rebecca Homkes, and Charles Sull. 2015. Why Strategy Execution Unravels – And What to Do About It. *Harvard Business Review, 93* (3), 58–66.

Swanson, Ana. 2022. China Continues to Fall Short of Promises to Protect Intellectual Property, U.S. Says. *The New York Times*. 27 April. Accessed 23 May 2022. www.nytimes.com/2022/04/27/business/economy/china-trade-intellectual-property.html.

Weybrecht, Giselle. 2011. *The Sustainable MBA: The Manager's Guide to Green Business*. John Wiley & Sons, Ltd., Chichester, UK,

Whiting, Kate. 2020. These Are the Top Job Skills of Tomorrow – And How Long it Takes to Learn Them. *The World Economic Forum*. 21 October. Accessed 17 May 2022. www.weforum.org/agenda/2020/10/top-10-work-skills-of-tomorrow-how-long-it-takes-to-learn-them/.

Who We Are. 2022. Who We Are. Fair Trade Certified. Accessed 23 May 2022. www.fairtradecertified.org/about-us.

Wowak, Adam J., John R. Busenbark, and Donald C. Hambrick. 2022. How Do Employees React When Their CEO Speaks Out? Intra- and Extra-Firm Implications of CEO Sociopolitical Activism. *Administrative Science Quarterly*, February, 1–41.

WRI & WBCSD. 2004. *The Greenhouse Gas Protocol: A Corporate Accounting and Reporting Standard, Revised Edition*. World Resources Institute and the World Business Council for Sustainable Development. ISBN: 1-56973-568-9.

Appendix 1
OUTLINE OF MARKETING PLAN

1 Executive Summary
2 Situation Analysis
   a Introduction. A description of the purpose and scope of the plan.
   b SWOT analysis.
3 Target market analysis
4 Marketing Objectives. The set of objectives that the marketing team hopes to achieve with its target market. Objectives must use the SMART format.
5 Marketing Strategy. For each objective, a separate and distinct marketing strategy must be created.
   a Product Strategy
      1 Description of the organization's offering and its value proposition.
      2 Selection of product objectives, strategy, and tactics.
   b Pricing Strategy
      1 Description of cost structure, elasticity of demand, competitive pricing, and consumer perceptions of pricing.
      2 Selection of pricing objectives, strategy, and tactics.
   c Place Strategy
      1 Description of how the value proposition will be physically delivered to customers.
      2 Selection of the place objectives, strategy, and tactics.
   d Promotional Strategy
      1 Description of the message that will be communicated to the target audience.
      2 Selection of the promotional objectives, strategy, and tactics.
6 Facilitating successful strategy execution
   a How will we organize for success?
   b How will the effort be monitored and results reported?
   c How will course corrections be accomplished?
7 Conclusion
8 References
9 Appendices

Appendix 2 ESSENTIALS OF MARKETING ANALYTICS

Contribution Margin

This metric is the amount of money that is made after variable costs are subtracted from total sales. Contribution margin is generally calculated in sales receipts (euros, dollars, etc.). Managers can also calculate contribution margin on a per unit basis or as a ratio. The contribution margin indicates how much profit is being made from the sale of each product, which can then help *contribute* to the company's other costs.

Contribution Margin = total sales revenue – total variable costs

EXAMPLE: A small manufacturing firm sells its product for €10 per unit and it costs €4 to produce each of these units. If the firm sells 20,000 units, its contribution margin would be:

Contribution Margin = €200,000 – €80,000

Contribution Margin = €120,000

Contribution Margin per unit = €10 – €4

Contribution Margin per unit = €6

Contribution Margin ratio = €6 / €10

Contribution Margin ratio = 60%

Gross Margin

Gross margin is a measure of how much revenue a company makes, after deducting the cost of producing, delivering, and servicing the product (cost of goods sold (COGS)). Gross margin is especially useful in comparing different products to one another, as well as a single product over time. Gross margin accounts for variable costs, as well as other costs involved in getting the product to the consumer. If, for example, the marketing team finds that it has a product with a decreasing gross margin over time, it may seek to find better ways to increase production efficiencies and decrease costs.

Gross Margin = total sales revenue – COGS

EXAMPLE: The same small manufacturing firm from above has additional costs of €1.50 per unit to deliver and service the product, bringing COGS per unit to €5.50 (€4.00 + €1.50).

Gross Margin = €200,000 – €110,000

Gross Margin = €90,000

Break-Even Analysis

This analysis takes a careful look at costs and revenues to determine the point at which total expenses = net revenue. With the very next sale after this break-even point, the organization will start to make a profit. This analysis helps answer questions such as how to price the product, how to better understand the product's cost structure, and how many units the organization needs to sell. Because it answers these fundamental questions, the Break-Even Analysis is one of the most frequently utilized tools in marketing decision-making. There are several variations of the Break-Even Analysis; the most common variations are:

Break-Even Quantity = fixed costs / (contribution margin per unit)

Break-Even Sales (€) = fixed costs / (contribution margin ratio)

EXAMPLE: Sarah is the VP of Marketing for a regional airline in the Fiji Islands, one of the many industries where fixed costs are very high. Her airline is contemplating a new daily route from Nadi, Fiji to Tokyo, Japan and Sarah needs to determine how many seats she needs to sell in order to make the route profitable. Fixed costs will include a wide variety of items, such as hangars, equipment, and even the airplanes. Long-term variable costs include maintenance on the airplanes, staffing costs, fuel costs, taxes, gate fees, and partnership fees. These variable costs change with the addition of a new flight service between these two cities, but they don't change with the number of passengers on the plane. For our purposes, actual variable costs include supplies (such as food, drinks, etc.), fees for ground crew (to handle more luggage), and possibly fuel costs (more passengers make the plane heavier, so more fuel is needed). In this example, fixed costs are €18,000 for a one-way trip from Nadi to Tokyo. A typical Boeing 737 has 143 seats. If the tickets sell for €525 each and the variable costs are €123 per seat, we know that the contribution margin is €402 (€525 – €123).

Break-Even Quantity = €18,000 / €402

Break-Even Quantity = 44.8

Note that since the airline cannot sell a partial seat, the break-even point would be 45 seats on this route. With a seating capacity of 143, there is plenty of room left for the airline to make a profit.

Break-Even Sales (€) = €18,000 / (€402/€525)

Break-Even Sales (€) = €23,508

Note that if the airline achieves total sales of €23,508 for this route, €18,000 will go to cover fixed costs while €5508 will cover variable costs. Remember that because we can only sell full seats and not partial seats, a quick check of our numbers reveals slightly different results from above. That is, 45 seats × €402 per seat margin = €18,090 to cover fixed costs (not €18,000).

RECAP: Sarah now knows that the introduction of the new route has the potential to be enormously profitable. If all of the seats are sold on these routes, the airline has the ability to make €39,396 per flight (98 seats remaining x €402 per seat contribution margin).

Conversion Rate

The conversion rate describes the percentage of individuals who perform the behavior we want them to perform. What percentage of visitors to our website click through on our special offer? What percentage of consumers sign up for our weekly newsletter? What percentage of online consumers who initiate a purchase follow through and complete that purchase? Incidentally, a surprising 70% of online shoppers abandon their carts before making their purchase. Why? Many are discouraged from completing their purchases because of too-high shipping costs, the requirement to set up an account, or because the checkout process is too long (Dopson 2021). Marketers are often interested in the different conversion rates for different promotional channels, such as in-store promotions, and mobile promotions, vs. online promotions.

Conversion Rate = # of individuals completing desired behavior / total number of individuals

EXAMPLE: Charlie is a director of digital marketing at an Irish company that specializes in upscale yoghurts and cheese. Charlie wants to know how many people actually complete a purchase after visiting the company's website. If 10,000 individuals visit the company's website and 400 complete a purchase, what is the conversion rate for this promotional channel?

Conversion Rate = 400 / 10,000

Conversion Rate = 4%

Market Potential

Often, a marketing manager will need to make an estimate of the total amount of profit or sales that are possible out of a given market segment. This analysis is often quite useful during the segmentation → targeting → positioning process because it allows comparisons between several different market segments. At the end of this analysis, the marketing manager will be armed with the information needed to help in the selection of a profitable target market.

Market Potential = total number of individuals in the population x size of the segment (%) x customer value

Note that the segment size is the proportion of the total population that a given market segment represents, while customer value is the amount of profit that can be expected from each individual customer.

EXAMPLE: Alex is the marketing manager for a new minor-league baseball team that is coming to a town of 150,000 residents. Alex has identified three market segments and is trying to determine which segment would be most profitable. Since there is not enough money in the marketing budget to target all of these segments, Alex must pick just one.

	Segment 1 18–25-year-Old Men Avid Sports Fans	Segment 2 18–25-year-old Women Avid Baseball Fans	Segment 3 18–50-year-olds Hispanic
Total population	150,000	150,000	150,000
Size of segment	15%	8%	18%
Customer value	€190	€390	€250
Market Potential	€4,275,000	€460,000	€6,750,000

RECAP: These results clearly indicate that it would be most beneficial to target the Hispanic market. Although these individuals spend less per person on baseball than women who are avid baseball fans, the market is so large that the market potential is much higher than the other segments.

Return On Investment (ROI)

The ROI analysis tells us whether or not an investment is worth it. Specifically, how much profit can we expect to make from a particular investment in advertising, new equipment, or something else? The ROI is one of the most widely-used metrics in marketing.

ROI = (net profit / cost of investment) x 100%

EXAMPLE: Carlos is facing a difficult situation and needs to make a decision quickly. One half of his marketing team wants to invest in new point-of-purchase material for all of the company's European locations. This material will require a fairly expensive upfront cost, but it is expected that it will catch consumers where they are making their purchase decisions – in the retail store. The other half of Carlos' team would like to launch a new advertising campaign. The campaign represents an important attempt to target a new market and is both creative and beautiful in its execution.

	New Point-of-Purchase Material	New Ad Campaign
Estimated sales for fiscal year	€410,000	€525,000
Cost of goods sold (COGS)	€160,000	€222,000
Net sales	€250,000	€303,000
Cost of investment	€200,000	€130,000
Net Profit	€50,000	€173,000
ROI	25%	133%

RECAP: On the face of it, this decision is not an easy one. The purchase of new point-of-purchase material will provide an attention-getting message in the retail store, but the cost of the new ad campaign is €70,000 lower. In looking at the results, it is clear that the new ad campaign is a better investment.

Market Share

Marketing managers often talk about their market share and often implement strategies designed to increase market share. Market share is the percent of sales in a given industry that are generated by given organization. Sportswear giant Nike, for example, is estimated to have a global market share of 27.4%. That is, for every euro spent on sports-related equipment, footwear, and clothing around the world, 27.4 cents are spent on Nike-branded products. Other big players in the market include Reebok, Adidas, Puma, and Under Armour (Sabanoglu 2021).

Market Share = (total sales for the company / total sales for the industry) x 100%

EXAMPLE: Chan operates a small stand at a farmer's market where he sells organic vegetables from his farm. The farmer's market is open once a week, and each week the farmer's market sells about €15,000 in items to locals and tourists. If Chan's average weekly sales receipts are €800, what is his market share?

Market Share = (800 / 15,000) x 100%

Market Share = 5.33%

Chan has a market share of 5.33% at the farmer's market.

Relative Market Share

Relative market share is slightly different. Here, a company's sales are compared to those of the largest competitor in the industry. Used in combination with market share, relative market share provides an indication of how well the company is doing with respect to its competitors.

Relative Market Share = company market share / largest competitor's market share

EXAMPLE: In looking at our example from above, it is hard to determine whether 5.33% market share is good or bad. Indeed, this is the case in many industries. A market share that is enviable in one industry might be cause for deep concern in another industry. If there are only a few vendors at the farmer's market, a market share of 5.33% is quite low. However, if there are many vendors, this market share might not be too bad. If our farmer, Chan, finds out that the largest vendor in the market has a 12% market share, what is Chan's relative market share?

Relative Market Share = 5.33 / 12

Relative Market Share = 44.42%

RECAP: By examining relative market share, Chan is now aware that he is a significant player in the market.

Percentage Increase or Decrease

This figure tells marketing decision-makers important information about the direction of their sales figures. It can also be used to track movement over time in other metrics, such as profits, advertising dollars spent, customer responses, etc. In examining trends that show an increase (or decrease) in sales, profits, etc. over time, decision-makers can spot long-term trends that are otherwise difficult to see when just looking at the raw numbers.

% Increase or Decrease = (Time2 sales – Time1 sales) / Time1 sales

Example: Maria is the marketing manager for a global company specializing in manufacturing windows for the residential housing market. In looking at her sales and profit figures for the previous 5 years, she found the following:

	2018	2019	2020	2021	2022
Sales (€000s)	754,087	822,044	919,234	998,252	1,009,376
Profit (€000s)	406,805	431,661	453,009	472,534	461,538

The percentage increase in sales from 2018 to 2019 is as follows:

% Increase in Sales = (€822,044–754,087) / €754,087

% Increase in Sales = 9.01%

The resulting increases (or decreases) in sales and profits are provided below:

	2018 to 2019	2019 to 2020	2020 to 2021	2021 to 2022
Increase in Sales	9.01%	11.82%	8.60%	1.11%
Increase in Profit	6.11%	4.95%	4.31%	-2.33%

RECAP: It is interesting to note that, although sales went up over the years, the increase in sales slowed considerably, especially in the last time frame. Importantly, profits have not kept pace with the increase in sales and indeed, there was a decrease in profits between 2021 and 2022. Maria and her team need to immediately investigate why sales are going up, but profits are going down.

Customer Lifetime Value (LTV)

This metric is based on the fundamental notion that it is more profitable to keep a customer than it is to find a new customer. Here, we calculate the value that the customer has to the organization over the entire time that the customer continues to buy products from us. Car makers make a concerted effort to target younger car buyers and then try to keep those customers as they get older, raise children, and then retire. Simply look at Honda's lineup of cars for different demographic groups. The Civic is targeted at Millennials, while the slightly pricier Accord is targeted to Generation X individuals. LTV is an important metric because it enables marketing decision-makers to determine which customers are 'most valuable' to the organization over the long term.

LTV = the customer's profit per year (€) x the number of years this person is our customer

Example: Jorge has been going to his favorite barber, Billy, every month for a haircut for 15 years and its likely he will continue for another 15 years. Billy calculates that each haircut at the shop nets him €20 in profit. Billy also has a family of four, the Garcias, who come to the shop once a month for haircuts. They just moved into the area 1 year ago but will only be here for about another year because they are making plans to move out of the area to be closer to their family. Jorge's and the Garcia family's LTV can be calculated as follows:

Jorge's LTV = €240 x 30 years = €7200

The Garcia Family's LTV = (€240 x 4 people) x 2 years = €3840

RECAP: Armed with this information, Billy the barber can see that, although he is making more money from the Garcia family per visit, they will be moving away in one more year. Although he certainly wants to provide a good haircut to them, Billy the barber might want to do what he can to make Jorge feel like he's appreciated. Billy might want to spend a little extra time with the haircut or offer him a complimentary shave every once in a while. Importantly, Billy should perform this same calculation with all of his customers so that he can assess the average LTV of all his customers as well as the LTV of his different customer segments.

Discounted Cash Flow

The Discounted Cash Flow converts expected future cash flows into today's currency; it is a measure of the present value of future cash flows. This analysis takes into account the "time value of money" and is done so that the marketing team can assess the viability of an expense, such as an investment in a new piece of manufacturing equipment. It is especially helpful in comparing two options against one another. In the formula below, future value represents the total value of the asset across all of the time it is viable. That is, if the new equipment is expected to last for 5 years, future value will include all of the revenue that can be attributed to this new piece of equipment for the next 5 years. Discount rate refers to the cost of the capital and n refers to the number of years we will be using this piece of equipment.

Discounted Cash Flow = future value / (1 + discount rate)^n

EXAMPLE: Ayesha is in the enviable position of having two promising ways in which she can spend €95,000 for her company. Option A will result in a one-time immediate payback of €118,000. Option B will result in a one-time payback of €125,000 next year. The cost of capital is 10%. Which, if any, option should Ayesha select?

Option B Discounted Cash Flow = €125,000 / (1 + 0.10)^1

Option B Discounted Cash Flow = €113,636

RECAP: In comparing the two options, Option A is clearly the best choice because Option A is worth €118,000 today, whereas Option B is worth €113,636 today. Both options will return more than the initial €95,000 investment.

Present Value

This metric is an assessment of today's value of an investment that was made in the past. It assumes that the investment has provided benefits to the organization over a period of time and that it has appreciated over time.

Present value = original value x $(1 + \text{interest rate})^n$

EXAMPLE: Silvia is the VP of Marketing for the Panama Canal. In looking back at all that she has accomplished over her career, one of her proudest moments was the completion of the €6,000,000 visitor's pavilion along the Canal's route 25 years ago. Over these years, it has provided visitors with a history of the Canal, information about its operations, and ample educational space. Assuming a 3% annual interest rate, what is the present value of this pavilion? Was the original investment worth it?

Present value = original value x $(1 + \text{interest rate})^n$

= €6,000,000 x $(1 + 0.03)^{25}$

= €12,562,668

RECAP: From a purely economic perspective, the visitor pavilion more than doubled in value over the 25-year period. On that measure alone, it was definitely worth the investment. In addition, the visitor's pavilion brought in extra revenue for the Canal (which is not incorporated into this calculation), provided jobs to locals, educated scores of school students and tourists about the Canal, and helped increase the reputation of the Canal.

Net Present Value (NPV)

This metric is an assessment of the stream of future cash flows, after taking into account the initial investment. It is similar to the Discounted Cash Flow, but it incorporates the original cost of the investment. Note that in the formula below, a required rate of return can be substituted for discount rate.

NPV = [future cash flow / $(1 + \text{discount rate})^n$] – initial investment

EXAMPLE: Hans is the VP of marketing for a small chain of German bakeries in northern Europe. He is trying to determine whether or not he should have new ovens, which are quite costly, installed in the bakeries, but will speed up production and thus, result in increases in sales. On a per-bakery basis, he expects that the new ovens will increase revenue by €4000 each year. The ovens, however, cost €40,000 and are expected to last 10 years. After that time, they will have no monetary value. If Hans requires a rate of return of 6%, what is the NPV for the ovens?

NPV = [€4000 x 10 years / $(1 + 0.06)^{10}$] – €40,000

NPV = €22,336 – €40,000

NPV = – €17,664

RECAP: Even though the new ovens seem to increase efficiency and sales, the NPV calculation indicates that the investment is not worth it.

References

Dopson, E. 2021. 30+ Shopping Cart Abandonment Statistics (and Strategies for Recouping Lost Sales). *Shopify*. 23 June. Accessed 12 July 2021. https://www.shopify.com/blog/shopping-cart-abandonment?prev_msid=9b6cdd27-ABEB-41F3-A289-6DD4B489D68E.

Sabanoglu, T. 2021. Forecast of Nike's Global Market Share in Athletic Footwear 2011–2025. *Statista*. 4 February. Accessed 10 July 2021. https://www.statista.com/statistics/216821/forecast-for-nikes-global-market-share-in-athletic-footwear-until-2017/.

Appendix 3
SUGAR-FREE PEZ? WHAT WILL KIDS THINK?

Diane M. Phillips

Christine Wismer,[1] Head of Marketing & Licensing at PEZ International, needed to make a decision quickly. In the fast-paced, competitive industry of candy, cookies, and other sweet treats ("confectionary"), companies needed to stay relevant and continuously innovate. Over the previous 2 years, PEZ had made a splash with its PEZPlay game. Now, however, Wismer needed to direct the next critical step for the brand. One opportunity was a response to the rising obesity levels in young children. Should PEZ offer a sugar-free candy? Healthcare professionals and parents seemed likely to approve, but would kids like it?

Background

PEZ International was founded in 1927 in Austria by Eduard Haas, III, who designed a peppermint candy to help people quit smoking. In 1949, a dispenser was designed to be very similar in size and shape to a cigarette lighter. Haas reasoned that the combination of the candies and the dispenser would simulate the "feel" of smoking, without the obvious harmful effects. Early on, the candies only came in one flavor: peppermint. In fact, the name PEZ is derived from the German word for peppermint (pfefferminz). Over the years, PEZ was sold throughout Europe in candy stores, grocery stores, and vending machines. In 1953, PEZ was introduced to the US. In order to appeal to American consumers, two important strategic changes were made. First, PEZ added several fruit flavors to appeal to the American desire for variety. Second, the product was repositioned as a "luxury candy" and free samples were provided to movie stars and other celebrities.

---

[1]The actual decision-maker preferred anonymity; Christine Wismer is a pseudonym.

Even President John Kennedy received an exclusive commemorative gift set of PEZ dispensers when he and his wife Jacqueline visited Vienna, Austria in 1961 (Internal company documents 2018).

As the product evolved from a simple candy into a toy with a beloved character that dispensed a piece of candy, decision-makers realized that the dispensers were just as important to consumers as the candy. PEZ first added a small hat to the top of the dispensers for the American market and then, in 1955, it introduced a Santa Claus head, which today is still the company's best-selling dispenser (Yurkevich 2015). In 1962, PEZ made its first foray into licensing when it obtained the rights from Disney to incorporate Mickey Mouse and Donald Duck heads on top of PEZ dispensers (Nieburg 2014). Except for a few small changes, "dispensers have basically been the same since the 1960s; they're sold in 80 countries around the world," explained Wismer. Thus, the product's positioning has shifted over the decades from a quit smoking aid, to a luxury candy, to a more mainstream, pop-culture product.

The company had two global locations: Orange, Connecticut and Traun, Austria. The Orange facility produced candy exclusively for the US and Canadian markets. This facility produced 12 million tablets of PEZ daily and used 50,000 pounds of sugar every 4 days – the size of an 18-wheeler truck. In the US alone, over 3 billion PEZ candies were consumed each year (Yurkevich 2015). Around the world, over 70 million PEZ dispensers were sold and 5 billion PEZ candies were consumed each year (internal company documents 2018). PEZ International was privately-held by the Haas family and had estimated annual sales in the US of $69.8 million (Mergent Intellect 2018).

Target Markets

Decision-makers at PEZ identified two core target markets: at about 90% of the total market, the first group was children, 3–8 years old. This target market had distinct challenges because both children and their parents were "targets" for the product. That is, children were the consumers of the product, but their parents were the customers who purchased the product. The second target market, at about 10% of the market, was made up of collectors. These people could be any age, but were united in their love for the PEZ brand and the characters.

Children and Parents

Marketing to the children and parents target market was a two-pronged effort. First, children 3–8 years old enjoyed the fun PEZ characters and the tasty little treats that the dispenser provided. Any active role they might play was in asking their parents for a specific dispenser or candy refills. From a marketing perspective, children needed to be excited about the characters and they needed to enjoy the candy treats. Second, the marketing team understood the need to also appeal to parents. Internal research at PEZ indicated that although parents felt nostalgia for the product and wanted to give their kids a little treat, they were concerned about the product's nutrition and health implications. PEZ estimated that 40% of all children/parents in this target market purchased PEZ on an annual basis. Further internal research indicated that, compared to girls, boys (and their parents) purchased more PEZ products. The annual customer value to the organization was $24 for boys and $19 for girls.[2]

[2]These numbers are estimates.

Collectors

In many ways, PEZ was considered a "cult brand," a brand that had a dedicated, passionate following of individuals. PEZ enthusiasts regularly attended collector meets, conventions, and auctions. These individuals were in the 20–70-year-old age range across all 80 countries where the product was distributed (Nieburg 2014). Just in the US, there were 10 different PEZ conventions each year for collectors (Seeds 2014). Legend has it that online auction site eBay was originally created to help the developer's wife buy and sell PEZ dispensers with other avid collectors (Rothman 2015). Hundreds of PEZ-dedicated collector and trading sites, YouTube channels, Facebook pages, and blogs are in existence. Although decision-makers at PEZ paid close attention to these collector activities and appreciated their passion, the company did not actively engage with them.

Marketing Highlights

The marketing team worked hard to keep consumers engaged with the brand. They did this by nurturing the brand as a cultural icon, engaging in selective licensing deals, and recently, launching the PEZPlay game.

Popular Culture Icon

PEZ has been a part of popular culture for many years, making numerous special-guest appearances on TV shows and movies. In *Ant-man and the Wasp* by Marvel Studios, a Hello Kitty dispenser played a critical role in one action scene. Kitty even appeared in the movie's trailer. It is important to note that PEZ never pays for any product placement. Instead, writers include PEZ in their scripts and then seek permission from PEZ to use the product in their creative works. PEZ also leverages a variety of cultural trends and events. For example, it created a special Prince Harry and Meghan Markle commemorative set to honor their May 2018 wedding and then auctioned it off for charity. The winning bid was $9893.33 and all proceeds went to the Make-A-Wish UK Foundation (PEZ Candy, Inc. 2018). Hard-to-find dispensers regularly received eye-popping sums at auction, but the highest price occurred in 2006 when the "Astronaut B" figurine sold for over $32,000. "In many respects, PEZ is seen as a cult brand," Wismer observed.

Licensing

In the US, unlicensed dispensers like Santa, the Easter Bunny, and a variety of other characters and animals, made up 50% of the company's sales. The other 50% of US sales came from dispensers with licensed images and the overwhelming majority of global sales were with licensed products. "What keeps it fresh is licenses – getting characters that kids love. If the license is good, sales go up," Wismer offered.

However, licensing decisions were quite complicated. "We need to know what will be popular about 1 year in advance, sometimes before the studios are even finished with the movies. We have to retool the machinery and get countless approvals. A lot of these decisions happen during the Licensing Expo in Las Vegas every year – it's a big trade show where manufacturers like us meet with representatives from the studios. Organizations like Disney and Warner Brothers attend and they describe their plans for upcoming characters and shows. Of course, it all has to fit with your own licensing plans. It's a hard decision, but sometimes you just get a feeling. For example, *Frozen* (by Disney) was a big surprise. We expected it to be popular, but no one in the industry expected it to be such a huge hit," explained Wismer.

Photo A3.1 Retail display for PEZ dispensers and refill packs

Source: courtesy, PEZ International

To appeal to the children and parent target market, "we mainly look for licenses for lower age groups and we try to identify around 10 assortments, or properties, per year. Each property is accompanied by about 4–6 characters. Disney's *Frozen*, for example, would be the 'property' and the characters would be *Elsa*, *Anna*, and *Olaf*. About 60% of the licenses are common between the US and the rest of the world; about 20% are only in the US; and about 20% are popular globally (but not in the US). The US is our biggest market. Germany is huge too. Japan is also a big market – we've been there since the 1970s," noted Wismer.

To appeal to collectors, the company created collector sets, such as a set containing the characters from *Harry Potter*, and the dinosaurs from *Jurassic World*. To maintain a sense of exclusivity and demand, these collector sets generally had limited runs of 300,000–400,000 units. Occasionally, production is increased, as was the case for *The Lord of the Rings* and *Elvis Presley*, when production increased to 450,000–500,000 units (Pacyniak 2010).

The PEZPlay Game

In August 2016, PEZ launched PEZPlay, an interactive gaming app for the global market (the US and Canadian market were not included). According to Wismer, "in the digital world, it is even more important to stay fresh. Kids are digital at a very young age." The primary target market for this effort was children 6–8 years old. Players simply downloaded the free app, which was available in English, French, German, and Spanish. Then, they scanned special codes on the inside of PEZ candy refill packages to get keys to unlock different characters and games. Players could also unlock keys by getting high scores or by uploading selfies and other pictures. When PEZPlay was first introduced, sales for the dispenser plus starter candy packs were growing. One of the team's goals, however, was to increase sales for the refill packs, which were stagnant. PEZPlay games were designed to be both educational and fun, with a variety of basic matching tasks, memory games, and pattern recognition puzzles. In addition to a bump in sales of refill packs, the team had two other objectives: strengthen engagement with the brand and modernize the brand image (see Photos A3.1 and A3.2).

To strengthen engagement, PEZPlay was designed to connect children and their parents over their shared relationship with the brand; kids would have fun and parents would feel nostalgic. The marketing team found ample evidence of increased engagement with the brand. By November 2018, there were 450,000 downloads of the app, 1.6 million scans of the game codes, and an average of 2.43 minutes spent playing the game[3] (Internal company documents 2018). Between the time spent playing, scanning, and purchasing, there were 65,000 additional hours of interaction with the brand. This was the equivalent of €3.1 million in advertising value. "Believe me, the investment was a lot less than that!" exclaimed Wismer.

[3] 2.43 represents the average "dwell time" for children playing the game. Dwell time is a metric used by app developers to indicate how much time users are engaged in an app. It is calculated by taking the total amount of time that the game is being used, divided by the total number of users over a given amount of time. According to the experts, 2.43 is very good.

Engagement, however, seemed to be unequal across different countries. First, most downloads were in the UK and Germany. This may have been, in part, due to the fact that PEZ structures its promotional budget on the percentage of sales method in each market. More sales mean that there is more money to spend on promoting new initiatives like PEZPlay, and that is exactly what happened in the UK and Germany. Second, children in Serbia and Croatia seemed to be the most engaged with the game; although fewer children downloaded the app, once they did, they made on average 8.3 and 8.4 scans of refill packs (see Table A3.1 below for engagement numbers).

Table A3.1 Engagement data per country

	Country	Total # of Scans	Scans per User
1	Germany	303,840	6.2
2	UK	262,998	5.8
3	France	118,880	5.1
4	Serbia	114,050	8.3
5	Croatia	91,677	8.4
6	Australia	90,197	4.1
7	Sweden	71,429	6.1
8	Austria	65,025	6.8
9	Norway	38,265	5.8
10	Netherlands	39,199	5.7

Source: courtesy, PEZ International

Photo A3.2 Screen shot of PEZPlay game

Source: courtesy, PEZ International

To modernize the brand image, PEZPlay connected the brand digitally to a growing area of interest: gaming. "There is a 'collectable' component to the game, but this time it's with the game codes, not new dispensers. They get a surprise each time and can collect and play one game after another," explained Wismer. Children over 13 were encouraged to upload selfies and other pictures, something they were already doing with other digital platforms. Within a few months of launch, more than 1.5 million pictures had been uploaded (Internal company documents 2018). Without changing the product itself, PEZPlay both increased engagement with its audience and modernized the brand's image.

Health Concerns

Next, the team decided to turn its attention to an issue that seemed to be getting significant attention: health and wellness. A full 62% of US children aged 6–11 liked to eat junk food as a treat and 61% ate snacks throughout the day (Mintel 2018b). In the US, childhood obesity had reached epidemic proportions, with more than 1 in 5 boys aged 6–11 obese (see Table A3.2). Childhood obesity leads to long-term health problems such as diabetes, asthma, sleep apnea, bone and joint problems, and heart disease, as well as social and emotional problems (Mintel 2018a).

Table A3.2 Prevalence of obesity in US children

Age	Girls	Boys
2–5 years old	13.5%	14.3%
6–11 years old	16.3%	20.4%

Source: Mintel (2018a)

Many parents, especially millennials, were taking the issue of childhood obesity quite seriously. Millennial parents (born between 1981 and 1996) (Dimock 2018) were empowered consumers. They utilized online research about products, had high expectations for quality and convenience, and were willing to utilize social media to share their consumption experiences. In the US, there were 11.6 million millennial households with children. These parents were increasingly looking for high-protein, low-fat, low-sugar options like nuts, bars, cheese, fruit, and vegetables (Fromm 2015).

Confectionary industry experts, including those at PEZ, were noticing: "Parents are concerned with sugar and its link to the obesity problem. PEZ actually addresses this concern quite well because the portions are small and fat free. None of our candy has any artificial sweeteners or color," explained Wismer. In an acknowledgment of parental concerns about health, PEZ partnered with Brush Buddies in 2018 and introduced the PEZ Poppin' toothbrush. Although it looked like an ordinary PEZ dispenser, a simple press of a button made a toothbrush pop up. The toothbrush was small enough to comfortably fit into a child's hand and the soft bristles were perfect for a child's teeth and gums (PR Newswire 2018). A sugar-free candy would be relatively easy and cost-effective for the company's in-house team to develop.

Despite some evidence that there would be a favorable reaction from the market to a sugar-free candy, a positive reaction was not guaranteed. Initial marketing research found very few requests or demands from parents for a sugar-free option. Wismer wondered whether kids would like the taste. Would parents still see the product as a "treat" for their kids? Would there still be a nostalgic or sentimental feeling among parents for a sugar-free product? Would her team, which was already fully engaged in the PEZPlay initiative, be able to split its time and attention with a new initiative?

Summary

As Wismer was considering her long-term strategic plan, she decided to seriously consider the possibility of responding to frequent reports about the growing global epidemic of childhood obesity. The US was its biggest customer and many parents were concerned. On the one hand, trends seemed to point toward a focus on health and wellness and it would be quite easy to add a variety of sugar-free candies to the product line, so parents who wanted to purchase them could easily do so. Because the product is part candy and part toy, children might not even notice the sugar-free candies in their favorite dispenser. Further, research indicated that compared to children who did not receive treats from their parents, children who did receive occasional treats developed healthier eating habits later in life. Thus, when done thoughtfully, parents could use the product to teach children important skills for how to live healthier lives (Birch, Fisher, and Davison 2003, Jansen, Mulkens, Emond, and Jansen 2008). Finally, millennial parents already utilized a variety of apps to track the activities and nutrition of their children, so a sugar-free line would easily fit into the everyday habits of these parents.

On the other hand, there would be additional packaging, marketing, and distribution costs involved. Further, the sugar-free candy might interfere with the nostalgic feelings that the marketing team tried to engender with its product. Parents who wanted to provide the same candy to their children that they themselves enjoyed might find it harder to feel nostalgic with the new product. Finally, and most importantly, how would kids react to the new product?

ASSIGNMENT QUESTIONS

1. Calculate the market potential for 6–11-year-old obese boys and girls in the US. Assume that there are 24.5 million children in this age group, evenly split between boys and girls.
2. Should Wismer and her team introduce a sugar-free version of the candy? Clearly state your recommendation and then support that recommendation with facts from the case and elsewhere.
3. For a parent with a child in PEZ's target market, what is the value proposition for this product? For a collector, what is the value proposition?
4. Carefully describe the company's four-part marketing mix.
5. Assuming that parents download the PEZPlay app and children play the app, Table A3.1 indicates that parent engagement is greater in the UK and Germany (there are more total scans), but child engagement is greatest in Serbia and Croatia (a greater number of scans per person). How could a marketing decision-maker use this information?
6. How successful was the PEZPlay initiative? Discuss in detail.
7. If the company decided against a new sugar-free line, what other options should Wismer consider for greater returns for the company?

References

Birch, L.L., Fisher, J.O., and Davison, K.K. 2003. Learning to overeat: Maternal use of restrictive feeding promotes girls' eating in the absence of hunger. *American Journal of Clinical Nutrition, 78* (2), 215–20.

Dimock, M. 2018. Defining generations: Where Millennials and post-Millennials begin. *Pew Research Center*. 1 March. Accessed 3 October 2018. www.pewresearch.org/fact-tank/2018/03/01/defining-generations-where-millennials-end-and-post-millennials-begin/.

Fromm, J. 2015. Snacking habits of Millennial parents are shaping the category for future generations. *Forbes*. 9 September. Accessed 20 September 2018. www.forbes.com/sites/jefffromm/2015/09/09/snacking-habits-of-millennial-parents-are-shaping-the-category-for-future-generations/#37e3e8b34183.

Internal company documents. 2018. Provided by Christine Wismer, PEZ International.

Jansen, E., Mulkens, S., Emond, Y., and Jansen, A. 2008. From the Garden of Eden to the land of plenty. Restriction of fruit and sweets intake leads to increased fruit and sweets consumption in children. *Appetite, 51* (3), 570–75.

Mergent Intellect. 2018. 30-184-7963. PEZ International, GMBH. *mergentintellect.com*. Accessed 3 October 2018. www.mergentintellect.com.ezproxy.sju.edu/index.php/search/companyDetails/301847963.

Mintel, Inc. 2018a. "Children and health - US - February 2018." *The Mintel Group, Ltd.*, London, UK, EC4V 6RN.

Mintel, Inc. 2018b. "Marketing to kids and Tweens - US - March 2018." *The Mintel Group, Ltd.*, London, UK, EC4V 6RN.

Nieburg, O. 2014. "PEZ returns to roots with adult proposition." *Confectionary News*, 5 February. Accessed 20 September 2018. www.confectionerynews.com/Article/2014/02/05/PEZ-re-enters-adult-market.

Pacyniak, B. 2010. "Working the PEZ plan." *Candy Industry, Northbrook, 175*(3), 16–18, 20, 22.

PEZ Candy, Inc. 2018. "PEZ Candy, Inc. royal dispenser auction raises over $9,500 for Make-A-Wish UK foundation." *Financial Services Monitor Worldwide*. 15 May. Accessed 7 September 2018. http://ezproxy.sju.edu/login?url=https://search-proquest-com.ezproxy.sju.edu/docview/2038636862?accountid=14071.

PR Newswire. 2018. "New PEZ Poppin' toothbrush collection from Brush Buddies brightens smiles." *PR Newswire*, 25 April. New York.

Rothman, L. 2015. "The small-scale story behind eBay's big bucks." *Time.com*. 11 September. pN. PAG.

Seeds, D. 2014. "Peppermint PEZ." *Smart Business Northern California, 8* (1), 5 December.

Yurkevich, V. 2015. "5 things you didn't know about the PEZ dispenser." *CNN Money*. 6 May. Accessed 5 September 2018. https://money.cnn.com/2015/05/06/smallbusiness/PEZ-dispenser/index.html.

HYDE IRISH WHISKEY: NEAT OR ROCKY ROAD TO NEW MARKETS?

Joe Bogue, Lana Repar and Conor Hyde

Conor Hyde had just joined a crowd of fellow sailors in the local pub in Cork, Ireland. During the chat about the day's sailing, Hyde noticed a group of Japanese tourists who were ordering Irish Whiskey and was bemused by their lack of awareness of the brands and the unique characteristics of Irish Whiskey. Finally, the Japanese tourists sat down, satisfied with their purchase of a top-selling Irish whiskey brand. They had missed the opportunity to taste an exclusive, small, local batch Irish Whiskey. As he sat back and sipped his glass of Hyde Whiskey, he thought again about the important decisions he had to make in introducing his own brand to a global marketplace. Life is golden, Hyde thought, as he looked at the beautiful amber whiskey in his glass.

Whiskey With an "e"[4]

Historians believe that Irish monks first started producing whiskey in the 6th century; it quickly became known as "the water of life." Over the centuries, it was exported around the world and enjoyed by millions of people. In the past few decades, Irish whiskey has undergone a surge in popularity, as consumers have increasingly sought authenticity and heritage in their drinks, appreciated

[4]*Whiskey* (with an e) refers to grain spirits distilled in Ireland and the United States; *whisky* (with no e) refers to spirits distilled anywhere else.

its superior sensory quality, and shifted their interest to cocktails. The global whiskey market was worth $6.14 billion in 2018 and was projected to reach $7.87 billion by 2023 (IWSR 2019).

Irish Whiskey sales are approximately €620m and account for 42% of Ireland's beverage exports (Bord Bia 2019). Irish Whiskey is triple distilled, unlike most whiskies, which are double or single distilled, giving it a smooth and sweet flavor. To be called "Irish Whiskey," it must be distilled and matured in Ireland for at least 3 years. Jameson was the biggest selling Irish Whiskey at 7.7 million cases, but sales of small-scale, craft distillery whiskies were also increasing (Bord Bia 2019).

Hyde Whiskey was a notable success story of the Irish Whiskey Renaissance, a resurgence in interest in small-batch whiskies. Since 1640, the Hyde family has sold only the very finest Irish Whiskey and Irish Stout in Bandon, County Cork. Conor Hyde was its Managing Director and was contemplating an expansion into global markets. To be successful, Hyde recognized that he had to satisfy consumers' needs and coordinate brand development, while also out-competing other Irish Whiskey (Jameson, Teeling, Tullamore Dew, etc.), Scotch Whisky (Johnnie Walker, Teachers, etc.), and American Whiskey (Jack Daniels, Jim Beam, etc.) manufacturers.

Photo A3.3 Hyde Whiskey bottles

Source: courtesy, Hyde Whiskey

Global expansion offered the possibility of profitable new markets, increased competitiveness, and access to new product and technology developments (Hollensen 2017). An important part of Hyde's success was leveraging the product's unique characteristics. Hyde Whiskey was a premium, small-batch, handcrafted whiskey that had won over 40 international awards for taste and innovation (see Photo A3.3). Hyde Whiskey was triple distilled in traditional copper and column stills, and a non-chill filter gave it a more complex, rich taste with a long smooth finish. As the whiskey finished and matured in wooden casks for 3–4 years, experts tasted and trialed each batch in order to identify the casks that had reached their unique "sweet spot" of maturation, ready for bottling. The creation of a consistent Hyde "house style" taste was essential to the company and its loyal consumers. The wood is an interactive organic material, which reacts on a molecular level on an ongoing basis with the whiskey spirit. Every wooden cask is unique and behaves very differently, so each one had to be monitored continually. To add specialty flavors, wooden casks from a variety of sources, such as bourbon, sherry, rum, and burgundy, were also used. In introducing his brand to the world, Hyde needed to make a variety of important decisions in four key areas: identifying lucrative new markets, determining the best distribution strategy, securing the most appropriate marketing research tools, and developing a promotional strategy and budget.

New Markets

Although Hyde Whiskey was a household name in Ireland, the brand was not well known on a global basis. Hyde was considering the following new markets: Australia, Japan, Canada, Russia, and India. A priority for Hyde was developing a marketing strategy for the entire global market in a way that encompassed numerous countries simultaneously, leveraging commonalities across markets, with occasional adaptation to market particularities (Jeannet and Hennessey 2004). This meant that Hyde Whiskey had to embrace a product standardization strategy and work on the "bigger picture," which involved finding connections, rather than differences, among markets.

Global whiskey consumption was forecasted to grow by 5.7% CAGR from 2018 to 2023, to almost 581 million nine-liter cases (IWSR 2019). India consumed nearly half the world's whiskey and in 2018 consumption in India grew by 10.5%, compared to 5% and 8% growth in the US and Japan, respectively (IWSR 2019). Whiskey was very popular in Australia and Canada, and increasing consumption was also being tracked in Japan and Russia (Vinepair 2019).

Hyde was particularly interested in insights about industry trends. One report identified an increased interest in holistic approaches to consumption, through convenience, transparency, value, and advanced technological solutions, but with a human touch (Mintel 2019). Further insights suggested that convenience, experience, technology, and mindful drinking were also important (IWSR 2018). In addition, younger consumers increasingly utilized online resources for information and purchases. They also were more open to "experiential drinking," as an important part of experiences and events, such as festivals. As he was considering new markets, Hyde turned his attention to distribution.

Distribution Strategy

Hyde's current distribution strategy included direct sales to retailers, bars and restaurants, as well as online purchases. About half of the retail price can be attributed to distribution, so the choice of distribution strategy was critical in ensuring that the product was competitively priced. Global distribution is especially challenging and, for small manufacturers, often depended on finding the right distributor and nurturing long-term relationships, "it's almost like a good marriage," Hyde explained.

The global distribution strategy hinged on identifying the most appropriate level of complexity, or the number of intermediaries, between producers and consumers. In determining channel complexity, Hyde needed to consider interactions among multiple geographically and temporally separated players, and their level of integration; channel loyalty; territory volatility; economic concerns of each party; relationship longevity (Jobber and Ellis-Chadwick 2020); and synergy with the company's broader objectives (Rosenbloom 2013) (see Table A3.3).

Table A3.3 Channel options for global markets

Characteristics	Key Cost Components	Advantages	Disadvantages
Option 1: Producer → Consumer			
• Selling directly to consumers • No intermediaries • Example: Dell computers	• Cutting out distributor/retailer profit margin • Cost of running a store and shipping	• Personal relationship with consumers • High control • Independence	• Unknown territory • Potentially strong competition • Increased costs
Option 2: Producer → retailer* → consumer			
• Selling directly to the retailer • Example: Tesco	• Retailer profit margin	• Convenient for consumers to see the product in the retail outlet	• Growing power of retailers • Limited control over product
Option 3: Producer → distributor → retailer* → consumer			
• Selling through two intermediaries • Traditional distribution model • Example: Small retailers	• Distributor profit margin	• For smaller order quantities • Good starting point for new markets	• Lack of communication with consumers • Dependency on the distributors
Option 4: Producer → agent → distributor → retailer* → consumer			
• Selling through three intermediaries • Example: When entering a foreign market	• Agent's commission	• An agent is familiar with the foreign market • An agent contacts distributors and retailers and handles sales	• Lack of control • Foreign language • Lack of communication with consumers
Option 5: Online: Producer → consumer			
• Selling directly to consumers • No intermediaries • Example: company website	• Cuts out distributor profit margin • Cost of shipping • Cost of maintaining a website and online shopping features	• Available 24/7/365 • Not dependent on location • Convenience • New trends	• Not shipping to some/many destinations • IT maintenance costs • Data security issues and IT errors

* For whiskey, "retail" includes the hospitality industry (bars and restaurants).

Source: adapted, in part, from Jobber and Ellis-Chadwick (2020)

Strategies with several intermediaries were common in this industry (Jobber and Ellis-Chadwick 2020) and an option that included retailing/hospitality was under serious consideration. Selling Hyde Whiskey in a retail setting offered several advantages. First, because consumers are able to interact with brands in a more experiential and meaningful way (Kantar 2019), consumers could more fully experience and appreciate the uniqueness of Hyde Whiskey. Second, consumers could easily compare different whiskies and become educated about the differences between brands. A third advantage is that consumers could purchase whiskey immediately, without waiting for delivery.

An important part of the distribution strategy decision rested on a deep understanding of the dynamics of the new market, including identification of market leaders and key channel players. This information could be obtained through market research or agents, who have specialized and extensive knowledge of these issues. However, relying on an agent can result in loss of control over the product and how it is marketed.

Finally, although an online option seemed obvious, there were two important downsides. First, shipping costs are usually paid by the consumer and can vary significantly around the world. Second, consumers would not be able to purchase the whiskey if they lived in countries where Hyde Whiskey did not ship. Because smaller companies like Hyde often offer limited shipping services, an online distribution strategy only works for consumers that are located in designated delivery areas.

To meet the expectations of today's global consumers, many companies opt for a multi-channel strategy (Bressolles and Lang 2019, Rosenbloom 2013). These increasing expectations are being driven by consumers spending more time online and by a redefinition of "shopping" (Chaffey and Ellis-Chadwick 2019). For example, momentum for "click and collect" options (order online and collect the product in-store) have increased dramatically, as have technologies that generate automatic product reorders. In addition, online subscription services, such as Amazon Prime, give consumers access to premium products and services, with big discounts (Kantar 2019). While the multi-channel strategy has many benefits, it would significantly increase wage costs, facility costs, and distribution fees (Ishfaq and Bajwa 2019). Hyde's next big decision centered on generating market-specific research.

Marketing Research

The importance of marketing research was amplified by a recent experience the team had with its efforts to export to the US market. Just as the team was about to launch its single-malt edition, a small oversight nearly ruined their efforts. Initially, Hyde Whiskey bottles were designed with a gold metal mark embossed with the Irish Harp facing from right to left. However, the Irish Government had previously registered this symbol of the Irish Government Seal of Office as an international trademark. Due to strong US–Irish connections and a long trading history, many industry professionals and officials would instantly recognize this mistake. Hyde Whiskey was asked to change the symbol on all its packaging or face the recall of thousands of bottles. In response, the team rotated the famous harp to face from left to right. Lesson learned: acquiring accurate, market-specific research is crucial (Hollensen 2017, Jeannet and Hennessey 2004). Hyde had a variety of marketing research options at his disposal to help provide specific data and insights into the marketplace of his choice (see Table A3.4).

Table A3.4 Marketing research alternatives

Research Element and Description	Required External Resources and Time for Completion	Cost in $USD*
Current beverage market and consumer trends. What is happening globally?	• Mintel Report • 8 days (3 hours per day) x 1 person	• Hourly wage: $22.00 • Per report: $4,500.00
Global beverage market leaders. Who are the key players and why? Various categories.	• Kantar Report • Communication with experts • 7 days (3 hours per day) x 1 person	• Hourly wage: $22.00 • Per report: $1,500.00
Economic situation in the country. Key economic indicators.	• Gallup Report • 5 days (2 hours per day) x 1 person	• Hourly wage: $22.00 • Per report: free
Direct competitors in the country. Their products, vision and mission, prices, market size, brand value, and marketing strategy.	• Nielsen tailored Report** • 3 days (2 hours per day) x 1 person	• Hourly wage: $22.00 • Subscription: $500.00 per month
Distribution channels in the country. Key distribution and retail options, benefits, and challenges.	• Kantar Report • 4 days (2 hours per day) x 1 person	• Hourly wage: $22.00 • Per report: $1,000.00
Legislation in the country. Regulations related to commercial trade, sale and promotion of whiskey.	• Gallup Report • 10 days (3 hours per day) x 1 person	• Hourly wage: $22.00 • Per report: free
Socio-demographic analysis of consumers in the country. Age and gender structure, education levels, disposable incomes spending patterns, values and technological access and literacy.	• Mintel Report • Gallup Report • 6 days (2 hours per day) x 1 person	• Hourly wage: $22.00 • Per Mintel Report: $4,300.00 • Per Gallup Report: free
Characteristics of whiskey drinkers in the country. Drinking habits, occasion of drinking, environment, and taste preferences.	• Nielsen tailored Report** • 3 days (2 hours per day) x 1 person	• Hourly wage: $22.00 • Subscription: $500.00 per month

Research Element and Description	Required External Resources and Time for Completion	Cost in $USD*
Primary research. Retail audits, interviews with stakeholders, consumer surveys, and focus groups.	• Survey tool: 1-year basis subscription*** • Booking place for focus groups: 1 room per focus group for 90 minutes • Transcription service: per focus group • 28 days (3 hours per day) x 2 persons	• Hourly wage: $25.00 • Survey tool: $75.00 per month • Booking: $50.00 per 90 minutes • Transcription: $100.00 per focus group
Analysis and reporting. Analysis of materials from secondary and primary research. Producing a written report.	• 35 days (4 hours per day) x 1 person	• Hourly wage: $22.00

* Costs are illustrative. **Cost of subscription to Nielsen is $500.00 per month, available only on a 12-month minimum basis. ***Cost of subscription for survey tool services is $75.00 per month, available only on a 12-month minimum basis.

Source: courtesy, Hyde Irish Whiskey

Developing a Promotional Strategy and Budget

The image of Ireland and whiskey fit one another – both are seen as lively, musical, fun, friendly, and casual. Irish whiskies were very suitable for those new to the whiskey category, open to exploration and those seeking a smooth-tasting whiskey. The marketing team identified four target audiences: *Generation X* (born between 1965 and 1980, grew up without the Internet, adapted to digital culture through their adulthood); *Millennials* (born between 1980 and 1995, the children of "Baby Boomers," familiar with digital technology); *Novices* (new to the whiskey category), and *Professionals* (loyal whiskey drinkers, gentlemen, and gentlewomen). The marketing team created key themes it hoped to communicate to these different audiences:

- Generation X → Inspiration/Variety/Surprise
- Millennials → Exploration/Adventure
- Novices → Fun/Conviviality/Ease of Mind/Healthy Living
- Professionals → Status/Distinction/Craft/Exclusive

Hyde Whiskey engaged in a range of promotional activities across these markets. First and most importantly, it maintained a consistent brand identity and backed it up with registering the Hyde Irish Whiskey trademark in several key global markets. Second, it communicated its unique cask flavor profiles; the broad range of flavors resonated with those who did not want a heavily peated, smokey, Scottish whiskey. Third, Hyde created aperitifs from lighter and smoother Irish whiskies, which offered a distinctive position in the marketplace. Finally, Hyde engaged with barkeepers and offered expert advice on sensory profiles, seasonal flavors/

combinations, and food pairings. These activities were supported with point-of-sale items (glasses, beermats, T-shirts, caps etc.), sales brochures/sell sheets, cocktail menu creation, brand ambassador activity, online brand influencer engagement, social media engagement, whiskey festivals, and whiskey trade shows (see Table A3.5).

Table A3.5 Types and costs of selected marketing activities and materials

Type	Quantity/Duration	Cost in $USD*
Brochures on Hyde Whiskey	Per brochure	• Design for all brochures (fixed cost): $200.00 • Print for one brochure: $0.10
Hyde Whiskey caps	Per cap	• One cap: $4.53
Stave platters	Per platter	• One platter: $12.80
Tent cards	Per tent	• One tent: $0.54
Beer mats	Per mat	• One mat: $0.13
Hyde Whiskey T-shirts	Per T-shirt	• One T-shirt: $4.15
Hyde Whiskey polo shirts	Per polo shirt	• One polo shirt: $10.40
70% Hyde dark chocolates	Per chocolate	• One chocolate: $1.64
Hyde Whiskey glass	Per glass	• One glass: $13.98
Coupons	Per coupon	• Value of one coupon: $20.00
Brand ambassadors	Hiring for 30-day duration	• Training: $100.00 • Compensation: $3,000.00
Rugby sponsorship	Sponsorship per event/match	• One match/event: $5,500.00
Hockey sponsorship	Sponsorship per event/match	• One match/event: $5,700.00
Trade Show	Per day	• One day costs: $1,000.00
Pull up banner	Per banner	• One banner: $35.00
Facebook campaign	For 30-day campaign	• Ads + awards: $1,500.00
Twitter campaign	For 30-day campaign	• Ads + awards: $1,000.00
Instagram campaign	For 30-day campaign	• Ads + awards: $1,750.00
Promotional video	60 seconds	• One video: $3,650.00
	Distribution Costs	
Distribution to Australian Market	Costs to ship materials (bulk)	• Costs: $2,435.00
Distribution to Japanese Market	Costs to ship materials (bulk)	• Costs: $1,585.00
Distribution to Canadian Market	Costs to ship materials (bulk)	• Costs: $2,038.00
Distribution to Russian Market	Costs to ship materials (bulk)	• Costs: $1,355.00
Distribution to Indian Market	Costs to ship materials (bulk)	• Costs: $1,683.00

Note: The costs of shipping materials (bulk) are shown for promotional materials shipping from Ireland to designated locations per one full container.

* Costs are illustrative.

Source: courtesy, Hyde Irish Whiskey

Summary

Since the very earliest days of Irish whiskey production, this golden drink has had a special place in the Irish psyche. Conor Hyde belonged to a new generation of Irish whiskey makers and carried the huge responsibility of introducing his whiskey to global markets. If his strategy was successful, tourists like those he saw at the pub would instantly recognize the Hyde brand as a premium quality, smooth-flavored, small-batch whiskey, with a great story to tell. Sláinte!

ASSIGNMENT QUESTIONS

1. Which market should Hyde Whiskey enter first (Australian, Japanese, Canadian, Russian, or Indian)? Which distribution strategy should Hyde and his team choose to optimize market entry? Justify your answer using Table A3.3.
2. Devise a market research strategy for Hyde Whiskey entering the Canadian market. Use Table A3.4 with the following limitations: 80 days and $20,000.00. Which elements did you decide to incorporate? Why?
3. What are some key components of Hyde Whiskey's brand identity?
4. Hyde Whiskey wants to run a Christmas marketing campaign in Japan. Using Table A3.5, create a marketing strategy for this market with the following limitations: 30-day campaign and a budget of $15,000.00. Create a timetable and calculate the costs of your marketing strategy.
5. Create a 1-year marketing strategy for Hyde Whiskey entering a market of your choice (Australian, Japanese, Canadian, Russian, or Indian). Using Table A3.5, outline what type of marketing activities/materials you would select with Hyde Whiskey entering one retail store, one exclusive store, and one bar-restaurant in your chosen market. Justify your answer. Calculate the cost of your marketing strategy using the figures provided in Table A3.5. Discuss your choices and costs.
6. Prepare a strategy for entering a new market for Hyde Whiskey. Include your choice of: (i) market, (ii) distribution strategy, (iii) market research, and (iv) marketing strategy. Justify your choices. Discuss why your choices are optimal for Hyde Whiskey.

References

Bord Bia. 2019. *Export Performance and Prospects 2018–2019*. Report. Accessed 27 July 2020. www.bordbia.ie/globalassets/performance--prospects-2018-2019/export-performance-prospects-2018-2019.pdf.

Bressolles, G. and Lang, G. 2019. KPIs for performance measurement of e-fulfillment systems in multi-channel retailing. *International Journal of Retail & Distribution Management*, Vol. ahead-of-print No. ahead-of-print. https://doi.org/10.1108/IJRDM-10-2017-0259.

Chaffey, D. and Ellis-Chadwick, F. 2019. *Digital Marketing*, 7th edition. Pearson Education, Ltd., Harlow, UK.

Hollensen, S. 2017. *Global Marketing*, 7th edition. Pearson Education, Ltd., Harlow, UK.

Ishfaq, R. and Bajwa, N. 2019. Profitability of online order fulfillment in multi-channel retailing. *European Journal of Operational Research*, 272, 1028–40.

IWSR. 2018. *IWSR Global Trends Report 2018. Convenience, experience, technology and mindful drinking revolutionize alcohol market trends.* Accessed 27 July 2020. www.theiwsr.com/wp-content/uploads/IWSR-Press-Release_Key-Global-Trends-2018_14August2018.pdf.

IWSR. 2019. *IWSR Global Trends Report 2019. The Trends that Defined 2019 for IWSR's Analysts.* Accessed 27 July 2020. www.theiwsr.com/the-trends-that-defined-2019/.

Jeannet, J.P. and Hennessey, H.D. 2004. *Global Marketing Strategies*, 6th edition. Houghton Mifflin Company, Boston, Massachusetts/New York.

Jobber, D. and Ellis-Chadwick, F. 2020. *Principles and Practice of* Marketing, 9th edition. McGraw-Hill Education, Maidenhead, UK.

Kantar. 2019. *Retail Predictions: Coming of Age in the 2020s.* Report. Accessed 27 July 2020. https://consulting.kantar.com/wp-content/uploads/2019/01/KantarConsulting_Retail_Predictions_2019.pdf.

Mintel. 2019. *Consumer Trends 2030. Seven Core Drivers of Consumer Behaviour that will Shape Global Markets over the next 10 years.* Report. Accessed 27 July 2020. www.mintel.com/global-consumer-trends.

Rosenbloom, B. 2013. *Marketing Channels. A Management View*, 8th edition. Toronto: South-Western Cengage Learning.

Vinepair. 2019. *The Countries that Drink the Most Whiskey.* Accessed 27 July 2020. https://vinepair.com/wine-blog/map-the-countries-that-drink-the-most-whiskey/.

THE SAVANNAH BANANAS: BRINGING FUN AND PROFIT BACK TO BASEBALL

Diane M. Phillips

"Whatever is normal, do the exact opposite," Jesse Cole, owner of The Savannah Bananas

It was the end of another long, exhausting day at historic Grayson Stadium in Savannah, Georgia, USA. Jared Orton, President of the Savannah Bananas, made his way back to his office after the day's post-game chat with the staff. As Orton leaned back, put his aching feet up on his desk, and took a long drink of cold water, he thought about the accounting report that was sitting on his desk – more revenue needed to be generated immediately.

The Strangest Name in Baseball

Baseball had a distinguished history in the beautiful, historic city of Savannah. In recent years, however, trouble had started to brew. In 2015, Savannah's Minor League Baseball (MiLB) team, the Savannah Sand Gnats, issued an ultimatum: build a new baseball stadium, or we're leaving. After several losing seasons, anemic attendance, and no enthusiasm, the City of Savannah said "no thanks" and the Sand Gnats left (Stock 2018).

At the same time, Jesse and Emily Cole, who had recently purchased another baseball team, found out about the trouble in Savannah. When they saw Grayson Stadium and learned that the franchise was for sale, they knew they had to buy it. Baseball legends Babe Ruth, Lou Gehrig, and Hank Aaron had all played in the 1926 stadium (Stock 2018) and it was still bursting with charm. Buying the franchise, however, would not be easy. Teams can cost from $250,000 to $1 million (George 2018). The couple was committed to the idea, and after selling their house and going into deep debt, made it happen (Stock 2018).

Their first decision was to abandon the traditional formula for running a baseball franchise and do something "out of the ordinary." Importantly, the team needed a new name. "Take our name, the Bananas. That was our first big foray into doing something weird ... and it worked! The city itself had no connection to bananas. We don't grow them here or process them here ... we are the only fruit-based baseball team anywhere. When we announced the name, it was polarizing in both ways. People thought, 'these people are ridiculous', but it was fun, different, exciting, a breath of fresh air," said Orton.

Team owner Jesse Cole's taste for the ridiculous didn't stop with the team's name. The team organized "an 'all you can eat' food truck festival for one price. We also did a morning only beer festival that started at 9am. These events were hugely successful. We *could* do things the same as everyone else, but we do the opposite," observed Orton. The team also celebrated "St. Patty's Day in July" with each of the team members sporting a bright yellow plaid kilt for the entire game. One player noted, "this is one of the coolest things I've ever done in baseball" (Gilbert 2018).

Fans First, Profits Second

The Bananas had a strong record of sellouts as well as one of the best records in the league. Part of this success was due to their "Fans First" philosophy.[5] The management team believed that if fans had a top-notch experience, profits would follow. Fans enjoyed the circus-like experience and Cole was a true master at orchestrating the activities while madly dashing around the stadium in a canary-yellow tuxedo (complete with yellow shoes and top hat). The organization took this circus mentality seriously: "we need to be a circus, and maybe a baseball game will break out," offered Cole (Stock 2018) (see Photo A3.4).

Photo A3.4 Team owner Jesse Cole orchestrating the fun

Source: Savannah Bananas, Malcolm Tully, photographer

The Financials of Baseball

The Savannah Bananas were part of the Coastal Plain League, a 16-member league comprised of players from collegiate baseball teams across the US. They played 26 games over the summer. Unlike their predecessors, the Bananas were not affiliated with a major league team. For most other teams, this would make it more difficult to draw a crowd. However, the Bananas were not like other teams.

[5]Fans First Entertainment is the umbrella organization that is owned by Jesse and Emily Cole. It controls both the Gastonia Grizzlies and the Savannah Bananas.

Traditionally, baseball teams drew revenue from four different sources: ticket sales, sponsorships and partnerships, concessions, and merchandise. The goal was to fill up the facility. Even if the seats were sold very cheaply, high attendance was needed so the team could make its money with concessions and merchandising. Greater numbers of fans in attendance also garnered higher advertising revenue.

Attending a Major League Baseball (MLB) game was very expensive, in part, because of higher operating expenses for state-of-the-art new stadiums. In contrast, for teams in the Minor League (MiLB) and Collegiate Leagues, most of the expenses were stadium lease agreements and operations. In MiLB, stadium leasing fees could easily exceed $1 million annually. Operating income for the top 30 teams in the MiLB averaged $2.2 million, or approximately 17% of revenue (Klebnikov 2016). For the Savannah Bananas and other Collegiate League teams, the financials were even more favorable. The lease on Grayson Stadium, for example, was only $20,000 per year. These savings could then be passed on to the fans.

Another advantage with a collegiate team like the Bananas was that because the players were current National Collegiate Athletic Association (NCAA) players, they could not be paid. Therefore, expenses were even lower – no salaries and no workers' compensation insurance were needed (George 2018). The Bananas did, however, provide players with a comfortable stay while they were in Savannah. The players stayed with host families, the majority of their equipment needs were provided, and transportation, food, and lodging at away games were covered. Players also received plenty of pregame and postgame meals.

In 2018, MLB attendance was down 6.5% (Brown 2018). Because of the high price and the long games, often averaging over 3 hours per game, the MLB formula was not conducive to affordable and fun family entertainment. Although fewer fans were attending MLB games, macro-level trends indicated a positive future for MiLB and Collegiate League games. More fans were attending these games and, since 2000, over 60 new MiLB ballparks had been opened around the country (Klebnikov 2016).

Pricing and Cost Structures

Three types of pricing structures are common in baseball: dynamic pricing, variable pricing, and fixed pricing. Orton needed to carefully consider each one.

Dynamic Pricing Strategy

With a dynamic pricing model, the price of the ticket varied, depending on current inventory (how many seats were left), the weather, the visiting team, how many days were left before the game, and the seat's location within the stadium. Dynamic pricing was widely used in a number of industries, such as the airline industry. In baseball, the San Francisco Giants were the first team in the MLB to utilize dynamic pricing (Parris, Drayer, and Shapiro 2012). A dynamic pricing strategy is especially beneficial in maximizing revenue when there is a fixed capacity of "product," such as when there are a fixed number of seats on a plane or in a stadium – the organization cannot make more if demand increases. Dynamic pricing is also appropriate when products are "perishable" – they can't be saved for later. Once the plane takes off, the ticket is worthless. Therefore, because of a need to put fans in seats (think merchandise, concessions, and advertising), it is better to sell a sharply discounted ticket than to not sell the ticket at all. The Los Angeles Dodgers had 28 pricing categories and the San Francisco Giants had 11. Since so many sports teams and other organizations used dynamic pricing, fans were used to it (Parris, et al. 2012). Initiating a dynamic pricing model would be relatively easy with the numerous software programs that were readily available. Further, a dynamic pricing strategy puts less pressure on the sales staff.

Variable Pricing Strategy

A variable pricing strategy sets different prices for tickets based on days of the week (weekdays are cheaper), the time of the season (midsummer is more expensive), and the opponent (the Yankees and Red Sox usually command higher prices). Unlike a dynamic pricing strategy that gives marketers the ability to make day-to-day or even moment-to-moment pricing changes, variable prices are set at the beginning of the season and remain unchanged for the duration of the season. This strategy did not need the support of sophisticated statistical formulas or software programs. Instead, most pricing decisions were based on sales data and a bit of gut feeling. A variable pricing strategy also had the advantage of not surprising fans with wildly-fluctuating prices.

Fixed Pricing Strategy

All MLB teams used either dynamic or variable pricing strategies (Best 2017). It is not surprising that, just as with everything else, the Savannah Bananas tried something completely different. For the 2016–18 seasons, the great majority of Bananas tickets were the same price all the time: $15. In addition, each ticket was a "loaded fixed price ticket," including parking and all-you-can-eat food at the concession stands. Fans could help themselves to as many chicken sandwiches, hotdogs, hamburgers, cheeseburgers, popcorn, cookies, soda, and water as they wanted. Why the fixed price pricing model? "We thought this was the greatest value for our fans. At other ballparks, the tickets might be $5 or $8, but it's a ridiculously negative experience because of the high cost of the food," noted Orton. For the Bananas, this pricing strategy was an integral part of the "Fans First" value proposition – a fun, family experience, without getting ripped off.

Sales Strategy

Grayson Stadium had a 4200-seat capacity and had a strong record of selling out all of its seats. At about 110,000 tickets per season, the Bananas were certainly on a winning streak with their own home crowd (Gilbert 2018). This was accomplished, in part, by the three full-time salespeople who had a 100% sell-out goal. This goal of consistent sell-outs may have been an extraordinarily high goal for the tiny three-person team, but one benefit was that the goal was *very clear* – there was no grey area regarding expectations. Rather than selling individual tickets via mass media advertising, the team focused its efforts on selling packages of tickets to organizations like local businesses, churches, and scouting organizations. About 90% of ticket sales came from four sources: 5 or 10 game packages, group tickets, season tickets, and the hospitality bullpen, which was designed for groups of 50–125 and provided access to no-wait lines for concessions. "For the remaining 10%, we want fans to wonder what they can do to also get that great deal. We tell them, 'get on the waitlist and you will have a shot!'" said Orton.

"As an organization, we have to commit to selling out every game. From the perspective of the fans, when there is always a ticket available, there is no rush," said Orton. This strategy of scarcity encouraged immediate purchases for fans who were afraid of missing out. Research confirms that scarcity increases perceived value and purchase intentions (Suri, Kholi, and Monroe 2007). A scarcity strategy works especially well with discretionary spending and specialty products, as was the case with the one-of-a-kind experience at the ballpark (Stock and Balachander 2005). Orton believed that scarcity motivated the Banana fans. "As an example, a few years ago, the Braves spent a huge amount of money on a new stadium. On opening night, the stadium was packed, but the second night, not so much. Part of the problem was they kept selling and selling ... standing room only, bench seats, all kinds of seats ... there were always more tickets available. There was no rush, no urgency for people to buy a ticket," explained Orton.

Bananas fans who couldn't get tickets were put on a wait list. "We now have 2000 people on our priority wait list. These people have the first chance of getting a ticket at any one of the remaining games," reported Orton. Each year when tickets become available, fans eagerly scoop up as many tickets as they can afford for the season. "This jump starts us in selling out the remaining games for the season. So, 1900 people get their tickets for next season, but 2000 additional people had to be put on the wait list. We will have 75% of our inventory sold by January. That's unheard of in the industry," said Orton. Preselling tickets provided a guaranteed cash flow to the organization.

Food Prices

The question now facing Orton centered around a report from the accounting department. Although most other costs associated with operations were remaining steady, food costs were about to increase dramatically because of a change in suppliers. At the same time, the price for an all-inclusive ticket at the park was still $15, the same price it had been for 3 years. In 2017, the team's average operating margin as a percentage of its revenue (earnings before interest, taxes, depreciation, and amortization) (EBITDA) was approximately 17%, in 2018 it was 16%, and by 2019 it had dropped to 15.5%.[6] This decrease was primarily due to rising food prices. Orton needed to take into account a few things when determining whether to change his pricing strategy. It was obvious that something needed to be done, but he first wanted to look at the competition's pricing, the cost structure of the concessions, and the food quality.

The first thing that Orton considered was competitive pricing. As a comparison, attending an MLB game was significantly more expensive and Orton concluded that there would be room for a slight increase in the fixed price ticket for the Bananas. One useful measure was the Fan Cost Index (FCI) which measured how much it cost a family of four to attend a game. It included four tickets, four sodas, two beers, four hotdogs, two ball caps, and parking. The Chicago Cubs had the most expensive FCI at $368.28, with the Boston Red Sox closely following at $345.88. The Arizona Diamondbacks were the most reasonable at $145.58. The Atlanta Braves, the closest Major League team to the Bananas, had an FCI of $217.84 (Hartweg 2018). By comparison, the average FCI for MiLB was $64.18 (Klebnikov 2016).

Next, Orton examined the concession stand cost structure. For all-you-can-eat (AYCE) tickets, there is an 86% redemption rate. That is, 86% of AYCE ticket holders attend the game for which they purchased the ticket. The non-AYCE tickets have a 95% redemption rate because these tickets are usually purchased in the last few days before game day or at the gate on game day. In examining the accounting department's report, Orton saw that the organization's all-in cost for food was as follows: hotdogs = $0.55, hamburgers/cheeseburgers = $1.22, and chicken sandwiches = $0.83. For the AYCE tickets, all consumption represents a cost to the organization. However, for the non-AYCE fans, these food items are purchased and the team makes a small amount of profit for each item sold (see Table A3.6).

[6]These numbers are estimates.

Table A3.6 Average per person consumption and price for food items

	Average AYCE per Person Consumption	Average Non-AYCE per Person Consumption	Price for Food Item
Hotdog	0.65	0.12	$3.00
Hamburger	0.35	0.02	$4.00
Cheeseburger	0.50	0.04	$5.00
Chicken sandwich	0.42	0.02	$4.00

Source: The Savannah Bananas

Since non-AYCE fans purchased very few food items, Orton was concerned that if prices increased at the concession stands, these fans might purchase even fewer items. In addition, the high price of food might diminish the experience and later dissuade them from purchasing the all-inclusive AYCE tickets. Finally, the thought of raising food prices was a complete contradiction to what he and owner Jesse Cole had been preaching all along – the fan experience needed to be optimized and paying high prices for food would detract from an optimal experience.

The last issue Orton needed to consider was how the quality of the food experience was consistent with the overall experience at the ballpark. The Bananas recently invested significant funds to improve food quality by improving the kitchens and purchasing several commercial grills that provided a better taste to the food, as well as easier prep and shorter cooking times. The goal was to have the fans wait no longer than 6 minutes in line; the sooner the fans could return to their seats, the sooner they could enjoy the experience again. "We know that we can't be the best at food and beverage, but if we can do our job and get them back and enjoying the entertainment, then their experience is really hitting through the roof," explained Orton (Rector 2018). Since fans were starting to notice the increased quality of the food, Orton wondered if they would be willing to pay a little more for their AYCE tickets.

Summary

The city of Savannah saw several baseball teams come and go over the decades. Then, the Bananas came to town. The ridiculous and unexpected became a key part of their standard operations and fans came in droves. The management team believed that if they gave fans a top-notch experience, profits would just naturally follow. However, is this really possible? Orton realized that operating revenues were decreasing and turned his focus to the organization's pricing strategy. Should the Savannah Bananas switch to a dynamic or variable pricing model, or maintain a fixed price strategy (with the option of increasing the price to, for example, $18 or $20)? Alternatively, should Orton push a 'why mess with perfection' approach and do nothing?

ASSIGNMENT QUESTIONS

1. Calculate the percentage change in operating revenue from 2017 to 2018 to 2019.
2. Examine the pricing and redemption figures in Table A3.6. Calculate the estimated cost of food for both AYCE and non-AYCE food consumption. Calculate the profit for non-AYCE food purchases. How could Orton use this information to make his decision?

3 Should the Savannah Bananas: (a) initiate a dynamic pricing model, (b) initiate a variable pricing model, (c) increase their fixed ticket prices, or (d) do nothing? Support your recommendation with evidence from the case and elsewhere.
4 Let's say that Orton decides that he will increase the AYCE ticket prices and/or the non-AYCE prices. What price would be ideal?
5 Identify the direct competitors as well as the indirect competitors for the Savannah Bananas.
6 Evaluate the "scarcity" sales strategy. In what ways might this be a good idea? In what ways might it be a detriment to the team?
7 The dynamic pricing model works well for organizations that have a fixed inventory, like the Savannah Bananas. Develop an argument for why it makes sense for the organization to increase its inventory by, for example, playing more games or constructing more seating.

References

Best, N. 2017. Yankees tickets now feature variable and dynamic pricing. *Newsday*. 7 March. Accessed 7 November 2018. www.newsday.com/sports/baseball/yankees/yankees-tickets-now-feature-variable-and-dynamic-pricing-1.13224207.

Brown, M. 2018. Inside the numbers: MLB's attendance is down 6.5%; Here's how it can be fixed. *Forbes*. 18 June. Accessed 11 October 2018. www.forbes.com/sites/maurybrown/2018/06/18/inside-the-numbers-mlbs-attendance-is-down-6-5-heres-how-it-can-be-fixed/#4884dfd739c2.

George, T. 2018. The "411" – Part 3 – Acquiring a Summer Collegiate Baseball Team. *The Sports Advisory Group*. Accessed 22 October 2018. www.thesportsadvisorygroup.com/resource-library/business-of-sports/411-part-3-acquiring-summer-collegiate-baseball-team/.

Gilbert, A. 2018. Bananas in kilts! Just be careful sliding into second base, fellas. *Connect Savannah*. 25 July. Accessed 9 October 2018. www.connectsavannah.com/savannah/bananas-in-kilts/Content?oid=9236093.

Hartweg, C. 2018. Fan Cost Index details 2.4% increase to attend MLB games. *Team Marketing Report*. Chicago. 23 April. Accessed 11 October 2018. www.teammarketing.com/.

Klebnikov, S. 2016. Minor League Baseball's most valuable teams. *Forbes*. 8 July. Accessed 11 October 2018. www.forbes.com/sites/sergeiklebnikov/2016/07/08/minor-league-baseballs-most-valuable-teams/#d0293e843b22.

Parris, D.L., Drayer, J., and Shapiro, S.L. (2012). Developing a pricing strategy for the Los Angeles Dodgers. *Sports Marketing Quarterly, 21* (4), 256–64.

Rector, E. 2018. Extra innings with Jared Orton, president of the Savannah Bananas. *MarketScale*. 1 October. Accessed 18 October 2018. https://marketscale.com/industries/sports-entertainment/extra-innings-with-jared-orton-president-of-the-savannah-bananas/.

Stock, A. and Balachander, S. 2005. The making of a "Hot Product": A signaling explanation for marketers' scarcity strategy. *Management Science, 51* (8), 1181–92.

Stock, M. 2018. From a dingy duplex to dancing baseball players: The birth of the Savannah Bananas. *WBUR News*, Boston's NPR News Station. 10 August. Accessed 9 October 2018. www.wbur.org/onlyagame/2018/08/10/savannah-bananas-baseball.

Suri, R., Kohli, C., and Monroe, K.B. 2007. The effects of perceived scarcity on consumers' processing of price information. *Journal of the Academy of Marketing Science, 35* (1), 89–100.

DAVID AND GOLIATH: THE EVOLUTION OF A STRATEGIC PARTNERSHIP IN WINE

Diane M. Phillips and Jason Keith Phillips

The stunning Meridiana Wine Estate consists of a beautiful stone villa, surrounded by 47 acres of precisely-planted and trellised grape vines. It was in this setting that founder and CEO Mark Miceli-Farrugia completely revolutionized Malta's wine sector with his innovative approach and unwavering dedication. After returning to his office on one recent afternoon, Mark[7] sat back and thought about the recent sale of the estate to his business partner of 24 years. In the end, was the Meridiana project a success? It depends on how one defines success.

The Tiny Nation of Malta

Located 90 miles off the coast of Sicily, mid-way between the Straits of Gibraltar and the Suez Canal, Malta is home to approximately 500,000 people. Malta's economy, primarily fueled by services and tourism, is stable with a low inflation rate (1.3%), low unemployment (4.6%), and steady GDP growth rate (6.7%). Many of the nation's social indicators are quite good; a citizen of Malta can count on a strong education, exceptional life expectancy, high literacy rates, and excellent health-care (CIA 2020). Because of its strategic location, Malta's history is characterized by waves of

[7]Mark Miceli-Farrugia prefers to be referred to as Mark.

invasions, occupation, and cultural change. Traces of human settlements date back 7000 years and waves of Phoenician, Roman, Byzantine, and Arabic people established settlements and cultures there. In 1530, the Knights of Malta took control and launched a golden age of art, architecture, and culture, much of which still exists today. In 1798, the British took control and held the nation until 1964 when Malta became a sovereign country (Visit Malta 2022. These shifting cultural waves left an indelible influence on Malta, as well as its winemaking techniques and perceptions.

Outdated Winemaking Techniques

A native of Malta, Mark made his career in the beverage industry, advancing to senior-level positions at several global beverage firms. His strong network of industry connections made him an important influencer in the world of wine and spirits. Mark always had a particular appreciation for wine. However, winemakers throughout Malta still relied on centuries-old techniques that made it impossible to produce high-quality wine there.

First, winemakers were not using proper wine-quality grapes. Indeed, the grape varieties were much better suited to be eaten fresh as table grapes. Another problem was that many of the growing techniques were just as out of date as the grape varieties. Local wine producers rarely utilized trellises, pruning, or irrigation for their vines. A final problem was a left-over system from the British government: little regulation of the wine sector. For more than two centuries, the British maintained a military contingent in Malta. The colonial government's objective was to control wine prices rather than wine quality. "As long as their servicemen got cheap wine, they were satisfied! It was absolute plonk!" Mark noted. Not surprisingly, the inferior grapes, outdated techniques, and inconsistent regulations combined to produce inferior-quality wines.

Poor Perceptions

When locals wanted to drink a good-quality wine, they often looked overseas. Local wine distributors and restaurants shared these perceptions; no one believed that a good, or even great, quality wine had a chance of being produced in Malta. Local banks refused to issue loans for the venture. "They said it had never been done before, why should we believe that you can do it?" Mark explained. Never deterred, Mark was convinced that premium-quality wine could be produced in Malta. Then, his wife Josette suggested a strategic move that would forever change Malta's wine-making industry: why not try to elicit the assistance of the most well-respected wine producer in the world? What happened next is a story of how "David" partnered with "Goliath."

Key Players

Just like the ancient story of David and Goliath, this partnership has one partner who is clearly more powerful than the other. However, unlike the old story, this partnership resulted in much more positive outcomes.

David: The Entrepreneur Miceli-Farrugia

Mark knew that some of the world's best wines were made in the rolling hills of Tuscany, Italy, where the climate and soil conditions were perfectly suited for growing the best quality grapes. Malta had a very similar climate and soil conditions and Mark hired some experts to help prove that point. One was an oenologist who was specialized in the finer techniques of wine-making, such as the selection and grafting of vines, cultivation, and fermentation procedures. The other was a local beverage distributor who believed that a market niche existed for premium-priced, high-quality Maltese wines. The next thing Mark needed was a powerful, well-connected, and well-financed business partner.

Goliath: Antinori Estates

By the time Mark started exploring partnership opportunities in the mid-1990s, the Antinori Family had been making and selling wine for 26 generations – since the year 1385. Today, the family still lives in its 15th century palace in Florence (Gibson 2017, Virbila 2014). A small, inconspicuous door with the word "vino" can still be found on the palace's ground floor. In previous centuries, people would knock on the door, hand over a few coins, and a cellar worker would fill a cup of wine for them (Frank 2016). Over the centuries, the Antinori Family has survived political upheavals, famine, plagues, wars, and a devastating flood. The Antinori name is synonymous with prestige and distinction. When Piero Antinori became CEO in 1966, most of the industry was focused on volume, not quality. To strengthen the brand, Antinori instituted strict quality improvements, shifted some production to organic standards, and initiated a variety of other global ventures. By the late 1990s, Antinori Estates started to expand beyond Italy and Europe (Frank 2016), and focused its sights on the US, Chile, Hungary, and Romania.

David *and* Goliath

Despite receiving countless invitations to establish strategic partnerships every year, Antinori carefully considered Mark's proposal for several reasons. First, and most importantly, he appreciated Mark's "vision and great enthusiasm," as well as his moves to assemble a team of experts. Second, Antinori saw that the soil and climate of Malta was very similar to that of nearby Sicily, which had a proven history of making fine wines. Finally, the Miceli-Farrugia family had an outstanding reputation as business people with high standards of integrity and Mark had a particularly strong reputation in the wine-importation business. According to Antinori, these three factors prompted him to give the venture serious consideration.

After visiting the 47-acre estate and meeting the team, Antinori agreed to the alliance. For Antinori, the final deciding issue was "the beauty of Malta, its great history, and the potential for tourism." In the beginning, he contributed his significant knowledge and expertise, but did not contribute any financial capital. In exchange, Antinori received 20% ownership in the business. According to Mark, "I wanted to entice him to become a participant in the company. I gave him 20% and he provided us with the technology."

Evolution of Strategic Alliances

Strategic partnerships are usually forged because they are mutually beneficial to both parties; they are maintained as long as both members continue to reap benefits. Partnerships in which a big, well-established firm works with a smaller firm are called *asymmetric strategic alliances*. Often, they have a contentious David vs. Goliath relationship – in the beginning, the smaller firm receives an infusion of much needed cash or expertise, but over time, the big firm reaps more advantages, often to the detriment of the smaller firm.

Just like any alliance, asymmetric strategic alliances evolve over time, but generally start out with both parties having a set of expectations. From the perspective of the big company, the benefits could be access to new ideas, technology, talent, and innovation. Because of this, it is not surprising that large firms with slow, bureaucratic structures often seek alliances with smaller, entrepreneurial firms (Alvarez and Barney 2001). A study by global consulting giant Accenture confirms that managers of large corporations expect to access skills, talent, and new markets (see Table A3.7).

Table A3.7 Benefits that large corporations expect from collaborating with entrepreneurs

Benefits	Percentage
Accessing specific skills and talent	53%
Entering new markets	50%
Improving return on in-house investment	48%
Accelerating disruptive innovation in your company	42%
Designing new products and services	40%
Enhancing company's brand/image	39%
Enhancing the entrepreneurial culture of your company	17%

Source: Accenture (2015)

The benefits to a small, entrepreneurial firm are generally focused on getting access to the larger corporation's expertise, processes, legitimacy, and capital. Oftentimes, a small firm simply will not be able to realize its full potential without a bigger, well-funded partner (Alvarez and Barney 2001) (see Table A3.8).

Table A3.8 Benefits which entrepreneurs expect from collaborating with large companies

Benefits	Percentage
Getting access to a large company's distribution network and customer base	49%
Being a supplier for large companies	45%
Securing investment from corporate venture funds	43%
Getting access to a large company's market knowledge	42%
Working together on joint innovation to develop new products and services	39%
Getting access to experts with specialized skills	34%
Benefiting from mentorship under accelerator/incubation programs	31%
Benefits from brand legitimization	17%

Source: Accenture (2015)

As the relationship evolves, the need for different skills also shifts. Specifically, creativity and technological know-how are most important in the early stages, whereas problem-solving skills, project management, and manufacturing capability are more important in the later stages of the project (Hogenhuis, Van Den Hende, and Hultink 2016) (see Figure A3.1).

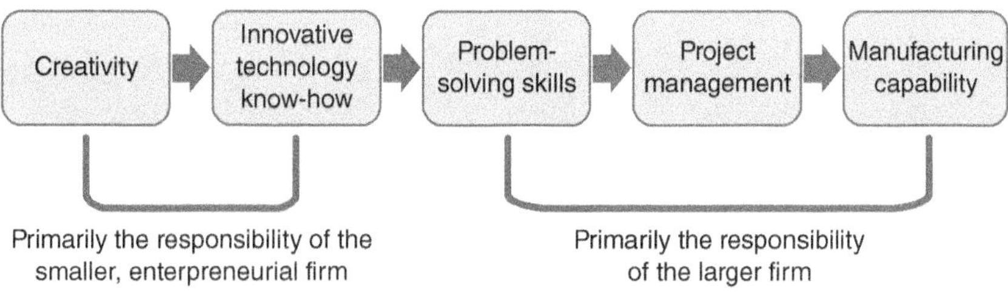

Figure A3.1 The evolution of a strategic alliance

Source: adapted from Hogenhuis, et al. (2016)

Because the bigger firm is often responsible for bringing new products to market and sustaining that effort over a period of time (Hogenhuis, et al. 2016), long-term financial benefits often go to the bigger firm (Alvarez and Barney 2001). When the only benefit the smaller firm has to offer is a new skill or innovation, it is particularly vulnerable (Alvaraz and Barney 2001). Unless the smaller, entrepreneurial firm can continue to contribute as the relationship evolves, Goliath firms have a tendency to gobble up the smaller, entrepreneurial Davids out there.

Evolution of the Meridiana Partnership

Just like other partnerships, Meridiana's strategic alliance evolved over time.

In the Beginning

At Antinori's urging, Mark obtained his vines from France. Thinking ahead to consumer demand, both agreed that the wines needed to be crafted from grapes that were well-known and respected – the "noble varieties" (Cabernet Sauvignon, Merlot, Syrah, and Chardonnay). Antinori introduced Mark to a variety of techniques to improve the soil, such as planting clover to add nitrogen, deep ploughing to encourage a deeper root structure, and adding organic fertilizer. Antinori also offered his expertise on a variety of other process and production improvements. Within a very short time, 90,000 vines were planted in precise, laser-guided rows, which would assist with later pruning, irrigation, and harvesting. In the end, five different varieties were planted. New vines typically take 2 years to become established and produce fruit, but to everyone's surprise, the soil, climate, and vines were so ideally matched that the first grapes started to appear in just 1 year. From the beginning, Antinori insisted that his name would not appear on the label. "His concern was that the project should prove itself on its own," remembered Mark. Mark agreed; from his perspective, the wine needed to be positioned as being completely grown and produced in Malta. Narrowly, he wanted locals to feel a sense of pride in the wine; more broadly, he wanted to challenge the existing perception within the global wine community that high-quality wines could not be produced in Malta (see Photo A3.5).

Photo A3.5 Meridiana Estates

Source: courtesy, Mark Miceli-Farrugia

Changing these long-held perceptions would not be easy, even locally. The Maltese have a cultural preference for foreign brands and often assume that local products are of inferior quality (de Aenlle 2004). The entire team set out to convince local restaurants, hotels, and distributors about Meridiana's superior quality and persuade them that it was worth its high price. "It was very difficult," Mark remembered, "we had to do a lot of wine-tastings. We had to convince the decision-makers in the trade. Every one. Every week! We invited them to the estate where they could see the beautiful stretch of vines and state-of the-art facility for themselves. They tried the wine and we gave them food – lots and lots of sandwiches!" he laughed. Pricing was an important part of its luxury image, so Meridiana was offered at more than twice the price of other Maltese wines. Soon, orders started to arrive and local restaurants recommended Meridiana wines on their menus; "that was when we really started breaking in," recalled Miceli-Farrugia.

As the Alliance Deepened

Over the next few years, as Meridiana started to produce and sell a consistently high-quality wine, the alliance strengthened because Antinori was convinced that Meridiana could live up to its potential. Antinori continued to provide expert help. For example, for the first several years, Meridiana would send samples of the wine to Antinori headquarters in Italy where experts would recommend the perfect combination of varieties for that year's harvest (e.g. 80% cabernet sauvignon and 20% merlot). After a few years, the Meridiana team was able to conduct this analysis on-site. Antinori soon provided €3 million and received another 20% ownership in the venture, for a total of 40%. This strengthened commitment from Antinori convinced local banks to also provide much-needed loans (€660,000) to further develop and expand the business.

At the same time, two important external factors influenced the alliance. The first was Malta's entry into the European Union (EU). Entry into the EU meant that many of the governmental protections designed to support Maltese companies would no longer be possible; they would now have to compete head-to-head with more experienced, better financed, and scalable firms. On 1 May 2004, Malta officially entered the EU and a flood of inexpensive foreign wine and grapes entered Malta, making it very difficult for local producers to survive. Sales of Meridiana's main competitor, Marsovin, dropped by 25%. Meridiana experienced no decrease in prices or sales – it continued to sell approximately 100,000 bottles per year (DeAenlle 2004), confirming that there was a market for high-quality, locally-made, premium-priced wines.

The second environmental factor impacting the alliance occurred when the Maltese government started to pursue Mark with several offers of global diplomatic posts. He eventually accepted a position as the Ambassador to the US, Canada, and the Commonwealth of The Bahamas in 2007. Leaving the team and his sister in charge of the day-to-day operations, he and Josette moved to Washington, DC for 4 years, where they enjoyed any occasion to share their wine with visiting business people and dignitaries. Even though his diplomatic duties kept him busy, he kept in regular contact with the estate and visited twice each year.

All Good Things Must Come to an End

Mark returned to Malta in mid-2011, ready to devote his full-time attention to Meridiana again. At this point, Meridiana was producing 200,000 bottles per year and receiving numerous international accolades. The alliance continued to be characterized by ongoing communication, joint decision-making, and capital investment. Importantly, both Mark and Antinori had a shared set of values revolving around long-term steady improvement of the vines, soil, and processes. Without the need to satisfy shareholders, Antinori could take a longer-term approach to the partnership. Further, as a result of the experience, Antinori started building a collection of individual estates located around the world to produce elite wines. He believed that "just because the company was centuries old did not mean it was safe. A company like ours is fragile because it is based on people, on passion" (Frank 2016). Antinori's strategy seemed to be working – the operation owned close to 30,000 acres of vineyards in Italy, was expanding to California and across Europe, produced more than 80 different wines (Gibson 2017), and made approximately €36 million in annual profit (Frank 2016).

As Antinori expanded and strengthened his business, Mark started to feel the weight of Meridiana's debt load. "Despite the fact that we were selling more wine, by the end of the day, we were spending €150,000 per year in finance charges. I wasn't taking a salary. It was becoming very, very expensive and the finance charges were mounting," Mark recalled. In the end, the remainder of the company was sold to Antinori in 2016. In exchange, he removed Meridiana's crushing debt load. "I wasn't looking for a lot," Mark recalled, "just to recover what I had put into it." Importantly, both parties agreed that Meridiana would continue to produce and sell Malta's highest-quality wine. The removal of the debt immediately improved the financial outlook of the firm (see Table A3.9).

Table A3.9 Meridiana income statements

	2018 (euros)	2017 (euros)
Revenue	1,406,985	1,260,725
Cost of sales	(789,961)	(724,213)
Gross profit	617,024	536,512
Administrative expenses	(99,734)	(107,317)
Selling and distribution expenses	(55,288)	(50,821)
Net other income	9,905	10,947
Operating profit	471,907	389,321
Finance costs	(10,520)	(22,984)
Profit before tax	461,387	366,337
Income tax charge	(206,046)	(160,872)
Profit for the year	255,341	205,465

Source: This financial statement was prepared by Ernst & Young and provided courtesy of Piero Antinori

Summary

By one estimate, close to 95% of new businesses fail. However, entrepreneurs are also uniquely qualified to understand that there are a myriad of financial *and* non-financial benefits to starting up a new business. Only an entrepreneur can truly understand the personal, financial, professional, and psychological costs of starting up a new business and seeing a dream come alive (Frankel 2016). After navigating a strategic alliance with one of the most distinguished wine operations in the world, Mark's decision to sell 100% of the estate to his business partner has left him weighing both the costs and the benefits of the project. In the end, could his decision to form an alliance with the Goliath of wines be considered a success?

ASSIGNMENT QUESTIONS

1. Identify the overriding goals for the alliance. From Mark's perspective, was the strategic alliance a success? From Antinori's perspective, was it a success? Create a comprehensive list of the extrinsic measures of success as well as the intrinsic measures of success that Mark could use to determine whether or not the venture was successful.
2. Calculate the gross profit margin and the net profit margin for 2017 and 2018. What do these numbers indicate about the financial health of Meridiana?
3. At the beginning of the partnership, what specific benefits did each partner expect to receive from the alliance? In the end, how well did each partner's benefits match their initial expectations?
4. Take a careful look at the evolution of the strategic alliance over time and compare what happened to the five steps outlined in Figure A3.1. For each step in the figure, in what way did each of the partners utilize that particular skill? Explain.
5. When the "David" in an asymmetric strategic alliance is able to contribute skills throughout the entire evolution of the relationship, the alliance ends up being a more collaborative "David and Goliath" relationship, as opposed to a "David vs. Goliath" relationship. According to Tables A3.7 and A3.8, how successful was this asymmetric strategic alliance? Looking again at Question 4 above, how successful was this asymmetric strategic alliance?

References

Accenture. 2015. *Harnessing the Power of Entrepreneurs to Open Innovation*. Accenture. Young Entrepreneurs' Alliance Summit, Turkey.

Alvarez, S.A. and Barney, J.B. 2001. How entrepreneurial firms can benefit from alliances with large partners. *Academy of Management Executive, 15* (1), 139–48.

Caruana Galizia, D. 1994. Antinori to back new Malta winery. *The Times of Malta*. 19 March. 25.

CIA. 2020. *The World Factbook*. Accessed 22 April 2020. www.cia.gov/library/publications/the-world-factbook/geos/mt.html.

DeAenlle, C. 2004. With EU membership, Malta finds its wine industry under assault. 14 August. *The New York Times*. Accessed May 28, 2020. www.nytimes.com/2004/08/14/business/worldbusiness/with-eu-membership-malta-finds-its-wine-industry.html.

Ernst & Young. 2019. *Independent Auditor's Report to the Shareholders of Meridiana Wine Estate Limited*. Ernst & Young Malta Limited, Certified Public Accountants. 14 June.

Frank, M. 2016. The Family Trust. *Wine Spectator*. 30 April. Accessed 22 March 2020. https://top100.winespectator.com/article/the-family-trust/.

Frankel, R. 2016. How do entrepreneurs define success? *Forbes*. 29 February. Accessed 4 June 2020. www.forbes.com/sites/ryanfrankel/2016/02/29/how-do-entrepreneurs-define-success/#4acffcbb6d4c.

Gibson, A. 2017. Albiera Antinori Talks Wine, Family, and Business. *Forbes*. 17 July. Accessed 22 March 2020. www.forbes.com/sites/ambergibson/2017/07/17/albiera-antinori/#dc5d01e1856e.

Hogenhuis, B.N., Van Den Hende, E.A., and Hultink, E.J. 2016. "When should large firms collaborate with young ventures?" *Research-Technology Management*. January–February. 39–46.

Virbila, I. 2014. More than 600 Years of Chianti History in Piero Antinori's New Book. *Los Angeles Times*. 8 September. Accessed 22 March 2020. www.latimes.com/food/dailydish/la-dd-antinori-chianti-book-20140908-story.html.

Visit Malta. 2022. History. Accessed 30 September 2022. https://www.visitmalta.com/en/a/history/.

DEAR TOURISTS, PLEASE STOP WALKING AROUND IN YOUR BIKINIS. LOVE, VENICE

Diane M. Phillips and Jason Keith Phillips

As she did most mornings, Chiara Amadi[8] bent down to pick up a pile of trash left on her doorstep the night before by some tourists. Amadi is a highly-placed official in the City of Venice and knows first-hand some of the frustrations of living there. Her job is to help the City maintain a thriving tourism industry, while also balancing the needs of tourists and the City's increasingly-small population. How can Amadi encourage more sustainable tourism so that the City she loves continues to thrive for generations to come? More specifically, should her overall marketing objective be limiting the number of tourists or better managing the tourists once they arrive?

The Floating City

Venice can trace its origins to the 6th century, when individuals found refuge from invading barbarians in the lagoon on the Italy's northeast coast. These individuals and their descendants formed a vibrant and prosperous city on 118 small islands, connected by over 400 bridges. Because much of the City sits at sea level, it seems to float on water. Founded in the 8th century, the Republic of Venice relied on the sea for its power and influence. It soon became one of the most important global maritime powers and flexed its maritime might against numerous political

---

[8]This official prefers to remain anonymous. Chiara Amadi is a pseudonym.

and economic foes. By the 9th and 10th centuries, Venice was one of most powerful economic forces in the world. Its ships returned with goods from the far stretches of the world, and traders, merchants, and bankers prospered. The City also became a center for artists, writers, church leaders, and politicians. When the remains of St. Mark were brought back from Alexandria, Egypt in 828 by crusaders and the City built a cathedral in his honor in 1094, Venice became an important stop for crusaders traveling to the Holy Land (History 2019). Over the following centuries, the streets of Venice were alive with a global array of foods, spices, and products, as well as languages, customs, fashion, and music.

By the 15th and 16th centuries, for the first time in history, people started to travel for pleasure and Venice became an important destination. Tourism became an important economic driver for the City by the 17th century, helped by wealthy tourists eager to participate in Carnival and a variety of other artistic and cultural activities. The tourism industry further grew as restaurants, hotels, and entertainment venues opened to accommodate the growing number of visitors (Cernanova 2015) (see Photo A3.6).

Photo A3.6 The City of Venice

Source: Courtesy, Diane M. Phillips

A City in Distress

Venice officials work hard to balance the needs of several important stakeholder groups, including its residents, tourists, and tourist-related businesses. However, between 26 and 30 million tourists visit Venice each year (Warren 2019) and, as a consequence, the floating city is experiencing some very serious difficulties. Residents are finding the living conditions so unbearable that about 2000 of them leave every year. By 2017, the population was about 54,000 and declining (Giuffrida 2017). According to some experts, three big problems contribute to Venice's distress: massive overcrowding by tourists, devastating flooding, and damage from cruise ships.

Overcrowding

Approximately 82,000 tourists visit the City each day (Warren 2019) and, especially during high season, long lines can be found at restaurants, museums, and other attractions. Hordes of tourists often create bottlenecks on bridges and in alleyways, public transit boats are standing-room-only, hotel rooms are scarce, trash starts to pile up, and everyone's nerves get frayed. If these tourists arrive by cruise ship (44,000 during peak times), the experience is particularly bad. "The people who come for just a few hours and see nothing – it's as much of a nightmare for them," said one local (Giuffrida 2017). Any effort to encourage sustainable tourism needed to consider the needs of the tourists and how their experience is negatively affected by overcrowding, long lines, crime, and expensive hotels and restaurants.

By far, the largest numbers of tourists each year come from the US – about 549,000. This is followed by the UK (292,000), France (227,000), Germany (186,000), and China (173,000)

(Annuario del Turismo 2017). These individuals demonstrate very different behaviors with respect to where they stay (see Table A3.10).

Table A3.10 Where international tourists stay in Venice (in 000s)

Global Region	Total Arrivals	Total Overnight Stays	Hotel Arrivals	Hotel Overnight Stays	Other* Arrivals	Other* Overnight Stays
Europe	2,053	5,505	1,393	3,554	660	1,951
The Americas	1,233	2,547	949	1,848	284	699
Asia	690	1,179	570	913	120	266
Israel & Middle East	81	181	63	135	18	46
Africa	48	122	36	84	12	38
Oceana	159	383	101	233	58	150

* Includes hostels, holiday homes, and residential homes for tourist use (e.g., Airbnb and others).

Source: Annuario del Turismo (2017, 40–41)

On average, tourists who stay in the City spend 2.32 nights in overnight accommodations (Annuario del Turismo 2017). Italian and international tourists demonstrate different behaviors with their overnight stays and these behaviors have changed over time (see Tables A3.11 and A3.12).

Table A3.11 Where Italian tourists stay in Venice, 2013–17 (in 000s)

Year	Total Arrivals	Total Overnight Stays	Hotel Arrivals	Hotel Overnight Stays	Other* Arrivals	Other Overnight Stays
2013	566	1,357	444	889	122	468
2014	595	1,501	465	1,063	130	438
2015	598	1,394	458	934	141	460
2016	651	1,528	496	1,005	154	524
2017	679	1,624	506	1,038	173	568

* Includes hostels, holiday homes, and residential homes for tourist use (e.g., Airbnb and others).

Source: Annuario del Turismo (2017, 32)

Table A3.12 Where international tourists stay in Venice, 2013–17 (in 000s)

Year	Total Arrivals	Total Overnight Stays	Hotel Arrivals	Hotel Overnight Stays	Other* Arrivals	Other* Overnight Stays
2013	3,686	8,421	3,000	6,357	686	2,064
2014	3,686	8,482	2,947	6,482	740	1,999
2015	3,898	8,788	3,068	6,596	830	2,193
2016	3,995	8,983	3,095	6,626	900	2,357
2017	4,356	10,061	3,203	6,907	1,153	3,154

* Includes hostels, holiday homes, and residential homes for tourist use (e.g., Airbnb and others).

Source: Annuario del Turismo (2017, 31)

Adding to the problem of the sheer numbers of tourists is the fact that many of them behave badly. In 2020, two German tourists were fined $395 each for swimming in Venice's Grand Canal (DiDonato and Woodyatt 2020). Other tourists, motivated by social media, take videos of themselves jumping into the canals or doing other outlandish things. Still others set up tents and sleep in public spaces, walk around in bare feet and bikinis, or have a picnic on the steps of cathedrals, museums, or even people's homes.

Devastating Floods

Venetians are used to periodic flooding and are certainly capable of handling the seasonal flooding period called "Acqua Alta," which runs from fall through spring. Hardy Venetians simply set up high-water walkways so that they can move about. Most buildings have protective gates on their doors and windows to prevent water from coming in. Citizens can check the Hi!Tide app to see how high the floodwaters are in different neighborhoods. However, the flooding in recent years had been unlike anything Venetians have ever seen. In October 2018, an especially bad storm combined with strong winds flooded 77% of the City. The water was waist-high in some areas and ranked as the fifth worst flooding event in recorded history (Giuffrida 2019). In November 2019, a sudden Aqua Alta resulted in water that reached its highest level in 50 years, the second worst in history. Lasting several days, the water reached two meters deep in some streets and inflicted severe damage to countless homes, churches, and other historic buildings. It the words of Venice's mayor, it "brought the city to its knees" (Provoledo 2019).

This unprecedented flooding is happening because of rising sea levels from climate change and the fact that Venice itself is sinking by a several millimeters each year. Climate scientists predict that in the future, Venice will experience more frequent and intense flooding events – flooding that historically occurred once every 100 years will occur once every 5–6 years (Fritz and Pitrelli 2018). Adding insult to injury, Venice's new flood-protection floodgates were inoperable when the 2018 and 2019 flood waters hit (Fritz and Pitrelli 2018, Provoledo 2019). Plagued by mismanagement and corruption, the €6 billion floodgates have had countless construction delays and breakdowns (Gerard-Sharp 2017).

Cruise Ships

The number and size of cruise ships visiting Venice has increased dramatically in recent years. They travel through the delicate canals at least six times per day, emitting air pollution, obliterating the view, and causing waves that damage the delicate buildings, their foundations, and other structures. They also damage the delicate ecological balance of the lagoon and scrape away the underlying sediment that stabilizes the islands (Warren 2019).

Global Overtourism

Overtourism occurs when there are too many people for the existing infrastructure (Street 2018a) and is by no means a problem unique to Venice. The number of international tourists grew from 278 million people in 1980, to 674 million in 2000, to 1.3 billion in 2017 (Pannett 2018), and may reach 3 billion by 2050 (Tourtellot 2018/2019). Unfortunately, this increase in tourism is pushing some local communities and residents to breaking point.

Around the world, some tourists behave quite badly by ignoring local customs and basic standards of behavior. In Spain, the Philippines, and Thailand, tourists simply drop their trash on the beaches (Street 2018a). In Rome, street drinking is common, as is taking a dip in the City's fountains (Street 2018b). Many tourists are unprepared or too inexperienced for their adventures. In New Zealand, one group of clueless hikers needed to be rescued when they tried to walk barefoot up Mount Ngauruhoe after it appeared in the *Lord of the Rings* movies (Pannett 2018). Few places in the world are immune from overtourism and sometimes, overcrowding and inexperience can turn deadly. During the summer of 2019, eleven people died trying to reach the top of Mt. Everest, the world's highest mountain. The deaths were blamed on the record number of hiking permits issued by the Nepalese government, which brought record numbers of climbers – many of them inexperienced – to the top of Everest, where they paused to take selfies and enjoy the view as others waited in line for their turn. The air is so thin at the top of Everest, that the last 1000 feet of the climb is a do-or-die race to get up and then get down, otherwise climbers run out of oxygen and die (Schultz, Gettleman, Mashal, and Sharma 2019). Although most climbers carry supplemental oxygen tanks, *any* delay can prove fatal (Pokharel, Stapleton, and Said-Moorhouse 2019).

Overtourism Drivers

Four factors drive overtourism: enabling technology, social media pressure, increasing affluence, and increasing population.

Enabling Technology

Technology has empowered tourists and reduced barriers to international travel. Mobile apps for language translation, currency exchange, and mapping help tourists easily navigate unfamiliar areas. Other services like Uber, Airbnb, and TripAdvisor allow tourists to plan and design their own trips. One of the biggest culprits of overtourism is Airbnb. Although there are many home- sharing services, Airbnb is the biggest, so it gets the most attention. Tourism industry experts in Amsterdam report that Airbnb was responsible for 12% of all its overnight bookings there in 2017; in Barcelona it was 18%; and in Kyoto it was 22%. Airbnb claims that 97% of the money goes to locals who list their homes (Manjoo 2018). Others claim that outside investors purchase property in tourist hotspots to reap the financial benefits, which drives up local property prices and drives out local homeowners.

Social Media

Social media also encourages international travel in two different respects. First, monitoring the social media posts of influencers and others helps would-be travelers become inspired and more comfortable by seeing people just like themselves experience all the world has to offer. Second, individuals post about the trip to their own social networks. Geotags help others see where the traveler has been and, importantly, getting likes, comments, and shares validates the tourist's experience.

Affluence

Around the world, individuals simply have more money to travel. The world's middle class is expected to top 4.2 billion people by 2022 (Tourtellot, 2018/2019). One respected global think-tank found that, for the first time ever, more than half of the world's citizens were now living in "middle class" conditions or better, with the ability to purchase a range of consumer products, indulge in various forms of entertainment, and take vacations (Kharas and Hamel 2018).

Increasing Population

Simply put, there are just more people on the planet now than ever before. In 2022, the global population surpassed 8 billion people and experts predict that by 2080, the global population will be 10.4 billion (UN 2022).

Reaction to Overtourism

Around the world, the problem of overtourism and its impacts was gathering a great deal of attention. "Tourist go home" graffiti started to appear and local residents staged protests and demonstrations. Worried local officials started to react. In Thailand and the Philippines, officials closed down several popular tourist beaches to allow for ecosystem recovery from the onslaught of people and their trash (Street, 2018a, Tourtellot, 2018/2019). In 2019, officials in Iceland banned any new permits for new hotel construction in its capital city of Reykjavik when they discovered that the number of tourists was *six times* the population of the entire country (Tourtellot, 2018/2019). Barcelona cracked down on the number of unlicensed Airbnb rentals (Coldwell 2017) and Iceland restricted Airbnb rentals to 90 days per year. In an effort to spread tourists out across the country, Peru launched an advertising campaign to promote attractions other than Machu Pichu (Street 2018a). In Rome, police officers started issuing citations for tourists who drank alcohol in the street or took a swim in the City's fountains (Street 2018b).

One of the stronger reactions came from the small Italian town of Matera, where in 2018, the mayor declared "We don't want tourists." The town council and many of its residents worried that the notoriety of the town's recent designation as a UNESCO World Heritage Site[9] would increase tourism and fundamentally change the town's character and authenticity. Officials responded by issuing tourism permits at €19 per person to participate in any festivities (such as art exhibitions or food and music festivals) celebrating UNESCO's recognition (Pergament 2018).

Because many tourist destinations are one-of-a-kind cultural and historical assets for all of humanity, the international community has also taken notice. The City of Venice got a wake-up call in 2014 when the World Monument Fund put Venice on its "watch list" because "large-scale cruising is pushing the City to an environmental tipping point and undermining the quality of life for its citizens" (Gerard-Sharp 2017; Warren 2019). Another hit occurred when UNESCO threatened to put Venice on its "in danger" list, a designation typically reserved for war-torn countries and desperately-poor sites in developing regions of the world (Gerard-Sharp 2017).

Venice officials needed to do something. In May 2018, they installed turnstiles to limit the number of tourists who could enter the City's residential areas, but locals become so irate that they tore down several of them. In early 2019, they contemplated a plan to charge daytrippers – people who arrived for the day, visited some of the top sights, and left – a small fee to enter the City. To control traffic during peak times, the fee could be increased (Giuffrida 2019). Implementation of the fees was put on hold during the pandemic, but the City planned to implement the €3 fee (€5 – €10 during peak times) in 2023 (CBS/AP 2022).

Summary

Amadi knew that a longer-term, more sustainable solution was needed – one that balanced the needs of tourism-related businesses, local citizens, and tourists. The first decision, however, was

[9]UNESCO is the United Nations Educational, Scientific, and Cultural Organization. It designates special areas as World Heritage Sites because of their unique cultural, scientific, or historic significance. This designation provides the area with international legal protections.

the overall marketing objective. Should she promote a plan to *limit* the number of tourists coming into the City or a plan that would better *manage* the tourists once they arrive? Each alternative involved different measures and represented different implications to stakeholders. Amadi and her family have called Venice home since the early 1700s, so she understood what was at stake – Venice must survive in order to inspire many more generations to come.

ASSIGNMENT QUESTIONS

1 Should the City of Venice work to *limit* the number of tourists or should it work to better *manage* the tourists? Support your answer with details from the case and elsewhere.
2 An overall objective of limiting tourists vs. managing tourists will result in very different marketing strategy decisions. For the objective you selected in question 1, create a detailed and thoughtful set of recommendations for each part of the marketing mix.
3 Tourists to Venice come from many different regions of the world. Use Table A3.10 to calculate the market share for tourists coming from each region, for both hotel arrivals and overnight stays as well as other arrivals and overnight stays. Create at least two managerially-relevant insights and recommendations based on these findings.
4 Using Tables A3.11 and A3.12, calculate the percentage change over the 5-year period in the number of Italian tourists and international tourists who stay in hotels and "other" accommodations. Create at least two managerially-relevant insights from these findings.
5 For each part of the Triple Bottom Line, describe two to three important issues that Amadi and the City of Venice must consider when making the decision about how to develop a sustainable solution to this problem.
6 Which part of the Triple Bottom Line should be most important to Amadi and the City of Venice – people, planet, or prosperity? Why? Support your answer with evidence from the case and elsewhere.

References

Annuario del Turismo. 2017. Città di Venezia, Assessorato al Turismo.

CBS/AP. 2022. Venice to Impose Fee on Day-Trippers to Preserve Historic City. 4 July. Accessed 1 October 2022. https://www.cbsnews.com/news/venice-unveils-mandatory-day-trippers-reservation-and-fee/.

Cernanova, I. 2015. Tourism in Early Modern Venice. *Vanderbilt Historical Review*, 24 November. Accessed 30 July 2019. http://vanderbilthistoricalreview.com/tourism-in-early-modern-venice/.

Cilluffo, A. and Ruiz, N.G. 2019. World's Population is Projected to Nearly Stop Growing by the End of the Century. *FactTank: News in the Numbers*. Pew Research Center. 17 June. Accessed 1 August 2019. www.pewresearch.org/fact-tank/2019/06/17/worlds-population-is-projected-to-nearly-stop-growing-by-the-end-of-the-century/.

Coldwell, W. 2017. First Venice and Barcelona: Now Anti-Tourism Marches Spread Across Europe. *The Guardian*. 10 August. Accessed 29 July 2019. www.theguardian.com/travel/2017/aug/10/anti-tourism-marches-spread-across-europe-venice-barcelona.

DiDonato, V. and Woodyatt, A. 2020. German tourists fined $790 for swimming in Venice's Grand Canal. *CNN Travel*. 5 June. Accessed 8 June 2020. www.cnn.com/travel/article/tourist-fine-italy-canal-intl-scli-grm/index.html.

Fritz, A. and Pitrelli, S. 2018. Three Quarters of Venice Just Flooded while its Costly Flood Gate Sits Unfinished. *The Washington Post*. 30 October. Accessed 30 July 2019. www.washingtonpost.com/weather/2018/10/30/three-quarters-venice-just-flooded-while-its-costly-flood-gate-sits-unfinished/?utm_term=.cedd46730b75.

Gerard-Sharp, L. 2017. Venice World Heritage Status Under Threat. *The Guardian*. 26 May. Accessed 30 July 2019. www.theguardian.com/travel/2017/may/26/venice-tourists-cruise-ships-pollution-italy-biennale.

Giuffrida, A. 2017. "Imagine Living with this Crap:" Tempers in Venice Boil Over in Tourist High Season. *The Guardian*. 22 July. Accessed 29 July 2019. www.theguardian.com/world/2017/jul/23/venice-tempers-boil-over-tourist-high-season.

Giuffrida, A. 2019. The Death of Venice? City's Battles with Tourism and Flooding Reach Crisis Level. *The Guardian*. 6 January. Accessed 30 July 2019. www.theguardian.com/world/2019/jan/06/venice-losing-fight-with-tourism-and-flooding.

History. 2019. Basilica di San Marco. Accessed 30 July 2019. www.basilicasanmarco.it.

Kharas, H. and Hamel, K. 2018. A Global Tipping Point: Half the World is Now Middle Class or Wealthier. *The Brookings Institute, Future Development*. 27 September. Accessed 1 August 2019. www.brookings.edu/blog/future-development/2018/09/27/a-global-tipping-point-half-the-world-is-now-middle-class-or-wealthier/.

Manjoo, F. 2018. "Overtourism" and the Role of Technology. *The New York Times*, Business/Financial Desk, 167(58070), 20 August, B1–B2.

Pannett, R. 2018. Anger over Tourists Swarming Vacation Hot Spots Sparks Global Backlash; In Venice, Barcelona, Thailand, and New Zealand, "Overtouristing" is Straining Local Infrastructure and Prompting Restrictions; The "Lord of the Rings" Effect. *Wall Street Journal* (Online). New York. 22 May, n/a.

Pergament, D. 2018. An Ancient Corner of Italy Finds the World on its Doorstep. *New York Times* (Online). New York. 3 December.

Pokharel, S., Stapleton, A., and Said-Moorhouse, L. 2019. Mount Everest Death Toll Rises to 11 Amid Overcrowding Concerns. *CNN World*. 28 May. Accessed 29 July 2019. www.cnn.com/2019/05/27/asia/mount-everest-deaths-intl/index.html.

Provoledo, E. 2019. Venice flooding brings city "to its knees." *The New York Times*. 13 November. Accessed 5 June 2020. www.nytimes.com/2019/11/13/world/europe/venice-flood.html.

Schultz, K., Gettleman, J., Mashal, M., and Sharma, B. 2019. It's "Like a Zoo" at Everest's Tip as Deaths Soar [Foreign Desk]. *The New York Times, Late Edition (East Coast)*. New York. 27 May. A1.

Street, F. 2018a. Can the World be Saved from Overtourism? *CNN Travel*, 3 October. Accessed 29 July 2019. www.cnn.com/travel/article/overtourism-solutions/index.html.

Street, F. 2018b. Rome Issues New Laws to Tackle Unruly Tourism. *CNN Travel*. 15 November. Accessed 29 July 2019. https://edition.cnn.com/travel/article/rome-unruly-tourists/index.html.

Tourtellot, J.B. 2018/2019. Why it Matters: Overtourism. *National Geographic Traveler, 35* (6), Washington, December/January, 30–31.

UN. 2022. 'World Population to Reach 8 Billion on 15 November 2022'. Department of Economic and Social Affairs. The United Nations. Accessed 30 November 2022, https://www.un.org/en/desa/world-population-reach-8-billion-15-november-2022.

Warren, K. 2019. Disappointing Photos Show What Venice Looks Like in Real Life, From Extreme Overcrowding and Devastating Floods to Pollution from Cruise Ships. *Business Insider*. 18 January. Accessed 29 July 2019. www.businessinsider.com/disappointing-photos-show-venice-italy-expectation-vs-reality-2018-12.

COFFEE AND CUSTOMER LOYALTY AT WAWA

Dena Caiozzo and Diane M. Phillips

Anyone living along the East Coast of the US has heard of Wawa, the chain of convenience stores famous for its friendly service, good coffee, made-to-order sandwiches, and competitively-priced gas. Wawa's marketing team was currently contemplating two options designed to increase customer loyalty: should Wawa provide free travel coffee mugs to its most frequent coffee customers, or to their infrequent coffee customers to encourage them to increase their coffee purchases? Enter Marketing Manager, Dena Caiozzo.

A Beloved Convenience Store

Wawa is a privately-run organization with 38,000 associates and $11 billion US in annual revenue (Mulligan 2021). Headquartered on the outskirts of Philadelphia, it was best known for its variety of fresh food and beverages, including coffee, build-to-order hoagies,[10] breakfast sandwiches, and specialty beverages. Its approximately 1000 stores offered a variety of packaged goods, convenience items, and fuel. Wawa had operations in six states including Pennsylvania, New Jersey, Delaware, Maryland, Virginia, and Florida. By 2021, Wawa was ranked #29 on the Forbes' list of largest privately-held companies in the US (Mulligan 2021).

Founded in 1803, Wawa had very humble beginnings and manufactured a variety of items over the years. By 1902, it opened a dairy processing plant in Wawa, Pennsylvania. The name "Wawa" originated from a local Native American name for the Canada Goose, which migrated through the area on its way south every fall. In 1964, the company opened its first retail store to sell its dairy products and in 1975, it introduced fresh-brewed coffee to busy customers. The company was one of America's most beloved convenience stores and regularly received accolades as an outstanding employer.

[10]"Hoagie" is the local Philadelphia term for a submarine or grinder sandwich – one with lunchmeat, cheese, lettuce, tomato, onion, and other toppings.

Wawa sold millions of built-to-order hoagies annually and, despite being more of a regional presence, was the sixth largest brewed coffee seller in the US (Parmley 2016), selling more than 195 million cups of coffee each year (Staff 2014). Wawa continued its geographical expansion goals with frequent new store openings in both traditional and new markets. At the same time, the marketing team developed new ways to engage with consumers through digital channels, including its mobile app and delivery service. Food and beverage made up more than half of Wawa's annual revenue (Parmley 2016).

Wawa Coffee

The Wawa coffee bar played a central role in the store layout and traffic. Up to a dozen carafes of freshly-brewed coffee, complete with a multitude of creamers, milks, sweeteners, and toppings, occupied a large footprint within the store. Customers served themselves the ready-to-drink coffee and could customize their drinks to their tastes. Core varieties such as regular, decaf, and hazelnut were offered year-round while limited time offerings were periodically introduced. Despite all of the choices, regular coffee was still the most popular variety. While most customers took a disposable cup to fill their ready-to-drink coffee, they had the option of using a refillable mug and would receive a small discount when doing so. In addition to fresh-brewed self-serve coffee, Wawa also offered lattes, macchiatos, cappuccinos, and iced coffees that were made to order by a team member. Brew-at-home varieties such as bagged coffee and K-Cups were also available on store shelves for consumers to purchase. Coffee was big business at Wawa.

Coffee Trends

Across America, coffee was extremely popular, with approximately 62% of adults drinking it daily. Older Americans were particularly fond of coffee – more than 68% of consumers over 60 consumed it daily (DeRupo 2017). The entire market was worth approximately \$16.7 billion and was expected to grow to \$18.9 billion by 2026. At home, Americans liked to brew their coffee from grounds (32%) or from coffee pods (19%) (Mintel 2021). The popularity of coffee may have been due, in part, to its health benefits. Studies have suggested, for example, that coffee can decrease cardiovascular disease (i.e., Andersen, et al. 2006), diabetes (Odegaard, et al. 2008), and stroke (Kokubo, et al. 2013). Coffee's all-important caffeine kick also makes it an essential part of the fast-paced lives of many consumers (Mintel 2021).

Coffee Promotions

Several times each year, Wawa launches coffee promotions, which are often focused on price (any size coffee for \$1.00) and are supported with advertising, including television, radio, and social media. Occasionally, the company offers free coffee for all customers – no coupon or ID required – for a day (for example, "Wawa Day" in April). The company estimates that it gives away 1.7 million free cups of coffee for events like these (Genovese 2016). These events generate media attention, enhance consumer enthusiasm, and increase sales.

Wawa Customers

Wawa enjoyed an almost fanatical following, with many customers claiming that they felt a strong sense of family when visiting the stores. It was not unusual for customers to stop in every day just to say "hello" and get their cup of coffee to start the day. When loyal customers traveled out of town, it was comforting to visit Wawa again when they returned; it was almost like going home. One customer likened the store to a friendly, all-American experience: "it's like, apple pie and Wawa, you know?" (Drankoski 2016).

An important element in building and maintaining customer loyalty at Wawa was its passionate group of team members. Unlike the quick turnover experienced at most convenience stores and fast-food outlets, it was not unusual for Wawa employees to stay for decades. This was, in part, due to the attractive set of benefits and employee stock ownership program, 41% of the company was owned by employees via this program (Drankoski 2016).

Another factor contributing to strong customer loyalty was the company's strong commitment to their local communities. For example, in coordination with the Children's Hospital of Philadelphia (CHOP), Wawa employees and volunteers staffed a coffee cart and offered free coffee to anyone visiting a child at the hospital. Overseeing many of these efforts, The Wawa Foundation was established to support three main priorities – health, hunger, and everyday heroes. Together, Wawa and the Foundation committed $50 million over 5 years to support these causes (Staff 2018).

Wawa customers demonstrated their loyalty and passion for the brand in a variety of ways. Couples got married in stores, had Wawa tattoos inked on their bodies, and created social media content about the brand. This loyalty is so strong that some have even described it as a "cult brand" (Mashable 2016). Marketing research firm Nielsen ranked Wawa number one in convenience store brand equity (Staff 2017), indicating that customers associated strong value with the brand, above and beyond that of a simple convenience store. Many customers visited daily, particularly morning coffee buyers. On average, a Wawa customer spent $7.42 per trip, far above the industry average of $4.12 at other convenience stores (Aspan 2018).

Customer Loyalty at Wawa

There are two different types of customer loyalty. *Attitudinal loyalty* is a positive inclination toward the brand; consumers like the brand, are committed to it, and believe in the brand's value proposition. *Behavioral loyalty* is based on what consumers actually do. It is often demonstrated by repeat, even habitual, purchases. Not surprisingly, both are highly correlated with one another – obviously, if customers have positive attitudes toward brands, they will likely buy those brands (Chaudhuri and Holbrook 2001). Distinguishing between these two types of loyalty is important because it provides marketers guidance on how to measure, track, and influence loyalty. When consumers exhibit attitudinal loyalty, they are willing to pay a higher price for the product. However, when consumers exhibit behavioral loyalty, sales and market share increase (Chaudhuri and Holbrook 2001).

Decision-makers at Wawa believed that their customers demonstrated both behavioral and attitudinal loyalty toward the brand. Behaviorally, the marketing team had quantitative data demonstrating that for some consumers, a trip to Wawa was a habit; some even visited several times each day. From an attitudinal perspective, qualitative data indicated that customers clearly loved the brand; they appreciated the good food and coffee, reasonable prices, atmosphere, and friendly staff.

The concept of customer lifetime value (LTV) suggests that it is far more profitable to keep your loyal customers satisfied than it is to recruit new customers. LTV aligns closely to the behavioral conceptualization of loyalty because it focuses on a consumer's purchasing patterns. LTV is measured by combining all of the revenue generated from a customer in one time period (a month, a year) and then multiplying that revenue by the amount of time the customer has a relationship with the firm (Peppers and Rogers 2011). The concept of LTV was a central component to the marketing team's discussions about the coffee promotion.

The Rewards Club program provided the company with a way to reward loyal shoppers for purchases they were already making. Just like its regular customers, members that signed up for the loyalty program represented a wide range of demographics. Millennials and Baby Boomers each comprised about one third of the registrations and gender was split almost evenly between men (49%) and women (51%). By far, the most commonly purchased item and the most redeemed reward was coffee.

The loyalty program was supported by Wawa's mobile app, which was introduced at the same time. The app allowed customers to find store locations, see current fuel prices, and view nutritional information. Upon joining the loyalty program, new members could select a free beverage as a thank you. After joining the program, members were offered a reward based on their spending such that each time a member reached $50 in eligible spending, they would receive a choice of three rewards. One big benefit to the Rewards program was the generation of vast amounts of data on Wawa's customer purchasing habits.

A few years after the loyalty program's launch, the marketing team, headed by Dena Caiozzo, faced a challenge. After several years of operation, the team wanted to leverage the loyalty data to drive optimal member engagement and help the company achieve its broader sales goals. With long-term coffee trends looking positive, people increasingly on-the-go, and deeply loyal customers, Caiozzo and her team set their sights on a coffee-related loyalty promotion.

The Idea

In examining the loyalty data, the marketing team wondered if Rewards members were aware that using a refillable mug would offer additional savings. The company sold four different sizes of refillable travel mugs and customers paid different prices for refills for those different sized mugs. The price to purchase a refillable travel mug for the most frequently-purchased size of coffee, 20oz, was $2.29. The team proposed sending a coupon to select Rewards Club members for a free 20oz mug. At the same time, a communications program could inform customers that using the mug for coffee refills would save money (see Table A3.13). It is important to note that Wawa would save about $0.09 for the cost of the take-away cup, sleeve, and lid for each refill purchase.[11] The key question was who should receive the offer. One alternative would be to send the offer to the highest-frequency coffee buyers in order to thank them for their loyalty and encourage even more coffee purchases. Alternatively, an offer could be sent to low-frequency coffee buyers to encourage more frequent purchases. The key decision criterion was straightforward: the free mug would go to the group of consumers that had the highest potential for increased sales.

Table A3.13 Coffee retail prices

Size	Regular Price	Refill Price
Coffee 12 oz	$1.45	$1.19
Coffee 16 oz	$1.55	$1.29
Coffee 20 oz	$1.69	$1.45
Coffee 24 oz	$1.79	$1.55

Source: courtesy, Wawa, Inc.

[11]The industry standard for these items is approximately $0.09.

The Experimental Set-Up

The overall marketing objective was to increase the number of monthly visits by Rewards Club members. The rationale was that once a customer entered the store to make a purchase, other items would likely be purchased too. Caiozzo and her team needed to examine the existing Rewards Club data more closely to help them make the decision about whether the free mug should go to low-frequency customers or high-frequency customers. Loyalty data would provide insights about Rewards Club members based on a customer's pattern of coffee purchases over the previous 2 months. The data would provide information about who made purchases, how often they purchased, what size coffee they purchased, and other items that were purchased at the same time. In all, the data would reveal whether the low-frequency or high-frequency group would generate more visits and thus increase overall sales.

In order to test both alternatives, the marketing team pulled a list of customers who had purchased coffee through the Rewards Club and broke out two tiers by frequency of visit: high and low. Then, a random sample of consumers was selected to be the test group and another sample was selected to be the control group. Low-frequency members would include coffee buyers with an average of 1–4 visits in the past 2 months, while high frequency coffee buyers averaged 30 to 60 visits in the same time frame. When conducting the analysis, the team also wanted to review coupon redemption rates, the number of visits, store-level spend, and product-specific spend, including sales of coffee. The team compared results for the test group with those of the control group (see Table A3.14).

Table A3.14 Experimental set-up

	Test Group	Control Group
Low-frequency customers: average 2.5 visits/month (range = 1–4 visits/month)	1000	1000
High-frequency customers: average 45 visits/month (range = 30–60 visits/month)	500	500

Source: courtesy, Wawa, Inc.

Research Assumptions

As with any research project, the researchers need to clarify some assumptions before proceeding. The first step was to estimate the redemption rates for the offer. Based on previous data, as well as the fact that the offer of a free coffee mug was relevant, high value, and long lasting, the team agreed that the redemption rate would likely be relatively high. Low-frequency members were expected to have a 30% redemption rate, while high-frequency members were expected to have a 60% redemption rate.

The second assumption was that low-frequency members would double their visits after getting the coffee mug, but the high-frequency members would only increase their visits by about 5%. These estimates were based on previous promotions with low- and high-frequency Rewards Club members. A key question here was whether the increase in low-frequency visits would be able to be sustained over the long term. Caiozzo reasoned that, compared to previous promotions, the increase in number of visits would be able to be sustained for at least a few months as customers got into the habit of using the new coffee mug on every visit.

The third assumption was that both low- and high-frequency Rewards Club members would sustain their same level of spending on other purchases. Since they were saving money on their coffee refills, they would actually be saving money and spending a little less per visit. For the 20oz coffee refill, members would pay $1.45 instead of $1.69 for each purchase. The team believed that customers would pocket the savings.

The fourth and final assumption was that customers would scan their Reward Club card on each visit.

Summary

Each of the two options represented benefits and risks. By choosing to send the offer to high-frequency coffee customers, Wawa would be demonstrating appreciation for their most frequent customers. At the same time, Wawa hoped that these high-frequency customers would become even more committed to the brand and spend even more money throughout their lifetime at Wawa. However, it was possible that these members visited the stores so frequently that there was little room for improvement. Moreover, if members did not change their habits other than to start using a reusable mug, the company could lose money as a result of the promotion.

The alternative was to send the offer of a free mug to low-frequency coffee buyers. These customers were only visiting Wawa one to four times per month, so there was a significant potential to increase the frequency of their visits. Perhaps the lower pricing for coffee refills would be attractive enough to drive those additional visits. At the same time, customers may not change the frequency of their visits, but instead, use the mug to spend less at each visit. "I remember debating this for quite some time. There was a good rationale for each decision. I think the only true way to answer the question was to test this in-market. Luckily, the loyalty program allowed us to do this to a small audience as a test before we would implement the promotion to a larger group, which would help us to spend our marketing dollars more efficiently. I was also hoping that this test could help demonstrate the value of the loyalty program to the organization," reflected Caiozzo.

ASSIGNMENT QUESTIONS

1. Calculate the overall break-even point for a customer who is purchasing a 20oz mug and getting refills.
2. Calculate the current amount of money that is spent at Wawa by low-frequency members and high-frequency members. Assume that low-frequency members visit 2.5 times per month and high-frequency members visit 45 times per month. If a customer continues to be loyal to Wawa for 20 years, what is the lifetime value of each of these customers?
3. Calculate the expected increase in the number of visits and the amount of coffee purchases for the low-frequency and the high-frequency members.
4. Should Wawa send its offer to low-frequency or high-frequency coffee buyers? Defend your decision with evidence from the case and elsewhere.
5. Evaluate the initial four research assumptions that were made by the marketing team. Are these reasonable? Should others be added?
6. The new promotion is based on behavioral loyalty. What kinds of promotions could Wawa initiate to increase attitudinal loyalty? Be creative.

References

Andersen, L.F., Jacobs Jr., D.R., Carlsen, M.H., and Blomhoff, R. 2006. Consumption of coffee is associated with reduced risk of death attributed to inflammatory and cardiovascular diseases in the Iowa Women's Health Study. *The American Journal of Clinical Nutrition, 83* (5), 1039–46.

Aspan, M. 2018. The inside story of Wawa, the beloved $10 billion convenience store chain taking over the East Coast. *Inc Magazine*. June. Accessed 4 June 2022. www.inc.com/magazine/201806/maria-aspan/wawa-convenience-store-pennsylvania.html.

Chaudhri, A. and Holbrook, M.B. 2001. The chain effects from brand trust and brand affect to brand performance: The role of brand loyalty. *Journal of Marketing, 65* (2), 81–93.

DeRupo, J. 2017. Daily coffee consumption up sharply. Press Release. The National Coffee Association. 25 March. Accessed 4 June 2022. www.ncausa.org/Portals/56/PDFs/Communication/NCA_NCDT2017.pdf?ver=2017-03-29-115235-727.

Drankoski, D. 2016. The cult of Wawa. *Mashable*. 9 March. Accessed 4 June 2022. https://mashable.com/2016/03/09/the-cult-of-wawa/#gWcwqlH3g5q3.

Forbes. 2020. America's best employers. *Forbes*. Accessed 4 June 2022. www.forbes.com/companies/wawa/.

Genovese, P. 2016. Wawa free coffee day 2016: How, when to get free coffee Thursday at Wawa. *NJ.com*. NJ Advance Media. 14 April. Accessed 4 June 2022. www.nj.com/entertainment/index.ssf/2016/04/free_coffee_at_wawa_today.html.

Kokubo, Y., Iso, H., Saito, I., Yamagishi, K., Yatsuya, H., Ishihara, J., Inoue, M., and Tsugane, S. 2013. The impact of green tea and coffee consumption on the reduced risk of stroke incidence in Japanese population: The Japan public health center-based study cohort. *Stroke. 14 March, 44*, 1369–74.

Mintel. 2021. Coffee and RTD Coffee – US – 2021. *Mintel Academic*. The Mintel Group, Ltd.

Mulligan, R. 2021. Wawa leads all Pennsylvania companies with $11B in revenue, tops rival Sheetz. *Philadelphia Business Journal*. 25 November. Accessed 4 June 2022. www.bizjournals.com/philadelphia/news/2021/11/25/wawa-leads-philadelphia-area-companies-on-forbes.html.

Odegaard, A.O., Pereira, M.A., Koh, W.P., Arakawa, K., Lee, H.P., and Yu, M.C. 2008. Coffee, tea, and incident type 2 diabetes: The Singapore Chinese Health Study. *The American Journal of Clinical Nutrition, 88* (4), 979–85.

Parmley, S. 2016. Wawa grows through its restaurant appeal. *Phillynews.com*. 15 April. Accessed 4 October 2022. www.philly.com/philly/business/20160415_How_Wawas_are_becoming_more_like_restaurants.html.

Peppers, D. and Rogers, M. 2011. *Managing Customer Relationships: A Strategic Framework*, 2nd edition., John Wiley & Sons, Inc., Hoboken, New Jersey.

Staff. 2014. The Wawa story. *Wawa.com*. Accessed 4 June 2022. http://s3.amazonaws.com/Wawa.com/TheWawaStory.pdf.

Staff. 2017. Wawa has highest brand equity in the convenience channel. *CS News*. 20 October. Accessed 4 June 2022. https://csnews.com/wawa-has-highest-brand-equity-convenience-channel.

Staff. 2018. Foundation Goal. *The Wawa Foundation*. Accessed 4 June 2022. www.thewawafoundation.org/wp-content/uploads/2018/04/Foundation_Goal.pdf.

IS "MAKING HISTORY" A MISSION IMPOSSIBLE TASK FOR COPA AIRLINES?

Diane M. Phillips

Spring of 2018: Panama had just made it past an incredibly hard elimination round and was heading to the World Cup of Football, to be held in Russia. Copa Airlines was the team's sponsor and was in the process of creating a promotional plan to support the team. As the advertising agency presented its plan to the marketing team,[12] there was an all-around sense of disappointment with the proposal to create a World Cup-themed song. Although it had merit, the team wanted something bigger, something splashier, something that would really make history. The problem was, senior management had just cut the marketing budget by two thirds. As the saying goes, should the marketing team "go big" or should they "go home?"

Football: Religion and Big Business

People around the world love football. "It arouses in the world collective passions that are unmatched by nothing short of war ... it gets presidents elected or thrown out, and it defines the way people think, for good or ill, about their countries" (Kuper 2002). Global tournaments like the World Cup and the Olympics allow small developing countries to go head-to-head with big superpowers, even if only on a football pitch. During the tournament's few weeks, billions of people watch the action, cheer for their teams, and even applaud other teams when they

[12]The actual decision-makers on the marketing team preferred anonymity.

make a spectacular play. They know the players, the coaches, and the team's history and heartaches. The credibility and fortunes of a nation and its football team are often intertwined and, in many countries, "to say football is a religion would be to downplay its importance" (Rogers 2016). A football win at the Olympics or World Cup will turn cities and small towns across the country into jubilant masses of cheering crowds, young couples will name their newborn babies after star players, and political leaders will announce national days of celebration. A country's football loss on the world stage is enough to make grown men cry.

Held every 4 years, the World Cup is the world's most watched sporting event. For the 2018 competition hosted by Russia, $11.8 billion was spent on construction and preparation. FIFA, the World Cup's governing body, made approximately $6 billion from the event, up 25% from the previous tournament in 2014. As many as 3.2 billion people worldwide were estimated to have watched the games (Sheetz 2018), with 1 billion tuning in for the final game. The World Cup is truly a global event, from both a cultural and an economic perspective (see Table A3.15).

Table A3.15 Economics of the World Cup

The World Cup is Big Business
Ticket prices ranged from a low of $50 for one of the opening matches, to a high of $1100 for a ticket to the final game.
Before the start of the games, 2.4 million tickets were sold, with approximately 870,000 purchased by Russians, 89,000 purchased by Americans, and 73,000 by Brazilians.
The first place team got $38 million in prize money, followed by $28 million for second place, and $24 million for third place.
TV broadcast rights for FIFA for 2015–2018 were approximately $3 billion; it was expected to increase to $3.5 billion for the next 4-year cycle.

Source: Badenhausen (2018)

Copa Airlines

Founded in 1947, the airline initially focused its efforts on the domestic market and several nearby countries. In 1980, Copa shifted its strategic focus on helping Panama become The Hub of the Americas, a logistical connection point between North and South America. With the support of the Panamanian government, Tocumen International Airport in Panama City was modernized and updated, allowing for bigger jets and more frequent flights (Our History 2022). The routing system was structured as a classic "hub and spoke" system with flights coming from numerous destinations to Tocumen and then being rerouted to other destinations. Very soon, Panama City and Tocumen Airport started to become the largest, busiest, and most important hub connecting the Americas and the Caribbean. With Copa Airlines as the biggest operator in Panama City, Copa Airlines was ideally positioned to take advantage of this growth. Copa Airlines responded by delivering one of the best on-time performances in the world, with close to 90% on-time arrivals. Despite intense competition, the company remained profitable, posting net profits for the 2 years preceding the country's trip to the World Cup (Copa Holdings 2018) (see Table A3.16).

Table A3.16 Copa Airlines statement of profit or loss for 2015–17 (in thousands of dollars)

	2017	2016	2015
Operating revenue:			
Passenger revenue	$2,462,419[13]	$2,155,167	$2,185,465
Cargo and mail revenue	55,290	53,989	56,738
Other operating revenue	9,847	12,696	11,507
Total operating revenues	2,527,556	2,221,852	2,253,710
Operating expenses:			
Fuel	572,746	528,996	603,760
Wages, salaries, benefits, other employee expenses	415,147	370,190	373,631
Passenger servicing	99,447	86,329	84,327
Airport facilities and handling charges	171,040	159,771	148,078
Sales and distribution	200,413	193,984	188,961
Maintenance, materials, and repairs	124,709	121,781	111,178
Depreciation and amortization	164,345	159,278	134,888
Flight operations	101,647	88,188	86,461
Aircraft rentals and other rentals	134,539	138,885	142,177
Cargo and courier expenses	7,375	6,099	6,471
Other operating and administrative expenses	96,087	92,215	105,484
Total operating expenses	2,087,495	1,945,716	1,985,416
Operating profit	440,061	276,136	268,294
Non-operating income (expense):			
Finance cost	(35,223)	(37,024)	(33,155)
Finance income	17,939	13,000	25,947
Gain (loss) on foreign currency fluctuations	(5,218)	13,043	(440,097)
Net change in fair value of derivatives	2,801	111,642	(11,572)
Other non-operating income (expense)	(2,337)	(3,982)	(1,632)
Total non-operating income (expense), net	(22,038)	96,679	(460,509)
Profit (loss) before taxes	418,023	372,815	(192,215)
Income tax expenses	(48,000)	(38,271)	(32,759)
Net profit (loss)	370,023	334,544	(224,974)

Source: Copa Holdings (2018)

[13] Panama's currency, the Balboa, is tied 1:1 to the US dollar. Therefore, these figures are expressed in US dollars.

The marketing team saw a strong link between the financial health of Copa Airlines and the country's position as The Hub of the Americas. Accordingly, the team wanted to ensure that key stakeholders in the government and around the country, like hotel, tourist, and travel trade organizations, would continue their strong support of Tocumen Airport as this important hub. Tocumen needed to rely on government funding for maintenance, upgrades, and expansions. "We are just as important to this country as the Panama Canal. Think about it, no one would do anything to hurt the Canal. We employ about the same number of people, but we also have a ripple effect with impacts on hotels, restaurants, and other attractions. A full 80% of tourist dollars in the country can be traced to Copa Airlines," observed one senior-level member of the marketing team.

The marketing team had three macro-level objectives that directed all of its efforts; each of Copa Airlines' marketing strategies was designed to fulfill at least one of them:

#1 – support Copa Airlines as a key driver for the national economy

#2 – as an important factor in the success of The Hub of the Americas, acknowledge Copa Airlines as a key asset for the country

#3 – position Copa Airlines as a symbol of national pride.

In developing its marketing strategy, the team also had to integrate one of four key levers – sports, music, education, or culture – in order to carry out these objectives. Simply put, each promotional strategy needed to incorporate one of these levers into its message. Copa Airlines used the educational lever, for example, in one of its strategies to carry out objective #3, pride. This particular strategy honored several top-performing local school children by giving them a special experience at the company's hangar at Tocumen Airport.

With the World Cup event, the marketing team identified two key priorities: changing some ill-informed and long-held brand perceptions about Copa Airlines, and leveraging the World Cup event to bring global recognition to the country, the team, and the brand.

Changing Brand Perceptions

Because of some disturbing marketing research results it had recently received, the team needed to first address brand perceptions. One of the key measures in the research report asked consumers to identify the "most recognizable" Panamanian brands. The results indicated that Copa Airlines was not even in the top half of the list. Copa Airlines was responsible for 5% of the country's GDP and 70% of the population used it for international flights, but somehow that didn't translate into recognition. One of the more frustrating findings was that global fruit and produce company Chiquita, which wasn't even Panamanian, got a higher recognition score than did Copa Airlines. The marketing team concluded that, although people in Panama generally knew about and respected Copa Airlines, they didn't have a strong emotional connection to the brand. This was very concerning to the marketing team, because of the need for broad-based public support for Tocumen Airport as a critical transportation hub.

The marketing team connected this rebranding effort to objective #1, to support Copa Airlines as a key driver of the country's economy. After extensive discussions with stakeholders, insights were developed, as was a two-pronged approach. First, no mass-advertising efforts were undertaken. Instead, the marketing team leveraged its already-existing strong relationships with employees, customers, government groups, and trade organizations. Discussions were held, visits were made, and reports were shared with these key stakeholders to demonstrate to them the important economic role played by Copa Airlines. Second, the team held a press conference to present its research findings about Copa Airlines' key role in the national economy, which generated substantial free media coverage. After these efforts, the team engaged in a follow-up study where they asked many of the same questions from before. Copa Airlines moved up from dead last on the list of most recognizable Panamanian brands to #2!

Making History

When faced with the difficult decision about what to do to leverage the excitement that the country was experiencing with the last-minute surprising win in the qualifying round of the 2018 World Cup, the marketing team's skills were put to the test. Panama's team was heading to Russia to compete in the World Cup championship and, to the marketing team's surprise, the company's top management cut the promotional budget that had been set aside for the World Cup by two thirds. The company's annual marketing budget is set by upper management using a percentage of revenue method and the annual marketing budget is between $7.58 and $10.11 million. Because of cost-cutting measures, the budget set aside for the World Cup was originally $300,000 but was cut to about $100,000. The marketing team knew that it needed to allocate $20,000–$40,000 of the budget for the production of radio, TV, and print ads. The majority of the remaining budget would be used for media placement.

One of the first things that the marketing team insisted upon was that their World Cup strategy needed to fulfill objective #3, pride. Secondly, both Copa Airlines' Senior Marketing Director and Brand Manager believed that if Copa Airlines did not have the capability to do a truly phenomenal job, it should not do anything at all; it was "either all or nothing."

Panama and football

At the time, Panama had a population of 4.3 million people, an annual GDP of $53.98 billion, and an annual inflation rate of 1.6%. Poverty was going down, literacy was going up, and numerous life and health indicators were improving (World Bank 2022). Importantly, the country had a stable, democratically-elected government and important steps were being taken to curb corruption.

Photo A3.7 Panama's 2018 World Cup team

Source: Shutterstock

Copa Airlines had been a long-time sponsor of the national football team, the longest, continuously-running sponsor in the entire international football league. For several years, the team was recruiting better players and had just hired a new coach; it was shaping up to be a bit of a "dream team." In 2015, Copa Airlines painted one of its planes with the team colors and, whenever possible, used the "team plane" to transport the team to its qualifying games. The airline even did some extra things for the team, such as picking it up when it was stranded by bad weather on one occasion and extending its stay by a few days on another occasion. The relationship between the team and Copa Airlines was mutually-beneficial and strong (see Photo A3.7).

The World Cup

In early 2018, as part of its annual preparations, the marketing team developed a marketing plan for the remote possibility that the national team would go to the World Cup. Panama had never been to a World Cup tournament, but 2018 felt like it might actually be the year. Having narrowly missed its chances in 2014, the team was stronger in 2018 but still had almost insurmountable odds. In order for them to make it to the World Cup, the US had to lose to Trinidad & Tobago, and Panama had to win against football powerhouse Costa Rica. No one believed that either one of these would happen, let alone both (Lowe 2018). At this point, the team was totally demoralized. What did Copa Airlines do? It sent the team plane to take the players to the last game against Costa Rica. One of the marketing team leaders recalled, "It was like saying, hey guys, we have your back. We're proud of you! Even if others are counting you out, Copa Airlines is still here behind you. You should have seen the players. There were tears in their eyes." In the final qualifying games, the impossible happened. The US lost and Panama won, sending Panama to the World Cup for the first time ever (Lowe 2018). Now the team and the entire country believed in miracles. Citizens took to the streets and celebrated with stamina and enthusiasm. The day after the qualifying game, the president declared a national holiday (Lowe 2018) – no one was going to work anyway – and the entire country set its sights on the games in Russia.

Marketing options

Unfortunately, the options were fairly limited after the marketing team was informed that its budget had been sliced. To put this into perspective, the difference between what Copa Airlines could spend and what other advertisers like beer and sportswear companies were spending was between 10 and 20 times. This was particularly challenging because Copa Airlines wanted to be a part of making history – for the company, the country, and the team. How could Copa Airlines compete with other advertisers for the attention, hearts, and minds of the Panamanian people and make history with only one third of the budget it was anticipating? Of all the things that were working against the team, there was one additional issue that increased the risk for Copa Airlines. As the country eagerly consumed information about the players, the upcoming competitors, and the games, the World Cup was expected to generate wall-to-wall free media coverage for the team and its biggest sponsor, Copa Airlines. If Copa Airlines could design something big and inspiring, it could benefit from the free media coverage and might actually "make history." Otherwise, the brand could be damaged by any half-hearted attempts at promotion. In fact, it might be better to do nothing than to do something just half-way. The marketing team concluded that they should either "go big" or "go home." The team identified four low-cost options:

1 The first option was to continue to do what it had already been doing. At the time, the thought was, "why mess with success?" Copa had already risen to prominence in the minds and hearts of Panamanians with its earlier brand-building efforts and support of the team, so very little extra effort was needed for the World Cup, aside from taking them to the games in Russia. Copa could continue to enjoy its earlier successes and the free media coverage that was bound to happen. This was the *de facto* "go home" option.

2 The second option was to accept the proposal of the ad agency, a very well-known firm with a strong record of excellence and success. They proposed that Copa work with a well-known musician to create a 30-second jingle; indeed, the agency had already lined up a rapper to do the work. This would touch on one of the four levers mentioned above and, if done correctly, might even tie in the sports and culture levers. This well-coordinated plan seemed to hold a lot of promise in fulfilling the three key objectives as well as three out of the four levers.
3 The third option was to launch a coordinated social media campaign, taking advantage of the excitement that was already being generated. Copa Airlines could insert some carefully-crafted social media messages and then rely on fans to share those messages far and wide across their own social networks. Compared to other nations, Panama had a fairly young population; the median age was about 29 (O'Neill 2021), and these young people were very tech-savvy. Copa Airlines could engage fans in content co-creation by inviting them to share their own stories about what the team meant to them.
4 The fourth option was to creatively utilize public relations (PR), the one element of the promotional mix that was free. Unfortunately, PR had one significant drawback: a company gives up significant control of the message when it relies on a news outlet to tell its story. However, as mentioned previously, Copa Airlines now was in the enviable position of having very positive brand equity around the country because of its earlier rebranding efforts. In addition, the country was currently in a very good mood, so it was unlikely that any negative PR would result.

In short, there were three "go big" options (e.g., the ad agency idea, social media, or PR) and one "go home" option (e.g., continue with what they were already doing).

Summary

Frustrated, the marketing team thought that they had been given an impossible task. How could Copa Airlines leverage the country's enthusiasm to further support the team as it made its way to its first World Cup appearance with just one third of the budget it had anticipated? With its extensive experience in strategy, branding, and relationships, they certainly had the tools to do the job. But they firmly believed that if they were going to do something, they needed to do it right. For them, it was a "go big" or "go home" decision.

ASSIGNMENT QUESTIONS

1 For each of the four options that the Copa Airlines' marketing team considered, provide a list of advantages and disadvantages. Be sure to discuss how well each option fits with the firm's marketing objectives.
2 Should the marketing team "go big" or should they "go home" and just follow through on the current plan of flying the team to the World Cup in Russia? Support your answer with facts and details from the case and elsewhere.

(Continued)

3. How well does the "make history" objective fit with the existing three objectives for Copa Airlines?
4. Regardless of which option is selected, how can the marketing team make sure that the promotion touches on the four levers? Be creative and be specific.
5. Evaluate Copa Airlines' current method for setting its marketing budget. What are some benefits and drawbacks of this approach?
6. Using the financial data in Table A3.16, calculate return on sales for 2015, 2016, and 2017. Based on these results, what conclusions can you draw about the financial health of Copa Airlines? What other measures might the marketing decision-maker be able to utilize to more accurately determine Copa Airlines' financial health?

References

Badenhausen, K. 2018. FIFA World Cup 2018: The money behind the biggest event in sports. *Forbes*. 14 June. Accessed 5 June 2022. www.forbes.com/sites/kurtbadenhausen/2018/06/14/world-cup-2018-the-money-behind-the-biggest-event-in-sports/?sh=27cab0a76973.

Copa Holdings. 2018. Annual Report, Form 20-F. *The United States Securities and Exchange Commission*. 18 April 2018.

Kuper, S. 2002. The world's game is not just a game. *New York Times Magazine*. 26 May. 36–9.

Lowe, S. 2018. "Like something handed down by God" – how Panama reached the World Cup. *The Guardian*. 17 June. Accessed 5 June 2022. www.theguardian.com/football/2018/jun/17/pananma-world-cup-finals-god-ballboys.

O'Neill, A. 2021. Panama: Average age of the population from 1950–2050 (median age in years). *Statista*. 8 September. Accessed 5 June 2022. www.statista.com/statistics/454394/average-age-of-the-population-in-panama/.

Our History. 2022. *Copa Airlines*. Accessed 5 June 2022. www.copaair.com/en/web/us/our-history.

Rogers, M. 2016. Brazil thirsts for Olympic football gold. *USA Today*. 4 August. Sports. 6.

Sheetz, M. 2018. Here's who is getting rich off the World Cup. *CNBC*. 14 June. Accessed 5 June 2022. www.cnbc.com/2018/06/14/the-business-of-the-world-cup--who-makes-money-and-how-much.html.

World Bank. 2022. Country Profile: Panama, Databank. *The World Bank*. Accessed 5 June 2022. https://data.worldbank.org/country/panama?view=chart.

PRICING AT THE PANAMA CANAL CAUSES GLOBAL RIPPLE EFFECTS

Diane M. Phillips

Silvia de Marucci, Executive Manager for Economic Analysis and Market Research at the Panama Canal, had an important decision to make. Shortly after the newly-expanded Panama Canal had officially opened, its biggest competitor, the Suez Canal, enacted a 65% price cut. Should de Marucci match the price cut or should she enact a different pricing strategy? Her decision would reverberate across the entire global shipping industry.

The Panama Canal

Shortly after the first Europeans arrived on the tiny isthmus of Panama, attempts were made to carve a canal that would connect the Atlantic and Pacific Oceans. The first serious effort was initiated by the French in 1880. Unfortunately, the weather, landscape, and dense tropical jungle proved too inhospitable. In addition, the project was plagued by mismanagement, labor shortages, inadequate equipment, and sickness. More than 20,000 people died, mainly due to mosquito-borne sicknesses such as yellow fever and malaria. By 1898, the French had abandoned their effort and sold the construction rights to the US. In 1904, the Americans started work by first reducing the prevalence of mosquitos by clearing away stagnant water and improving sanitation. In 1914, the Panama Canal was officially opened, shortening the trip between East and West by about 8000 miles and 2 weeks (ACP 2022).

The Canal was a feat of engineering genius. Fresh water from a man-made lake flowed into a series of locks as ships took the 8–11-hour trip from one ocean to the other (ACP 2017). No pumps or electricity were needed to move the massive volume of water needed for each ship and the gates that closed the locks were so finely balanced that they could be operated by a hand crank (Bogdanich, Williams, and Méndez 2016).

On 31 December 1999, control and ownership of the Canal was transitioned to Panama (ACP 2018). Since that time, the "Autoridad del Canal de Panamá" (ACP), or the Panama Canal Authority, has operated with expertise and efficiency. At the time of the transition, global maritime trade was accelerating and much larger container ships, some too big to traverse the Canal, were being built and put into service. Because of this, in 2016, a newly-expanded Canal which was 40% longer and 60% wider was added to accommodate these bigger ships (ACP 2018).

The Canal's Far-Reaching Impacts

Over 160 countries use the Canal, using 144 different routes, that arrive at or depart from 1,700 ports around the world (ACP 2018). There were between 13,000 and 14,000 transits per year and the Canal was responsible for 3.4% of global maritime trade (ACP 2018). It is not surprising that most consumers in developed economies own numerous products that have passed through the Panama Canal. The Canal is also an indispensable component of Panama's economic and geopolitical standing (ACP 2018), generating $4 billion in annual revenues and $2 billion in profits for the country (ACP 2021). In addition to the Canal's significant economic and consumer impacts, it has also had a considerable influence on global shipbuilding, ports, and maritime procedures.

Shipbuilding

When the ACP announced the size and dimensions for the construction of the newly-expanded Canal, shipbuilders around the world started building ships to fit the new specifications. In a tribute to the importance of the Canal, ships that fit within the maximum dimensions of the original Canal are called "Panamax" vessels and bigger ships that fit the new Canal are called "NeoPanamax" vessels.

Global ports

Because of the greater number of NeoPanamax vessels traversing the world's seas, ports around the world needed to be retrofitted to accommodate them. Ports needed to deepen harbors, raise bridges, and outfit their ports with new cranes, warehouses, and docks (Phillips 2016, Whelan 2016). Operations at the Panama Canal also influenced global shipping traffic patterns. For example, ports along the West Coast of the US experienced less traffic, while their East Coast counterparts saw more traffic after the 2016 opening. Why this shift? Previously, 70% of the shipments from Asia to the US docked in California. The cargo was loaded onto trains and trucks, which then distributed the items across the country. After 2016, NeoPanamax vessels from Asia could now sail straight through the Canal to East Coast destinations, providing significant cost savings. Experts predicted that 25% of shipments from Asia to the US would eventually shift their routes directly to the East Coast (Taves 2014).

Maritime procedures

The Canal has also had far-reaching impacts on global maritime shipping procedures and protocols. One example is the Panama Canal Universal Measurement System (PC/UMS), a global standard of measurement based on a ship's cargo capacity. Another example is the way in which shipping companies have altered their own internal procedures to be more synergistic with the Canal's procedures. For example, to prevent delays and ensure more efficient transits, the ACP implemented a policy stating that once a ship reached the Canal waters, it needed to be ready to transit through the Canal – no delays for maintenance, refueling, or changing the crew. "Because of this, many of our customers made changes to their policies so that they didn't waste time doing these maintenance-related tasks. They needed to perform these tasks before they reached the Canal waters, because once they do reach our waters, their own policies now say they need to be ready to transit the Canal at any time," explained de Marucci.

The Business of the Canal

When de Marucci first arrived at the ACP in 1995, all operations at the Canal reported directly to the Pentagon in Washington, DC because of the Canal's military, geo-strategic, and economic importance. Almost immediately after the transfer to Panama, the Canal switched to a for-profit model, which meant that de Marucci and her team had to start implementing some very basic principles of marketing strategy, such as identifying the Canal's target market, communicating its value proposition, and determining its marketing mix.

Defining and Segmenting Customers

One of the first tasks was to segment the market. "One of the first questions we asked was, who are our customers? We had data on cargo, type of ship, origination port, all of that, but we didn't know who our customers really were. We really started with nothing. One of the first things we did was gather more data. We asked questions like, what company are you from, who are the owners, what is in the shipment, what ports have you already visited, who else has chartered this vessel, and who else has leased this vessel?" remembered de Marucci. "We also purchased some data and even visited some of our customers to find out what they needed. Which is more important to them: just a simple transit or speed? We started to form relationships with them for the first time." As a result of this work, the team segmented the market by value and by need.

Segmenting by Value (Value *of* the Customer)

When segmenting by value (how much is this customer worth to us?), the team created four key target markets, each based on the type of ship and its cargo:

1 Liquid Bulk (33% of ACP revenue) – includes liquified petroleum gas and natural gas (LNG), crude oil, and liquid chemicals.
2 Dry Bulk (22%) – these ships carry dry commodity products such as coal or corn.
3 Liners (33%) – includes container ships, refrigerated ships, and general cargo ships.
4 Especialized Services (9%)[14] – includes vehicle transport ships and passenger ships.

Table A3.17 depicts the increase in business between 2017 and 2018 and Table A3.18 depicts the increase in tonnage and revenue between 2013 and 2018.

[14]The remaining 3% is made up of other miscellaneous shipments.

Table A3.17 Increasing traffic and volume of shipments at the Panama Canal, 2017–18, by market segment. Tonnage is depicted using PC/UMS

	Transits: 2018	Transits: 2017	Tonnage: 2018	Tonnage: 2017
Liquid Bulk	4028	3625	130,280	105,405
Dry Bulk	2686	2915	73,739	79,135
Liners	4041	4085	175,067	160,579
Especialized Services	1090	1041	60,955	56,618
Other	354	326	1138	1033
Total	12,199	11,992	441,177	402,770

Source: courtesy, Silvia de Marucci

Table A3.18 Panama Canal volume and revenue for 2013–18

	2018	2017	2016	2015	2014	2013
Tonnage in millions (PC/UMS)	441.2	402.8	330.4	340.8	326.8	320.6
Revenue in billions of dollars	3.11	2.85	2.48	2.61	2.63	2.41

Sources: Internal documents (de Marucci), ACP Annual Reports (see www.panCanal.com/eng/general/reporte-anual/index.html) and ACP Audited Financial Statements (www.panCanal.com/eng/general/fin-statements/index.html).

Segmenting by Need (Value *to* the Customer)

Marketers also segment by need (what does the customer need from us?). For de Marucci and her team, segmenting by need identified two clear targets:

1 Liners and Containers (58% of the market) – these ships are able to carry thousands of individual shipping containers at a time, each with a wide variety of items such as vehicles, commodity products, and consumer products. The old locks accommodate ships that carry 8000 containers, while the new locks can accommodate ships that can carry about 14,800 containers. These shippers have a fixed schedule each week and visit several ports along the voyage. Shipping giants Costco and Maersk were the biggest players in this segment. Their key need is quick and efficient transit time.

2 Trampers (42% of the market) – this category of ships does not have a fixed schedule and could be thought of as "globe trotters." They usually carry commodities and change course from time-to-time, depending on changes in futures and pricing. Oil tankers, for example, fall into this category. Sometimes, a shipper or trader "buys the shipment and sends it off to Japan, but half way there, the global price of oil fluctuates and the cargo is sold to someone else who now wants it in Australia," explained de Marucci. Because these ships sometimes make changes mid-voyage, their most important need was flexibility in scheduling.

The result of this two-layered segmentation strategy gave ACP a foundation for its new pricing policy (described in the price section below).

Product

The Canal provides safe, fast, and efficient passage between the Atlantic and Pacific. The fact that the Canal has been operating for 100+ years is a testament to its durability and engineering genius. The Canal also offers a variety of other services. One important service is the use of an ACP-certified pilot that boards the ship and navigates it through the two sets of locks (2.5–3.0 hours each), making the transit both faster and safer. Although the ship's captain remains on the bridge, the Panama Canal is the only place in the world where a captain is required by law to give up control of the ship. Another important service that ACP provides is a variety of free data and statistics, including data about the weather and tides. The ACP also provides expertise and assistance with a variety of forms, codes, certifications, and inspections. Finally, for the community, the ACP provides mooring facilities at the lake for passenger vessels to disembark, electricity that it sells back to the grid, and potable water which it sells to local villages.

Price

Many shippers decline to use the Panama Canal and instead make the trip around Cape Horn (the southern tip of South America) or the Cape of Good Hope (Africa). However, because of the punishing currents and storms in these regions, these trips are very dangerous. The trips also require extra fuel and time. A trip around Cape Horn, for example, will save the Canal's transit fee but will cost about two more weeks of time as well as tens of thousands of dollars in extra fuel. In all, the trip around Cape Horn might save the shipping company about 8.5%. All told, with the extra time, money, and risk, it is easy to see why many shippers prefer the Canal.

Based on its unique value proposition, the ACP announced a new tiered pricing policy in 2013. "Customers were very angry because they were not used to this. But, we provided a service that had few competitors," explained de Marucci. The resulting pricing strategy provided bigger discounts to containers that were on a fixed and predictable schedule, while trampers paid a premium for flexible scheduling. Combining the size of the ship with their specific needs and the value of the cargo, the broad pricing categories were as follows (ACP 2018):

Size of Ship:

- Panamax vessels: $140,000–$400,000.
- NeoPanamax vessels: $500,000–$1,200,000.

Type of Ship:

- Containers & Liners: $300,000–$1,000,000.
- Trampers: $180,000–$520,000.

In order to book a timeslot to transit the Canal, all ships need to pay a booking fee. The booking fee to transit the NeoPanamax locks is $35,000. If ships choose to not book a timeslot, they need to wait until an open timeslot is available. Most times, they can transit on the same day they arrive. If a tramper, which needs to maintain flexibility and therefore will rarely book a timeslot, shows up at the Canal and needs to transit immediately, it can still obtain a timeslot by buying one at auction. When there is increased traffic and demand for slots, auction prices can increase dramatically. The record price paid at auction for a timeslot was $375,000. In addition to transit costs and booking fees (if applicable), ships also pay a variety of other fees that amount to an additional 11–18%. When the pricing policy was implemented, the ACP Administrator met with some of the Canal's biggest customers to explain the new policies.

Logistics

If the physical operations of the Canal are a wonder to behold, another feat of genius is the complex logistical processes that coordinate and schedule the ships through the Canal. The enhanced vessel traffic-management system is a state-of-the-art portal that integrates real-time information from a variety of different sources, such as weather, maritime information, and routing information. It also combines data from all of the ships as they approach and exit the Canal so decision-makers can track and even alter shipping routes and transits, if needed.

The ACP's real-time global satellite tracking system allows global shipping decision-makers to track ships as they visit ports and move around the world. This was the system that alerted de Marucci's team about an increasing number of ships being re-routed from Asia around the Cape of Good Hope (Africa) or through the Suez Canal in 2014–16 because of a delay in the opening of the newly-expanded Canal.[15] This critical information helped generate insights into the needs of their customers, which was then utilized to encourage these customers to return once the newly-expanded Canal was opened. Shortly after the new Canal opened, most customers indeed returned.

Promotion

Promotion of the Canal was focused on two key audiences: the general public and shipping customers. When communicating with the general public, the team relied heavily on a beautifully-integrated website that provided vast amounts of information on the Canal's operations, history, and sustainability. The transparent and easy-to-navigate website had several videos, as well as up-to-date information, newsletters, and press releases on a variety of topics related to the Canal's operations and pricing.

When communicating with customers, de Marucci regularly gave presentations at industry conferences and meetings to discuss a variety of topics related to the Canal, global shipping trends, and innovations. Importantly, the team worked to build relationships with its customers by calling and visiting them to discuss their needs. "This was the first time we had ever done that and we're more than 100 years old! They were really surprised," de Marucci reflected. De Marucci credits these efforts at relationship building as critical to the success of both the Canal and its customers. When the ACP needs to implement any price increases, these strong relationships have proven essential to implementation. Of course, no customer will applaud a price increase, but once the rationale for the increase is provided, the implementation goes smoothly. "When we increase tolls, there has to be a public hearing, which is required by law. But, one thing that is not required, is a personal consultation with our customers. We do that. They give us feedback and tell us what the effect will be on their business. For example, they

[15]Originally scheduled to open in 2014, construction and labor problems caused the opening of the expanded Canal to be delayed for 2 years till 2016.

will tell us it is not a good time because demand is down or oil prices are high. Sometimes they are actually ok with an increase if they can pass it along to their customers. We even provide them the ability to do that in the way we bill them for the transit," offered de Marucci.

Competitive Attack

The Suez Canal connects the Mediterranean Sea to the Indian Ocean via the Red Sea. Completed in 1869, it is 120 miles long and connects Europe and countries surrounding the Mediterranean with India, Asia, and East Africa. Originally under the control of the British and French, in 1956, the Suez Canal reverted to Egyptian control (SCA 2017a). In 2015, the Suez Canal underwent an $8.5 billion project to widen and deepen the waterway, which almost doubled the volume of ships that could traverse it. Proponents said that it would eventually account for up to a third of Egypt's economy and, importantly, would restore the country's global prestige after political unrest and allegations of corruption. The Suez Canal accounted for approximately 8% of the world's maritime trade (Kholaif 2015), and at the time of its expansion project, produced annual revenues of approximately $5.3 billion, which were expected to increase to $13.226 billion by 2023 (SCA 2017b).

In late 2016, citing a number of factors such as a slowdown in global trade and lower oil prices (which made it more economically feasible for ships to travel around the Cape of Good Hope), the Suez Canal instituted a 50% selective price drop (Staff 2017). With the waiver of other fees, the effective price drop for some container ships was 65%. This price reduction was specifically targeted at ships taking the Asia to US East Coast routes, the same routes that the Panama Canal was hoping to attract back after its new expansion. Because of the timing and the fact that container ships made up approximately 50% of the new Panama Canal's revenues, de Marucci and her team interpreted this as a direct competitive attack. In determining how to respond, the team needed to keep two additional issues in mind. First, it needed to comply with the requirements of its neutrality treaty. Because of the Canal's global economic and strategic importance, individuals who crafted the 1999 treaty which shifted control of the Canal to Panama had the foresight to include a neutrality agreement: (1) operations at the Canal needed to be fair, (2) tolls needed to be reasonable, and (3) all customers needed to be treated equally. Second, the team was reminded that the Suez Canal has a much lower cost structure and higher margins as compared to the Panama Canal. Indeed, the Panama Canal spends millions of dollars annually on the maintenance of its locks, navigational channels, and equipment. The Suez, by contrast, merely needs to periodically dredge silt out of its waterways.

Summary

At the time of the Suez price attack, the Panama Canal was running efficiently and effectively. Customers were happy with the Canal's expanded capacity, the closer relationship that had been forged with the ACP, better service, and a much more equitable and transparent pricing policy. De Marucci and her team needed to develop a response to the well-timed and targeted price cut that the Suez Canal had recently instituted. Should she suggest a similar cut in price (65%), a smaller price cut (perhaps 35%), or no price cut at all?

ASSIGNMENT QUESTIONS

1. How should Silvia de Marucci and her team respond to the aggressive price reduction at the Suez Canal? Be specific and support your recommendation with facts from the case and elsewhere.
2. What are the benefits to a company of segmenting the market by need vs. segmenting the market by value?
3. Calculate the ROI for the $5.4 billion expansion project at the Canal. How many years will it take for the ACP to break even on this investment? Be sure to list out the assumptions that were made in performing these calculations.
4. Evaluate the current pricing strategy at the Panama Canal. Which pricing strategy does the Canal's strategy most closely resemble? What role does transparency play in the Canal's pricing strategy?
5. Evaluate the three options that de Marucci is considering, by providing a list of "pros" and "cons" for (1) a 65% price reduction, (2) a somewhat lower price reduction (perhaps 35%), and (3) doing nothing.
6. Much of the discussion revolves around the *price* to transit the Canal. Discuss the *value* that the Canal provides to its customers. What are the various dimensions of this value? How could de Marucci and her team communicate its value proposition?

References

ACP. 2022. Learn About the History of the Panama Canal. *The Panama Canal Authority (ACP)*. Accessed 6 June 2022. https://pancanal.com/en/history-of-the-panama-canal/#:~:text=The%20Panama%20Canal%20Authority%20(ACP,and%20modernization%20of%20the%20Canal.

ACP. 2021. Autoridad del Canal de Panamá: Financial Statements. *KPMG*, Panamá, República de Panamá. 30 September.

ACP. 2018. Miraflores Visitor Center, *The Panama Canal Authority (ACP)*.

Bogdanich, Walt, Jacqueline Williams, and Ana Graciela Méndez, A.G. 2016. The New Panama Canal: A Risky Bet (foreign desk). *New York Times, Late Edition (East Coast)*. New York. 23 June. A1.

Kholaif, Dahlia. 2015. Egypt Prepares to Inaugurate Expanded Suez Canal; Project Cost $8.5 Billion, Stirred Patriotic Fervor. *The Wall Street Journal* (Online). New York. 5 August. n/a.

Phillips, Erica E. 2016. South Carolina Will Get Boost from Expanded Panama Canal; Inland Greenville-Spartanburg Region, Called the Upstate, Gears Up for Business Boom. *The Wall Street Journal* (Online). New York. 23 June. n/a.

SCA. 2017a. Canal History. *The Suez Canal Authority*. Accessed 6 June 2022. www.suezCanal.gov.eg/English/About/SuezCanal/Pages/CanalHistory.aspx,

SCA. 2017b. New Suez Canal. *The Suez Canal Authority*, Accessed 6 June 2022. www.suezCanal.gov.eg/English/About/SuezCanal/Pages/NewSuezCanal.aspx.

Staff. 2017. Egypt Cuts Transit Fees Through Suez Canal by Half. *Middle East Observer*. Accessed 6 June 2022. www.middleeastobserver.org/2017/08/18/39187/.

Taves, Max. 2014. Ports Prep for Canal Traffic – Panama Expansion Could Reroute Cargo to Houston, Baltimore, Other US Cities. *Wall Street Journal, Eastern Edition*. New York. 9 July. C8.

Whelan, Robbie. 2016. As Expanded Panama Canal Prepares to Open, New York Isn't Ready; Delayed Bayonne Bridge Project Means East Coast's Busiest Port Can't Receive Biggest Ships. *Wall Street Journal* (Online). New York. 22 June. n/a.

INTRODUCING THE BLAA: IRELAND'S SOON-TO-BE MOST FAMOUS TINY ROLL

Diane M. Phillips

Walsh's Bakehouse in Waterford, Ireland specializes in making a humble, often under-appreciated bread called the "blaa" and Dermot Walsh is its third-generation co-owner. Walsh was currently contemplating two exciting opportunities. One option was exporting to the United Arab Emirates (UAE), where European products were strongly sought-after and thus achieved a higher price and margin. The other option was to engage in intensive distribution within Ireland, where the business landscape was more familiar, but the price and margins were much smaller. Unfortunately, he could select only one.

History and Legacy of the Blaa

Walsh's Bakehouse in Waterford, Ireland was founded in 1921 by Dermot's grandfather and has been a staple in the local community ever since. "Our family has been at it for over 100 years now," Walsh remarked. Walsh's Bakehouse specializes in making the blaa, Waterford's most famous bread, which can trace its origins back to the 17th century when French Huguenots settled in the Waterford area. The small, white bread roll is made from refined wheat flour and was seen as something suitable for factory workers, farmers, and laborers to bring to work in their lunch packs. They are soft on the inside, with a slightly crispy outside, and dusted with flour (see Photo A3.8). Blaas were for everyday people, not the upper class. They "were never sold in hotels or restaurants. Ever. They were just sold in the shops and that was it. Men would buy them on the way to work," Walsh explained. Over the years, the Walsh brothers worked hard to expand their customer base. Through a series of carefully considered moves, the blaa moved from a lowly, insignificant part of the business to the product upon which the future of the bakery hinged.

Faced with the decision about whether to pursue the Emirates market or the Irish market, Walsh's most important decision criterion was the profit potential of the deal. The blaa would have a higher price point and margin in the Emirates market, but the volume would be smaller.

Photo A3.8 The Waterford Blaa

Source: courtesy, Dermot Walsh

Alternatively, the Irish market would demand a higher volume, but a lower price point and margin. Although both alternatives held significant promise, as a small operation, Walsh could select just one. In the lead-up to the decision, the brothers had already made several important decisions regarding the product, erected a barrier to entry, and learned more about their existing target markets.

Believing in the Blaa

When the brothers realized how truly unique the blaa was, "it was an eye-opening experience. We realized the answer was right there all the time. It was September 2006. At that point, we were about to cut 20–25% of the bakery's workforce and refocus the business. The market was shrinking. We looked at lots of products as a way to bring things back," Walsh recalled. For example, the brothers traveled to an international baker's convention in France in order to find something new and unique to bring back to the bakery. "At that time, we were looking for a product that would appeal to an Irish audience and continental breads[16] were growing in popularity," he related. Then, in 2008, the Terra Madre food festival came to Waterford. With close connections to the Slow Food Movement, the festival sought to promote local, healthy, and socially-just production of food. "It was just people who believed in properly-made regional foods, all of the good things that had been overlooked here in Ireland for quite a few years. We had kind of turned our back on local food. That festival was a kickstart. We participated in the festival by not only having a booth but also providing blaas as the bread of choice because they were a local delicacy and there was a big gathering of national and international people there. Then, a few of the local chefs who were there decided to put blaas on their menus! Soon, other chefs were using blaas in their menus too. It was at that stage that we said to ourselves, 'we might be on to something here!'" Walsh recalled.

Also in 2008, "we went to farmers markets and we approached vendors who were making their own hand-made burgers and sausages. We asked if they would start using our bread. We first started giving it to them free of charge and seeing what the feedback was from their customers. Every bit of feedback we got was absolutely positive. For about a year or two, I spent my Fridays and Saturdays driving all over the country trying to get people to try my blaas!" Walsh remembered.

Although the brothers considered other bakery products, they kept coming back to the lowly blaa. "We wouldn't have said 'no' to these other options, but the blaas were just better for us. We were good at making blaas; we know how to make them and how to make them in volume. When we sat down and looked at our strengths and weaknesses, we realized that our main strength was that we had been making this product for years."

[16]"Continental breads" refers to breads that are made on the main continent of Europe, as opposed to the islands of Great Britain and Ireland.

Erecting a Barrier to Entry

To protect the product from imitators, the brothers pursued Protected Geographical Indication (PGI) Certification for the blaa. The European Commission certifies a product as PGI when there is an especially strong "relationship between the specific geographic region and the name of the product, where a particular quality, reputation, or other characteristic is essentially attributable to its geographical origin" (PGI 2022). In order to obtain certification, the product must have simple ingredients and must be produced with traditional skills and knowledge. Ireland's leading food council, Bord Bia, had been trying to identify a sufficiently high-profile product within the food community and in 2009 zeroed-in on the blaa. "Once we applied for it, everything changed because once you send in your initial application, you are covered by PGI legislation until they either refuse or accept your application. There was a lot of publicity about the application and that in turn gave us even further momentum." According to Walsh, there are about 1200 manufacturers from 28 countries that have PGI designations.

In 2013, the Waterford Blaa was awarded the coveted PGI certification by the European Commission, joining other products such as champagne and Parma ham. Only three other products in the Republic of Ireland and two in Northern Ireland have achieved the exclusive PGI designation (Digby 2013). This designation protects the blaa from imitators, and only three bakeries in the world – all from Waterford – can produce the "blaa." Further, all bakers making the blaa must be certified members of the Waterford Blaa Bakers Association.

Walsh believed that the certification would be a key point of differentiation for international markets. Because of the ability to place the PGI logo on the package, customers could be assured of its exclusivity and quality. "What do we get out of it? Legal protection. No one from outside the area can make our product – it gives us a competitive advantage," Walsh explained.

Target Markets

Before Walsh could consider which market to pursue, he needed to first consider the potential impact on each of his two existing markets: Ireland and select markets in Europe.

The Irish market

Ireland was the largest market for blaas; customers could get them fresh, packaged, or frozen. The fresh product was purchased in large quantities by people on their way to work each morning. About 10,000–12,000 fresh blaas were sold straight from the Waterford Bakehouse every day. The fresh product had also recently been made available in select outlets throughout Ireland. "We linked up with one of the biggest bakeries in Ireland because they have their own national distribution network. It is relatively easy for us because we just need to deliver to a central location by about 1:00am every morning. They'll distribute it to various depots, load them onto the various vans by about 5:00–6:00am, and drive them to the various supermarkets around the country. All within about a 14–16-hour period from when the product is made, so the product is still nice and fresh," explained Walsh. Walsh's sold 30,000 fresh blaas per week through this distribution channel.

Foodservice outlets throughout Ireland purchased packaged blaas, where they were often warmed up, stuffed with a variety of fillings, or otherwise incorporated into different recipes.

Finally, boxes of frozen blaas were also distributed across Ireland to some of the bigger foodservice operations. The bakehouse shipped about seven containers of frozen blaas per week throughout Ireland (at 78,000 blaas per container).

The European market

Walsh's Bakehouse also sold blaas to the UK, France, and Germany. For these markets, the product was either delivered in packages or frozen. A total of 500,000 blaas per year were sold to the European market, the great majority of which were sold to the UK (about 90%). "For all of these markets, PGI is the reason why we're able to get these contracts," offered Walsh. See Table A3.19 for the cost structure related to manufacturing and shipping blaas.

Table A3.19 Net contribution margin for various package sizes of blaas (in euros)

	Recommended Retailer Price*	Retailer Margin	Net to Walsh's	Per Unit Cost	Distribution Cost	Net Contribution
Fresh: 4-pack traditional	2.20	35%	1.43	0.30	0.45	0.69
Fresh: 6-pack traditional	2.75	35%	1.79	0.43	0.54	0.83
Fresh: 4-pack large	2.50	35%	1.63	0.38	0.49	0.76
Fresh: 6-pack small	2.40	35%	1.56	0.31	0.47	0.79
Single blaa sold loose	0.45	39%	0.27	0.07	0.00	0.21
Food Service vc: Traditional boxed	18.50	0%	18.50	8.07	1.17	9.27
Food Service vc: Large boxed	16.50	0%	16.50	8.44	1.17	6.89
Food Service vc: Small boxed	19.50	0%	19.50	9.59	1.17	8.74
Frozen: 6-pack boxed	22.00	0%	22.00	7.95	1.17	12.89

* All prices are in euros. Any small differences in amounts are due to rounding errors.

Source: courtesy, Dermot Walsh

Exporting to the United Arab Emirates

This was not the first time Walsh's Bakehouse had targeted the UAE. "A few years ago, we had a distributor that was bringing the blaa to foodservice outlets in Dubai and Abu Dhabi. But, we were having a lot of quality control problems because their refrigeration units were not being used consistently. The end result was that the frozen blaas were being left out in the heat. That just can't happen. So, we severed our relationship with them. A few years after that, they went out of business. Now, with the help of Bord Bia we've found another distributor with an Irish connection. They already sell Irish butter, dairy products, cheese, and saltbread there. Bord Bia does a lot of the on-the-ground work like visiting the facilities, checking for quality control throughout the process, and helping to make connections. Their help is invaluable," Walsh recalled. The UAE is attractive for a number of reasons, including several positive economic indicators, a strong customer preference for European products, and very promising projected volumes and pricing.

Favorable Economics and Customer Situation

At the time, the UAE was home to 9.89 million people and had a GNI per capita PPP[17] of $66,690 (World Bank 2020a), compared to $71,040 for Ireland (World Bank 2020b), and $64,210 for the US (World Bank 2020c). Approximately 88% of the population were foreign-born, with the majority of those individuals coming from India (38%). The median age was 38.4 years old and 87.5% of the population lived in urban centers, including 3.0 million in Dubai and 1.5 million in Abu Dhabi (the capital). Although oil was the original source of much of its wealth, by 2018, the country had diversified enough that only 30% of its income came from oil. The UAE was especially attractive for foreign direct investment because it had a number of free trade zones, which offered 100% foreign ownership and a 0% tax rate. UAE citizens enjoyed a 1.6% unemployment rate and an inflation rate below 3% (CIA World Factbook 2022a).

UAE customers exhibited a strong preference for European products. "Consumers there want something that is not mass produced, something different. It gives them some bit of exclusivity," offered Walsh. After leaving the bakery, the product spends 6 weeks at sea before it reaches the UAE. "If they want more, we can also send them a shipment by air – that tells you how much money they're getting for it over there!"

More than 80% of the UAE's food was imported. In addition, the UAE functioned as an important food distribution hub in this part of the world: a significant amount of food travels to the UAE and is then re-exported to other neighboring countries in the Middle East, Gulf States, East Africa, and India (Export Solutions 2019). If Walsh's Bakehouse started exporting to the UAE again, there would be significant potential for sales to other parts of the Arab world.

Projected Volume and Pricing

The distribution company that was identified by Bord Bia was so anxious to sign a contract with Walsh's Bakehouse, it had already forged an agreement with one of the most well-known high-end food retailers in the country, Spinney's, where the blaa would easily sell for a premium price because it would be offered alongside other premium Western-sourced products. The suggested retail price for a 6-pack of frozen blaas would be €24.00. To start, the distributor would be able to take 1 container every 5 weeks and would charge €3 per unit for distribution.

Expanding in Ireland

Walsh's blaas were already being sold in the Irish domestic market in fresh, packaged, and frozen form. However, Walsh was in discussions with Supervalu, the country's largest grocery and food distributor, to carry fresh blaas. The company had 223 full-service Supervalu grocery stores (About Supervalu 2022) as well as 480 Centra mini-convenience stores throughout Ireland (About 2022). Unlike Spinney's, Supervalu and Centra stores were much more value-oriented in their pricing and product selection. The Irish market was certainly very attractive

[17]This measure used by the World Bank refers to a country's per capita Gross National Income (GNI), which is measured by all of the income generated by resident producers, taxes, and primary income earned abroad by residents. This figure is expressed in purchasing power parity (PPP), which is measured in international dollars (the same value of the US dollar). PPP estimates the purchasing power that is required for a similar "basket of goods" in different countries, while smoothing out the effects of different exchange rates, interest rates, and trade policies.

primarily because the culture, distribution system, language, invoicing, etc. were already familiar and easy to navigate. In addition, the Irish economy was on an upswing, Irish consumers were demonstrating a resurgence of pride in local products and production, and importantly, the predicted volumes and pricing were quite attractive.

Irish Economy

Ireland had a population of approximately 5.275 million and a full 82.2% of the residents were native Irish. The median age was 37.8 years old and 64.2% of the population lived in urban centers, primarily the city of Dublin, which was home to 1.26 million people (CIA World Factbook 2022b). The Irish economy was primarily driven by services, manufacturing, and technology. By the time Walsh was making his decision, the Irish economy had recovered nicely after the world financial crisis of 2008–2009 and its associated debt problems. The country's GDP real growth rate was 5.9%, the unemployment rate was 5.0%, and the rate of inflation was a mere 0.9% (CIA World Factbook 2018b).

Local Pride

Importantly, Irish consumers had a strongly positive attitude toward local food and artisanal food, and were likely to buy it. Tired of fast-paced industrial food production and consumption, the Slow Food Movement celebrated local food culture, sustainable production, and authenticity. Food tourism was also starting to become more popular as some people found it enjoyable to visit small agricultural operations (Allen 2009) as well as breweries, distilleries, bakeries, and other manufacturing facilities. Irish consumers believed that purchasing local food helped to support the local community (78% agreed) and that it was fresher than other alternatives (74% agreed). Seventy-two percent of Irish consumers thought that local food was high quality, 67% believed it was made with 100% Irish ingredients, 67% thought it was made with natural ingredients, 65% thought it was better quality than ordinary food, and 64% thought it was made/produced by small scale producers. Interestingly, the most preferred retailer to obtain local food was Supervalu (Bord Bia 2017).

Projected Volume and Pricing

The plan proposed to launch the blaa as a fresh product with Supervalu in a phased-in approach, starting with 80 stores and eventually expanding to all 223 stores. The Walsh brothers hoped that if the blaa was successful at Supervalu, it would also be carried in a majority (or even all) of the Centra stores. In the first 6 months, sales were projected to double from the current 30,000 blaas per week to 60,000 per week. In the second 6 months after the deal was signed, sales were projected to double again to 120,000 per week.

An important factor in the decision to pursue the Ireland/Supervalu option was the newly-constructed bakery that had been completed in the summer of 2017 and quadrupled its output. The bakehouse was currently running two shifts per day and Walsh was confident that the new bakehouse would be able to handle any increase in volume with the addition of a third shift. Indeed, the new modern bakehouse could handle the volumes for either of the alternatives that Walsh was considering. See Table A3.20 for variable costs for the fresh product.

Table A3.20 Cost structure for various package sizes of blaas (in euros)

	Ingredients	Packaging	Utilities	Labor	Total per Unit Variable Cost
Fresh: 4-pack traditional	0.080	0.030	0.035	0.150	0.295
Fresh: 6-pack traditional	0.120	0.030	0.050	0.225	0.425
Fresh: 4-pack large	0.100	0.030	0.040	0.210	0.380
Fresh: 6-pack small	0.090	0.030	0.035	0.150	0.305
Single blaa sold loose	0.020	0.000	0.010	0.038	0.068

* All prices are in euros. Any small differences in amounts are due to rounding errors.

Source: courtesy, Dermot Walsh

The Irish distributor planned to charge 50 cents per unit to pick up the shipments from the bakehouse, deliver them to several centralized distribution centers, and then deliver them to Supervalu stores all around Ireland. The suggested retail prices would be the same as indicated in Table A3.19. Walsh reflected on the importance of finding a good distributor with which to partner: "the distribution decision is really critical because we're really good at making blaas, but we're not so good at transportation. If we don't have a good distributor, it will destroy our brand equity. A lot relies on them."

Summary

As he reflected on the two options, Walsh saw another benefit to increased production at the bakehouse – increased employment in his beloved city of Waterford. Walsh's Bakehouse had been an indispensable component in the life of Waterford for three generations and he hoped that it would continue in that role for many more generations. Fortunately for Walsh, he had two very promising opportunities from which to select.

ASSIGNMENT QUESTIONS

1. For each of the products listed in Table A3.19, calculate the net contribution margin as a percentage of the selling price to the seller. From this information, develop at least two insights that would be useful for Dermot Walsh as he is making his decision about whether to pursue the Emirates deal or the Ireland deal.
2. Calculate the projected 1-year profit for Walsh's Bakehouse for the Emirates/Spinney's deal and for the Ireland/Supervalu deal. We know that the Emirates and Spinney's will only be taking the frozen product, while Supervalu will be taking four versions of the fresh product.

(Continued)

For your calculations for the Ireland/Supervalu option, assume that each of the four versions will represent 25% of the sales by volume. Which option should Walsh pursue? Why? Support your recommendation with facts from the case and elsewhere.

3 Provide a detailed list of "pros and cons" of the Emirates deal and another list of "pros and cons" for the Supervalu deal.

4 In determining which market to pursue, Walsh's most important decision criterion was the profit potential. Discuss the importance of creating a set of decision criteria. What are some other decision criteria that he could have also considered?

5 There are several ways for an organization to enter a new foreign market. Which market entry strategy is Walsh contemplating for his entry into the UAE? Is this the appropriate strategy? Why/why not?

References

About. 2022. Centra – Live Every Day. Accessed 6 June 2022. https://centra.ie/about.

About Supervalu. 2022. About Supervalu. Accessed 6 June 2022. https://supervalu.ie/about.

Allen, D. 2009. *Submission to the 2020 Agri Food Committee. FoodHarvest 2020.* Slow Food Ireland.

Bord Bia. 2017. *Local Food: Understanding Consumer Attitudes.* The Thinking House – Bord Bia Insight Centre. A Research Report in Collaboration with Coyne Research. February 2017. Accessed 6 June 2022. www.bordbia.ie/globalassets/bordbia.ie/industry/marketing-reports/consumer-reports/local-food-report-february-2017.pdf.

CIA World Factbook. 2022a. The World Factbook: Middle East: United Arab Emirates. *CIA World Factbook.* Accessed 6 June 2022. www.cia.gov/the-world-factbook/countries/united-arab-emirates/#people-and-society.

CIA World Factbook. 2022b. The World Factbook: Europe: Ireland. *CIA World Factbook.* Accessed 6 June 2022. www.cia.gov/the-world-factbook/countries/ireland/.

Digby, M.C. 2013. Waterford Blaa Awarded Special Status by the EU. *The Irish Times.* 19 November. Accessed 6 June 2022. www.irishtimes.com/life-and-style/food-and-drink/waterford-blaa-awarded-special-status-by-eu-1.1599966.

Export Solutions. 2019. Gulfood – February 2020, Dubai. Accessed 6 June 2022. www.exportsolutions.com.au/gulfood/.

PGI. 2022. Protected Geographical Indication (PGI). Geographical Indications. Aims of EU Quality Schemes. *The European Commission.* Accessed 6 June 2022. https://ec.europa.eu/info/food-farming-fisheries/food-safety-and-quality/certification/quality-labels/quality-schemes-explained_en.

World Bank. 2020a. Country Profile – United Arab Emirates. *World Bank Data.* Accessed 6 June 2020. https://databank.worldbank.org/views/reports/reportwidget.aspx?Report_Name=CountryProfile&Id=b450fd57&tbar=y&dd=y&inf=n&zm=n&country=ARE.

World Bank. 2020b. Country Profile – Ireland. *World Bank Data.* Accessed 6 June 2022. https://databank.worldbank.org/views/reports/reportwidget.aspx?Report_Name=CountryProfile&Id=b450fd57&tbar=y&dd=y&inf=n&zm=n&country=IRL.

World Bank. 2020c. Country Profile – United States. *World Bank Data.* Accessed 6 June 2022. https://databank.worldbank.org/views/reports/reportwidget.aspx?Report_Name=CountryProfile&Id=b450fd57&tbar=y&dd=y&inf=n&zm=n&country=usa.

BUGS IN THE SUPPLY CHAIN: GROWING THE EDIBLE INSECT MARKET

Emily M. Moscato

Mohammed Ashour, CEO of Aspire Food Group (Aspire), and his team were sitting in his office to discuss the company's future. Ashour, an Ontario Canada native, founded the company in graduate school at McGill University based on the concept of improving human and planet welfare through producing sustainable protein products for people. The idea won the Hult Prize in 2013 and $1 million in seed money. The source of this protein? Crickets. Today, Aspire's leadership team has a critical decision to make regarding the company's supply chain. Should they focus on building farming technology and become an ingredient supplier? Or should they continue to forward integrate and build demand in the consumer market? There was a thoughtful pause in discussion. Some team members leaned forward and focused their gaze at the whiteboard. Ashour was having an oddly déjà vu moment as he sat pondering the options with his team. "This is exactly a set-up for a business case study," he thought, as he conjured up a vivid memory of analyzing case studies in graduate school. He knew what to do next: "first, we look at the data."

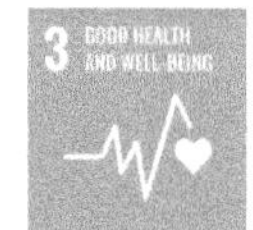

Introduction

As the world grapples with climate instability and a growing population, new perspectives have opened possibilities in the food system. Edible insects for humans and other animal consumption fit into this renewed entrepreneurial, sustainable focus. Edible insects, such as crickets, have many sought-after advantages in the marketplace. First, insects are an excellent source of protein and protein continues to be a food trend that attracts consumers. Other nutritional advantages of insect proteins are their high calcium, amino acids, and other vitamin content (Van Huis et al. 2013). Second, they can be tasty. Whole roasted insects have a similar taste and crunch profile to sunflower seeds. Cricket powder (the most common type) has a subtle nutty taste and combines well with familiar baked goods, smoothies and protein shakes, and many other sweet and savory dishes. Third, insects are safer to consume than traditional livestock; edible insects have a lower risk of harboring pathogens (such as E. coli) or transmitting zoonotic diseases to humans. Lastly, edible insects are more efficient that warm-blooded traditional livestock (see Table A3.21). Insects convert food to protein more economically, have a much lower land footprint and water usage, and their greenhouse gas production is tiny, compared to larger livestock. Moreover, improvements in insect farming continue to create better balanced living conditions that increase production efficiency and insect welfare. Despite these positive attributes, the edible insect food sector works hard to overcome the "ick" factor, convince the market of the product's benefits, build demand, and secure a consistent, quality supply chain. This is the context in which Aspire Food Group, a leader in the edible insect market, finds itself.

Table A3.21 Efficiencies of production: Feed and water requirements to produce 1kg of animal protein

	Feed (kg)	Water (liters)	% of animal edible
Beef	10	22,000–43,000	40
Pork	5	3,500	55
Chicken	2.5	2,300	55
Crickets	1.7	52*	80

*Estimated from Morales-Ramos et al. (2018).

Source: Van Huis et al. (2013)

Aspire is in a solid space. In its mission to improve the food system, Aspire has focused on creating capacity. It has patented farming and harvesting technologies and has built a consumer brand with growing equity. Recently, however, Ashour was approached by a large pet food manufacturer interested in Aspire becoming a supplier for their premium lines of pet food. It is an attractive offer, but it required a shift in focus away from Aspire's current strategy. The leadership team needs to decide where to build their capabilities: do they focus solely on creating supply or do they continue to develop supply efficiencies while also building a viable consumer brand? Being in a relatively new market means limited supply because of higher costs in all areas: research and development, technology, automation, logistics, developing partnerships, working with legislation, and product promotion. This, in turn, translates to higher consumer prices, which decreases demand and discourages growth in supply. To break this inertia, the industry must build stronger demand and attract capital investment.

In the simplest terms, Ashour saw the problem as a basic issue of supply and demand. Why invest in increasing supply if the demand is not there? Importantly, damage to the nascent industry – and Aspire as a forerunner in the market – would be significant if demand increases and the company could not deliver the necessary supply. Of course, the team knew that no decision is that simple. Like all marketing strategy decisions, simple issues are leveled with considerations of supply chain, as well as consumer attitudes, behaviors, tastes, preferences, awareness, and accessibility. Moreover, consumers, supply chain members, and policy makers needed to be educated about the product. Finally, government regulations needed to be considered.

On the Relevance of Insects

Worldwide, there is growing interest in the edible insect market as a sustainable food source for humans and animals. The 2013 treatise published by the United Nations' Food and Agricultural Organization (UN FAO) entitled *Edible Insects: Future Prospects for Food and Feed Security* (Huis et al. 2013), provided an impetus for further research and interest in marketing insects. Currently, there are over 2000 insects that are recognized as suitable for human consumption (Jongema 2017). Projections for the global insect protein market are optimistic with the largest demand growth in the feed sector (fish, poultry, pigs, and pet food), with forecasts estimating compound annual growth rate (CAGR) of 39%, reaching $72 billion by 2030 (Persistence Market Research 2020a). The pet food market has seen growth in premiumization, treats, and food toppers, with sales increasing by 20% between 2016 and 2020 – outpacing growth in the human food market (when omitting the short-term impact of the global Covid-19 pandemic) (Mintel 2020). The pet food market is growing worldwide as pets are increasingly seen as "members" of the family in some cultures. Further, to be consistent with their values, some owners seek out sustainable pet food, and are willing to pay higher prices for that food. A survey of US pet owners finds 28% of adult respondents were interested in sustainably sourced pet food; a full 31% (the highest category) of young pet owners (aged 18–34) are attracted to sustainability claims (Mintel 2020).

Projections for the human market are more moderate with CAGR of 5%, with the market forecasted to reach $925 million by 2030 (Persistence Market Research 2020b). Although the size of the human sector is dwarfed by that of the feed sector, there are considerable growth opportunities and attractive margins for food-grade crickets. Additionally, insect byproducts (chitin and frass, valued products in pharmaceuticals and fertilizer, respectively) also generate revenue for producers. Entomo Farms in Ontario, Canada is an example of a company that concentrates on supply, describing itself as "a global leader in the cultivation of cricket flour, cricket powder, and insect protein; delivering the planet's most sustainable food source" (https://entomofarms.com). Chirps is an example of a company focused on the consumer market. With the slogan "eat bugs," it sells a line of high-protein cricket powder tortilla chips, cookie mixes, and protein powder (https://eatchirps.com/). Another example is the startup BugFoundation, acquired by Kupfer Innovative Food in September 2021, which sells "insekten burger," patties made from buffalo worms, at over 4,000 German supermarkets and discounters (Münster 2021). In addition, several established food manufacturers have expanded lines to produce products containing edible insects. For example, Fazer Bakery of Finland created a bread loaf with "70 ground crickets," motivated by their commitment to source sustainable ingredients and promote ecology throughout the food system (Fazer Group 2018). As one might expect, the novelty of insect-based products stirs up significant publicity. Unfortunately, publicity is not a good predictor of sales.

Many insect entrepreneurs come from non-food industry backgrounds and have faced steep learning curves. The inability to locate consistent supply and inconsistencies in the product are difficult enough for established companies. Ashour and his team are no exception, but they do have the advantage of developing technology and focusing on manufacturing along with building the consumer market. While several businesses have found sustainable success in the industry, the list of entrepreneurs that have exited the marketplace is long (list available at Bugburger.se). One problem is that companies have had to scramble to find supply while building demand. This caused bottlenecks and inconsistent product quality. Moreover, products needed to have an attractive price point that would allow consumers to integrate the product into their weekly meals or snacks, but also allow adequate margins for the manufacturer. When trying to establish a market, the struggle over supply and demand can cause significant disruptions, but this can also open possibilities for companies with strategic partnerships, technical acumen, and foresight.

Consumers and the Consumer Market

Decision-makers at Aspire must remind themselves that insects remain a novelty to many consumers. Westerners are especially reluctant to incorporate insects into their diet because of socialization and acquired distaste: insects are not part of traditional Western diets and are therefore subject to cultural bias. Historically, in Europe and much of northern Africa, larger animals, birds, and fish were in abundance, making people less likely to seek insects as sources of protein. Adding to the problem of widespread acceptance in Western cultures is the fact that many countries have enacted regulations to control for "defect" amounts of insects and other adulterants that are allowable in common products such as chocolate, pasta, and peanut butter (see https://inspection.canada.ca/ for examples). In other parts of the world, however, some insects are traditional and celebrated food sources. It is estimated that over two billion people regularly (intentionally!) eat insects (Van Huis et al. 2013). Whether it is intentional or not, everyone on the planet consumes *some* insects.

Since edible insects are not customary in Western diets, the food categories in which new products position themselves range significantly. Products that incorporate edible insects include snack bars, tortilla chips, cookies, breads, Bolognese sauce, dried pasta, snack mixes, sausages, and burgers. The unique selling proposition for these products has primarily been high protein. A survey of UK consumers 16 and older found that 21% would be interested in trying a high-protein product made with insect proteins. In this survey, a third of younger Millennials (under 35) and Gen Z (16–25) were interested, with 43% of men under 35 saying they would be willing to try it (Mintel 2018). Since snack consumption has grown worldwide, another attractive market for edible insects is the snack category. In the US, for example, nearly 50% of adults report having a morning snack at least a few times a week and about 60% snack as often in the afternoons or evenings (Mintel 2021a). Since snacks are typically ready-to-eat and consumers are more variety seeking with snacks, edible-insects in snacks may be an easier entry point for consumers, compared to replacing center-of-the-plate proteins.

The rise of availability and interest in edible insects coincides with an increased interest in reducing meat consumption because of ecological, animal welfare, and personal health concerns. More than 75% of US consumers say that they try to act in a way that is not harmful to the environment (Young 2020). Many consumers are increasingly adapting "flexitarian" diets by having meals without a meat dish or adapting vegetarian or vegan diets. Although insects would not qualify as vegetarian, many consumers who are motivated by these concerns find edible insects a suitable alternative. Farmed insects allow for better animal welfare through strategic control of living conditions and humane killing methods, such as freezing.

Insects are part of the animal kingdom, yet in legislation that benefits the edible insect market, the US and Canada currently categorize insects as fruits and vegetables, which lessens the regulation required. While current regulation mostly favors edible insects, obstacles and biases reduce edible insects' acceptance as safe food products. Certain retailers, for example Whole Foods and Trader Joe's in the US, have requested Generally Regarded as Safe (GRAS) determination from the Food and Drug Administration (FDA) before they will sell insect-based products. Although humans have eaten insects for millennia, it is expected that the FDA will require rigorous testing before edible insects will receive GRAS. Rigorous testing necessitates significant time, expertise, and financing. For these reasons, start-ups in this space are reluctant to seek GRAS for their products (Nagy 2020).

Food safety in the European Union (EU) and the UK operate in a similar way. Edible insects in the EU are governed by "novel food" legislation. This requires the European Food Safety

Authority (EFSA) to review applications for all food categories not used for human consumption "to a significant degree" within the EU before 15 May 1997 (Regulation (EU) No 2015/2283). However, the Netherlands, Belgium, Denmark, Finland, and the UK (then part of the EU) argued that insects were exempt because animal products do not require novel food authorization, and these member countries continued to allow edible insect production. In January 2018, a streamlined application process for novel foods was issued with regulation specifying that all edible insects required review. Within the UK, the process was further complicated by Brexit. Companies that had started the EU application found they had to reapply and start the regulation process from the beginning. In December 2021, the house cricket *acheta domesticus* was the third edible insect to reach the final authorizing step as a novel food in the EU. Slowly, more edible insects and products containing edible insects are being approved across Europe, opening the market to companies inside the EU, as well as companies from across Asia and the Americas.

Aspire's History and Growth

Since its inception in 2013, Aspire has made a name for itself as an innovative, data-driven leader in the edible insect market. Ashour and his team first established operations in Canada, US, Mexico, and Ghana to produce crickets and palm weevil larva. They have since centralized operations in North America with a highly-automated facility able to produce 45,000kg of food-grade crickets each year. Aspire sought to support its original initiative to solve food insecurity and promote ecology using data, technology, and automation at a level that is unique in the industry. As an early player in the industry, Aspire looked to other foods and industries to uncover insights and benchmark best practices in the consumer market. Initially, Aspire created the brand "Aketta" to produce protein bars, cricket powder, dry-roasted crickets, and granola. The name Aketta is a phonetic spelling derived from the scientific name *acheta domesticus* crickets farmed by Aspire. These branding efforts helped build awareness and gain acceptance of edible insects with consumers, distributors, and retailers.

Because of its success, Aspire acquired another cricket-based consumer brand, EXO, in 2018. The acquisition included EXO's technologies, its snack bar product lines, and significantly higher brand equity in the consumer market. The EXO brand focused on the consumer market interested in "clean ingredients" and eating to support fitness goals. EXO's primary product is its protein bars (the average performance protein bar costs $2.99 at retail). With retail margins at 35%, the wholesale revenue per bar to EXO is $1.94 (EXO's variable costs are half of the wholesale price) (see Table A3.22). The snack bar market in the US was worth around $7 billion in 2019 and was estimated to grow to over $7.9 billion by 2025 (Mintel 2021b). EXO sells its bars – with flavors including coconut, peanut butter and jelly, and blueberry muffin – primarily through its website and has a strong social media presence. In 2019, Aspire negotiated entrance into several H-E-B supermarkets – a well-regarded supermarket chain with stores throughout Texas and parts of Mexico. Having studied the successes and failures of other edible insect and unique food companies that have a supermarket presence, Aspire decided to use self-contained displays containing products and signage to sell the EXO brand in H-E-B. Aspire also supported its supermarket expansion with regular in-store taste tests. The growth of EXO in the retail space was somewhat hampered by the global Covid-19 pandemic, but the brand met or exceeded all sales goals at H-E-B stores.

In addition to using their crickets in the EXO brand, Aspire supplies food-grade cricket powder to other brands in the market. On its face, this may appear to be helping the competition, but the use of these ingredients is limited to consumer brands without supply capabilities. As Ashour sees it, the reliability and quality of Aspire's cricket supply bolsters the entire market as it grows demand. The EXO brand as the "face" of Aspire continues to grow but Ashour and his team are left questioning the brand's direction. The newness of the market means that Aspire has little information on which consumer segments and which products offered the best growth potential. The snack bar market was initially chosen because of accessibility, but the market itself is quite crowded. Would cricket powder have better consumer acceptance if incorporated into a different food? Similarly, other consumer segments – families with young children, eco-conscious consumers, adventure and outdoor enthusiasts, and consumers with food sensitivity or allergies – are all attractive possibilities for developing more sustainable market demand. The opportunities in the consumer market are many and Aspire is in a good position to capitalize on them.

Decision Point

Aspire must determine where to focus its efforts for long-term success. Each direction has both opportunities and risks. With the first option, Aspire would focus its efforts on the consumer market, where EXO aready enjoys favorable brand equity and it can achieve higher margins. Currently, the brand is only used on protein bars, but research indicates there are other segments and product development opportunties to leverage.

The second option is for Aspire to concentrate on the supply side and contract with a major pet food manufacturer. In order to fulfill the needs of the contract to be a supplier in the pet food ingredients market, Aspire would need to increase its capacity by 110-fold and produce 4.95 million kg of crickets annually (see Table A3.22). This would require a new facility with the estimated cost of $72 million. Ashour believes he has a good shot at securing a business grant from the Canadian government, which would help to fund part of the building project. As a supplier of raw ingredients, this would reduce the pressure to support a consumer brand. It would focus efforts away from the human food market but may also hurt the chances of infiltrating the consumer market if consumers forge strong associations between insects and pet food. Is there a way to separate the pet and human markets from one another? Would such an endeavor be worth it for the company? Each direction has its risks, rewards, and trade-offs. With these dynamics in mind, Ashour and his team are ready to evaluate the evidence and determine Aspire's path forward.

Table A3.22 Financial Information

	Consumer Brand EXO Bars*	Supplier Only Pet-food Cricket Powder (1kg)*
Retail Price	$2.99	--
Wholesale Price	$1.94	$12.15
Variable Costs	$0.97	$10.32
Fixed Costs	$2,011,740	$9,398,858.00

*All figures are in USD.

Source: Moscato

ASSIGNMENT QUESTIONS

1. Examine the edible insect market:
   a. Why is there interest in developing the edible insect as a food source?
   b. Conduct a PESTLE analysis to identify the macro-environmental conditions for Aspire and the edible insect market.
   c. What are Aspire's competitive advantages?
2. Identify the advantages and challenges for each strategic option: the consumer market and the supplier market.
3. Calculate the break-even point (in dollars and units) for both the consumer protein bar market and the dog food ingredient market. Generally speaking, what is the purpose of a break-even analysis? Discuss the benefits and shortcomings of this analysis.
4. Which course of action should the marketing team at Aspire select? Support your answer with information from the case and elsewhere.
5. In the future, would you eat "dog food?" In what ways could Aspire safeguard the human edible insect market against any negative associations with a pet food brand?

References

Fazer Group. 2018. *Fazer Sirkkaleipä cricket bread wins bronze in the Cannes Lions contest.* [Press Release] 3 July. www.fazergroup.com/media/news/Fazer-Sirkkaleipa-cricket-bread-wins-bronze-in-the-Cannes-Lions-contest/

Huis, et. al. 2013. Edible Insects: Future Prospects for Food and Feed Security. FAO Forestry Paper 171. Food and Agriculture Organization of the United Nations. Rome. Accessed 29 December 2022. https://www.fao.org/3/i3253e/i3253e.pdf

Jongema, Y. 2017. *List of edible insects of the world.* 1 April 2017. Wageningen University & Research. www.wur.nl/en/Research-Results/Chair-groups/Plant-Sciences/Laboratory-of-Entomology/Edible-insects/Worldwide-species-list.htm.

Mintel. 2018. *Attitudes towards Sports Nutrition – UK.* Industry Report. Accessed through Academic License.

Mintel. 2020. *Pet Food – US, 2020.* Industry Report. Accessed through Academic License.

Mintel. 2021a. *How America Eats – US.* Industry Report. Accessed through Academic License.

Mintel. 2021b. *Snack, Nutrition and Performance Bars – US.* Industry Report. Accessed through Academic License.

Morales-Ramos, J.A., Rojas, M.G., and Dossey, A.T. 2018. Age-dependent food utilisation of Acheta domesticus (Orthoptera: Gryllidae) in small groups at two temperatures. *Journal of Insects as Food and Feed, 4* (1), 51–60.

Münster, L.M. 2021. *Insect burger start-up acquired by Kupfer Innovative Food.* News. Startbase. 22 September. www.startbase.com/news/insekten-burger-start-up-von-kupfer-innovative-food-uebernommen/

Nagy, M. 2020. *Insects for Food Use Is Permitted by Enforcement Discretion in U.S.* 28 October. thefutureofedibleinsects.com/category/regulations/

Persistence Market Research. 2020a. *Edible Insects For Animal Feed Market.* Industry Report. Persistence Market Research. www.persistencemarketresearch.com/market-research/edible-insects-for-animal-feed-market/toc

Persistence Market Research. 2020b. *Edible Insects For Human Consumption Market.* Industry Report. Persistence Market Research. www.persistencemarketresearch.com/market-research/edible-insects-for-human-consumption-market.asp

Van Huis, A., Van Itterbeeck, J., Klunder, H., Mertens, E., Halloran, A., Muir, G., and Vantomme, P. 2013. *Edible insects: Future prospects for food and feed security.* (No. 171). Food and Agriculture Organization of the United Nations. www.fao.org/3/i3253e/i3253e.pdf

Young, E. 2020. *Surroundings 2021: Sustainable Spaces* [Trend Report]. Mintel. Accessed through Academic License.

RIDING THE WAVE OF THE NATURAL HAIR MOVEMENT: BRAND EXTENSION AT CURLS, LLC.

Tyrha M. Lindsey-Warren and Diane M. Phillips

Mahisha Dellinger knew how to take big ideas and turn them into big money. Dellinger is the founder and CEO of Curls, a hair-care company designed to meet the specific needs of women of color who want a natural look for their hair. Her timing could not have been more perfect. Her line of hair-care products coincided with a movement toward more natural styles of hair and Curls soon became a multimillion-dollar brand, sold in some of the top-name retailers in the US, Canada, Brazil, Africa, and the United Kingdom. Because of this success, some top global beauty brands were introducing their own products for natural hair styles, such as Dove's "Love Your Curls" brand and Revlon's "Realistic" line. In order to stay ahead, Dellinger was currently considering two options: introduce a new oral vitamin designed for hair, skin, and nail health, or introduce a line of men's hair care products.

Hair and its Cultural Meaning

In Western cultures, the ideal image of female beauty is a young, thin, White woman with long flowing hair (Dawson and Peluchette 2019, Griffin 2019, Ndichu and Upadhyaya 2019, Rock 2019, Rudman and McLean 2016, Scott-Ward 2018, Versey 2014). Because of this, Black women have a complicated relationship with their hair and often face discrimination.

Hair Discrimination

Even today, there is very real discrimination against natural hairstyles. In the US, a student wrestler was forced to cut his dreadlocks because his hairstyle did not conform to the league's standards. An auditorium full of shocked onlookers watched as an official took a pair of scissors and cut off the student's offending locs (Onanuga 2020). Another male student in Texas received disciplinary action over his long dreadlocks. The school board cited a 30-year-old policy requiring a male student's hair to be cut so that it fell above the ears and shirt collar. The school removed him from class, prevented him from attending the prom, and threatened to not allow him to participate in the school's graduation ceremony (Cox 2020). In the UK, a 12-year-old boy with dreads was removed from his classroom and put into isolation. With the help of a non-profit human rights group, the boy's family went to court and it was found that the school had discriminated against the boy. The verdict hinged on the fact that a person's race or religious beliefs should not prevent them from receiving an education (Edkins 2018).

Women often experience discrimination too. Compared to others, Black women are 30% more likely to be formally reminded of workplace appearance policies and 83% more likely to be judged harshly on their looks (Akutekha 2020). Women report that their hair is often viewed by others as untidy, unprofessional, and even delinquent, violent, and dangerous (Ndichu and Upadhyaya 2019). Recently, however, a cultural shift seems to be occurring. Corporations are changing their policies for employees, and even the US military has changed its policies to allow women recruits to wear braids and locs (Griffin 2019). In addition, the CROWN Act (Creating a Respectful and Open World for Natural Hair), a prohibition against discrimination based on natural hairstyles, is gaining momentum around the US (The Crown Act 2020).

Women and their Hair

To say that a Black woman's hair is central to her self-concept and self-esteem may underestimate its importance in a Black woman's life. Regardless of hairstyle, only 48% of Black women believe their hair looks its best most of the time and 15% believe others judge them negatively because of their hairstyle. Spending significant amounts of time and money doesn't seem to matter much in the love–hate relationship many Black women have with their hair – just 53% of women with relaxed hair (e.g., straight hair) feel confident that their hair looks its best most of the time (Mintel 2019b). Research indicates that natural styles like braids or afros are considered less serious, less professional, less competent, and even "angry." Not surprisingly, many Black women adopt Eurocentric hairstyles in order to avoid the hassle and criticism. This pressure to conform can have a significant influence on a woman's self-concept and self-identity (Dawson and Peluchette 2019).

The Natural Hair Movement

By the early 2020s, the natural hair movement was starting to gain traction. This shift was accompanied by some developments in pop culture, such as the popularity of *Hair Love*, an animated film that won an Academy Award in 2018. The charming short animation shows a frustrated dad trying to style his daughter's hair (Akutekha 2020). Key influencers are helping natural hair become more mainstream, with actors like Lupita Ny'ongo regularly opting for natural styles (Ndichu and Upadhyaya 2019). Global tennis legend Serena Williams wears a natural style, as do A-list celebrities Halle Berry and Alicia Keys. The number of online communities centered around natural styles has also exploded, offering support and validation to women who opt for natural hair (Versey 2014). By 2018, sales of at-home relaxer kits plummeted by

22.7%. That year, less than half of Black women (47%) wore their hair in a non-natural style, while 77% wore a natural style (note that women often change styles). This trend was mostly driven by younger consumers who wanted a more natural look, as well as innovative and convenient products (Mintel 2018). At least two factors have influenced the move toward natural hairstyles: health and economics.

Health Motivations

Harsh chemicals and heat used on the hair cause dryness and breakage, as well as more serious effects such as burns, hair loss, and even blindness (Dawson and Peluchette 2019). Relaxers contain a chemical called sodium hydroxide, which can cause baldness and burns. If inhaled, it can cause permanent damage to the lungs (Rock 2009). Relaxers also contain chemicals that are hormone disruptors (Scott-Ward 2018), which can cause cancer, diseases of the reproductive system, disruptions in immune function, and metabolic problems (NIH 2020).

Another underappreciated health consequence concerns a woman's reluctance to engage in physical exercise after having her hair professionally styled. Because Black women spend so much time, effort, and money on their hair, they often do not exercise for fear of sweating too much, getting their hair wet, or otherwise disturbing their hair. By contrast, women who wear natural hairstyles are much more likely to have healthier lifestyles and exercise (Versey 2014). Women who switch to natural styles feel good about themselves: 67% are confident that their hair looks its best most of the time, compared to 48% of other women with other styles (Mintel 2019b).

Economic Considerations

Black women often undergo hours in the salon chair getting their hair styled. An elaborate style may take 6–8 hours and cost several thousand dollars. Extensions, for example, can cost several thousand dollars. In addition, the woman has to return every 1–2 weeks to get her hair washed and conditioned and return again in 6 weeks to have her hair redone (Rock 2009). A weave can cost up to $2000 to purchase the hair and up to $300 to install it (Turner and Green 2018). Even for everyday maintenance, Black women often have a multi-step hair care regimen: shampoo, co-wash, conditioner, deep conditioner, treatment, and styler. Indeed, 43% of Black women use five or more haircare products at home and collectively spend $2.51 billion in the US each year; this figure is expected to increase to $2.656 billion by 2023 (Mintel 2018).[18]

Perfect Timing

After several years successfully climbing the corporate ladder at such well-known companies as Intel and Pfizer (Raimonde 2019), Mahisha Dellinger decided to set her sights on the health and beauty industry. Her first move was to hire a chemist to help create a line of haircare products for women of color. Compared to other demographics, Black women's hair needs extra treatment and care because it is dry and prone to breakage (Turner and Green 2018). After contributing $40,000 in savings to the effort, an ideal formulation was identified – and the Curls brand was born! Working out of her garage, she made $86,000 in sales her first year selling the product to salons and online. For the first 3 years, Dellinger did not take a salary (Raimonde 2019), but in

[18]These numbers are far lower than actual expenditures because they do not include wigs, weaves, products purchased at salons, services done at salons or by individuals, hair accessories, extensions, or electric haircare tools (Turner and Green 2018).

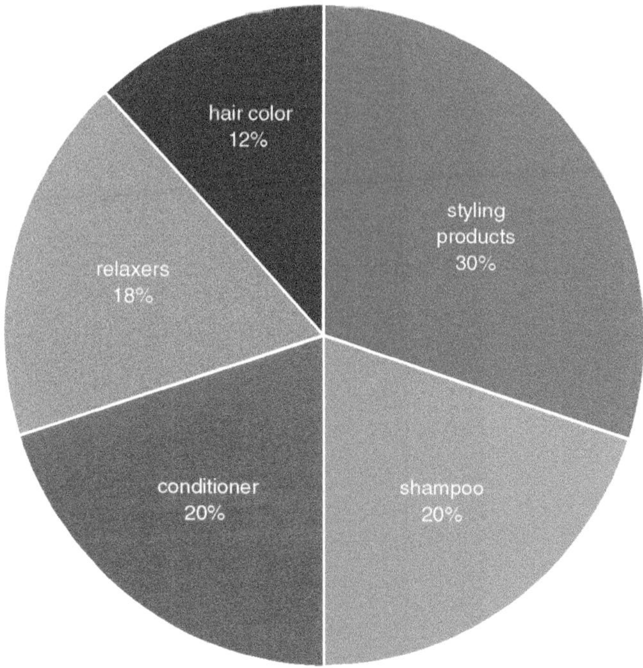

Figure A3.2 Expenditures in the ethnic haircare market

Source: derived from Mintel (2018)

2009, "Target called and wanted to carry my product" (Bryant 2017). The timing could not have been more perfect. "The market was extremely competitive with new entrants entering the industry every day," but demand was increasing even faster, explained Dellinger. By 2010, Curls products were in all US Target stores (Gumbs 2019). Soon, Walmart, CVS, and RiteAid followed. Dellinger made $360,000 in her second year, $600,000 in her third year (Holmes 2013), and according to Dellinger, by 2017, Curls was a multimillion-dollar business (see Figure A3.2).

Curls offered an inclusive line of different products for every need. Its Blueberry Bliss Collection was specifically designed to repair, restore, and grow damaged hair. All told, the company had over 40 award-winning organic hair care products for babies, kids, women, and professionals (see Photo A3.9 below).

Photo A3.9 Curls Blueberry Bliss product line

Source: courtesy, L.A.I. Communications

As the company achieved mass-market distribution, sales increased dramatically. The company experienced a substantial dip in sales in 2014 (see Figure A3.3), but in 2015, Curls introduced the new Blueberry Bliss Collection, which offered tremendous health benefits for the hair. Dellinger realized that continuous innovation was necessary for Curls to survive against the big global brands. At first, the Blueberry Bliss Collection was sold exclusively at Target as well as on the Curls website. Within one year, sales of the initial three products in the line nearly doubled. According to Dellinger, "Target was ecstatic regarding the success of the line and wanted more products." So, in 2016, Dellinger added three more products to the line.

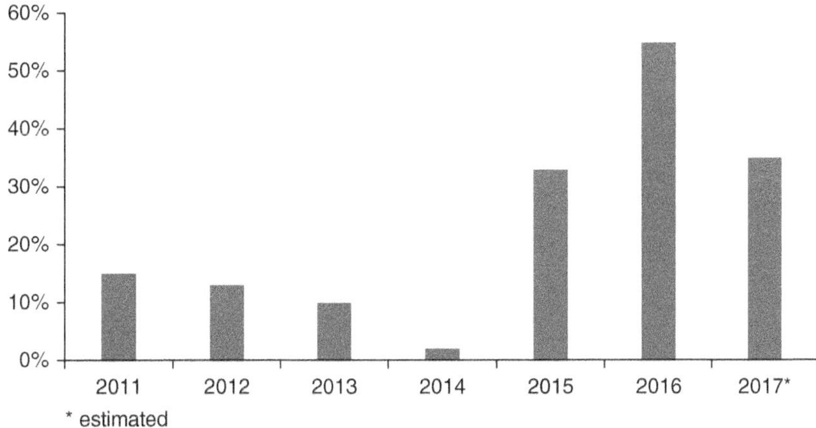

Figure A3.3 Revenue growth at Curls

Source: Hoopfer (2016)

Competitive Pressure

The beauty market is very lucrative; the average retail markup is 80% and operating margins are impressive. Global industry leader L'Oréal has an impressive operating margin of 17.3% (Haber 2015). The ethnic beauty market is even more attractive, with the category growing at an impressive 10% annual clip (Jones 2016). Black women account for 85% of all money spent on beauty industry sales, even though they make up only about 7% of the US population (Turner and Green 2018). In total, the Black haircare market was estimated to be worth $2.5 billion[19] (Gumbs 2019). Perhaps because of the tremendous opportunities, competition is tough (Bates 2014). New products are regularly introduced and many niche brands are being acquired by global industry giants. L'Oréal, for example, owns Carol's Daughter and Dark and Lovely, while Revlon owns Crème of Nature (Turner and Green 2018). With the onslaught of new products and increasing consolidation, smaller independent companies have difficulty staying relevant and financially viable.

Smaller brands like Curls are at a particular disadvantage because of the massive amounts of money that big brands can spend on marketing. When she first introduced her products, social media was an emerging platform and Dellinger relied on grassroots promotional tactics, such as events at salons and hair shows, as well as word-of-mouth. Later, with the rise of social media, key influencers were able to communicate the product's benefits both domestically and internationally. Social media platforms and online communities proved to be especially powerful

[19]This figure does not include wigs, weaves, products purchased at salons, services done at salons or by individuals, hair accessories, extensions, or electric haircare tools.

because busy women could access them anytime and anywhere. Importantly, they offered emotional support, information, validation, and empowerment (Versey 2014). Dellinger was convinced that this form of communication with her customers would continue to be an important key to her success (Meisel 2015). To facilitate this, Curls connected with social media influencers and others to communicate the brand's key benefits and points of differentiation.

Dellinger also relied heavily on PR to spread the word about Curls. Inspired by her business acumen and success, Dellinger's story appeared on CBS' *The Talk*, CNBC's *Street Signs*, *The Scene* by CondeNast, *Bloomberg*, *The Real*, *News One Now with Roland Martin*, and *The New York Times*. In addition, her story appeared in magazines such as *InStyle*, *Essence*, *Glamour*, *Ebony*, *Juicy*, *Redbook*, *Lucky*, *Seventeen*, *Vibe*, *Black Enterprise*, *Elle*, *Modern Salon*, *Woman's World*, and *Parents*, along with a host of beauty and salon trade publications. A-List celebrities like Halle Berry, Alicia Keys, Nia Long, Tia Mowry, Blair Underwood, Ashanti, and Yvette Nicole Brown also spoke out about using Curls products.

As another indicator of her success, Dellinger regularly received offers to buy the company from some of the industry's biggest names. Carol's Daughter sold to L'Oréal in 2014 and other niche brands were also being pursued. Unfortunately, the L'Oréal deal received a lot of negative press. Black women felt a strong sense of loyalty to the brand and felt betrayed by the sale (Bates 2014). Although the offers were certainly tempting, Dellinger was not yet ready to leave. "Over the years, I have worked incredibly hard to grow my business and have had several offers for Curls, but I didn't sell because I felt that I had something left that I wanted to achieve," she reflected.

Despite these successes, Dellinger did not become complacent. She relocated her operations from California to Dallas, Texas, a regional hub for manufacturing of personal care products. The move allowed her to better scale production and it allowed for very short flights to the headquarters of most of her retail partners (Haber 2015). She also introduced several new lines, such as Curly Q for kids, Poppin' Pineapple with extra vitamins, and Green Vegan, a line of vegan haircare products. Dellinger realized that she needed to do something even more innovative to stay ahead of the global brands and was contemplating two alternatives. The first alternative would be consistent with her emphasis on health and wellness; she could introduce a line of oral vitamins that promote healthy skin, hair, and nails. Alternatively, she could leverage her knowledge and expertise in haircare to introduce a line of men's products.

Expand into Health and Wellness

None of Curls' direct competitors were in the health and wellness category and Dellinger believed the expansion would allow her to broaden the definition of her brand beyond just topical haircare. The US market for vitamins and health supplements was strong and growing. Approximately 50% of American adults took a daily multivitamin, 83% took some type of daily vitamin, more than half took a mineral supplement, and one third took calcium. Total sales in the category in 2019 were approximately $26 billion and were growing at about 5.2% per year. By 2024, sales were expected to reach $32 billion (Mintel 2019a). Since nutrient deficiencies and hormone imbalance often lead to hair loss, Dellinger believed a new vitamin or supplement addressing those problems would complement the line and would promote health from the inside–out. She estimated that she might be able to capture 10% of the US market and sell a 1-month supply for $25 per month. She did have several concerns, however. Although herbal supplements and vitamins did not need FDA approval, Dellinger needed to ensure that the product met her customers' high standards for performance. Another concern was whether the addition of a vitamin or supplement might cannibalize her existing products – consumers might wonder if it was necessary to buy both an oral vitamin *and* an array of topical haircare products.

Introduce a Line of Men's Products

In a recent study of Black men, 73% said that the haircare products they buy work as expected and 60% said that they use haircare products specifically formulated for Black hair. Unfortunately, 58% also believed that all haircare products deliver the same results regardless of price (Mintel 2019b), indicating a reluctance to spend money on specialized products. A strong majority of Black men (over 80%) wear their hair in a very short natural style, which they believe is a more conservative look; 34% wear their hair in "naturalized" (or non-conformist) styles like twists, locs, or cornrows (men change their hairstyles too) (Mintel 2019b). Research indicates that the target market is most likely aged 35+, who make more than $75,000 in household income, work full time, have graduated from college, are married or with a partner, and are a father. This group represents 51% of all Black men (Mintel 2019b). Dellinger thinks she could capture 8% of the market and that men will likely spend $35 per month on their haircare regimen. She was concerned, however. How willing would men be to purchase and use their wives' or girlfriends' haircare brand?

Summary

Looking toward the future, Dellinger was "confident that the movement of going natural is here to stay and we will continue to see more women embracing their natural texture" (Meisel 2015). With a strong record of success in innovation, Dellinger was ready for her biggest bet yet. Should she pursue a new oral vitamin designed to improve the health and vitality of a woman's hair, skin, and nails? Alternatively, should she pursue the men's natural haircare market?

ASSIGNMENT QUESTIONS

1. Should Dellinger develop a new product line of vitamins for women or should she develop a line of men's haircare products? Support your recommendation with evidence from the case and elsewhere.
2. Dellinger is contemplating two alternatives to expand and develop her product line. However, another alternative would be to sell the company while it is performing so well – to go out on top, so to speak. How viable is this alternative? Discuss.
3. Estimate the market potential (in $) for both the vitamin market and the men's haircare market in the US. Be sure to list the assumptions that were made in creating these estimates.
4. The Ansoff Matrix (chapter 8) is used to help create a set of product objectives. Which type of objective would Denlinger be pursuing with the vitamin product? Describe some general advantages and disadvantages of this objective that Dellinger will need to consider when making her decision. Which type of objective would be pursued with the men's products? Describe some general advantages and disadvantages of this objective.
5. Where does the Blueberry Bliss line sit on the Product Life Cycle curve? Discuss. Given this placement, create a four-part marketing strategy (product, price, place, promotion) that Dellinger could employ to manage this line.

References

Akutekha, E. 2020. How the natural hair movement has failed black women. *Huffpost.* Style & Beauty section. 16 March. Accessed 7 June 2022. www.huffpost.com/entry/natural-hair-movement-failed-black-women_l_5e5ff246c5b6985ec91a4c70.

Bates, K.G. 2014. A black cosmetic company sells, or sells out? *NPR. Morning Edition.* 24 October. Accessed 7 June 2022. www.npr.org/sections/codeswitch/2014/10/24/358263731/a-black-cosmetic-company-sells-or-sells-out.

Bryant, A. 2017. Becoming a leader of your own life. *The New York Times.* Section BU. Sunday. 1 January. Accessed 9 June 2020 through academic license.

Cox, C. 2020. Texas teen banned by high school from attending graduation after refusing to cut dreadlocks. *USA Today.* 24 January. Accessed 7 June 2022. www.usatoday.com/story/news/nation/2020/01/24/black-texas-teen-barred-high-school-after-graduation-not-cutting-dreadlocks/4562210002/.

Dawson, G.A. Karl, K.A., and Peluchette, J.V. 2019. Hair matters: Toward understanding natural black hair bias in the workplace. *Journal of Leadership & Organizational Studies, 26* (3), 389–401.

Edkins, G. 2018. Young Rastafarian Boy, 12, WINS racial discrimination case against Church of England school that wanted him to shave off his dreadlocks or remain in isolation. *The Daily Mail.* 12 September. Accessed 7 June 2022. www.dailymail.co.uk/news/article-6161817/Rastafarian-boy-12-wins-discrimination-case-dreadlocks-ban.html.

Griffin, C. 2019. How natural black hair at work became a civil rights issue. *JSTOR Daily.* Politics & Government Section. ITHAKA. 3 July. Accessed 7 June 2022. https://daily.jstor.org/how-natural-black-hair-at-work-became-a-civil-rights-issue/.

Gumbs, A. 2019. Mahisha Dellinger became a multimillion-dollar beauty maven. *Black Enterprise, 49* (4), January/March. 10.

Haber, H. 2015. Inside the Dallas beauty business. *D CEO.* September. Accessed 7 June 2022. www.dmagazine.com/publications/d-ceo/2015/september/inside-the-dallas-beauty-business/.

Holmes, T.E. 2013. Natural hair is big business. *Black Enterprise, 43* (6). January/February. 93–8.

Hoopfer, E. 2016. She started in her garage, now she has a multimillion-dollar company in DFT. What's next? *Dallas Business Journal.* 2 June. Subscription access only. Accessed 7 June 2022. www.bizjournals.com/dallas/news/2016/06/02/she-started-in-her-garage-now-she-has-a-multi.html.

Jones, L. 2016. Experts: Cultivate diversity in beauty. *Mass Market Retailers.* 23 May. Accessed 7 June 2022. www.massmarketretailers.com/experts-cultivate-diversity-beauty/.

Meisel, M. 2015. Illustrious advancements: Ethnic hair care and skin care companies are having success at every level. *Happi.* 1 April. Accessed 7 June 2022. www.happi.com/issues/2015-04-01/view_features/illustrious-advancements/.

Mintel. 2018. *Mintel's Black Haircare – US.* September 2018.

Mintel. 2019a. *Vitamins and Minerals – US.* September 2019.

Mintel. 2019b. *Black Haircare – US.* August 2019.

Ndichu, E.G. and Upadhyaya, S. 2019. "Going natural": Black women's identity project shifts in hair care practices. *Consumption, Markets & Culture, 22* (1), February, 44–67.

NIH. 2020. Endocrine disruptors. National Institute of Environmental Health Sciences. Health & Education. Accessed 7 June 2022. www.niehs.nih.gov/health/topics/agents/endocrine/index.cfm#:~:text=When%20absorbed%20in%20the%20body,production%20of%20hormones%20(right).

Onanuga, T. 2020. "What does Hair Love's Oscar success say about diversity in Hollywood?" The Guardian. Movies section. February 25. Accessed 29 December 2022. https://www.theguardian.com/film/2020/feb/25/what-hair-love-oscar-success-diversity-hollywood

Raimonde, O. 2019. This mom was denied a small business loan. Here's how she built a multimillion-dollar hair care business anyway. *Money*. 1 August. Accessed 7 June 2022. https://money.com/this-mom-was-denied-a-small-business-loan-heres-how-she-built-a-multimillion-dollar-hair-care-business-anyway/.

Rock, C. 2009. *Good Hair*. HBO Films.

Rudman, L.A. and McLean, M.C. 2016. The role of appearance stigma in implicit racial ingroup bias. *Group Processes & Intergroup Relations, 19* (3), 374–93.

Rudolph, Thomas & Nagengast, Liane & Nitsch, Frauke. (2015). Einkaufstourismus Schweiz 2015 : Eine Studie zu den aktuellen Entwicklungen des Einkaufstourismus, St. Gallen: Universität St.Gallen.

Scott-Ward, G. 2018. *Back to Natural: A Documentary Film*.

The Crown Act. The 2020. About. Accessed 7 June 2022. www.thecrownact.com/about.

Turner, A. and Green, D. 2018. The black hair care industry billions – but the US is missing out on the market. *CNBC*. Household Products Section. 17 August. Accessed 7 June 2022. www.cnbc.com/2018/08/17/black-hair-care-wigs-weaves-extensions-salons.html.

Versey, H.S. 2014. Centering perspectives on black women, hair politics, and physical activity. *American Journal of Public Health, 104* (5), 810–15.

EMMI: HOW A SWISS DAIRY COMPANY CONQUERED THE US MARKET

Kristina Kleinlercher and Thomas Rudolph

Emmi, Switzerland's largest dairy company, has had a long and winding road in its efforts to crack the US market. Starting in 2009, the margin, market relevance, and growth potential prompted Emmi to strengthen its footprint in this huge, but highly competitive market. Indeed, the US was Emmi's largest foreign market, generating approximately 12% of the company's overall sales. At the end of another exhausting but successful day of contract negotiations, Urs Riedener, CEO of the Emmi Group, leaned back in his desk chair and reflected on Emmi's efforts to conquer the US market.

The Stagnating Swiss Market

Emmi is Switzerland's largest milk processor and one of the leading global companies for premium dairy products. What started in 1907 as a milk association of 62 different cooperatives now had 6000 employees, partnerships with 300 different cheese dairies, more than 20 global acquisitions, and 2018 global sales in excess of $3 billion[20] (Emmi Annual Report 2018). Riedener, who became CEO of Emmi in 2008, played a leading role in its expansion.

By the early 2000s, declining milk consumption and stagnating sales prompted the company to look abroad for growth opportunities. In 2008, the average Swiss customer consumed 75 liters

[20]Unless otherwise specified, all financial figures are in USD.

of milk per year, but by 2018, per capita milk consumption dropped to only 50 liters (Theiler 2019). On the supply side, an increasing number of low-cost competitors and substitute products based on soy, almond, or rice milk were entering the Swiss market, causing intense pressure on prices. The situation with cheese had also been intense, as an increasing number of imports and private-label cheeses jeopardized Emmi's retail shelf space and intensified price pressure. According to Riedener, the amount of cheese imports increased by 36% between 2009 and 2017, while per capita consumption remained stable. In addition, Swiss shoppers were increasingly crossing into nearby countries to do their grocery shopping; many found particularly attractive prices in Austria, Germany, France, and Italy (Rudolph, et al. 2015).

Entering the US Market

Starting in 2005, the company committed to international expansion, despite identifying only a limited number of markets compatible with Emmi's commitment to product innovation and high production standards. All indications were that the US was a promising new avenue for Emmi's international growth – a market that is not only the origin of worldwide food trends, but is also 40 times bigger than that of Switzerland.

A firm's first entry into a new market is typically accomplished with exporting. Later, firms increase their commitment by entering into contractual agreements, strategic alliances, or direct investment (Pan and Tse 2000). With the goal to position itself as a product leader in the US, Emmi chose a similar path. Although Emmi started exporting Swiss dairy products to the US as early as the first half of the 20th century, in 2009, management decided to acquire its first US dairy firm. With an increasing number of partnerships and acquisitions, Emmi gradually increased its market knowledge in the US, enabling the company to offer a wide range of premium and specialty dairy products that cater specifically to US customer preferences.

By the early 2020s, Emmi had utilized this gradual entry strategy in several foreign markets and had become a successful multinational company with subsidiaries in 13 different countries. Emmi's subsidiaries have a strong company culture and allegiance, sharing the same values toward environmental, social, and economic sustainability, as well as humane treatment of animals, employee engagement, and preservation of long-standing traditions. Emmi allows its subsidiaries to continue to operate in the same way they had done before their merger with Emmi. However, Emmi offers significant support, such as updating production sites with the latest technology and offering industry best practice knowledge through group strategic initiatives (Raaflaub 2015).

In 2018, for the first time in company history, sales from international markets accounted for more than 50% of Emmi's group sales. Emmi's Americas division generated sales of more than $1 billion, which represented an organic growth of 5.6%. The US is Emmi's largest foreign market, followed by Spain, Germany, and Tunisia (Emmi Annual Report 2018). Emmi utilized three different strategies in the US market: 1) direct export of products from Switzerland, 2) the Emmi Roth specialty cheese division, and 3) the California Collection, a conglomerate focusing on goat milk, organic, and lactose-free products.

Emmi's Exports

Dairy products produced in Switzerland and exported to other countries represent 10% of Emmi's sales. Consumers around the world cherish the *Swissness* of Emmi's products because they represent the values of high quality, precision, and performance. Riedener estimated that if Swiss milk production volume stayed constant, "one quarter of Swiss milk will always have to be exported to other countries in order to stay competitive" (Best 2016). Of the many Emmi dairy products that are exported to the US, the most popular are traditional and exclusive cheeses, artisan cave-aged cheeses, and hot fondues. Emmi cheeses are available at restaurants, grocery deli counters, fine cheese shops, and high-end supermarkets.

At the core of Emmi's success is a strong belief in sustainable agriculture and respect for the people, animals, and land. Emmi has a close working relationship with the Swiss farms that supply the milk for its cheeses, most of which are family farms with fewer than 30 cows. Use of genetically modified organism (GMO) feed is strictly forbidden and Emmi adheres to strict quality controls, environmental directives, and guidelines throughout the production process. Emmi controls the entire value chain for its cheese products from sourcing the fresh Swiss milk, to producing the cheese in various sizes and shapes, setting its prices, and engaging with individual customers.

Although Emmi had been able to steadily increase sales from exports to the US (with almost 7000 tons of exported goods in 2018), the company recently had some additional challenges. For instance, ensuring profitability with certified AOP (Appellation d'Origine Protegée) cheeses in the US has proven difficult. The Swiss Federal Office of Agriculture certifies products, such as cheese or wine, that meet very stringent requirements regarding quality, origin, and production (AOP-IGP 2019). Because of limitations on production and processing in 2018, Emmi had to purchase one of its most popular cheeses, Le Gruyère AOP, from another supplier before further aging and refining. This reduced Emmi's margins and volume; Emmi exported just over 2500 tons of Le Gruyère AOP to the US that year.

Another challenge occurred in 2004 when Emmi introduced chilled coffee drinks made from freshly brewed high-quality coffee beans and Swiss milk. What started as a simple idea became a successful global product sold in 10 different varieties to 15 foreign markets. Emmi's success with Caffè Latte encouraged it to introduce the chilled coffee drink to the US. Unfortunately, some unexpected difficulties arose: (1) logistics and the refrigerated supply chain were complicated, as the quality of Caffè Latte is very sensitive to temperature changes; (2) retailers were reluctant to offer dedicated, refrigerated spaces; (3) marketing was expensive because customers were not familiar with the product; and (4) US companies such as Starbucks began to offer chilled coffee as well. In the end, Emmi decided to withdraw Caffè Latte from the US market. Today, Emmi is the market leader for cold coffee products in Western Europe (Weinmann 2019), and Caffè Latte is one of Emmi's bestselling products in Switzerland and abroad, with steadily increasing sales volumes (Emmi Annual Report 2018).

Emmi Roth and Specialty Cheeses

In 1911, Swiss entrepreneur Otto Roth immigrated to the US state of Wisconsin and founded an import agency for Swiss cheeses. Eighty years later, the company began to produce its own cheeses, using locally-sourced, high-quality, local milk. Wisconsin has a long history and tradition of cheese production, with small family-owned farms and cheese factories throughout the region. In 2009, Emmi purchased Roth Käse USA and became Emmi Roth. Today, Emmi Roth is one of the largest producers of specialty cheese in the US, and is known for its award-winning cheeses such as Grand Cru® and Buttermilk Blue®, as well as everyday favorites such as Havarti and Gouda. Emmi Roth sources milk from 150 small family farms within a 60-mile radius, where treating cows with bovine growth hormones to increase milk production is strictly forbidden (Emmi Roth 2019a).

Guided by Emmi's strong social, ecological, and economic values, Emmi Roth invests heavily in social and environmental concerns. For instance, in 2018, Emmi Roth added 1600 solar panels to its cheesemaking plant in Platteville, Wisconsin, that supply 15% of the facility's annual electrical usage. These panels reduce the company's annual carbon footprint by 14,000 tons (Emmi Roth

2018). In 2018, Emmi invested in social sustainability by donating a food truck which visits the school district of nearby Madison, offering free or reduced-price lunches to students while educating them about the benefits of fresh, healthy, and locally-produced food (Cotant 2018).

Emmi Roth cheeses are positioned as premium products, consistent with Emmi corporate positioning. The premium specialty cheese market in the US is extremely competitive. In order to compete with major players such as Saputo (Canada) or Lactalis (France), Emmi Roth continues to invest significant resources in anticipating emerging market trends and strengthening its niche products. Emmi Roth cheeses are available across the US in both retail settings (supermarkets, specialty cheese shops, and deli departments), and the foodservice industry (restaurants). Emmi Roth is especially well-known for its excellent foodservice department, which is characterized by its reliable delivery and excellent customer service. Emmi Roth even employs chefs who work with key accounts to develop new recipes and menus that feature its cheeses. This channel accounts for approximately 60% of its sales.

Emmi Roth was an early entrant in the organic category. In 2017, the company launched a line of cheeses made with 100% fresh, locally-sourced organic milk (Emmi Roth 2017). It was also ahead of the curve in blue cheese. In 2019, Emmi Roth acquired the Great Lakes Cheese blue cheese plant in Seymour, Wisconsin. In keeping with the Emmi Group's corporate philosophy and policies, Emmi Roth offered continued employment to all employees at the Seymour location. This enabled Emmi Roth to maintain access to a talented group of cheesemakers to quickly expand its blue cheese production and maintain its existing customer base. Importantly, this acquisition helped Emmi Roth to develop innovative blue cheese products and new packaging solutions (Emmi Roth 2019b). Other recent innovations include blue cheese crumbles (Emmi Roth 2019c) and Roth Chèvre, a fresh and earthy goat cheese (Emmi Roth 2019d). With continuous product innovations, Emmi Roth expects to further strengthen its position in the US cheese market.

The California Collection

With a median household income well above the US average and an abundance of health-conscious consumers (Data USA 2017), California is home to many consumers who are dedicated to seasonal, healthy, and local food. California is known for its progressive social stance and is home to the innovative contributions of Silicon Valley and the tech industry. In short, California brings significant disruptive influence to the entire country. Because of this, Emmi set its sights on California. Emmi's California Collection features a set of premium brands and diverse product offerings (milk, yogurt, cheese, and the fermented milk-based product kefir) that are on the cutting edge of nationwide food trends. As of 2019, Emmi owned four companies in California: Cowgirl Creamery, Cypress Grove, Meyenberg, and Redwood Hill. In line with Emmi's strategic goal to strengthen its niche business, all of these companies focus on goat milk, lactose-free, and/or organic dairy products.

Goat milk products

With Cypress Grove, Redwood Hill, and Meyenberg, Emmi controls a strong position in the goat dairy business in the western half of the US. This market is especially attractive because it addresses the needs of people who are allergic to cow dairy products. Not only is goat milk more easily digestible, it contains 18% more calcium, 43% more potassium, 40% more magnesium, and 104% more Vitamin A than whole cow's milk. Furthermore, not only do goats require less water per gallon of milk produced, they produce nearly 20 times less methane per kilogram of body weight than dairy cows. However, goat milk is more challenging to handle than cow's milk. Goat milk is more fragile and its composition can be easily damaged unless handled carefully. An additional complication is that supply and demand for goat milk products are not well aligned. Production peaks in spring and is lowest in winter. However, demand is generally highest during the winter (Archwamety 2017). In all, Emmi's goat milk products address trends for healthy fats, high protein, probiotic, and low sugar.

An additional value of goat milk products is that they generate higher profit margins than conventional cow's milk products. According to the US market research company IRI, goat cheese volume sales have gained steadily since 2013. More than 10 million pounds of goat milk cheese are sold annually in the US (Archwamety 2017). Goat cheeses are especially popular among Millennials and households with annual income greater than $100,000 (Archwamety 2017). While the earthy-flavored Chèvre continues to be the most popular goat cheese in the US (with approximately 50% market share), varieties and quality levels of goat cheese have increased substantially in the last decade (Archwamety 2017).

Despite its steady growth, however, goat milk cheese holds only a small share of the total cheese sold in the US, and remains a niche market for Emmi, generating approximately 5% of the group's total sales. Emmi first entered this niche in 2010, when it acquired Cypress Grove in Arcata, California, one of the first major goat cheese producers in the US. After the acquisition, Emmi built a new goat dairy to significantly increase milk supply, a new state-of-the-art creamery to increase cheesemaking capacity, and launched a new marketing communications plan designed to educate stakeholders about goat milk production. Cypress Grove's sales quickly grew from $10 million to $30 million. The company is known for its tireless commitment to quality and has won numerous awards for its cheese. The 3-week aged Humboldt Fog is the company's signature cheese, making up about 40% of Cypress Grove's US sales. The strength of the company is enhanced by Cypress Grove's exceptionally loyal and passionate customer base. In keeping with other Emmi brands, Cypress Grove uses a premium pricing strategy. Its cheeses cost between $56 and $77 per kilogram, whereas cheaper mass-market goat cheeses are available for as low as $11 per kilogram.

In 2015, Emmi acquired Redwood Hill Farm, an award-winning producer of goat milk cheese, fresh milk, butter, kefir, and yogurt. In keeping with the company's commitment to sustainability, Redwood Hill's creamery runs completely on renewable energy and each farm that supplies its goat milk must prove that it is certified in treating its animals humanely (Humane Farm Animal Care 2018). In addition, the company prints sustainability-related information on their product labels and recently redesigned its yoghurt and kefir cups to reduce the use of plastic and maximize the use of recyclable material per cup. According to Riedener, this initiative decreased Redwood Hill's consumption of plastic by 40 tons per year (see Photo A3.10) (Emmi Annual Report 2018).

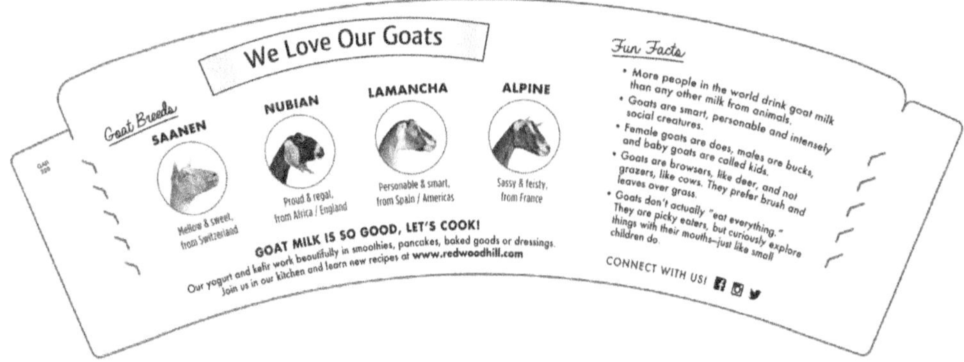

Photo A3.10 Redwood Hill's yogurt and kefir cup labels

Source: courtesy, Emmi, Inc.

To further increase its goat milk business and benefit from synergies between subsidiaries, Emmi acquired Meyenberg in 2017, a California company that controls a significant portion of the goat milk sold in the US. Meyenberg sources goat milk from over 20 West Coast dairies, all of which are passionate about treating their goats well and providing customers with high-quality premium goat milk, butter, and cheddar cheese.

Lactose-free and organic products

With its acquisition of Redwood Hill in 2015, Emmi decided to further commit to the lactose-free dairy niche. Launched in 2010 as an affiliated brand of Redwood Hill, Green Valley is the most significant line of lactose-free cow dairy products in the US. Approximately 30–50 million American adults (i.e., 12% of the US population) suffer from lactose intolerance (Green Valley 2019). With a deep commitment to offering delicious dairy products to this segment of the population, Green Valley offers yogurt, kefir, sour cream, cream cheese, butter, and cottage cheese made from lactose-free milk. Because working with lactose-free milk and cultures is difficult, Redwood Hills' experience in handling delicate goat milk was an important factor in the success of Green Valley's growth.

In 2016, Emmi strengthened its position in the organic cheese market by purchasing Cowgirl Creamery. Cows on organic dairy farms have open access to pasture, may not be treated with bovine growth hormones, are given no antibiotics, and are fed only grass and feed that have not been treated with pesticides. When Cowgirl Creamery got its start in 1994, the goal was to create fresh and artisan cheese made from organic cow milk. More than two decades later, the award-winning Cowgirl Creamery sells cheese in two proprietary stores, over 500 retail stores, farmers markets, restaurants, and chain supermarkets across the country (Krähenbühl 2016).

Summary

Emmi's annual sales forecasts for its Americas division continued to increase at an encouraging 4-6%. Despite continued pressure on Emmi's margins, its strong positioning as a product leader, continuous investment in innovation, and high production standards gave Emmi the ability to offer its customers a compelling value proposition. With such a strong record of success, Riedener is confident that Emmi will continue to thrive well into the future.

ASSIGNMENT QUESTIONS

1. Emmi decided to utilize acquisitions to increase its footprint in the US. What would have happened if Emmi had decided to focus on contractual agreements such as licensing? Compare the advantages and disadvantages of the two market entry strategies in the US.
2. Emmi is looking for new firms to acquire in the US in order to further strengthen its market position. Identify the characteristics that such a firm should have in order to suit Emmi's positioning, product portfolio, and company values. Screen the US market for potential candidates, propose two to three different firms, and provide reasoning for your choices.
3. In 2012, Emmi failed to successfully introduce Caffè Latte to the US market. Use the information from the case and other sources to develop a strategy for Emmi to introduce Caffè Latte to the US market today.

(Continued)

a. Assess the competitive landscape for Caffè Latte in the US, elaborating on its target market and unique selling proposition (USP) and develop a distribution, logistics, and marketing strategy.
b. Calculate the market potential (in sales $) for this product and provide a list of the assumptions you made in performing this calculation.

4. Assuming a stable goat cheese market from 2017 onwards, calculate Cypress Grove's market share volume in the US today.
5. Compare Emmi's business strategy in the US with one from a leading dairy firm of your choice in the US market (e.g., Lactalis or Saputo). Conduct a SWOT Analysis for both firms and compare their product portfolios. Draw insights from your analyses and derive concrete action recommendations for Emmi on how to increase its competitive advantage in the US market.

References

AOP-IGP. 2019. Definition AOP-IGP. Accessed 7 June 2022. www.aop-igp.ch/de/ueber-aop-igp/definition-aop-igp/.

Archwamety, R. 2017. Cheese of the Month – January 2017: Goat's milk cheese gaining in demand, quality, variety. *Cheese Market News*. January. Accessed 7 June 2022. www.cheesemarketnews.com/articlearch/cheese/13jan17.html.

Best, D. 2016. Emmi CEO Urs Riedener on 2017, M&A strategy and Brexit – the just-food interview, part two. *Just-food*. 2 September. Accessed 7 June 2022. www.just-food.com/interviews/emmi-ceo-urs-riedener-on-2017-ma-strategy-and-brexit-the-just-food-interview-part-two/.

Cotant, P. 2018. Farm to school food truck launched at Madison high schools. *Wisconsin State Journal*. 16 April. Accessed 7 June 2022. https://madison.com/wsj/news/local/education/local_schools/farm-to-school-food-truck-launched-at-madison-high-schools/article_bca27e1b-10d4-5d34-a566-8e2c9981e50d.html.

Data USA. 2017. California. *Data USA*. Accessed 7 June 2022. https://datausa.io/profile/geo/california.

Emmi Annual Report. 2018. *Annual Report 2018*. Accessed 7 June 2022. https://report.emmi.com/2018/de/downloads/.

Emmi Roth. 2017. Emmi Roth launches new Roth® Organics cheese line. Press Release. 20 January. Accessed 7 June 2022. www.emmiroth.com/emmi-roth-usa-launches-new-rothr-organics-cheese-line/.

Emmi Roth. 2018. Emmi Roth adds 1,600 solar panels to Platteville, Wisconsin, plant in efforts to reduce carbon footprint. Press Release. 19 September. Accessed 7 June 2022. www.emmiroth.com/emmi-roth-adds-1600-solar-panels-to-platteville-wisconsin-plant-in-efforts-to-reduce-carbon-footprint/.

Emmi Roth. 2019a. Great-tasting cheese starts with the highest quality milk. Accessed 7 June 2022. www.emmiroth.com/our-company/our-farmers/.

Emmi Roth. 2019b. Emmi Roth acquires Great Lakes Cheese's Seymour plant. Press Release. 4 January. Accessed 7 June 2022. www.emmiroth.com/emmi-roth-acquires-great-lakes-cheeses-seymour-plant/.

Emmi Roth. 2019c. Roth® Cheese adds Chèvre to its collection of specialty cheeses. Press Release. 18 May. Accessed 7 June 2022. www.emmiroth.com/roth-cheese-reinvigorates-the-blue-cheese-category-with-new-flavor-ups-blue-cheese-crumbles/.

Emmi Roth. 2019d. Roth® Cheese reinvigorates the blue cheese category with new Flavor Ups™ Blue Cheese Crumbles. Press Release. 18 May. Accessed 7 June 2022. www.emmiroth.com/roth-cheese-reinvigorates-the-blue-cheese-category-with-new-flavor-ups-blue-cheese-crumbles/.

Green Valley. 2019. Our story. *Green Valley Creamery*. Accessed 7 June 2022. https://greenvalleylactosefree.com/our-story.

Humane Farm Animal Care. 2018. *Humane Farm Animal Care Standards: Dairy, Fiber, and Meat Goats*. March 2013. A report published by Humane Farm Animal Care. Middleburg, Virginia. Accessed 7 June 2022. https://certifiedhumane.org/wp-content/uploads/Std19.Goat_.3H.pdf.

Krähenbühl, Samuel. 2016. Emmi expandiert weiter in den USA. *Schweizer Bauer*. 17 May. Accessed 7 June 2022. www.schweizerbauer.ch/politik--wirtschaft/agrarwirtschaft/emmi-expandiert-weiter-in-den-usa-28718.html.

Pan, Y. and Tse, D.K. 2000. The hierarchical model of market entry modes. *Journal of International Business Studies, 31* (4), 535–54.

Raaflaub, Martin. 2015. Unruhe in Emmis Auslandportfolio. *Schweizer Bauer*. 8 May. Accessed 7 June 2022. www.schweizerbauer.ch/markt--preise/marktmeldungen/unruhe-in-emmis-auslandportfolio-22288.html.

Rudolph, Thomas, Nagengast, Liane, and Nitsch, Frauke 2015. *Einkaufstourismus Schweiz 2015: Eine Studie zu den aktuellen Entwicklungen des Einkaufstourismus*. St. Gallen: Universität St.Gallen.

Theiler, Lucia. 2019. Changing consumption habits: Milk does it – but not like it used to. *Schweizer Radio und Fernsehen*. 5 May. Accessed 7 June 2022. www.srf.ch/news/wirtschaft/veraenderte-konsumgewohnheiten-milch-macht-s-aber-nicht-mehr-so-wie-frueher.

Weinmann, Benjamin. 2019. Neuer Name für Caffè Latté: Emmi tauft seinen Verkaufsschlager um. *Luzerner Zeitung*. 18 April. Accessed 7 June 2022. www.luzernerzeitung.ch/wirtschaft/probleme-beim-verkaufsschlager-ld.1112055.

BUILDING BRAND ENGAGEMENT: THE SYDNEY OPERA HOUSE IS SO MUCH MORE THAN TOP HATS AND TIARAS

Diane M. Phillips

For Christina Erskine, General Manager of Marketing for the Sydney Opera House (SOH), it was not the first time that her marketing research agency had provided some head-scratching results. Although the local community had a very strong love for, appreciation for, and pride in the SOH, around 25% of "Sydneysiders" do not attend events there. Given the local Sydney market was the backbone to SOH's revenue and attendance, why weren't more locals visiting the venue? At the same time, revenue from tourism was strong and growing. Should SOH continue to pursue Sydneysiders, or should the organization shift its focus to the lucrative tourist market?

Iconic Cultural Status

For thousands of years, the land on which the Sydney Opera House stands was a gathering place for Australia's First Peoples. In 1788, some of the first European settlers to set foot in Australia arrived on 11 ships from Great Britain carrying supplies, soldiers, and convicts. Known as the First Fleet, it was never expected that this rag-tag group of people would lay the foundations of a modern city, but that is indeed what happened. Over the years, Sydney continued to expand and grow in prominence. In 1973, a new opera house was built with an innovative exterior of curved lines and nested white "sails." Australians were initially skeptical, but it quickly became one of the most recognized landmarks in Australia and around the world. Architecturally, the Opera House was a marvel of shape and dimension; artistically, it was an inseparable part of the artistic performance and experience; and culturally, it cemented Sydney's place among other centers of global art and culture, like London and Paris. In 2007, it received recognition as an UNESCO[21] World Heritage Site, placing it alongside some of the most iconic structures in the world, including the Taj Mahal and the Great Wall of China. As one UNESCO official noted, "it stands by itself as one of the indisputable masterpieces of human creativity, not only in the 20th century but in the history of humankind" (Our Story 2022). The SOH is Australia's number one tourist attraction. Even after the global Covid-19 pandemic and economic slowdown, 8.2 million people visited the precinct, admired the view, and snapped pictures. Each year, the SOH staged more than 2000 events and performances and welcomed 1.5 million guests (Our Story 2022) (see Figure A3.11).

Photo A3.11 Sydney Opera House

Source: courtesy, Diane M. Phillips

Sydney Opera House's Economic Impact

Original estimates for the cost of construction were $7 million[22] and it was expected to take 4 years to complete. To say that these estimates were optimistic is an understatement. The final cost was $102 million and it took 14 years to complete the building and the six performance venues inside. In the end, a large part of the final cost was funded by a state lottery; it was officially opened in 1973 by Queen Elizabeth II (Our Story 2022). In 2018, the SOH contributed an estimated $1.2 billion to the Australian economy, including direct sales from tickets, bars, restaurants, and shops, as well as indirect economic benefits through its supply chains into other sectors. In all, 8,698 full-time equivalent jobs could be attributed directly and indirectly to the SOH. Overall, the Opera House was worth $6.2 billion in cultural, economic, and iconic value (Deloitte 2018).

---

[21]UNESCO is the United Nations Educational, Scientific, and Cultural Organization. It designates special areas as World Heritage Sites because of their unique cultural, scientific, or historic significance. This designation provides the area with international legal protections.

[22]All monetary figures are in Australian dollars.

Challenges of Marketing the Sydney Opera House

Erskine headed a 45-person marketing team, tasked with increasing engagement with SOH's various audiences for a broad range of programming – from kids' shows to contemporary music, comedy to opera, dance to musicals. Three key strategic goals guided the team's efforts, each with several action-oriented priorities (Internal documents 2018) (see Table A3.23).

Table A3.23 Strategic goals for the marketing team

Goal 1 – be led by our customers and actionable insights	Goal 2 – develop inspiring content to engage customers	Goal 3 – drive sustainable growth
a. listen to and better understand our audiences, visitors, and customers	a. tell a holistic brand story for the Sydney Opera House that helps people recognize what we stand for	a. improve the performance of our owned channels and campaigns
b. prioritize and leverage our data and tools	b. create structures and systems to maximize content discovery	b. attract new customers, retain them, and increase their value to SOH
c. empower staff to turn data insights into action-oriented customer insights	c. place customer experience thinking at the heart of creative decisions	c. explore new growth channels, partners, and technologies

Source: courtesy, SOH Marketing Team

In addition to the goals and priorities, the team was also guided by the SOH Brand Framework which included five content pillars. The team focused on "content connection," explained Erskine, "it's all about telling a consistent story and making sure that the sum of the hundreds of things we do every year as a brand add up to something more, building a narrative under each of our five key pillars." The thematic pillars represented key concepts that needed to be communicated; they acted as a guiding force for all of the team's creative and content-related brand decisions (Internal documents 2018). To ensure the most effective use of budget, a focus on research and planning was essential; the team needed to make sure their "dollars cut deep and went far. All of our brand work starts with insights from research, then we find connection to these five key pillars," confirmed Erskine (see Table A3.24).

Table A3.24 Five thematic pillars

Connection	To feel a sense of unity with the city, country and world, and all the communities within them.
Escapism	To be transported, to forget your normal self through engaging creativity, in all its forms
Challenge	To be taken to the edge, to feel an encouraging push
Inspiration	To be inspired by creativity to see the world differently
Transformation	To appreciate the greater potential to improve with innovative pathways

Source: courtesy, SOH Marketing Team

Brand Hurdles: Preconceptions

With any new initiative, the marketing team needed to be careful to not disrupt the strong loyalty felt by current guests. The team knew that it needed to walk a fine line between appealing to its current customer base, while also being edgy and relevant enough to attract a new, younger crowd. The most recent marketing research report found a consistent and less than favorable trend in perceptions. Individuals with a low level of engagement with the SOH said that it was (Internal documents 2018):

- a place mostly for traditional art forms
- not a place for "someone like me"
- not affordable

This finding was especially frustrating for the team because the Opera House actually had a wide variety of different shows that appealed to diverse audiences. Further, many of the ticket prices were very affordable. Unfortunately, these preconceptions were held by the local market *and* tourist market.

Drivers to Address Preconceptions

The marketing team realized that there were both cognitive and affective underpinnings to these perceptions and developed a set of "drivers" that would be important levers to reverse those preconceptions. Essentially, the team believed that it needed to address cognitive (or thinking) preconceptions as well as affective (or feeling) preconceptions in any new branding initiatives (see Table A3.25).

Table A3.25 Think and feel drivers to changing preconceptions

Think Drivers	Feel Drivers
• is a place where I feel comfortable and proud	• exciting
• is a place for someone like me	• inspiring
• encourages me to try new things	• passionate
• embraces new and traditional art forms	• friendly
• offers the best selection of experiences	• fun
• enhances my experience of the arts	• diverse
• offers good value for the money	• welcoming
	• leader
	• innovative

Source: courtesy, SOH Marketing Team

Increasing Engagement

The marketing team also realized that success depended on improving the digital customer experience and access to inspiring content. So, between 2015 and 2017, it underwent a digital transformation, updating marketing technologies, platforms, and strategies. The first step was updating the website to be more user-friendly, interactive, and engaging. In parallel, the marketing team worked to update the SOH brand identity, starting with revolutionizing the capabilities of the in-house creative team and developing guidelines and assets for the team to utilize. Central to the effort was ensuring that "our streaming customers had experiences with our content that were just as bold and inspiring as those having physical ones at the Opera House." According to Erskine, this transformation was "not just a project, it was a fundamental shift in the way the team thought about digital content and technologies, encouraging staff to really think about the customer and care about how they experience the same brand both physically and virtually."

In one effort, the SOH "inked a deal with Netflix for *Stranger Things* to premiere season 2 in Australia at the same time it premiered in the US." The goal was to leverage the *Stranger Things* brand to drive relevancy with the SOH brand, acquire new customers, and share digital content about the experience. The talented in-house production team transformed the Opera House's open areas and foyers into immersive sets and scenes from the popular series; fans were given free tickets. Erskine reflected, "events like these allow us to look at culture that is often consumed alone or in a home environment – gaming, podcasts, television – and bring audiences together to share in a *collective* experience ... there is nothing that super fans love more than coming together to geek out on their shared love of a show like this" (Chambers 2017).

At the same time that the Sydney Opera House was going through its digital and brand transformation, the team continued to focus on two key target markets. The first was the local Sydney audience, 25% of whom had not yet visited. The second was national and international tourists. For both of these markets, SOH was already in a strong position. Guided tours, particularly popular with the tourist market, had grown 72% between FY14 and FY18. According to Erskine, the performance venues inside the SOH averaged an annual occupancy of around 80%. However, there was still opportunity for growth and the team knew it needed to forge strong connections to the core SOH brand in order for it to work. Guests needed to connect to the Opera House as well as the show. This insight was critical, because research had revealed that 38% of the "value" in seeing a show at the Sydney Opera House was actually due to the venue itself; patrons didn't just go to see a given performer, many went *because* that performer was at the Opera House (Deloitte 2013). To leverage this insight, the team believed that it needed to invite people to share content around creating memories and experiences at the SOH. "When social media lights up with these shared experiences, the earned media value often far exceeds the media spend" (Chambers 2017). Thus, to engage its two target markets with the SOH brand, social media and content co-creation were critical, as was the critical connection with the venue.

Another piece of data that was meaningful to Erskine was that tourists spent, on average, $194 per transaction, while Sydneysiders spent about $207 per transaction. So, although Sydneysiders had a reputation for being quite frugal, when it came to seeing a performance, they were willing to pay.

Targeting Tourists

In 2018, there were 10.9 million visitors to the Sydney Opera House precinct, including about 9 million people in the "tourist" target market (the remaining 1.9 million visitors to the precinct were business people and locals). Tourists were responsible for the purchase of 450,000 tickets to performances and 490,000 tours of the facility (Deloitte 2018).[23] The team dubbed the rest of these visitors "selfie tourists" because of their desire to take a few pictures and then

[23]Although difficult to estimate, the team believed that there were about 9 million people in the tourist target market.

head off to see other sites around the city without truly engaging with the SOH. These individuals represented a huge opportunity because people were literally at the Opera House front door – walking around the building, but not going inside. The team decided to break though that reluctancy barrier and simply invite people to come in and have a look around.

In 2016, the "Come on In" campaign was born. Selfie tourists just did what they normally did – took pictures and posted them to their social media accounts. However, at the same time, people working at the Opera House and their agency at the time, DDB Sydney, were monitoring social media traffic and content. They sent an immediate personalized response to the tourists, some with an invite to come inside and have a unique experience for free. Hundreds of surprised people got messages such as, "hey Lisa, liked your picture, come on in and ..." Staff members would meet that person at a specified door and they would get a personalized experience inside – from a backstage tour to a cocktail-making class, from watching a rehearsal to learning acrobatic movements with cabaret performers (Internal documents 2018). "It had to be a top-tier experience," offered Erskine.

The team initially had three broad objectives for the campaign:

1 Drive awareness and reappraisal of the Sydney Opera House being a destination that everyone talks about through leveraging our extensive social media reach.
2 Increase conversion of on-site visitors to customers and advocates.
3 Increase ticket sales for shows, tours, food and beverage, and retail.

Outcomes for key performance indicators (KPIs) exceeded expectations (Internal documents 2018):

- approximately 5.3 million people saw a new side of SOH:
  - paid social media reach = 2.3 million people
  - organic social media reach (influencer + consumer followers) = 1.1 million people
  - PR reach = 1.9 million people
- 540,000 total social footprint (included email subscribers, Instagram, Facebook, and Twitter)
- weekly Facebook reach of 5.5 million, equaling a 7% engagement rate[24]
- on social media, sentiment was 96% positive during the campaign, and in PR, the sentiment was 100% positive
- engagement on SOH's social channels jumped by 30%
- cost per view (CPV) on paid social media was $0.03, well below the industry benchmark of $0.10.

The marketing team was pleased with the results from the campaign,[25] and it went on to win a Gold Lion and three Silver Lions in the Cannes International Festival of Creativity in the Mobile category. Next, the team turned its sights toward creating a campaign targeting locals.

[24]Engagement rate is a metric used by Facebook and is the percentage of total people reached who have interacted with a SOH Facebook post in any form, including likes, comments, shares, clicks, or video views.
[25]The team produced a wrap-video for "Come on In" which can be found here: www.youtube.com/watch?v=Vr8ZRW4-yvU&feature=youtu.be

Targeting Sydneysiders

What's a Sydneysider? If you have to ask, you haven't spent much time in Sydney. People living in Sydney ("Sydneysiders") are proud of their city but are notoriously hard to please and frequently complain about a lot of things, including the high cost of the city and long commutes (Hildebrand 2013). More than 5.4 million people reside in Sydney, about 20% of Australia's total population of about 25.8 million people (Australian Bureau of Statistics 2022). Many Sydneysiders thought that the Opera House was too "elite." This impression was compounded by the name: the Sydney Opera House. To tackle this preconception head-on, the team created a promotional campaign targeted at 29–35-year-old Sydneysiders. Together with their creative agency, the team created a content-focused campaign on a media channel where the audience was already active: Facebook Messenger. The goal was to encourage greater engagement with the brand by increasing SOH's voice and presence on Messenger by highlighting lesser-known SOH stories about the Opera House.

The "Seal BOT" campaign was launched in May 2018 with much fanfare, including a giant inflatable seal that floated next to the Sydney Opera House in Sydney Harbor for a day. Why seals? Since 2014, a wild long-nosed fur seal had made frequent visits to the steps immediately outside the Opera House to take a nap and relax in the sun (Joyce 2018). Curious locals would keep their distance, but would take pictures and watch as the seal slept, stretched, and engaged in some antics. Locals dubbed the seal "Benny" and started to become quite fond of him. The team believed that a Benny-themed chatbot could be a fun and entertaining way to reach a younger target market.

Seal BOT operated via Facebook Messenger and was designed to address any SOH-related preconceptions by giving users a laugh and having them discover unexpected content. Users could find out information about seals, random and little-known facts about upcoming shows, the history of the SOH, and inside stories of celebrity encounters (Green 2018). In the months after the launch, the results were encouraging. More than 5,000 people had interacted with the chatbot for an average of more than 2 minutes, the reach of the owned and paid social media campaign was 1.2m people, and the Net Promoter Score (NPS) taken from users came close to reaching the SOH's all time high score (Internal documents 2018). However, AI technology and functionality were changing so rapidly, by the time of the rollout, people were becoming less inclined to use chatbots. In the end, although the Seal BOT was deemed successful, the team thought they could do better.

Summary

The marketing team continued to believe that Sydneysiders presented an important potential for an increase in customer lifetime value for the SOH. After all, they lived in the city and once they understood the benefits and breadth of experiences available, they could turn into reliable, repeat guests. Tourists, by contrast, generally visited once and then were gone, and many of them made the decision about what they were going to do in Sydney only days before they actually did it – not a reliable source of revenue and engagement in a strategic sense, but a very valuable one nonetheless. Investing in brand building appeals for tourists, therefore, might result in a one-time bump in attendance and engagement, but would likely not have any long-term benefits. On the other hand, targeting the estimated 9 million tourists each year did offer a lot of promise. The Opera House only needed to attract a tiny fraction of these visitors. Moving forward, should the marketing team target national and international tourists, or should it target Sydneysiders with brand building campaigns?

ASSIGNMENT QUESTIONS

1. Should the SOH pursue the Sydneysider audience or should it shift its focus to the national and international tourist market? What is the market potential for the tourist market vs. the untapped Sydneysider market? Support your answer with details from the case and elsewhere.
2. Identify some unique challenges for the performing arts in marketing live shows and experiences to audiences. In what ways might the job of marketing the SOH be *easier*, compared to other performing arts venues?
3. In 1973, construction costs for the Sydney Opera House were $102 million. Thinking just in economic terms, calculate the present value of the Opera House in 2018, 45 years later, assuming a 4% annual interest rate. With the 2018 Deloitte report claiming that the value of the Opera House was $6.2 billion, was the initial investment worth it? Discuss.
4. Evaluate the extent to which the "Come on In" campaign and the "Seal BOT" campaign address "think drivers" and "feel drivers."
5. Evaluate the success of the "Come on In" campaign: (a) To what extent does it fulfill each one of the five thematic pillars? (b) Are the KPIs used for the "Come on In" campaign appropriate? (c) Are there others that could be added?

References

Australian Bureau of Statistics. 2022. Population. *Australian Bureau of Statistics*. Accessed 7 June 2022. www.abs.gov.au/statistics/people/population/regional-population/2020-21.

Chambers, P. 2017. The rise of experiential marketing: why TV fans want more than streaming. *AdNews*. 11 October. Accessed 7 June 2022. www.adnews.com.au/news/the-rise-of-experiential-marketing-why-tv-fans-want-more-than-streaming.

Deloitte. 2013. How do you value an icon? The Sydney Opera House: economic, cultural and digital value. *Deloitte Sydney*, a member of Deloitte Touche Tohmatsu, Ltd., Sydney, New South Wales, Australia.

Deloitte. 2018. Revaluing our icon: Midpoint in Sydney Opera House's decade of renewal. *Deloitte Sydney*, a member of Deloitte Touche Tohmatsu, Ltd., Sydney, New South Wales, Australia.

Green, R. 2018. Sydney Opera House makes a splash with seal chatbot campaign via The Works + On Message. *Campaign Brief*. 8 May. Accessed 7 June 2022. www.campaignbrief.com/2018/05/sydney-opera-house-makes-a-spl.html.

Hildebrand, J. 2013. 25 ways to tell if you're a true Sydneysider and prove how much better we are than Melbourne. *The Daily Telegraph*. 8 August. Accessed 7 June 2022. www.dailytelegraph.com.au/news/nsw/ways-to-tell-if-you8217re-a-true-sydneysider-and-prove-how-much-better-we-are-than-melbourne/news-story/dcec91f67e78fd99ce730bd97a94aa3f.

Joyce, E. 2018. You can now talk to the Sydney Opera House seal. *TimeOut*. 7 May. Accessed 7 June 2022. www.timeout.com/sydney/news/you-can-now-talk-to-the-sydney-opera-house-seal-050718.

Our Story. 2022. House history: The story of Sydney Opera House. The Sydney Opera House. Accessed 7 June 2022. www.sydneyoperahouse.com/our-story.html.

CAN CHAMPAGNE BECOME AN EVERYDAY DRINK? *SHOULD* IT?

Diane M. Phillips

At 25 years old, Clara Dechelle was the third-generation owner of a small champagne estate and was looking forward to an especially abundant and good-tasting product this year. A recent report by France's most important trade union for growers of champagne grapes, however, made her pause. The union was launching a €12 million campaign to reposition champagne as an everyday drink. Would consumers accept this new product positioning? What impact would this repositioning have on the long-held image of champagne as a luxury product?

France's Champagne Region

Just 1 hour northeast of Paris sits the only place in the world where one can grow the grapes that are needed for the creation of champagne. It was here that in the early 17th century, a French Benedictine monk named Dom Perignon perfected the process by which wine was turned into sparkling wine (Beardsley 2018, Faith 2016). In 1843, champagne producers organized to protect the integrity of their product and in 1936, strict protections were codified into law – only the sparkling wines coming from the Champagne Region of France have the right to be called champagne (Comité Champagne 2022). This law specified the exact types of grapes that can be used, as well as methods of pruning, hand-picked harvesting, and production (Comité Champagne 2022). The region is so unique that UNESCO recognizes the champagne hillsides, houses, and cellars as a World Heritage Site (Faith 2016, The Wines of Champagne 2018).[26] The region produces, on average, 300 million bottles per year (Beardsley 2018, The Wines of Champagne 2018).

[26]UNESCO is the United Nations Educational, Scientific, and Cultural Organization. It designates special areas as World Heritage Sites because of their unique cultural, scientific, or historic significance. This designation provides the area with international legal protections.

France's biggest and most important trade organization for champagne producers is called the Comité Champagne. The overall goal of the organization is to defend the integrity of champagne and the Champagne Region by increasing the economic success of its growers and producers (Faith 2016). To do this, the Comité Champagne regulates the supply and demand of the product, ensures that growers and producers are following the appropriate regulations, and manages the AOC (appellation d'origine controlée), the official certification from the French government that the product was produced in accordance with the law.

While the Champagne Region makes up only 0.5% of the world's vineyards, it accounts for 10% of the global consumption of sparkling wine volume and 36% by value. At the time that Dechelle was making her decision, the region's production was worth €4.9 billion; 51.3% of the production volume was exported. The most important market for champagne is the US, which makes up about 12% of the overall global market for champagne (Comité Champagne 2022) (see Table A3.26).

Table A3.26 Champagne's top global markets

	2018 Ranking	Revenue in Millions of Euros (Excluding Taxes)	Millions of Bottles
1	USA	577.1	23.7
2	United Kingdom	406.2	26.8
3	Japan	318.8	13.6
4	Germany	203.0	12.1
5	Italy	158.6	7.4
6	Belgium	144.9	9.1
7	Australia	123.3	8.4
8	Switzerland	120.9	5.8

Source: Comité Champagne, 2018

The Champagne Region experienced several years of remarkably good harvests between 2017 and 2019 due, in part, to climate change. Long-time residents, producers, and climate scientists have noted that the entire region has become drier, hotter, and sunnier since the beginning of the 21st century. Overall, climate change has resulted in devastating agricultural losses throughout Europe. Indeed, the 2019 European heatwaves brought temperatures to 45°C in southern France and turned some grapes into raisins right on the vine (Mercer 2019). Further north, however, these changes just happen to be ideal growing conditions for the three varieties of grapes that are essential for the production of champagne. Although the grapes need to be harvested a full 2 weeks earlier than normal and workers need to avoid the hottest parts of the day during the harvest (Mercer 2019), for now, climate change is resulting in increased production and a tastier product (Beardsley 2018, Faith 2016). The Champagne Region has 15,800 smaller, independent producers and 320 big producers (Comité Champagne 2022).

Negociants vs. Independent Producers

The first broad category of champagne producers is made up of big producers, or "negociants." Because they do not have the number of vines needed to sustain their massive production needs, they purchase grapes from a variety of smaller, independent producers. Then, negociants blend these grapes with their own and put their own label on the product. This arrangement is beneficial for both the negociants and the independent producers. The negociants are able to obtain the grapes for their product and the independent producers are able to have a reliable outlet for their grape production without the added responsibility of buying and maintaining expensive bottling, labeling, or other equipment.

One of the biggest negociants is Moët & Chandon, which is under the umbrella of luxury brand conglomerate Louis Vuitton Moët Hennessy (LVMH). Moët has been producing champagne since 1743 and was the first champagne producer to be listed on the French Stock Exchange. The Moët & Chandon brand controls the Dom Perignon brand, the world's most profitable luxury brand of wine (Faith 2016). Together, all of the champagnes under the LVMH umbrella account for 40% of all global champagne sales (Faith 2016).

Independent producers, by contrast, make up the majority of the producers in the Champagne Region. Although the AOC certification dictates a very strict set of regulations for champagne production, it does allow some flexibility for different tastes and consistencies, depending on the grape blends, the exact location of the fields, and annual growing conditions. This difference between negociants and independent producers means that the smaller, independent producers usually have more freedom to develop different blends, which expands the variety of different tastes and, potentially, appeals to variety-seeking consumers. By contrast, a customer who buys a bottle of Moët knows exactly what to expect; it is very "reliable" (Faith 2016). In the end, the relationship between the negociants and independent producers is mutually beneficial and allows the champagne industry to access the supply of grapes needed for consistent and reliable production, as well as innovative blends that appeal to a variety of tastes.

Dechelle Estates

Dechelle Estates was started by Clara Dechelle's grandparents in 1902. Throughout the region, it is not unusual to trace estate ownership back seven or more generations. "I am only the third generation of winemakers here – we're fairly new," said Dechelle. Dechelle Estates is an independent producer, with its own equipment and branding, and a maximum production of 90,000 bottles per year. Most years, it produces 50,000 bottles and sells the remaining grapes to negociants at €6.5 per kilogram; each bottle requires 1.2 kilograms of grapes. Customers purchase Dechelle champagne at the estate, online, and at several local wine and champagne shops.

French consumers take extreme care with their champagne purchases. "Back when my parents ran things, people used to come out to our estate and stock up for a whole year – they would fill up the back of the car. Back then, it wouldn't bother a family to spend €400 in 1 day for a few cases to fill up the car. They understood that the price really didn't matter too much because you had champagne for the whole year. People would make a whole weekend event out of going to get their champagne for the year. It was a family trip. Today, people are not loyal to one house any more. Also, they don't have as much money as they had before. The economy is tight for everyone. We still have many faithful customers but it is not so simple anymore," explained Dechelle.

Dechelle identified two emerging trends in consumer purchasing behaviors. First, consumers are less willing to pay a high price for champagne. Instead, many purchase sparkling wine. Some sparkling wine has an AOC designation ("crémant"), meaning that it was produced with grapes grown outside the Champagne Region, but according to the AOC regulations. These crémants offer a fairly good quality for a lower price. Unfortunately, sparkling wine is not regulated, so the quality can vary quite considerably. Second, fewer customers are brand loyal; they like the challenge of discovering new tastes and brands. Dechelle Estates was well positioned to handle these shifts. Its prices are very competitive, starting at €18.80 per bottle, and it produces champagnes with a variety of tastes, which reflect annual differences in the growing season, as well as special-release blends and textures.

The Economics of Champagne Production

Because of higher costs, champagne producers must charge a higher price than other sparkling wine producers. Many of the production costs are a result of regulations. "For example, harvesting is only allowed to be done by hand, so the labor costs are very high," said Dechelle. Another contributor to costs is equipment. Moët & Chandon, for example, has its own equipment. Dechelle Estates is one of the smaller producers that also has its own equipment. "A lot of costs go into the production of champagne, such as the cost of the bottle, cost of the grapes, labeling, corks, and of course the investment in bigger materials and machinery like the labeling machine, tanks, and the bottle turner," explained Dechelle. Price, however, is not necessarily an indicator of quality. Some of the best quality champagnes come from smaller producers who charge more reasonable prices (see Table A3.27).

Table A3.27 Cost structure for independents and negociants

	Cost per Bottle for Independent Producers (in Euros)	Cost per Bottle for Negociants (in Euros)
Grape Production/Acquisition	3.7	7.2
Champagne Production	2.5	2.5
Other Costs (including labor and debt)	3.0	0.0*
Marketing Costs	0.9	4.8
Total Costs	10.1	14.5

* For negociants, "other costs" are incorporated into the other cost categories of grape production/acquisition, champagne production, and marketing costs.

Sources: Comité Champagne (2022) and Dechelle (2019)

Champagne's Luxury Image

By the 18th century, champagne had become particularly popular with the aristocracy in Europe (Faith 2016). Around this time, champagne solidified its luxury image because of two crucial developments. First, the aristocracy and upper classes were captivated by the story of how the bubbly drink was perfected by Dom Perignon. The image of a French monk toiling away to produce the world's most luxurious drink achieved almost mythic status. Second, there was a widely-held belief that champagne was an aphrodisiac. Indeed, French King Louis XIV and the royal court at Versailles were infatuated with champagne, served it during his many raucous parties, and rarely drank anything else (Rokka 2017).

Through skillful marketing, by the mid 1800s, champagne's luxury image became inextricably entwined with the Champagne Region (Comité Champagne 2022, Rokka 2017).

By the 1870s, champagne was being marketed around the world as a luxury product (Faith 2016) and was especially popular among the wealthy, as well as with artists, musicians, and other cultural elites (Rokka 2017). By the mid-19th century, champagne was consumed across Europe, Russia, the US, and Canada (Faith 2016).

Although the luxury image of champagne has been solidified and reinforced around the world with skillful marketing strategies, the marketing of champagne in France remains exceptionally difficult. The 1991 Evin Law bans any alcohol advertising that contains "positive, evocative images and messages that associate alcohol with pleasure, glamour, success, sport, performance, sex, opinion leaders, etc." Instead, alcohol advertising must be informative and depict only objective qualities of the product, such as the type of grape used or foods with which it can be paired. All ads must also contain a warning that says alcohol consumption is a danger to one's health. Violations are met with stiff fines (Gallopel-Morvan, et al. 2015). Even though food and wine are an integral part of France's culture and history, this law is one of Europe's strictest.

Champagne is enjoyed by people all around the world and has become an indispensable part of life's most important events and celebrations – people use champagne to make a toast at a wedding, to christen a ship, to celebrate the team's big win, and to celebrate life's milestones. Recent evidence, however, seems to indicate that champagne's positioning may be becoming more "democratized" (Rokka 2017). Champagne is becoming consumed more often for all kinds of occasions. For example, some of the biggest producers have experimented with different packaging, such as champagne in cans, to allow customers to bring champagne to a variety of venues that don't allow glass, such as the beach (Daniel 2019). Champagne is also becoming more of a summertime drink with modest sales increases during the summer season. Producers have responded by offering special summer and limited-time editions.

The Concept of Terroir

Some products are simply more desirable *because* they come from a specific place. Champagne is one of them. Other examples are Irish whiskey, Cuban cigars, and Vermont maple syrup. Sure, consumers can get these products from other locations, but they are especially tasty and sought-after when they come from a specific place. This is the basis of the concept of *terroir*. Every place or region has two separate characteristics related to its location. The first is soil composition, weather, and climate. Distinct minerals, clay, and microorganisms in the soil, as well as the number of sunny days, the amount and timing of rain, the amount of humidity in the air, the coolness of the nights, and angle of the sun all imbue food and beverage products with a unique taste, composition, and texture. The second component of terroir encompasses a region's unique social and cultural characteristics – the people, history, and shared values of the place. This human element of terroir includes the work ethic of the people, their shared values, language, and philosophy, as well as a shared set of skills and methods that were likely passed down through many generations (Charters, Spielmann, and Babin 2017).

From a marketing perspective, terroir is part of the "place" component of the marketing mix, the one component that is most difficult to change. Terroir is impossible for a competitor to copy, so it serves as a barrier to market entry and allows for higher prices. In sum, terroir can be part of the brand's value proposition and sustainable competitive advantage (Charters, et al. 2017). Independent champagne producers are ideally suited to take advantage of the concept of terroir. The climate, soil, and physical characteristics of the Champagne Region, as well as the history and expertise of the people working there, combine to make a truly special product. The two biggest players in promoting the luxury terroir image of champagne are the General Syndicate of Wine Growers (SGV) and The Comité Champagne.

The SGV

Formed in 1904, the SGV is the most important independent trade union for growers of champagne grapes and often works in collaboration with the Comité Champagne. In 2018, SGV launched a campaign to promote champagne as an everyday drink. The president of SGV explained, "Champagne is for all the people, for all the moments, not just for ceremonial occasions.

[We believe] that champagne is wonderful, and you can make an occasion wonderful by drinking champagne." The 3 year campaign was designed to make champagne more accessible and egalitarian for younger buyers who were starting to learn about and appreciate champagne (Woodward 2019). The target market was young French people, 25–45 years old (Schmitt 2019).

The tagline of the campaign was, "suitable for any occasion." Outdoor and print ads depicted a glass of champagne on an unadorned table next to a variety of commonplace foods, such as a hard-boiled egg or cheese. Importantly, the campaign was designed to promote the champagne category, rather than any specific champagne brand[27] (Schmitt 2019). SGV pledged €12 million over 3 years to the effort that launched in France, and quickly expanded to Belgium, Luxembourg, and Italy (Schmitt 2019). Part of SGV's effort was to appeal to millennials who want authenticity, unique experiences, and confirmation through social media. For millennials who are not used to drinking it, champagne is unique. Thus, SGV's efforts to promote the category, to encourage an everyday image, and leverage the millennial drive for authenticity and variety were predicted to be a recipe for success. Like most independent producers, Dechelle was already a member of SGV and thus had access to the campaign's marketing materials and other resources.

The Comité Champagne

Unfortunately, the Comité Champagne strongly disagreed with SGV's efforts, called it "desacralization" of the category, and claimed it would be the "devaluation of the champagne category" (Schmitt 2019). Therefore, the Comité Champagne and most of the big negociants chose to not participate. Instead, rather than supporting a category-based campaign, the negociants decided to continue with their own marketing and branding campaigns (Schmitt 2019, Woodward 2019).

Marketing Research

At the same time Clara Dechelle was contemplating the decision about whether to follow the advice of the SGV and promote the estate's champagne as an everyday drink, her younger sister was working on her master's thesis at a nearby university and had some results from a small-scale marketing research study to share with the family (see Table A3.28).

Table A3.28 Marketing research results

How often do you drink champagne?*	Never = 2.6% Rarely = 49.5% Several times a month = 43.4% Several times a week = 4.6%
How often do you buy champagne?	Never = 19.9% Rarely = 60.7% Several times a month = 18.9% Several times a week = 0.5%

(Continued)

[27]Examples of the campaign can be seen here:www.thedrinksbusiness.com/2019/02/generic-marketing-for-champagne-courts-controversy/

Table A3.28 (Continued)

How many different champagne brands have you tried in your life?	None = 1.0% One brand only = 1.0% 2 brands = 5.1% 3 to 5 brands = 13.3% Less than 10 brands[28] = 14.3% More than 10 different brands = 65.3%
Which of the following best describes your opinion?	I don't pay attention to the brands = 16.3% I drink many different champagne brands = 36.7% I have my favorite 2–3 brands = 34.7% I drink champagne from one single producer only = 3.6% I haven't found the champagne to fully satisfy me yet = 8.7%
Which adjective best describes your vision of the champagne industry?	Innovative = 9.5% Prestigious = 44.7% Healthy = 5.5% Environment friendly = 5.5% Old = 9.7% Aging = 9.7% Collaborative = 8.4% Other = 6.8%
Most important product attribute?	Good value for the money = 27% Tasty = 25% Natural ingredients = 14.8% Good customer reviews = 12.2% Label design = 9.7% Brand prestige = 6.1% Good customer service = 5.1%

* The 295 respondents for this study were recruited from online wine forums and blogs

Source: Dechelle (2019)

Summary

Clara Dechelle needed to decide whether to participate in the SGV's marketing campaign to broaden champagne's appeal or continue to leverage the luxury image for which champagne is known. On the one hand, she would be able to tap into the resources of France's largest and most prestigious champagne grower's trade union. They had data to back up their strategy and the millennial market seemed to be an ideal target. On the other hand, could such an approach damage the luxury image of champagne in general, and Dechelle Estates in particular?

[28]Unfortunately, the choices here are non-exclusive.

ASSIGNMENT QUESTIONS

1. Should Dechelle Estates follow the advice of the SGV and try to market its champagne as an everyday drink? Support your recommendation with evidence from the case and elsewhere.
2. Carefully define Dechelle's core target market for champagne from Dechelle Estates, both psychographically and demographically.
3. What is product positioning? For the target market identified in #2 above, (a) identify the two most important product attributes for champagne and (b) construct a 2 x 2 positioning map for champagne. Be sure to identify where Dechelle Estates is likely to be located, as well as at least three other brands. For each brand, discuss your rationale for the location you selected.
4. What is branding? What are the benefits and drawbacks to a luxury branding positioning?
5. Calculate the estimated sales and profit for the champagne from Dechelle Estates. Assume a volume of 90,000 bottles. List your key assumptions in the calculation of this figure.
6. What does it mean when we say that small champagne producers are ideally suited to take advantage of the concept of terroir? Do you agree or disagree? Support your conclusion with evidence from the case and elsewhere.

References

Beardsley, E. 2018. Champagne Makers Bubble Over a Bumper Crop Caused by European Drought. *National Public Radio*. 13 September. Accessed 7 June 2022. https://apple.news/A0U7_YfcQR_KBuWlbzmnGQA.

Charters, S., Spielmann, N. and Babin, B.J. 2017. The Nature and Value of Terroir Products. *European Journal of Marketing, 51* (4), 748–71.

Comité Champagne. 2022. *Champagnes Only Come from Champagne, France*. The Comité Champagne. Accessed 7 June 2022. www.champagne.fr/en/.

Dechelle, A. 2019. *The power of language in marketing and advertisement in Champagne domain*. Academic thesis. Neoma Business School: Technology & Management Program.

Faith, N. 2016. *The Story of Champagne*. Infinite Ideas, Ltd. Oxford, UK.

Gallopel-Morvan, K., Diouf, J.F., Lecas, F., Riguad A., and David, N. 2015. Restrictions on Alcohol Marketing in France: The Evin Law. Presentation to the *Alcohol Policy Network in Europe*. 6 October. Edinburgh, Scotland.

Mercer, C. 2019. "Unprecedented" French Heatwave Affects Vineyard Work. *Decanter*. 26 June: 1.

Rokka, J. 2017. Champagne: Marketplace Icon. *Consumption Markets & Culture, 20* (3), 275–83.

Schmitt, P. 2019. Generic Marketing for Champagne Courts Controversy. *The Drinks Business*. 6 February. Accessed 7 June 2022. www.thedrinksbusiness.com/2019/02/generic-marketing-for-champagne-courts-controversy/.

Woodward, G. 2019. Bubbling Over. *Harpers Wine & Spirit*. March. 19.

INDEX